Symbol	Definition	Symbol	Definition
H_1 and H_2	Alternative hypotheses. 153	r	Pearson product-moment correlation coefficient. 240
HSD	Tukey's "honestly significant difference." 408	r^2	Proportion of variance accounted for. 255
i	1. Index of summation. 44 2. Width of a class interval. 49	r_{12}	Correlation between Measures 1 and 2. 317
LCL and UCL	Lower and upper confidence limits. 189	r_s	Spearman rank-order correlation coefficient. 282
Mdn	The point on a measurement scale—not necessarily a score—that divides a frequency distribution in half. 49	r_b	Biserial correlation coefficient. 296
Mode	The most frequently occurring score. 54	r_{pb}	Point-biserial correlation coefficient. 292
MS_B	Mean square between groups; between-groups variance. 388	r_t	Tetrachoric correlation coefficient. 292
MS_W	Mean square within groups; within-groups variance. 388	$r_\alpha(m,df)$	Standardized (Studentized) range for a given significance level (α), number of means (m), and degrees of freedom (df). 403
N	Number of individuals. 29	$R_\alpha(m,df)$	Critical value of the range in raw-score units for a given significance level (α), number of means (m), and degrees of freedom (df). 403
n_s	Size of a sample space. 106		
p	Binomial probability of success. 136		
p_c	Common probability of success in independent binomial samples. 226	R_A and R_B	Sum of the A and B ranks in the Mann-Whitney U test. 216
p_e	Population proportion; expected proportion. 421	R_i	Marginal total for a row in an r by c contingency table. 297
p_o	Observed proportion in a sample. 421	S	Corrected estimate of population standard deviation. 177
p_j	Simple percentage of cases within a score interval. 84	$S_{\bar{x}}$	Standard error of the mean. 178
p_w	Simple percentage within the score interval being transformed to a percentile rank. 84	$S_{\bar{Y}|\bar{X}}$	Corrected standard error of estimate. 269
P_1 and P_2	Observed proportions of success in two binomial samples. 226	$S_{Y'}$	Standard error of Y' values. 269
		S_{Yf}	Standard error of future Y values. 271
PR	Percentile rank. 82	S^2	Unbiased estimate of population variance. 177
q	Binomial probability of failure. 136	S_B^2	Variance between groups. 385
q_c	Common probability of failure in independent binomial samples. 226	S_W^2	Variance within groups. 382
Q_1 and Q_3	First and third quartiles. 88	SD	Standard deviation of a sample. 64
Q	Semi-interquartile range. 88	$SD_{Y|X}$	Standard error of estimate. 256
R	A rank on an ordinal scale. 82	SD^2	Variance of a sample. 68

(continued on back endpaper)

Using Statistics for Psychological Research

Using Statistics for Psychological Research
An Introduction

James Thomas Walker
University of Missouri — St. Louis

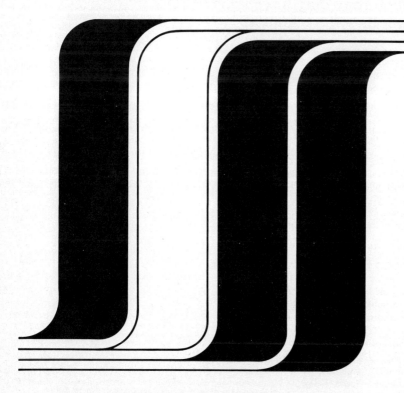

HOLT, RINEHART AND WINSTON
New York   Chicago   San Francisco   Philadelphia
Montreal   Toronto   London   Sydney
Tokyo   Mexico City   Rio de Janeiro   Madrid

Publisher   John L. Michel
Senior Acquistions Editor   Nedah Abbott
Senior Developmental Editor   Rosalind Sackoff
Senior Project Manager   Arlene D. Katz
Production Manager   Lula Als
Art Director   Lou Scardino
Managing Editor   Edward Cone
Text Design   Caliber Design Planning, Inc.
Cover Design   Albert D'Agostino

To my teachers, students, colleagues, and friends,
mutually intersecting sets of people who have taught me in many ways,
some of them less than they may have wished,
and others more than they have known.

Library of Congress Cataloging in Publication Data
Walker, James T.
   Using Statistics for Psychological Research
   Bibliography: p. 573
   Includes index.
   1. Psychometrics.   2. Psychology — Research.   I. Title.
BF39.W34   1985   519.5'02415   84-6662

ISBN 0-03-063591-8

CBS COLLEGE PUBLISHING
Holt, Rinehart and Winston
The Dryden Press
Saunders College Publishing

Preface

This is a sophomore- or junior-level text for use following an introductory course in psychology or one of the social or behavioral sciences.

Research methods in the behavioral sciences are *quantitative* methods that require the manipulation of quantitative ideas. Nevertheless, logical thinking plays a greater role than mathematics in designing experiments and observations, and even in analyzing the results. A college algebra course, or its equivalent, will provide sufficient background for understanding and using the procedures presented in this text. Appendix A provides a review of basic algebraic operations. I suggest that you read that appendix early, and then refer to it whenever you need to refresh yourself.

This book is designed to be used in any of three situations: (1) in a free-standing one-semester *statistics* course; (2) in a sequence consisting of a *statistics* course followed by a course in *research methods* or *experimental psychology;* (3) in a one-year integrated course in *statistics and research methods.* Since the validity of a statistical test rests squarely on the procedures used in gathering the data, the topic of experimental design is introduced in the first chapter. Discussions of design problems and statistical procedures are interwoven throughout the remainder of the book. Rather than supplanting any of the detailed treatments of statistical tests, the material on experimental design supplements those treatments.

In a free-standing statistics course that may or may not be followed by a course in research methods, the material on experimental design will promote the appreciation of the place of statistics in the overall research enterprise. If a statistics course is part of a quantitative sequence, then this text can be used in a subsequent course in research methods, where the material on designing experiments and observations can be emphasized more strongly. In that case, or in a one-year integrated course, supplementary readings in the philosophy of science and in some content areas can be useful. Some of the references cited in the text will be helpful in that respect.

This book is largely organized within a framework consisting of the kinds of research questions that we ask — for example, whether a single mean differs from some expected value, or whether there is any difference between two independent groups, or any correlation between two variables. Where a chapter is devoted to several methods of answering a particular kind of question, the nature of the measurement scale — nominal, ordinal, interval, or ratio — provides another level of organization. Nonparametric tests are presented within that framework, rather than being relegated to a separate, disjointed chapter.

Exercises and study questions are provided at the end of each chapter. Detailed answers are given in the back of the book, and the solution to each problem is laid out completely. The *Student Workbook* provides additional exercises and answers, sets out the major learning objectives, and provides a self-test of the key terms and concepts introduced in each chapter.

A small, inexpensive calculator will be very useful in working the problems and exercises, even if you have access to calculators or computers in a statistics laboratory on your campus. A calculator that will add, subtract, multiply, divide, square, and take square roots, and that has two or three memories, will be sufficient at this stage. Indeed, a more sophisticated calculator that is too highly automated will not teach you as much as a more modest machine.

The *Instructor's Manual* provides a great many questions and problems that are suitable for examinations, and exercises suitable for homework or laboratory assignments. Additionally, it describes a number of experiments and observations that have proven useful as laboratory exercises in the above situations.

I am pleased to acknowledge the help of my colleagues at the University of Missouri — St. Louis, John J. Boswell, Alan G. Krasnoff, and Dominic J. Zerbolio, Jr., who read all or parts of the manuscript. I greatly appreciate their advice, criticism, and encouragement. The University of Missouri provided a sabbatical leave at a critical juncture, and provided support in many other ways, for all of which I am grateful.

This book has profited greatly from the careful reading and thoughtful comments of the following reviewers: Edwin Brainerd, James E. Carlson, Edward Cobb, David Dailey, Lorraine Davis, William Frederickson, Arthur Gutman, Terry Libukman, Robert Malgady, Stuart Miller, and John Seamon. I greatly appreciate the efforts, interest, and concern of the editorial staff at Holt, Rinehart, and Winston — particularly Arlene Katz, Daniel Loch, Nedah Abbott, and Rosalind Sackoff. If our finished product somehow falls short of absolute perfection, then I apologize in advance for whatever errors, inadequacies, or impenetrable passages may remain in spite of all of our best efforts.

I am grateful to the Literary Executor of the late Sir Ronald A. Fisher, F. R. S., to Dr. Frank Yates, F. R. S., and to Longman Group Ltd., London, for permission to reprint Tables III and IV from their book *Statistical Tables for Biological, Agricultural and Medical Research* (6th edition, 1974). I also appreciate the generous permission of many other authors and publishers to reprint or adapt tables and other materials. Sources are acknowledged and identified in all of those cases.

In writing this book, I kept two principal functions of a textbook in mind: First, I have designed this book to *teach,* and second, to serve as a *reference* after you have finished using it in your present course. The statistical tables, symbol list, extensive subject index, and the body of the text itself have all been organized with those two ends in mind. I hope this book will serve those two purposes and remain useful to you over many years to come.

James Thomas Walker

St. Louis
August, 1984

Contents

---

6   Random Variables and Probability Experiments   103

No—

Description and Measurement

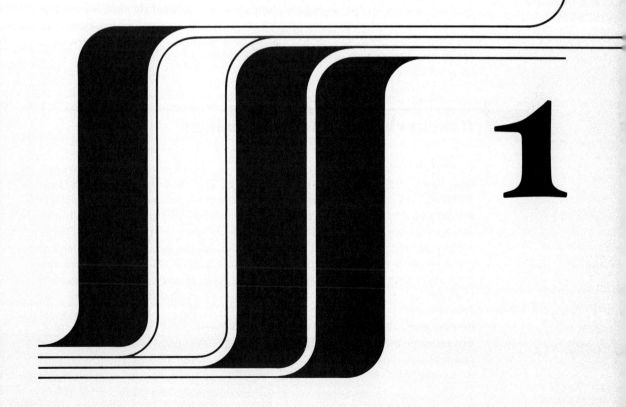

1

Since this is a book about research methods in psychology, you are entitled to know at the outset what I think the field of psychology is about, and what I hope this book will help you accomplish. My definition of psychology is a fairly conventional one: The study of the behavior and experience of organisms. But like most definitions, this one is not entirely satisfactory. Some psychologists will object to the word **experience** in my definition, arguing in the tradition of Behaviorism (Watson, 1913) that psychology is the study of **behavior,** and nothing more. And they are right, in an important sense.

While there has been a great resurgence of interest in consciousness and other facets of experience (for example, Ornstein, 1972; Gazzaniga & LeDoux, 1978), it is quite true that everything we think we know about the inner experience of another person — the person's thoughts, feelings, beliefs, yearnings — is an **inference from behavior,** a judgment based on directly observable actions (Hebb, 1972). What a person *says,* of course, is behavior, and so is whatever a person *does,* including the kinds of physiological behaviors that can be observed only by instruments of one sort or another.

You have been an observer of human and animal behavior all your life, and you have made a great many inferences about individuals and groups from their behavior. The sole purpose of this book is to help you draw inferences — that is, reach conclusions, make judgments — more systematically than you may have done thus far.

If you have not already acquired the habit of reading the preface of each of your textbooks, this is a good time to begin cultivating that habit. The preface of this text is designed to give you and your instructor an overview of the plan of the book, and some reassurances about the level of mathematical difficulty. The preface also offers some suggestions on how to use this book most effectively.

 # Research Goals in Psychology

Research in the field of psychology is the process of generating new knowledge in order to attain four principal goals: The **description, prediction, control,** and **understanding** of behavior and experience. These four goals are arranged in ascending order of their usual difficulty of attainment, but in some situations it may be more difficult to achieve control than to achieve understanding. To speak of control as one of the goals of psychological research may be very disquieting to some people. Most of us have the conviction that we are free agents, and we have an even stronger conviction that this is as it should be (but see Skinner's book *Beyond Freedom and Dignity,* 1971, on this point). We resist the notion of a psychologist — or anyone else — attempting to control our behavior, and perhaps I have confirmed some of your worst fears by arguing that control is indeed one of the goals of psychological research. But a great many people already control many facets of our behavior, and very few of those exercising control are psychologists. Most people pay their taxes—often against their will—and obey most of our laws, and some people are called upon to risk their lives in one situation or another. Most of us have long since accepted a certain amount of control over our lives as one of the demands of civilization.

Unfortunately, the field of psychology has been only moderately successful in controlling human behavior. I wish we knew enough to control the behavior of those violent, antisocial people who threaten our well-being and our lives. Better yet, I wish we knew enough to allow those people to modify their own behavior along more beneficial lines, for their own good and ours. I have, of course, made a great many value judgments about various kinds of behavior and human institutions. I value rational discourse over violence, learning over ignorance, and civilization over its alternatives. And I see as one of the important tasks of psychological research the acquisition of knowledge that may help us maintain and strengthen our civilization and preserve and enhance our humanity.

Psychology as a Science

You have no doubt recognized that the four goals of psychological research listed in the preceding section are widely shared in other fields. Indeed, the aims of psychological research are precisely the aims of *science* in general (Bachrach, 1981). At first blush, the field of psychology may not appear to be very scientific, even though we share the goals of science. Certainly, our predictions leave much to be desired, and our control over behavior is very poor in comparison with the control which physical scientists exercise over their segments of the universe. Our apparatus, for the most part, is much less complicated—and much less costly—than the equipment used in many other fields. But the hallmark of a science is the application of the **scientific method,** a set of procedures for generating and testing hypotheses, rather than the study of any particular content area, or the use of any particular kind of apparatus.

Hypothesis Testing. A *testable hypothesis* about some aspect of the universe is a statement that can potentially be rejected as a result of observation or experimentation. For example, we might formulate the following hypothesis: There is no significant difference between the performance of men and women on Task A. To test that hypothesis, we have only to observe the performance of men and women on the task, taking certain precautions that we will describe later. We will also describe in *great* detail exactly what is meant by a significant difference.

Hypothesis testing plays a great role in achieving the goals of prediction, control, and understanding. We will have occasion to deal extensively with the generation and testing of hypotheses. Psychology is concerned with testable hypotheses about behavior, and about experience as inferred from behavior, and thus the field of psychology lends itself to many of the methods that have proven useful in other fields of research. Bachrach (1981) provides an excellent discussion of psychology as a science, and Hempel (1966) offers an excellent treatment of the scientific method in general.

Relationships among the Goals of Science

While the goals of science are highly interrelated, it is often possible to achieve some of these goals without being able to achieve the others. The early astronomers, for example, were able to make elegant predictions, and even achieve some degree of understanding, without being able to exercise any control whatever over astronomical events. In the field of psychology, we can control learning—at least to the extent that we know something about the effects of reinforcement and motivation—but the neurophysiological bases of this most important process are simply not understood in any satisfying way. We have no more than a few glimmerings of the kinds of neural mechanisms that may account for learning.

The diagram in Figure 1-1 shows some of the interrelations among the goals of science. For the most part, development in a science moves in the direction indicated by the heavy vertical arrows. Description comes first, then prediction, and then perhaps control and understanding. Description, even in the absence of control or prediction, suggests at least some degree of understanding, hence the light arrow from description directly to understanding. In some instances, notably in astronomy, prediction may lead to some degree of understanding with little possibility of control, hence the direct arrow from prediction to understanding. Understanding greatly facilitates control and prediction, and to some extent facilitates even the most fundamental goal of description, as shown by the downward pointing arrows in the diagram. Thus, the goals of science interact with each other in a kind of positive feedback loop, facilitating and feeding on each other. To the scientist, understanding represents the most esthetically satisfying goal of all, and a highly useful goal in a purely practical sense. And now abideth description, predic-

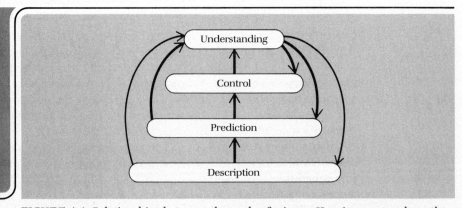

FIGURE 1-1. Relationships between the goals of science. Heavier arrows show the more usual pathways.

tion, control, and understanding, these four, and the greatest of these is understanding.

The Role of Measurement

We ordinarily think of description as a kind of verbal process whereby we attach words, as labels, to things. But numbers — as well as words — can serve as descriptions, and for many purposes, numbers provide much better descriptions than words. **Measurement** is simply the process of attaching numbers to things in meaningful ways. Many of the things we measure are quite concrete and can be measured in terms of physical dimensions such as length and weight, but other things, such as temperature, represent higher levels of abstraction. Temperature cannot be directly observed, but must be inferred from the length of a column of mercury or colored alcohol in a thermometer, or from some "pointer reading." Thus, temperature is an inference from the behavior of a thermometer in much the way that your judgment about what another person thinks or feels is an inference from the behavior of the person.

The oldest — and one of the most successful — of the sciences is astronomy. The field of astronomy has achieved a very high level of understanding, and we will briefly consider the course of its evolution from its humble beginnings as an essentially descriptive enterprise. Psychology and astronomy are very different, and yet we will see that there may be a common thread running through the two fields.

Description and Prediction in Astronomy

Good description is fundamental to achieving the other goals of science. To begin at the beginning, the first step in the oldest of the sciences was the description of the lighted objects in the heavens. The earliest descriptions were *qualitative,* that is, celestial bodies were classified into categories such as stars, tiny points of light that remained fixed relative to each other; planets, brighter objects that wandered about against the background of the fixed stars; and the sun and moon. Descriptions became increasingly *quantitative* as the science of astronomy developed. The brightness of the stars was measured with great precision, and the size, distance, and even the mass of the planets was determined. Prediction in astronomy has been highly successful for a very long time. No one is surprised to learn the precise path and time schedule of the next total eclipse of the sun. Such accurate predictions depend on highly accurate quantitative measurements of the celestial objects involved: The size of the moon and the sun, their distances from the earth and each other, and a great many other things.

Control and Understanding.   In a sense, we have even achieved a bit of control over some astronomical events. We have landed men on the moon, and we have placed artificial satellites in orbit around the earth, the moon, and at least three planets besides the earth as of this writing, so we have made some things happen at astronomical distances from the earth. Astronomers have also been successful in achieving, at least in part, the goal of understanding. We have come to understand that the earth is not the center of the universe—or even the solar system—but is instead a modest-sized planet revolving around a modest-sized star some distance from the center of a galaxy of 100 billion or so other stars.

Description and Prediction in Psychology

It is a long leap from astronomy to psychology, and yet there are many parallels between the development of the two fields. Description is fundamental in psychology, just as in astronomy. Before a study of the behavior and experience of organisms can proceed, the organisms and their behavior must be described. The earliest descriptions of people, like those of celestial bodies, were qualitative. The ancient Greeks recognized four personality types: *Choleric,* quick to anger; *melancholic,* sad; *phlegmatic,* slow, lethargic; and *sanguine,* warm, confident. Each personality type supposedly resulted from an excess of a particular body fluid, but the associations between personality types and the specific body fluids, which the Greeks hypothesized, have not held up in the light of later findings. Although the Greeks were better astronomers and mathematicians than physiological psychologists, it is none the less quite clear today that body chemistry—the action of hormones and the like—profoundly influences behavior.

Qualitative and Quantitative Descriptions.   We still make extensive use of *qualitative descriptions,* such as our categories of mental disorders—schizophrenia, manic-depressive psychosis, and so on—but as the study of behavior has progressed, descriptions have tended to become more and more *quantitative.* For example, counting the number of hallucinations a psychotic reports per day provides a quantitative description of one aspect of psychotic behavior. Changes in the number of reported hallucinations may provide a rather fine-grained description of a psychotic's behavior during the course of therapy. A declining frequency of such reports would indicate at the very least a quantitative change in *behavior,* though not necessarily a decrease in the hallucinations themselves.

We often describe people as bright, dull, or average when we observe them in situations where we suppose intelligent behavior is required. Broad classifications of this sort have proven useful, since we can predict to some extent that people who show intelligent behavior in one situation, perhaps in school, will *tend* to do so in other similar situations. For example, a bright student who handles numbers well in school would be more likely to be a successful accountant than a student who has chronic troubles with addition and subtraction.

Using only three descriptive categories—bright, dull, and average—represents a very coarse kind of classification. There may be great differences between people near the top of the average category and people near the bottom of that category. We might improve our predictions by dividing our very broad categories into narrower ones—for example, very bright and fairly bright, high average and low average, and so on. We could make our categories narrower still by attaching numbers to the students, based on their grades or on their performance on various standardized tests, such as scholastic aptitude, achievement, and IQ tests.[1] Using numbers provides us with very fine-grained descriptions of behavior, and the better our descriptions, the better predictions we can make, and the greater our progress toward understanding behavior. There is a very strong historical trend toward greater use of quantitative measurements in all of the sciences, and psychology is no exception in this respect.

Numbers and People

Research methods in psychology turn out to be quantitative methods. It sometimes comes as a surprise that numbers and measurement processes play such a large role in the field of psychology, and some students are dismayed as well as surprised. After a lecture by one of my colleagues, a student who had been teaching elementary school for some time said to the instructor, "You're trying to reduce people to a bunch of numbers, but my pupils are all real, flesh-and-blood children." I can admire that teacher's humane concern, but there is no necessary reason why numbers should be any more dehumanizing than any other kind of description. Indeed, since numbers provide finer-grained descriptions than some of our broader, coarser verbal categories, we could argue that numbers represent more precise, fairer, and thus more humane descriptions of people. Some time ago, E. L. Thorndike (1940) argued, essentially, that anything that exists at all exists in some quantity, and can therefore be measured. Extending Thorndike's argument, any human trait, behavior, experience, or desire that really exists can be measured. While we recognize the great difficulties in measuring such human attributes as personality traits, or even aptitudes and intelligence, quantitative methods have proven useful in psychology. The great success of the physical sciences is due in no small part to their skillful and widespread use of quantitative methods, and we have every reason to believe that such methods will continue yielding dividends in the field of psychology.

Some important human characteristics can be measured very easily. We can measure height and weight, for example, and we can attach numbers to

---

[1] Such psychological tests have received a rather bad press in recent years, partly because of their use in controversial employment situations and university admissions, and partly because of the role IQ measurements have played in the heredity-environment controversy. A special issue of the *American Psychologist* (Glaser & Bond, 1981) deals with many of those conceptual and practical problems in testing. At this stage, you will be able to appreciate some of those discussions, and the material on correlation and regression in Chapter 10 will give you additional insight.

people on these dimensions in highly meaningful ways. To say that a person is 76 inches tall and weighs 150 pounds conveys much more information than simply describing the person as tall and thin. Quantitative measurements greatly facilitate some kinds of comparisons that we can make between people, but there are pitfalls to be avoided. For example, we all know that a person six feet tall is 20% taller than a person five feet tall, and someone who weighs 200 pounds is twice as heavy as someone who weighs only 100 pounds. Those comparisons are obvious to all of us, but does a student who has a Scholastic Aptitude Test score of 600 have twice as much scholastic aptitude as a student having a score of 300? The answer here is, We don't know, *not* because of the poor quality of the test, but rather because of some characteristics of measurement scales. There are important differences between the measurement scales associated on the one hand with height and weight, and with many test measurements on the other. Some kinds of arithmetic operations cannot be performed on some scales, and as a result, measurement scales determine the kinds of arithmetic comparisons we can make and also determine the kinds of statistical procedures we can use.

Measurement Scales

There are four principal measurement scales with which we will be concerned (Stevens, 1951). The scales are described below, and they are listed in order in Table 1-1, where their systematic relationships may be more apparent. Moving upward through the list in Table 1-1, each scale has one more

TABLE 1-1.   Relationships between Measurement Scales: Each Higher-Level Scale Permits One More Operation Than the Next Lowest Scale.

		Permissible Operations			
Scale	*Classifying*	*Placing in Order*	*Determining Differences*	*Determining Ratios*	*Examples*
Ratio	X	X	X	X	Age, reaction time, height, weight, number of responses, Kelvin temperature
Interval	X	X	X		IQ, aptitude tests, calendar time, Fahrenheit and Celsius temperature
Ordinal	X	X			Preferences, or any set of ranks on any kind of measurements
Nominal	X				Sex, political party, ethnic group, many model numbers

attribute than the next lowest scale. Be sure to look at this table carefully after you have read the descriptions of the scales.

Nominal Scale.   Numbers on a **nominal measurement scale** are used simply as labels — identification tags. The nominal scale is nothing more than a set of *names,* or categories, which may be identified by numbers on occasion. For example, it might be convenient to use the number 1 to designate one of the sexes and the number 2 to designate the other, especially if we were using a computer to help tabulate or analyze data. Numbers used in this way have no more quantitative meaning than the letters F and M, or the geneticists' symbols ♀ and ♂. It would make little sense to describe a class made up of half men and half women as having an average sex of 1.5! Political party affiliation also represents a nominal scale. We could assign, for convenience, the numbers 1, 2, and 3 to Democrats, Republicans, and Independents, but again, the numbers merely stand for the names of categories. College majors, such as psychology, English, and electrical engineering comprise a nominal scale, and so does sex, as we have noted earlier. We can ask some interesting questions about relationships between these nominal variables. For example: Is there any relationship between sex and college major? And if there is a relationship — if a greater proportion of one sex is found in one field or another — what are the implications? We will develop some methods of answering questions of this nature and other kinds of questions involving nominal scales in later sections.

Ordinal Scale.   If we place the students in a graduating class in descending order of academic performance based on grades and assign to them the numbers 1, 2, . . . , N, then the numbers comprise an **ordinal scale.** The largest number, N, is assigned to the lowest ranking student and represents the lowest level of academic performance in that class. The numbers comprising an ordinal scale have some quantitative meaning, in that the students having higher ranks (smaller numbers) possess more of the attribute under consideration. Thus, values on an ordinal scale have the property of **transitivity;** that is, if student Smith is higher than Jones, and Jones is higher than Brown, then Smith is also higher than Brown. Suppose those three students rank 1, 2, and 3 in their class. Is there as much difference between Smith and Jones as between Jones and Brown? It is tempting to say yes, since the difference between the numbers 1 and 2 is exactly equal to the difference between 2 and 3, but we simply cannot answer the above question without more information — or perhaps at all, in any exacting sense. Rank in class is determined by calculating for each student a grade-point average (GPA) by assigning the number 4 to an A, 3 to a B, and so on, through a zero for an F. Different schools may use somewhat different methods, but the GPA is a quantitative index of academic performance, *as measured by grades.* Students in a graduating class are then placed in descending order of GPA and assigned ranks. Suppose our three students, above, constitute the entire graduating class of a very small school. Their hypothetical GPAs and ranks in class are shown in Table 1-2, and the data are shown graphically in Figure 1-2. On the GPA scale, the difference between Smith and Jones is much less than the difference between Jones and Brown, and thus the differences

TABLE 1-2.   GPA and Rank in Class for a Hypothetical Class of Three Students.

Name	GPA	Rank
Smith	3.90	1
Jones	3.80	2
Brown	2.10	3

between these students on the GPA scale do not compare closely with the corresponding differences between their ranks in class. If you knew only the ranks of the students, you would have no way of knowing that the first two are superb and nearly indistinguishable on GPA while the third is quite marginal. We can further illustrate this difficulty with an ordinal scale by considering the following questions: What would the ranks of these three students be if Brown were also a superb student with a GPA of 3.70; or if Smith and Jones had GPAs of only 2.3 and 2.2 respectively? Under those conditions the ranks would be unchanged. Thus, our ordinal scale is highly ambiguous, yielding identical ranks under widely differing conditions. However, ranks in a large graduating class ordinarily convey somewhat more information than the ranks in our very small, contrived example. But in no case could we say that a student ranking in the upper 10% of a class is twice as good a student as someone ranking in the upper 20%.

An ordinal scale does not necessarily consist of a set of ranked individuals in every case. For example, consider the following categories of juvenile crime and deliquency: Truancy, shoplifting, armed robbery. Those categories of misbehavior are arranged in increasing order of severity, and while we might assign to them the numbers 1, 2, and 3, we have no assurance that the difference between truancy and shoplifting is equal to the difference between shoplifting and armed robbery. Over a period of a year in any major city, we would expect to observe a large number of juveniles charged with each of the above offenses. Thus, a great many individuals would each level of such an ordinal scale, and in effect, there would be a great many ties in such a distribution.

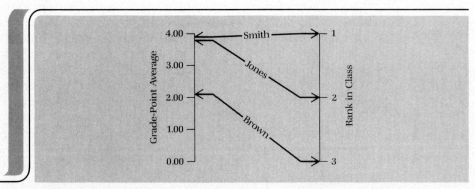

FIGURE 1-2. Relationships between grade-point average and rank in class.

Interval Scale.   Consider the years of the calendar. Did the same amount of time pass between the years 1900 and 1910 as between 1910 and 1920? The answer is yes, neglecting the very slight lengthening of the year by an amount principally of interest to astronomers and physicists. The years, which comprise the intervals of our calendar, are equal in length, and a scale having such equal intervals is called an **interval scale.** Now, consider another question. In 200 A.D., was the world twice as old as it was in 100 A.D.? Of course not, even though the number 200 is twice as large as 100. The fact that the earth already had *some* age at the time of the birth of Christ, the zero point on our calendar scale, keeps us from being able to answer questions about *ratios* between calendar years — that is, questions about how many times larger one number is than another. It matters not at all whether the age of the earth at the birth of Christ was closer to the cosmologists' estimate of about 5 billion years, or Archbishop Usher's estimate of 4,004. A zero point on a calendar scale is thus an **arbitrary zero,** and by this we mean that calendar time could be reckoned just as well from some other point, as long as people could agree on some other zero.

The Fahrenheit and Celsius (Centigrade) temperature scales are examples of other interval scales. Water freezes at 0° C and boils at sea level at 100° C, so the Celsius scale is more elegant in many respects than the Fahrenheit. Looking at the Celsius scale in Figure 1-3, it is tempting to suppose that 100° C is twice as hot as 50° C. But look at the corresponding temperatures on the Fahrenheit scale, where 212° F corresponds with 100° C, and 122° F with 50° C. We would certainly not make the mistake of supposing that 212° F is twice as hot as 122° F! The problem here is identical to the problem with our calendar time scale: The zero points on both temperature scales are arbitrary, so we cannot make ratio comparisons between temperatures on these scales. We could make up a great many other temperature scales, each having an arbitrary zero, if we cared to. For example, we could choose our human body temperature as a zero point for a new temperature

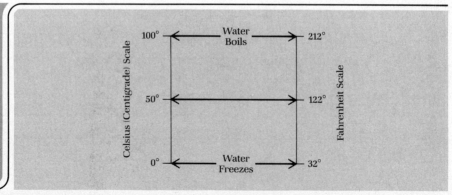

FIGURE 1-3. Some corresponding temperatures on two scales. Is 100° C twice as hot as 50° C? And is 212° F twice as hot as 122° F?

scale. We will offer some examples of psychological measurements on interval scales after we have presented the ratio scale, below.

Ratio Scale.   Some measurements allow us to make ratio comparisons between quantities. A person who weighs 200 pounds *is* twice as heavy as someone who weighs 100, and a person who has $200 indeed has twice as much money as someone who has only $100. These comparisons are possible because both money and weight represent ratio scales. The essential feature of a **ratio scale** is an **absolute,** or **meaningful zero,** that is, a zero point on the measurement scale that corresponds with zero amount of whatever is being measured. Zero money is no money at all, and zero weight means no weight at all. These absolute, meaningful zero points on ratio scales are very different from the arbitrary zeroes of interval scales. Does the zero of the Celsius thermometer scale correspond with zero amount of temperature? Certainly not, since the Fahrenheit zero represents *less* temperature than the Celsius zero. But neither does the Fahrenheit zero correspond with zero amount of temperature, since we often observe lower temperatures. However, the Kelvin, or absolute scale does have an absolute zero, which is equal to $-273.16°$ C. The freezing point of water on the Kelvin scale is $273.16°$ K, and the boiling point is $373.16°$ K. Absolute zero is the point at which molecular motion theoretically ceases, and in effect there is no more temperature left at that point. If you have had a course in chemistry or physics, you may remember that the Kelvin scale is very useful for some purposes.

Psychological Measurements on Interval and Ratio Scales

So far, our discussion of interval and ratio scales has been rather abstract, so we will now relate these scales to some psychological measurements. Consider an examination given in some course or other — perhaps an overly familiar kind of psychological measurement. If such a test is well constructed, the resulting scores constitute an interval scale *at best.* Why not a ratio scale? Isn't it true that a student who gets 80 questions right has indeed answered twice as many questions correctly as a student who gets only 40 right? And isn't it true that a student who gets a score of zero[1] has answered no questions at all correctly, so why doesn't that performance represent an absolute, meaningful zero? We can resolve some of these problems if we consider what it is that an examination is supposed to measure. In giving an exam, an instructor attempts to measure knowledge of the subject matter, or perhaps some sort of performance mastery. The examination is a sample of behavior from which we attempt to judge the amount of knowledge inside the student's head, and thus our judgment is an inference from the student's

---

[1] Perhaps the astute reader will recognize that I am not talking about a multiple-choice examination here, since the probability of a zero performance on such an examination of any substantial length is exceedingly small. We will have more to say on this topic later.

examination behavior. If a student gets a score of zero, can we draw the clear inference that his knowledge is zero? Maybe such a student knows *something* about the course—if only the instructor could find a sufficiently easy question to ask. The point is, we can never be sure that the zero point on an examination scale corresponds with an absolute zero amount of knowledge, so we are in no position to say that the student with a score of 80 is twice as good a student, or knows twice as much about the course, as the student with a score of 40.

Various standardized tests, such as scholastic aptitude, achievement, and IQ tests, also represent interval scales at best. The IQ test, like an examination in a course, does not have an absolute zero. A performance of zero on an IQ test would indeed represent a very low level of intelligence, but perhaps a person with a score of zero could demonstrate *some* level of performance if only the tester could find a sufficiently easy task. Since the IQ scale lacks an absolute zero, we could never say, for example, that a person with an IQ of 120 is twice as bright as someone with an IQ of 60. There is even some question of whether IQ measurements constitute an interval scale or the lower-caliber ordinal scale.

There are some psychological measurements that constitute ratio scales. Reaction time—the time between the presentation of a stimulus and the subject's response—represents a ratio scale, and so does the age of an organism. The preceding time scales represent elapsed time, and there are meaningful, absolute zeroes on both of these scales, while the scale of calendar time possesses only an arbitrary zero. It is true that a zero reaction time does not exist, since no organism can react instantaneously, but reaction times constitute a ratio scale, nevertheless. The zero on this scale is highly meaningful, and what it means is that zero on the scale corresponds with zero amount of reaction time. It matters not at all that we can never observe a zero reaction time, any more than it matters that we can never observe a person having a zero height. A person who requires 300 milliseconds to react to a stimulus is twice as slow as a person who requires only 150, just as a person six feet tall is twice as tall as a person three feet tall. Some other examples of ratio scales are the number of responses in an operant conditioning situation, the time required to learn a motor skill, and the number of nonsense syllables acquired in a verbal learning task.

Choosing a Measurement Scale.   If the ratio scale is the highest-caliber measurement scale, then why not use this scale for all our measurements? The answer should be clear: Some kinds of measurements do not have a meaningful, absolute zero, and we cannot simply decide to use a ratio scale unless our data meet this essential requirement. On the other hand, if our data do meet the requirements of the ratio scale, we could choose to use a lower-caliber measurement scale. For example, height is a ratio scale where the numbers are highly meaningful, but for some purposes it might be sufficient merely to take into account the order of people's heights, rather than their absolute magnitudes, or it might be sufficient simply to designate the people as short or tall. In the first case, we would have degraded our ratio scale to an ordinal scale, and in the second case, to a nominal scale. The calendar time scale is an interval scale, which historians often degrade to an ordinal scale (early, middle, late) or to a nominal scale (the Dark Ages, the Colonial Period, the Era of Good Feeling). The general principle is that any higher-level scale can be reduced to any lower-level scale. Referring to Table 1-1, any scale higher in this table can in effect be converted to any lower scale, since every higher scale contains all of the attributes of every lower scale. But we lose information when we degrade any of the higher measurement scales. Telling you the rank order of three people's heights conveys much less information than giving you the ratio scale measurements of 71, 68, and 62 inches. But for some purposes, when we may not be keenly interested in great precision, lower-caliber scales may be sufficient.

Observations and Experiments

A **variable** is a quantitative characteristic of a person, any other object, or event, that can take on different values. Gathering quantitative information — making measurements — thus consists of finding the values of one or more variables. Height and weight are variables that are measured on ratio scales, while sex, political party affiliation, and occupation are variables that are measured on nominal scales. As we noted earlier, nominal measurements are not quantitative in the same sense as higher-caliber measurements, but we will nevertheless find it useful to apply the term variable to any characteristic that can take on different values regardless of the kind of measurement scale.

There are two fundamental ways of gathering information: **Observation** is the process of measuring variables just as they occur in nature, without directly or deliberately influencing their values; and **experimentation** is the process of manipulating one or more variables in order to produce some possible effect. Thus, experimentation is a more active process than observation.

Observing Correlations

We can observe throughout the year that the temperature is related to the length of the day, higher temperatures being associated with longer days. Such a relationship between variables is called a **correlation.** Not every longer day in the spring or summer is necessarily warmer than every shorter day in the fall or winter, but in the main, there is a substantial correlation between the temperature variable and the length-of-day variable. There is also a substantial correlation between height and weight. Tall people tend to be heavier, though not every tall person is heavier than every short person. There is also a correlation between sex and height, although some women are taller than some men. We can also observe that students who perform better on tests of academic aptitude tend to perform better in school, though not every student who does well on such tests does well in school, nor does every student who does poorly on aptitude tests do poorly in school.

Correlation and Causality.   When we see a correlation between variables, we are often tempted to suppose that one of the variables causes the other. We are of course very much interested in questions of **causality** — questions of what we can do to control events, to produce desired results. But a correlation does not necessarily mean that one variable *causes* the other, that is, that either of the variables produces or leads to the other. The following example should serve to put you on guard against drawing causal inferences from correlations. Do you know there is a correlation between the rate of ice-cream consumption per day and the rate of drownings in the United States? As ice-cream consumption goes up, so do the number of drownings. Before you conclude that eating ice cream somehow interferes with a swimmer's ability to stay afloat, think of the relationship between ice-cream consumption, drownings, and a third variable — the time of year. More ice cream is consumed in the summer, and more people swim in the summer — and when more people swim, more drown. The lesson to be learned from our preposterous example is an important one: Correlation does not imply causality — that is, the existence of a correlation does not necessarily mean that either of the variables causes the other.

If we are unable to conclude that either variable causes the other when we observe a correlation, then it may appear that observing any relationship between variables is an idle exercise, but that is not the case. If there is a causal relationship between two variables, then there will be an observable correlation in most cases, and if there is no causal relationship, then there will be no correlation. Thus, the presence of a correlation is ambiguous, since the variables may or may not be causally related. But if there is no correlation between two variables, then we can draw the stronger, less ambiguous inference that there is *no* causal relationship — that is, that neither variable causes the other under the conditions prevailing at the time of our observations.

Correlational methods are used extensively in many areas of psychology, so we will have a great deal to say about correlation in later sections of this text. We will develop techniques of expressing the degree of relationship between variables in several ways.

The Experimental Method

The experimental method is surely one of the foundations of science. The process of manipulating things and observing the results has played a great role in the development of all of the sciences. For example, we have learned a great many useful things about the behavior of gases through experiments conducted over the last 300 years or more. As the experimenter raises the temperature of a gas, if its pressure is kept constant, then its volume increases. Further, as the temperature and volume of a gas increase, the density decreases, and thus a warm gas tends to rise. Outside the laboratory, rising masses of warm air produce many of our most important weather phenomena — often with great human consequences on a global scale.

Causal Inferences. In the gas experiment above, manipulating — changing — the temperature variable affects the volume variable, and the density as well. If the experimenter has directly changed only the temperature of the gas, then we can draw the inference — and here we mean the firm conclusion — that changing the temperature of a gas *causes* its volume to change. Strong inferences about causality can be drawn from experiments, in contrast with the much weaker inferences that can be drawn from observations.

Independent and Dependent Variables. The essence of the experimental method is the process of manipulating an **independent variable** and then measuring the resulting changes in a **dependent variable.** The values of the independent variable are manipulated — that is, assigned, or created — at the will of the experimenter, and those manipulations produce the resulting values of the dependent variable. Thus, the observed values of the dependent variable *depend* on the experimenter's choice of values of the independent variable. In the gas experiment described above, temperature is the independent variable and volume is a dependent variable. Since the density of a gas also changes as a function of temperature, we could also consider density as a dependent variable. In many experiments, manipulating a single independent variable produces changes in more than one dependent variable. When we observe that changing the value of an independent variable results in a change in a dependent variable, if everything else has been controlled, then we can conclude that the two variables are causally related.

The experimental method is used in virtually every area of psychology. In a learning experiment, for example, if the experimenter provides each of five different groups of subjects with a different amount of practice time on a learning task, then the subjects receiving greater amounts of practice will ordinarily perform better. In this experiment, the practice variable has been manipulated. The different **levels** — values — of the practice variable chosen by the experimenter result in different levels of performance; thus, practice is the independent variable and performance is the dependent variable.

Instead of providing different groups of subjects with different amounts of practice, an experimenter might use a single group of subjects. In that experimental design, the performance of each subject would be measured several times, after successively larger amounts of practice. In later chapters, we will discuss the relative merits of making repeated measurements on the same group of subjects versus the procedure of using independent groups, where each group receives a different level of the independent variable.

Some Final Words

As you read this text, and as you read anything in the field of psychology, try to keep the goals of science always in mind. Much of this chapter has been devoted to the measurement process, which plays an important part in achieving the fundamental goal of description and in achieving the higher goals of research as well. In later chapters, we will be concerned with carrying out observations and experiments in order to achieve the goals of prediction and control. Our ultimate concern is the goal of understanding, which is the highest goal of all. When all is said and done, the goals of scientific research are no different from the goals of any actively thinking person. The sole aim of this text is to provide some of the tools that can help you achieve those goals in the field of psychology, and perhaps in some other areas as well.

Technical Terms Used in This Chapter

All of the terms used in a technical sense in the present chapter are listed below. It is essential that you know these terms. Statistics, like every other subject matter, has a special vocabulary. The *ideas* of statistics and research methods — like the ideas of every other field — are expressed largely in *words,* even though we will make extensive use of mathematical symbols. Since words are the building blocks of ideas, if you are to understand the ideas presented in this text, you must first understand the words. To some extent, learning any new subject is similar to learning a new language. You may find it useful to write a brief definition for each of the terms listed below, and then check your definitions against those in the text. The terms are listed approximately in the order of their occurrence. You can also use the list of terms as an aid in the exercise of *comparing* and *contrasting* ideas — that is, in noting the ways in which ideas are similar and different. For example, what are the similarities and differences between ratio and interval scales, between experiments and observations, and between the fields of physics and psychology?

Behavior	**Testable hypothesis**
Experience	**Measurement**
Inference from behavior	**Nominal scale**
Research	**Ordinal scale**
Description	**Interval scale**
Prediction	**Ratio scale**
Control	**Transitivity**
Understanding	**Arbitrary zero**
Scientific method	**Absolute zero**
Science	**Meaningful zero**

Variable	**Causality**
Observation	**Independent variable**
Experimentation	**Dependent variable**
Correlation	**Level**

EXERCISES AND STUDY QUESTIONS

1. What do we mean by *qualitative* and *quantitative* description? What roles have these varieties of description played in psychology and in the other sciences?

2. What is arbitrary about an arbitrary zero on a measurement scale, and what is absolute about an absolute zero?

3. If a ratio scale represents the best, highest-caliber measurement scale, then why would a psychologist — or any other researcher — ever use one of the lower-grade scales?

4. In answering the following questions, identify the measurement scales, and briefly justify your answers:

   a. Is a man who weighs 230 pounds twice as heavy as a woman who weighs 115?

   b. Consider the Douglas DC-3, a very successful airplane that was the workhorse of commercial aviation for many years after its introduction in 1936. Now consider the DC-9, a widely used jet airliner at present. Is the DC-9 three times as large as the DC-3?

   c. In studying political party preference, a social psychologist assigns the number 0 to Independents, 1 to Democrats, and 2 to Republicans. Is there as much difference between Independents and Democrats as there is between Democrats and Republicans?

   d. The Boeing 727, 737, and 747 are three widely used airliners. Is there as much difference between a 727 and 737 as there is between a 737 and a 747? Is the difference between a 727 and a 747 *twice* as great as the difference between a 727 and a 737?

   e. Assuming that an IQ test measures intelligence, is a person with an IQ of 120 twice as intelligent as a person with an IQ of 60?

   f. Assuming that a course examination is a fair measure of what has been learned, does a student with a score of 80 know twice as much as a student with a score of 40?

   g. A rat in a Skinner box presses the bar at a rate of 5 presses per minute. Another rat presses at a rate of 10 presses per minute. Is the second rat pressing at twice as great a rate as the first?

   h. Are two pounds of feathers twice as heavy as one pound of lead?

   i. Consider the winners of the gold, silver, and bronze medals in an Olympic event. Is there as much difference between the performance of the gold and silver medalists as there is between the silver and bronze?

   j. In a visual reaction-time experiment, the experimenter flashes a light and the subject presses a button as quickly as possible. One person has a reaction time of 150 milliseconds, and another a reaction time of 300 milliseconds. Is the first person twice as fast as the second?

   k. In the above question, would it be possible to observe a reaction time of zero? What would such a reaction time mean, and what bearing would that have on your answer to the above question?

5. What is the principal advantage of experiments over observations? Given that advantage of experimentation, why would any researcher ever use any other method?

6. The population of the United States has grown substantially over many years, but the area of the country and our territories has remained essentially constant. Thus, the population density — that is, people per square mile — has increased substantially. The crime rate has also increased substantially, as measured by serious crimes per 1,000 people. Therefore, the increase in population density has been a factor in the increase in major crimes. Support, refute, or qualify that conclusion.

7. A cognitive psychologist is interested in assessing the effects of group size on problem solving. Subjects are given problems to solve under three conditions: (1) working alone; (2) in pairs; (3) in groups of three people. The psychologist notes the number of correct solutions under those conditions. Identify the independent and dependent variables in this experiment.

8. What do we mean by manipulating an independent variable, and why is this such an important idea?

Frequency Distributions: Graphical Methods

2

In the previous chapter, we saw that measurement — the process of attaching numbers to things in meaningful ways — was a kind of descriptive process. We discussed measurement scales largely in terms of their uses in describing individual people or things. In the present chapter, we will develop some graphical methods of presenting groups of measurements.

Groups

A **group** is a set of individuals sharing some common characteristic. The individuals in a **naturally occurring group,** for example, share a common characteristic such as age, sex, or occupation. In an **experimentally determined group,** the individuals share a common value of some independent variable assigned to them through the manipulations of an experimenter. The results of a great many kinds of observations and experiments consist of comparisons between groups — naturally occurring ones, or experimental and control groups manipulated by an experimenter.

A **frequency distribution** is a set of **scores,** measurements, on a group of subjects arranged so as to show the number of cases, or **frequency,** occurring within each region of the measurement scale. Frequency distributions provide the basis for all of the comparisons that we will make between different groups, and between different sets of measurements on the same group of subjects. As you will see, the field of statistics nearly reduces to the study of frequency distributions.

Samples and Populations

There are two fundamental reasons for our interest in groups. First, a group may be of interest in and of itself, as in the case of a specific class of students taking a specific course. Secondly, we often wish to consider a group as a **sample,** a subset of objects drawn from a **population,** which is the total set of things under consideration. A population might consist of all the people in the world, all the people in the United States, or indeed, any collection of people, animals, or other things that we might wish to consider.

Descriptive and Inferential Statistics.   The early chapters in this text are devoted principally to **descriptive statistics,** the process of determining the quantitative characteristics of samples. In later chapters, we will deal extensively with **inferential statistics,** the process of making judgments about populations based on observation of samples. No psychological study, or any other kind of research, has ever utilized as subjects all of the people in the world, so everything we think we know about the general principles of human behavior is based on the observation of samples. Indeed, our strongest motivation for conducting research is to learn things that we can apply to people in general — that is, things that we can generalize to a population.

Displaying Frequency Distributions

A frequency distribution can be presented in the form of a table or as a graph. Each kind of presentation has its own advantages, which we will point out shortly. We will use a great many graphs in this text, and you will find a great many in the psychological research literature, so it will pay you to look at each of our graphs carefully and thoughtfully. To paraphrase an old Chinese proverb, one graph can be worth a thousand words.

Role of the Measurement Scale

To a great extent, the measurement scale in a particular frequency distribution determines our choice of a graphical method of presentation — hence the organization of the remainder of this chapter. Graphical methods appropriate for use with the different measurement scales are presented below.

Nominal Scales

Bar Graphs. The various areas of the field of psychology, which are shown in Table 2-1, constitute a nominal scale. The scores on such a measurement scale are not at all quantitative, since they consist merely of the categories *Clinical, Experimental,* and so on. The numbers of psychologists

TABLE 2-1. Distribution of Psychologists in the United States by Specialty Areas in 1978.

Data from Stapp and Fulcher (1981). Copyright 1981 by the American Psychological Association. Adapted by permission of the publisher and author.

Specialty	Frequency	Percentage
Clinical	19,250	43%
Counseling	5,093	11
Educational	2,359	5
Experimental	2,208	5
Industrial	2,644	6
School	3,037	7
Social	1,886	4
Other	8,311	19
Total	44,788	100%

falling in the various categories are shown in the column headed *Frequency,* and the percentages of the group falling in those categories are shown in the *Percentage* column. Figure 2-1 shows the preceding data in the form of a **bar graph,** a display where the length of each bar represents the frequency, or the percentage of cases in each category. In that figure, the categories are listed in alphabetical order down the vertical dimension. Frequencies are shown along the horizontal dimension at the top of the graph, and percent-

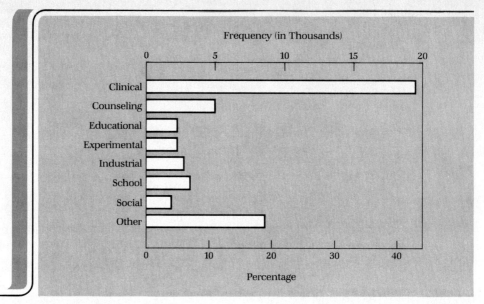

FIGURE 2-1. Bar graph showing American psychologists by specialty areas (data from Table 2-1).

ages along that dimension at the bottom. The gaps between bars are intended to indicate that the nominal scale is not a continuous dimension, but rather a set of discontinuous categories.

The bar graph in Figure 2-1 shows at a glance how the different areas of psychology compare in size. Table 2-1 shows the same information more precisely, in that frequencies are given to the nearest person, but for many purposes a bar graph offers a sufficiently precise presentation of the information.

There are a great many variations on the bar-graph theme. Sometimes the categories of the nominal scale are placed along the horizontal dimension and the frequencies along the vertical, and sometimes percentages or proportions are used instead of actual frequencies. In the popular press, rows of small human figures may be used to indicate the populations of different countries or census tracts, and stacks of symbolic coins may be used to indicate the income of different groups.

Pie Charts. Figure 2-2 shows the same data as the bar graph in Figure 2-1 in the form of a **pie chart.** In that display, the area of each **sector** — each slice of the pie — represents the percentage of cases in a given category.

To construct a pie chart, we need to consider the proportion of the area of a circle contained in any particular sector. The **central angle** of a sector is the angle between the two radii, that is, the angle at the point of the pie slice. The area of any sector is directly proportional to the central angle, and since there are 360 degrees of angle in a circle, the proportion of total area contained

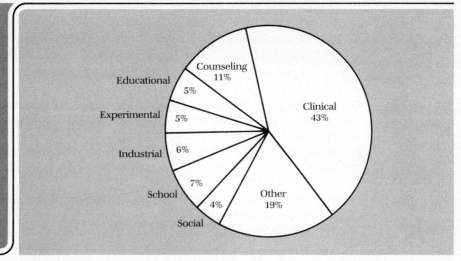

FIGURE 2-2. Pie chart showing American psychologists by specialty areas (same data as Figure 2-1 and Table 2-1).

in any sector is

$$\text{Proportion} = \frac{CA}{360},$$

where CA is the central angle of a sector in degrees. For example, a slice of pie having a central angle of $90°$ contains $90/360 = 1/4 = .25 = 25\%$ of the total pie. We can solve the above equation for the size of central angle needed to represent any given proportion. Thus,

$$CA = \text{Proportion}(360).$$

If we find the proportion of cases in each category in the frequency distribution by dividing each frequency by N, the total number of cases, then multiplying each proportion by 360 yields the central angle in degrees for the sector representing each category.

A pie chart may give a somewhat better picture of percentages or proportions than a bar graph does. However, bar graphs are more suitable where we are more concerned with actual numbers—frequencies—in a distribution and less concerned with percentages falling in the various categories. In most of the research literature, bar graphs are used more often than pie charts.

A Digression: Why Study Statistics?

To digress a bit, consider some of the implications of the data in Figures 2-1 and 2-2. Clinical psychology represents the largest specialty area in the field. Some clinical psychologists are members of university faculties, where they spend their time teaching and doing research, but most clinicians are either employed by agencies concerned with the treatment of mental disorders and behavioral problems or are employed in private clinical practice. In short, most clinical psychologists are concerned with helping people. Of what possible value could a number of courses in statistics and research methods be to a person who intends only to help people, and who has no intention of doing any research beyond whatever may be required to earn an advanced degree? And perhaps more to the point, what about the undergraduate student who has no intention of becoming a professional psychologist? Why should courses such as the one you are presently taking be required for all psychology majors? The answers to these questions are straightforward: Every professional psychologist and every psychology student as well is a *consumer* of research, though not always a *producer,* and to be an intelligent, critical consumer of research findings requires some knowledge and appreciation of how such findings are generated. We are swimming — if not drowning — in a flood of research findings from every field of science, some of which may have implications stretching beyond our imagination. As we will see, the facts do not always speak for themselves, but rather may require a considerable amount of interpretation. It behooves every thinking person to acquire some of the tools which are necessary for the critical interpretation of research findings.

Back to Graphical Methods: Drawing Some Conclusions

Returning to our development of graphical methods, Figure 2-3 shows a slightly more complicated bar graph showing the percentages of men and

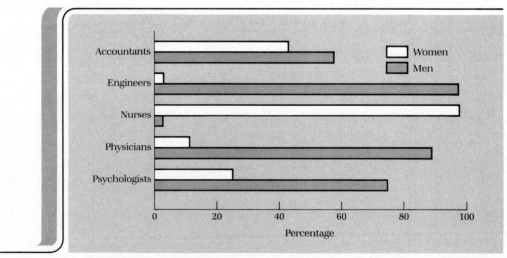

FIGURE 2-3. Bar graph showing distribution of professional people by sex and profession. Data from the *Statistical Abstract of the U. S., 1979,* and from National Research Council.

women in several different professions. We can see a number of things in this sample of professional people. Although the world's population is nearly equally divided between women and men, women are underrepresented in all of the professions in this sample except nursing. We can also see at a glance that there are proportionally fewer women in some professions than others. As an exercise in descriptive statistics, our bar graph is quite successful. Some important quantitative characteristics of a large sample of professional people are quite clear, but what do these things mean? Looking at the data—the facts—we might be tempted to conclude, for example, that the profession of psychology is less biased against women than is the engineering profession. But before reaching such a conclusion, we need to ask several questions. Is the difference between the representation of women in psychology and engineering **statistically significant**—that is, not merely due to chance? Questions of this sort, concerning the role of chance, fall within the domain of inferential statistics. We will deal extensively with such issues in later chapters, but for now, consider the following multiple-choice question:

Assume that women are indeed significantly better represented in psychology than engineering. What can we conclude on the basis of this observation?

A. Psychologists are less biased than engineers.
B. Women have little aptitude for engineering.
C. Girls are discouraged by society from developing interests in the kinds of studies that might prepare them for engineering careers.
D. In the absence of additional information, none of the above conclusions can be drawn.

We will answer the above question after the following brief discussion. The bar graph in Figure 2-3 shows the association between two variables, sex and profession. The sex variable is **dichotomous,** two-valued, while the profession variable has many values, each of which represents a category on a nominal measurement scale. Knowing one of these variables allows you to make an informed guess about the other. For example, if I tell you that a specific professional person is a man, then that person is much more likely to be a doctor than a nurse, or if I tell you that a person is an engineer, then that person is less likely to be a woman. But *why* are doctors men and nurses women, for the most part? Unfortunately, the information in our bar graph provides no answer to this question or to any similar question. A correlation between variables is well worth knowing about, and may suggest a great many other research questions, but as we have noted, a correlation offers no explanation of the *cause* of the relationship between variables. In the multiple-choice question, above, each of the first three choices represents a possible cause of the observed relationship between sex and profession, but since none of those conclusions is warranted *on the basis of the information in the bar graph,* choice D is the correct one. Based on other observations that we have all made, we may feel very strongly that choice C has a great deal of merit, but if we had no information beyond that presented in the bar graph, that conclusion—or any other besides choice D—would be unwarranted. This discussion has been a brief preview of some of the problems we will encounter in later chapters.

Ordinal Scales

A moment's reflection will convince you that it is not necessary to prepare any graphical frequency distribution for a set of ranks. Consider a class of students arranged in rank order. Since there is only one student per rank, each point on the scale has a frequency of one—ignoring for the present the possibility of tied ranks, a problem which we will deal with later. Thus, every set of ranks would have the same kind of frequency distribution, consisting of bars of unit height, so presenting such a distribution would serve no useful purpose.

In other situations, frequency distributions of ordinal data can be very useful. For example, arranging several categories of crimes in ascending order of severity yields an ordinal scale. A bar graph or pie chart showing the frequency or percentages of various crimes can be very informative. Any graphical method that is suitable for displaying nominal data can also be used with an ordinal scale.

Interval and Ratio Scales

Fortunately, the same graphical and numerical methods can be used with both of the above measurement scales. Table 2-2 shows a frequency distribution of examination scores in a class of several students. To prepare a frequency distribution of this sort, list the possible scores in descending order in Column 1, and then go through the class roll, marking a tally in Column 2 for each student alongside the appropriate score in Column 1. Each number in

TABLE 2-2. Frequency Distribution of Test Scores for a Class of 30 Students. (Data are shown graphically in Figures 2-4 through 2-6.)

Score X	Tally	Frequency f
22		
21	/	1
20		
19	//	2
18	~~////~~	5
17	~~////~~ /	6
16	~~////~~ ~~////~~	10
15	////	4
14	/	1
13	/	1
12		
		$N = 30 = \Sigma f$

Column 3 is the frequency, f, of occurrence of the particular score with which it is associated, that is, the number of times the score is represented in the distribution. It is very easy to make mistakes in handling data in this way, so you should cultivate very early the habit of checking your work carefully. There is a simple check that provides some indication of the accuracy of your work at this point: The sum of the numbers in the f column must equal the number of students who took the examination. We can express this relationship in the form of a simple equation:

$$\Sigma f = N, \tag{2-1}$$

where Σ (big Greek *sigma*) means that we sum — add up — all the values of f, and $N =$ the number of students. Σ is the **summation operator,** so do not make the mistake of supposing that Σf means Σ times f. We will deal more fully with summation operations in later sections, and we will also deal with the remaining columns and other aspects of Table 2-2.

Histograms. The tally column in Table 2-2 provides a kind of graphical representation of the frequency distribution, since each mark stands for one individual score, but the histogram in Figure 2-4 provides a better pictorial presentation. The scores are located on the horizontal axis, and the height of each bar indicates the frequency of each score. In a histogram, frequency is nearly always plotted on the vertical axis, although in many bar graphs frequency is often shown on the horizontal axis. The bars of a histogram are drawn immediately adjacent to each other because a histo-

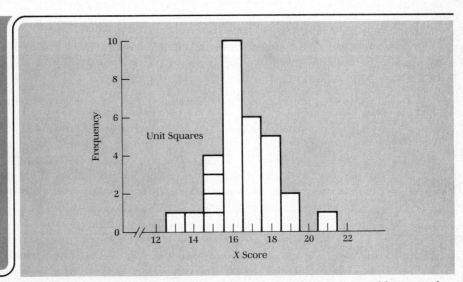

FIGURE 2-4. Histogram showing the frequency distribution from Table 2-2. Each small square associated with a score of 15 has a unit area, and thus the total area of the histogram is equal to 30, the total N of the distribution.

gram represents a frequency distribution associated with an interval or ratio scale, and there are no gaps between adjacent intervals on these scales. Each bar in this histogram can be considered as a stack of squares, where each square represents a single score in the distribution. The individual squares are shown for some of the scores in Figure 2-4, although this is not usually done. If each of the squares has a **unit area,** an area equal to 1.00, then the total area of the histogram is equal to N, the total number of scores. The proportion of scores falling above or below some particular score in a distribution is often of great interest, as we will see, and that proportion of scores is exactly equal to the proportion of the area of a histogram falling above or below the point of interest. For example, in Figure 2-4 we can readily see that about half of the scores are higher than 16.

In many cases, it will not be possible to represent each individual in a histogram by a square of unit area, since in a large distribution the resulting bars would be far too high to fit on a page. For example, if there were 300 students — rather than 30 — in the frequency distribution in Table 2-2, then in order to show that larger distribution in a histogram, we would need to compress the vertical scale considerably. The unit squares would then be compressed into flattened rectangles, each representing a single person in the distribution. If we consider each of those flattened rectangles as having a unit area, then the total area of the histogram is equal to N, no matter how large N may be, and no matter how much we may have compressed the vertical scale.

While the vertical scales of histograms and of other graphs are largely arbitrary, many writers have suggested following the **three-quarters rule,** a convention holding that the vertical extent of a graph should be about three-fourths as great as the horizontal extent. This convention represents no law of nature — or even of mathematics — and is often disregarded for one good reason or another, but the rule does provide a useful guide. Frequency distributions prepared in accordance with the three-quarters rule convey the most information with the least distortion, in most situations.

Frequency Polygons.   The histogram in Figure 2-4 is reproduced in Figure 2-5, where we have placed a dot at the midpoint of the top of each bar. We have also placed a dot on the horizontal axis at a score of 1, indicating a frequency of zero for that score. Connecting adjacent dots with a series of straight lines yields a **frequency polygon,** a many-sided closed figure. The straight lines cut off a number of triangular areas from the tops of the bars, but every such area exactly fits into a vacant area within the frequency polygon, as shown in Figure 2-5. Thus the area of the frequency polygon is exactly equal to the area of the histogram. Figure 2-6 shows the frequency polygon by itself. Notice that we have placed a dot on this horizontal axis just below the lowest score in the distribution and another just above the highest, thus indicating a frequency of zero for the two scores just outside the distribution. If these two points were not included, the frequency polygon would not be a closed figure having the same area as the histogram. We will very shortly develop a number of numerical methods of dealing with fre-

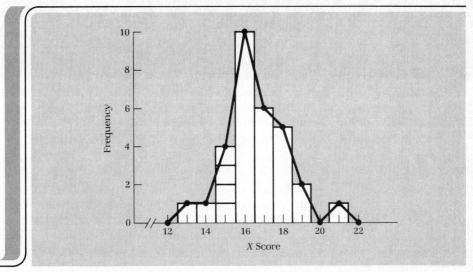

FIGURE 2-5. Same histogram as in Figure 2-4. Connecting the dots yields a frequency polygon. Each triangular portion of the histogram lying above and outside the frequency polygon exactly fits into a vacant area lying inside and below. Thus, the area of the frequency polygon is the same as that of the histogram.

quency distributions, but you will nevertheless often find it useful to work up a distribution in graphic form. A frequency polygon can be drawn more quickly than a histogram, and is therefore a more useful representation for many purposes.

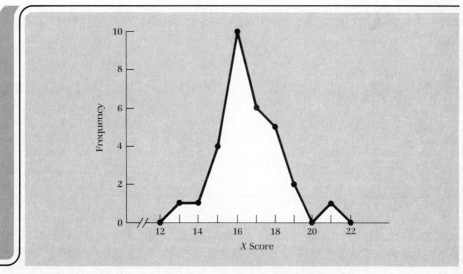

FIGURE 2-6. Frequency polygon in Figure 2-5 shown by itself.

A problem arises when the highest (or lowest) score actually occurring in a distribution is the highest (or lowest) score possible. For example, suppose that several students got perfect examination scores, say 20 out of 20 possible points on a multiple-choice examination. The frequency polygon for such a distribution is shown in Figure 2-7. It is unrealistic to place a dot on the horizontal axis indicating a zero frequency for a score of 21 points, since this might suggest that such a score would be possible. Thus, we are left with a frequency polygon that is not really a polygon at all, since it is not a closed figure, but this is usually preferable to incorporating an impossible score into our distribution.

Class Intervals.   In the frequency distributions we have considered so far, we have plotted the frequency of each score when constructing a histogram or frequency polygon. Sometimes it is more useful to group the scores into a number of **class intervals** of equal width, and then plot the frequency of scores falling within each of the class intervals. Figure 2-8 shows a distribution of scores where the histogram conveys little information about the shape of the distribution. A set of examination scores in a small class will often yield such a histogram.

If the scores in the above distribution are divided into class intervals of 30–39, 40–49, and so on, as in Figure 2-9, then the shape of the distribution becomes much more apparent. Scores near the middle of the distribution are much more frequent than scores near the ends, and this can be seen more readily when the scores are grouped into class intervals. As a rule, if the scores

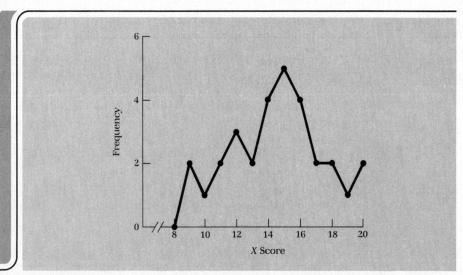

FIGURE 2-7. Frequency polygon where the highest possible score, 20, has a non-zero frequency. Strictly speaking, frequency polygon is a misnomer here, since the plot of this distribution does not form a closed figure.

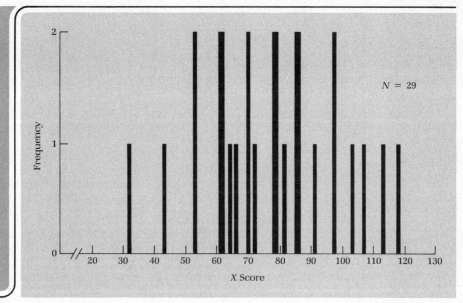

FIGURE 2-8. Histogram showing a distribution having a large number of units on the scoring scale and a small frequency for each score. The same distribution is replotted using class intervals in Figure 2-9. Which figure conveys more information about the shape of the distribution?

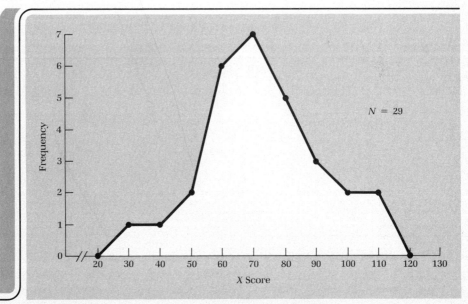

FIGURE 2-9. Frequency polygon showing the scores in Figure 2-8 grouped into class intervals. Compare this figure with that earlier one.

in a frequency distribution cover a range of a great many scale units, and if the frequency of each score is rather small — as in the present case — then it is useful to group the scores into class intervals before plotting the distribution. The scoring scale should be divided into about 9 to 11 class intervals of equal width, and thus the width of the class intervals will be determined by the number of units on the scoring scale. There is no hard-and-fast rule about the number of class intervals to use, but it turns out that about 9 to 11 intervals will often yield frequency polygons and histograms that are fairly easy to interpret.

A Stem-and-Leaf Display.   Figure 2-10 shows the same data as Figure 2-9 in the form of a **stem-and-leaf display** (Tukey, 1977). The numbers to the left of the vertical line represent the *tens* and *hundreds* places in the exam scores, and the digits to the right of the line are the *units*. The vertical scale represents the **stem** of the display, and each unit digit represents a **leaf** hanging on that stem. For example, there are six scores in the class interval 60–69, namely 61, 61, 62, 62, 64, and 66. Thus, the unit digits 1 and 2 are displayed twice in that class interval, and the digits 4 and 6 each appear once. Each unit digit — each leaf — occupies a unit area, and thus the total area of a stem-and-leaf display is equal to *N*, as is the area of a conventional histogram or frequency polygon. Indeed, you can think of a stem-and-leaf display as a **digital histogram,** if you prefer a more descriptive term.

The digital histogram in Figure 2-10 conveys as much information about the shape of the distribution as does the frequency polygon in Figure 2-9, and in addition gives the value of every individual score. For example, the frequency polygon has a height of 5 units at a score of 8, but that display gives

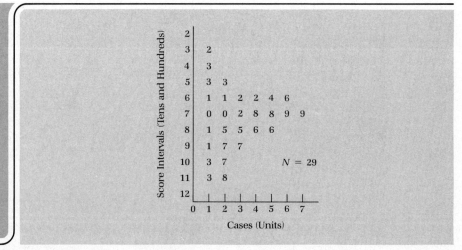

FIGURE 2-10. Stem-and-leaf display, or digital histogram (same data as in Figures 2-8 and 2-9).

no indication of the precise values of those 5 cases. On the other hand, the digital histogram gives the value of every case in the distribution.

A digital histogram is very easy to prepare. Begin by listing the *tens* and *hundreds* digits for the set of scores in descending order, as in Figure 2-10. Instead of merely tallying the number of instances of each score, list the value of the last digit for each case to the right of the vertical line, and then arrange those digits in ascending order as in Figure 2-10. For a number of other clever ways of displaying frequency distributions, see Tukey's book, *Exploratory Data Analysis.*

Some Distinctive Features of Frequency Distributions

The graph of a frequency distribution displays visually many of the characteristic features of the distribution. Like the features of the human face, those characteristics of frequency distributions often allow us to discriminate different distributions by visual inspection. The **central location** of a distribution is a point on the measurement scale that characterizes the middle, the center, of a distribution. Most of the scores in a frequency distribution tend to be found near the center, and indeed, measures of central location are often called measures of **central tendency.** The most commonly used measures of central location are the **mean, median,** and **mode,** in that order. The *mean* is a kind of average, the *median* is a point on the measurement scale that divides the cases in a distribution in half, and the *mode* is the most frequently occurring score. The next chapter describes those measures in detail.

In Figures 2-11A and 2-11B, as you can see by visual inspection, most of the scores in both distributions are located around a scale value of 5. Since 5 is the most frequently occurring score, the mode is equal to 5 in both of those distributions. The mean — symbolized $\overline{X}$ (read "X bar") — and the median are also equal to 5 in 2-11A and B. Thus, all three measures of central location are equal in those two distributions. But in other distributions in Figure 2-11, some of the measures of central location differ from each other.

Although the distributions in Figures 2-11A and B have identical measures of central location, those distributions certainly are not identical in all respects. Distribution A is more peaked, and B is flatter. More of the scores in Distribution A are closer to the central location, while the scores in B are spread over a larger range. Thus, Distributions A and B differ in terms of **dispersion,** the extent to which the scores spread out on the measurement scale. Figure 2-11B has the greater dispersion, since more of the scores are located farther from the center in that distribution. The **standard deviation,** symbolized *SD*, is a measure of dispersion described in detail in Chapter 4. The larger standard deviation of Distribution B reflects the greater degree of dispersion in that distribution.

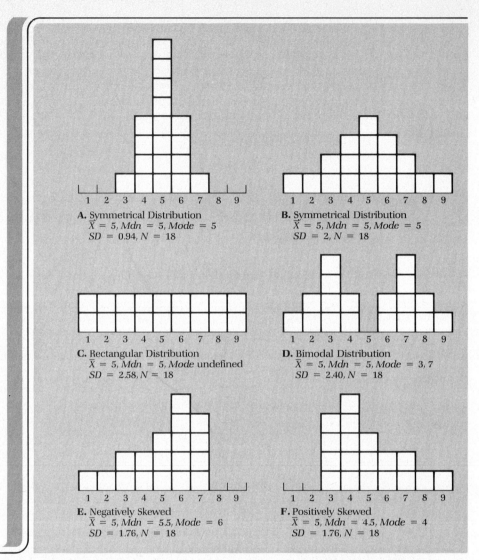

FIGURE 2-11. Several frequency distributions all having the same number of cases ($N = 18$) and the same mean ($\overline{X} = 5$) but different dispersions, as shown by the differing standard deviations (*SDs*). Shapes of distributions also differ greatly. Distributions **A** through **D** are symmetrical, **E** and **F** are asymmetrical.

The **shape of a distribution** has to do with whether the scores pile up at some point or other, or whether they may be essentially evenly distributed across the measurement scale. Figure 2-11A is relatively high-peaked, B is less so; C is a flat-topped, rectangular distribution; and D has two peaks, and is thus a **bimodal** distribution. All of the preceding distributions are symmetrical, since their left and right halves are mirror images of each other. In a symmetrical distribution having a single peak, the mean, median, and mode are all equal. The distributions in 2-11E and F are asymmetrical, and are said to be **skewed.** When the mean is smaller than the median (*Mdn*), the quantity $(\overline{X} - Mdn)$ is negative, and the distribution is said to be **negatively skewed,** as in 2-11E. When the mean is larger than the median, $(\overline{X} - Mdn)$ is positive, and the distribution is **positively skewed,** as in 2-11F. We will see later that the symmetry of some distributions is a very useful property. We will refer to Figure 2-11 several times in the next chapter, and we will provide better explanations of the measures of central location and dispersion than we have offered here.

Comparisons between Groups

We have already made some comparisons between two groups, professional men and women, in our discussion of Figure 2-3. In fact, that bar graph consists of two separate frequency distributions, one for men and one for women. Comparing two naturally occurring groups, such as men and women, constitutes an observation, as we defined that term in the last chapter. Comparing experimental and control groups, where one group has received a treatment of some kind and the other has not, constitutes an experiment. We will often have occasion to compare the frequency distributions of different groups using the graphical methods developed here and also using numerical methods, which we will develop later.

   In making comparisons between groups, we are really comparing features of different frequency distributions. We are usually interested in comparing measures of central location, but in order to do so we also need to take into account measures of dispersion. In the next two chapters, we will develop several numerical measures of central location and dispersion. In later chapters, we will use those measures in our development of inferential statistics, the methods of answering questions about differences between groups and about differences between observed and expected measurements.

Terms and Symbols Introduced in This Chapter

As we noted at the end of Chapter 1, learning the technical vocabulary is an essential step in understanding any subject matter. We have introduced a few symbols in the present chapter, and it is equally essential to learn the meaning of these symbols. Be sure that you can define each of the terms and symbols listed below. Check your definitions against the text. It is not necessary, or desirable, to parrot each definition word for word — indeed, it is better to be able to rephrase definitions in equivalent forms. You should also spend some time comparing and contrasting our terms and symbols. For example, how are the mean, median, and mode similar and different, and what are the similarities and differences between histograms, frequency polygons, and bar graphs?

Group	**Unit area**
Naturally occurring group	**Three-quarters rule**
Experimentally determined	**Frequency polygon**
group	**Class intervals**
Frequency distribution	**Central location**
Score	**Central tendency**
Frequency	**Mean, median,** and **mode**
Sample	**Dispersion**
Population	**Standard deviation**
Descriptive statistics	**Shape of a distribution**
Inferential statistics	**Bimodal**
Bar graph	**Positively** and **negatively**
Pie chart	**skewed**
Sector	Σ
Central angle	*f*
Statistically significant	*N*
Dichotomous	$\bar{X}$
Summation operator	*Mdn*
Histogram	*SD*

EXERCISES AND STUDY QUESTIONS

1. The following distributions are the heights in inches of a group of men and a group of women:

Men:	70	76	71	68	73	68	75	72	70	70	75	69	71	73	73	71	67	72	69	73	71
Women:	61	64	64	69	67	64	64	67	60	65	62	65	66	65	63	66					

Plot a histogram showing each distribution on the same axes. Notice that the distributions overlap.

2. Plot a frequency polygon showing each of the above distributions on the same axes, using different symbols for men and women. What are the relative advantages of frequency polygons versus histograms in this situation?

3. The following data on serious crimes against persons are from *Uniform Crime Reports for the United States, 1979,* published by the Federal Bureau of Investigation, Washington, D. C. The table shows the number of cases where guns were used or not used in three categories of major crimes. Draw a bar graph showing these data.

	Murder	Aggravated Assault	Robbery	Row Totals
Gun	13,582	141,269	185,352	340,203
No gun	7,874	472,944	281,529	762,347
Column totals	21,456	614,213	466,881	1,102,550

4. For each of the categories of crimes in the above data — murder, aggravated assault, robbery — find the percentages of crimes committed with and without a gun. Draw a bar graph showing those percentages, and compare with the bar graph showing frequencies of crimes in Exercise 3, above.

5. Is there any relationship, or association, between the category of crimes in the above data and the use of a gun? What is the nature of that association, if any? Which bar graph, the one showing frequencies or percentages, is most helpful in answering these questions?

6. Since murders are more frequently committed with guns, particularly with handguns, does the availability of guns lead to a greater number of murders? If we decreased the number of handguns, would the number of murders decrease? Or do those people who intend to commit murder merely seek out the most effective means of killing another person? In other words, do guns cause murder, or does the intent to murder cause a would-be killer to use a gun?

7. The National Institute of Mental Health reports the percentages of first admissions to mental hospitals falling in the following categories:

Alcoholic disorders	18%
Brain syndromes	11
Depressive disorders	10
Personality disorders	10
Schizophrenia	30
All others	21
	100%

Construct a pie chart showing the above data.

8. The scores below represent a distribution of examination points earned in a course, out of a total of 200 possible points.

159	121	85	157	147	129	144	150	144	128	107	171	116	109	164	95	190	152	180	169
92	168	147	150	189	126	147	135	145	118	126	105	138	133	143	153	168	112	124	

Show the distribution in the form of a digital histogram, or a stem-and-leaf display.

Measures of Central Location

3

The present chapter, like the last one, is really about frequency distributions. Visually inspecting frequency polygons and histograms can tell us a great deal about the important features of frequency distributions, but numerical methods allow us to develop refined measures of these features. In the present chapter, we will develop numerical measures of central location, and in the next chapter, we will develop measures of dispersion, another important aspect of frequency distributions.

The Principal Measures

As we noted earlier, the **central location** of a distribution is the point on the measurement scale around which most of the scores are found. The principal measures of central location are the **mean, median,** and **mode.** We will define each of these measures in one of the following sections. Each measure of central location is a kind of **average,** but each may convey somewhat different information about a frequency distribution. The mean is the most widely used measure, but in some situations we will see that the mean has some undesirable characteristics. The median, especially, and to some extent the mode, can be useful in some of those situations.

The concept of central location applies most directly to measurements on ratio and interval scales, and less directly to ordinal and nominal scales. We will discuss the role of the measurement scale in the interpretation of measures of central location after we have discussed those measures in detail.

Measures of central location can be directly calculated for samples, where every individual can be observed and measured. Such measures exist, of course, in populations, but we seldom have access to all of the members of a population. If we did, then we could in principle directly calculate the measures of central location, but in practice, we must usually estimate these measures from observed values in samples. We will deal with this estimation process, an exercise in inferential statistics, in later chapters. For the present, we will confine ourselves to finding measures of central location in samples where we know the value of every score.

The Mean

Consider the distribution of scores shown in Table 3-1. The scores represent different values of a variable which we will designate as X. The subscripts on

TABLE 3-1.   Ungrouped Distribution of Test Scores as They Might be Listed from an Alphabetical Class Roll.

Symbolic scores:	X_1	X_2	X_3	X_4	X_5	X_6	X_7	X_8	X_9
Observed values:	5	8	6	4	4	6	3	5	4

$$\bar{X} = \frac{\Sigma X}{N} = \frac{45}{9} = 5.00.$$

the Xs serve as identification tags, or serial numbers, and we will make use of these subscripts shortly. Notice that the subscripts are arranged in ascending order, but the values of the scores do not appear to be in any particular order. We might observe such an arrangement of scores if we simply listed test scores serially from an alphabetized class roll. The *mean* of a distribution is equal to the sum of the scores divided by the number of scores in the distribution. In symbols,

$$\text{Mean} = \overline{X} = \frac{\Sigma X}{N}, \tag{3-1}$$

where $\overline{X}$ (read "X bar") is the symbol for the mean, ΣX (read "sum X") is the sum of the scores, and N is the number of scores. Substituting values for the symbols in Equation 3-1 yields a mean of 5.00, as shown in the sample computation in Table 3-1. It is customary to compute a mean to two more decimal places than appear in the data, so we express our mean as 5.00 even though it has an integer value of 5.

Rounding. In most of the distributions of real data you will work with, the mean, median, and other statistics will seldom take on integer values — as they often have in the contrived distributions that we have used for illustrative purposes. Thus, it is usually necessary to round off statistics to some reasonable, manageable number of decimal places, customarily two more places than appear in the data. For example, examination scores are typically integers, whole numbers, and thus we would compute the mean to at least four decimal places and round off to two places. If you have access to an electronic calculator with a floating-decimal mode of operation, you should do all of your computations in this mode of operation. The calculator will usually give you many places to the right of the decimal, thus promoting a high degree of precision in your calculations. If you are doing calculations by hand, it is sufficient to carry out your calculations to two more places than the number you are going to retain in your final result. You can then round off your final result to the desired number of places. A decimal remainder less than 5 is dropped. The digit preceding a decimal remainder of more than 5 is rounded up to the next higher digit. For example, if we wish to round the number 4.385001 to two decimal places, since the decimal remainder, 5001, is greater than 5, we round up to 4.39, as in Table 3-2. What do we do with a remainder of exactly 5? If we always dropped such a remainder, or always

TABLE 3-2.   Some Examples of Rounding.

Computation:	23.1713	39.9851	4.385000	4.385001	4.375000	0.1250	0.2950
Rounded:	23.17	39.99	4.38	4.39	4.38	0.12	0.30

rounded up, we would introduce a slight bias into our results over the long run. We can avoid this bias by adopting the following convention: A remainder of exactly 5 is dropped if the preceding digit is even, and if odd, the preceding digit is rounded up. Thus, half the time we will drop a remainder of exactly 5, and half the time we will round up. Table 3-2 shows some examples of rounding.

Summation Operations.   Notice that the sum of the scores in Table 3-1 is equal to 45, which is the sum of *all* the individual scores in the distribution. Some of the scores occur more than once, and each score is added into the sum as many times as it occurs in the distribution. Finding ΣX by adding each score as many times as it occurs is easy in a small distribution, but more tedious in larger ones. There is a better method of finding the mean of a larger frequency distribution, but in order to develop this method, we will need to delve a bit more deeply into summation operations. We are going to formalize the summation operations we have carried out thus far, and our motive in doing so is not to make something very simple into something complicated, but rather to lay the groundwork for the extensive use we will make of summation operations.

The summation of a set of scores can be represented as follows:

$$\sum_{i=1}^{N} X_i = X_1 + X_2 + X_3 + \cdots + X_N. \tag{3-2}$$

Each of the Xs in the above equation — each of the individual scores — is identified by a subscript representing a specific value of the **index of summation**, i. The summation operator instructs us to add up the values of X associated with all of the values of the index of summation, beginning with the first value of the index, 1, and continuing through its last value, N. The dots, above, represent scores that are present in the distribution but omitted from our listing. The values of any such omitted scores are of course used in finding the sum of the distribution. Equation 3-2 is read, "The sum from $i = 1$ through N of X sub i is equal to X_1 plus X_2 plus X_3 plus the remaining values of X through X sub N." Substituting the values from Table 3-1 in the above equation yields

$$\sum_{i=1}^{9} X_i = 5 + 8 + 6 + 4 + 4 + 6 + 3 + 5 + 4 = 45.$$

A simple listing of individual scores, as in Table 3-1, represents a set of **ungrouped data.** If the frequencies of the scores are tabulated, as in Table 3-3, then we have a set of **grouped data.** Formula 3-1 is convenient for finding the mean of a fairly small ungrouped distribution, but larger frequency distributions can be handled more conveniently if they are first arranged in the form of grouped data. We will derive a formula for finding the mean of a set of grouped data, and we will illustrate some additional principles of summation in the process.

We begin by arranging the individual scores in our distribution in ascending order and collecting terms:

$$\sum_{i=1}^{9} X_i = 3 + 4 + 4 + 4 + 5 + 5 + 6 + 6 + 8$$

$$= 1(3) + 3(4) + 2(5) + 2(6) + 1(8) = 45. \tag{3-3}$$

TABLE 3-3. Grouped Distribution of Test Scores (same data as Figure 3-1).

Index of Summation j	Score X_j	Simple Frequency f_j	Cumulative Frequency cf_j	Frequency Times Score $f_j X_j$
5	8	1	9	8
4	6	2	8	12
3	$X_{LL} = 4.5$ 5	$f_w = 2$	6	10
2	4	3	$cf_b = 4$	12
1	3	1	1	3

$$\sum_{j=1}^{5} f_j = N = 9 \qquad\qquad \sum_{j=1}^{5} f_j X_j = 45$$

By Formula 3-5,

$$\overline{X} = \frac{\sum_{j=1}^{m} f_j X_j}{N} = \frac{\sum_{j=1}^{5} f_j X_j}{9} = \frac{45}{9} = 5.00.$$

By Formula 3-7,

$$Mdn = X_{LL} + i\left(\frac{\frac{N}{2} - cf_b}{f_w}\right) = 4.5 + 1\left(\frac{\frac{9}{2} - 4}{2}\right) = 4.5 + \frac{.5}{2} = 4.75,$$

where X_{LL} = Lower limit of interval containing median,

f_w = Frequency within interval containing median,

cf_b = Cumulative frequency below interval containing median,

and i = Interval width (here, $i = 1$).

Each of the multipliers in the above equation is the frequency of occurrence of a particular value of X, that is, a particular score value. In general — and by this we mean *ever and always,* not just "most of the time," as in everyday speech — we can express the sum of a set of scores as

$$f_1 X_1 + f_2 X_2 + f_3 X_3 + \cdots + f_m X_m = \sum_{j=1}^{m} f_j X_j. \qquad (3\text{-}4)$$

The Xs in Equation 3-4 no longer stand for individual **cases** — the scores of specific individuals — as previously. Instead, the Xs here represent the different **values** of scores — the different values of the variable X — which occur in the distribution. For example, even though Smith and Jones both may have scores of 5, the value of their score appears only once in Equation 3-3, where it is multiplied by two. In general, each value of X occuring in a distribution appears only once in Equation 3-4, where it is multiplied by the frequency, f_j, of cases having that value. We have used a different index of summation, j rather than i, to help indicate that we are summing across different values of X rather than across individual scores, as previously. The maximum value, m, of the index of summation will always be less than N, the total number of individual cases, since some scores occur more than once in a set of grouped data. The summation operator in Equation 3-4 instructs us to multiply each value of X by its frequency and to sum the values of these products across all of the m different values of X. Each f is listed in the third column of Table 3-3, and each of the products, f_jX_j, appears in the last column of that table.

By definition, the mean is the sum of a set of scores divided by the number of scores. Since we have developed an expression for the sum of a set of grouped data, Equation 3-4, we can now derive the formula for the mean by dividing that expression by N:

$$\bar{X} = \frac{\sum_{j=1}^{m} f_jX_j}{N}. \tag{3-5}$$

There is a sample computation of the mean using the above formula in Table 3-3. The computation of the median, also shown in Table 3-3, will be explained in a later section.

Ordinarily, when there is no likelihood of confusion, we will drop the index of summation and the subscripts and write the above formula as

$$\bar{X} = \frac{\sum fX}{N}. \tag{3-6}$$

However, it will sometimes be necessary to use the complete, formal summation notation when we are developing new ideas. I emphasize that we will do this not to make simple things complicated, but rather to set out as clearly as possible the ideas we will develop.

For distributions that are small or of moderate size, the ungrouped procedure for finding the mean is at least as convenient as the grouped-data procedure using Formula 3-5 or 3-6. If you have a small calculator, Formula 3-1 works well for moderate-sized distributions, even though each score must be entered as many times as it occurs. However, an exercise at the end of the chapter will make clear the value of the grouped-data procedure in a large distribution — actually, a *huge* one — where entering each score individually would be out of the question for human hands using paper and pencil or a small calculator. Of course, a large-scale computer can easily handle large sets of data using ungrouped procedures.

The Median

The *median* is that point on a scale of scores which divides the cases in a distribution into numerically equal upper and lower halves. There are as many scores above the median as below, so in a sense, the median represents the midpoint of a distribution. Consider the three distributions shown in Table 3-4. These distributions are identical, except for the highest score in each. The scores in each distribution are arranged in ascending order, and in each case the median is 4, since there are as many scores above as below a score of 4. We defined the median, above, as a *point* on a scoring scale, and while it happens that the median in each of the distributions in Table 3-4 corresponds with a score of 4, we will see shortly that the median in some cases does not correspond with any score found in distribution.

TABLE 3-4.   Three Distributions Differing Only in Their Extreme Scores. Mean of Each Distribution is Influenced by a Single Extreme Score, but Median is Not.

Distribution	X_1	X_2	X_3	X_4	X_5	$\overline{X}$	Mdn
1	1	2	4	5	8	4	4
2	1	2	4	5	23	7	4
3	1	2	4	5	148	32	4

The means as well as medians are listed in Table 3-4. While the medians are identical for the three distributions, the means differ considerably. The differences between means are due to a single extreme score in each distribution. The mean is greatly influenced by a single extreme score, while the median is not influenced at all. In the case of Distribution 3, especially, the median may provide a better indication of the central location than the mean provides.

Finding the median is very easy in distributions where each score occurs only once, as in Table 3-4. Arrange the scores in ascending order, and if there are an odd number, then the median is the middle score. If there are an even number of scores, as below, then the median

$$2 \quad 4 \quad 5 \quad 9$$
$$\uparrow$$
$$Mdn = 4.5$$

lies halfway between the two scores closest to the middle of the distribution. In this case, the median corresponds with a point on the scoring scale, 4.5, rather than with any score actually found in the distribution. Remember that it is always necessary to arrange the scores in numerical order in finding the median. It would make no sense at all to list the scores serially from a class roll in alphabetic order and then take the midpoint of such a list as the median.

Most of the frequency distributions you will have occasion to work with will be in the form of grouped data, since there will usually be several identical scores in a distribution of any size. We will develop methods of finding the median of a set of grouped data. The data from Table 3-3 are shown in another way in Figure 3-1 (top). Suppose the data represent test scores that can take on integer values only. A variable whose possible values are separated by finite steps—such as whole numbers, or some smaller or larger interval—is a **discrete variable,** as opposed to a **continuous variable,** whose possible values may be infinitely close together.

The underlying achievement variable, which we attempt to measure with our discrete test scores, is no doubt a continuous variable in the way that height is continuous, even though we typically measure height in discrete inches. The height of a person 67.3 inches tall is typically rounded down to 67 inches, and a height of 66.8 inches is rounded up to 67 inches. Consider the two students who made scores of 5. If achievement is a continuous variable, then these two students probably differ slightly in achievement, just as two people who give their height as 67 inches are probably not *exactly* the same

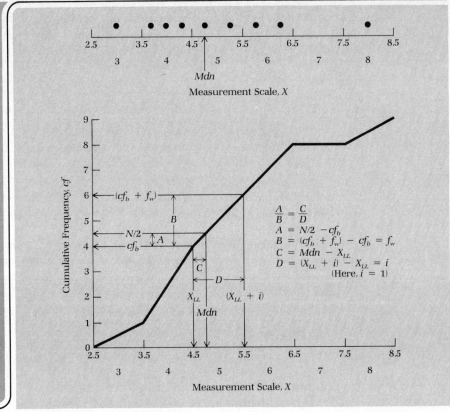

FIGURE 3-1. Same distribution as in Table 3-3. Top: Each dot represents one individual. All individuals having the same score are regarded as evenly distributed through that score interval. Bottom: Cumulative frequency at the limits of score intervals. *A, B, C,* and *D* are lengths of line segments. Other symbols are defined in Table 3-3 and in text. Median is found by interpolation.

height. It is useful to consider the score of 5 as an interval extending from exactly 4.5 to 5.5, and to consider our two students as evenly distributed through this **score interval,** as shown in Figure 3-1 (top). Every score is regarded as an interval extending from a **lower limit** of .5 below to an **upper limit** of .5 above the value of the score, and all of the cases falling within a given score interval are regarded as evenly distributed through that interval. The median, then, is 4.75, the measurement scale value associated with the fifth student in the distribution, since there are a total of nine students. This method of finding the median will always work, but since it becomes tedious with larger distributions, we will develop a general formula for finding the median of a set of grouped data.

In Table 3-3, the **cumulative frequency, cf_j,** associated with any score is equal to the number of cases in that score interval, the **simple frequency, f_j,** plus the number falling below the interval. Thus, the cumulative frequency associated with a particular score is equal to the number of scores that are less than or equal to the particular score. Column 4 in Table 3-3 shows the cumulative frequency associated with each score in our distribution. To find these cumulative frequencies, start with the lowest score in the distribution. Since there are no scores below the lowest score, its cumulative frequency is the same as its simple frequency. The cumulative frequency of each successively higher score is found by adding its simple frequency to the cumulative frequency of the score just below. Note that the cumulative frequency of the highest score in any distribution is always equal to N. In formal terms, the cumulative frequency, cf_k, associated with any score, X_k, is

$$cf_k = f_k + cf_{(k-1)} = \sum_{j=1}^{k} f_j.$$

Since the median divides a distribution into an upper and lower half, the cumulative frequency at the median is exactly $N/2$. Referring to the cumulative frequency column in Table 3-3, we can see that the median must lie somewhere in the score interval from 4.5 to 5.5, since the cumulative frequency below that interval, cf_b, is equal to four — less than half the cases — and the cumulative frequency through the interval itself is equal to six — more than half the cases. Thus, the interval containing the median is the lowest interval within which the cumulative frequency, cf, exceeds $N/2$. The lower limit of that interval is X_{LL}, and the upper limit is $(X_{LL} + i)$, where i is the interval width. Referring to Figure 3-1, our problem is to find the median by interpolation, that is, to find that point on the measurement scale between X_{LL} and $(X_{LL} + i)$ where the cumulative frequency is exactly $N/2$. We can write the following proportionality between the lengths of the line segments shown in Figure 3-1:

$$\frac{A}{B} = \frac{C}{D}.$$

Line segments A and B represent distance on the cumulative frequency scale, and C and D distances on the measurement scale, the scale of scores. Substituting, from Figure 3-1,

$$\frac{\frac{N}{2} - cf_b}{f_w} = \frac{Mdn - X_{LL}}{i},$$

where f_w is the simple frequency in the interval containing the median. Solving for the median yields our general formula:

$$i\left(\frac{\frac{N}{2} - cf_b}{f_w}\right) = Mdn - X_{LL},$$

$$Mdn = X_{LL} + i\left(\frac{\frac{N}{2} - cf_b}{f_w}\right), \qquad \text{where } f_w \neq 0. \tag{3-7}$$

Formula 3-7 cannot be used if the frequency in the interval containing the median is zero, since division by zero is not a permissible operation (see Appendix A on that point). If f_w is equal to zero, then the median is simply the midpoint of the interval containing the zero frequency. Some examples will be given shortly.

Table 3-3 demonstrates the computation of the median using the above formula. In that distribution, the interval width i is equal to 1, and could thus be disregarded in using Formula 3-7, since i appears as a multiplier in that formula. But where scores are grouped into class intervals, as in Table 3-5, the interval width must be used in that formula. Table 3-5 demonstrates the

TABLE 3-5.   Computing the Mean and Median of a Distribution Grouped into Class Intervals.

Index of Summation j	Class Interval $i = 3$	Midpoint of Interval X_j	Simple Frequency of Interval f_j	Cumulative Frequency of Interval cf_j	Frequency Times Midpoint $f_j X_j$
6	16 – 18	17	1	13	17
5	13 – 15	14	2	12	28
4	10 – 12	11	3	10	33
3	7 – 9	$X_m = 8$	$f_w = 4$	7	32
2	4 – 6	5	2	$cf_b = 3$	10
1	1 – 3	2	1	1	2

$X_{LL} = 6.5$

$$\sum_{j=1}^{6} f_j = N = 13 \qquad\qquad \sum_{j=1}^{6} f_j X_j = 122$$

Here, X_j = midpoint of class interval,
and X_m = midpoint of interval containing the median.
By Formula 3-5

$$\overline{X} = \frac{\sum_{j=1}^{k} f_j X_j}{N} = \frac{\sum_{j=1}^{6} f_j X_j}{13} = \frac{122}{13} = 9.38.$$

By Formula 3-7,

$$Mdn = X_{LL} + i\left(\frac{\frac{N}{2} - cf_b}{f_w}\right) = 6.5 + 3\left(\frac{\frac{13}{2} - 3}{4}\right) = 6.5 + 3\left(\frac{3.5}{4}\right) = 9.12.$$

computation of the median where the interval width is 3. The lower limit, X_{LL}, of the interval containing the median is .5 below the lowermost score in that interval. Another way of finding X_{LL} is to use the following formula:

$$X_{LL} = X_m - \frac{1}{2}(i), \tag{3-8}$$

where X_m is the midpoint of the interval containing the median. This formula provides a check on the value of X_{LL} as found by the previously described method. Formula 3-8, in conjunction with Formula 3-7, also makes it possible to find the median of a distribution where i is less than 1, as for example, in a distribution of reaction times measured to the nearest .01 second and a distribution of heights measured to the nearest .5 inch.

We can also compute the mean of a distribution grouped into class intervals of any size, including sizes less than 1. Referring to Table 3-5, multiply the midpoint of each class interval by the frequency of scores falling in that interval, sum the resulting products, and divide by N. Table 3-5 demonstrates that procedure.

If you have access to the frequencies of individual scores, it is better to use such a distribution for all computations. When we carry out computations using class intervals, we must make the assumption that the scores are evenly distributed throughout each class interval, just as we made the earlier assumption that the scores were evenly distributed through score intervals, as in Figure 3-1. But when we group a distribution of individual scores into class intervals, we can often see that some of the scores are *not* evenly distributed through some of the class intervals. In such a case, the mean computed by using class intervals will differ from the mean computed by using individual scores. And if the scores are not evenly distributed through the class interval containing the median, then the class-interval median will differ from the individual-score median. While class intervals are very useful for graphical representations, we lose some of the detailed information in a frequency distribution when we use class intervals, and hence our computations suffer a loss of precision. You should always use the best data available for any computations.

It is sometimes possible, even with grouped data, to find the median by inspection, but it is seldom possible to find the mean so easily. Table 3-6 shows four distributions where the median can be found easily without using Formula 3-7. Indeed, in some of these cases, the formula could not be used

TABLE 3-6. Finding the Median by Inspection in Four Distributions.

Score X_j	Distribution 1 f_j	Distribution 2 f_j	Distribution 3 f_j	Distribution 4 f_j
12		2	1	1
11		1		2
10	1	4	2	
9		3		1
8	1	5 $\quad Mdn = 7.5$	1	
7	2	6	$Mdn = 7$	3
6	$Mdn = 6 \quad$ 1	4	3	
5	3	2		$Mdn = 5.5$
4	1	2		2
3		1	1	3
2				1
1				1
	$N = 9$	$N = 30$	$N = 8$	$N = 14$

without modification. There is no problem in applying the formula to Distribution 1, although it is unnecessary. But in Distribution 2, the median falls at 7.5, which is a point defining the limit of two score intervals. In order to use our formula, we have to determine X_{LL}, the lower limit of the interval containing the median — but which interval is this, 6.5–7.5 or 7.5–8.5? We noted earlier that the interval containing the median is the lowest interval where the cumulative frequency exceeds $N/2$, and by this criterion 7.5–8.5 is that interval. In Distribution 3, there is an empty interval, 6.5–7.5, below which — and above which — 50% of the scores are found. This empty interval thus divides the distribution in half, and its midpoint is the median. Using Formula 3-7 here would lead to disaster, through division by zero, a forbidden operation yielding mathematical nonsense. The same problem arises in Distribution 4, where the median lies within an empty interval from 4.5–6.5. Where Formula 3-7 cannot be applied, the median can be found easily by inspecting the cumulative frequencies.

Comparing the Mean and Median

The mean and median are always equal in symmetrical distributions but may differ considerably in asymmetrical ones. Figure 2-11 shows a number of distributions where the mean and median are sometimes the same and sometimes different. We have seen in Table 3-4 that a single extreme score can result in a great difference between these measures. In concrete terms, the contrived distribution in Table 3-7 shows how the mean and median income

TABLE 3-7.   Distribution of Earnings in a Small Business.

		Employee		
1	2	3	4	5
$8,000	$9,000	$10,000	$11,000	$62,000
	Mdn =	$10,000	$\bar{X}$ =	$20,000

can differ in a small business where one employee, perhaps a highly successful salesman, has an extremely high income. In such a case, the difference between these two measures of central location might lead to some interesting misunderstandings about the "average" earnings of workers in this small business. Most of the workers — all but the highly paid salesman — might argue that they were grossly underpaid. But the owner might point out that the mean income was $20,000, which might be substantially above the industry-wide mean. A worker could argue, however, that the median of $10,000 in this case more properly reflects the earnings of the "average" worker. Perhaps our contrived example merely confirms what you have long suspected — that anyone with an axe to grind can always support his position with a well-chosen statistic. Who is correct here, labor or management? The answer is, neither in one sense, and both in another. Both are using perfectly correct — but different — measures of central location, but neither is conveying a complete picture of the distribution of earnings in that small business.

Skewed Distributions. Figure 3-2 shows an example drawn from the real world, the number of children under age 18, living at home, in the 1980 U.S. Census. The distribution is quite asymmetrical, and the mean and median differ greatly. As mentioned in Chapter 2, such a distribution is said to be *skewed*, and the direction of skew is in the direction of the long tail of the distribution. When the long tail is to the right, toward the high end of the measurement scale, a distribution is **positively skewed,** and when the long tail is to the left, a distribution is **negatively skewed.** In a more formal sense, a skew results when extreme scores displace the mean away from the median. The sign of the skew — positive or negative — is determined by subtracting the median from the mean, always in that order, as below:

$$\text{Skew} = \bar{X} - Mdn. \tag{3-9}$$

We will be principally concerned with determining the sign of the skew, and for our purposes, Formula 3-9 will be sufficient. But there are more elegant methods for finding the quantitative degree of skew, which are described in more advanced texts.

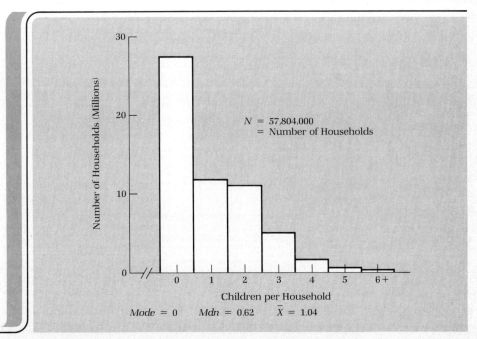

FIGURE 3-2. Children under 18 years of age living at home (data from U.S. Census of 1980).

Some Physical Analogies.   Figure 2-11, in the last chapter, shows two skewed distributions in the form of histograms. Notice that in each case the median exactly divides the area of the distribution into equal upper and lower halves, as it must, since the area of a histogram or frequency polygon is proportional to the number of cases in the distribution. Suppose we constructed a physical model of the distribution in Figure 2-11E, by stacking blocks on a long board, letting each block represent one of the cases in the frequency distribution. Such a model is illustrated in Figure 3-3. If we balanced the board — like a see-saw, or laboratory balance — we would find that the **balance point** corresponds precisely with the mean. Since the median divides the number of cases exactly in half, it may seem surprising that the median is not the balance point in this skewed distribution. But it will be easy to show a little later that the mean is the balance point. Indeed, we leave the proof of this weighty principle as an exercise at the end of Chapter 4.

The Mode

This measure of central location is the most frequently occurring score in a distribution. Thus, the mode always corresponds to an actual score found in a distribution, while the mean and median do not necessarily represent actual scores. More often than not, these last two measures of central tendency will take noninteger values even in discrete distributions. For example, in Figure 3-2, the mean number of children at home is 1.04, and the median is 0.62. But,

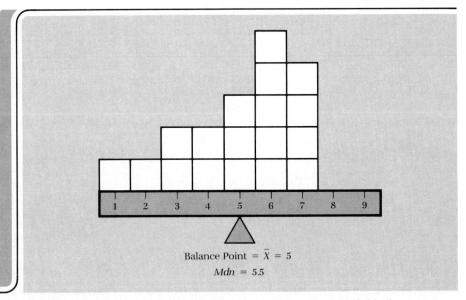

FIGURE 3-3. Physical model of distribution in Figure 2-11E. Each block represents a case in the distribution.

of course, children come only in whole numbers. The mode in that distribution is zero, since by far the largest number of households had no children living at home in 1980. In some respects, the mode is a more representative measure than the mean or the median, since there were 27,433,000 households having zero children at home, but not a single one having 0.62 or 1.04 children.

Bimodality and Types of People. Sometimes there are two most frequently occurring scores, as in Figure 2-11D, where the distribution is called **bimodal.** In some bimodal distributions, the two peaks may differ in height, and the two most frequently occurring scores may differ in frequency. A bimodal distribution suggests that there may be two different **types** of people represented in the distribution, one type having predominantly higher scores and the other predominantly lower scores. For example, the sex variable contributes to bimodality on several physical dimensions, such as height and weight, and on some cognitive dimensions, such as verbal comprehension (favoring women) and quantitative skills (favoring men). But most human traits are **unimodally distributed,** having a single peak near the middle of the distribution.

Many kinds of aptitude tests, course examinations, and other psychological measurements are unimodally distributed. While there may be great differences between the people in the high and low extremes of a distribution, a unimodal dimension represents a spectrum of finely graded values rather than distinct types of people—a continuous interval scale rather than a nominal scale having discrete categories. A small distribution is likely to appear quite jagged, having several peaks and valleys. But if a larger sample is taken, then the peaks and valleys tend to be smoothed out, leaving an essentially unimodal distribution.

The Role of the Measurement Scale

By now it should be obvious that some measures of central location are more suitable for use with some measurement scales than with others. For example, in a survey of voter preferences, Democratic, Republican, and Independent preferences would represent categories on a nominal scale. If you found the greatest frequency of voters in a particular congressional district expressing a Democratic preference, then that category would represent the mode, and it would be reasonable to describe the *modal,* or most typical voter in that district as a Democrat. On the other hand, if you have assigned the numbers 1, 2, and 3 to the Democratic, Republican, and Independent categories, it would not make much sense to describe the mean preference as 1.68, or any other such number, nor would it be useful to find the median of a distribution on a nominal scale. Indeed, the assignment of numbers to the categories on a nominal scale is entirely arbitrary, and so is the numerical value of any measure of central location calculated in such a distribution.

In a set of ranks, the concept of the mode is useless, since all ranks occur with a frequency of 1, unless some ranks are tied. The mean is also of little value, since the mean of any set of ranks is equal to $(N + 1)/2$ in the absence of ties, and so is the median. In some other cases, however, the mode of a distribution on an ordinal scale can be useful. For example, the following crimes against persons are arranged in increasing order of severity: Robbery, aggravated assault, murder. It is informative to know that the modal crime in that distribution is aggravated assault, rather than robbery or murder. But if we assigned those crimes the numbers 1, 2, and 3, it would not be particularly instructive to calculate the mean or the median.

All of our measures of central location convey more information in distributions that are measured on interval and ratio scales, the two highest-caliber measurement scales. In the next chapter, measures of central location will play a great role in our development of the concept of dispersion. Thus, the nature of the measurement scale enters into the development and interpretation of measures of dispersion as well as measures of central location.

Terms and Symbols

Some of the following terms and symbols were introduced in Chapter 2. All of those, and many new ones, are used extensively in the present chapter — and most will be used again and again in chapters yet to come. Our future discourse in the language of statistics and research methods will depend heavily on your mastery of the vocabulary of this new language.

Central location	**Cumulative frequency**
Mean	**Positively** and **negatively**
Median	**skewed**
Mode	**Balance point**
Average	**Bimodality**
Rounding	**Types**
Summation operations	**Unimodally distributed**
Index of summation	$\overline{X}$
Grouped data	ΣX
Ungrouped data	N
Cases	f_j
Values	cf_b
Discrete variable	cf_k
Continuous variable	X_{LL}
Score interval	f_w
Lower and upper limit	X_m
Simple frequency	

EXERCISES AND STUDY QUESTIONS

1. A group of 18 subjects is given 2 minutes to construct as many words as possible from a set of scrambled letters. Each subject's performance is listed below in terms of words correct:

   4 4 6 6 5 5 3 5 5 5 6 4 6 7 5 5 4 5

   a. Find the mean performance using the ungrouped-data procedure, Formula 3-1.
   b. Arrange the scores into a grouped frequency distribution.
   c. Find the mean using the grouped-data procedure, Formula 3-5.
   d. Is the distribution symmetrical or skewed?
   e. Find the mode and median by inspection.
   f. Find the median using Formula 3-7.
   g. Draw a frequency polygon showing the distribution, and indicate the mean on the frequency polygon.

2. A second group of 18 subjects performs the same task as in Exercise 1 above. Their scores are listed below.

   6 3 5 4 6 5 8 7 6 5 3 4 2 1 4 5 9 7

   a. Find the mean using Formula 3-1.
   b. Arrange the scores into a grouped frequency distribution.
   c. Find the mode and median by inspection.
   d. Draw a frequency polygon, and show the mean on your graph. Use the same horizontal and vertical scales as in Exercise 1 in order to facilitate comparisons.

3. We now compare the frequency distributions in Exercises 1 and 2 above. Which distribution has the best subject? Which has the worst? Is one distribution better overall than the other, and if so, which one, and why? Or is neither distribution better than the other, and how so?

4. In what essential respects are the two distributions above similar, and in what respects are they different?

5. Now suppose a third group of 18 subjects performs the same task as in the preceding exercises. Their scores are listed below.

   6 2 4 4 7 3 6 7 7 5 6 5 6 1 5 7 6 3

   a. Find the mean using the ungrouped-data procedure.
   b. Arrange the scores into a grouped frequency distribution.
   c. Find the mode.
   d. Find the median using Formula 3-7.
   e. Is the distribution skewed, and if so, which way? How do you know?
   f. Draw a frequency polygon and show the mean, mode, and median. Use the same horizontal and vertical scales as in preceding exercises.

6. Now suppose that yet another group of 18 subjects performs our scrambled-letters task. Here are their scores:

3 9 7 4 5 6 3 4 7 5 6 4 4 4 3 8 3 5

For the present distribution, do everything listed in Items a through f in Exercise 5 above.

7. Comparing the frequency distributions in Exercises 5 and 6 above, in what respects are those distributions similar, and in what respects are they different? Which distribution is better overall, and how so?

8. Compare the usefulness of the mean, median, and mode as measures of central location in the distributions in Exercises 5 and 6.

9. Consider the performance of one more group of 18 subjects on our scrambled-letters task, shown below.

9 1 7 6 2 3 7 8 6 3 8 4 7 3 7 2 4 3

   a. Arrange the scores into a grouped frequency distribution.
   b. Find the modes, and find the mean and median by inspection.
   c. What problem would arise if you tried to use Formula 3-7 to find the median?
   d. Draw a frequency polygon and indicate the modes, mean, and median.
   e. What is the term used to describe this frequency distribution? What might account for the nature of such a distribution?

10. The following distribution is the number of children under 18 years of age living in each household, from the U.S. Census of 1980.

Number of Children	Frequency of Households (Nearest 1,000)
6 or more	277,000
5	549,000
4	1,745,000
3	4,913,000
2	11,005,000
1	11,882,000
0	27,433,000
	N = 57,804,000 = Number of Households

   a. Find the mode, and find the median using Formula 3-7.
   b. Find the mean using the grouped-data procedure. Notice that the highest number of children is 6 *or more*. For the purpose of finding the mean, treat the data as though there were no more than 6 children in any household.
   c. Since the data provide no information on the number of households having more than 6 children, there is a certain amount of imprecision in our information. What effect does this imprecision have on the mode, median, and mean?

    d. Is the distribution skewed? Which way?

    e. Draw a frequency polygon and show the mean, mode, and median. Compare with the histogram in Figure 3-2.

11. In general, which measure of central location

    a. best represents the score of a typical individual in a frequency distribution?

    b. represents the "balance point" of a distribution?

    c. is usually taken as the "average"?

    d. always corresponds to a score occurring in the distribution?

    e. divides the area of a frequency polygon in half?

    f. takes the value of every score in a distribution into account?

    g. is *least* influenced by a few very large scores?

    h. is *most* influenced by a few very large scores?

    i. divides the number of cases in a distribution in half?

12. Consider the distribution of personal income in the United States. Most incomes are located near the middle of the distribution, but there are a great many people with extremely low incomes, and a much smaller number with extremely high incomes.

    a. What is the shape of the distribution of incomes?

    b. What proportion of incomes (more than half, or less than half) are below the mean?

    c. What proportion of incomes are below the median?

    d. Draw a frequency polygon roughly illustrating the distribution of incomes under the above conditions. Show the mean, mode, and median.

13. Suppose that we have somehow managed to greatly reduce poverty in the United States, so that there are now very few people with extremely low incomes, and a much larger number with extremely high incomes. Respond to items a through d in the preceding question under the present hypothetical conditions.

Measures of Dispersion

4

The present chapter, like the last two, deals with frequency distributions, with groups of scores. In this chapter we will be concerned with calculating measures of dispersion in samples, where we know the value of every score. Later, we will develop methods of estimating these measures in populations, where we do not know the value of every score. We will see that such estimates play a great role in inferential statistics.

The Nature of Dispersion

As we noted earlier, distributions having identical measures of central location may differ greatly in dispersion. Most of the scores in a distribution tend to be located near the middle, but some scores may spread over a wide region of the measurement scale. The **dispersion** of a distribution is the extent to which the scores spread out on the measurement scale. **Variability** is a synonym for dispersion.

We have previously described measures of central location, indicating where the middle of a distribution lies on the measurement scale. Although measures of central location are often called measures of central tendency, these measures do *not* represent the tendency of the scores in a distribution to be tightly clustered, as opposed to being spread widely over the measurement scale. The value of the mean, for example—whether high or low on the measurement scale—gives no indication of the degree of dispersion in a frequency distribution. Thus, the ideas of central location and dispersion represent two very different aspects of frequency distributions, but you should not suppose that one of these ideas is the opposite of the other.

In comparison with measures of central location, the concept of dispersion appears unfamiliar and abstract. But in the next chapter, we will use measures of dispersion in a very concrete way, in answering the question of how large or small a particular score is in relation to other scores in its distribution. In later chapters, we will make extensive use of measures of dispersion in analyzing the results of experiments and observations. There is much dispersion—much variability—in most of the data in the biological and social sciences, and indeed, as will become evident in later chapters, this fact is one of the principal reasons why the tools of statistics are so widely applied in these fields.

The Range

The **range** is the difference between the upper limit of the highest score and the lower limit of the lowest score in a distribution. Thus, letting X_{max} and X_{min} equal the highest and lowest scores,

$$\text{Range} = (X_{max} + .5) - (X_{min} - .5) = (X_{max} - X_{min}) + 1.$$

It might appear simpler to define the range as the highest score minus the lowest, as some writers have done, but such a definition would yield a range covering one less score interval than the distribution itself covers. By our definition, however, a distribution consisting of the scores 5 and 6 has a range of two, and it is clear that this distribution occupies two score intervals.

At first glance, the range is an appealing measure of dispersion. It is simple, straightforward, and easy to visualize. Unfortunately, the range is not very stable from sample to sample, and thus is not a very useful measure of dispersion. Since the range of a sample is determined by just two scores, the range is strongly subject to chance fluctuations. By this we mean that if we drew a number of different samples of the same size from a population, we should expect to observe rather markedly different ranges in the different samples. Every descriptive statistic, that is, every measure we observe in a sample, is to some extent subject to chance fluctuations, but some measures are less stable than others. We will seldom use the range as a measure of dispersion.

The Average Deviation

Most of the scores in a distribution are located fairly close to the mean, while some are a considerable distance away on the measurement scale. On the average, how far away from the mean are the scores in a distribution? The **average deviation, AD,** answers that question:

$$AD = \frac{\Sigma|X - \bar{X}|}{N},$$ (4-1)

where $|X - \bar{X}|$ is the **absolute value** of a score minus the mean. To find the average deviation, we subtract the mean from each score, and we make all the differences positive, changing the negative signs wherever they occur. We then sum the resulting absolute values of the differences and divide by N. Each value of $|X - \bar{X}|$ is the absolute value of the **deviation** of a score from the mean of the distribution. Thus, in words, the *average deviation* is the mean of the absolute deviations from the mean. Formula 4-1 is suitable for ungrouped data. The following formula, where f is the frequency of each score, is for use with grouped data:

$$AD = \frac{\Sigma f|X - \bar{X}|}{N}.$$ (4-2)

A sample computation of the AD is shown in Table 4-1.

The AD is a better measure of dispersion than the range, since the AD takes all the scores into account. However, for reasons which we can best explain later, the standard deviation is the most widely used measure of dispersion.

TABLE 4-1.   Computation of Measures of Dispersion.

X	f	fX	$|X - \bar{X}|$	$f|X - \bar{X}|$	$(X - \bar{X})$	$(X - \bar{X})^2$	$f(X - \bar{X})^2$	X^2	fX^2
9	1	9	4	4	4	16	16	81	81
8	1	8	3	3	3	9	9	64	64
7	2	14	2	4	2	4	8	49	98
6	4	24	1	4	1	1	4	36	144
5	5	25	0	0	0	0	0	25	125
4	4	16	1	4	−1	1	4	16	64
3	2	6	2	4	−2	4	8	9	18
2	1	2	3	3	−3	9	9	4	4
1	1	1	4	4	−4	16	16	1	1
$N = 21$		105		$\Sigma f|X - \bar{X}| = 30$			$\Sigma f(X - \bar{X})^2 = 74$		$\Sigma fX^2 = 599$

$$= \Sigma fX \qquad \bar{X} = \frac{\Sigma fX}{N} = \frac{105}{21} = 5$$

Average deviation $= AD = \dfrac{\Sigma f|X - \bar{X}|}{N} = \dfrac{30}{21} = 1.43.$

Conceptual formulas:

Variance $= SD^2 = \dfrac{\Sigma f(X - \bar{X})^2}{N} = \dfrac{74}{21} = 3.52.$

Standard deviation $= SD = \sqrt{\dfrac{\Sigma f(X - \bar{X})^2}{N}} = \sqrt{\dfrac{74}{21}} = \sqrt{3.52} = 1.88.$

Computational (raw-score) formulas:

Variance $= SD^2 = \dfrac{\Sigma fX^2 - \dfrac{(\Sigma fX)^2}{N}}{N} = \dfrac{599 - \dfrac{105^2}{21}}{21} = \dfrac{599 - 525}{21} = \dfrac{74}{21} = 3.52.$

Standard deviation $= SD = \sqrt{\dfrac{\Sigma fX^2 - \dfrac{(\Sigma fX)^2}{N}}{N}} = \sqrt{\dfrac{599 - \dfrac{105^2}{21}}{21}} = \sqrt{\dfrac{74}{21}} = \sqrt{3.52} = 1.88.$

The Standard Deviation

The following formula defines the **standard deviation** for a set of un-grouped data:

$$\text{Standard deviation} = SD = \sqrt{\frac{\Sigma(X - \bar{X})^2}{N}}, \tag{4-3}$$

where $X - \bar{X}$ is the deviation between a score and the mean of the distribution, the summation is across all of the scores, and N is the number of scores. The subtraction is always carried out in the indicated direction, and thus some deviations will be positive and others negative. Each deviation is squared, the squared deviations are summed and divided by N, and the positive square root is then taken. In words, the standard deviation is the positive square root of the mean of the squared deviations from the mean. There exists a squared deviation $(X - \bar{X})^2$ for each score, and thus summing those squared deviations and dividing by N yields the mean of the squared deviations. Taking the positive square root of that quantity then yields the standard deviation. Although every positive number has a negative as well as a positive square root, as noted in the math review in Appendix A, we define the standard deviation as the positive square root of the quantity under the radical.

For grouped data in a frequency distribution,

$$SD = \sqrt{\frac{\Sigma f(X - \overline{X})^2}{N}}, \tag{4-4}$$

where f is the frequency of each value of X, and the other symbols are defined as above.

Formulas 4-3 and 4-4 are **conceptual formulas,** that is, equations that define the standard deviation. Very shortly we will develop **computational formulas** that are mathematically equivalent, and more convenient for calculations. Computational formulas also reduce rounding errors where the mean is not an integer. Although computational formulas are more convenient, and usually more precise, we have used the conceptual formula for illustrative purposes to compute the standard deviation in Table 4-1.

Notice in the above formulas that every deviation is squared in finding the standard deviation, and every negative deviation thereby becomes positive. Thus, it might appear that it makes no difference in finding any particular deviation whether the mean is subtracted from the score or the score from the mean, since the squared deviation will have a positive sign and the same magnitude in either case. But we will deal with deviations in some other situations where the sign is important, and where the order of subtraction does make a difference, so it will be useful for you to cultivate the habit of finding a deviation by subtracting the mean from the score.

Why bother to *square* the deviations in finding the standard deviation? If we merely summed the deviations, retaining the sign of each one, then the resulting measure would always be zero, since the sum of the deviations from the mean is always equal to zero — as you will be able to show after we have developed a few more principles of summation. We might overcome that difficulty by summing the absolute values of the deviations from the mean and dividing by N, but that would yield the average deviation, a measure of dispersion we have already developed. For now, suffice it to say that there are reasons why the standard deviation will prove to be a more useful measure of dispersion, even though it involves a little more arithmetic.

Computational Formulas. It is of course possible to use a conceptual formula for the purpose of computing a statistic, as we have done in Table 4-1. But a conceptual formula suffers a great disadvantage: The deviation of each score from the mean must be found by subtraction, and when the mean is a noninteger that has been rounded, each deviation will then contain the same rounding error as the mean. A rounding error is not a mistake that we have made in our arithmetic, but rather the difference between the true value of the mean and its value to however many decimal places we have chosen to use. Some numbers cannot be expressed precisely as decimals no matter how many places we use. Thus, a mean is usually subject to rounding error. Furthermore, in carrying out the large number of subtractions required in a large distribution, it is easy to make arithmetic errors. The following computational formula for ungrouped data utilizes raw scores, and thus avoids the above difficulties:

$$SD = \sqrt{\frac{\sum X^2 - \dfrac{(\sum X)^2}{N}}{N}}, \qquad (4\text{-}5)$$

where $\sum X^2$ is the sum of individual squared scores and $(\sum X)^2$ is the sum of scores, the quantity squared.

In formula 4-5, the first term of the numerator, $\sum X^2$, instructs us to square each value of X and to sum the resulting individually squared values. The next term instructs us to find the sum of the individual X values, square that *sum,* and divide by N. Note that $\sum X^2 \neq (\sum X)^2$. In words, the sum of the individually squared scores is not equal to the squared sum of the scores.

Formula 4-6 is a computational formula for grouped data:

$$SD = \sqrt{\frac{\sum fX^2 - \dfrac{(\sum fX)^2}{N}}{N}}. \qquad (4\text{-}6)$$

In the above formula, to find the first term in the numerator, we square each individual score, multiply the squared score by the frequency of the score, and sum the resulting products across the set of scores. In the second term $\sum fX$ is the sum of all the scores. We find that quantity just as in the past, square it, and divide by N.

As a partial check on your calculations, the numerator under the radical can never be negative. That fact is not obvious in looking at Formula 4-5 or 4-6, but Conceptual Formula 4-3 should make it clear that the numerator must always be positive, or zero, since the numerator is the sum of a number of squared quantities. While the computational formulas are much easier to use for calculations, the first conceptual formula is a better aid to understanding. For example, it is cumbersome to state Formula 4-5 in words, but quite easy to state Conceptual Formula 4-3 in a verbally satisfying and meaningful way.

Using a Calculator.   It has become highly desirable — if not essential — for people involved in any kind of quantitative work to have access to an electronic calculator. You will find it very useful to have a small calculator of your own, although I cannot offer specific advice on *which* calculator to buy, since the field is in such a state of flux. There are many small inexpensive calculators that will do most of the statistical operations you will need to carry out. Many small calculators have several memories, which allow you to accumulate intermediate results to several decimal places, and to manipulate those results in a complicated formula without having to take any numbers out of the machine until the final result is calculated. An electronic calculator should always be operated in the floating-decimal mode, if you have a choice, so that the machine will retain as many places to the right of the decimal as possible during all of the intermediate calculations. You can then round your final result to the desired number of places.

Representing the Standard Deviation Graphically. The standard deviation is measured in the same units as the scores in a distribution, and thus we can represent the *SD* as a specific length of line segment along the measurement scale. Figure 4-1 shows the data from Table 4-1 as a frequency polygon. A vertical line is erected on the horizontal measurement scale at the mean. It is important to understand that the mean is a point on the measurement scale, and is thus located on the horizontal axis. Do not suppose that the mean is represented by the height of the vertical line in the middle of the distribution, or by the point at the top of that vertical line.

We have also erected a vertical line perpendicular to the horizontal measurement scale at a point 1 *SD* above the mean, and another 1 *SD* below the mean. The standard deviation is not represented by lengths of these vertical lines, or by the points at the top of these lines, but rather by the horizontal distance between these lines and the mean. We have erected these

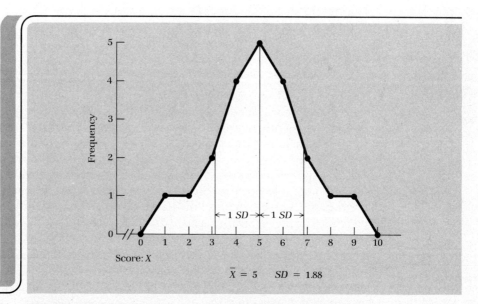

FIGURE 4-1. Frequency polygon showing data from Table 4-1. Mean is located on horizontal axis, not at top of vertical line. Horizontal line segments indicate magnitude of standard deviation. Vertical lines indicate points on horizontal axis 1 *SD* above and 1 *SD* below mean.

lines because we will be greatly interested in the proportion of the area of the frequency polygon lying within various regions of the scoring scale measured in standard deviation units — that is, regions of the scale measured in terms of the length of the standard deviation. As you can see, the ulk of the area of the frequency polygon in Figure 4-1 lies within ± 1 *SD* of the mean. We will find later that about 68% of the cases in many distributions, regardless of the actual value of the standard deviation, are located within ± 1 *SD* of the mean. We will make extensive use of that fact in assessing the relative standing of individuals within groups and also in connection with inferential statistics.

The Variance

The **variance** is the mean of the squared deviations from the mean, and is thus equal to the square of the standard deviation:

$$\text{Variance} = SD^2 = \frac{\Sigma(X - \bar{X})^2}{N}. \tag{4-7}$$

The raw-score computational formula for the variance in an ungrouped distribution is the following:

$$\text{Variance} = SD^2 = \frac{\Sigma X^2 - \dfrac{(\Sigma X)^2}{N}}{N}. \tag{4-8}$$

For grouped data, the computational formula is

$$\text{Variance} = SD^2 = \frac{\Sigma f X^2 - \dfrac{(\Sigma f X)^2}{N}}{N}, \tag{4-9}$$

where the symbols are defined as in Formula 4-6.

Since the variance and standard deviation are so closely related — one measure being the square of the other — it might appear that one or the other of those measures is unnecessary. But the standard deviation has the advantage of being expressed in the same units as the measurement scale, and thus can be represented as the length of a line segment along the horizontal dimension of a frequency polygon or histogram. The variance, on the other hand, is equal to the square of the standard deviation, and thus would have to be represented graphically as an area — that is, as the square of a length. For our present purposes, the standard deviation can be illustrated more readily. There are other differences between the variance and standard deviation, which we will explain in later chapters, so there is considerable justification for having two such closely related measures of dispersion where it might appear that one would do.

Do not use the terms *variance* and *variability* interchangeably. Variability is a synonym for dispersion, while the variance is one specific measure of dispersion — among several other measures — that is defined precisely by Formula 4-7.

Summation Operations

We need to develop some additional summation principles for several reasons — for example, to show that our conceptual and computational formulas, which appear so different, are in fact precisely equivalent. You may be willing to take my word for that, but that would be a mistake. We will make extensive use of summation operations in developing a great many fundamental ideas, as well as computational formulas, and you will find it helpful to understand these operations as fully as possible.

Variables and Constants

A **variable** is any quantity that can take different values. For example, a distribution of scores represents the measurement of some particular variable in a group of subjects. We have seen that summation operations involving variables have figured prominently in our calculations of measures of central location and dispersion.

A **constant** is a quantity that takes only a single value. In many instances, summation operations involve constants as well as variables. For example, the mean of a set of scores is a constant. Thus, finding the standard deviation and the variance involves subtracting a constant from each score in a distribution, squaring the resulting deviation, and summing across the set of scores.

Transformed Scores.   Altering each of the scores in a distribution in some systematic way yields a set of **transformed scores.** For example, algebraically adding a constant to each score in a distribution is one kind of transformation, and multiplying each score by a constant is another. In the following sections, we will apply the principles of summation operations to distributions of transformed scores. Beginning in the next chapter, we will make extensive use of several varieties of transformed scores in many contexts.

Summation of a Variable: ΣX.   We have already developed the basic summation operations in Chapter 3. Equation 3-2 gives the summation of a set of scores, a set of values of the variable X. That equation is reproduced below, and identified here as Equation 4-10 for the purposes of our present development.

$$\sum_{i=1}^{N} X_i = \underbrace{X_1 + X_2 + \cdots + X_N}_{N \text{ terms}}. \tag{4-10}$$

We will shortly make use of the fact that there are N terms on the right side of 4-10, as noted above.

Summation of Two Variables: $\Sigma(X + Y)$. We will often have occasion to deal with situations that require summing expressions containing more than one variable. As a concrete example, some tests of academic achievement consist of separately scored subtests of verbal (V) and quantitative (Q) achievement. A student's overall score is the sum of two variables, the V and Q scores. This operation looks a bit like adding apples and oranges — an operation probably forbidden to you in about the fifth grade — but in some instances, the results can be useful. The summation operator, below, instructs us to add the first values of X and Y to find the first term in the summation, to add the second values to find the second term, and so on through all of the N values of X and Y:

$$\sum_{i=1}^{N} (X_i + Y_i) = (X_1 + Y_1) + (X_2 + Y_2) + \cdots + (X_N + Y_N).$$

Dropping parentheses and rearranging terms,

$$\sum_{i=1}^{N} (X_i + Y_i) = \underbrace{X_1 + X_2 + \cdots + X_N}_{N \text{ terms}} + \underbrace{Y_1 + Y_2 + \cdots + Y_N}_{N \text{ terms}}.$$

Since the N terms, above, involving X are equal to ΣX — as in Equation 4-10 — and the N terms involving Y are equal to ΣY, it follows that

$$\sum_{i=1}^{N} (X_i + Y_i) = \sum_{i=1}^{N} X_i + \sum_{i=1}^{N} Y_i. \tag{4-11}$$

Thus, we can see that the summation operator obeys the **distributive law,** that is, the operator applies individually to the additive (or subtractive) terms in a parenthetic expression. (There is a brief review of algebraic operations involving parentheses in Appendix A.) While the summation operator can be distributed across additive terms in parentheses, the operator cannot be distributed individually across multiplicative terms. Thus, $\Sigma XY \neq \Sigma X \Sigma Y \neq \Sigma X + \Sigma Y$.

Summation of a Variable Plus a Constant: $\Sigma(X + c)$. Suppose we have a distribution of scores, and suppose we algebraically add a constant, c, to each score. We will derive a general expression for the summation of such a set of scores. By the distributive law,

$$\sum_{i=1}^{N} (X_i + c) = \sum_{i=1}^{N} X_i + \sum_{i=1}^{N} c. \tag{4-12}$$

We now have the problem of finding the summation of a constant, Σc. Notice that there is no subscript on the constant c in the above equation. The subscript on X indicates that X is a variable, which can take on different values, but since c is a constant, and thus has only one value, no subscript is used on c. If we expand the left side of the above equation, we can gain some insight into the summation of a constant.

$$\sum_{i=1}^{N} (X_i + c) = (X_1 + c) + (X_2 + c) + \cdots + (X_N + c). \tag{4-13}$$

Each of the N terms on the right side of Equation 4-13 represents one of the transformed scores. Dropping parentheses and rearranging the N variable terms and the N instances of the constant c,

$$\sum_{i=1}^{N} (X_i + c) = \underbrace{X_1 + X_2 + \cdots + X_N}_{N \text{ terms}} + \underbrace{c + c + \cdots + c}_{N \text{ terms}}.$$

Substituting from Equation 4-10, and collecting the N instances of c,

$$\sum_{i=1}^{N} (X_i + c) = \sum_{i=1}^{N} X_i + Nc. \tag{4-14}$$

The last term in Equation 4-14, Nc, is an expression for the summation of a constant, a result which we can also get by subtracting Equation 4-12 from 4-14 and transposing. Thus,

$$\sum_{i=1}^{N} c = Nc. \tag{4-15}$$

Summation of a Constant Times a Variable: ΣcX. Suppose we generate a transformed distribution of scores by multiplying each score by a constant, always using the same constant as a multiplier. We will now derive a general method of finding ΣcX. The summation operator, below, instructs us to multiply each value of X by the constant c, and to sum the resulting products across the set of scores.

$$\sum_{i=1}^{N} cX_i = cX_1 + cX_2 + \cdots + cX_N$$

$$= c(X_1 + X_2 + \cdots + X_N).$$

Since the expression in parentheses, above, is equal to ΣX, we have

$$\sum_{i=1}^{N} cX_i = c \sum_{i=1}^{N} X_i. \tag{4-16}$$

We will find Equation 4-16 very useful in many contexts.

Equivalence of Conceptual and Computational Formulas

We will now use the principles of summation operations to show that the conceptual and computational formulas for the variance are precisely equivalent. Our demonstration will consist of showing that Formula 4-8 can be derived from 4-7. Beginning with 4-7, squaring and then distributing the summation operator across the resulting terms, we have

$$SD^2 = \frac{\Sigma(X - \bar{X})^2}{N} = \frac{\Sigma(X^2 - 2X\bar{X} + \bar{X}^2)}{N} = \frac{\Sigma X^2 - \Sigma 2X\bar{X} + \Sigma\bar{X}^2}{N}. \tag{4-17}$$

Consider the term ΣX^2 in 4-17, above. Since the mean, $\overline{X}$, is a constant for any particular distribution,

$$\Sigma \overline{X}^2 = N\overline{X}^2 = N\frac{(\Sigma X)^2}{N^2} = \frac{(\Sigma X)^2}{N}. \qquad (4\text{-}18)$$

Now consider the term $\Sigma 2X\overline{X}$ in 4-17. Rearranging, and noting that $2\overline{X}$ is a constant, and that $\overline{X} = \Sigma X/N$, we can write

$$\Sigma 2X\overline{X} = \Sigma 2\overline{X}X = 2\overline{X}\Sigma X = 2\frac{\Sigma X}{N}\Sigma X = 2\frac{(\Sigma X)^2}{N}. \qquad (4\text{-}19)$$

Substituting 4-18 and 4-19 for $\Sigma \overline{X}^2$ and $\Sigma 2X\overline{X}$ in 4-17,

$$SD^2 = \frac{\Sigma X^2 - 2\dfrac{(\Sigma X)^2}{N} + \dfrac{(\Sigma X)^2}{N}}{N} = \frac{\Sigma X^2 - \dfrac{(\Sigma X)^2}{N}}{N}. \qquad (4\text{-}20)$$

Since 4-20 is identical to 4-7, we have shown that our conceptual and computational formulas are precisely equivalent — for the variance, and for the standard deviation as well — and we have also brought a number of the principles of summation operations into play.

Computers and Statistics

It may have occurred to you that in this day and age, a computer — or even a moderately sophisticated calculator — should be capable of handling a great many statistical operations. Indeed, computers have taken much of the drudgery out of many kinds of statistical work, especially calculations involving large amounts of data, or very complicated operations. Because of their great speed and enormous capacity, computers have made it possible to carry out routinely many kinds of analyses that were seldom attempted in the past. But it would be a mistake to suppose that computers have therefore rendered statistics courses, and textbooks, obsolete. Computers and calculators can free us from a certain amount of drudgery, but as yet, they do not do much of our thinking for us. There is simply no way to put a set of raw data into the hopper of a machine and grind out meaningful results, as we might get sausage out of a meat grinder. There is no substitute for understanding the fundamentals of statistics and research methods.

Some Results of Transforming Scores

By transforming a set of scores, we mean modifying each score in some systematic way, for example, by adding a constant to each score, or multiplying each by a constant. Like most other ideas we have introduced, the concept of a set of transformed scores will be useful in the here-and-now and also useful in the future. Working with transformed scores will help sharpen your present understanding of summation operations, and your appreciation of the nature of measures of central location and dispersion. In future chapters, transformed scores will play a great role in our development of several statistical procedures. Indeed, a number of statistical tests are little more than exercises in transforming sets of scores, as we will see.

We will be particularly interested in seeing what happens to the mean, variance, and standard deviation when a set of scores is transformed. Table 4-2 shows an original distribution and two sets of transformed scores. The scores in Distribution 1, the original set, were transformed, converted, into Distribution 2 by adding a constant to each of the scores. Distribution 3 consists of each of the scores in Distribution 1 multiplied by a constant. Table 4-2 shows the measures of central location and dispersion in the original set of scores and in the two transformations. We will now show what happens in general to those measures when those two kinds of transformations are carried out.

TABLE 4-2. A Distribution and Two Transformations.

Distribution	X_1	X_2	X_3	X_4	X_5	$\overline{X}$	SD^2	SD
1. Original values	5	3	1	4	7	4	4	2
2. Adding a constant, $c = 2$	7	5	3	6	9	6	4	2
3. Multiplying by 2	10	6	2	8	14	8	16	4

Adding a Constant

In some cases, it is useful to symbolize the mean of a set of scores as **Mean(X),** rather than $\overline{X}$. Where we have transformed a set of scores by adding a constant, each transformed score is equal to $X + c$, and the mean of the transformed scores is $Mean(X + c)$. Thus,

$$Mean(X + c) = \frac{\Sigma(X + c)}{N} = \frac{\Sigma X}{N} + \frac{\Sigma c}{N} = \overline{X} + \frac{Nc}{N} = \overline{X} + c. \tag{4-21}$$

Equation 4-21 shows that algebraically adding a constant to each score in a distribution changes the mean by the value of the constant.

We now consider the effect that adding a constant has on the variance and standard deviation. Letting the expression **Var(X + c)** represent the variance of a set of transformed scores,

$$Var(X + c) = \frac{\Sigma[(X + c) - Mean(X + c)]^2}{N}.$$

Substituting 4-21 for $Mean(X + c)$,

$$Var(X + c) = \frac{\Sigma[(X + c) - (\overline{X} + c)]^2}{N} = \frac{\Sigma(X - \overline{X})^2}{N}$$

$$= Var(X) = SD_X^2. \tag{4-22}$$

The above equation shows that adding a constant to each score in a distribution does not change the variance at all.

Since the standard deviation is the square root of the variance, and since we have just shown that algebraically adding a constant to each score has no effect on the variance, that operation also has no effect on the standard deviation. Letting **$SD(X + c)$** represent the standard deviation of a set of transformed scores,

$$SD(X + c) = SD(X) = SD_X. \tag{4-23}$$

Multiplying by a Constant

Where each score is multiplied by a constant,

$$Mean(cX) = \frac{\Sigma cX}{N} = \frac{c\Sigma X}{N} = c\overline{X}. \tag{4-24}$$

Thus, multiplying each score by a constant multiplies the mean by the value of that constant.

The variance of cX is

$$Var(cX) = \frac{\Sigma[(cX - Mean(cX)]^2}{N}.$$

Substituting 4-24 for $Mean(cX)$,

$$Var(cX) = \frac{\Sigma[cX - c\overline{X}]^2}{N} = \frac{\Sigma[c(X - \overline{X})]^2}{N}$$

$$= \frac{\Sigma c^2(X - \overline{X})^2}{N} = \frac{c^2\Sigma(X - \overline{X})^2}{N} = c^2Var(X) = c^2SD_X^2. \tag{4-25}$$

Thus, where each score is multiplied by a constant, the variance is multiplied by the square of that constant.

Since the standard deviation is the square root of the variance,

$$SD(cX) = \sqrt{Var(cX)} = \sqrt{c^2Var(X)} = c\sqrt{Var(X)} = cSD_X. \tag{4-26}$$

Thus, multiplying each score by a constant multiplies the standard deviation by the absolute value of that constant.

TABLE 4-3.   The Effects of Some Transformations on Measures of Central Location and Dispersion.

Transformation	Effect		
Adding a constant	$Mean(X + c)$	$= Mean(X) + c$	$= \overline{X} + c$
	$Var(X + c)$	$= Var(X)$	$= SD_X^2$
	$SD(X + c)$	$= SD(X)$	$= SD_X$
Multiplying by a constant	$Mean(cX)$	$= c\,Mean(X)$	$= c\overline{X}$
	$Var(cX)$	$= c^2Var(X)$	$= c^2SD_X^2$
	$SD(cX)$	$= c\,SD(X)$	$= c\,SD_X$

Table 4-3 lists the effects of the above transformations in general on the mean, standard deviation, and variance. Concrete examples of those effects are shown in Table 4-2. In the next chapter, we will develop several methods of comparing individuals with other members of their reference groups. Those methods will depend heavily on the use of transformed scores.

Terms and Symbols

Make sure that you can define the following terms and symbols, and understand the ideas they represent. Spend some time comparing and contrasting these ideas.

Dispersion	**Constant**
Variability	**Transformed scores**
Range	*AD*
Deviation	*SD*
Average deviation	SD^2
Absolute value	ΣX^2
Standard deviation	$(\Sigma X)^2$
Conceptual formula	$\Sigma f X^2$
Computational formula	$(\Sigma f X)^2$
Variance	*Mean*(X)
Variable	*Var*(X)
Distributive law	*SD*(X)

EXERCISES AND STUDY QUESTIONS

1. The scores below represent the performance of the 18 subjects on the scrambled-letters task in Exercise 1 at the end of Chapter 3:

4 4 6 6 5 5 3 5 5 5 6 4 6 7 5 5 4 5

a. Find the range.
b. Find the average deviation using Formula 4-1, the ungrouped-data procedure.
c. Find the standard deviation using the raw-score computational Formula 4-5 for ungrouped data.
d. Find the variance. Referring to Formula 4-8, the variance is the square of the standard deviation. Thus, the variance is the quantity under the radical in Exercise 1c above.
e. Plot a frequency polygon, or use the one you drew in Exercise 1 at the end of Chapter 3. Erect a vertical line at the mean, and erect vertical lines 1 *SD* below and above the mean.

2. The following distribution is the performance of the 18 subjects in Exercise 2 in Chapter 3:

6 3 5 4 6 5 8 7 6 5 3 4 2 1 4 5 9 7

   a. Arrange the scores into a grouped frequency distribution.
   b. Find the range.
   c. Find the average deviation using the grouped-data procedure, Formula 4-2.
   d. Find the standard deviation using the raw-score computational Formula 4-4 for grouped data.
   e. Find the variance. Formula 4-9 shows that the variance is the quantity under the radical in Exercise 2d above.
   f. Plot a frequency polygon, or use the one you drew in Exercise 2 in Chapter 3. Erect vertical lines at the mean and at the points 1 *SD* above and below the mean.

3. a. In Exercise 1, about what proportion of the area of your frequency polygon lies beyond 1 *SD* above the mean?
   b. In Exercise 2, estimate the proportion of the area of your frequency polygon lying beyond 1 *SD* above the mean.
   c. The distributions in Exercises 1 and 2 above are shown as histograms in Figures 2-11A and 2-11B. Referring to those histograms, you should be able to find more precisely the area in each lying beyond 1 *SD* above the mean. How do those areas compare?

4. Two bowlers have the same average of 178 for their last 100 games. Bowler A's distribution of scores has a standard deviation of 16, and bowler B has a standard deviation of 22.
   a. Which bowler is more consistent? How so?
   b. Which bowler is more likely to bowl a 200 game, or higher?

5. Two violinists' pitch perception is tested using a 440 Hertz standard tone, equal to the frequency of an A string on a violin. The tone is presented, turned off, and then each musician adjusts the frequency of an audio generator to match the pitch of the tone. In 50 trials, violinist A has a mean of 439.8 and an *AD* of .73 Hertz, and violinist B has a mean of 440.2 and an *AD* of .32 Hertz. Which musician has the better pitch perception? Explain.

6. Using the principles of summation, show that in general the sum of the deviations from the mean is equal to zero.

7. Table 4-3 shows the effect that multiplying each score by a constant has on the mean, variance, and standard deviation. How are those measures affected if we *divide* each score in a distribution by a constant?

8. There are 50 questions on a *midterm* exam in a particular course. The mean and *SD* are 36.12 and 6.20 on the midterm. There are 100 questions on the *final* exam. What are the values of the mean, standard deviation, and variance on the final exam under the following conditions?
   a. Each student's score on the final exam is exactly 30 points higher than on the midterm.

    b. Each student earns 50% more points on the final than on the midterm exam.

    c. Each student answers the same proportion of questions correctly on the final as on the midterm.

9. In Chapter 1, we briefly discussed the notion of correlation, or relationship between variables. What is the nature of the correlation between midterm and final exam scores under conditions a, b, and c above?

The Individual and the Group

5

As early as Chapter 1, we began developing methods of attaching numbers to individuals. We went on to develop numerical measures of group characteristics. We will now be concerned with finding the relative standing of individuals within their groups. An individual measurement of any kind becomes more meaningful in comparison with a group of such measurements. In fact, some measurements are truly meaningful *only* in relation to a group.

In the present chapter, we will develop methods of comparing the relative standing of individuals *within* groups. In later chapters, we will use these concepts extensively in making comparisons *between* different groups, that is, in comparing one group as a whole with another. Such comparisons —for example, between control and experimental groups—represent one of the pillars of psychological research, and indeed, scientific research in general.

A Preview

Suppose a student makes a score of 26 on an examination. Is that a high score, a low score, or about average? That individual measurement tells you very little, in the absence of other information about the examination. If there were only 27 possible points, a score of 26 might represent a superb performance— unless the exam were so easy that everyone else got all 27 questions right. If there were 100 multiple-choice questions, each having four alternatives, then we might conclude that a student making a score of 26 knows essentially nothing about the material covered on the test, since that score is within one point of the performance expected by chance alone. (We will considerably amplify some of these ideas in later chapters.) Thus, we must have additional information about a distribution before an individual score can tell us much about the caliber of the individual's performance.

Suppose, again, that a student has made a score of 26—this time on an essay exam having 38 possible points. You could find the student's percentage score by dividing 26 by 38 and multiplying by 100, but unless you knew the scores of the other students, you would gain little information by transforming the score to a percentage. If you knew, however, that the mean was 24.03, then you could see at once that a score of 26 is somewhat above the mean. But is this score a high performance, or a mediocre one attained or exceeded by a substantial number of students? We almost seem to be asking, How high is *up*? But we are not quite posing such an unanswerable question. We will see that deciding whether a given score is high, low, or mediocre depends as much on the dispersion of the distribution as on the score's location above or below the mean.

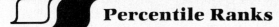

Percentile Ranks

We introduced the notion of ranks in Chapter 1, where we noted that a set of ranks constitutes an ordinal scale. No matter whether we have ranked a set of height measurements (a ratio scale) or a set of test scores (an interval scale), the resulting ranks themselves constitute an ordinal scale. The **percentile rank** of a score is the percentage of the distribution lying below the midpoint of the score interval. There is a close relationship between the ranks of a set of scores and the percentile ranks. Indeed, the latter measures also comprise an ordinal scale. We will often use the shorter term **percentile** when we mean *percentile rank,* but you should always keep in mind that percentiles constitute an ordinal scale regardless of the nature of the underlying measurement scale.

Figure 5-1 shows a distribution of five scores ranging from the value of 2 through 8. Notice that there are some empty intervals on the measurement scale, intervals for scores of 4 and 7. Moving downward in Figure 5-1, we have transformed the scores into a set of ranks. Notice that every interval on the rank scale is occupied by a case—there are no empty intervals as on the original measurement scale. The scale of ranks gives no hint that there is a

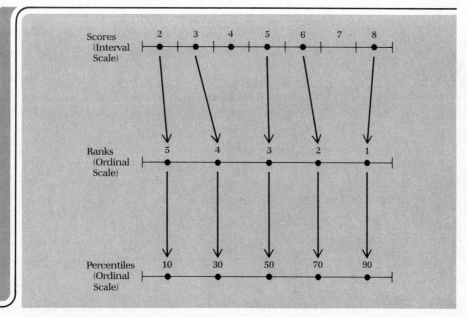

FIGURE 5-1. Relationships between scores, ranks, and percentiles. Each dot represents one individual. Moving downward, scores are transformed into ranks, and ranks into percentiles.

greater difference between Ranks 1 and 2 than between 2 and 3. Thus, we have lost some of the information contained in our original set of scores. But in another sense, we have gained. If we tell you that a particular individual ranks second out of five, then you know more about the person's relative standing than if we tell you only the score. Notice that the size of a distribution must be taken into account in order to translate a rank into a meaningful measure of relative standing. For example, which would probably represent the better performance, ranking second out of five, or second out of five hundred? The percentile rank takes the size of the distribution into account and provides in a single number a measure of relative standing.

Transforming Ranks to Percentiles

We consider a scale of ranks as consisting of intervals, like other measures we have previously considered. The scale of ranks in Figure 5-1 shows the limits of each interval. Notice that small-numbered ranks are associated with large score values, since it is customary to assign Rank 1 to the highest score and Rank N to the lowest. Now, what percentile does Rank 1 represent? It is tempting to say the 100th percentile, since all of the other ranks are lower — that is, numerically greater. But only four out of five ranks — 80% of the distribution — lie below the lower limit of Rank 1. Since the percentile of a rank, like that of any other measure, is the percentage of cases lying below the *midpoint* of its interval, we must find the percentage of cases lying below the midpoint of Rank 1. Since each rank represents only one case, the cumulative frequency below the lower limit of a rank, cf_b, is the following:

$$cf_b = N - R, \tag{5-1}$$

where N is the number of ranks, and R is a specific rank. For example, in Figure 5-1, cf_b is 4 for Rank 1 and 2 for Rank 3.

To find the cumulative frequency below the midpoint of R, cf_R, we must add .5 to cf_b, since half of the case represented by Rank R is considered to lie below the midpoint of the interval containing R. Thus, substituting Equation 5-1 for cf_b,

$$cf_R = cf_b + .5 = N - R + .5. \tag{5-2}$$

Dividing cf_R by N gives the proportion of the distribution below the midpoint of R, and multiplying that proportion by 100 gives the percentile rank, PR:

$$PR = \frac{cf_R}{N} 100.$$

Substituting Equation 5-2 for cf_R then yields the following working formula, which gives the percentile of any rank in terms of R and N. Thus,

$$PR = \frac{N - R + .5}{N} 100. \tag{5-3}$$

What meaning can we attach to the 0th (read, "zeroth") and 100th percentiles? To begin with, no score actually occurring in a distribution can ever fall precisely at either of these percentiles. The **0th percentile** corresponds to that point on the measurement scale below which 0% of the distribution occurs, and thus, this percentile corresponds with the lower limit of the lowermost nonempty interval of the measurement scale, as shown in Figure 5-1. The **100th percentile,** the point below which 100% of the distribution occurs, corresponds with the upper limit of the highest nonempty interval of the measurement scale. In practice, the percentiles of the lowest and highest scores in large distributions can approach—but never equal— zero and 100, respectively.

Tied Ranks. Formula 5-3 is a completely general formula which always allows us to convert ranks to percentiles, even when there are ties between some of the scores, as in Table 5-1. If Smith and Jones both have

TABLE 5-1.   Distribution of Scores With Ties.

			Ties				Ties	
Scores	4	6	7	7	7	8	9	9
Ranks, as in the absence of ties	8	7	6	5	4	3	2	1
Means of tied ranks				5			1.5	
Means substituted for tied ranks			5	5	5		1.5	1.5
Ranks, with ties	8	7	5	5	5	3	1.5	1.5

scores of 9, then their scores are tied, and it would be unreasonable to rank one of these persons above the other. But Smith and Jones both rank higher than the next highest person in the distribution, who should receive a rank of 3 regardless of whether Smith and Jones are tied. We can then consider Smith and Jones as falling at the midpoint of the interval containing Ranks 1 and 2, and we can assign both persons a rank of 1.5. We can treat the three tied scores of 7 analogously. When a tie occurs, we assign to each individual within the tie the mean of the ranks that would have been assigned in the absence of a tie. As you can see in Table 5-1, this procedure is simpler than it can be made to sound in words. But why not simply assign Smith and Jones the rank of 1, since they are tied, and the next highest person the rank of 2, and so on? Unfortunately, this apparently simpler procedure would yield ranks with a maximum value less than N, and as a result, Formula 5-3 could not be used. It would not be at all straightforward to convert such a set of ranks to percentiles, and thus, some of the conceptual value of the ranks would be lost. Difficulties would also arise in comparing the ranks of the same individuals on different variables, a problem we will deal with in Chapter 11.

Transforming Scores Directly to Percentiles

While Formula 5-3 will always work, the procedure first requires transforming a set of scores to ranks, a process that is time consuming and error prone, especially in sizable distributions where there are many ties. It is conceptually useful to see the close relationship between ranks and percentiles, as in the previous section, but computations are more efficient when raw scores are directly transformed to percentiles.

The scores shown as a list in Table 5-1 are shown in the form of a frequency distribution in Table 5-2. The **simple percentage, p_j,** within each

TABLE 5-2.   Grouped Distribution of Scores from Table 5-1.

Index of Summation j		Score X_j	Frequency Simple Frequency f_j	Frequency Cumulative Frequency cf_j		Percentage Simple Percentage p_j	Percentage Cumulative Percentage cp_j
5		9	2	8		25.0%	100.0%
4		8	1	6		12.5	75.0
3	$X_{LL} = 6.5$	7	$f_w = 3$	5	$p_w = 37.5$		62.5
2		6	1	$cf_b = 2$		12.5	$cp_b = 25.0$
1		4	1	1		12.5	12.5

$$\Sigma f = N = 8 \qquad\qquad \Sigma p = 100.0\%$$

To find percentile of a score of 7 using Formula 5-5,

$$PR = \left(\frac{cf_b + .5f_w}{N}\right)100 = \left(\frac{2 + .5(3)}{8}\right)100 = \frac{3.5}{8}\,100 = .4375(100)$$

$$= 43.75\text{th percentile.}$$

To find the score at a given percentile—the 50th, for example—use Formula 5-7, where X_{LL} is the lower limit of the lowest interval in which the cumulative percentage exceeds PR:

$$X_{PR} = X_{LL} + i\left(\frac{\dfrac{PR}{100}N - cf_b}{f_w}\right) = 6.5 + 1\left(\frac{\dfrac{50}{100}8 - 2}{3}\right) = 6.5 + \frac{.5(8) - 2}{3}$$

$$= 6.5 + \frac{2}{3} = 6.5 + .67 = 7.17.$$

score interval is equal to the simple frequency of the score, f_j, divided by N and multiplied by 100. The **cumulative percentage, cp_j,** associated with a particular score, X_j, is the percentage of scores that are equal to or less than the particular score. Thus, the simple percentage and cumulative percentage of any score, X_j, are given by

$$p_j = \frac{f_j}{N}\,100, \qquad \text{and} \qquad cp_j = \frac{cf_j}{N}\,100.$$

The data from Table 5-2 are shown graphically in Figure 5-2. Notice that Figure 5-2 is very similar to Figure 3-1, which we used in developing procedures for finding the median in Chapter 3. There is a very close relationship,

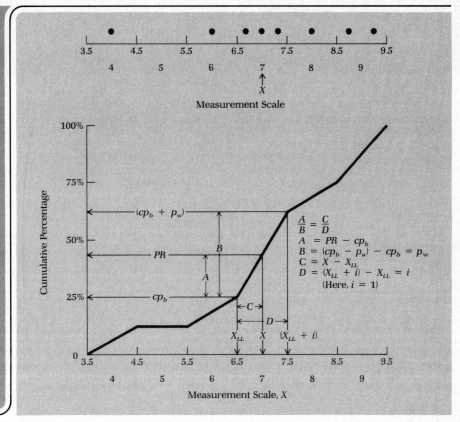

FIGURE 5-2. Same distribution as in Table 5-2. Top: Each dot represents one individual. All individuals having the same score are regarded as evenly distributed through that score interval. Bottom: Cumulative frequency at the limits of score intervals. *A*, *B*, *C*, and *D* are lengths of line segments. Other symbols are defined in Table 5-2 and in text. Percentile at a given score, and score at a given percentile, are found by interpolation. (Compare this figure with Figure 3-1, Chapter 3.)

as we will see, between the median and the concepts we are presently developing. We will consider the problem of directly finding the percentile of a score of 7 in our distribution, and we will develop a general method of transforming scores directly to percentiles.

There are three cases in our distribution having a score of 7. As before, we will consider any cases having the same score to be evenly distributed through that score interval, as shown in Figure 5-2 (top). Referring to the cumulative percentage graph in Figure 5-2 (bottom), we can write the following proportionality between the lengths of line segments *A* and *B* on the cumulative percentage scale and *C* and *D* on the measurement scale:

$$\frac{A}{B} = \frac{C}{D}.$$

Substituting from Figure 5-2,

$$\frac{PR - cp_b}{p_w} = \frac{X - X_{LL}}{i}, \qquad\qquad (5\text{-}4)$$

where the symbols are as defined in Figure 5-2 (bottom). When we are finding the PR of a particular score, X in the above equation is the middle of a score interval, and thus the right side of Equation 5-4 is equal to .5 regardless of the value of the score. Substituting,

$$\frac{PR - cp_b}{p_w} = .5.$$

Solving for PR,

$$PR - cp_b = .5p_w, \qquad \text{and} \qquad PR = cp_b + .5p_w.$$

In actual calculations, it is not necessary to find cumulative percentages. Since it is easier to work with frequencies than to work with percentages, we will express cp_b and p_w in the above equation in terms of frequencies. Thus,

$$PR = \frac{cf_b}{N}\,100 + .5\,\frac{f_w}{N}\,100$$

$$= \frac{cf_b + .5f_w}{N}\,100. \qquad\qquad (5\text{-}5)$$

Formula 5-5 allows us to find directly the percentile rank, PR, of a score without first having to convert the scores in the distribution to ranks. Thus, the above formula represents a procedure for transforming any measurement scale — any scale of scores — directly to the percentile scale. A sample computation is shown in Table 5-2.

Finding the Score at a Given Percentile.   It is sometimes useful to find the point on the measurement scale associated with a given percentile. This operation is the inverse of that described in the last section. Here, the question is, What point on the scoring scale corresponds with a given percentile — say the 50th, or the 1st, or the 5th? Questions of this sort will play an important role in our later development of the principles of inferential statistics.

Referring to Figure 5-2, we developed a method in the last section for finding the unknown PR associated with a given (known) score. We will now turn the problem around, and we will find the unknown score — strictly speaking, the unknown *point* on the measurement scale — associated with a given percentile. We will designate such an unknown point as X_{PR}, where the subscript PR indicates any given percentile, as X_{50th}, or X_{1st}, or X_{5th}. We will replace X with X_{PR} in Figure 5-2 and in Equation 5-4, and then solve for X_{PR}. In the equation below, PR is the value of the given percentile, and X_{LL} is the lower limit of the lowest score interval within which the cumulative percentage exceeds PR:

$$\frac{PR - cp_b}{p_w} = \frac{X_{PR} - X_{LL}}{i}.$$

Since it is easier to work with frequencies than percentages, we will express cp_b and p_w in terms of frequencies. Thus,

$$\frac{PR - \dfrac{cf_b}{N} 100}{\dfrac{f_w}{N} 100} = \frac{X_{PR} - X_{LL}}{i}. \tag{5-6}$$

Since X_{PR}—unlike X—is not necessarily at the middle of a score interval, the right side of Equation 5-6, above—unlike 5-5—is not necessarily equal to $1/2$. Continuing,

$$X_{PR} - X_{LL} = i \left(\frac{PR - \dfrac{cf_b}{N} 100}{\dfrac{f_w}{N} 100} \right).$$

Multiplying the numerator and denominator by $N/100$, and transposing X_{LL} yields the desired formula:

$$X_{PR} = X_{LL} + i \left(\frac{\dfrac{PR}{100} N - cf_b}{f_w} \right). \tag{5-7}$$

In the above formula, X_{LL} can be found using cumulative frequencies rather than cumulative percentages. X_{LL} is the lower limit of the lowest score interval where the cumulative frequency exceeds $\dfrac{PR}{100} N$. A sample computation using Formula 5-7 is shown in Table 5-2.

Some Percentiles of Special Interest

The 50th Percentile. The point on the scale of scores, X_{50th}, corresponding to the **50th percentile,** is often of great interest. This is the point below which 50% of the distribution occurs. Substituting the 50th percentile for PR in Equation 5-7,

$$X_{50th} = X_{LL} + i \left(\frac{\dfrac{N}{2} - cf_b}{f_w} \right). \tag{5-8}$$

The right side of 5-8 is identical to the right side of 3-7, the formula for the median, and thus

$$X_{50th} = Mdn.$$

Since 50% of the cases in a distribution lie below X_{50th}, it follows that 50% lie above, so X_{50th} and the median are one and the same. Our formula for the median is thus a special case of Formula 5-7, where we have set PR equal to 50.

The 25th and 75th percentiles. These percentiles respresent, respectively, the points below which one quarter and three quarters of a distribution occur. These points on the measurement scale are called the first and third **quartiles,** and they are usually designated as $\boldsymbol{Q_1}$ and $\boldsymbol{Q_3}$. Using our notation, above,

$$Q_1 = X_{25th}, \quad \text{and} \quad Q_3 = X_{75th}.$$

Thus, we can use Formula 5-7 to find the values of Q_1 and Q_3. The range between the values of Q_1 and Q_3 has been used to derive an alternative measure of dispersion. In a distribution where the scores are tightly clustered — where there is little dispersion — Q_1 and Q_3 will be relatively close together, but where the scores are widely dispersed, those points on the measurement scale will be more widely separated. The **semi-interquartile range, Q,** sometimes shortened to **quartile range,** is equal to half of the difference between the values of Q_1 and Q_3:

$$Q = \frac{Q_1 + Q_3}{2}.$$

We have not yet mentioned $\boldsymbol{Q_2}$, the second quartile. It should be apparent that this point is precisely equal to the median. In an asymmetrical distribution, Q_2 will be closer to Q_1 or Q_3, depending on the direction of skew. In skewed distributions, Q is less influenced by the values of extreme scores than is the standard deviation, and thus Q may be a more useful measure of dispersion in some situations.

Some Other Terms.   The term **decile** is sometimes used to express a percentile as a multiple of ten. For example, a score at the 1st decile is at the 10th percentile, and so on. Some writers have used the term **centile** instead of percentile, but we will use the latter, more widely preferred term.

The Normal Distribution

In this section we will develop a method of finding the relative standing of an individual, based on the normal distribution. Many different kinds of psychological measurements, and other kinds of biological measurements as well, are normally distributed. For example the typical frequency polygon of a

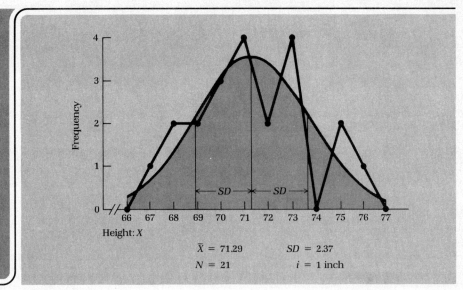

FIGURE 5-3. Frequency polygon showing the heights of a sample of 21 men to the nearest inch. If N were allowed to become infinitely large, and if height were measured with an infinitely small interval width, i, then the frequency polygon would approach the smooth normal curve as a limit.

distribution of heights has a peak near the middle and a low tail at each end. Such a frequency polygon approximates a normal distribution, the smooth, bell-shaped curve shown in Figure 5-3.

The frequency polygon in Figure 5-3 shows the height of a sample of N men measured to the nearest inch. Such a frequency polygon consists of a number of straight-line segments—unlike the smooth, continuous, normal curve. Now suppose that we let the class interval width, i, become smaller and smaller—that is, suppose we measure height more and more precisely, not just to the nearest inch—and suppose at the same time that we let N increase without limit, that is, we measure the height of more and more men. As N becomes infinitely large and i becomes infinitely small, the frequency polygon approaches as a limit the smooth curve of the normal distribution. Thus, a normal curve represents a theoretical population of an infinite number of cases, since we let N become infinite, and an infinite number of values of X, since X becomes a continuous variable as i becomes infinitely small. Such an infinite population is a theoretical construct that does not exist in the real world, but this construct is nevertheless a very useful idea. Later, we will find it useful to consider any frequency distribution of size N as a sample drawn from an infinite population. We have used the symbols $\overline{X}$ and SD for the mean and standard deviation of a sample, and we will use μ_x and σ_x as in Figure 5-4, for the mean and standard deviation of the normal curve. That curve represents the distribution of an infinite population, and thus μ and σ are the mean and standard deviation of such a population.

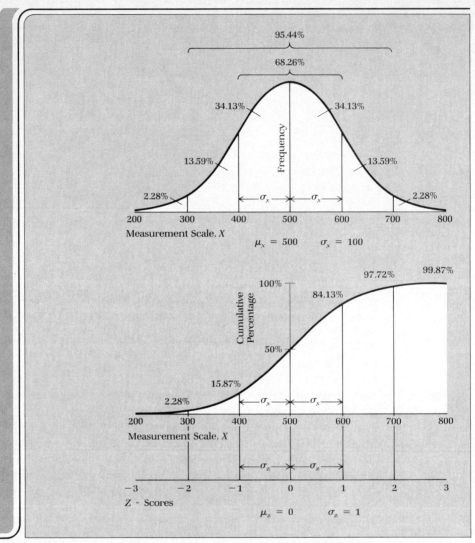

FIGURE 5-4. Top: Normal distribution showing percentages of area under curve in several regions. Bottom: Cumulative percentage curve shows percentage of cases below each point on measurement scale. Z-scores are explained in text.

The particular normal distribution in Figure 5-4 has a mean of 500 and a standard deviation of 100. In every normal curve the values of X extend without limit from minus infinity to plus infinity. Although Figure 5-4 shows only the central region of the measurement scale, that region contains the overwhelming proportion of the cases in the distribution. Suppose this normal distribution represents a very large set of scores on a test of academic aptitude. As Figure 5-4 shows, 68.26% of the individual scores are within the range from 400–600, that is, within ±1 σ of the mean; and 95.44% of the individual scores are within the range from 300–700, within ±2 σ of the mean. Now here is an exceedingly important fact: In every normal distribution, no matter what the values of the mean and standard deviation (μ and σ) may be, 68.26% of the scores are within ± 1 σ of the mean; and 95.44% of the scores are within ± 2 σ of the mean. We will explain shortly where these percentages come from, and how we can use them.

The Area Under a Curve

In Chapter 2, we noted that the area of a histogram or a frequency polygon is equal to Ni, and thus the total area is proportional to the total number of cases in the distribution. It is useful to let the area of a frequency polygon, and the **area under a normal curve,** represent the total *percentage* of the cases in a distribution — that is, 100% rather than the *number* of cases. In Figure 5-4 (top), the area under the normal curve is divided into a number of subareas by vertical lines erected on the measurement scale at one and two standard deviations below the mean and at the same distances above the mean. These subareas are **mutually exclusive and exhaustive,** that is, they do not overlap, and they account for 100% of the total area. The percentage of the area under the curve bounded by any particular region of the measurement scale is equal to the percentage of cases in the distribution having scores in that region. For example, 68.26% of the area under the curve is bounded by the region of the measurement scale extending from 400–600, that is, from 1 σ below the mean to 1 σ above, and the same percentage of individual scores also occur within that region. Notice that the curve is symmetrical, and thus half the area within ± 1 σ of the mean is above the mean and half is below.

Figure 5-4 (bottom) shows the cumulative percentage of the area under the normal curve at each point on the measurement scale. The height of the ordinate at any point gives the percentage of the area under the normal curve below that point. For example, the ordinate at 400 is 15.87%, and the ordinate at 500 is exactly 50%, as it should be at the mean of a symmetrical distribution. We are now able to find the percentiles of some selected scores, and we will shortly develop methods of finding the percentile of any score in any normal distribution.

Percentiles of Some Selected Scores. Consider a student having a test score of 400, a score one standard deviation below the mean. What is the student's percentile? Referring to Figure 5-4 (top), we can find the percentile by finding the percentage of the area below 400, and we can do this by adding 2.28% and 13.59% to get 15.87%, which represents the 15.87th percentile. Alternatively, we can refer to Figure 5-4 (bottom), where this addition has already been done for us in the cumulative percentage graph. The ordinate of the cumulative percentage curve at 400 is 15.87%, representing the desired 15.87th percentile. Now consider a score of 600, one standard deviation above the mean. We can find the percentage of scores below 600 by adding the percentages of the areas under the normal curve below that point: 2.28% + 13.59% + 34.13% + 34.13% = 84.13%. The ordinate of the cumulative percentage curve also gives the desired percentage. In any normal distribution, no matter what the value of the mean and standard deviation, a score 1 σ below the mean is at the 16th percentile (rounding up) and a score 1 σ above the mean is at the 84th percentile (rounding down).

Now consider the percentile of a score of 550, which is only 1/2 standard deviation above the mean. We could find the approximate percentile by using the cumulative percentage graph. We could erect a vertical line perpendicular to the measurement scale at 550, and the height of the resulting ordinate would give the required percentile. But graphical methods are not very precise, so we will develop some numerical methods of using the normal distribution. In the process, we will explain the origin of those percentages in Figure 5-4, which seem to have materialized out of thin air.

The Equation of the Normal Distribution

Not every smooth, bell-shaped curve represents a normal distribution, since there are other kinds of such curves. A normal distribution is a member of a family of curves generated by a specific equation, presented below. I hasten to say that we will develop some simple methods of using normal distributions, even though the equation, below, may appear rather formidable:

$$h = \frac{1}{\sigma\sqrt{2\pi}}\, e^{-\frac{1}{2}\left(\frac{X-\mu}{\sigma}\right)^2}, \tag{5-9}$$

where h = the height (ordinate) of the curve at any point, X; X = any point on the horizontal measurement scale; π = a constant (small Greek *pi*), approximately 3.1416; e = a constant, approximately 2.7183; μ = a parameter (small Greek *mu*), the mean of the distribution; and σ = a parameter (small Greek *sigma*), the standard deviation of the distribution.

Some definitions and explanations are in order. There are two *variables* in the above equation, h and X. The value of the **dependent variable,** h, is determined by — dependent upon — the value of the **independent variable,** X. The constant π is the familiar constant from geometry, the ratio of the circumference of a circle to the diameter. (It may not be instantly obvious that this geometrical constant has anything to do with statistics, but π has a way of turning up in a number of mathematical contexts.) The nature of the constant e need not concern us beyond noting that its value is approximately 2.7183. We can only give the values of e and π approximately because both constants are irrational numbers having nonterminating portions to the right of the decimal. The mean and standard deviation, μ and σ, are constant within any given normal distribution but are different in other normal distributions. Thus, Equation 5-9 is the equation of a **family of curves,** each of which represents a normal distribution. Any particular normal distribution, having a specific mean and a specific standard deviation, is generated by entering those values of μ and σ in Equation 5-9 and then solving for h at all values of X. Some normal distributions having different values of μ and σ are shown in Figure 5-5.

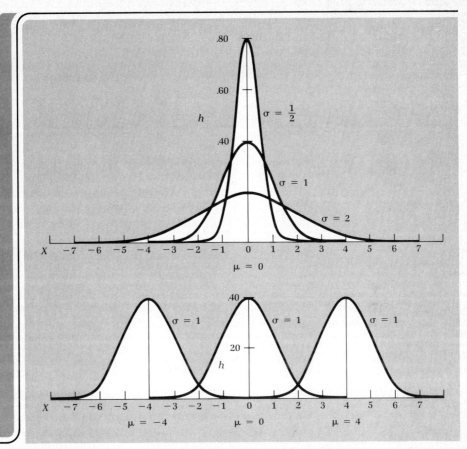

FIGURE 5-5. Top: Normal distributions having the same mean, but different standard deviations. Bottom: Normal distributions having the same standard deviations, but different means.

A constant, such as μ or σ, which can take on different values and thereby generate different curves relating h and X, is called a **parameter.** It can be proven mathematically that the parameters μ and σ appearing in Equation 5-9 are indeed the mean and standard deviation of the normal distribution, but such a proof would take us beyond the scope of this text. The fact that σ appears as a parameter in the equation for the normal distribution is one of the reasons why the standard deviation and the variance are the most widely used measures of dispersion.

The Standard Normal Distribution

The **standard normal distribution** is a special member of the family of normal curves having a mean of 0 and a standard deviation of 1. Using procedures to be described shortly, we can transform the scores in any normal distribution having any given mean and standard deviation into the

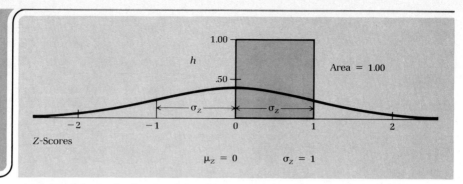

FIGURE 5-6. Standard normal distribution, equal vertical and horizontal scales. Area under the curve is equal to area of shaded square. Vertical scale is usually greatly exaggerated in most illustrations of normal curves.

standard normal distribution. Such a transformation is very useful in several contexts.

We will use the symbol **Z** to stand for a score in the standard normal distribution. We can find the equation of a set of **Z-scores** — that is, the equation of the standard normal distribution — by substituting Z for X in Equation 5-9, and substituting 0 and 1 for μ and σ. Thus,

$$h = \frac{1}{1\sqrt{2\pi}} e^{-\frac{1}{2}\left(\frac{Z-0}{1}\right)^2} = \frac{1}{\sqrt{2\pi}} e^{-\frac{1}{2}Z^2} \tag{5-10}$$

Equation 5-10 shows the nature of the normal curve more clearly than 5-9. As Z becomes very large — in either the positive or negative direction — h becomes very small, and the tails of the curve approach the horizontal axis as an **asymptote,** that is, more and more closely without ever reaching the axis. You will see that this is true if you note that the exponent of e is always negative whether Z is negative or positive, since Z^2 is always positive and is multiplied by $-1/2$. (There is a brief review of exponents in Appendix A.) Even though the curve never touches the horizontal axis, there exists an *area under the curve,* which is equal to 1.00 in the standard normal distribution and in the other normal distributions generated by Equation 5-9. Finding the area under such a curve is an exercise in integral calculus, but it is not at all necessary to have had a calculus course in order to understand the uses we will make of the normal distribution.[1]

The standard normal distribution is shown in Figure 5-6, where the vertical and horizontal scales are equal. The total area under the curve is equal to the area of the unit square shown in the figure. When the vertical and horizontal scales are in the same sized units, the standard normal distribution

[1] If you have some background in calculus, then you may be able to integrate Equation 5-10, perhaps with the help of Mood (1950). By doing so, you will see that the area under the curve is indeed equal to 1.00, and you will also see how it is that π enters into the equation of the normal distribution.

is rather flat, and other normal distributions with larger standard deviations are even flatter. When we illustrate a normal distribution, we will usually exaggerate the vertical scale greatly so that the graph will more nearly conform to the three-quarters rule of Chapter 2.

Transforming a Distribution to Z-Scores. The proportions of the area under the standard normal curve lying below any Z-score of interest have been calculated, and are shown in Table A in the back of the book. Thus, if we could transform an X score in a normal distribution into a Z-score, then we could find the proportion of the area below that value of Z in Table A. Multiplying that proportion by 100 would then give the percentile of the score — that is, the relative standing of the score in relation to the population.

The following equation is a definition of Z, and also provides a transformation of any value of X into a Z-score:

$$Z = \frac{X - \mu}{\sigma}, \tag{5-11}$$

where X is a raw score, and μ and σ are the mean and standard deviation of X.

By considering our discussion of transformations in Chapter 4, you can see how it is that applying the above equation to each value of X in a set of scores will result in a transformed distribution having a mean of 0 and a standard deviation of 1. As we showed earlier, adding or substracting a constant from each score in a distribution will change the mean by the value of that constant. In Equation 5-11, subtracting μ from each X score generates a new distribution having a mean of 0, and then multiplying each value of $(X - \mu)$ by $1/\sigma$ multiplies the standard deviation by that factor, and thus yields a standard deviation of 1 in the transformed distribution of Z-scores.

Equation 5-11 will transform any set of scores — whether normally distributed or not — into a distribution of Z-scores. But if the Xs are not normally distributed, then neither are the resulting Z-scores. Indeed, transforming to Z-scores merely changes the units of the horizontal measurement scale without altering the shape of a distribution in any way. That fact has considerable bearing on our use of Z-scores in finding percentile ranks, as we will explain.

Percentiles from Z-Scores. We will now explain how to find the percentile of any value of X by using the Z-score. Suppose a student has a test score of 600 in a population where the mean is 500 and the standard deviation 100. The Z-score is calculated in Table 5-3. The proportion of the area under the standard normal distribution lying below that Z-score is then found in Table A, Column 2. Multiplying that proportion by 100 then gives the percentile shown in Table 5-3. The Z-score for a test score of 400 is also calculated in that table. Notice that this Z-score is negative. The numerator of a Z-score is the deviation of an X value from the mean, and as we noted earlier, the mean is always subtracted from X. A negative deviation, and the

TABLE 5-3. Z-Scores and Percentiles in a Population Where the Mean and Standard Deviation Are 500 and 100, Respectively.

X	Z	Area below Z in Table A	PR
600	1.00	.8413	84.13th
500	0	.5000	50th
400	−1.00	.1587	15.87th

By Formula 5-11, $Z = \dfrac{X - \mu}{\sigma}$. Here, $\mu = 500$, $\sigma = 100$.

$$Z_{600} = \frac{600 - 500}{100} = 1.00; \qquad Z_{400} = \frac{400 - 500}{100} = -1.00.$$

resulting negative Z-score, indicates that a score is below the mean. Thus the sign of the Z-score must be taken into account in using Table A, where Column 3 shows the proportion of the area below negative Z-scores. Converting that proportion to a percentage, as before, yields the desired percentile. A test score of 500, exactly equal to the mean of the population, yields a Z-score of 0, corresponding to the 50th percentile.

In Table A, Column 2 gives the proportion of the area below a positive Z value, and since the normal distribution is symmetrical, that area is the same as the area above (to the right of) a negative Z value. Thus, there are two headings for Column 2: *Area below +Z,* and *Area above −Z.* Column 3 gives the proportion of the area above a positive Z and below (to the left of) a negative Z. Notice that the areas on the same lines in Columns 2 and 3 all add up to 1.00, since the areas above and below any point constitute the total area under the curve. Figure 5-7 illustrates the relationship between areas and percentiles for the Z-scores in Table 5-3.

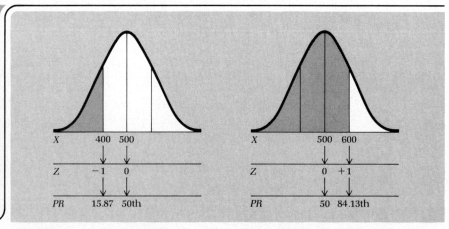

FIGURE 5-7. Test scores, Z-scores, and percentile ranks from Table 5-3. Shaded areas are proportions below Z-scores found in Table A.

Using Z-scores to find percentiles may appear very cumbersome, but notice that we can find the percentile of any score in a distribution without knowing the frequency of any of the individual scores, or even the size of the distribution. If we are dealing with a normally distributed population, then we need know only the mean and standard deviation in order to find the percentile of any score — that is, the relative standing of any given individual in relation to the other individuals in the population.

Z-Scores in a Sample. So far, we have dealt with Z-scores in a normally distributed population. We now consider Z-scores in a sample. Finding the relative standing of an individual in a sample, whether by using Z-scores or calculating percentiles by our earlier method, is not quite the same thing as finding the relative standing of that individual in the population from which the sample was drawn. Of course, we should expect an individual at the 90th percentile in a sample to rank high in the population as well, but as we noted earlier, sample statistics — the quantitative characteristics of samples — are subject to chance fluctuations. We will develop methods of estimating the relative standing of individuals in populations based on the observation of samples. These methods will play an important role in our later development of inferential statistics.

If a sample has been drawn from a normally distributed population, then we can use Z-scores to find the percentile rank of any score in the sample. When we do not know the mean and standard deviation of the population — as is often the case — we use the observed sample mean and standard deviation in place of those unknown population parameters. In that case, the Z-score is

$$Z = \frac{X - \bar{X}}{SD}. \tag{5-12}$$

Figure 5-3 shows a frequency distribution of heights in a small sample of young men. Table 5-4 shows the percentiles for heights based on Z-scores

TABLE 5-4. Essentially Normal Distribution of Heights Shown in Figure 5-3. Percentile Ranks by Formula 5-5, and by Z-Scores Using Formula 5-12.

X	f	PR	Z	PR$_Z$
76	1	97.62	1.99	97.67
75	2	90.48	1.57	94.18
73	4	76.19	.72	76.42
72	2	61.90	.30	61.79
71	4	47.62	−.12	45.22
70	3	30.95	−.54	29.46
69	2	19.05	−.97	16.60
68	2	9.52	−1.39	8.23
67	1	2.38	−1.81	3.51

$\Sigma f = N = 21$

$\bar{X} = 71.29 \qquad Mdn = 71.12 \qquad SD = 2.37$

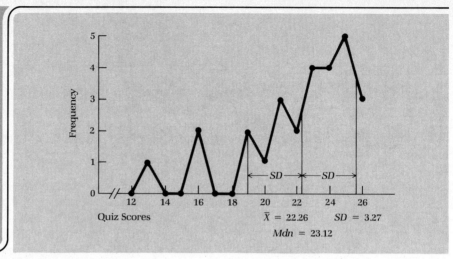

FIGURE 5-8. Skewed distribution of scores on an easy quiz, 26 possible points (data from Table 5-5).

found by Formula 5-12. For comparison, the percentiles of those heights were also found by Formula 5-5. Notice that the percentiles found by those two methods compare fairly closely.

Figure 5-8 shows a distribution of scores on a very easy quiz having a total of 26 points. The scores are bunched near the top of the scale, and thus the distribution is negatively skewed. Notice that the mean is less than the median, indicating the direction of skew.

Table 5-5 shows the percentiles for the quiz scores found by Formula 5-5 and also by Z-scores using Formula 5-12. The discrepancies between the percentiles found by those two methods are much greater here than in the

TABLE 5-5. Skewed Distribution of Quiz Scores Shown in Figure 5-8. Percentile Ranks by Formula 5-5, and by Z-Scores Using Formula 5-12. Compare Discrepancies Between Percentiles Here with Discrepancies in Table 5-4.

X	f	PR	z	PR_z
26	3	94.44	1.14	87.29
25	5	79.63	.84	79.95
24	4	62.96	.53	70.19
23	4	48.15	.23	59.10
22	2	37.04	−.08	46.81
21	3	27.78	−.39	34.83
20	1	20.37	−.69	24.51
19	2	14.81	−1.00	15.87
16	2	7.41	−1.91	2.81
13	1	1.85	−2.83	.23

$\Sigma f = N = 27$

$\bar{X} = 22.26 \qquad Mdn = 23.12 \qquad SD = 3.27$

essentially normal distribution of heights in Table 5-4. When we use Z-scores to find percentiles, we do so under the assumption that we are dealing with an essentially normal distribution. If a distribution is not normal, then percentiles found by Z-scores may differ greatly from the true values of the percentiles by Formula 5-5. Although we can transform any distribution into a set of Z-scores, that will not convert a nonnormal distribution into a normal one.

A Forward Look

In the present chapter, we have developed methods of finding the relative standing of individuals within a group. Later, we will extend those methods to making comparisons between different groups, and we will develop tests of the statistical significance of those comparisons. Thus, we will make extensive use of those ideas in several new contexts. We have touched on the role of chance in determining the characteristics of samples, and we will find this an important theme running through everything that is to follow.

Terms and Symbols

Although I have not provided a summary at the end of each chapter in this text, you can easily — and profitably — construct your own chapter summary by carefully reviewing, comparing, and contrasting the following terms and symbols, and the ideas they represent.

Percentile	**Parameter**
Percentile rank	**Family of curves**
Transforming ranks and scores	**Standard normal distribution**
Simple percentage	**Asymptote**
Cumulative percentage	**Z-score**
Score at a percentile	R
50th percentile	cf_b
Quartile	cf_R
Semi-interquartile range	PR
Quartile range	**0th percentile**
Decile	**100th percentile**
Centile	p_j
Area under a curve	f_j
Mutually exclusive and exhaustive	cp_j
Dependent variable	cf_j
Independent variable	p_w
Constant	i
	X_{LL}

X_{PR} σ

Q π

Q_1 e

Q_2 Z

Q_3 $\overline{X}$

h SD

μ

EXERCISES AND STUDY QUESTIONS

1. General Eisenhower ranked 61st out of 164 in his graduating class at West Point, and Private Schmidt ranked 61st out of 164 in his high school graduating class.

   a. Find General Eisenhower's percentile rank in his West Point class, which of course is identical to Private Schmidt's percentile rank in *his* class.

   b. Whose performance more likely represents a higher level of scholastic accomplishment, the general's, or the private's, or is there any difference?

2. A 22-year-old professional basketball player's height is at the 50th percentile in his association, and a 22-year-old college player's height is at the 50th percentile in his conference.

   a. Which man is more likely the taller?

   b. Draw some general conclusions about comparing percentile ranks in different distributions.

3. Briefly explain your answers to the following:

   a. Is a man at the 60th percentile in height twice as tall as a man at the 30th percentile?

   b. Does a person at the 60th percentile in income make twice as much money as a person at the 30th percentile?

   c. A group of juvenile offenders in a rehabilitation program are rated in terms of aggressiveness. Is a juvenile at the 60th percentile twice as aggressive as a juvenile at the 30th?

4. The Wechsler Adult Intelligence Scale (WAIS) is an IQ test having a mean of 100 and a standard deviation of 15. Person A has an IQ of 98, and person B an IQ of 119.

   a. Find the percentiles of the IQs above.

   b. Compare the IQs of person A and person B.

5. We now reconsider the two bowlers in Exercise 4 in the last chapter. Both bowlers have a mean of 178 in their last 100 games. Bowler A has an *SD* of 16, and bowler B an *SD* of 22. Assuming that each bowler's distribution of scores is approximately normal, do the following for each bowler:

   a. Find the percentile of a score of 194, and the percentile of a score of 200.

   b. Find the probability that each bowler's next game will be 194 or higher, and the probability that the next game will be 200 or higher. (*HINT:* Since past performance is the best guide to predicting the future, consider the proportion of each bowler's last 100 games that met or exceeded the performance levels above.)

6. In a normal distribution, what is the precise relationship between the following measures of dispersion: *AD*, *SD*, and *Q*. (*HINT:* Consider some of the areas under the normal curve in Table A.)

7. Suppose that the graduating classes at two high schools have the same mean and standard deviation on the Scholastic Aptitude Test (SAT). Thus, the students in those two schools are equally able, on the average — at least to the extent that the SAT provides a measure of scholastic ability. Now suppose that one school has a small graduating class of 100, and the other a large graduating class of 1,000. Student A ranks 51st in the class of 100, and student B ranks 51st in the class of 1,000. Compare those two students.

8. Suppose you have just made a score of 81 on a psychology exam where the mean is 72.40 and the *SD* 9.21. By a strange coincidence, a friend of yours has made a score of 81 on a political science exam, and by an even stranger coincidence the mean on that exam is also 72.40, but the *SD* is 14.87. Your friend insists that his performance is as good as yours. Do you agree, or disagree? Support your argument with some computations and elegant reasoning.

9. Consider the following combinations of Z-scores for height and weight of adult males. What would a man look like having each of the following Z-scores?
    a. $Z_H = -1.20$; $Z_W = 1.20$.
    b. $Z_H = 0.00$; $Z_W = 0.00$.
    c. $Z_H = 1.20$; $Z_W = -1.20$.
    d. $Z_H = -1.20$; $Z_W = -1.20$.
    e. $Z_H = 1.20$; $Z_W = 1.20$.

10. Using the histogram in Figure 2-11F (Chapter 2), make up a table showing the data in a grouped frequency distribution.
    a. Find the percentile rank of each score using Formula 5-5.
    b. Using the values of $\overline{X}$ and *SD* given in the figure, find the Z-score for each score.
    c. Using the Z-score procedure, find the percentile rank of each score.
    d. Explain the discrepancies between the percentiles found by the formula and by Z-scores. Which percentiles are more "accurate"?

11. a. Draw a frequency polygon showing the distribution of *raw scores* in the above exercise.
    b. Draw a frequency polygon showing the distribution of *Z-scores* in the above exercise, using the same horizontal scale as in your distribution of raw scores.
    c. Compare the shapes of your two frequency polygons.
    d. Generalize your findings here: When you transform a skewed distribution to a set of Z-scores, does that convert such a distribution into a normal distribution?

Random Variables and Probability Experiments

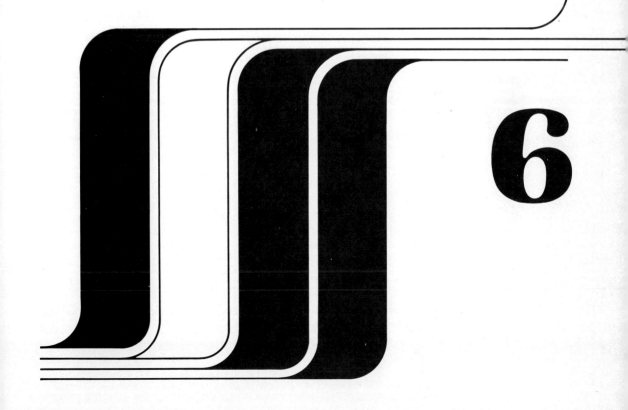

6

A variable, as we said earlier, is any kind of measurement that can take on different values. Test scores, number of correct responses in a maze, and reaction times are some examples of variables that are of interest in psychology. The major goal of psychological research is to understand the relationships between the variables that characterize human and animal behavior. For example, when we say that greater practice leads to greater learning, what we mean is that we believe there is a very high probability of a lawful, orderly relationship between the practice variable and the learning variable. We have every expectation that people who practice a task more will perform better, at least *most* of the people most of the time. Nevertheless, we will find it useful to consider any kind of measurement of human or animal behavior as a **random variable,** a variable whose value is determined by chance. Initially, the concept of chance—randomness—seems antithetical to the goals of science. How could we ever predict one variable from another, or hope to understand any facet of behavior if all of our measurements were truly random variables? Law and order are the very opposite of chance and randomness. Nevertheless, we design all of our observations and experiments to test the hypothesis that there is *no* lawful relationship between variables, that chance alone is at work. If we find a very low probability that chance alone can account for the observed results, then we reject the hypothesis that chance alone is at work and decide in favor of the probable operation of law and order. This direction of reasoning may seem to be putting the cart before the horse, but it turns out to be a useful way to proceed. This line of reasoning requires that we consider many kinds of measurements *as though* they were determined by chance—that is, as though they were random variables.

Probability Experiments

A **probability experiment** is any experiment where the **outcome,** the result, is determined by chance. Tossing a coin is perhaps the simplest example of a probability experiment. It may not be instantly obvious that analyzing such an experiment could be of any help in understanding human or animal behavior. But we will see that the analysis of probability experiments is the very cornerstone of inferential statistics.

In tossing a **fair coin,** *Heads* and *Tails* have an even chance of coming up. Rolling a fair die, where each of the six sides has an equal chance of turning up, is another example of a probability experiment. A single toss of a coin or a single roll of a die is called a **trial.** The possible outcomes of any trial are **mutually exclusive and exhaustive**—that is, the outcomes do not overlap in any way and they account for all possible results of the trial. In rolling a single die, if the number 6 comes up on a particular trial, then the numbers 1 through 5 are excluded on that trial; and if a coin comes up *Heads,* then *Tails* is excluded on that particular trial. We will decide beforehand not to count any trial where the coin lands on edge, sticks to the ceiling, disappears, or fails in any other way to come up *Heads* or *Tails;* nor will we count any trial where the die fails to show unequivocally one of the numbers 1 through 6. Thus, *Heads* and *Tails,* in the case of the coin, and the numbers 1 through 6, in the case of the die, exhaust the possible outcomes of a single trial.

A probability experiment can consist of a single trial or of many multiple trials, for example, where a single coin can be tossed several times, or where several coins can be tossed at once. As we will see, these two kinds of multiple trials are formally identical — as long as the successive as well as the simultaneous trials are **independent** — that is, do not influence each other in any way. We will clarify the concept of independence in a later section.

Events and Sample Spaces

In a probability experiment, a **simple event** is an outcome that can occur in one and only one way. For example, in rolling a single die, each of the numbers 1 through 6 is a simple event. A **compound event** is an outcome that can occur in more than one way. For example, we observe the compound event *Odd* if 1, 3, or 5 comes up on a single die. The **sample space** of a probability experiment is the list of all the mutually exclusive and exhaustive events that can occur in the experiment. Table 6-1A shows the sample space

TABLE 6-1. Rolling a Single Die.

A. Sample space for simple events.

	E_1	E_2	E_3	E_4	E_5	E_6
Simple events	1	2	3	4	5	6
Probabilities	$\frac{1}{6}$	$\frac{1}{6}$	$\frac{1}{6}$	$\frac{1}{6}$	$\frac{1}{6}$	$\frac{1}{6}$

B. Simple events resulting in some selected compound events.

Simple events	Compound events	Probability
1 3 5	Odd	$\frac{1}{2}$
2 4 6	Even	$\frac{1}{2}$
1 2	2 or less	$\frac{1}{3}$
4 5 6	4 or more	$\frac{1}{2}$

for a probability experiment consisting of rolling a single die and observing the particular number that turns up.

Table 6-1B shows some selected compound events that can occur in a probability experiment with a single die. It is not correct to think of a compound event as being made up, composed, of simple events. Rather, a compound event occurs if any one of a number of simple events occurs. Some of the compound events in Table 6-1B are mutually exclusive and exhaustive, and some are not. The events *Odd* and *Even* are mutually exclusive and exhaustive, and thus constitute a sample space for a probability experiment if we are interested only in whether the die comes up *Odd* or *Even* and not interested in the particular number which comes up. Since the events *Even* and *2 or less* overlap, they are not mutually exclusive, and thus do not constitute a sample space; nor do the events *2 or less* and *4 or more*, since those events are not exhaustive, though mutually exclusive.

Probability. The **probability** of any event is the proportion of times we expect the event to occur in a large number of repetitions of a probability experiment. In the long run, any event should occur in the same proportion as the event occurs in the sample space for the experiment. Thus, we can take the sample space as a kind of model representing the expected results of a large number or repetitions of a probability experiment. We define the probability of any event, simple or compound, as

$$P(E_i) = \frac{\text{Number of ways } E_i \text{ can occur}}{\text{Number of simple events in sample space}}, \qquad (6\text{-}1)$$

where $P(E_i)$ is the probability of the particular event, E_i. (Do not mistake $P(E_i)$ for P *times* E_i.) For the present, we will assume that all of the simple events within a sample space are equally probable. Since a simple event can occur in only one way, the probability of any simple event is

$$P(\text{Any simple event}) = \frac{1}{n_s}, \qquad (6\text{-}2)$$

where n_s is the number of simple events in the sample space. The probabilities shown in Table 6-1 were found using Formula 6-2. The probabilities of the compound events in that table were found using Formula 6-1. For example, since the event *4 or more* can occur in three different ways,

$$P(4 \text{ or more}) = \frac{3}{6} = \frac{1}{2} = .5.$$

It is also true that the probability of the compound event *4 or more* is equal to the sum of the probabilities of 4, 5, and 6, the simple events resulting in that compound event:

$$P(4 \text{ or more}) = P(4) + P(5) + P(6) = \frac{1}{6} + \frac{1}{6} + \frac{1}{6} = \frac{1}{2} = .5.$$

In general,

$$P(\text{Any compound event}, E_C) = \Sigma P(\text{Simple events resulting in } E_C). \qquad (6\text{-}3)$$

We will always express a probability as a single number, never in the form of **odds**. For example, we will state a probability as $1/2$ or .5—never as even odds—or .95—never 19 to 1. Our decimal or fractional notation will prove much more convenient.

Multiple Trials. We will now consider a more complicated probability experiment, tossing two coins simultaneously. We will designate the coins as Coin 1 and Coin 2. The sample space for this experiment is shown in Table

TABLE 6-2. Identical Sample Spaces for Two Probability Experiments. Random Variable X = Number of Heads. Values of X are in Parentheses. The Compound Event X = 1 is Enclosed in Each Sample Space.

A. Two Coins, Simultaneous Tosses.

Coin 2:

(Trial 2)

		H	T
Coin 1: (Trial 1)	H	H H (2)	H T (1)
	T	T H (1)	T T (0)

B. One Coin, Two Successive Tosses.

2nd toss:

(Trial 2)

		H	T
1st toss: (Trial 1)	H	H H (2)	H T (1)
	T	T H (1)	T T (0)

6-2A. Each coin is regarded as a trial, and while there are two trials in this experiment, each outcome listed in the sample space is a simple event. For example, the event *HT* can occur in one and only one way: Coin 1 must come up *Heads* and Coin 2 must come up *Tails*. The event *HT* is not the same simple event as *TH*, since the latter event is *Tails* on Coin 1 and *Heads* on Coin 2. Thus, there are four simple events in the sample space for this probability experiment, and by Formula 6-2, the probability of each simple event is 1/4.

Consider each of the two coins separately for a moment. Each coin represents a trial. The coins are tossed simultaneously in a fair, unbiased manner such that neither influences the other, and thus, the trials are said to be independent. Knowing the outcome of one trial tells us nothing about the outcome of the other. Suppose that I toss the two coins. I look at them, and I tell you that Coin 1 came up *Heads,* and I ask you to guess the outcome for Coin 2. Since the two coins are completely independent, knowing the outcome for Coin 1 is of no help whatever in allowing you to guess the outcome for Coin 2 — all of which may seem obvious in this context, but may appear less so in some other situations, as we shall see.

Now, consider a slightly different probability experiment, tossing a single coin twice. Here, we have an experiment consisting of two trials with a single coin. We toss the coin once, write down the results for Trial 1, and then toss the coin again and write down the results for Trial 2. We always toss the coin in an unbiased manner, so that *Heads* and *Tails* have an even chance of coming up on Trial 2 regardless of the outcome on Trial 1. Thus, the trials here are also independent, as in our earlier experiment where two coins were tossed simultaneously. Table 6-2B shows the sample space for our present probability experiment. The combined results of Trials 1 and 2 constitute a simple event in our two-coin experiment, even though we can consider each trial as a simple event in a one-coin experiment. The sample space here is identical to the sample space for tossing two coins simultaneously. In any probability experiment of any number of trials, it matters not at all whether the trials are simultaneous or successive, as long as the trials are independent.

Random Variables and Compound Events. There is a shorthand way of describing the results of a probability experiment that is especially useful where compound events are concerned. We define the random variable X as the number of heads occurring in our two-coin experiment. Since X can take on integer values only, the random variable X is discrete, as opposed to continuous. The numbers in parentheses in Tables 6-2A and 6-2B are the values of X associated with the simple events in each sample space. We could just as well define X in terms of the number of *Tails,* since there is no special magic in *Heads.* The only requirement is that we be consistent. We can consider our coin-tossing experiment as an exercise in observing a value of the random variable X, a variable whose value is determined by chance. Thus, each value of X represents an event, an outcome of a probability experiment. Each time we perform the probability experiment — that is, each time we toss the two coins simultaneously or toss the single coin twice — we observe one and only one value of X. All of the possible values of X are mutually exclusive and exhaustive, and thus constitute a sample space for a probability experiment consisting of observing a value of X. Two of these events, $X = 0$ and $X = 2$, are simple events that can occur in only one way, but the event $X = 1$ is a compound event that can occur in two ways. The event $X = 1$ is the same event as *Heads on one coin,* and thus, $X = 1$ is a kind of shorthand expression for the longer verbal expression *Heads on one coin.* The values of the random variable X also provide a quantitative description of all the possible outcomes of our probability experiment. We will find such quantitative descriptions extremely useful.

Table 6-3 shows the sample space for a probability experiment consisting of rolling two dice. As in the experiments with two coins, it makes no difference whether we actually use two dice or roll a single die successively, as long as the single die is rolled in an unbiased manner so that each of the six sides has the same probability of coming up. Whether we use one die or two, our experiment consists of two independent trials. Each of the 36 simple events in the sample space can occur in only one way, and every event is different from every other event. For example, the simple event *1,2* is not the same simple event as *2,1.* In this experiment, we let the random variable X equal the sum of the numbers on the two dice. The values of X are in parentheses in Table 6-3. The values of X equal to 2 and 12 can each occur in only one way, namely *1,1* and *6,6,* which represent simple events. All of the other values of X can occur in two or more ways, and thus represent compound events. Three compound events, $X = 4$, $X = 7$, and $X \geq 10$, are shown in Table 6-3.

Table 6-4 shows the different values, X_j, which the random variable X can take on. The frequency, f_j, is the number of simple events that produce a particular value of X, that is, a particular X_j. Since f_j is the number of ways that any particular value of X can occur, we can also find the probability of any value of X by Formula 6-1. We can also find the probability of any value of X by referring to Table 6-3 and summing the probabilities of the simple events that produce that value of X. The compound event $X \geq 10$ is a kind of event that will presently become very important in our development of inferential

TABLE 6-3.   Sample Space for Rolling Two Dice. Random Variable X = Sum of Numbers on Dice. Values of X are in Parentheses. Compound Events $X = 4$, $X = 7$, and $X \geq 10$ are Indicated by Enclosures.

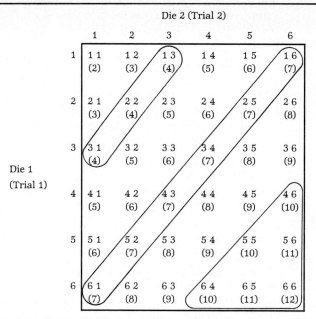

TABLE 6-4.   Values, Frequencies, and Probabilities of the Random Variable X, the Sum of the Numbers on Two Dice.

X_j	2	3	4	5	6	7	8	9	10	11	12
f_j	1	2	3	4	5	6	5	4	3	2	1
$P(X_j)$	$\frac{1}{36}$	$\frac{2}{36}$	$\frac{3}{36}$	$\frac{4}{36}$	$\frac{5}{36}$	$\frac{6}{36}$	$\frac{5}{36}$	$\frac{4}{36}$	$\frac{3}{36}$	$\frac{2}{36}$	$\frac{1}{36}$

$$\Sigma P_j = \frac{36}{36} = 1.00$$

statistics. The event $X \geq 10$ occurs if X equals 10, 11, or 12; thus, the probability that $X \geq 10$ is the sum of the probabilities of those events. There are six simple events that result in the compound event $X \geq 10$, and thus P($X \geq$ 10) = 6/36.

The values of the random variable X shown in Tables 6-3 and 6-4 are mutually exclusive and exhaustive. Any time the two dice are rolled, one and only one value of X occurs. Thus, the set of values of X constitutes a sample space for the probability experiment consisting of observing a value of X. But notice that the events in that sample space are not equally probable.

The Size of a Sample Space.   So far, we have considered two probability experiments, each consisting of two trials. In each case, it is very easy to list all of the simple events in the sample space, and if we know the size of a sample space, we can find the probability of each simple event by Formula 6-2. But in an experiment involving a larger number of trials, the size of the sample space is not so readily apparent. We will develop a general method for finding the size of the sample space for a probability experiment having any number of trials.

In our first probability experiment, each of the two trials was a toss of a coin. There were two possible outcomes per trial, and there were $2^2 = 4$ simple events in the sample space. In our second experiment, each of the two trials was a roll of a die. There were six possible outcomes per trial and there were $6^2 = 36$ simple events in the sample space. In general, where there are N trials, each having K outcomes, the size of the sample space is given by

$$\text{Size of sample space} = n_s = K^N. \qquad (6\text{-}4)$$

We can then find the probability of any simple event by substituting K^N for n_s in Formula 6-2:

$$P(\text{Any simple event}) = \frac{1}{K^N}. \qquad (6\text{-}5)$$

For example, suppose we toss ten coins at once, or equivalently, one coin ten times. What is the probability of tossing ten *Heads?* Since the sequence of ten *Heads* represents one of the simple events in the sample space of our probability experiment, Formula 6-5 gives the probability:

$$P(10\ \text{Heads}) = \frac{1}{2^{10}} = \frac{1}{1{,}024}.$$

The probability of ten *Tails* in a row — indeed, the probability of any particular sequence of *Heads* and *Tails* in ten trials — is also $1/1{,}024$, since each possible sequence is one of the 1,024 simple events in the sample space. It may appear paradoxical, but the sequence $H\,H\,H\,H\,H\,H\,H\,H\,H\,H$ is no more unusual — no less probable — than $H\,T\,T\,H\,T\,H\,H\,T\,T\,T$, or $T\,H\,T\,T\,T\,H\,T\,H\,H\,T$, or any other of the possible simple events in the probability experiment.

Some Properties of Probabilities

Probability of an Impossible Event.   If the sides of a single die are numbered 1 through 6, what is the probability of a 7 appearing? It is of course impossible for a seven to occur with our particular six-sided die, but it will be instructive to attach a number to the probability of that outcome. Since 7 is not listed in the sample space in Table 6-1, there are zero ways for a 7 to occur. Using Formula 6-1,

$$P(7) = \frac{0}{6} = 0.$$

Any event not listed in the sample space for a probability experiment is an **impossible event** which has a probability of zero.

Probability of an Absolutely Certain Event. If a coin has heads on both sides, what is the probability of *Heads* coming up? It is absolutely certain that such a coin will always come up *Heads* — ruling out the bizarre outcomes we mentioned earlier. Our two-headed coin has two sides, and each side represents a possible outcome. Thus, the sample space for a single trial consists of the two simple events H and H, since *Heads* can occur in two ways, either on Side 1 or 2. By Formula 6-1,

$$P(\textit{Heads with 2-headed coin}) = \frac{2}{2} = 1.$$

Thus, the probability of an absolutely certain event is 1.

Summing Probabilities. It is useful to know that the sum of the probabilities of all the events in any sample space — whether for a single trial, or for any kind of probability experiment — is equal to 1. For a sample space consisting of simple events, we can sum the probabilities using Formula 6-2, remembering that $1/n_s$ is a constant. Thus,

$$\sum_{i=1}^{n_s} P(E_i) = \sum_{i=1}^{n_s} \frac{1}{n_s} = n_s \frac{1}{n_s} = 1.$$

For a sample space consisting of mutually exclusive and exhaustive compound events, the sum of the probabilities is also 1, since the probability of each compound event is the sum of the probabilities of a number of mutually exclusive and exhaustive simple events.

Two Important Properties. The probability of an impossible event and an absolutely certain one, which we found previously, represent limits on the values that probabilities can take on. Since there is no event less probable than an impossible one, or more probable than an absolutely certain one, no probability can be less than zero or greater than 1. We list below those two important properties of all probabilities:

$$0 \le P \le 1, \qquad \text{and} \tag{6-6}$$

$$\Sigma P = 1. \tag{6-7}$$

Expression 6-6 is read, "P is less than or equal to one, and greater than or equal to zero." In Equation 6-7, the summation is understood to be across all the probabilities of all the outcomes in the sample space. We will make extensive use of the property shown in Equation 6-7 in connection with inferential statistics.

Expected Value of a Random Variable

The **expected value** of a random variable is the average value of the variable in the long run. For a random variable X, the expected value is symbolized **$E(X)$**. If we carried out a probability experiment a very large number of times, each time observing the value of a random variable, then the mean of that very large number of observations would represent the expected value of the random variable. For example, if we let X equal the number that turns up on a single roll of a single die, then we could roll the die again and again and find the mean of X in the long run — over a very large number of rolls.

The expected value is exactly equal to the mean of the population of Xs — that is, the mean of the infinite number of values of X that we could observe in an infinite number of rolls of the die. We have used the symbol μ for the mean of a population and thus

$$E(X) = \mu.$$

Of course, an infinite population exists only as a concept — as an idea — but such a construct turns out to be a very useful figment of our imagination. Fortunately, we can find the expected value of a random variable without taking an infinite amount of time to run an infinite number of probability experiments.

We can calculate the expected value of a random variable by using the sample space. Since the sample space is the enumeration of all possible outcomes of a probability experiment, no matter how many times we perform the experiment no outcome can occur other than those outcomes listed in the sample space. Further, we expect *in the long run* that the relative frequency of occurrence of the possible outcomes of an experiment will be the same as the relative frequency, the probability, of those outcomes in the sample space. Thus, the expected value of a random variable is the mean of the set of values occurring in the sample space.

Earlier, we described a probability experiment consisting of rolling two dice, where the random variable X equals the sum of the numbers turning up. The sample space for that experiment is shown in Table 6-3. We will find the expected value of X by finding the mean of X in the sample space. Noting that the size of the sample space n_s is equal to 36, we write

$$E(X) = \frac{\sum_{i=1}^{n_s} X_i}{n_s} = \frac{1}{36}(2 + 3 + 3 + 4 + 4 + 4 + 5 + 5 + 5 + 5 + 6 + 6 + 6$$
$$+ 6 + 6 + 7 + 7 + 7 + 7 + 7 + 7 + 8 + 8 + 8 + 8 + 8$$
$$+ 9 + 9 + 9 + 9 + 10 + 10 + 10 + 11 + 11 + 12).$$

Collecting terms and distributing the multiplier,

$$E(X) = \frac{1}{36}[1(2) + 2(3) + 3(4) + 4(5) + 5(6) + 6(7) + 5(8) + 4(9) + 3(10)$$
$$+ 2(11) + 1(12)]$$
$$= \frac{1}{36}(2) + \frac{2}{36}(3) + \frac{3}{36}(4) + \frac{4}{36}(5) + \frac{5}{36}(6) + \frac{6}{36}(7) + \frac{5}{36}(8)$$
$$+ \frac{4}{36}(9) + \frac{3}{36}(10) + \frac{2}{36}(11) + \frac{1}{36}(12) = 7. \tag{6-8}$$

Notice that each of the terms in Equation 6-8 consists of a value of the random variable X multiplied by the *probability* of observing that value — that is, the frequency of that value of X divided by the size of the sample space. Thus, we can rewrite the above equation in the following form,

$$E(X) = X_1 P(X_1) + X_2 P(X_2) + \cdots + X_{11} P(X_{11}) = \sum_{j=1}^{11} X_j P(X_j),$$

where the subscripts refer to the 11 different values of X that occur in the sample space, the values of 2 through 12. Generalizing the above equation allows us to find the expected value — that is, the mean — of any discrete random variable. Thus,

$$\mu = E(X) = \sum_{j=1}^{k} X_j P(X_j), \tag{6-9}$$

where j indicates a particular value of X, $P(X_j)$ is the probability of that value, and k is the number of different values of X. Using the methods developed earlier in this chapter, we can determine the sample space for a random variable, and we can find the probability associated with each value. We can use Equation 6-9 to find the expected value of the random variable. In effect, when we use that formula, we are finding the mean of the set of values of the random variable in the sample space.[1]

The expected value of a random variable plays a great role in hypothesis testing. If the **null hypothesis** is true — that is, if chance alone is at work in determining the outcome of an experiment — then the **observed value** of a random variable, the value actually occurring in the experiment, should not differ significantly from the expected value. Indeed, the comparison between observed and expected values is the very essence of hypothesis testing, as we will see. Whenever we find a sufficiently large discrepancy between the observed and expected values, we will reject the null hypothesis in favor of an **alternative hypothesis,** a statement that something besides chance is at work in determining the outcome of the experiment. We will devote much space in later chapters to the topic of hypothesis testing.

Variance of a Random Variable

The **variance of a random variable** is defined as the expected value of the squared deviations from the mean, that is, the average of the quantity $(X - \mu)^2$ in the long run. Since we have used the symbol σ for the standard

---

[1] Expression 6-9 applies only to discrete random variables. The expected value of a continuous random variable, such as the normal distribution, is

$$E(X) = \int_{-\infty}^{+\infty} X f(X) dX.$$

If you have had some calculus, you may be able to see some similarity between the above integral and Expression 6-9. If you haven't had any calculus, don't worry about it.

deviation of a random variable, the variance is σ^2. Thus,

$$\sigma^2 = E(X - \mu)^2. \tag{6-10}$$

We can utilize the sample space to find the variance of a discrete random variable in essentially the same way as we found the mean. Indeed, the variance of a random variable *is* the mean of the squared deviations from the mean calculated for the set of values in the sample space. The squared deviation, $(X - \mu)^2$ is itself a random variable. Thus, the variance of X is the expected value of the random variable $(X - \mu)^2$, and by Equation 6-9,

$$\sigma^2 = E(X - \mu)^2 = \sum_{j=1}^{k} (X_j - \mu)^2 P(X_j - \mu)^2, \tag{6-11}$$

where the summation is across all of the k different values of X in the sample space.

Now, what is the probability of $(X_j - \mu)^2$? Each value of $(X_j - \mu)^2$ is a value of a random variable that occurs in the sample space of squared deviations with the same frequency that X_j occurs in the sample space for X. Thus,

$$P(X - \mu)^2 = P(X_j),$$

where $P(X_j)$ is equal to the frequency of X_j in the sample space divided by the size of the sample space. Substituting in Equation 6-11,

$$\sigma^2 = E(X - \mu)^2 = \sum_{j=1}^{k} (X_j - \mu)^2 P(X_j). \tag{6-12}$$

We will make extensive use of the variance and expected value of random variables in developing the principles of hypothesis testing in later chapters. The variance of a random variable must be taken into account in deciding whether the discrepancy between an observed and expected value is sufficiently large to warrant rejection of the null hypothesis.

Set Theory and Conditional Probability

Independent and Nonindependent Events

Two events are said to be **independent** if neither influences the other. Simultaneous tosses of two fair coins, and successive tosses of a single fair coin, represent independent events. In a two-coin experiment, knowing that the first coin has come up *Heads* provides no information on whether the second has come up *Heads* or *Tails*. Given that *Heads* has occurred on Coin 1, the probability of *Heads* on Coin 2 is still 1/2, which is the same as the probability of *Heads* on Coin 2 in the absence of any information about Coin 1. If Events A and B are independent, then the probability of A, given that B has occurred, is the same as the probability of A. But if A and B are **nonindepen-**

dent events, then the probability of A, given that B has occurred, is not equal to the probability of A. In symbols,

For independent events, $\qquad P(A|B) = P(A);$ $\qquad\qquad$ (6-13)

for nonindependent events, $\qquad P(A|B) \neq P(A).$ $\qquad\qquad$ (6-14)

The expression $P(A|B)$ represents the **conditional probability** of A, and is read, "the probability of A given B." (Do not confuse $A|B$ with A divided by B.) The conditional probability of Event A given B is the probability of Event A under the condition that Event B *has already occurred*. Equation 6-13 holds true *if and only if* Events A and B are independent — that is, if the events are independent, then the equation is true, and if the equation is true, then the events are independent. Thus, Equation 6-13 provides a test of the independence of events. We will shortly examine some situations where that equation does not hold true, where events are *nonindependent*.

Figure 6-1 shows some compound events associated with a probability experiment consisting of rolling a single die. Consider the two events, *Odd* and *2 or less* in Figure 6-1A. The simple events resulting in the compound event *Odd* are enclosed in one circle, and the simple events resulting in the compound event *2 or less* are enclosed in another. Notice that the two circles intersect — that is, overlap. The simple event *1* is contained within both circles, and thus, when the number 1 turns up, the compound events *Odd* and *2 or less* also occur. Each of the four illustrations in Figure 6-1 is a **Venn diagram,** after the English logician John Venn (1834–1923).

The simple events resulting in any compound event constitute a **set,** which is any collection of things having some property in common. The

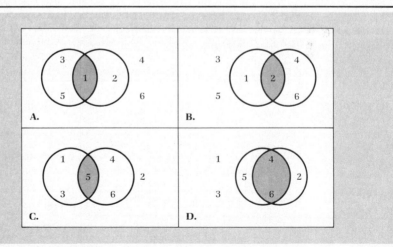

FIGURE 6-1. Venn diagrams showing compound events associated with the sample space for a single die. Intersects are shaded. **A:** Independent events *Odd* and *2 or less.* **B:** Independent events *Even* and *2 or less.* **C:** Dependent events *Odd* and *4 or more.* **D:** Dependent events *Even* and *4 or more.*

simple events *1*, *3*, and *5* share the common property of being odd numbers, and thus comprise a set. Similarly, the events *1* and *2* share the property of being numbers that are equal to 2 or less, and also comprise a set. The events *4* and *6* are contained within neither of the above sets, but the event *1* is contained within both. The **intersection, or intersect,** of two sets consists of those things that are members of both sets. Thus, the event *1* represents the intersection of the two sets *Odd* and *2 or less,* since the number 1 is both odd and less than or equal to 2. Here, the simple event *1* results in the **joint occurrence** of the compound events *Odd* and *2 or less.* The **union** of two sets consists of those things that are included in one set, or the other, or both. Events *1*, *2*, *3*, and *5* represent the union of the sets *Odd* and *2 or less.* In symbols, the union of two sets is written $A \cup B$, which is read "*A* union *B*." The intersection of two sets is written $A \cap B$, which is read "*A* intersect *B*."

As we note in the caption for Figure 6-1, the events *Odd* and *2 or less* are independent. By Formula 6-1, the probability of *Odd* is equal to $3/6 = 1/2$. Now, what is the probability of *Odd* given that the event *2 or less* has occurred — that is, given that we have rolled the die and that the number 1 or 2 has turned up? There are two simple events resulting in the compound event *2 or less,* and only one of these events also results in the event *Odd*. By Formula 6-1,

$$P(Odd|2\ or\ less) = \frac{\text{Number of ways } Odd \text{ and } 2\ or\ less \text{ can occur jointly}}{\text{Number of ways } 2\ or\ less \text{ can occur}}$$

$$= \frac{1}{2} = P(Odd).$$

Since the probability of the event *Odd* remains unchanged when we are given the information that the event *2 or less* has occurred, those two events are independent. It is also true that $P(2\ or\ less|Odd) = P(2\ or\ less)$. Similarly, referring to Figure 6-1B,

$$P(2\ or\ less|Even) = \frac{\text{Number of ways } 2\ or\ less \text{ and } Even \text{ can occur jointly}}{\text{Number or ways } Even \text{ can occur}}$$

$$= \frac{1}{3} = P(2\ or\ less).$$

Thus, the events *2 or less* and *Even* are independent.

Referring to Figure 6-1C, the probability of *4 or more* is $3/6 = 1/2$ by Formula 6-1. Now, what is the probability of *4 or more,* given that we have rolled the die and an odd number has turned up?

$$P(4\ or\ more|Odd) = \frac{\text{Number of ways } 4\ or\ more \text{ and } Odd \text{ can occur jointly}}{\text{Number of ways } Odd \text{ can occur}}$$

$$= \frac{1}{3} \neq P(4\ or\ more) = \frac{3}{6} = \frac{1}{2}.$$

Thus, the events *4 or more* and *Odd* are nonindependent. Knowing that the event *Odd* has occurred changes our assessment of the probability of *4 or more.*

Prior and Posterior Probability. The conditional probability of an event is sometimes called the **posterior,** or **a posteriori probability.** The posterior probability of an event is the probability of that event under the condition that the probability experiment has already been performed and some other event has occurred. The **prior,** or **a priori probability** of an event is the probability of that event before an experiment is performed. Thus, the prior probability of *4 or more* is 1/2, but if we know that the event *Odd* has occurred, then the probability of *4 or more* changes to 1/3. Thus, the posterior probability of an event is its probability in the light of partial information about the outcome of a probability experiment.

Referring to Figure 6-1D,

$$P(Even|4 \text{ or more}) = \frac{\text{Number of ways } Even \text{ and } 4 \text{ or more can occur jointly}}{\text{Number of ways } 4 \text{ or more can occur}}$$

$$= \frac{2}{3} \neq P(Even),$$

and thus, the events *Even* and *4 or more* are nonindependent. If the die has been rolled and you know that a 4, 5, or 6 has turned up, then the a posteriori probability of an even number is 2/3, while the a priori probability was only 1/2. If two events are nonindependent, then they are **related,** or **associated,** in the sense that the probability of one event changes when it is known that the other has occurred.

It will be useful to develop an expression for the probability of the intersection of two sets, that is the joint occurrence of two events. In the above equation the number of ways *Even* and *4 or more* can occur jointly is equal to the number of simple events in *Even* ∩ *4 or more.* Substituting,

$$P(Even|4 \text{ or more}) = \frac{\text{Number of simple events in } Even \cap 4 \text{ or more}}{\text{Number of ways } 4 \text{ or more can occur}}.$$

Dividing the numerator and denominator by the *Number of simple events* in the sample space yields, by Formula 6-1,

$$P(Even|4 \text{ or more}) = \frac{\dfrac{\text{Number of simple events in } Even \cap 4 \text{ or more}}{\text{Number of simple events in sample space}}}{\dfrac{\text{Number of ways } 4 \text{ or more can occur}}{\text{Number of simple events in sample space}}}$$

$$= \frac{P(Even \cap 4 \text{ or more})}{P(4 \text{ or more})}.$$

In general,

$$P(A|B) = \frac{A \cap B}{B} \quad \text{and} \quad P(B|A) = \frac{A \cap B}{A}. \tag{6-15}$$

Dividing the numerators and denominators, above, by the total number of simple events in the sample space,

$$P(A|B) = \frac{P(A \cap B)}{P(B)} \quad \text{and} \quad P(B|A) = \frac{P(A \cap B)}{P(A)}. \quad \text{(6-16)}$$

Thus, $P(A \cap B) = P(A|B)P(B) = P(B|A)P(A).$ (6-17)

Joint Occurrence of Independent Events.   Equation 6-17 gives the probability of the joint occurrence of any two events, whether independent or nonindependent. In the special case where A and B are independent,

$$P(A \cap B) = P(A)P(B),$$

since in that special case $P(A|B) = P(A)$. The probability of the joint occurrence of the events A, B, and C is the probability of their intersection, $P(A \cap B \cap C)$, which we can rewrite as $P[(A \cap B) \cap C]$. If the events are independent, then

$$P[(A \cap B) \cap C] = P(A \cap B)P(C) = P(A)P(B)P(C).$$

In general, the probability of the joint occurrence of any number of independent events is the product of their probabilities:

$$P\left[\begin{array}{c} \text{Joint occurrence of} \\ N \text{ independent events} \end{array}\right] = P(E_1)P(E_2) \cdots P(E_N). \quad \text{(6-18)}$$

What is the probability of rolling three 4s in a row with a single die? Remember, the situation here is precisely the same as though we were rolling three dice simultaneously. Since the successive trials are independent, we can consider three 4s in a row as the joint occurrence of three independent events each having a probability of 1/6. Thus, by Formula 6-18,

$$P(3 \text{ 4s}) = \frac{1}{6}\frac{1}{6}\frac{1}{6} = \frac{1}{216}.$$

We can also obtain the above result by Formula 6-5 and thus Formula 6-18 may appear redundant. But consider the joint occurrence of compound events having different probabilities, a situation where 6-5 cannot be used. For example, suppose we roll two dice three times. What is the probability of rolling 7, 8, and 9 *in that order?* The successive rolls are independent, and thus the required probability can be found by substituting the probabilities from Table 6-4 in Formula 6-18:

$$P(7, 8, 9) = \frac{6}{36}\frac{5}{36}\frac{4}{36} = \frac{120}{46,656} = .0026.$$

The Gambler's Fallacy.   Consider the probability of tossing 5 *Heads* in a row with a fair coin. By Formula 6-5

$$P(5 \text{ Heads}) = \frac{1}{2^5} = \frac{1}{32}.$$

Thus, *5 Heads in a row* is a rather rare event. Now, suppose you have just observed four tosses of a coin, and all four have come up *Heads*. Is there now a greater probability of *Tails* on the next toss? The **gambler's fallacy** holds that there is — that after a run of *Heads*, or *Tails*, the opposite result becomes more probable. If the gambler's fallacy were true, the coin would have to remember its past, or would have to be changed physically in some way as a result of its experience. But the coin has no memory, and no such physical change occurs, nor is there any "law of averages" that somehow changes the probabilities of independent events in the light of what has happened in the past. Successive, unbiased tosses of a fair coin are independent, and thus the probability of *Tails* on any toss is exactly 1/2, no matter how many *Heads* in a row have occurred previously. Since the event *Tails on 5th trial* and the event *4 Heads in a row* are independent, it follows from Equation 6-13 that

$$P(\text{Tails on 5th trial}|4 \text{ Heads in a row}) = P(\text{Tails on 5th trial}) = 1/2.$$

Knowing that the coin has come up *4 Heads in a row* does not alter the conditional probability of *Tails on 5th trial*, even though the probability of *5 Heads in a row* is only 1/32. We can add a further paradox by noting that the probability of the sequence *H H H H T* is only 1/32, even though we just found that the probability of *Tails on 5th trial* given *4 Heads in a row* was 1/2. You can easily resolve this seeming paradox if you distinguish between a priori and a posteriori (conditional) probabilities. The a priori probability of *H H H H T*, the probability before the die is rolled, can be considered as the probability of the joint occurrence of two independent events, *4 Heads in a row* and *Tails on 5th trial*. By Formula 6-18, that prior probability is 1/32, but *after* we have observed *4 Heads in a row*, the posterior (conditional) probability of *Tails on 5th trial* is 1/2. A failure to understand the gambler's fallacy can have interesting consequences in some situations.

Probabilities of Intersects and Unions

In rolling a single die, what is the probability of getting an odd number, or rolling a number less than or equal to 2? We are concerned here with an event that is contained within the set *Odd*, or within the set *2 or less*, or that is contained within both sets. The event of interest here represents the union of those sets. Referring to Figure 6-1A, the simple events *1, 3,* and *5* are contained in the set *Odd*, and the simple events *1* and *2* are contained within the set *2 or less*. Formula 6-1 gives a probability of 3/6 = 1/2 for the first set and 2/6 = 1/3 for the second. It is tempting to suppose that the probability of the union of these sets would be 1/2 + 1/3 = 5/6. But inspection of Figure 6-1A shows that only four simple events, *1, 2, 3,* and *5* are contained within the set *Odd*, within the set *2 or less*, or within both sets. Thus, the probability of the union is 4/6, not 5/6. The problem can be resolved by noting that we found the probability of *Odd* by counting the number of simple events in that set, namely *1, 3,* and *5*, and dividing that number by the size of the sample space. Similarly, we found the probability of *2 or less* by counting the number of simple events in that set, namely *1*, and *2*. Notice that the simple event *1*, representing the intersection of the sets, was counted once in each set, and was thus counted twice. We can find the number of events in the union of two sets by adding the number in each set and subtracting the number in the intersection. In general,

$$A \cup B = A + B - A \cap B, \tag{6-19}$$

and it follows that

$$P(A \cup B) = P(A) + P(B) - P(A \cap B). \tag{6-20}$$

Using the above formula,

$$P(Odd \text{ or } 2 \text{ or less}) = P(Odd \cup 2 \text{ or less})$$

$$= P(Odd) + P(2 \text{ or less}) - P(Odd \cap 2 \text{ or less})$$

$$= \frac{3}{6} + \frac{2}{6} - \frac{1}{6} = \frac{4}{6} = \frac{2}{3}.$$

Operations involving unions of sets can be carried out without regard to whether the sets represent independent or nonindependent events. Thus, we could find the probability of *Even* $\cup$ *4 or more*, where the sets represent related events, by the same formula we used above, where the sets represented independent events.

Operations with Several Sets.   Figure 6-2 shows three sets, containing *Small objects, Black objects,* and *Triangles.* Each set contains four objects. How many objects are there in the union of the three sets? By counting, we can see that the answer is 7. We will now develop a formal method for finding the union of three sets. We will begin by treating $(A \cup B)$ as a set and then finding $(A \cup B)$ union C. Thus, we reduce a three-set problem to a more familiar problem involving two sets:

$$A \cup B \cup C = (A \cup B) \cup C = (A + B - A \cap B) \cup C$$

$$= (A + B - A \cap B) + C - (A + B - A \cap B) \cap C$$

$$= A + B + C - A \cap B - A \cap C - B \cap C + A \cap B \cap C. \tag{6-21}$$

The above method can be extended to the union of any number of sets.

Substituting the number of objects in the three sets in Figure 6-2 in Equation 6-21 yields a value of 7 for *Small* $\cup$ *Black* $\cup$ *Triangles*, the same value we found by counting. There are eight objects in the sample space in Figure 6-2; thus, if we divide each of the terms in Equation 6-21 by 8, we can find the probability of each term. For example,

$$P(\text{Small} \cup \text{Black} \cup \text{Triangles}) = \frac{7}{8}.$$

Thus, if we carried out a probability experiment consisting of randomly drawing one of the objects shown in Figure 6-2, the probability is 7/8 of

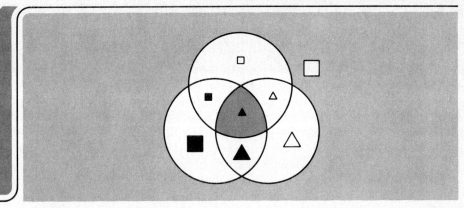

FIGURE 6-2. Venn diagram showing three sets: *Small objects, Black objects,* and *Triangles; S ∩ B ∩ T* is shaded.

drawing a small object *or* a black object *or* a triangle. Similarly,

$$P(\text{Small} \cap \text{Black} \cap \text{Triangles}) = \frac{1}{8}.$$

Thus, the probability of randomly drawing an object that is small *and* black *and* a triangle is 1/8. The union operation is associated with the word *or* in ordinary speech, and the intersection operation is associated with the word *and.* When we use multiple adjectives to describe an object — a small black triangle, for example — we are indicating that the object is contained within the intersection of two or more sets.

Intersection and Independence. If two events have no intersect, are they independent? It is tempting to say yes, since two such events do not overlap in any way, but the answer is no. Consider the sample space for rolling a single die. If you construct a Venn diagram showing the sets *Odd* and *Even,* you will find no intersection between these two compound events because there does not exist a simple event that is both *Odd* and *Even.* The events *Odd* and *Even* are related, nonindependent events, in that if one has occurred on a given roll of the die, then the other cannot have occurred on that roll. In terms of conditional probability, the probability of *Odd* is 1/2, but the probability of *Odd* given that *Even* has occurred is zero. Since $P(\text{Odd}|\text{Even}) \neq P(\text{Odd})$, the events *Odd* and *Even* do not pass the test for independence provided by Equation 6-13. By similiar reasoning, the simple events in any sample space are nonindependent. In a single toss of a coin, *Heads* and *Tails* are nonindependent since if one occurs the other cannot occur *on that toss.* Successive tosses are of course independent — a point on which we will expand presently. All events that have no intersection are nonindependent, but the converse is not true. As we saw in Figure 6-1, some events that intersect are independent and some are nonindependent.

Some Conditional Probabilities in the Real World

Figure 6-3 shows some of the results of a large study of 36,975 male smokers who were paired with 36,975 nonsmokers (Hammond, 1964). The smokers and nonsmokers were matched in terms of age, race, marital status, education, and many other variables. The Venn diagram in Figure 6-3 shows the total number of deaths that occurred during the 34 months of the study. The two largest rectangles in that diagram represent the number of deaths of smokers and nonsmokers from all causes, and the shaded rectangle represents the deaths from lung cancer. The areas of all of those rectangles are proportional to the number of deaths. Notice that the overwhelming proportion of men who died of lung cancer were smokers. Thus, given that a man died of lung cancer, the probability that the man was a smoker is

$$P(\text{Smoker}|\text{Lung cancer death}) = \frac{110}{122} = .90,$$

and the probability that the man was a nonsmoker is

$$P(\text{Nonsmoker}|\text{Lung cancer death}) = \frac{12}{122} = .10.$$

Now consider the probability of a smoker and a nonsmoker dying of lung cancer during the 34-month period of the study. The probability of a smoker dying of lung cancer is

$$P(\text{Dying of lung cancer}|\text{Smoker}) = \frac{110}{36,975} = .0030,$$

and for a nonsmoker, the probability is

$$P(\text{Dying of lung cancer}|\text{Nonsmoker}) = \frac{12}{36,975} = .00032.$$

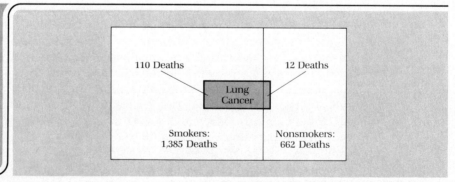

FIGURE 6-3. Venn diagram showing number of deaths among 36,975 matched pairs of smokers and nonsmokers. Shaded rectangle shows deaths from lung cancer. Areas of all rectangles are proportional to number of deaths. Data are from Hammond (1964).

Neither of the above probabilities may strike you as very impressive, but notice that for a smoker the probability of dying of lung cancer is more than nine times greater than for a nonsmoker. Furthermore, bear in mind that those small probabilities are associated with observations made over a rather short period of time — 34 months.

It is clear that smoking and dying of lung cancer are nonindependent events, and it is fairly easy to see the nature of the possible causal connection between smoking and lung disorders. We will now consider the relationship between smoking and dying of *all* causes. Figure 6-3 shows that there were 2,047 total deaths among the matched pairs of smokers and nonsmokers during the period of the study. Thus, the prior probability of dying from any cause — that is, the probability of dying without regard to smoking or not smoking — is the following:

$$P(\text{Dying}) = \frac{2,047}{73,950} = .028.$$

The conditional probability of a smoker dying during the period of the study is

$$P(\text{Dying}|\text{Smoker}) = \frac{1,385}{36,975} = .037,$$

and the conditional probability of a nonsmoker dying from any cause is

$$P(\text{Dying}|\text{Nonsmoker}) = \frac{662}{36,975} = .018.$$

Since P(Dying) ≠ P(Dying|Smoker), Smoking and Dying of any cause are nonindependent events. Notice also that the conditional probability of a smoker dying is more than twice as great as that of a nonsmoker. That is not to say that nonsmokers are any less likely to die eventually — since in the long run we are *all* dead, as the British economist John Maynard Keynes (1883 – 1946) put it. But the data show clearly that smokers are likely to die earlier from all causes than nonsmokers. For an extensive review of the research literature, see *Smoking and Health: A Report of the Surgeon General*, U.S. Department of Health, Education and Welfare, 1979.

Permutations and Combinations

The ideas to be presented here will play a direct role in our development of the binomial distribution in the next chapter. We will go on to use the binomial extensively in our development of inferential statistics. However, permutations and combinations are useful in their own right.

So far, the probability experiments we have dealt with have involved **sampling with replacement.** To explain what this means, we will consider a slight modification of our experiment with dice. Instead of using dice, we write one of the numbers 1 through 6 on each of six slips of paper. We place the slips of paper in a hat, mix them thoroughly, and draw one at random, without looking. Such a procedure is identical, in a formal sense, to the procedure of rolling one die. We write down the number we have just drawn. We put the number back in the hat, mix the numbers thoroughly, and once again draw a number without looking. Drawing a number constitutes one trial in a probability experiment, and the procedure can be repeated as many times as desired. Since every number is replaced after being drawn, this procedure is called sampling with replacement. Drawing two numbers with replacement, one after the other, is formally identical to our experiment consisting of rolling two dice, or rolling a single die successively.

Now consider another modification of our experiment. This time, we draw one of the six numbers out of the hat, and we do not replace the number. We draw another, and another, and so on until the numbers are all gone. The order in which the numbers are drawn is the event of interest here. This procedure is called **sampling without replacement.** If we have a set of N things, we can sample all N things without replacement, or we can sample some smaller number of things. A **permutation** is the order in which a set of S things are drawn without replacement from a set of N things, where $S \leq N$. We are interested in the number of permutations of N things taken S at a time, that is, the number of possible orders in which S things can be drawn from a set of N things. We symbolize the number of permutations as

Number of permutations of N things taken S at a time $= P_S^N$.

We will first consider the situation where $S = N$. Here, we are interested in the number of permutations of N things taken N at a time, that is, the number of orders in which N things can be arranged. Consider the letters A, B, and C taken all three at a time. In making up a sequence of letters, the first letter can be chosen in three ways — that is, from among three letters; the second in two ways — from among the two remaining letters; and the third can be chosen in only one way. Thus, there are $3 \cdot 2 \cdot 1 = 3! = 6$ permutations of 3 things taken 3 at a time. (You may find it helpful to write out the 6 possible permutations of 3 letters taken 3 at a time.) The expression 3! is read, "three **factorial,**" and is the product of the integers 1 through 3. In general,

$$P_N^N = N! \tag{6-22}$$

where $N! = N(N-1)(N-2) \cdots (3)(2)1$, which is the product of the integers 1 through N.

We will now consider the situation where $S < N$. How many permutations are there of the digits 1, 2, 3, 4, 5, and 6 taken 4 at a time? The first digit can be chosen in 6 ways, the second in 5, the third in 4, and the fourth in 3 ways. Thus,

$$P_4^6 = 6 \cdot 5 \cdot 4 \cdot 3 = 360. \tag{6-23}$$

Notice the factors on the right side of Equation 6-24. The first factor is N, the next is $(N - 1)$, the next is $(N - 2)$, and the last factor is $(N - 3)$, which is equal to $(N - S + 1)$. In general, the number of permutations of N things taken S at a time is the product of the integers N through $(N - S + 1)$.

$$P_S^N = N(N - 1)(N - 2) \cdots (N - S + 1). \tag{6-24}$$

The dots, above, indicate the omission of the factors from $(N - S + 2)$ through $(N - 3)$ inclusive. Equation 6-24 will always allow us to find P_S^N, but we can derive a more convenient expression by multiplying and dividing the right side of the equation by the product of the integers 1 through $(N - S)$. Thus,

$$P_S^N = \frac{N(N - 1)(N - 2) \cdots (N - S + 1)(N - S) \cdots (3)(2)1}{(N - S) \cdots (3)(2)1}.$$

The numerator, above, is equal to $N!$ and the denominator is equal to $(N - S)!$ Thus, the above equation simplifies to the following general formula for the number of permutations of N things taken S at a time:

$$P_S^N = \frac{N!}{(N - S)!}. \tag{6-25}$$

In Equation 6-25, the expression $(N - S)! \neq N! - S!$

A **combination** is a set of S things, without regard to order, chosen without replacement from a set of N things, where $S \leq N$. Consider the four digits, 1, 2, 3, and 4. We will first consider the number of *permutations* of these 4 digits taken 3 at a time. Using Equation 6-25,

$$P_3^4 = \frac{4!}{(4 - 3)!} = \frac{4 \cdot 3 \cdot 2 \cdot 1}{1!} = \frac{24}{1} = 24.$$

Table 6-5 shows the 24 possible permutations of these four digits taken three at a time. There are four columns of six permutations each in Table 6-5. Each column lists the permutations of a different set of three digits. There are only four possible sets of three different digits that can be chosen from four digits, and these four sets of three different digits are the combinations shown in the bottom row of Table 6-5. By definition, order is of no consequence in a combination, so each of the six permutations in any column in Table 6-5 represents the single combination shown below that column. Thus, for each

TABLE 6-5. Permutations and Combinations of 4 Digits Taken 3 at a Time. Each Column Shows Permutations and Combinations for a Different Set of 3 Digits.

	1 2 3	1 2 4	1 3 4	2 3 4
	1 3 2	1 4 2	1 4 3	2 4 3
Permutations:	2 1 3	2 1 4	3 1 4	3 2 4
$P_3^4 = 24$	2 3 1	2 4 1	3 4 1	3 4 2
	3 1 2	4 1 2	4 1 3	4 2 3
	3 2 1	4 2 1	4 3 1	4 3 2
Combinations:				
$C_3^4 = 4$	1 2 3	1 2 4	1 3 4	2 3 4

combination of 4 things taken 3 at a time, there are 3! permutations of 4 things taken 3 at a time. In general, dividing the number of permutations of N things taken S at a time by $S!$ gives the number of combinations of N things taken S at a time:

$$C_S^N = \frac{P_S^N}{S!} = \frac{\frac{N!}{(N-S)!}}{S!} = \frac{N!}{S!(N-S)!}. \tag{6-26}$$

We can show that the number of combinations of N things taken S at a time is equal to the number of combinations of N things taken $(N-S)$ at a time. We will find this property of combinations useful when we deal with the binomial distribution. Substituting $(N-S)$ for S in Formula 6-26,

$$C_{(N-S)}^N = \frac{N!}{(N-S)![N-(N-S)]!} = \frac{N!}{(N-S)!S!}.$$

Thus,

$$C_{(N-S)}^N = C_S^N. \tag{6-27}$$

What is the number of combinations of N things taken N at a time, that is, what is C_S^N when $S = N$? There is only one way to take N things, without regard for order, from a set of N things, and that is to take all N things. Thus $C_N^N = 1$. Now, we will see what result Formula 6-26 gives in this case:

$$C_N^N = \frac{N!}{N!(N-N)!} = \frac{N!}{N!\,0!}. \tag{6-28}$$

Applying Formula 6-27 here leads to an expression of zero factorial in the denominator of Equation 6-28. It may not be entirely obvious from our earlier discussion of factorials exactly what the value of **0!** may be. But if zero factorial were equal to zero, then Equation 6-28 would entail division by zero—an impermissible mathematical operation. Furthermore, if Formula 6-26 is to yield the same value of C_N^N that we arrived at through our logical argument, above, then it must be true that

$$0! = 1. \tag{6-29}$$

An Experiment Involving Permutations

Suppose we give a small child the letters A, B, C, D, and E, perhaps on a set of cards. We ask the child to put the letters in proper order, and he does. Now, does the child know the correct order of the first five letters of the alphabet? It is of course possible to arrange the letters correctly just by chance, but how probable would a correct performance be unless the child knew the correct order? We can answer these questions by making the tentative assumption that the child does not know the order of the letters. Under that assumption, the child's performance will be a probability experiment completely determined by chance, and in that case the child might as well draw the letters out of a hat without looking at them. If we first find the number of possible ways that five letters can be arranged in order, that is, the number of permutations of 5 things taken 5 at a time, then we can find the probability of a correct performance by chance alone. By Formula 6-22,

$$P_5^5 = 5! = 5 \cdot 4 \cdot 3 \cdot 2 \cdot 1 = 120.$$

There are 120 possible ways of arranging the five letters in order, and only one of these ways is correct. Thus, the probability of choosing by chance the one proper order is given by Formula 6-1:

$$P(\text{Proper order}) = \frac{\text{Number of ways proper order can occur}}{\text{Number of possible orders}}$$

$$= \frac{1}{P_5^5} = \frac{1}{120} = .0083.$$

The probability of 1/120 means that if the child randomly drew the letters out of a hat 120 times, only once should we expect to see the letters drawn in the proper order, $A\ B\ C\ D\ E$. Under the assumption that the child does not know the correct order, a correct performance would be a rare event having a probability of 1/120. Having observed a correct performance, we are inclined to reject the now unlikely assumption that the child knows nothing in favor of the more likely notion that he or she knows the proper order of the first five letters of the alphabet. An important question now arises: How low must the probability of an observed result be before we can reject the assumption that chance alone is at work? We will answer this question in the next section.

Testing the Null Hypothesis. The tentative assumption that chance alone has determined the outcome of an experiment is known as the *null hypothesis,* as we noted earlier. In the preceding example, the null hypothesis is the tentative assumption that the child does not know the correct order of the five letters. Indeed, the word *null,* from the Latin, literally means *nothing* — that is, no knowledge in our case. Under the tentative assumption that the null hypothesis is true, the child's performance will be determined completely by chance. The *alternative hypothesis* is the statement that something besides chance is at work in an experiment — in our present case, the statement that the child knows the correct order of the letters.

Analyzing the results of any experiment reduces to an exercise in deciding whether to reject or not reject the null hypothesis in favor of the alternative hypothesis (Fisher, 1935). If the observed results of an experiment have a probability of less than or equal to .05 (1/20), then we reject the null hypothesis, and the results are said to be **statistically significant.** When the observed results under the null hypothesis are as *im*probable as .05 or less, we will decide in favor of the alternative hypothesis as the more likely explanation for the outcome of the experiment. When we reject the null hypothesis at the .05 level, we can be .95 (95%) confident that our results are not just due to chance. The probability of .05, at or below which the null hypothesis is rejected, is called the **α *level*** (small Greek *alpha*). There is no mathematical basis for our choice of an α level—rather, the conventional α level of .05 represents a very wide consensus among researchers and statisticians, a point we will amplify later.

In the experiment with the letters, the probability of the observed outcome under the null hypothesis was only .0083, a value far below the α level of .05. Thus, we reject the null hypothesis, the assumption that the child does not know the correct order, in favor of the hypothesis that he or she does know the order. Our reasoning here represents little more than a slight refinement of the kind of reasoning any thinking person goes through in order to choose between competing explanations for observed outcomes. We will develop these ideas further in later chapters.

An Experiment Involving Combinations

Figure 6-4 shows seven objects that can be used in a simple experiment in concept formation, that is, the process of deciding which kinds of things go together. Suppose we ask a subject to choose the four things that go together best. As you can see, the shapes of the objects differ on the round-angular dimension. Suppose the subject selects the four angular objects. What is the probability of selecting those four objects by chance alone? Order is unimportant here, since it does not matter which angular object the subject selects first, or second, and so on. The number of ways of selecting 4 things from a set of 7 things is the number of combinations of 7 things taken 4 at a time. By Formula 6-26,

$$C_4^7 = \frac{7!}{4!(7-4)!} = \frac{7!}{4!3!} = \frac{7\cdot6\cdot5\cdot4\cdot3\cdot2\cdot1}{4\cdot3\cdot2\cdot1\cdot3\cdot2\cdot1} = \frac{7\cdot6\cdot5}{3\cdot2\cdot1} = 7\cdot5 = 35.$$

Notice in the above calculations that it is possible to do considerable canceling, and thus it is not necessary to calculate the value of 7! Because of the amount of canceling that is possible, working with permutations and combinations is not so laborious as it might appear. Under the null hypothesis, the probability of choosing the one correct combination of four things is given by Formula 6-1:

$$P(\text{Correct combination}) = \frac{1}{C_4^7} = \frac{1}{35} = .0286.$$

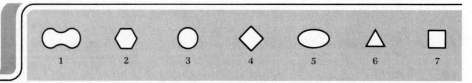

FIGURE 6-4. Seven shapes that can be used in a simple experiment in concept formation.

Since the above probability is less than .05, we reject the null hypothesis in favor of the alternative hypothesis that the subject has formed the concept *Angular things go together.*

Suppose we ask another subject to choose the three things that go together best. Three of the seven shapes are rounded, and here, we need to know the number of combinations of 7 things taken 3 at a time. By Formula 6-26,

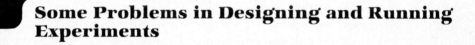

$$C_3^7 = \frac{7!}{3!(7-3)!} = \frac{7!}{3!4!} = \frac{7 \cdot 6 \cdot 5 \cdot 4 \cdot 3 \cdot 2 \cdot 1}{3 \cdot 2 \cdot 1 \cdot 4 \cdot 3 \cdot 2 \cdot 1} = \frac{7 \cdot 6 \cdot 5}{3 \cdot 2 \cdot 1} = 7 \cdot 5 = 35.$$

Notice that the number of combinations of 7 things taken 3 at a time is equal to the number of 7 things taken 4 at a time, as Formula 6-27 shows. Thus, the probability of choosing the 3 things out of 7 that go together is equal to the probability of choosing the 4 things out of 7 that go together. *Taking* some number of things from a set always involves *leaving* some number of things. Thus, taking any number of things from a set always involves dividing the things into two mutually exclusive and exhaustive categories, the things *taken* and the things *left*. That notion is useful even when we take all of the N things in a set, in which case there are N things in the *taken* category and zero in the *left* category. We will make use of those ideas in the next chapter in dealing with the binominal distribution.

Some Problems in Designing and Running Experiments

The experiments we have just described appear quite straightforward. However, there are a great many problems that can arise in the design and execution of experiments that can render the results ambiguous, uninterpretable, and therefore useless — or worse yet, misleading. Fortunately, with planning and forethought, you can avoid many of the pitfalls that await the unwary. We will describe some of those difficulties in the context of the present experiments, and we will discuss design problems more extensively in Chapter 13.

Confounding

Consider the experiment where we asked the small child to place the first five letters of the alphabet in order. Suppose you printed the letters by hand on five equal-sized cards, as in Figure 6-5A, and suppose as you progressed from A to E, you inadvertently allowed your letters to become smaller and smaller. The size of the letters is now **confounded** with their order. If the child placed the letters in order, we would not be able to tell from that performance whether the child was responding to the alphabetic order of the letters, or placing the

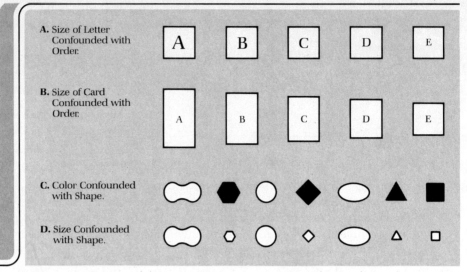

A. Size of Letter
Confounded with
Order.

B. Size of Card
Confounded with
Order.

C. Color Confounded
with Shape.

D. Size Confounded
with Shape.

FIGURE 6-5. Some possible confounds in the experiments involving permutations and combinations.

letters in order of their size, from largest to smallest. Now suppose you printed the letters all the same size, but on cards that get progressively smaller, as in Figure 6-5B. Here, the size of the card is confounded with the alphabetic order. The child could solve the problem even if the cards were turned face down — simply by choosing the largest card first, and then the next largest, and so on.

Color and shape are confounded in Figure 6-5C. If a child were asked to choose the four objects that belong together, and if the child chose the four angular shapes, we could not tell whether the child was responding to the angular shape or to the black color. Even if we *told* the child to choose the four angular shapes, the child could respond "correctly" on the basis of color without understanding the concept of angularity at all. In Figure 6-5D, where size and shape are confounded, similar difficulties would arise.

Whenever two variables are confounded — size and alphabetic order, or color and shape, for example — either variable can account for the results of an experiment. When confounding occurs, the results of an experiment or a set of observations are ambiguous: We simply cannot tell what the subject is responding to. Perhaps you would argue that only a very dull or careless experimenter could possibly design an experiment with such obvious flaws as I have just described. But there are more subtle ways in which confounding and other design flaws can occur, as we will see in later chapters.

Procedural Flaws

A **design flaw** — such as confounding — is a shortcoming that is built into an experiment, while a **procedural flaw** is a shortcoming in the way the experiment is run. For example, if the experimenter smiles, nods, or otherwise shows approval as the subject is about to choose one of the correct shapes in the concept formation experiment, the subject may be quick to pick up such a cue. In a study of concept formation, we are not interested in learning instead that the child may be able to detect the experimenter's approval when he or she is about to make a correct choice.

Epilog

The present chapter may have appeared quite abstract in part, perhaps rather far removed from the real world. Our concern with chance and probability may have left you feeling that we have attempted to reduce human behavior to a random process like rolling dice or drawing slips of paper out of a hat. But that is not the case. On the contrary, we must understand the workings of chance in order to *rule out* random processes in our attempts to understand and explain behavior. To that end, we have introduced some of the concepts of hypothesis testing, a set of ideas that we will develop extensively in later chapters, which will take us closer to our goal of understanding human behavior.

Terms and Symbols

Presenting the ideas in this chapter has required a great many new terms and symbols. When you have learned these terms and symbols, you will have gone a long way toward understanding the ideas they represent.

Random variable	**Expected value**
Probability experiment	**Observed value**
Outcome	**Null hypothesis**
Fair coin	**Alternative hypothesis**
Trial	**Variance of a random variable**
Mutually exclusive and exhaustive	**Nonindependent events**
Independent	**Conditional probability**
Simple event	**Venn diagram**
Compound event	**Set**
Sample space	**Intersection**
Probability	**Union**
Odds	**Joint occurrence**
Multiple trials	**Posterior probability**
Impossible event	**A posteriori**
Certain event	**Prior probability**
	A priori

Related events	n_s
Gambler's fallacy	$E(X)$
Permutation	μ
Combination	σ^2
Sampling with replacement	$(X - \mu)^2$
Sampling without replacement	$P(X_j)$
Factorial	$P(A|B)$
Statistically significant	$A \cap B$
Alpha level	$A \cup B$
Confounding	P_S^N
Design flaw	$N!$
Procedural flaw	C_S^N
$P(E_i)$	$0!$

EXERCISES AND STUDY QUESTIONS

1. In the human species, the probability of a live male birth is about .51, and the probability of a live female birth is about .49. Suppose a family has 5 children. What is the probability of the following?
   a. 5 boys.
   b. 5 girls.
   c. 5 children of the same sex.

2. Deuteranopia, a red-green color defect, is a sex-linked recessive trait carried on the X chromosome. If a mother is a carrier of deuteranopia, then each of her sons has a .5 probability of being a deuteranope. (A father, even a deuteranopic one, plays no role in determing the red-green color vision of a *son*.)
   a. Suppose a mother who is a carrier has 3 sons. What is the probability that all 3 will be deuteranopic?
   b. Suppose a mother has had 2 deuteranopic sons. If the mother then has another son, what is the probability that all 3 will be deuteranopic?

3. The following table shows some of the results of the 1970 U.S. Census.

	Male	Female	Total
74 years or less	95,933,568	99,648,312	195,581,880
75 years or more	2,978,624	4,651,422	7,630,046
	98,912,192	104,299,734	203,211,926

Construct a rectangular Venn diagram (similar to Figure 6-3) showing the above information graphically. It is more convenient to work with percentages than with frequencies in constructing such a display. Draw your diagram as carefully and accurately as possible, making sure that the area of each region is proportional to the size of the group of people that it represents. A scale graduated in millimeters will be very useful here, or millimeter-ruled graph paper can also be used.

4. Consider a probability experiment consisting of randomly drawing a person from the population in the 1970 U.S. Census (see above table). What is the probability of drawing each of the following?
   a. A male.
   b. A female.
   c. A person 75 years or older.
   d. A male 75 years or older.
   e. A female 75 years or older.
   f. Suppose we have just drawn a male from the population. What is the probability that we have drawn a man at least 75 years old?
   g. Suppose we have just drawn a female from the population. What is the probability that we have drawn a woman at least 75 years old?
   h. Are the events *Female* and *75 or older* independent?
   i. Is there an association between sex and longevity in the census data, and if so, what kind of association?

5. A conventional deck of cards consists of 4 suits of 13 cards each. There are 13 cards in a bridge hand. What is the probability of each of the following hands? (The problems in this exercise are easy to set up, but tedious to solve without a calculator.)
   a. 13 spades.
   b. 13 cards of the same suit.
   c. 13 hearts or 13 diamonds.
   d. 13 red cards.

6. A *flush* is a poker hand consisting of any 5 cards of the same suit.
   a. How many possible heart flushes are there?
   b. What is the probability of a heart flush?
   c. What is the probability of a flush in any suit?

7. In five-card draw poker, each player is dealt 5 cards. A player can discard any of his original cards face down and then replace each discard with a new card drawn from the deck. Suppose a player is dealt 3 hearts and 2 diamonds. The player discards the diamonds and draws two new cards. What is the probability of filling out a heart flush?

8. Compare and contrast the probabilities in Exercises 6b and 7 above, using the terms and concepts that we have developed.

9. Two clinical psychologists independently rank a group of 5 paranoid schizophrenics on judged severity of symptoms after assessment interviews. Suppose the two sets of ranks agree perfectly.
   a. State the null and alternative hypotheses.
   b. Do you reject the null hypothesis?
   c. Are the results statistically significant? Explain what that means.

10. A social psychologist has developed a new method aimed at identifying potential parole violators. Out of a group of 6 recent parolees, 2 violated their parole within three months. The parole board asks the psychologist

to identify the 2 violators, if possible, on the basis of their preparole records. Suppose the psychologist correctly identifies the violators.

a. State the null and alternative hypotheses.

b. Indicate whether you reject the null hypothesis.

c. Are the results statistically significant, and if not, what should the researcher do?

d. What is the probability that a totally unskilled observer could pick the names of the 2 violators without ever seeing any of the parolees' records?

Probability Distributions and Hypothesis Testing

In this chapter, we will develop methods of comparing the observed value of a random variable in a probability experiment with the value expected under the null hypothesis. For example, consider a well-constructed multiple-choice examination. A student who is totally ignorant of the subject matter is forced to guess on every question. In that case, the examination is a probability experiment, and the student's score is a random variable wholly determined by chance. We can find the probability of an observed score under the assumption that the null hypothesis is true, and if that probability is very low, we will reject the null hypothesis in favor of an alternative hypothesis. Rejecting the null hypothesis here is equivalent to rejecting the idea that the multiple-choice examination is a probability experiment whose outcome is wholly determined by chance. If the outcome is not completely determined by chance, then the student knows something about the subject matter. We will extend these methods to the evaluation of many other kinds of variables in many situations. We will begin by considering the binomial probability experiment.

The Binomial Distribution

The Binomial Probability Experiment

A **binomial trial** has two mutually exclusive and exhaustive outcomes, **success** and **failure.** If you were tossing a coin and betting on *Heads,* then *Heads* would represent success and *Tails* would represent failure. If you were betting on *Tails,* then *Tails* would represent success. Thus, success and failure are arbitrary in this context. In tossing a fair coin, the probability of success is equal to the probability of failure, but as we will see shortly, those probabilities are not always equal in other situations. We will reserve the symbols p and q for the probabilities of success and failure, respectively, in a binomial trial.

Rolling a single fair die, where each of the six sides has the same chance of turning up, can also be considered as a binomial trial — even though the die has six sides. If you were betting that the number 1 would come up, then 1 would represent success and any of the other numbers, 2 through 6, would represent failure. Any number that you are betting on — or that you have singled out for special attention — represents success, and all the other numbers represent failure. Thus, in the case of a six-sided die, success and failure are mutually exclusive and exhaustive — just as in the case of a two-sided coin — but with the die, failure can occur in five different ways. Here, $p = 1/6$ and $q = 5/6$.

Answering a single multiple-choice examination question where the student knows absolutely nothing about the subject matter is a further example of a binomial trial. Suppose the question has four choices, only one of which is correct. If choice A is the right answer, then A represents success and the other choices, B, C, and D, represent failure. As in our earlier examples, success and failure are mutually exclusive and exhaustive, but failure here can occur in three different ways, and thus $p = 1/4$ and $q = 3/4$.

In a **binomial experiment** there are N independent binomial trials. The probabilities of success and failure, p and q, remain constant across all N trials. We let the **binomial random variable** X equal the number of successes occurring in N binomial trials. Thus, X is a discrete variable, which can take on any integer value from zero through N, inclusive. The purpose of carrying out a binomial probability experiment is to observe a value of the binomial random variable X. Each time a binomial experiment is performed one and only one value of X occurs. Table 7-1 summarizes the requirements for the binomial experiment. The last requirement in that table is discussed in a later section.

TABLE 7-1. Requirements for the Binomial Experiment.

1. There are N identical independent trials.
2. Each trial has two mutually exclusive and exhaustive possible outcomes, *success* and *failure*. Classification of the outcomes requires only a nominal scale of measurement.
3. The probabilities of success and failure, p and q, do not change across trials.
4. $p + q = 1$.
5. The binomial random variable X is equal to the number of successes in N trials.
6. For the normal approximation to the binomial, $Np \geq 5$ *and* $Nq \geq 5$.

A **probability distribution** is the set of probabilities associated with the values of a random variable. The **binomial distribution** is the set of probabilities associated with the values of the binomial random variable X. In the present chapter, we will develop methods of finding the probability of any value of X, given the number of binomial trials and the values of p and q. Several kinds of probability distributions will play a very great role in our development of inferential statistics.

A Binomial Example. Suppose we gave a multiple-choice examination to a hypothetical student who knows absolutely nothing about the subject matter. For such a student, every answer would be a guess. We will assume that the student answers every question. The student may choose answers at random, or choose all B alternatives, or all Cs, or whatever, but the student would do just as well to choose by tossing a coin or rolling a die. Contrary to some of the student folklore, in a reasonably well constructed multiple-choice exam, there is no "pattern" to the right answers, nor is the right answer more often the longest, or the shortest, nor is B or C more often correct. Some students would reject any answer containing the word *never,* arguing that a statement containing the word *never* is never true. But the only strategy that will lead to a better-than-chance performance is the strategy of knowing some of the right answers — or at least being able to eliminate some of the wrong ones.

We will suppose that our examination has four questions, and that each question has four choices, only one of which is right. In this context, right and wrong correspond to success and failure, and thus each question represents a binomial trial where $p = 1/4$ and $q = 3/4$. Our null hypothesis is the assumption that the student is totally ignorant of the subject matter, and our alternative hypothesis is the statement that the student knows something. We will symbolize the null hypothesis by H_0 (read "H zero") and we will symbolize the alternative hypothesis by H_1 (read "H one"). We will develop methods of choosing between H_0 and H_1 given any possible outcome of our binomial probability experiment, and we will extend these methods to the analysis of many other kinds of probability experiments.

Table 7-2 lists the 16 possible combinations of right and wrong answers to the four questions. For example, Combination 2 represents the event where Questions 1, 2, and 3 are right and 4 is wrong. There are three other combinations, namely, Combinations 3, 4, and 5, where there are also three questions right and one wrong. As Table 7-2 shows, there are four and only four ways that three questions can be answered right and one answered wrong, and each of these ways is one of the possible combinations of 4 things taken 3 at a time.

The 16 possible combinations of right and wrong answers shown in Table 7-2 are mutually exclusive and exhaustive, and since each can occur in only one way, each combination can be regarded as a simple event. For example, the only way Combination 2 can occur is for Questions 1, 2, and 3 to be answered right and 4 to be answered wrong. But you might argue that Question 4 can be answered wrong in three different ways, since there are three incorrect alternatives. However, in a binomial experiment we are not ordinarily concerned with the specific way in which a question is answered incorrectly, but rather with whether the question is right or wrong. Thus, we can regard each possible combination of right and wrong answers as a simple event. In our previous discussions of sample spaces, all of the simple events were equally probable, but in our binomial sample space the simple events are not necessarily equally probable, as we will see.

Each combination of answers produces a value of the binomial random variable X listed in the column headed X_i. Each X_i represents the joint occurrence of four independent events, namely the successes and failures (right and wrong answers) in the four independent trials (questions) in the binomial experiment. Thus, we can find the probability of any X_i associated with any combination of right and wrong answers by using Formula 6-18. The column headed $P(X_i)$ gives the probability of each combination — that is, each simple event — as the product of the probabilities of the right and wrong answers making up that combination. Notice that the sum of those probabilities is 1.00, as required by Equation 6-7. For any combination having X successes, there are always $(N - X)$ failures, and thus the following expression gives the probability of any combination of successes and failures in N binomial trials:

$$P \begin{bmatrix} \text{Any one combination of} \\ X \text{ successes and } (N - X) \text{ failures} \end{bmatrix} = p^X q^{(N-X)}. \qquad (7\text{-}1)$$

TABLE 7-2. Outcomes of a Binomial Experiment Having Four Trials (Questions); $N = 4$, $p = 1/4$, $q = 3/4$.

Combination	Right and Wrong Answers to Questions: 1	2	3	4	X_i	$P(X_i) = p^x q^{(N-x)}$	X_j	$f_j = C_x^N$	$P(X_j) = C_x^N p^x q^{(N-x)}$
1	R	R	R	R	4	$pppp = p^4 q^0 = \dfrac{1}{256}$	4	1	$1p^4 q^0 = \dfrac{1}{256}$
2	R	R	R	W	3	$pppq = p^3 q^1 = \dfrac{3}{256}$			
3	R	R	W	R	3	$ppqp = p^3 q^1 = \dfrac{3}{256}$			
4	R	W	R	R	3	$pqpp = p^3 q^1 = \dfrac{3}{256}$	3	4	$4p^3 q^1 = \dfrac{12}{256}$
5	W	R	R	R	3	$qppp = p^3 q^1 = \dfrac{3}{256}$			
6	R	R	W	W	2	$ppqq = p^2 q^2 = \dfrac{9}{256}$			
7	R	W	R	W	2	$pqpq = p^2 q^2 = \dfrac{9}{256}$			
8	W	R	R	W	2	$qppq = p^2 q^2 = \dfrac{9}{256}$			
9	R	W	W	R	2	$pqqp = p^2 q^2 = \dfrac{9}{256}$	2	6	$6p^2 q^2 = \dfrac{54}{256}$
10	W	R	W	R	2	$qpqp = p^2 q^2 = \dfrac{9}{256}$			
11	W	W	R	R	2	$qqpp = p^2 q^2 = \dfrac{9}{256}$			
12	R	W	W	W	1	$pqqq = p^1 q^3 = \dfrac{27}{256}$			
13	W	R	W	W	1	$qpqq = p^1 q^3 = \dfrac{27}{256}$			
14	W	W	R	W	1	$qqpq = p^1 q^3 = \dfrac{27}{256}$	1	4	$4p^1 q^3 = \dfrac{108}{256}$
15	W	W	W	R	1	$qqqp = p^1 q^3 = \dfrac{27}{256}$			
16	W	W	W	W	0	$qqqq = p^0 q^4 = \dfrac{81}{256}$	0	1	$1p^0 q^4 = \dfrac{81}{256}$
						$\Sigma P(X_i) = \dfrac{256}{256} = 1$			$\Sigma P(X_j) = \dfrac{256}{256} = 1$

It is clear that Equation 7-1 gives the probabilities of Combinations 2 through 15 in Table 7-2, but what about Combinations 1 and 16, where the probabilities are p^4 and q^4, respectively? By Expression 7-1, the probability of Combination 1, where there are four successes and no failures, is $p^4 q^0$, and since a constant raised to the zeroth power is equal to 1, this probability is equal to p^4. (Operations with exponents are reviewed in Appendix A.) Similarly, the probability of Combination 16, where there are four failures and no successes, is $p^0 q^4 = q^4$.

In some cases in Table 7-2, several combinations of right and wrong answers produce the same value of the random variable X. For example, Combinations 2 through 5 all result in $X = 3$, and thus $X = 3$ is a compound event that can occur in four ways. Notice that the value of 3 is listed four times in the sample space for the experiment in the column headed X_i. The individual values of X are collected into a frequency distribution in the columns headed X_j and f_j, which show, respectively, the different values that X can take on and the frequencies of those values in the sample space. Each frequency, f_j, is the number of ways of answering X questions right and $(N - X)$ wrong, which is equal to the number of combinations of N things taken X at a time, that is, C_X^N. We noted earlier that the probability of a compound event is the sum of the probabilities of the simple events resulting in that compound event. Thus, for example, the probability of the compound event $X = 3$ is the sum of the probabilities of Combinations 2, 3, 4, and 5. Each of those four simple events results in the compound event $X = 3$, and each has the same probability, namely 3/256. The column headed f_j gives the frequency of occurrence of the simple events resulting in $X = 3$. Multiplying that frequency, 4, by the probability of each simple event, 3/256, gives the probability of the compound event $X = 3$, namely 12/256, which is listed in the column headed $P(X_j)$. That column lists all the probabilities associated with all the possible values of X. Notice that the sum of those probabilities is 1.00.

It follows that we can now give a general expression for the probability of X successes in N binomial trials. Thus,

$$P(X) = C_X^N p^X q^{(N-X)}, \tag{7-2}$$

where X is the number of successes, and p and q are the probabilities of success and failure.

The binomial random variable X can take on the values from 0 through 1 inclusive, and thus there are $(N + 1)$ different possible values of X in a binomial experiment. Each time we perform a binomial experiment consisting of N trials, we observe one and only one value of X. We can find the probability of each value of X by Equation 7-2. Finding the total set of such probabilities, each associated with a particular value of X, is exactly equivalent to expanding the binomial

$$(p + q)^N.$$

The binomial expansion above yields $(N + 1)$ terms, which are identical to the terms that Equation 7-2 yields when the $(N + 1)$ different values of X are entered into that equation. Since $p + q = 1$, it follows that $(p + q)^N = 1$ also, and thus we see that the sum of the terms in the binomial expansion is equal to the sum of the probabilities found by Equation 7-2.

Testing the Null Hypothesis

Returning to our multiple-choice examination, suppose a student got all four questions right. In Table 7-2, the column headed $P(X_j)$ shows that the probability of this performance is only .0039 under H_0, the assumption of total ignorance of the subject matter. Since that probability is well below the α level of .05, we reject H_0 in favor of H_1, that is, we accept the alternative hypothesis that the student knows something about the subject matter. Having rejected H_0, and having used an α level of .05, we can describe our results as **statistically significant at the .05 level.**

If H_0 were correct, the probability of getting all four questions right would be only .0039 — less than one chance in a hundred. Thus, our observed performance calls H_0 seriously into question. Of course, it is *possible* that a totally ignorant student could answer all four questions right, but such a result would be highly improbable. In hypothesis testing, we calculate the probability of an observed result under the assumption that H_0 is true. If that probability is very low, then the credibility of H_0 is also very low, and in that case, we reject H_0 in favor of H_1. In effect, hypothesis testing is an exercise in assessing the credibility — the believability — of the null hypothesis.

Now, what is the lowest score a student could make on our examination and still demonstrate some knowledge of the subject matter at the .05 level of significance? Table 7-2 shows that the probability of getting *exactly* three questions right is .0469, and since that probability is less than .05, it might be tempting to consider a score of 3 statistically significant. But the question we have asked requires finding the lowest member of a set of scores such that the probability of getting that lowest score *or* any higher score is less than or equal to .05. For a totally ignorant student, the probability of getting three or four right is equal to $P(3) + P(4) = .0469 + .0039 = .0508$, since the values of the binomial random variable X are mutually exclusive and exhaustive. We can also note that $P(3 \text{ or } 4)$ represents the probability of a union of events. By Formula 6-20, remembering that mutually exclusive events have no intersect,

$$P(3 \text{ or } 4) = P(3 \cup 4) = P(3) + P(4) - P(3 \cap 4) = P(3) + P(4).$$

Since a totally ignorant student would have a probability of .0508 of getting three or four questions right, and since .0508 exceeds our α level of .05, we cannot reject H_0 when we observe a score of three right. It is true that .0508 is *almost* equal to .05, but we can reject H_0 if and only if the calculated probability of our observed result is less than or exactly equal to .05. In order to allow us to reject the null hypothesis of total ignorance at the .05 level of statistical significance, a student would have to get all four questions correct on our very short multiple-choice exam.

We can state our null and alternative hypotheses in the following quantitative ways:

$$H_0: p = \frac{1}{4};$$

$$H_1: p > \frac{1}{4}.$$

We have said nothing about q, the probability of failure, in the above statements of our hypotheses, because attaching a value to p also determines the value of q (remember, $p + q = 1$). Our quantitative statement of the null hypothesis, above, is implied by our verbal statement that the student taking our exam knows nothing about the subject matter, since in that case the probability of success — getting a question right — will be equal to 1/4. Our alternative hypothesis is the quantitative statement that the probability of success is greater than 1/4.

The Idea of a Critical Value. We will now consider a true-false exam having 16 questions, where each question has only two alternatives — true or false. Here, we will also find the lowest score that will allow a student to show some knowledge of the subject matter at the .05 level of significance. The binomial random variable X can take on values from zero through 16 inclusive in this case. Using Formula 7-2, we can find the probability associated with each value of X. Table 7-3 shows the probability distribution of the

TABLE 7-3. Binomial Probability Distribution for $N = 16$, $p = 1/2$, $q = 1/2$, Showing Critical Value for a 1-Tailed Test.

	X_j	$P(X_j)$	$cum\ P(X_j) = P(X \leq X_j)$
	16	.0000153	1.0000000
	15	.0002441	.9999847
	14	.0018311	.9997406
	13	.0085449	.9979095
Critical → value	12	.0277710 $< .05$	.9893646
	11	.0666504	.9615936
	10	.1221924	.8949432
	9	.1745605	.7727508
	8	.1963806	.5981903
	7	.1745605	.4018097
	6	.1221924	.2272492
	5	.0666504	.1050568
	4	.0277710	.0384064
	3	.0085449	.0106354
	2	.0018311	.0020905
	1	.0002441	.0002594
	0	.0000153	.0000153

binomial random variable for our exam. The third column of that table shows the cumulative probability associated with each X_j, each value of X. For each X_j, the **cumulative probability**, $cum\ P(X_j)$, is equal to the probability of that particular value of X plus the probabilities of all lower values of X. Thus, the cumulative probability associated with any value of X is the probability of getting a score of X_j or *lower* just due to chance. In symbols,

$$cum\ P(X_j) = P(X \leq X_j). \tag{7-3}$$

The above equation states that the cumulative probability associated with any particular value, X_j, is the probability of observing an X that is less than or equal to that particular value. Notice that the cumulative probability of a score of 16 is 1.0000000. We noted in the previous chapter that the probability of an absolutely certain event was equal to 1.00; here, if we give a student our exam, then we are certain to observe a score of 16 or less[1].

Now, consider a score of 12 on our true-false exam. What is the probability of getting a score of 12 or more just due to chance? Referring to Table 7-3, we can find the desired probability by summing the probabilities of scores from 12 through 16 inclusive. We can also find the probability of 12 or more using the cumulative probabilities in the third column of Table 7-3. Since the events *12 or more* and *11 or less* are mutually exclusive and exhaustive,

$$P(X \geq 12) = 1 - P(X \leq 11) = 1 - .9615936 = .0384064.$$

We would reject H_0 if we observed any one of the scores from 12 through 16, since $P(X \geq 12)$ is less than .05. We could not reject H_0 if we observed a score of 11, since $P(X \geq 11) = .1050568$, a value greater than .05. Thus, a score of 12 is the lowest value in a region of scores within which we would reject H_0. In general, the **critical region** of a random variable is a range of values of the variable within which H_0 is rejected, and the **critical value** is the least extreme value within the critical region. We reject H_0 whenever we observe a value of a random variable that equals or exceeds the critical value. In our 16-question true-false exam, the critical value of X is a score of 12, and the critical region extends from 12 through 16 inclusive.

1-Tailed Tests. In evaluating our true-false exam performance, where there are only two alternatives per question, we can state our null and alternative hypotheses as follows:

$$H_0: p = \frac{1}{2};$$

$$H_1: p > \frac{1}{2}.$$

Notice that the above hypotheses are stated in terms of the expected value of p, rather than X — even though our test statistic is the binomial random variable X, the number of successes observed in N trials. Observing a value of X greater than or equal to the critical value allows us to reject the null hypothesis, above, which states that $p = 1/2$.

Figure 7-1 shows the probability distribution of our true-false exam in the form of a histogram. The probability associated with the critical region is shown in gray. In evaluating an examination performance, we are ordinarily interested only in high scores. A student demonstrates knowledge of the subject matter by allowing us to decide that p is significantly *greater* than its expected value under H_0. Thus, we reject H_0 and accept H_1 when we observe a value of the random variable X near the high end of the probability distribu-

---

[1] We have carried the probabilities in Table 7-3 to seven decimal places in order to show that the probabilities indeed sum to 1.0000000. Less than 7-place accuracy here would not yield a sum of exactly 1.0000000 because of slight rounding errors. Ordinarily, we will use fewer decimal places.

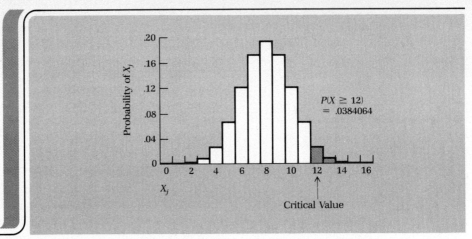

FIGURE 7-1. Binomial probability distribution for $N = 16$, $p = 1/2$, $q = 1/2$. Data are shown in Table 7-3. Those values of X associated with the shaded area are the critical region for a 1-tailed test at the .05 level.

tion, that is, in the *upper tail* of the distribution. In this case, we are carrying out a **1-tailed test.** Here, the lower tail of the probability distribution is of no interest. It is true that we could define a region of scores in the lower tail where the probabilities would sum to less than .05, but what would it mean if we observed a score falling in that region? Such a score would certainly not imply any knowledge of the subject matter — unless the student was playing games, deliberately answering questions wrong. Thus, in evaluating a performance where one end of the scoring dimension is clearly to be preferred over the other, we ordinarily run a 1-tailed test. We ordinarily have no interest in learning that a student has been so spectacularly unlucky as to make a score significantly *lower* than we would expect just by chance.

2-Tailed Tests.   In our early discussions of probability experiments in Chapter 6, we introduced the notion of a fair coin. We are now in a position to test a coin for possible bias. If a coin is fair, then *Heads* and *Tails* are equally probable. If we let p equal the probability of *Heads* and q the probability of *Tails* (or vice versa, if you prefer), then $p = q$, unless the coin is biased. Our null hypothesis is the statement that the coin is not biased, and it would seem that our alternative hypothesis would simply be the statement that the coin *is* biased. But our coin could be biased in one of two ways — in favor of *Heads* or in favor of *Tails*. Thus, there are *two* alternative hypotheses in this situation. Since we have let p equal the probability of *Heads*, p could be greater than q or less than q, depending on whether the coin is biased in favor of *Heads* or *Tails*. We can state our null and alternative hypotheses as below:

H_0: $p = q$;

H_1: $p > q$;

H_2: $p < q$.

Suppose we toss a coin 12 times. How many *Heads* would allow us to reject the null hypothesis of no bias in favor of one of the above alternative hypotheses? If we let the binomial random variable X equal the number of *Heads* in 12 tosses of the coin, then our problem is to choose two critical values of X, a high value that will define a critical region in the upper tail of the distribution, and a low value that will define a critical region in the lower tail of the distribution. If we observed a high value of X in the upper critical region, then we would decide in favor of H_1, a bias favoring *Heads*. Observing a low value of X, a value in the lower critical region, would lead us to decide in favor of H_2, a bias favoring *Tails*. We choose a high critical value, $\boldsymbol{CV_1}$, and a low critical value, $\boldsymbol{CV_2}$, such that the probability of X falling in the high critical region *or* the low critical region is less than or equal to .05. We are dealing here with the probability of the union of two sets, one representing the event $(X \geq CV_1)$ and the other the event $(X \leq CV_2)$. By Formula 6-20 the probability of the union of these events is

$$P[(X \geq CV_1) \cup (X \leq CV_2)] = P(X \geq CV_1) + P(X \leq CV_2) - P[(X \geq CV_1) \cap (X \leq CV_2)]$$
$$= P(X \geq CV_1) + P(X \leq CV_2).$$

Since observing a value of X in the high critical region and observing a value in the low critical region are mutually exclusive events, the probability of their intersect is zero, and thus the probability of the intersect vanishes from the equation above. Since we will reject the null hypothesis of no bias in our coin if we observe a value of X falling in either critical region, the above equation gives the probability of rejecting the null hypothesis *when the null hypothesis is true,* a point that we will elaborate later. Thus, we write

$$P(\text{Rejecting } H_0) = [P(X \geq CV_1) + P(X \leq CV_2)] \leq .05.$$

The above equation allows us to find CV_1 and CV_2 such that the probability of rejecting H_0 in favor of either alternative is less than or equal to our α-level probability of .05. We must choose critical values that will place half of our α probability in the upper tail and half in the lower tail of the distribution. Thus, we must choose critical values such that the probability associated with each of the two critical regions will approach .025 as closely as possible, but not exceed that probability. In Table 7-4, we note that the cumulative probability of $X = 2$ is .0192, which is the probability of observing a value of $X \leq 2$. Since the cumulative probability of $X = 3$ is .0729, a value greater than .025, the lower critical value of X is 2. Since the binomial distribution is symmetrical when $p = q$, as in our special case here, the probability of observing a value of $X \geq 10$ is also .0192. The values of 2 and 10 bear a symmetrical relationship to each other, since each is the same distance from the midpoint of the distribution. We can also find the probability of $X \geq 10$ using the cumulative probabilities in Table 7-4, as below:

$$P(X \geq 10) = 1 - P(X \leq 9) = 1 - .9806 = .0194.$$

(The probability of $X \geq 10$, which we found by using the cumulative probability, is not precisely the same as the probability of $X \leq 2$ because of

TABLE 7-4.   Binomial Probability Distribution for $N = 12$, $p = 1/2$, $q = 1/2$, Showing Critical Values for a 2-Tailed Test at the .05 Level. Cumulative Probabilities do not Sum to 1.0000 Because of Rounding Error.

	X_j	$P(X_j)$	$cum\ P(X_j) = P(X \le X_j)$
	12	.0002	.9998
	11	.0029	.9996
$CV_1 \rightarrow$	10	.0161	.9967
	9	.0537	.9806
	8	.1208	.9269
	7	.1934	.8061
	6	.2256	.6127
	5	.1934	.3871
	4	.1208	.1937
	3	.0537	.0729
$CV_2 \rightarrow$	2	.0161	.0192
	1	.0029	.0031
	0	.0002	.0002

rounding error.) The values of 10 and 2 found above satisfy our requirements for CV_1 and CV_2, the upper and lower critical values of X, since

$$P(X \ge 10) + P(X \le 2) = .0384 \le .05.$$

Figure 7-2 shows the binomial probability distribution for our present situation. The two critical regions are shown in the upper and lower tails of the histogram.

The Effects of Sample Size

Is there any difference between the frequency of human male and female births? We can consider a human birth as a binomial trial, where p is the probability of one sex and q the probability of the other. (It makes no difference which sex we designate as a "success.") Our null hypothesis is the statement that $p = q$, or that $p = 1/2$, and clearly we should carry out a 2-tailed test, since the frequency of either male or female births could be greater. How large a sample of births should we observe in order to answer our question? As we look around us, we can see that there appears to be no great difference between the numbers of male and female births. Would it be reasonable to observe the next 12 births at a local hospital and expect to answer our question? We have already determined the critical values for a 2-tailed test where $N = 12$ and where H_0 is the statement that $p = q$. Table 7-4 shows that X, the number of male or female births in a sample of 12 births, would have to be as large as 10 or as small as 2 in order to reject H_0. Dividing those values of X by N gives the proportion of male or female births we should have to observe in our sample in order to reject H_0, namely .833 or .166. Thus, p would have to be as large as .833 or as small as .166 in order to allow us to decide in favor of H_1 or H_2. But all of our experience tells us that if there is any difference between the proportion of male and female births, the difference is surely rather small. Intuitively, a larger sample would appear to be more

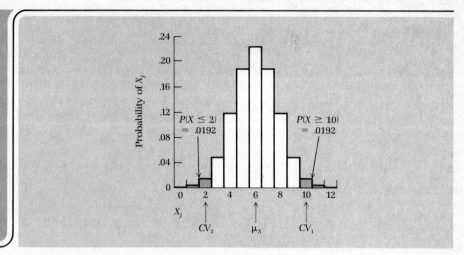

FIGURE 7-2. Binomial probability distribution for $N = 12$, $p = 1/2$, $q = 1/2$. Data are shown in Table 7-4. Critical regions for a 2-tailed test at the .05 level are those values of X associated with the shaded areas.

appropriate for our investigation of the small difference which we expect to observe between p and q.

Suppose we observe a sample of 10,000 births. In principle, we could find critical values in the upper and lower tails of the binomial probability distribution for $N = 10,000$, just as we have for smaller values of N. But in practice, the calculations would be very tedious — to say the least. Tables of binomial probabilities could be prepared (indeed, have been prepared), but such tables can be very cumbersome to use. Fortunately, there exists a simple way of dealing with binomial probabilities in large samples, a method that uses the standard normal distribution. For the present, we will put aside our discussion of the proportion of male and female births, and we will return to this problem when we have developed some better methods of dealing with large binomial distributions.

Expected Value and Variance of the Binomial Random Variable X

In order to develop methods of dealing with distributions where N is large, it will be useful to find expressions for the **expected value** — that is, the mean — and for the **variance** of the binomial distribution. The binomial random variable X is equal to the number of successes in N independent binomial trials. If we let the **random variable T** represent the outcome of a single binomial trial, where T takes on values of 1 and 0 for success and failure, respectively, then X is a sum of N independent random variables. Thus,

$$X = T_1 + T_2 + T_3 + \cdots + T_N,$$

where $T = 1$ for success, and $T = 0$ for failure. We can find the mean of the random variable X, symbolized μ_X, by taking the expected values of both sides of the above equation. Thus,

$$\mu_X = E(X) = E(T_1 + T_2 + T_3 + \cdots + T_N). \tag{7-4}$$

Intuitively, it would appear that we should be able to distribute the expectation operator on the right side of 7-4 across the terms in parentheses, and indeed we can. Thus,

$$\mu_X = E(X) = E(T_1) + E(T_2) + E(T_3) + \cdots + E(T_N). \tag{7-5}$$

We can find the mean of the random variable T, symbolized μ_T, by using Equation 6-9. Since T can take only the values of 1 and 0, representing success and failure, and since the probabilities of those values are respectively p and q, then it follows that

$$\mu_T = E(T) = \Sigma TP(T) = 1p + 0q = p, \tag{7-6}$$

where μ_T is the mean of the random variable T, and p and q are the binomial probabilities of success and failure.

Since the binomial probability experiment requires that p and q remain constant across trials, all of the Ts in Equation 7-5 representing the outcomes of the trials have identical expected values, namely p. Substituting in that equation and collecting terms

$$\mu_X = E(X) = E(T_1) + E(T_2) + E(T_3) + \cdots + E(T_N) = \underbrace{p + p + p + \cdots + p}_{N \text{ terms}} = Np.$$

Thus, we have the important result that

$$\mu_X = E(X) = Np, \tag{7-7}$$

and thus the expected value of the binomial random variable X — that is, the expected number of successes in N trials — is equal to N times the probability of success.

We will now find the variance of the binomial random variable X. Since X is the sum of the outcomes of the N binomial trials, the variance of X is the variance of that sum. Thus,

$$\sigma_X^2 = Var(X) = Var(T_1 + T_2 + T_3 + \cdots + T_N). \tag{7-8}$$

By analogy with our development of the expected value of X, you might expect to be able to distribute the variance operator on the right side of Equation 7-8 across the terms in parentheses. That can indeed be done in our present situation, where the Ts represent binomial trials that are independent random variables. (In other cases, the variance of a sum of nonindependent variables must be found differently, as explained in Appendix B.) Continuing,

$$\sigma_X^2 = Var(X) = Var(T_1) + Var(T_2) + Var(T_3) + \cdots + Var(T_N) \tag{7-9}$$

Thus, the variance of a sum of *independent* random variables is the sum of the variances of the individual variables.

We will now find the variance of T, in order to find the variance of X. Beginning with Equation 6-11,

$$\sigma_T^2 = Var(T) = E(T - \mu_T)^2 = E(T - p)^2 = E(T^2 - 2pT + p^2) = E(T^2) - 2pE(T) + E(p^2).$$

Since p^2, above, is a constant, $E(p^2) = p^2$, and thus

$$\sigma_T^2 = Var(T) = E(T^2) - 2pE(T) + p^2 = E(T^2) - 2pp + p^2 = E(T^2) - p^2. \qquad (7\text{-}10)$$

Since T can take on only the values 0 and 1, it follows that $T^2 = T$ for all possible values of T — all two of them — and thus $E(T^2) = E(T)$. Substituting in Equation 7-10, and continuing,

$$\sigma_T^2 = Var(T) = E(T) - p^2 = p - p^2 = p(1 - p) = pq. \qquad (7\text{-}11)$$

Remembering that p and q remain constant across all of the trials in a binomial experiment, the variances of all the Ts in Equation 7-9 are identical, since each variance is equal to pq. Substituting in that equation and collecting terms,

$$\sigma_X^2 = Var(X) = Var(T_1) + Var(T_2) + Var(T_3) + \cdots + Var(T_N)$$

$$= \underbrace{pq + pq + pq + \cdots + pq}_{N \text{ terms}}$$

$$= Npq. \qquad (7\text{-}12)$$

Having developed expressions for the expected value and variance of the binomial random variable, we are now ready to return to our discussion of applications of the binomial to larger samples.

The Normal Approximation to the Binomial

Probability and the Area under a Curve

As we noted in Chapter 2, if a frequency distribution is shown in the form of a histogram where the height of each bar represents the frequency of a particular score and the bar width is equal to 1, then the area of the histogram is equal to N, the total number of cases in the distribution. If we divide the frequency of each score by N, then we find the probability of that score in accordance with Formula 6-1. Plotting a histogram showing the probability — rather than the frequency — of each score yields a probability distribution. Figure 7-3 shows several binomial probability distributions, each for a different value of N. If the length of each score unit on the horizontal axis of a probability distribution is taken as 1, then the area of any particular rectangle in the distribution is equal to 1 times the probability of the particular score for that rectangle, and it follows that the *area* of such a rectangle is equal to the *probability* of the score. Summing the areas (probabilities) for all such rectangles, it follows that the total area of any probability distribution is equal to 1.00, in accordance with Equation 6-7. It is very useful to let áreas represent

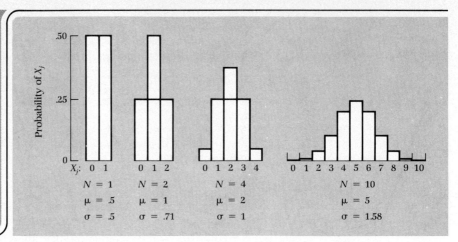

FIGURE 7-3. Binomial probability distributions for different values of N; $p = q = 1/2$ in all cases *here*. As N increases, the binomial distribution approaches the normal distribution.

the probabilities associated with particular values of random variables. For example, in Figures 7-1 and 7-2, the probabilities associated with the critical regions for some statistical tests are shown as areas shaded in gray. In Figure 7-1, the probability of observing a value of X greater than or equal to the critical value of 12 is equal to the proportion of the total area under the curve located at and above a value of 12.

In Figure 7-3, all of the binomial probability distributions have areas of 1.00. As the number of binomial trials increases, the standard deviation increases, but the area of each distribution is exactly 1.00. If we let N become infinitely large and at the same time let the length of each unit on the horizontal scale of scores become infinitely small, then the histogram representing the binomial probability distribution very closely approaches the normal distribution. As N becomes infinite, we say that the binomial distribution approaches the normal distribution as a *limit*. We can consider the area under the normal distribution as consisting of an infinite number of rectangles each having a height of h — the ordinate of the normal curve at any point — and an infinitely small width. It is possible to show that the sum of the areas of those rectangles is equal to 1.00, and thus the area under the normal distribution — as we noted in Chapter 5 — is equal to 1.00.

Comparing the Binomial and the Normal Distribution. In Figure 7-4 the histogram shows the binomial probability distribution for $N = 10$ and $p = q = .5$. The height of each bar is equal to the probability of observing a particular value of the binomial random variable X. For that distribution,

$$\mu_X = Np = 10(.5) = 5 \qquad \text{and} \qquad \sigma_X = \sqrt{Npq} = \sqrt{10(.5)(.5)} = 1.58.$$

The smooth curve in Figure 7-4 is a normal distribution having the same

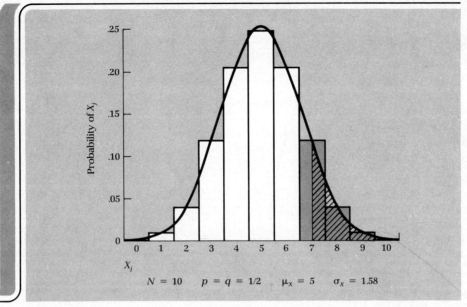

$N = 10 \qquad p = q = 1/2 \qquad \mu_x = 5 \qquad \sigma_x = 1.58$

FIGURE 7-4. Normal curve fitted to binomial probability distribution. Shaded area is exact binomial probability that $X \geq 7$. Cross-hatched area is normal curve probability that $X \geq 7$. Notice that cross-hatched area is substantially smaller than shaded area. See text for explanation.

mean and standard deviation as the above binomial distribution. That normal curve was plotted using Equation 5-9. Notice that the height of the smooth curve is very close to the height of each bar at each value of X. Thus, in that respect, the normal distribution fits the binomial distribution very closely.

Now consider the binomial probability of observing a value of $X \geq 7$. That probability corresponds to the area of the shaded bars in Figure 7-4, and is equal to .1719. Now, what proportion of the area under the normal curve lies beyond an X value of 7? That area is shown by cross-hatching in Figure 7-4. We can find that area by utilizing the standard normal distribution — that is, by transforming the X value of 7 to a Z-score. Using Equation 5-11,

$$Z = \frac{X - \mu_x}{\sigma_x} = \frac{X - Np}{\sqrt{Npq}} = \frac{7 - 10(.5)}{\sqrt{10(.5)(.5)}} = \frac{7 - 5}{\sqrt{2.5}} = \frac{2}{1.58} = 1.27. \quad (7\text{-}13)$$

Referring to Table A, Column 3 shows that the proportion of the area above a positive Z value of 1.27 is .1020. Thus, there is a considerable discrepancy between the probability found using the normal distribution and the actual binomial probability. In our present case, the normal probability underestimates the exact binomial probability by more than 40%. We will resolve that discrepancy in the next section.

The Correction for Continuity.   Referring to Figure 7-4, the normal curve probability which we calculated for a score of 7 is the cross-hatched area lying above a *point* of 7 on the scale of scores. As we noted in Chapter 3, a score is considered as occupying an interval on a continuous scale. Even in the case of a discrete random variable such as the binomial, we consider each value of X as occupying an interval rather than a point — indeed, we must do so if we are to let the area of a histogram represent probability. Since a score of 7 extends from 6.5 to 7.5, if we find the area under the normal curve above a point of 6.5, then that area will very closely approximate the actual binomial probability that $X \geq 7$. Thus, we substract .5 from the score of 7, and find the Z-score of the resulting point on the measurement scale:

$$Z = \frac{(X - .5) - Np}{\sqrt{Npq}} = \frac{(7 - .5) - 10(.5)}{\sqrt{10(.5)(.5)}} = \frac{6.5 - 5}{1.58} = .95. \qquad (7\text{-}14)$$

The proportion of the area beyond a positive Z-score of .95 is found in Table A. That probability, and the actual binomial probability of a score of 7 or more, are shown below for comparison:

Normal probability $= A_Z = A_{.95} = .1711$;

Binomial probability $= P(X \geq 7) = .1719$;

where A_Z is the area beyond a given Z-score. Thus, the normal probability above is a close approximation to the exact binomial probability.

Now consider the binomial probability of getting a score of 3 or less.

$$Z = \frac{(X + .5) - Np}{\sqrt{Npq}} = \frac{(3 + .5) - 10(.5)}{\sqrt{10(.5)(.5)}} = \frac{3.5 - 5}{1.58} = -.95. \qquad (7\text{-}15)$$

The exact binomial probability of a score of 3 or less is .1719, and the normal approximation to that probability is .1711.

There is a general rule, which we can now extract from Equations 7-14 and 7-15. In the first case, where X is greater than its expected value, Np, we subtracted .5 from the value of X. In the second case, where X is less than Np, we added .5 to the value of X. Thus, the rule is to reduce the magnitude of the deviation between X and Np, whether the deviation is positive or negative. Adding or subtracting .5 represents a **correction for continuity,** which results in improved agreement between the normal probability associated with Z and the exact binomial probability. The correction for continuity is necessary because we are using a continuous distribution — the normal — to approximate the probabilities associated with a discrete distribution — the binomial. The following equation, incorporating the correction for continuity, represents one form of the **normal approximation to the binomial:**

$$Z = \frac{(X \pm .5) - Np}{\sqrt{Npq}}; \quad + .5 \text{ if } X \leq Np, \quad - .5 \text{ if } X \geq Np. \qquad (7\text{-}16)$$

There is a small ambiguity in applying the correction for continuity in Equation 7-16 when X is exactly equal to its expected value, Np: Should you add or subtract the correction? When X is exactly equal to Np, adding .5 results in a value of Z that gives the probability of observing a value of X less than or equal to Np; subtracting .5 gives the probability of observing an X greater than or equal to Np. In so far as hypothesis testing in concerned, a value of X equal to Np is of little interest, since we reject the null hypothesis only when we observe an extreme value of a statistic.

Whether X is greater than or less than Np, the effect of the correction for continuity is to reduce the absolute magnitude of the deviation between X and Np. Thus, we can rewrite Equation 7-16 in a form that may be easier to use:

$$Z = \frac{|X - Np| - .5}{\sqrt{Npq}} \tag{7-17}$$

The expression $|X - Np|$ in the above equation is the absolute value of the deviation of X from its expected value — that is, the value of the deviation without regard to sign. The correction for continuity in 7-17 always requires *subtracting* .5, and thus that equation offers fewer opportunities than 7-16 for making mistakes. You can easily satisfy yourself that both of those equations yield identical values of Z, except for sign, and thus the two procedures yield identical normal approximations to binomial probabilities.

Large Binomial Samples

A 2-Tailed Test. We will now return to the question we asked earlier about the relative frequency of male and female human births. Our null hypothesis is the statement that there is no difference between the male and female frequencies, and thus $p = q = .5$. Since either the male or the female frequency could be larger, we will carry out a 2-tailed test. We can state the null and alternative hypotheses symbolically:

H_0: $p = .5$;

H_1: $p > .5$;

H_2: $p < .5$.

We will observe a sample of 10,000 births, and we will use the normal approximation to the binomial to test our null hypothesis at the .05 level. Before making our observations, we will determine the critical values of Z at or beyond which we will reject H_0 in favor of H_1 or H_2. Figure 7-5 (right) shows that for a 2-tailed test at an α level of .05, the α probability must be divided equally between the two tails of the curve so that each tail contains an area equal to $\alpha/2$, an area that is bounded by one of the critical values. The critical values are determined by consulting Table A. The problem is to find the positive value of Z that will cut off an area in the upper tail of the curve equal to $\alpha/2$, and the negative value of Z that will cut off a similar area in the lower tail of the curve. In Table A, Column 3 shows that .025 of the area lies above a Z of $+1.96$ and .025 lies below a Z of -1.96. Thus, those values of Z are

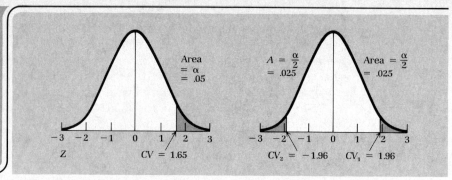

FIGURE 7-5. Standard normal distribution showing critical values of Z for a 1-tailed test at the .05 level (left) and for a 2-tailed test at the .05 level (right). In the first case, all of the α probability is located in one tail of the curve. In the second case, half of the α probability is located in each tail.

respectively CV_1 and CV_2, the critical values that will lead to our rejection of H_0 in favor of H_1 or H_2, respectively.

The critical value for a 1-tailed test at the .05 level, as in Figure 7-5 (left) is found similarly, except in this case we find the value of Z that cuts off an area equal to the entire α probability of .05. For a 1-tailed test, we place the critical region in the upper or lower tail of the curve, depending on whether our alternative hypothesis states that $p > .5$ or $p < .5$.

Now in a sample of 10,000 births, suppose we observe 4,877 females and 5,123 males. We let the binomial random variable X equal the number of female births, p equal the probability of a female birth, and q the probability of a male birth. Using Equation 7-17 to find the normal approximation to the binomial,

$$Z = \frac{|X - Np| - .5}{\sqrt{Npq}}$$

$$= \frac{|4{,}877 - 10{,}000(.5)| - .5}{\sqrt{10{,}000(.5)(.5)}} = \frac{|4{,}877 - 5{,}000| - .5}{\sqrt{2{,}500}}$$

$$= \frac{|-123| - .5}{50} = \frac{122.5}{50} = 2.45 \qquad (7\text{-}18)$$

The proportion of the area under the standard normal distribution lying beyond the above Z value is found in Table A. Thus,

$$A_Z = A_{2.45} = .0071; \quad .025 = \frac{\alpha}{2}. \qquad (7\text{-}19)$$

The value of Z in Equation 7-18 exceeds CV_1, since $2.45 > 1.96$. Notice also that the value of $A_{2.45}$, the probability beyond a Z value of 2.45, is only .0071, which is substantially less than .025.

Having now rejected the null hypothesis, which alternative hypothesis should we accept? In Equation 7-18, the deviation of the observed value of X from the expected value is a negative number, -123, which indicates that the observed number of the female births is less than the expected number. Since the expected number of female births is equal to the mean of the binomial distribution, we have observed a value of X in the lower tail of the distribution. It follows that the observed proportion of female births is significantly less than the male proportion, and thus, we accept H_2, the alternative hypothesis that states that $p < q$. In working with the absolute value of the deviation in 7-18 we lose the sign on the resulting value of Z, but we can tell whether the Z value is in the upper or lower tail of the distribution by noting whether X is greater than or less than Np.

We said earlier that it does not matter whether we let p equal the number of female births or the number of male births. In the latter case, we would let the random variable X equal the number of male births. Formula 7-17 would yield identical results, in that we would conclude that the proportion of male births is significantly *greater* than .5.

Significance Probability. We have described the results of our observation of a sample of 10,000 births as showing that the proportion of male births is significantly higher than the proportion of female births — but we need to qualify carefully what we mean by statistical significance. We can find the observed proportions of male and female births by dividing the observed frequencies in our sample by our sample size; those observed proportions are, respectively, .5123 and .4877. (Over a period of many years, the actual proportion of male births in the U.S. population has been about .5125.) Under our null hypothesis, $p = q = .5$. If H_0 were true, it would be very unlikely that we would observe a proportion of male births as high as .5123 — indeed, we have shown that the probability of observing a proportion that high or higher in 10,000 births is only .0071, a probability of less than 1 chance in a hundred. If H_0 were true, and if we observed a hundred different samples of 10,000 births each, only about once in those hundred samples should we expect to observe a proportion of male births as high or higher than .5123. But is there any tremendous difference between the observed proportions of male and female births — about 51% and 49% respectively? As you observe the people you have seen around you, are you aware of that difference? The fact that binomial proportions may differ significantly in the statistical sense is no guarantee that there will be any great and readily apparent difference between the observed frequencies of success and failure, even in a large sample. We will have much more to say about the meaning of statistical significance in later chapters.

A 1-Tailed Test. Suppose a student takes a 60-question multple-choice examination where there are four choices per question. The student makes a score of 22. Does the student know anything, or might that performance have occurred just by chance? We will use the normal approximation to the binomial to carry out a 1-tailed test at the .05 level. In evaluating an examination performance, we are interested only in the upper tail of the curve, as we have argued earlier. Our null and alternative hypotheses are the following:

$$H_0: p = \frac{1}{4};$$

$$H_1: p > \frac{1}{4}.$$

Notice that H_0, above, is the statement that $p = 1/4$, *not* the statement that $p = q$, since the probabilities of success and failure in the present situation are respectively 1/4 and 3/4. Since we are carrying out a 1-tailed test, we will place all of our α probability in the upper tail of the curve. Thus, refering to Table A, the critical value of Z for our test is 1.65. Applying Equation 7-17,

$$Z_X = \frac{|X - Np| - .5}{\sqrt{Npq}} = \frac{|22 - 60(.25)| - .5}{\sqrt{60(.25)(.75)}} = \frac{6.5}{3.35} = 1.94.$$

Since the above value of Z exceeds the critical value of 1.65, we reject H_0 in favor of H_1. Would you be able to reject the null hypothesis if we had erroneously decided to run a 2-tailed test in this situation?

Some Restrictions on the Normal Approximation

For a reasonably large N, the normal approximation yields probabilities that are very close to the actual binomial probabilities, but when N is small — especially when p and q are not equal — the approximation is not very good and should not be used. The normal approximation should be used only when *both* of the following conditions are met:

$$Np \geq 5, \qquad \text{and} \qquad Nq \geq 5. \tag{7-20}$$

Fortunately, the above conditions are usually met in those situations where the binomial would be most tedious to calculate. When those conditions are not met, as when N is small, the calculation of the actual binomial probabilities is usually easy and straightforward.

Some Final Words

We have developed an important probability distribution — the binomial — in the present chapter, and we have also developed the fundamentals of hypothesis testing. In later chapters, we will devote a great deal of space to hypothesis testing, but we will need to add only a little to the fundamental ideas we have developed here.

Terms and Symbols

Most of the following terms and symbols were introduced in the present chapter, although some were introduced earlier. All of these ideas have played important roles in our present developments, and will continue to be of great importance in the future.

Binomial distribution	**Normal approximation to the**
Binomial trial	**binomial**
Success and failure	p and q
Binomial experiment	$C_X^N p^x q^{(N-x)}$
Binomial random variable X	$(p + q)^N$
Probability distribution	$Cum\ P(X_j)$
Null hypothesis	H_0
Alternative hypotheses	H_1
Statistical significance	H_2
.05 level	μ_x
Critical value	$E(X)$
Cumulative probability	σ_X^2
Critical region	$Var(X)$
1-tailed test	μ_T
2-tailed test	$E(T)$
Expected value	σ_T^2
Variance	Z
Random variable T	f_j
Independent random variables	α
Area under a curve	CV_1
Significance probability	CV_2
Binomial coefficient	A_Z
Correction for continuity	

EXERCISES AND STUDY QUESTIONS

1. Are there more left-handed or right-handed people? Suppose you select a random sample of 10 people, and you find 2 left-handers and 8 right-handers.

   a. Formulate the null and alternative hypotheses in words and symbols.

   b. Should this be a 1 or 2-tailed test? Why? Should your answer to this question be determined by the data above, that is, by the results of your observations?

   c. Justify the use of the normal approximation to the binomial in the present case.

d. Carry out a test. Do you reject H_0? What does rejection or nonrejection of the null hypothesis mean here?

2. In Exercise 1, above, suppose you had drawn a larger sample of 20 people, and suppose you found 4 left-handers and 16 right-handers in that sample — that is, exactly the same proportion of left- and right-handers as in your smaller sample.

   a. Justify the use of the normal approximation to the binomial.

   b. Carry out a test, indicating whether you reject H_0, and indicating what that decision means.

   c. Compare the results of the present test with the results in Exercise 1, above. What bearing does the sample size have on the probability of detecting a difference between the proportion of left- and right-handers? Would you expect the effects of sample size to generalize to other situations?

3. In the Jefferson National Expansion Memorial, a national park on the west bank of the Mississippi River in St. Louis, Missouri, there stands an enormous Arch of gleaming stainless steel. The Arch is 630 feet tall — taller than the Washington Monument — and 630 feet wide at the base, measured across the outside of the legs. Thus, the horizontal and vertical dimensions of the Arch are equal in length. But do those dimensions *look* equal in the figure below?

   Suppose we show a picture of the Arch, a full frontal view, to 12 subjects. Each person is asked to indicate whether the horizontal or vertical dimension looks longer. Judgments of equality are discouraged by asking any subject who initially makes such a judgment to look at the picture very carefully, and see if one dimension looks *even slightly longer* than the other. The results below indicate the longer-appearing dimension for each subject. Is there an illusion in the perception of the Arch?

Subject	1	2	3	4	5	6	7	8	9	10	11	12
Response	V	V	V	H	V	V	V	V	V	V	V	V

   a. Formulate the null and alternative hypotheses in words and symbols.

   b. Should this be a 1- or 2-tailed test? Why? Should your answer to this

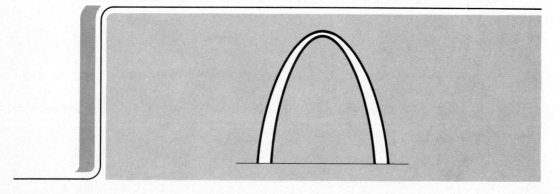

question be determined by the above data, by the responses of the subjects?

   c. Justify the use of the normal approximation to the binomial in the present case.

   d. Do you reject H_0? What does rejection or nonrejection of the null hypothesis mean here?

4. Suppose the results of the study in Exercise 3, above, had come out slightly differently. For example, suppose that one subject could see no difference at all in the apparent length of the horizontal and vertical dimensions, insisting that those dimensions appeared precisely equal. Those possible results are shown below:

Horizontal longer	1
Vertical longer	10
Equal horizontal and vertical	1

   a. What special difficulty arises in using the binomial to test the present results, and how can that difficulty be overcome?

   b. Justify using the normal approximation to the binomial, and carry out a test.

   c. Compare the statistical significance of the present test with the test in Exercise 1, above.

5. A student makes a score of 10 on a 20-item true-false exam. The instructor gives the student an F, arguing that the student appears to know absolutely nothing about the subject matter. The student argues that he really knew the answers to the 10 questions he got right, but says he had to guess the answers to the remaining 10 questions, and insists that unfortunately he guessed all of those questions wrong. The student goes on to argue that perhaps he should receive a minimal passing grade since he knew half the material on the exam. Evaluate the instructor's and the student's arguments by appropriate statistical tests and reasoning.

6. The *oddity problem*, an exercise in concept formation, has been studied in several animal species, for example, monkeys, pigeons, and young children (Harlow, 1949). Several oddity problems are shown in the figure below. In each case, choosing the odd or different member of a trio of

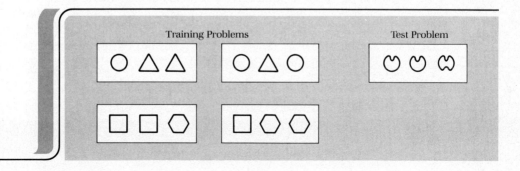

objects results in reinforcement—for example, a bit of chocolate for a young child. A group of 16 children are each given 6 trials on each of the above training problems. The spatial location of the odd object is randomized on each trial. Notice that Problem 2 is a reversal of Problem 1, since the circle is correct in the first case and incorrect in the second; Problems 3 and 4 are similarly related. After the training problems, each child is given a single trial on the test problem above, and 13 of the 16 children choose correctly.

  a. Formulate the null and alternative hypotheses in words and symbols.
  b. Should this be a 1- or 2-tailed test? Explain.
  c. Justify treating this study as a binomial probability experiment, and justify the use of the normal approximation.
  d. Do you reject H_0? Explain what that means.

7. A very insightful researcher might point out a small flaw in the study in Exercise 6 above. The correct object in the test problem is a disk having two indentations while each incorrect object has only a single indentation, and thus the correct one is more *complex,* and furthermore resembles the letter *H*. Since children, and other people as well, have been shown to prefer complexity, the insightful researcher might argue that the test problem offers two bases for a correct choice, *oddity* and *complexity,* and that we have no way of knowing the basis for any subject's choice, as the experiment now stands.

  a. What is the term that applies here, where either of two variables could account for the results of an experiment or observation?
  b. How could the study be modified, very slightly, to overcome this difficulty?

8. Suppose in conducting the study in Exercise 6, above, the researcher had access to a total of 16 young children as potential subjects, perhaps in a small nursery school. During the course of the experiment, 2 subjects became upset and were dismissed before getting through the training problems. Of the remaining 14 subjects, 11 solved the test problem correctly.

  a. Is the normal approximation to the binomial appropriate here? If not, why not?
  b. Analyze the results using an alternative procedure.

9. Two students, Smith and Jones, have just made scores of 6 and 9 respectively on a 10-question true-false exam in statistics. Smith argues that he should receive a passing grade since his pattern of right and wrong answers—shown below, question by question—is a very rare event under the null hypothesis:

Smith's answers: R W W R R W W R R R;

P(Smith's pattern) < .001.

Smith calculates that the probability of obtaining his particular pattern of answers just by chance is less than .001, and furthermore, points out that the pattern of Jones's answers, shown below, also has the same probability under the null hypothesis:

Jones's answers: R R R R R R R R W R;

P(Jones's pattern) < .001.

Smith goes on to argue that his performance is as rare an event as Jones's under the null hypothesis, and therefore demonstrates an equally significant level of performance.

Jones is unconvinced, pointing out that the *pattern* of right and wrong answers is of little concern on an exam. Arguing that it is the *score* that counts, Jones calculates the exact binomial probabilities of the two exam scores, below, using a single term in the binomial expansion to find the probability of each score.

P(Smith's score) = .205;   P(Jones's score) = .00977.

Jones goes on to argue that his performance is statistically significant at the .01 level by a 1-tailed test, while Smith's performance does not even approach significance.

a. Verify the above probabilities of the patterns of answers and the exact binomial probabilities of the exam scores.

b. Evaluate Smith and Jones's arguments. In what sense are both right? What important point has Jones missed, as well as Smith?

10. Can rats learn to discriminate between a lighter and a darker shade of gray? The door to one arm of a Y-maze is lighter, and the door to the other is darker. For some rats, the light door is correct and is reinforced, and for other rats the darker door is correct. The left-right locations of the lighter and darker doors are presented randomly from trial to trial. The experimenter has decided that a rat that eventually learns to make 9 correct responses out of a block of 10 trials will be considered to have learned the discrimination. Indeed, a criterion of 9 out of 10 correct has been adopted as a standard in many kinds of two-choice experiments.

a. Evaluate the experimenter's criterion of 9 out of 10 correct as a standard for deciding whether an individual animal has learned the discrimination. Is that an arbitrary standard, or is it logically defensible on statistical grounds?

b. Suppose the lighter door is always on the left, and the darker on the right. In an experiment using 20 rats, half are reinforced for choosing the lighter door and half for choosing the darker. What difficulty arises here in interpreting the results of this experiment?

c. Suppose the left-right positions of the lighter and darker doors are randomized across trials, but suppose the darker door is always reinforced. What difficulty arises here?

Testing a Single Mean

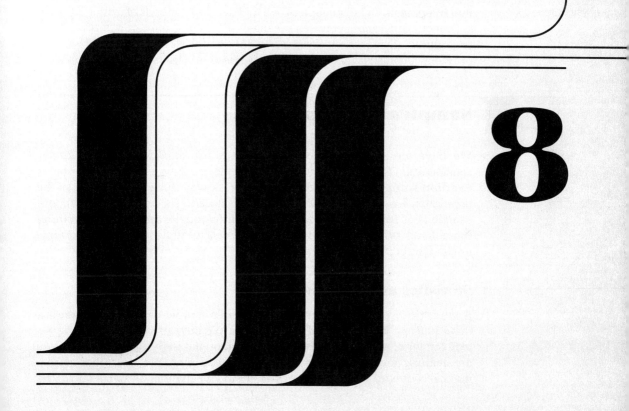

8

So far, we have developed methods of hypothesis testing in a variety of probability experiments involving permutations, combinations, and the binomial distribution. All of those experiments involved discrete random variables that could take only integer values. But there are many situations that do not conform to the requirements for the probability experiments that we have described previously. For example, a subject's reaction time—the time between the onset of a signal and the subject's response—is a continuous variable that can take on an infinite number of positive values. Similarly, the distance between two people engaging in some kind of social interaction represents another continuous variable, and so does the perceived magnitude of a visual illusion.

In the present chapter, we will develop methods of testing hypotheses involving continuous random variables, and also discrete variables that do not meet the requirements of our earlier probability experiments. These methods will require measurements that constitute interval or ratio scales. In the last chapter, we explained the use of the binomial distribution in connection with nominal scales, and in later chapters we will present additional methods of hypothesis testing suitable for use with nominal and ordinal scales.

In the present context, a probability experiment will consist of observing a random variable in a sample of some number of subjects, and then comparing the observed value of the sample mean with the expected value under the null hypothesis. In later chapters, we will develop methods of testing hypotheses about differences between means of different groups of subjects. These procedures all represent exercises in inferential statistics—the process of drawing conclusions about populations based on observations of samples.

Samples and Populations

We have already defined a population as the total set of things under consideration for some purpose, and a sample as a subset of the population. A **random sample** is a sample chosen in such a way that every member of the population has an equal chance of being chosen. The concept of a random sample is of fundamental importance in inferential statistics. In everything that follows, whenever we use the term *sample* we will mean *random sample* unless we specify otherwise.

Statistics and Parameters

A **statistic** is a quantitative characteristic of a sample, and a **parameter** is a quantitative characteristic of a population. We have used the term *statistics* to mean what a large part of this book is about, but in the present context, we are defining the term slightly differently—and more precisely. In a mathematical context, a parameter is a constant in an equation. Indeed, μ and σ, the mean and standard deviation of the normal distribution, appear as parameters in the equation of that distribution, reproduced below:

$$h = \frac{1}{\sigma\sqrt{2\pi}}\, e^{-\frac{1}{2}\left(\frac{x-\mu}{\sigma}\right)^2}. \tag{5-9}$$

Statistics and parameters will play a great role in our development of inferential statistics. Indeed, the whole of inferential statistics nearly reduces to the process of drawing conclusions about the values of population parameters based on observations of sample statistics. To help differentiate between parameters and statistics, we will use Greek letters to stand for population parameters, μ and σ, for example, and Roman letters to stand for sample statistics, such as $\overline{X}$ and SD.

Sampling a Population Where μ and σ Are Known

Some faculty members seem to take almost as much pride in the caliber of their students as the alumni take in the prowess of the football team. Comparing the caliber of psychology students across different institutions provides almost endless opportunities for intercollegiate competition. Besides adding a small element of excitement to the academic life, such comparisons may provide some insight into the educational process.

Suppose 10 graduating seniors in a particular psychology department have applied for admission to several graduate schools. One of the criteria for admission to most graduate programs in psychology is a satisfactory performance on the Graduate Record Examination (GRE), consisting of high-level tests of verbal and quantitative aptitude and an advanced test of academic achievement in the area of psychology. The faculty is very pleased to note that the mean quantitative aptitude score of their 10 graduating seniors is 604, while the mean of the 851,915 students taking the GRE during a recent three-year period was 512, and the standard deviation was 134. But in the midst of their rejoicing over the high caliber of their graduating seniors, one of the more sophisticated faculty members raises the question of whether their students differ *significantly* from the population mean, that is, the mean of all the students taking the GRE.

The Sampling Distribution

Suppose we have a population consisting of an infinite number of elements, where each element is a value of the random variable X, and where μ and σ are known. Our population of 851,915 GRE scores is so large as to be considered infinite for our present purposes. We consider our 10 graduating seniors as a random sample drawn from that population, and thus our 10 GRE scores comprise a probability experiment consisting of 10 trials, where each trial is an observation of the random variable X. We are primarily interested in $\overline{X}$, the sample mean, rather than the individual values of X.

Now suppose we draw another random sample of size 10, and we calculate the mean of the second sample. Would you expect the means of the two samples to be identical? Intuitively, we should expect the means to be fairly close to each other, but it would be most unlikely to observe identical means in the two samples. Thus, $\overline{X}$, the sample mean, is a random variable — a quantity that takes on different values in different random samples. If we drew all possible samples of size 10, and if we calculated the mean of each sample, then we would generate a **sampling distribution** — that is, a distribution of sample means analogous to distributions of other random variables.

The expected value of the sampling distribution is the mean of the sample means in the long run, where each sample is of some specific size, say 10, as in our present example. The standard deviation of the sampling distribution is a measure of the dispersion of the sample means around their expected value, that is, around their central location. Where there is any possibility of confusion, we will use subscripts to indicate whether we are dealing with the expected value and standard deviation of the sampling distribution, $\mu_{\overline{x}}$ and $\sigma_{\overline{x}}$, or of the individual values of the random variable X, μ_x and σ_x. As you may suppose, and as we will demonstrate shortly, $\mu_{\overline{x}}$ is exactly equal to μ_x. We will also find the relationship between $\sigma_{\overline{x}}$ and σ_x. The parameters of the sampling distribution will prove very useful in a great many contexts.

Critical Ratios

If the sample means were normally distributed, and if we could find the expected value and standard deviation of the sampling distribution, $\mu_{\overline{x}}$ and $\sigma_{\overline{x}}$, then we could find the Z-score associated with any observed value of $\overline{X}$, as below:

$$Z_{\overline{x}} = \frac{\overline{X} - \mu_{\overline{x}}}{\sigma_{\overline{x}}}, \tag{8-1}$$

where $Z_{\overline{x}}$ is the Z-score associated with the sample mean, $\overline{X}$. We could then find the probability associated with the above Z-score using the standard normal distribution, and that probability would give us the relative standing of the observed mean in the sampling distribution — that is, in the distribution of the means of all possible random samples of a specified size that could be drawn from the population.

The right side of Equation 8-1, above, is a ratio of two quantities. The numerator of that ratio is the deviation of a sample statistic, $\overline{X}$, from its expected value, $\mu_{\overline{x}}$, which is the expected value of the sampling distribution. The denominator of the above ratio is $\sigma_{\overline{x}}$, the standard deviation of the sampling distribution. Any ratio of the form of Equation 8-1, that is, the deviation of a sample statistic from its expected value divided by its standard deviation, is a **critical ratio.** We will develop several kinds of critical ratios for use in hypothesis testing.

The normal approximation to the binomial, Equation 7-17, represents a critical ratio that we have already utilized:

$$Z_X = \frac{|X - \mu_X| - .5}{\sigma_X} = \frac{|X - Np| - .5}{\sqrt{Npq}}. \tag{7-17}$$

Equation 7-17 is quite analogous to 8-1 in that each equation is a critical ratio consisting of the difference between an observed and expected value of a random variable divided by its standard deviation. Because of the correction for continuity in 7-17, there are superficial differences between the two equations, but the similarities are more fundamental than the differences. We will develop expressions for the expected value and standard deviation of the sampling distribution, and we will then be able to use critical ratios comparable to Equation 8-1 for hypothesis testing in much the way we have used the normal approximation to the binomial.

Expected Value of the Sample Mean

We now find the expected value of the sampling distribution, that is, the expected value of the sample mean, remembering that the mean is a random variable that can take on different values in different samples. In the following expression for the sample mean, each of the individual values of X represents one observation of the random variable X:

$$\bar{X} = \frac{\Sigma X}{N} = \frac{1}{N}(X_1 + X_2 + \cdots + X_N).$$

Taking expected values,

$$\mu_{\bar{X}} = E(\bar{X}) = E\left[\frac{1}{N}(X_1 + X_2 + \cdots + X_N)\right]. \tag{8-2}$$

In Equation 8-2 above, the expected value of $\bar{X}$ is equal to the expected value of a constant, $1/N$, times a sum of random variables, the individual observations of X. Distributing the expectation across the sum of random variables,

$$E(\bar{X}) = \frac{1}{N}[E(X_1) + E(X_2) + \cdots + E(X_N)]. \tag{8-3}$$

Since the individual X values represent subjects drawn from the same population, the expected values of all the Xs are equal. Thus,

$$E(X_1) = E(X_2) = \cdots = E(X_N) = E(X).$$

Substituting in 8-3,

$$E(\bar{X}) = \frac{1}{N}[E(X) + E(X) + \cdots + E(X)] = \frac{1}{N}(\mu_X + \mu_X + \cdots + \mu_X).$$

Since there are N terms in parentheses,

$$\mu_{\bar{x}} = E(\bar{X}) = \frac{1}{N}(N\mu_x) = \mu_x. \tag{8-4}$$

Recalling that the expected value of a random variable is the mean of the variable in the long run, Equation 8-4 gives us some important information: If we draw a large number of samples of size N from an infinite population having a mean μ_x, then the mean of the sampling distribution — the **mean of the sample means** — which we should expect to observe in the long run, is exactly equal to μ_x, the mean of the population of Xs. Since the expected value of $\bar{X}$ is exactly equal to μ_x, $\bar{X}$ is an **unbiased estimator** of the population mean. In situations where we do not know the value of μ_x, we can use $\bar{X}$ to estimate the parameter. Since $\bar{X}$ is an unbiased estimator, that statistic will neither under- nor overestimate the population mean in the long run. (For an excellent treatment of the algebra of expected values, see Hays, 1981, p. 625.)

Notice that in deriving Equation 8-4 we have said nothing about the distribution of the population we have sampled. Equation 8-4 holds true for any population — normally distributed, skewed, bimodal, or whatever — as long as the population is of infinite size and has a finite variance.

Variance of the Sampling Distribution

Since the sample mean is a random variable, the distribution of sample means has a measure of central location $\mu_{\bar{x}}$, and measures of dispersion, $\sigma_{\bar{x}}$ and $\sigma_{\bar{x}}^2$, respectively the standard deviation and variance of the sample means. The standard deviation of the sample means, usually called the **standard error of the mean,** is a measure of the dispersion of the means for a particular sample size — that is, a measure of the extent to which the sample means tend to spread out from their measure of central location. We will now find the **variance of the sample mean.**

We begin with the following familiar expression for the mean of a sample of size N:

$$\bar{X} = \frac{\Sigma X}{N} = \frac{1}{N}(X_1 + X_2 + \cdots + X_N).$$

The variance of $\bar{X}$ is

$$\sigma_{\bar{x}}^2 = Var(\bar{X}) = Var\left[\frac{1}{N}(X_1 + X_2 + \cdots + X_N)\right]. \tag{8-5}$$

The right side of 8-5, above, is the variance of a constant $(1/N)$ times a variable (the sum of the Xs in parentheses). We showed in Chapter 4 that the variance of a constant times a variable was equal to the square of the constant times the variance of the variable. Thus,

$$Var(\bar{X}) = \frac{1}{N^2}[Var(X_1 + X_2 + \cdots + X_N)].$$

Each value of X, above, represents the outcome of one trial — the observation of one subject — in a probability experiment consisting of drawing a random sample of size N from our population. Since the trials are independent — as they must be, if our sample is a random sample — the expression in parentheses above is a sum of independent random variables, and thus we can distribute the variance operator across the independent terms in that sum:

$$Var(\overline{X}) = \frac{1}{N^2} [Var(X_1) + Var(X_2) + \cdots + Var(X_N)]. \tag{8-6}$$

As we argued earlier, the individual X values, above, represent independent observations of the same random variable. Thus,

$$Var(X_1) = Var(X_2) = \cdots = Var(X_N) = Var(X) = \sigma_X^2.$$

Substituting in 8-6, and noting that there are N terms in parentheses, below,

$$Var(\overline{X}) = \frac{1}{N^2} (\sigma_X^2 + \sigma_X^2 + \cdots + \sigma_X^2) = \frac{1}{N^2} (N\sigma_X^2) = \frac{1}{N} \sigma_X^2.$$

Thus,

$$\begin{array}{l} \text{Variance} \\ \text{of sample mean} \end{array} = \sigma_{\overline{X}}^2 = Var(\overline{X}) = \frac{\sigma_X^2}{N}, \tag{8-7}$$

$$\text{and} \quad \begin{array}{l} \text{Standard error} \\ \text{of sample mean} \end{array} = \sigma_{\overline{X}} = \frac{\sigma_X}{\sqrt{N}}. \tag{8-8}$$

Like Equation 8-4, Equations 8-7 and 8-8 hold true without regard to the form of the population distribution — whether normally distributed or not — as long as the population has a finite variance of known value.

The Central Limit Theorem

In order to utilize the critical ratio in Equation 8-1 for testing hypotheses about sample means, we need to assure ourselves that the distribution of sample means is a normal distribution, or reasonably nearly so. The **central limit theorem** states that for samples of size N, as N increases, the distribution of sample means approaches as a limit a normal distribution having a mean of μ_X and a variance of σ_X^2/N. The central limit theorem is quite remarkable in that, as N increases, the distribution of sample means approaches a normal distribution without regard to the form of the population from which the samples are drawn: It is only necessary that the population have a finite variance.

We will not be able to prove the central limit theorem, but we can show that the theorem is reasonable intuitively, and we can offer the results of a simple empirical experiment in support of the theorem. Figure 8-1 (top) shows the probability distribution for rolling a single die. Figure 8-1 (middle) shows the results of Experiment 1, rolling a die 100 times. That experiment can be

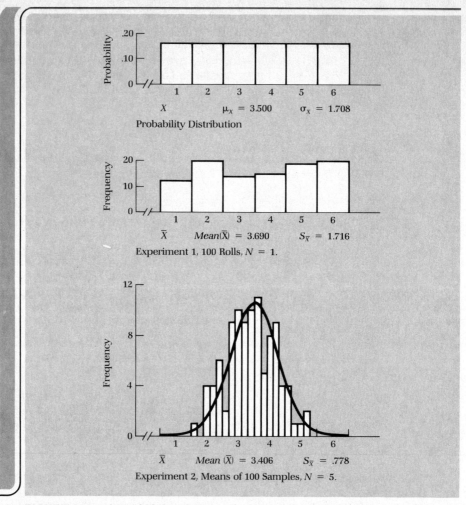

FIGURE 8-1. Top: Probability distribution for rolling a single die. Middle: Observed frequency distribution of 100 rolls of a single die — in effect, a sampling experiment where $N = 1$. Bottom: Observed frequency distribution of the means of 100 . samples, each consisting of 5 rolls of a single die. Normal distribution is superimposed for comparison.

considered as a sampling experiment where $N = 1$, where each roll of the die constitutes a sample of size 1. Figure 8-1 (bottom) shows the results of Experiment 2, a sampling experiment where each sample consists of rolling a die 5 times; the figure shows the frequency distribution of the means of 100 random samples.[1] In Experiment 1, where $N = 1$, the frequency distribution

[1] The sampling experiments described here and shown in Figure 8-2 were actually computer simulations, rather than experiments carried out with a real die. The fact is, it is more difficult to carry out unbiased, random sampling experiments in the real world than you might suppose. Thus, computer simulations of probability experiments can be very useful.

is essentially rectangular — like the probability distribution. But in Experiment 2, where $N = 5$, the frequency distribution is very different from the rectangular probability distribution. Indeed, the frequency distribution there has a peak near the middle and lower tails at each end — like the superimposed normal curve. Thus, when we draw samples from a population having a rectangular probability distribution, even for a sample size no larger than 5, the distribution of sample means begins to take on the appearance of a normal distribution.

The expected value and standard deviation of the random variable X were found using Formulas 6-9 and 6-12. The expected value and standard deviation of $\overline{X}$, the sample mean, were found in Experiments 1 and 2 using Formulas 8-4 and 8-8. (In Figure 8-1 we have introduced a new symbol, $S_{\overline{X}}$, which we will use for the standard error — the standard deviation — of the sample mean. We will fully explain this symbol shortly.) Table 8-1 shows the above expected values and the observed values in Experiments 1 and 2 for comparison.

TABLE 8-1. **Observed and Expected Values in Sampling Experiments in Figure 8-1.**

	Observed	Expected
Experiment 1 ($N = 1$)		
Mean ($\overline{X}$)	3.690	3.500
$SD_{\overline{x}}$	1.716	1.708
Experiment 2 ($N = 2$)		
Mean ($\overline{X}$)	3.406	3.500
$SD_{\overline{x}}$	.778	.764

The central limit theorem may appear paradoxical at first, but we can dispel some of the apparent paradox if we consider some samples of size 2 drawn from our rectangler population. There is only one way the mean of a sample of size 2 can be equal to 1: The sample must consist of the values (1, 1). But there are two ways the mean of such a sample can be equal to 1.5: The sample can consist of the values (1, 2) or (2, 1). And there are three ways the sample mean can equal 2, namely, (1, 3), (3, 1), and (2, 2). Thus, the probability of observing a mean of 2 is greater than the probability of a mean of 1.

Our present sampling experiment is essentially identical to the probability experiment involving rolling two dice or one die twice, which was described in Chapter 6. Table 6-3 gives the sample space for the sum of the numbers turning up on two dice, and Table 6-4 gives the probability distribution associated with that sample space. The sample space in Table 6-3 corresponds precisely with the list of all possible samples of size 2 that can be drawn from our present population; thus, dividing each of the sums in Table 6-4 by 2 yields the distribution of means of all possible samples of size 2. Figure 8-2 gives the probability distribution from Table 6-4 of the means of all possible samples of size 2. The triangular probability distribution in Figure 8-2 is very different from the rectangular distribution in Figure 8-1 (top). Like the normal distribution, the distribution in Figure 8-2 has a peak near the

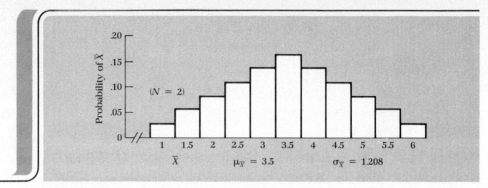

FIGURE 8-2. Probability distribution for means of samples of size 2, where each sample consists of 2 rolls of a single die. Compare with the probability distribution for 1 roll of the die in Figure 8-1 (top).

middle and lower tails at each end. As you can see, the probability distribution of sample means in Figure 8-2 — even for a sample size as small as 2 — has begun to approach the normal distribution. For larger sample sizes — as in Figure 8-1, for example — the distribution of sample means approaches the normal distribution more and more closely.

Where N is as large as about 30, the distribution of sample means closely approaches the normal distribution without regard to the nature of the population distribution — as long as the variance is finite. We will refer to a sample where $N \geq 30$ as a *large sample*. For smaller sample sizes — even as small as *one* — if the population is normally distributed, then the sample means will also be normally distributed.

The Z Test of a Single Mean

Since the central limit theorem indicates that the means of large samples are essentially normally distributed, and since we have found expressions for the expected value and standard error of the mean, we can now use Equation 8-1 to test hypotheses about the mean of a sample from *any* population — normal or not — where $N \geq 30$. Where a population is normally distributed, we can use Equation 8-1 for *any* size of sample, including the case where $N = 1$.

We now return to our earlier question regarding the evaluation of a group of GRE scores: Does the mean quantitative aptitude score for the 10 graduating seniors, 604, differ significantly from 512, the mean of the population of students previously taking the test? We are dealing with a small sample here, but we will be able to use a Z test, since the population of test scores is normally distributed. In effect, we are asking whether the 10 students are drawn from the general population of students taking the GRE, or from a different population having special characteristics. If the psychology department graduating those 10 seniors has been truly successful in attracting high-caliber students, then its students are drawn from a population having a higher mean aptitude than the general population of students.

On the other hand, if a department is less successful in attracting high-caliber applicants, then its students will be drawn from a population having a mean below that of the general population of students taking the GRE. Our null hypothesis is the following:

$H_0: \mu = \mu_0$.

In the above equation, μ is the mean of the population from which our 10 students were drawn, and μ_0 is the mean of the general population of students taking the GRE. Should we carry out a one- or two-tailed test? While the faculty in any department in a university would be pleased and delighted to find that its graduates were significantly higher in aptitude than the general mean, the faculty would also be keenly interested in the possibility that its students might be significantly below the general mean. Thus, we will carry out a two-tailed test, where our alternative hypotheses are the following.

$H_1: \mu > \mu_0$;

$H_2: \mu < \mu_0$.

Returning to Equation 8-1, and substituting from 8-4 and 8-8,

$$Z_{\bar{X}} = \frac{\bar{X} - \mu_{\bar{X}}}{\sigma_{\bar{X}}} = \frac{\bar{X} - \mu_X}{\dfrac{\sigma_X}{\sqrt{N}}}.$$

Noting that μ_X is the mean of X in the general population, μ_X is the expected value of X under the null hypothesis, and thus

$$Z_{\bar{X}} = \frac{\bar{X} - \mu_0}{\sigma_{\bar{X}}} = \frac{\bar{X} - \mu_0}{\dfrac{\sigma_X}{\sqrt{N}}}. \tag{8-9}$$

Substituting values in Equation 8-9,

$$Z_{\bar{X}} = \frac{604 - 512}{\dfrac{134}{\sqrt{10}}} = \frac{92}{\dfrac{134}{3.1623}} = \frac{92}{42.3745} = 2.17.$$

From Table A, the critical value of Z for a 2-tailed test at the .05 level of significance is 1.96. Since our observed value of $Z_{\bar{X}}$ is greater than the critical value, we reject H_0 in favor of H_1. Thus, the 10 graduating seniors differ significantly from the general population of students taking the GRE, and we conclude that those 10 students likely represent a sample drawn from a population having a mean significantly greater than 512.

The Z Test and Percentiles. There is a close relationship between the process of hypothesis testing and the process of finding the percentile rank of a score, which we developed in Chapter 5. Consider the observed value of $Z_{\bar{X}}$ in the above example, 2.17. Table A shows that the probability of observing a value of $Z_{\bar{x}}$ as great as 2.17 is .0150. That probability is the proportion of the standard normal distribution lying above a Z of 2.17, and by subtraction, .9850 of the distribution lies below that value of Z. Multiplying a proportion by 100 yields a percentage, and thus the percentile rank of our observed value of $\bar{X}$ is 98.5. Here is what that means: If we drew samples of size 10 again and again from the population of quantitative GRE scores, then in the long run 98.5% of the means of those samples should be less than 604, the value of our observed mean. Since we should expect only rarely to observe a mean as great as 604 in a sample drawn from a population having a mean of 512, we reject the hypothesis that our 10 students were drawn from that population in favor of the alternative hypothesis that they were drawn from a more select population having a higher mean. Our best estimate of that higher mean is 604, the observed value of the sample mean.

Figure 8-3 shows the relationships between our distribution of sample means, Z-scores, and percentile ranks. Critical values, at or beyond which we reject H_0, are shown for all three of the measurement scales in Figure 8-3. On the percentile scale, notice that physically equal lengths do not correspond to equal percentile differences. For example, the distances are approximately

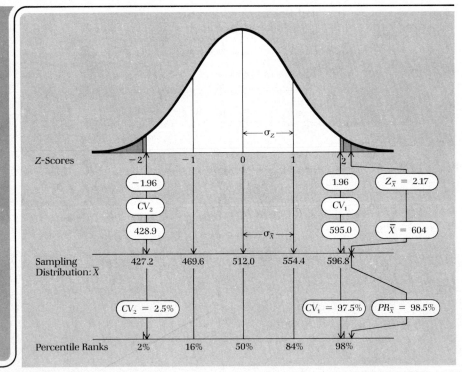

FIGURE 8-3. Relationships between the distribution of sample means (middle); Z-scores (top), and percentile ranks (bottom). On the scale of percentile ranks, notice that physically equal distances do not correspond to equal percentile differences. Shaded areas are each equal to $\alpha/2 = .025$.

physically equal from 2 to 16%, and from 16 to 50%, but the first of those distances represents a percentile difference of 14, and the second a percentile difference of 34. As we explained in Chapter 5, percentile ranks constitute an ordinal scale, which lacks the property of equal intervals.

Requirements for the Z Test. We have mentioned a number of requirements for the Z test in several places in the preceding pages. Since the requirements for Z overlap to a great extent with those for the t test, we will discuss the requirements for both tests in detail after we have presented the t test. The requirements for the Z test are presented in Table 8-4 and are discussed in the adjacent portions of the text.

Sampling a Population Where σ is Unknown

Figure 8-4 shows the Ponzo illusion, one of the classical visual illusions. For most observers, the upper horizontal line looks longer than the lower one, although both lines are the same length. Visual illusions are more than just curiosities, in that the study of some illusions has yielded insights into the nature of some important perceptual processes.

Suppose you were the first person to observe the illusion illustrated in Figure 8-4. To you, the upper line looks longer (we will say), but will other people see the illusion as you do? You construct an apparatus to measure the illusion. In your apparatus, the upper line is 100 mm long, and its length is held constant. The length of the lower line can be adjusted until it looks equal to the length of the upper line. You measure the illusion in a sample of 10 subjects. If your subjects see the illusion, then the mean setting of the lower line should be significantly greater than 100 mm. Suppose the mean and standard deviation of your measurements are 112.70 mm and 10.68 mm respectively. Since we have supposed that the illusion has never before been measured, you have no way of knowing the true value of the mean and standard deviation in the population of possible subjects for whom the

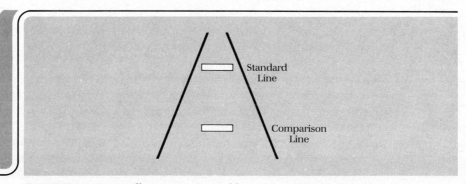

FIGURE 8-4. Ponzo illusion. Horizontal lines are equal in length.

illusion could — in principle — be measured. But those population parameters can be *estimated* from your sample observations. Indeed, one of the principal reasons for making such observations *is* the estimation of population parameters.

We can easily determine the value of the population mean under the null hypothesis, that is, under the assumption that no illusion exists. If there is no illusion, then the mean setting of the line length in the total population of subjects will be 100 mm. Our null hypothesis is the statement that the mean of the population from which our sample was drawn is equal to 100 mm. In symbols,

$$H_0 : \mu = \mu_0 .$$

We can test the above null hypothesis by deciding whether the observed mean of our sample, 112.70, is significantly different from 100. It is tempting to proceed by utilizing the critical ratio in Equation 8-9. It looks as though we should be able to substitute our sample standard deviation, SD_x for the population standard deviation, σ_x, in that critical ratio, but a problem arises. The critical ratio in 8-9 is a Z-score. Correctly interpreting the probabilities associated with that Z-score depends on whether $Z_{\bar{x}}$ is normally distributed. We have seen that the central limit theorem assures us that $\bar{X}$ will be approximately normally distributed for samples of reasonable size, but if we substitute an *estimate* of the population standard deviation for the *known value* of that parameter in the critical ratio in Equation 8-9, then $Z_{\bar{x}}$ will not be normally distributed. The consequence would not be particularly disastrous for "large" samples of 30 or more cases, but for smaller samples, we would seriously underestimate the probabilities associated with our critical ratio, and we would erroneously reject the null hypothesis far too frequently. Fortunately, there is a solution to the problem of hypothesis testing using a small sample when the population standard deviation is not known.

Estimating the Population Variance and Standard Deviation

If we do not know the value of σ_x, the standard deviation of the population, then we must estimate that parameter in order to test hypotheses about $\bar{X}$, an observed sample mean. As we show in Appendix B, the sample variance and standard deviation are **biased estimators** of the population variance and standard deviation, in contrast with the sample mean, which is an **unbiased estimator** of the population mean. In the long run, the expected values of the sample variance and standard deviation are systematically less than the value of the corresponding population parameters. Multiplying the sample variance, SD^2, by a correction factor equal to $N/(N-1)$ yields an *unbiased estimator* of the population variance; we will use the symbol S^2 to stand for that unbiased estimator. When we say that S^2 is an unbiased estimator of the population variance, we mean that the expected value of S^2 is exactly equal to σ^2. The following formula, which is derived in Appendix B, is a computational formula for S^2:

$$\text{Unbiased estimator of population variance} = S^2 = \frac{\Sigma X^2 - \frac{(\Sigma X)^2}{N}}{N-1}. \tag{8-10}$$

Taking the square root of S^2, or multiplying the sample standard deviation, SD, by $\sqrt{N/(N-1)}$, yields a quantity which we will designate **S** and define as the **corrected estimator of the population standard deviation.** Surprisingly — perhaps — as we explain in Appendix B, the expected value of S is a little less than the value of σ. Thus, S turns out to be a slightly biased estimator of the population standard deviation — though a better estimator than SD, the uncorrected sample standard deviation. The following is a computational formula for S:

$$\text{Corrected estimator of population standard deviation} = S = \sqrt{\frac{\Sigma X^2 - \frac{(\Sigma X)^2}{N}}{N-1}}. \tag{8-11}$$

Since the population standard deviation, σ, is exactly equal to the square root of the population variance, σ^2, and since S is exactly equal to the square root of S^2, it may seem curious that S^2 is an unbiased estimator of σ^2 while S is a slightly biased estimator of σ. The reason for this small paradox may not be instantly obvious, so we have provided a brief explanation in Appendix B. Removing the bias from S is somewhat cumbersome, and since the small amount of remaining bias is negligible for most purposes, most statisticians disregard it. The fact that S is a slightly biased estimator of the population standard deviation will not interfere in any way with our use of S in developing the t test in the next section.

Formulas 8-10 and 8-11, above, are identical to our earlier computational formulas for the sample variance and standard deviation except in one respect: In the above formulas, the term $N-1$ appears in the denominators instead of N. The simple expedient of dividing by $N-1$, rather than by N, provides an unbiased estimator of the population variance, and a corrected estimator of the population standard deviation.

Much of the remainder of this text will be devoted to inferential statistics — the process of estimating population parameters, and drawing other conclusions about populations. Thus, S and S^2, as estimators of population parameters, will play a greater role in our future discussions than will SD and SD^2, which are the standard deviation and variance observed in specific samples. To save words in our future discussions, we will ordinarily refer to S and S^2 as the standard deviation and variance, letting those simpler terms stand for the more cumbersome "corrected estimator of the population standard deviation" and "unbiased estimator of the population variance."

The *t* Distribution

The following equation defines the **t ratio:**

$$t = \frac{\bar{X} - \mu_{\bar{x}}}{S_{\bar{x}}} = \frac{\bar{X} - \mu_0}{\frac{S_x}{\sqrt{N}}} = \frac{\bar{X} - \mu_0}{\sqrt{\frac{S_x^2}{N}}}. \tag{8-12}$$

In the above equation, the quantity $S_{\bar{x}}$ is a **corrected estimator of the standard error of the sample mean.** We will ordinarily refer to $S_{\bar{x}}$ simply as the standard error of the mean. In the present situation, the population standard deviation is not known, and thus the standard error of the mean must be estimated. Thus,

$$\begin{matrix} \text{Standard error} \\ \text{of the mean} \end{matrix} = S_{\bar{x}} = \frac{est\ \sigma_x}{\sqrt{N}} = \frac{S_x}{\sqrt{N}} = \sqrt{\frac{S_x^2}{N}}, \tag{8-13}$$

where σ is unknown.

The *t* ratio in 8-12 is equal to the deviation of an observed sample mean from the population mean divided by the standard error of the mean. Thus, the *t* ratio is analogous in many respects to the critical ratios in Equations 8-1 and 8-9, where σ was known. As we have noted earlier, $\bar{X}$ is a random variable which can take on different values in different samples. Thus, the numerator of the *t* ratio is a continuous random variable identical to the numerator of the Z ratio in 8-1. But the denominator of the *t* ratio is also a random variable, while the denominator of the Z ratio is a constant. The random variable Z is normally distributed, but *t* is not. The *t* distribution was described in 1908 by W. S. Gosset, writing under the pen-name "Student." The distribution is sometimes called *Student's t,* not because of its great popularity — or notoriety — among generations of students, but because of Gosset's pseudonym.

The probabilities associated with the values of the random variable *t* have been calculated, and those probabilities are presented in Table B. Thus, the *t* distribution, like the standard normal distribution, can be used in testing hypotheses. We will describe some of the characteristics of the *t* distribution, and then we will explain the use of Table B.

The equation below gives the probability density function of *t*:

$$h = C\left[1 + \frac{t^2}{df}\right]^{-\frac{(df+1)}{2}}, \tag{8-14}$$

where h is the height (ordinate) of the curve; t is the value of the *t* ratio, which can take on any value from $-\infty$ to $+\infty$; *df* is the number of degrees of freedom, explained below, in this case equal to $N - 1$; and C is a constant that depends only on the value of df. Fortunately, you will not have to solve that equation in order to use the *t* distribution.

Degrees of Freedom. Suppose we draw a sample of three cases from a population, and suppose we ask, How many of our three values are free to vary? To clarify what we mean by being free to vary, we will consider a concrete example. Suppose I have drawn a sample of three men, and I tell you the heights of the first two men were 68 and 66 inches, and I ask you to guess the height of the third man. If you know that the mean height of adult American males is about 69 inches at present, you would probably guess the height of the third man in our sample to be 69 inches. But does it help to know the heights of the first two men? If I have drawn a random sample, then each of the values in our sample is independent of every other value. The point is, all of the values in our samples are free to vary within the limits of the population, so you have no way of knowing the height of the third man, given the heights of the first two.

Now, suppose the heights of the three men in our sample are 68, 66, and 70 inches. We will now consider S^2, the sample variance. We could find S^2 by using Computational Formula 8-10, but in our present example, it will be more instructive to use Conceptual Formula B-9 from Appendix B:

$$S^2 = \frac{\Sigma X^2 - \dfrac{(\Sigma X)^2}{N}}{N-1} = \frac{\Sigma(X - \overline{X})^2}{N-1}. \qquad (8\text{-}15)$$

We will now use the above formula to calculate the variance of our sample.

$$S^2 = \frac{\Sigma(X - \overline{X})^2}{N-1} = \frac{(68-68)^2 + (66-68)^2 + (70-68)^2}{3-1}$$

$$= \frac{0^2 + (-2)^2 + 2^2}{2} = \frac{4+4}{2} = 4.$$

Notice that in finding each of the above deviations, the sample mean is always subtracted from the score, and the sign is retained. When the deviations are squared, any negative signs of course disappear, but the signs are of some importance before the deviations are squared. As we noted in Chapter 4 — and left as an exercise for you — the sum of the deviations from the mean of a sample is always equal to zero. That fact bears directly on our present discussion.

If I told you the mean height in our sample of three men — 68 inches — and if I told you any two of the heights, you would be able to find the third. Since $\Sigma(X - \overline{X}) = 0$, only two of the deviations from the sample mean are free to vary, and thus knowing the values of any two deviations determines at once the value of the third. Since the variance is a function of the squared deviations from the mean, only two of those deviations are free to vary. The number of **degrees of freedom** associated with the variance is equal to the number of deviations that are free to vary. In general, the variance and standard deviation of a sample have only $N - 1$ degrees of freedom, since only $N - 1$ of the deviations from the sample mean are free to vary. H. M. Walker (1940) offers an excellent discussion of degrees of freedom.

The number of degrees of freedom, which we will abbreviate df, appears as a parameter in the equation for the t distribution and also appears as a parameter in some other probability distributions which are useful in hypothesis testing. Since the constant C in Equation 8-14 is a function of df, the t distribution is a family of curves determined by the single parameter df. Although we cannot fully explain the nature of the constant C within the scope of the present text, we can nevertheless describe the important features of the t curve, and we can use the t distribution to good advantage in a great many situations.

Some Characteristics of the t Curve. We can learn something about the shape of the t curve by referring to Equation 8-14. Since df is a parameter of that equation, the shape of the t curve depends on the sample size. Holding df (and hence C) constant, we will examine the value of h for different values of t. Notice that t appears as a squared variable in the expression within brackets, and notice that the bracketed expression is raised to a negative power, $-(df + 1)/2$. When $t = 0$, $h = C$. But for all other values of t, positive or negative, h is less than C. Thus, the height of the t curve is at a maximum for $t = 0$. Since h is a function of t^2, the height of the curve is the same for positive and negative values of t, and thus the curve is symmetrical. As t becomes infinitely large in the positive or negative direction, h approaches zero. Since the t curve is symmetrical, and since h reaches a maximum at $t = 0$, the expected value of the t distribution is zero.

Figure 8-5 shows the t distribution for 2 df and 10 df, and the normal curve for comparison. Both distributions are bell-shaped curves having expected values of zero, but there are differences as well as similarities between the two distributions. The tails of the t curve are higher, and that has important consequences. We will make additional comparisons between

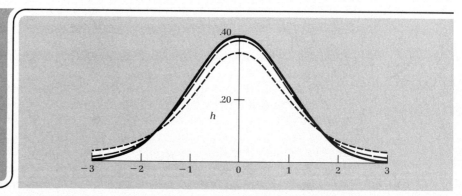

FIGURE 8-5. The t distribution for 2 df (short dashes), 10 df (long dashes), and the standard normal distribution (solid line). Notice that a greater proportion of the area under each t curve is located in the tails of the distributions.

those distributions after we have dealt with the use of the t ratio in hypothesis testing.

Calculating the t Statistic. The observed value of the t ratio in a particular sample — that is, the calculated value of t — is sometimes called the **t statistic.** The process of using the t statistic in hypothesis testing consists of comparing the observed value of that sample statistic with its expected value of zero. Since we have developed a computational formula for S_x^2, the sample variance, we can use the rightmost expression in Equation 8-12 to calculate the t ratio. Some small hand calculators have a routine that automatically finds the mean and standard deviation of a sample. If you have access to such a machine, Formula 8-12 will be a very useful computational formula. (If your machine gives you SD_X instead of S_X, remember that $S_X = SD_X\sqrt{N/(N-1)}$.)

We will derive another useful computational formula for t. Substituting Equation 8-11 for S_X in Equation 8-12,

$$t = \frac{\overline{X} - \mu_{\overline{x}}}{S_{\overline{x}}} = \frac{\overline{X} - \mu_0}{\dfrac{\sqrt{\dfrac{\Sigma X^2 - \dfrac{(\Sigma X)^2}{N}}{N-1}}}{\sqrt{N}}} = \frac{\overline{X} - \mu_0}{\sqrt{\dfrac{\Sigma X^2 - \dfrac{(\Sigma X)^2}{N}}{N(N-1)}}},$$

$$df = N - 1. \tag{8-16}$$

Since t is a function of the standard deviation of a sample, the t statistic above has the same number of degrees of freedom, df, as the standard deviation has, namely $N - 1$. Shortly, we will explain the use of df in working with the t statistic.

We will now return to the problem of the visual illusion which we put aside earlier. Table 8-2 shows the results of measuring the illusion in a sample of 10 subjects. Each subject adjusted the length of the comparison line (see Figure 8-4) to appear equal to the length of the standard line. The length of the standard line was held constant at 100 mm. The observed value of the sample mean in Table 8-2 is 112.7 mm. Under the assumption that there is no illusion — that is, under the null hypothesis — the expected value of the sample mean is 100 mm. Table 8-2 illustrates the direct calculation of the t statistic using computational Formula 8-16. It would, of course, be possible to calculate t by first using 8-11 to find S, then using 8-13 to find $S_{\overline{x}}$, and finally using 8-12 to find t. Formula 8-16 merely combines those operations as a matter of convenience.

In describing the results of an experiment, it is useful to present the standard deviation as well as the mean. When you use Formula 8-16 to calculate t, it is not necessary to calculate the standard deviation separately. Multiplying the denominator of the t statistic in 8-16 by $\sqrt{N}$ yields S.

$$S = \text{Denominator}_t \sqrt{N}. \tag{8-17}$$

Table 8-2 illustrates the use of the above formula.

TABLE 8-2.   Illusion Data, Calculation of t Test.

Subject Number	Comparison Length, mm X	X^2
1	110	12100
2	128	16384
3	127	16129
4	113	12769
5	88	7744
6	106	11236
7	115	13225
8	117	13689
9	109	11881
10	114	12996

$$\Sigma X = 1127 \qquad \Sigma X^2 = 128153$$

$$N = 10 \qquad \bar{X} = 112.70 \qquad SD = 10.68 \qquad S = 11.26$$

By Formula 8-16,

$$t = \frac{\bar{X} - \mu_0}{\sqrt{\dfrac{\Sigma X^2 - \dfrac{(\Sigma X)^2}{N}}{N(N-1)}}}, \qquad \begin{aligned} df &= N - 1 \\ &= 9. \end{aligned} \qquad \begin{aligned} &H_0: \mu = \mu_0 = 100 \text{ mm} \\ &H_1: \mu > \mu_0 \\ &H_2: \mu < \mu_0 \end{aligned}$$

$$= \frac{112.70 - 100}{\sqrt{\dfrac{128153 - \dfrac{1127^2}{10}}{10(9)}}} = \frac{12.70}{\sqrt{\dfrac{128153 - \dfrac{1270129}{10}}{90}}} = \frac{12.70}{\sqrt{\dfrac{128153 - 127012.9}{90}}}$$

$$= \frac{12.70}{\sqrt{\dfrac{1140.1}{90}}} = \frac{12.70}{\sqrt{12.6678}} = \frac{12.70}{3.5592} = 3.57 = t_{observed}.$$

From Table B, $CV_{.05} = \pm 2.262$. Since $t_{obs} > +2.262$, Reject H_0 at the .05 level in favor of H_1.

By Formula 8-17, $S = $ Denominator$_t \sqrt{N}$

$$= 3.5592 \sqrt{10} = 3.5592(3.16) = 11.26.$$

The observed (calculated) value of our t statistic in Table 8-2 is 3.57, while the expected value of t under the null hypothesis is zero. Should we carry out a one- or two-tailed test? If the subjects in our experiment saw the upper line in Figure 8-3 as *shorter,* rather than longer, that would certainly constitute a visual illusion — and perhaps even a more interesting illusion than the one we typically observe. If the Ponzo illusion were unknown, and if you were carrying out the first investigation of this phenomenon, you would certainly be interested in either of the possible alternative hypotheses, longer or shorter. Thus, a two-tailed test is appropriate here — and indeed, appropriate in any situation where the experimenter is unwilling, or unable, to exclude one of the directional alternatives from consideration.

The t statistic can take on negative as well as positive values. Where an observed mean is greater than its expected value, as in our present case, t is positive, but where an observed mean is less than its expected value, t is negative. Thus, the sign of the t statistic indicates which of the alternative hypotheses is to be accepted in the event the null hypothesis is rejected. Table B shows critical values of t for several different levels of significance (α levels) and different numbers of df. The table shows only positive t values, but since the t distribution is symmetrical and has an expected value of zero, the same significance levels are associated with positive and negative values of the same magnitude. To find the critical values of any t statistic, first locate the number of df associated with that statistic in the first column of Table B. (In our present situation, $df = N - 1$. We will later use some other kinds of t ratios where the degrees of freedom are determined in other ways.) For a given df, the critical values are all located on the same line in the table. The column headings give the significance probability levels associated with the critical values. Notice that there is one set of column headings for critical values for one-tailed tests and another set of headings for two-tailed tests. As in the standard normal distribution, or the binomial, the significance probabilities are areas under the curve. For a two-tailed test, half of the significance probability, that is, $\alpha/2$, is located in each tail of the curve.

Since $df = 9$ in our present case, the critical value of t for a two-tailed test at the .05 level of probability is 2.262. Our observed value of t is 3.57, and since our observed t is significantly greater than its expected value of zero, we reject the null hypothesis that our sample was drawn from a population having a mean of 100 mm in favor of the alternative hypothesis that our sample was drawn from a population having a mean greater than 100 mm. Not only does the observed value of t — that is, the value we calculated from our sample — exceed the critical value for a test at the .05 level, but it also exceeds the critical value for a two-tailed test at the .01 level, namely 3.250. Some statisticians recommend that a level of significance probability be adopted before an experiment is carried out, and that the null hypothesis be tested only at that level. Those statisticians would recommend, for example, that we choose a significance level, say, of .05, before collecting our data, and that we simply report our present results as significant at the .05 level. But our results are *more* significant than that. A significance level is the probability that the results of an experiment are due to chance alone, and thus a low significance level is better than a higher one. To say that our results are significant at the .05 level is true, but they are also significant at the .01 level — which is even more significant. In practice, most researchers ordinarily do not choose a significance level in advance. The usual practice is to find the level of probability associated with a calculated t value, or some other statistic, after the data are collected. By convention, as we explained in Chapter 6, an α level of .05 is the highest level of probability at which results are considered statistically significant. As a rule, results that are significant at the .06 or the .10 level, for example, are not considered worthy of being reported to the scientific community.

Comparing *t* and the Standard Normal Distribution.   As we have noted, both distributions have a mean of zero. The variance of the standard normal distribution is 1, but the variance of *t* is greater than 1. Although both distributions are bell-shaped curves, there are important differences between their shapes. The area under each curve is equal to 1.00, but the distribution of the area is different for each curve. The *t* curve has more of its area—probability—located in its tails, as Figure 8-5 shows. Thus, extreme values are more likely to be observed in the *t* distribution than the same extreme values in the standard normal distribution. In terms of hypothesis testing, that means that if we use a *Z* test where a *t* test is really appropriate, then we increase the risk of rejecting the null hypothesis when we should not.

Table 8-3 compares the critical values of *Z* and *t* for various degrees of freedom for two-tailed tests at the .05 level. Unlike *t*, the critical values of *Z* do not change for different sample sizes. Table 8-3 shows that if you were erroneously using a *Z* test where you should have used a *t* test, and if you observed a *Z* of 1.960, then for a sample of any size shown in that table—except one of infinite size—you would erroneously reject the null hypothesis.

TABLE 8-3.   Comparisons Between Critical Values of *t* and *Z* at .05 level.

df:	2	4	6	8	10	20	120	∞
t:	4.303	2.776	2.447	2.306	2.228	2.086	1.980	1.960
Z:				1.960				

Requirements for *Z* and *t* Tests, One-Sample Case

Table 8-4 lists the requirements that must be met in order to use *Z* or *t* in hypothesis testing. In the present situation, we are concerned with the **one-sample case,** that is, comparing the mean of a single sample with the value expected under the null hypothesis. Later, when we develop other kinds of *Z* and *t* tests, we will extend and modify some of the requirements listed in Table 8-4. In some statistics texts, the requirements that must be met in order to use a particular test are referred to as the **assumptions** underlying the test.

The requirements for *Z* and *t* are discussed in the following sections,

TABLE 8-4.   Requirements for *Z* and *t* Tests of a Single Mean.

1. Interval or ratio measurement scale for the random variable X.
2. Approximately normal distribution of X. Most important for small samples, of little importance when N ≥ 30, approximately.
3. Each value of X observed in a sample must be independent of every other observed value of X.
4. For *Z*: σ, the population standard deviation, must be known.
   For *t*: σ is unknown and must be estimated from S, the sample standard deviation.

where the numbers correspond with those listed in Table 8-4. Notice that the same requirements, except the last one, apply to both Z and t.

1. Interval or Ratio Scale. Both Z and t require the calculation of a sample mean. If we had only an ordinal scale — that is, a set of ranks — the value of a mean would be determined simply by the number of cases in a sample. As we noted in our earliest discussion of measurement scales in Chapter 1, a nominal scale uses numbers only as labels to identify categories. For example, if we were studying political party affiliation in a particular city or geographic area, and if we assigned the numbers 1, 2, and 3 to Democrats, Republicans, and Independents, then it would make little sense to calculate the mean and standard deviation of a sample of registered voters.

2. Normal Distribution. The central limit theorem assures us that the distribution of $\overline{X}$ will closely approximate the normal distribution as N increases, whether X is normally distributed or not. Thus, where a Z test is appropriate — where we know the value of μ and σ — we need not be greatly concerned about departures from a normal distribution, as long as our sample is on the order of about 30 cases or so. A Z test can also be used for very small samples — including the limiting case where $N = 1$ — but where the sample size is small, X must be normally distributed. (The special case where $N = 1$ corresponds closely with our use of a Z-score in Chapter 5 to determine an individual's place in a group — that is, the individual's percentile rank.)

Where we do not know the value of σ, a t test is appropriate. Gosset's development of the t test was based on the assumption of a normal distribution, but he thought it likely that only extreme departures from normality would affect the test adversely, an opinion held by later workers as well (for example, Boneau, 1960).

3. Independence. Both Z and t tests are based on distributions of the means of random samples. Since by definition every element in a population has an equal chance of being represented in a random sample, it follows that every element in such a sample must be chosen independently of every other element. Nonindependence can arise in several ways. For example, consider our illusion experiment. The set of measurements in Table 8-2 represents one measure of the illusion for each of 10 subjects. Suppose we had measured the illusion three times for each subject. Would we then have a sample of 30 independent measurements? The answer is no, because the repeated measures on each subject would be *related,* not independent. We should expect each subject who experiences a large amount of illusion to yield fairly consistently high measurements on all three trials, and each subject who experiences little illusion to yield fairly consistently low measurements. Thus, the three measurements on each subject would be related to each other. If we made the erroneous assumption that we had 30 rather than 10 independent measurements in our sample, we would increase the risk of erroneously rejecting the null hypothesis, since the critical value for 29 df is less than the critical value for 9 df. We will have more to say later about a number of such problems in the design and interpretation of experiments.

4. Known vs Estimated Population Standard Deviation. As we have noted earlier, a Z test is appropriate where σ is known. Where the population standard deviation must be estimated from a sample, a t test is appropriate. While it is true, as we noted earlier, that the t distribution approaches the normal distribution as the sample size increases, it is appropriate to use t whenever σ is unknown, regardless of the sample size. Even for large samples of 100 or more cases, the critical value of t is greater than the critical value of Z, and thus using Z where t is appropriate increases the probability of erroneously rejecting H_0. As you can see by looking at the bottom line of Table B, the critical values of t are precisely equal to the critical values of Z only for an infinite number of degrees of freedom.

 # Errors in Hypothesis Testing

How often are we correct when we reject the null hypothesis, and how often are we wrong? We can also ask how often we are right or wrong when we do not reject the null hypothesis. If the null hypothesis is *true,* and if we do not reject it, then we have made a correct decision. But if we reject the null hypothesis when it is true, then we have made a particular kind of error — a **Type 1 error.** If the null hypothesis is *false,* and if we reject it, then we have made a correct decision. But if we fail to reject the null hypothesis when it is false, then we have made a **Type 2 error.** Thus, there are two possible states of nature — H_0 can be true or false — and there are two possible decisions to be made — reject or do not reject H_0. Table 8-5 lays out the four possible combinations of decisions and states of nature: There are two ways to be right, and two ways to be wrong.

We can easily assess the probability of making a Type 1 error, that is, rejecting H_0 when it is in fact true. That probability is exactly equal to α, the level of significance probability at or below which we have decided to reject H_0. We can also find the probability of making a correct decision given that H_0

TABLE 8-5.   Possible States of Nature and Decisions Based on Statistical Tests.

| | | Possible decisions based on test: | |
		Do not reject H_0	Reject H_0
Possible states of nature:	H_0 is true	Correct decision. $P(\text{Correct}\|H_0\text{ true})$ $=1-\alpha$	Type 1 error. $P(\text{Error}\|H_0\text{ true})$ $=\alpha$
	H_0 is false	Type 2 error. $P(\text{Error}\|H_0\text{ false})$ $=\beta$	Correct decision. $P(\text{Correct}\|H_0\text{ false})$ $=1-\beta$

is true: That probability is equal to **1 − α.** Since we would like to reduce errors as much as possible, why not reduce the α level substantially, say to .001, or even to .0001? When H_0 is true, the probability of making a Type 1 error can be made as small as we like by setting the α level very low. But when H_0 is *false,* what happens if we have chosen a very low α level? Unfortunately, choosing a very low level of significance probability *increases* the probability of a Type 2 error. Perhaps the solution to our present dilemma might be to choose a very low α level when H_0 is true and a more moderate level when H_0 is false. But such a "solution" begs the question, since the whole point of running a statistical test in the first place is to make some decision about the probable truth or falsity of the null hypothesis. If we had any way of knowing whether H_0 was true or false, we wouldn't need to run a statistical test. The best we can do is to choose a value of α that will hold the probability of a Type 1 error *and* a Type 2 error to acceptable levels.

In the discussion that follows, we assume that we are dealing with a normal distribution where we know the value of σ, the population standard deviation. The ideas we are about to develop also apply where the population standard deviation is unknown and must be estimated from a sample.

Figure 8-6 graphically illustrates the relationship between the various probabilities associated with hypothesis testing. The curve on the left is the distribution of sample means when the null hypothesis, H_0, is true. The mean of that distribution is μ_0. For a two-tailed test, CV_1 and CV_2 are the critical values of the sample mean at or beyond which H_0 is rejected in favor of H_1 or H_2. Given that H_0 is true, it follows that (1) $\mu = \mu_0$; (2) the conditional probability of rejecting H_0 (making a Type 1 error) is equal to the probability in the two shaded areas in the tails of that curve, each area representing a probability of $\alpha/2$; and (3) the conditional probability of not rejecting H_0

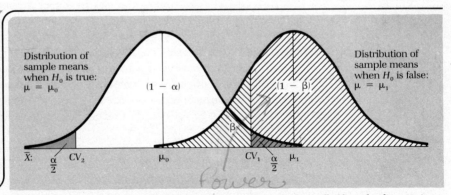

FIGURE 8-6. Distribution of sample means when H_0 is true (left) and when H_0 is false (right). CV_1 and CV_2 are the critical values of the sample mean at or beyond which H_0 is rejected. When H_0 is true, probability of a Type 1 error—incorrectly rejecting H_0—is equal to α, and probability of a correct decision—not rejecting H_0—is equal to 1 − α. When H_0 is false, probability of a Type 2 error—failing to reject H_0—is equal to β, and probability of a correct decision is equal to 1 − β.

(making a correct decision) is equal to **$1 - \alpha$**, which is the white area under the curve.

The curve on the right in Figure 8-6 is the distribution of sample means when H_0 is false and H_1 is true. The mean of that distribution is equal to μ_1, which is greater than μ_0. Given that H_1 is true, and given that $\mu = \mu_1$, it follows that (1) the conditional probability of making a Type 2 error (not rejecting H_0) is equal to β, the cross-hatched area below CV_1 and above CV_2; and (2) the conditional probability of making a correct decision (rejecting H_0) is equal to **$1 - \beta$**, the cross-hatched area above CV_1.

Now consider what happens to the other conditional probabilities when we change α, the significance level for our test of the null hypothesis. Suppose that CV_1 and CV_2 in Figure 8-6 are the critical values for a test of H_0 at the .05 level of significance, and suppose we decide to carry out a test at the .01 level instead. The critical values for the .01 level are located farther away from μ_0 — farther out in the tails of the curve — and thus CV_1 will be located closer to μ_1. If the null hypothesis is true, then we reduce the probability of a Type 1 error as we move the critical values farther away from μ_0, as we do when we choose a lower α level. But if H_0 is false, and if the true value of the mean is μ_1, then as we lower our α level and CV_1 moves to the right, the area equal to β increases and the area equal to $1 - \beta$ decreases. Thus, Figure 8-6 shows that as we lower our α level, not only do we decrease the probability of making a Type 1 error, but we *increase* the probability of a Type 2 error, and thus *decrease* the probability of rejecting the null hypothesis if it is in fact false.

Power of a Test

The **power** of a statistical test is the probability of rejecting the null hypothesis when it is in fact false, and thus the power of a test is equal to $1 - \beta$. Power is a measure of the ability of a test to detect a specified difference between μ_0 and μ_1 — that is, a specified different between the hypothesized value of μ under H_0 and under H_1. We can choose our α level — and thereby fix the probability of a Type 1 error — without referring to any specific value of μ_1 or μ_2, but we cannot determine the power of a test without referring to a specific value of μ under one of the alternative hypotheses. In Figure 8-6, if μ_1 were located at some other point — closer to μ_0, or farther away — then the areas representing β and $1 - \beta$ would be larger or smaller than they are in our present example.

The size of a sample also influences the power of a test. In Figure 8-6, the standard deviation of each distribution of sample means is the standard error of the mean. Since that quantity is equal to $\sigma/\sqrt{N}$, increasing the sample size decreases the dispersion of each distribution. For a larger sample size, the values of $\overline{X}$ in each distribution in Figure 8-6 would cluster more tightly around the mean of the distribution. The critical values would be located closer to μ_0, and thus if H_1 were true, and if μ_1 were the true value of μ, then β would be less, and the power of the test would be greater.

It would be possible to adopt a significance level so very low that CV_1 would be located in the extreme right tail of the distribution under H_0. In that case, CV_1 would also be to the right of (higher than) μ_1. We could choose a significance level so low, resulting in a critical value so high, that we would almost never reject H_0 even if it were false and H_1 true. There would be little point in carrying out a statistical test — or indeed, in running an experiment — since our decision not to reject H_0 would essentially be a foregone conclusion. In most situations, most researchers feel that the conventional significance level of .05 provides reasonable protection against an excessive number of Type 1 and Type 2 errors.

Confidence Intervals for the Mean

Besides carrying out a statistical test of the null hypothesis, we are usually interested in estimating the value of the population mean. We have noted that the observed mean of a sample is an unbiased estimator of the population mean, but we have also pointed out that the sample mean is a random variable. Thus, it is most unlikely that any particular sample mean will exactly equal the population mean. Based on observing a single sample, how much is the sample mean likely to differ from the true value of the population mean?

The **confidence interval** is a range of values within which we expect μ to lie with some high level of probability, usually .95 or .99. The **upper** and **lower confidence limits,** which we will abbreviate **UCL** and **LCL,** are the upper and lower bounds of the confidence interval. The **level of confidence** is the probability that the true value of μ is contained within the confidence interval. Our problem is to find the confidence limits associated with a particular level of confidence — .95, for example — as in the following equation:

$$P[LCL \leq \mu \leq UCL] = .95. \tag{8-18}$$

In words, the above equation says that the probability that μ is greater than or equal to LCL and less than or equal to UCL is .95. The range of values from LCL to UCL inclusive is the .95, or the 95% confidence interval for the population mean. We will develop a general procedure for finding confidence intervals for the mean, and then we will apply that procedure to our observation of GRE scores and to our measurements of the visual illusion we discussed earlier.

Confidence Intervals Where σ Is Known

Suppose we have a population where we know the value of σ, as in our population of GRE scores, for example. Now suppose that we draw a random sample of some particular size from that population, and we calculate the sample mean, $\overline{X}$. The value of Z associated with $\overline{X}$ is the following:

$$Z_{\overline{X}} = \frac{\overline{X} - \mu}{\sigma_{\overline{X}}},$$

where μ is the true value of the population mean. If we were to carry out a two-tailed Z test at a significance level equal to α, then the probability of observing a value of Z greater than the higher critical value would be $\alpha/2$, and the probability of observing a value less than the lower critical value (a negative value of Z) would also be $\alpha/2$. Thus, the probability of observing a value of Z contained within the interval from the lower to the higher critical value is $1 - \alpha$. In the following equation, $\mathbf{Z_{\alpha/2}}$ (read "Z sub alpha over 2") and $-\mathbf{Z_{\alpha/2}}$ are respectively the higher and lower critical values for a two-tailed test at a significance level equal to μ:

$$P[-Z_{\alpha/2} \le Z \le Z_{\alpha/2}] = 1 - \alpha. \tag{8-19}$$

The above equation gives the probability that an observed value of Z will lie within the interval bounded by the upper and lower critical values, and thus that interval is a confidence interval for Z. The probability equal to $1 - \alpha$ is the level of confidence associated with that confidence interval. The confidence limits for Z in Equation 8-18 are the following:

$$LCL_{(1-\alpha)} = -Z_{\alpha/2};$$

$$UCL_{(1-\alpha)} = Z_{\alpha/2}.$$

The subscripts on LCL and UCL in the above equation are the probability associated with the confidence interval. Setting the level of α in 8-19 fixes the confidence level, determines the critical values of Z, and thus determines the size of the confidence interval.

We will use Equation 8-19 to develop an expression for the confidence interval for the population mean. Substituting for Z,

$$P\left[-Z_{\alpha/2} \le \frac{\overline{X} - \mu}{\sigma_{\overline{X}}} \le Z_{\alpha/2}\right] = 1 - \alpha = P\left[-Z_{\alpha/2}\,\sigma_{\overline{X}} \le (\overline{X} - \mu) \le Z_{\alpha/2}\,\sigma_{\overline{X}}\right] = 1 - \alpha$$

$$= P[(-\overline{X} - Z_{\alpha/2}\,\sigma_{\overline{X}}) \le -\mu \le (\overline{X} + Z_{\alpha/2}\,\sigma_{\overline{X}})]$$

$$= 1 - \alpha.$$

The next step involves multiplying the inequality by -1, an operation described in Appendix A. Thus,

$$P[(\overline{X} - Z_{\alpha/2}\,\sigma_{\overline{X}}) \le \mu \le (\overline{X} + Z_{\alpha/2}\,\sigma_{\overline{X}})] = 1 - \alpha. \tag{8-20}$$

From 8-20, the confidence limits for the population mean are

$$LCL_{(1-\alpha)} = \overline{X} - Z_{\alpha/2}\,\sigma_{\overline{X}} = \overline{X} - Z_{\alpha/2}\frac{\sigma_x}{\sqrt{N}}; \tag{8-21}$$

$$UCL_{(1-\alpha)} = \overline{X} + Z_{\alpha/2}\,\sigma_{\overline{X}} = \overline{X} + Z_{\alpha/2}\frac{\sigma_x}{\sqrt{N}}. \tag{8-22}$$

We will now return to our GRE scores and we will find the .95 and .99 confidence intervals for the mean. From Table A, the critical values of Z for a two-tailed test at the .05 level are ± 1.96. Substituting those values for $\pm Z_{\alpha/2}$, and substituting the values of $\overline{X}$ and σ_x in 8-21 and 8-22,

$$LCL_{.95} = 604 - 1.96 \frac{134}{\sqrt{10}} = 520.95;$$

$$UCL_{.95} = 604 + 1.96 \frac{134}{\sqrt{10}} = 687.05.$$

Substituting the above confidence limits in 8-20 yields the 95%, or the .95, confidence interval for the population mean — that is, the mean of the above-average population from which our sample of 10 students was chosen. Thus,

$$P(520.95 \le \mu \le 687.05) = .95.$$

The above equation states that the probability is .95 that μ, the population mean, lies within the interval from 520.95 to 687.05. The value of μ under our null hypothesis, which we tested earlier, was 512. The observed sample mean, 604, was sufficiently high to allow us to reject H_0 at the .05 level of significance. Notice that our .95 confidence interval does not contain the value 512, or *any* value less than 520.95. If the null hypothesis is rejected at a significance level of .05 in a two-tailed test, it is always true that μ_0 — the expected value of the population mean under the null hypothesis — will lie outside the .95 confidence interval for the mean.

Confidence Intervals Where σ Is Unknown

Where the standard deviation of the population is unknown, it is appropriate to use t rather than Z in constructing confidence intervals for the population mean. By analogy with Equation 8-19,

$$P(-t_{\alpha/2} \le t \le t_{\alpha/2}) = 1 - \alpha. \tag{8-23}$$

In the above equation, $t_{\alpha/2}$ and $-t_{\alpha/2}$ are, respectively, the upper and lower critical values for a two-tailed test at a significance level of α. Thus, Equation 8-23 gives the $(1 - \alpha)$ confidence interval for t. Substituting for t, and continuing as in our earlier development,

$$P(-t_{\alpha/2} \le \frac{\overline{X} - \mu}{S_{\overline{X}}} \le t_{\alpha/2}) = 1 - \alpha; \tag{8-24}$$

$$LCL_{(1-\alpha)} = \overline{X} - t_{\alpha/2} S_{\overline{X}} = \overline{X} - t_{\alpha/2} \frac{S_x}{\sqrt{N}}; \tag{8-25}$$

$$UCL_{(1-\alpha)} = \overline{X} + t_{\alpha/2} S_{\overline{X}} = \overline{X} + t_{\alpha/2} \frac{S_x}{\sqrt{N}}; \tag{8-26}$$

$$P[(\overline{X} - t_{\alpha/2} S_{\overline{X}}) \le \mu \le (\overline{X} + t_{\alpha/2} S_{\overline{X}})] = 1 - \alpha. \tag{8-27}$$

Returning to our visual illusion measurements, we will find the 95% and the 99% confidence intervals for the mean. The necessary quantities for our calculations are in Table 8-2. For a two-tailed test, the critical value CV_α is equal to $t_{\alpha/2}$. Substituting $CV_{.05}$, $\overline{X}$, and S from Table 8-2 in Equations 8-25 and 8-26,

$$LCL_{.95} = 112.70 - 2.262 \frac{11.26}{\sqrt{10}} = 104.65;$$

$$UCL_{.95} = 112.70 + 2.262 \frac{11.26}{\sqrt{10}} = 120.75.$$

Substituting the above confidence limits in Equation 8-20 yields the 95%, or the .95, confidence interval for the population mean:

$$P(104.65 \leq \mu \leq 120.75) = .95.$$

The above equation states that the probability is .95 that μ, the population mean, lies within the interval from 104.65 mm to 120.75 mm. The value of μ under the null hypothesis was 100 mm, and our observed value of $\overline{X}$, 112.70, was sufficiently high to allow us to reject H_0 at the .05 level — and even at the .01 level of significance. Notice that our .95 confidence interval does not contain the null value of 100 mm, or any other value less than 104.65.

For purposes of comparison, we will find the .99 confidence interval for the population mean. From Table B, the critical value for t with 9 df for a two-tailed test at the .01 level is 3.250. Substituting in Equations 8-25 and 8-26,

$$LCL_{.99} = 112.70 - 3.250 \frac{11.26}{\sqrt{10}} = 101.13;$$

$$UCL_{.99} = 112.70 + 3.250 \frac{11.26}{\sqrt{10}} = 124.27;$$

$$P(101.13 \leq \mu \leq 124.27) = .99.$$

Notice that the .99 confidence interval, like the .95 confidence interval, does not contain the value of μ_0, 100 mm. Since we rejected H_0 at the .01 level, we should expect the .99 confidence interval to exclude the value of μ_0, as it does. Notice also that a confidence level of .99 produces a larger confidence interval than a level of .95.

Confidence intervals based on t are quite analogous to confidence intervals based on Z. Whether we use Z or t in constructing a confidence interval depends on which of those statistical tests we would use in testing the null hypothesis. Where σ, the population standard deviation is known, it is appropriate to use Z in hypothesis testing and in constructing confidence intervals. But where σ is unknown, and must be estimated from a sample, it is appropriate to use t in constructing confidence intervals as well as in hypothesis testing.

Confidence Intervals and Hypothesis Testing

Finding the confidence interval for the population mean is a procedure that usefully supplements a test of the null hypothesis. In hypothesis testing, we compare the observed value of $\overline{X}$ with a single value of μ_0 expected under the null hypothesis. If we reject H_0 and accept H_1, we reject the notion that the population mean is equal to μ_0 in favor of the notion that μ is greater than μ_0. If we have rejected H_0 at the .05 level, and if we then construct a 95% confidence interval for μ, it will always be true that μ_0 will lie outside that confidence interval. We can then state that the probability is .95 that μ is not only greater than μ_0, the single value of μ under the null hypothesis, but also greater than all of the possible values of μ between μ_0 and the lower confidence limit for the mean. In effect, constructing a confidence interval for the mean allows us to test simultaneously all of the potential values of μ_0 lying outside the confidence interval.

In dealing with confidence intervals, it may appear as though we are treating the population mean, μ, as if it were a variable and $\overline{X}$, the sample mean, as if it were a constant. But it is the sample mean $\overline{X}$ that is the variable, which will take on different values in different samples drawn from the same population. Since any confidence interval is based on some particular value of $\overline{X}$, which in turn depends on the values of X observed in a particular sample, the confidence interval for the population mean will vary from sample to sample. Figure 8-7 shows the 95% confidence intervals based on 20 random samples drawn from the population of GRE scores that we discussed earlier. As it happens, 19 of those 20 confidence intervals contain the true value of μ, the population mean. There is of course no guarantee that *any* of the .95 confidence intervals will contain the true value of the mean, since the .95 confidence level represents a probability which is less than absolute certainty. We should not expect many of our 95% confidence intervals to fail to bracket the population mean, and indeed, in only one case in our example does one of the 20 random samples yield a confidence interval which does not contain the population mean.

The heavy bar in Figure 8-7 is the .95 confidence interval for the mean based on our earlier observation of the GRE scores of a group of 10 graduating

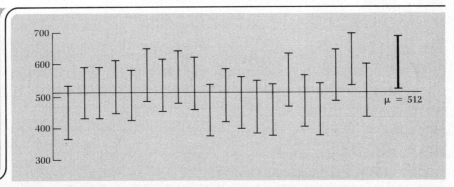

FIGURE 8-7. Light bars are the .95 confidence intervals for the mean based on 20 random samples drawn from a population where $\mu = 512$ and $\sigma = 134$. Heavy bar is the confidence interval for the mean based on the observation of 10 students (see text).

seniors. That confidence interval was found by applying Equations 8-25 and 8-26:

$$LCL_{.95} = \bar{X} - Z_{.025} \frac{\sigma_x}{\sqrt{N}} = 604 - 1.96 \frac{134}{\sqrt{10}} = 521;$$

$$UCL_{.95} = \bar{X} + Z_{.025} \frac{\sigma_x}{\sqrt{N}} = 604 + 1.96 \frac{134}{\sqrt{10}} = 697.$$

Since we rejected the null hypothesis at the .05 level in our earlier discussion, we should not expect the confidence interval, above, to contain the population mean of 512. But the confidence interval in one of the 20 random samples also fails to contain the population mean. The mean of that random sample was 618, which is even higher than the mean score of the students, 604. The point is, if the mean of a random sample can differ significantly from the population mean, how do we know whether the mean of the 10 graduating seniors *really* differs from the population mean? The answer is simple: We don't really know. We can only say that the probability of observing a value of $\bar{X}$ as high as 604 is less than .05 if the population mean is 512. Having observed a value of the sample mean, 604, that represents a rare event under the hypothesis that $\mu = 512$, we reject that hypothesis in favor of the alternative hypothesis, that our students were drawn from a different population having a higher mean than the general population of students taking the GRE. But wouldn't we also reject H_0 if there was really no difference between the caliber of our student population and the general population of students taking the GRE, and if we happened to observe—just by chance alone—a sample of students having a mean of 604—or 618, like one of our 20 random samples? The answer is yes, and in that case, we would make a Type 1 error. We can never eliminate the possibility of making incorrect decisions, but we can adopt procedures that will hold the probabilities of Type 1 and Type 2 errors to acceptable levels.

Terms and Symbols

Spend some time comparing and contrasting the following terms and symbols, and especially the ideas they represent. The tests that we have introduced in this chapter are very useful in their own right, and furthermore, the ideas that we have presented here will be very important in our development of other kinds of tests in later chapters.

Random sample	**Standard error of the mean**
Population	**Central limit theorem**
Statistic	**1-tailed test**
Parameter	**2-tailed test**
Critical ratio	**Critical value**
Mean of the sample means	**Unbiased estimator**
Variance of the sample mean	**Biased estimator**

Corrected estimator	$\overline{X}$
Degrees of freedom	SD
***t* statistic**	S
Assumptions	$S_{\overline{x}}$
Type 1 error	SD^2
Type 2 error	S^2
Power	t
Confidence interval	df
Confidence limits	CV_1 and CV_2
Sampling distribution	α
μ_x	β
σ_x	$1 - \alpha$
σ_x^2	$1 - \beta$
$\mu_{\overline{x}}$	LCL and UCL
$\sigma_{\overline{x}}$	$Z_{\alpha/2}$
$\sigma_{\overline{x}}^2$	$t_{\alpha/2}$
$Z_{\overline{x}}$	

EXERCISES AND STUDY QUESTIONS

1. In developing the principles of summation in Chapter 4, we noted that $\Sigma c = Nc$. At that point, treating the sample mean as a constant, we also noted that $\Sigma \overline{X} = N\overline{X}$. In the present chapter, we have treated the sample mean as a random variable. Is there an inconsistency here? Explain.

2. What is the central limit theorem, and what bearing does it have on the Z test of a mean?

3. The State Department of Education has devised a new test of basic education skills for all high-school seniors called the State-Wide Educational Achievement Test, or the SWEAT. Last year, the mean and standard deviation were 100 and 20 for all of the students taking the test. For the 112 graduating seniors at Boskydell East High School the mean SWEAT score was 103.49. Do the students at Boskydell East differ significantly from the statewide mean?

   a. Justify the use of a Z test taking into account the nature of the measurement scale and other requirements.

   b. Formulate the null and alternative hypotheses in words and symbols.

   c. Should this be a 1 or 2-tailed test? Why? Should you base your decision here on the observed value of the sample mean?

   d. Indicate whether you reject or do not reject H_0, and explain what that means.

   e. Find the 95% confidence interval for the mean. Does that confidence interval contain 100? Should it?

4. There are 201 graduating seniors at Boskydell West High School. By a strange coincidence, their mean score on the SWEAT is also 103.49,

exactly the same as the mean at Boskydell East in Exercise 3, above. Do the students at Boskydell West differ significantly from the state-wide mean of 100?

   a. Formulate the null and alternative hypotheses in words and symbols.
   b. Indicate whether you reject H_0.
   c. Find the 95% confidence interval for the mean. Does that interval contain 100? Should it? Why, or why not?
   d. Find the 99% confidence interval. Does that interval contain 100? Should it? Why, or why not?
   e. Compare the sizes of the 95% and 99% confidence intervals. Which is larger? Which should be larger?

5. Compare the results of the tests in Exercises 3 and 4 above.
   a. For any given value of an observed sample mean, what bearing does the sample size have on the probability of rejecting H_0?
   b. What is the *power* of a test, and what bearing does the sample size have on power?
   c. What is the effect of sample size on the size of the confidence interval?

6. On the average, do gamblers win or lose when they play the slot machines in Las Vegas? Suppose we observed 12 randomly chosen slot-machine players during a period of 1 hour. Their wins (positive signs) and losses (negative signs) are shown below to the nearest dollar:

Persons	1	2	3	4	5	6	7	8	9	10	11	12
Wins and losses	12	-97	-43	47	-63	-90	17	6	-74	9	-81	-34

   a. Justify the use of a t test, taking into account the nature of the measurement scale and other requirements.
   b. Formulate the null and alternative hypotheses in words and symbols.
   c. Justify your decision to use a 1 or 2-tailed test.
   d. Indicate whether you reject H_0. Explain the meaning of the sign on your observed t ratio.
   e. Find the 95% and 99% confidence intervals for the mean. Which of those intervals contains zero? Which should, if either?

7. Suppose we now consider the observations in Exercise 6, above, as a binomial probability experiment where each person either wins or loses.
   a. Justify using the normal approximation to the binomial.
   b. Formulate the null and alternative hypotheses in words and symbols. Explain whether this should be a 1 or 2-tailed test.
   c. Indicate whether you reject H_0 by the normal approximation.
   d. Compare the present results with the t test in the preceding exercise. Is there any inconsistency between the results of the two tests? Which test is more appropriate, which is more powerful, and how so?

8. A version of the Müller-Lyer illusion is shown below. The left and right portions of the horizontal line are equal in length, although the left looks

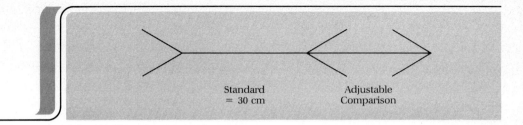

Standard
= 30 cm

Adjustable
Comparison

longer to most people. Suppose we have an apparatus constructed so that the *standard*, the left portion of the horizontal line, remains constant at a length of 30 cm. The subject's task is to adjust the length of the *comparison*, the right portion of the horizontal line, so that it appears to match the length of the standard. The results in a group of 10 subjects are shown below in cm. Carry out the most appropriate test.

34.2   33.3   33.6   35.7   28.5   33.0   32.1   33.6   32.4   33.9

a. Formulate the null and alternative hypotheses in words and symbols.
b. What is the actual value of μ_0, the population mean under H_0?
c. Indicate whether you reject or do not reject H_0, and indicate the level of statistical significance.
d. Find the 99% confidence interval for the mean. Does that interval contain μ_0? Should it?

9. The results of the Müller-Lyer illusion observations in Exercise 8 are highly statistically significant. Suppose the experimenter draws the conclusion that the configuration of the fins — the diagonal lines — causes the comparison to look shorter than the standard. As the experiment stands, is that conclusion entirely justified, or is another interpretation possible?

10. Suppose you are an educational researcher. You have developed a theory that most students have unrealistic expectations which lead them to overestimate their test performances. You have just carried out a study using a 2-tailed statistical test, and a standard test instrument such as the GRE, and indeed, students tended to overestimate their performances, but not statistically significantly. Discuss each of the following possible alternatives open to you at this point:

a. Do a 1-tailed test on the present results, and if significant, consider your theory supported.
b. Discard the present results, do another study using 10 subjects, and run a 1-tailed test this time.
c. Discard the present results, do another study using 10 subjects, using the same instrument, and run a 2-tailed test. If that study is not statistically significant, discard those results and continue testing samples of 10 subjects until you find statistically significant results by a 2-tailed test.

    d. Do another study using a substantially larger number of subjects, perhaps pooling the new subjects with the existing ones — as long as you have no reason to believe the new sample represents a different student population. In any case, run a 2-tailed test.

    e. Develop a more sensitive measure of students' expectations.

    f. Discard your theory, since results that are not statistically significant are due only to chance.

Comparing Two
Independent Groups

9

Comparing measurements of independent groups of subjects is a process that represents one of the very foundations of the experimental method — not only in the field of psychology, but in many other fields as well. **Independent groups** are random samples of different subjects, sometimes drawn from the same population, and sometimes from different populations. For example, if we wanted to compare two methods of teaching second-grade reading, we might select two random samples of second-graders, teach each of the two groups by a different method, and then compare their mean performance on a common test of reading achievement.

In many situations, we are interested in comparing measurements made on different kinds of subjects, that is, subjects drawn from different populations. For example, we might be interested in the mean level of education among management and nonmanagement personnel in a particular profession or in the proportion of men and women in two different professions.

The appropriate procedure for comparing two groups depends on the nature of the measurement scale — ratio, interval, ordinal, or nominal — and also depends on whether the value of the population standard deviation is known. Thus, the four varieties of measurement scales provide a framework for the organization of this chapter, and for much of the remainder of this text as well.

Interval and Ratio Scales

Differences Between Means Where σ Is Known

Suppose we are interested in comparing the level of academic achievement in two groups of graduating seniors in psychology, one at University A, the other at University B. The Advanced Test in Psychology (AT), a part of the Graduate Record Examination, was taken by 18,666 students in a recent two-year period. The mean AT score was 529, and the standard deviation was 91. At University A, the 25 students who took the AT made a mean score of 559, while at University B, the mean score for 36 students was 512. Is there a significant difference between the mean AT score for graduating seniors at University A and University B?

Since we know the mean and standard deviation in the population of students having previously taken the test, it might occur to you to test each of the observed means against the population mean of 529. Perhaps, you might argue, if the mean for University A differs significantly from the population mean and the mean for University B does not, then the students at the two universities must differ from each other. But it is possible for the two groups to differ significantly from each other even though neither differs from the population mean — indeed, that turns out to be the case in our present example. It is also possible for both groups to differ from the population mean and not differ from each other. Thus, we need to develop additional methods for testing the statistical significance of differences between the means of two groups.

The Z Test of a Difference Between Means. We will proceed by developing an expression analogous to the critical ratio for the Z test of a single mean in Chapter 8. We let $\overline{D}$ represent the difference between $\overline{X}_1$ and $\overline{X}_2$, the means of two independent samples. Thus,

$$\overline{D} = \overline{X}_1 - \overline{X}_2. \tag{9-1}$$

We have noted previously that a sample mean is a random variable that can take on different values in different samples, and thus $\overline{D}$, the difference between two independent sample means, is also a random variable. In our present discussion it does not matter whether $\overline{X}_1$ and $\overline{X}_2$ are drawn from different populations having different means and standard deviations, or from the same population, as long as both samples are random and each is independent of the other. If we drew two random samples again and again, each time finding the value of $\overline{D}$, we could — in principle — determine the sampling distribution of $\overline{D}$, that is, its expected value and standard deviation. Further, $\overline{X}_1$ and $\overline{X}_2$ will be normally distributed if each sample is drawn from a normal population, or if each sample size is approximately 30 or larger. In either case, $\overline{D}$ will also be normally distributed. Thus, if we can find expressions for the expected value and standard deviation of $\overline{D}$, respectively $\mu_{\overline{D}}$ and $\sigma_{\overline{D}}$, then we can use the following critical ratio to test hypotheses about differences between two sample means:

$$Z_{\overline{D}} = \frac{\overline{D} - \mu_{\overline{D}}}{\sigma_{\overline{D}}}, \tag{9-2}$$

where $Z_{\overline{D}}$ is the Z-score associated with an observed value of $\overline{D}$.

The critical ratio, above, can be used to test the following hypotheses:

$H_0: \mu = \mu_0 = \mu_{\overline{D}} = (\mu_1 - \mu_2);$

$H_1: \quad \mu > (\mu_1 - \mu_2);$

$H_2: \quad \mu < (\mu_1 - \mu_2).$

In testing the difference between two sample means, the value of μ_0 under the null hypothesis is equal to the difference between the means of the two populations from which the samples were drawn. We are usually interested in testing the hypothesis that there is no difference between the means of those populations, and in that special case $\mu_1 = \mu_2$, and thus $\mu_0 = 0$. We will return to this point a little later.

Expected Value of a Difference Between Sample Means. The **expected value** of a difference between two random variables is equal to the difference between their expected values. Thus,

$$\mu_{\overline{D}} = E(\overline{D}) = E(\overline{X}_1 - \overline{X}_2) = E(\overline{X}_1) - E(\overline{X}_2).$$

We showed in the last chapter that $E(\overline{X}) = E(X) = \mu$, and thus

$$\mu_{\overline{D}} = E(X_1) - E(X_2) = \mu_1 - \mu_2. \tag{9-3}$$

Standard Deviation of a Difference Between Sample Means. Counterintuitively, the variance of a difference between two independent random variables is equal to the *sum* of their variances — as we will show. By Equation 6-10,

$$\sigma_{\overline{D}}^2 = E(\overline{D} - \mu_{\overline{D}})^2.$$

Substituting $\mu_{\overline{D}}$ from Equation 9-3, above, and continuing,

$$
\begin{aligned}
E[(\overline{X}_1 - \overline{X}_2) - (\mu_1 - \mu_2)]^2 &= E[(\overline{X}_1 - \mu_1) - (\overline{X}_2 - \mu_2)]^2 \\
&= E[(\overline{X}_1 - \mu_1)^2 + (\overline{X}_2 - \mu_2)^2 \\
&\quad - 2(\overline{X}_1 - \mu_1)(\overline{X}_2 - \mu_2)] \\
&= E(\overline{X}_1 - \mu_1)^2 + E(\overline{X}_2 - \mu_2)^2 \\
&\quad - 2E[(\overline{X}_1 - \mu_1)(\overline{X}_2 - \mu_2)]. \tag{9-4}
\end{aligned}
$$

The last term in Equation 9-4 is equal to zero where we are dealing with the means of independent samples. That term is a function of the **correlation** between sample means — that is, a measure of the extent to which we could predict the value of $\overline{X}_2$, given an **observed value** of $\overline{X}_1$. If two samples are independent, then there is no correlation between their means, and the last term in 9-4 vanishes. You will be able to appreciate this point better after studying the materials on correlation in Chapter 10, but for now, it is sufficient to note that Equation 9-4 simplifies considerably. Thus,

$$\sigma_{\overline{D}}^2 = \sigma_{\overline{X}_1}^2 + \sigma_{\overline{X}_2}^2, \tag{9-5}$$

where $\sigma_{\overline{X}_1}^2$ and $\sigma_{\overline{X}_2}^2$ are the variances of the sample means.

Taking the square root of Expression 9-5 yields the **standard error of the difference between means,** which is the standard deviation of the difference between the means of all possible pairs of samples of sizes N_1 and N_2 that could be drawn from Populations 1 and 2. Thus,

$$
\begin{array}{l}
\text{Standard error} \\
\text{of the difference} \\
\text{between means}
\end{array}
= \sigma_{\overline{D}} = \sqrt{\sigma_{\overline{X}_1}^2 + \sigma_{\overline{X}_2}^2} = \sqrt{\dfrac{\sigma_1^2}{N_1} + \dfrac{\sigma_2^2}{N_2}}, \tag{9-6}
$$

where σ_1^2 and σ_2^2 are the variances of Populations 1 and 2, $\sigma_{\overline{X}_1}^2$ and $\sigma_{\overline{X}_2}^2$ are the variances of the sample means, and N_1 and N_2 are the sample sizes. Substituting in Equation 9-2,

$$
Z_{\overline{D}} = \frac{(\overline{X}_1 - \overline{X}_2) - (\mu_1 - \mu_2)}{\sqrt{\dfrac{\sigma_1^2}{N_1} + \dfrac{\sigma_2^2}{N_2}}}, \qquad
\begin{array}{l}
\text{where } \sigma_1 \text{ and } \sigma_2 \text{ are known,} \\
\text{and } \mathrm{H}_0 \text{ is } \mu_0 = \mu_{\overline{D}} = \mu_1 - \mu_2.
\end{array}
\tag{9-7}
$$

The critical ratio above provides a test of the null hypothesis that an observed difference between sample means does not differ significantly from μ_0. In general, μ_1 and μ_2 may be equal or unequal, and thus μ_0 may or may not be equal to zero. But we are usually interested in the question of whether two samples were drawn from the same population, and in that case $\mu_1 = \mu_2$, and thus $\mu_0 = 0$. If $\bar{X}_1$ and $\bar{X}_2$ are the means of independent random samples drawn from the same population, then it also follows that $\sigma_1 = \sigma_2 = \sigma$. Rewriting Formula 9-7 then yields

$$Z_{\bar{D}} = \frac{\bar{X}_1 - \bar{X}_2}{\sqrt{\sigma^2\left(\dfrac{1}{N_1} + \dfrac{1}{N_2}\right)}}, \qquad \begin{array}{l} \text{where } \sigma \text{ is known,} \\ \text{and } H_0 \text{ is } \mu_0 = \mu_1 - \mu_2 = 0. \end{array} \tag{9-8}$$

Equation 9-8 represents the critical ratio that we will use in testing hypotheses about differences between means where we know the value of σ, the standard deviation of the population. Formula 9-7 shows that we can also test hypotheses about differences between means drawn from *different* populations having different expected values and standard deviations. But in practice, we are nearly always interested in testing the null hypothesis that two samples were drawn from the same population.

Calculating Z for Independent Samples. Returning to the problem of testing the difference between the mean AT scores at University A and University B, we formulate the following null hypothesis and two alternative hypotheses:

$H_0: \mu_1 = \mu_2;$

$H_1: \mu_1 > \mu_2;$

$H_2: \mu_1 < \mu_2.$

The null hypothesis, above, seems reasonable enough, but since we have already observed that $\bar{X}_1$ (the mean for University A) is greater than $\bar{X}_2$, why not test only the alternative hypothesis that says $\mu_1 > \mu_2$? Testing only H_1 would constitute a one-tailed test, and the critical value of Z would be lower than for a two-tailed test, thus making it easier to reject H_0. But the decision to carry out a one- or two-tailed test should be made before any data are collected, and once made should be adhered to. In the present situation, we would be just as impressed if the mean for University B were significantly higher than the mean for University A, and thus a two-tailed test is clearly appropriate.

The calculation of Z is shown in Table 9-1. In the present example, the observed value of Z was positive and greater than the upper critical value for a two-tailed test at the .05 level, so we reject H_0 in favor of H_1, the alternative hypothesis stating that $\mu_1 > \mu_2$. If we had observed a negative value of Z more extreme than the lower critical value — that is, farther away from the mean — then we would have rejected H_0 in favor of H_2.

TABLE 9-1.   Z Test of a Difference Between Independent Sample Means.

Advanced Test in Psychology: $\mu = 529$

$\sigma = 91$

University A: $\overline{X}_1 = 559$ University B: $\overline{X}_2 = 512$

$N_1 = 25$ $N_2 = 36$

By Formula 9-8,

$$Z_{\overline{D}} = \frac{\overline{X}_1 - \overline{X}_2}{\sqrt{\sigma^2 \left(\frac{1}{N_1} + \frac{1}{N_2}\right)}} = \frac{559 - 512}{\sqrt{\frac{91^2}{25} + \frac{91^2}{36}}} = \frac{47}{\sqrt{\frac{8281}{25} + \frac{8281}{36}}}$$

$$= \frac{47}{\sqrt{561.268}} = \frac{47}{23.691} = 1.98 = Z_{observed}.$$

$H_0: \mu_1 = \mu_2$ Two-tailed critical values from Table A:

$H_1: \mu_1 > \mu_2$ $LCV_{.05} = -1.96$, $UCV_{.05} = +1.96$.

$H_2: \mu_1 < \mu_2$ Since $1.98 > 1.96$, $Z_{obs} > UCV_{.05}$.

Therefore, reject H_0 in favor of H_1 at .05 level.

Requirements for the Z Test

The requirements for the Z test in the present situation — the assumptions underlying the test — are listed in Table 9-2 and are discussed under the numbered headings below. The requirements for the Z test of a difference between means are very similar to the requirements for the Z test of a single mean shown in Table 8-4.

TABLE 9-2.   Requirements for Z Test of a Difference Between Means of Two Independent Samples.

1. Interval or ratio measurement scale.
2. Approximately normal distribution if $N_1 < 30$ or $N_2 < 30$ (not required for larger sample sizes).
3. Each value of X_1 and X_2 must be independent of every other value within each sample and between samples.
4. The population standard deviation must be known.

1. Interval or Ratio Scales.   The same considerations apply here as in our earlier discussion of the test of a single mean. If a difference between means is to be quantitatively interpretable, then we must have at least interval scales for the measurements of both samples.

2. Normal Distributions.   The Z test is based on the assumption that the difference between sample means is normally distributed. But if we are dealing with two small samples from different populations, one of which is not normally distributed, then the difference between the means of those small samples will not be normally distributed. For large samples, where the Ns are as large as 30, regardless of the form of the distributions, that problem vanishes because of the central limit theorem. The same considerations of sample sizes apply to independent samples from a single population.

3. Independence. Both samples must be random samples, which means that the cases *within* each sample must be independent of each other, and the cases must all be independent *between* samples as well. Thus, in the two-sample test, the assumptions of independence can be violated in the following ways, among others: (1) By including multiple measurements on one individual in the same sample and treating those measurements as though they represented different individuals; and (2) by including measurements on the same individuals in both samples. (In Chapter 12 we will present methods of dealing with *repeated measures*, that is, measurements on the same group of individuals under two conditions.)

4. Known Standard Deviations. Where independent samples are drawn from two different populations, both standard deviations, σ_1 and σ_2, must be known, though not necessarily equal. Where the null hypothesis states that both independent samples are drawn from the same population, the standard deviation of that population must be known. Where σ is unknown, and must be estimated from the sample data, as in the next section, a t test of the difference between means is the appropriate procedure.

Differences Between Means Where σ Is Unknown

In most cases, we do not know the value of the population standard deviation when we are interested in testing a difference between sample means. For example, suppose we wanted to carry out an experiment to compare a new method of teaching a statistics course with a standard method. Suppose we have a class of 23 students, which we divide into two randomized groups of 11 and 12 students. (We will explain randomization procedures in detail in Chapter 13.) One group of students, the experimental group, is subjected to the new method of teaching; the other group, the control group, is taught by the standard method. At the end of the semester, both groups are given the same final examination.

The situation here is very different from the earlier situation where we compared the performance of two groups of students on the Advanced Test in Psychology, a standardized test that has been given to many thousands of people. In the present case, we are dealing with a specially constructed examination covering a statistics course. A population of scores on such an examination ordinarily does not exist. However, there does exist a population of students to whom we could give our exam, at least in principle. Thus, we can consider a hypothetical population of exam scores in much the way we have considered hypothetical populations of coin tosses and the like. We will develop a method of testing the hypothesis that the performances of our two groups, the experimental and control groups, do not differ significantly and thus represent random samples drawn from the same hypothetical population of exam scores.

The *t* Test of a Difference Between Means.   Where we do not know the value of σ, the population standard deviation, we must estimate its value from sample data. Substituting the **estimated standard error of the difference between means, $S_{\bar{D}}$,** in Equation 9-2 yields the *t* ratio for a test of that difference:

$$t = \frac{\bar{D} - \mu_{\bar{D}}}{S_{\bar{D}}}. \tag{9-9}$$

Equation 9-9 differs from 9-2 only in the use of an estimate in the place of the known value of $\sigma_{\bar{D}}$. Continuing as in our earlier development of the Z test, Equation 9-10, below, is analogous to 9-8:

$$t = \frac{\bar{X}_1 - \bar{X}_2}{\sqrt{S^2\left(\frac{1}{N_1} + \frac{1}{N_2}\right)}}, \qquad \text{where } \sigma \text{ is unknown,} \atop \text{and } H_0 \text{ is } \mu_0 = \mu_1 - \mu_2 = 0. \tag{9-10}$$

A problem immediately arises in connection with Formula 9-10, above: How do we find the value of S^2, the unbiased estimate of the population variance? Where we are testing the difference between means, we have two samples, and thus we have *two* estimates of σ^2, namely S_1^2 and S_2^2, the variance of the two samples. Since S_1^2 and S_2^2 will very seldom be exactly equal, we have to solve the problem of reconciling those two estimates of the population variance. We can derive an **unbiased estimator of the population variance** by weighting the sample variances in proportion to their respective degree of freedom, as below:

$$\text{Unbiased estimator of} \atop \text{population variance} = S^2 = \frac{(N_1 - 1)S_1^2 + (N_2 - 1)S_2^2}{(N_1 - 1) + (N_2 - 1)}. \tag{9-11}$$

It is easy to show that Equation 9-11 is indeed an unbiased estimator of the population variance. Taking expected values,

$$E(S^2) = E\left[\frac{(N_1 - 1)S_1^2 + (N_2 - 1)S_2^2}{(N_1 - 1) + (N_2 - 1)}\right] = \frac{(N_1 - 1)E(S_1^2) + (N_2 - 1)E(S_2^2)}{N_1 + N_2 - 2}.$$

Since S_1^2 and S_2^2 are unbiased estimators of σ_X^2, the above expression is equal to

$$\frac{(N_1 - 1)\sigma^2 + (N_2 - 1)\sigma^2}{N_1 + N_2 - 2} = \frac{(N_1 + N_2 - 2)\sigma^2}{N_1 + N_2 - 2} = \sigma^2.$$

Thus, we have shown that the expected value of Expression 9-11 is equal to σ^2, and thus our expression for S^2 is an unbiased estimator of the population variance. In the present context, S^2 is found by combining, or **pooling,** the weighted values of S_1^2 and S_2^2, and is often called a **pooled estimate** of the population variance.

We can derive a computational formula for t by substituting Expression 9-11 for S^2 in 9-10:

$$t = \frac{\bar{X}_1 - \bar{X}_2}{\sqrt{\dfrac{(N_1 - 1)S_1^2 + (N_2 - 1)S_2^2}{N_1 + N_2 - 2}\left(\dfrac{1}{N_1} + \dfrac{1}{N_2}\right)}}, \qquad df = N_1 + N_2 - 2. \qquad (9\text{-}12)$$

The number of degrees of freedom, **df**, associated with the t ratio above can be found by considering the df of each of the sample variances entering into that t ratio. (The concept of df was explained in Chapter 8.) Each of the terms in parentheses in 9-11 is the df of one of the sample variances. Of the observations used in calculating S_1^2 and S_2^2, only $(N_1 - 1)$ and $(N_2 - 1)$, respectively, are free to vary. Thus, of the observations entering into the calculation of S^2, only $(N_1 + N_2 - 2)$ are free to vary.

The above formula defines the t ratio in terms of the sample variances. If you have access to a small hand calculator that will automatically calculate the mean and standard deviation of a sample, then Formula 9-12 will be very useful. If your machine calculates SD instead of S, remember that $S = SD\sqrt{N/(N-1)}$.

Using Computational Formula 9-12 requires multiplying each sample variance by its df, but finding a sample variance in the first place requires *dividing* the sum of the squared deviations from the sample mean by the df. Thus, there are some arithmetic operations in that computational formula that can be eliminated. We will derive a computational formula for t which will not require that we first calculate the sample variances, S_1^2 and S_2^2.

We will define the **sum of squares** for each sample, **SS_1** and **SS_2**, as the sum of the squared deviations from the sample mean, and we will note the relationship between the sum of squares and the sample variance. Thus,

$$S_1^2 = \frac{\Sigma(X_1 - \bar{X}_1)^2}{N_1 - 1} = \frac{SS_1}{N_1 - 1}, \qquad \text{and} \qquad S_2^2 = \frac{\Sigma(X_2 - \bar{X}_2)^2}{N_2 - 1} = \frac{SS_2}{N_2 - 1}.$$

Substituting Computational Formula 8-10 for S_1^2 and S_2^2 in the above equations and solving for SS_1 and SS_2 yields the following computational formulas for the sums of squares:

$$SS_1 = (N_1 - 1)S_1^2 = \Sigma X_1^2 - \frac{(\Sigma X_1)^2}{N_1}; \qquad (9\text{-}13)$$

$$SS_2 = (N_2 - 1)S_2^2 = \Sigma X_2^2 - \frac{(\Sigma X_2)^2}{N_2}. \qquad (9\text{-}14)$$

Substituting SS_1 and SS_2 for $(N_1 - 1)S_1^2$ and $(N_2 - 1)S_2^2$ in Formula 9-12 yields the following computational formula for the t ratio:

$$t = \frac{\bar{X}_1 - \bar{X}_2}{\sqrt{\dfrac{\Sigma X_1^2 - \dfrac{(\Sigma X_1)^2}{N_1} + \Sigma X_2^2 - \dfrac{(\Sigma X_2)^2}{N_2}}{N_1 + N_2 - 2}\left(\dfrac{1}{N_1} + \dfrac{1}{N_2}\right)}}, \qquad df = N_1 + N_2 - 2.$$

$$\qquad (9\text{-}15)$$

Although Formula 9-15 may appear rather formidable, it offers some computational advantages over 9-12. There is a little less arithmetic involved in 9-15, and thus fewer opportunities for rounding errors to occur.

We can also express 9-15 in the following way:

$$t = \frac{\bar{X}_1 - \bar{X}_2}{\sqrt{\dfrac{SS_1 + SS_2}{N_1 + N_2 - 2}\left(\dfrac{1}{N_1} + \dfrac{1}{N_2}\right)}}, \quad df = N_1 + N_2 - 2 \tag{9-16}$$

Formula 9-16 is somewhat more compact than 9-15, but in order to use 9-16, the sums of squares must first be found by 9-13 and 9-14.

A word of caution may be in order regarding the sum of squares. Do not confuse SS, the sum of the squared deviations from the mean, with ΣX^2, the sum of the squared scores. Remember,

$$SS = \Sigma(X - \bar{X})^2, \quad \text{and thus} \quad SS \neq \Sigma X^2.$$

You will also need to remember, as we have mentioned earlier, that

$$\Sigma X^2 \neq (\Sigma X)^2.$$

Equal Sample Sizes. The computational formulas that we have developed so far can be used whether the sample sizes are equal or unequal, but where the two samples are the same size, the t formula can be simplified considerably. Letting $N_1 = N_2 = N_G$, where N_G is the number of subjects per group, and substituting in the quantity under the radical in 9-16,

$$\frac{SS_1 + SS_2}{N_G + N_G - 2}\left(\frac{1}{N_G} + \frac{1}{N_G}\right) = \frac{SS_1 + SS_2}{2(N_G - 1)}\frac{2}{N_G} = \frac{SS_1 + SS_2}{N_G(N_G - 1)}. \tag{9-17}$$

Substituting 9-17 in 9-16,

$$t = \frac{\bar{X}_1 - \bar{X}_2}{\sqrt{\dfrac{SS_1 + SS_2}{N_G(N_G - 1)}}}, \quad \begin{array}{l}\text{where } N_1 = N_2 = N_G, \\ df = 2(N_G - 1).\end{array} \tag{9-18}$$

Equation 9-18 expresses the t ratio in terms of the sums of squares, SS_1 and SS_2. Using the above formula requires that we first calculate the values of SS_1 and SS_2. Substituting formulas 9-13 and 9-14 for the sums of squares in 9-18 yields the following formula for the t ratio:

$$t = \frac{\bar{X}_1 - \bar{X}_2}{\sqrt{\dfrac{\Sigma X_1^2 - \dfrac{(\Sigma X_1)^2}{N_1} + \Sigma X_2^2 - \dfrac{(\Sigma X_2)^2}{N_2}}{N_G(N_G - 1)}}}, \quad \begin{array}{l}\text{where } N_1 = N_2 = N_G, \\ df = 2(N_G - 1).\end{array} \tag{9-19}$$

The above formula, like 9-15, offers the advantage of combining in a single equation all of the operations entering into the calculation of the t ratio.

As we noted earlier, in some cases it is useful to express t in terms of the sample variances, S_1^2 and S_2^2. Beginning with the quantity under the radical in 9-18,

$$\frac{SS_1 + SS_2}{N_G(N_G - 1)} = \frac{1}{N_G}\left(\frac{SS_1}{N_G - 1} + \frac{SS_2}{N_G - 1}\right) = \frac{1}{N_G}(S_1^2 + S_2^2) = \frac{S_1^2 + S_2^2}{N_G}. \qquad (9\text{-}20)$$

Substituting 9-20 for the quantity under the radical in 9-18,

$$t = \frac{\overline{X}_1 - \overline{X}_2}{\sqrt{\dfrac{S_1^2 + S_1^2}{N_G}}}, \qquad \begin{array}{l}\text{where } N_1 = N_2 = N_G, \\ df = 2(N_G - 1).\end{array} \qquad (9\text{-}21)$$

It may appear that we have developed a number of superfluous computational formulas, but each formula has its uses. Formulas 9-12, 9-15, and 9-16 yield identical results, but one or another of those formulas may be more useful in a specific case — depending partly on the kind of calculator that may be available to you, and partly on your personal preference. The preceding formulas can be used whether the sample sizes are equal or unequal, but where $N_1 = N_2$, Formulas 9-18, 9-19, and 9-21 require less arithmetic.

Calculating the t Statistic. Returning to our experiment comparing a new teaching method with a standard one, should we use a one- or a two-tailed test? Perhaps you might argue that we are interested in only one of the possible outcomes of the experiment, the case where the new method is significantly better, since we would simply continue using the standard method otherwise. Further, since the critical value for a one-tailed test is lower, such a test has greater power at a given α level than a two-tailed test — that is, greater sensitivity, greater ability to detect a difference between means if the one-tailed alternative hypothesis is in fact true. Thus, a one-tailed test may be appropriate if you are *completely* uninterested in knowing whether the new method might be significantly *worse* than the standard one — but if you have the slightest interest in that possible outcome, then a two-tailed test is appropriate. In most research situations, before an experiment is performed, we may have strong convictions about the probability — or desirability — of a particular one-tailed outcome. But in our quest for understanding, we are usually prepared to be impressed by significant results in the opposite direction. Taking the broad view, we formulate the following null hypothesis and two alternative hypotheses:

$H_0: \mu_1 = \mu_2;$

$H_1: \mu_1 > \mu_2;$

$H_2: \mu_1 < \mu_2.$

The results of the experiment are shown in Table 9-3. The individual exam scores for the experimental group are shown under the column headed X_1, and the scores for the control group are shown under X_2. Since the two samples are of different sizes, we will use Formula 9-15.

TABLE 9-3. *t* **Test of a Difference Between Two Independent Means, Unequal *N*s.**

Experimental Group (New Method)		Control Group (Standard Method)	
X_1	X_1^2	X_2	X_2^2
17	289	9	81
13	169	10	100
11	121	15	225
14	196	12	144
11	121	17	289
16	256	12	144
12	144	7	49
19	361	13	169
18	324	11	121
16	256	9	81
15	225	12	144
12	144		

$\Sigma X_1 = 174$ $\quad\quad \Sigma X_1^2 = 2606$ $\quad\quad \Sigma X_2 = 127$ $\quad\quad \Sigma X_2^2 = 1547$

$\overline{X}_1 = 14.500$ $\quad\quad N_1 = 12$ $\quad\quad\quad \overline{X}_2 = 11.545$ $\quad\quad N_2 = 11$

Applying Formula 9-15,

$$t = \frac{\overline{X}_1 - \overline{X}_2}{\sqrt{\frac{\Sigma X_1^2 - \frac{(\Sigma X_1)^2}{N_1} + \Sigma X_2^2 - \frac{(\Sigma X_2)^2}{N_2}}{N_1 + N_2 - 2}\left(\frac{1}{N_1} + \frac{1}{N_2}\right)}} \qquad \begin{aligned} df &= N_1 + N_2 - 2 \\ &= 12 + 11 - 2 = 21 \end{aligned}$$

$$= \frac{14.500 - 11.545}{\sqrt{\frac{2606 - \frac{174^2}{12} + 1547 - \frac{127^2}{11}}{12 + 11 - 2}\left(\frac{1}{12} + \frac{1}{11}\right)}}$$

$$= \frac{2.955}{\sqrt{\frac{163.727}{21}(.174)}} = \frac{2.955}{\sqrt{1.357}} = \frac{2.955}{1.165} = 2.537 = t_{observed}.$$

$H_0: \mu_1 = \mu_2$

$H_1: \mu_1 > \mu_2$

$H_2: \mu_1 < \mu_2$

Two-tailed critical values from Table B:

$LCV_{.05} = -2.080,$ $\quad UCV_{.05} = +2.080.$

Since $2.537 > 2.080,$ $\quad t_{obs} > UCV_{.05}.$

Therefore, reject H_0 in favor of H_1 at .05 level.

The first step is to arrange the individual scores from the two groups in two columns, as in Table 9-3. Add up the individual scores to find ΣX_1 and ΣX_2, and then find $\overline{X}_1$ and $\overline{X}_2$. Square the individual scores, and enter the squared scores in a separate column for each group. Add up the squared scores to find ΣX_1^2 and ΣX_2^2. At this point, the preceding quantities, together with N_1 and N_2, are entered into the t formula.

Many small calculators will accumulate ΣX^2 and ΣX. If you have access to such a machine, you can save yourself the tedium of entering all of the squared scores in columns, as in Table 9-3. Many small calculators have several memory registers, so it is possible to store many of your intermediate results without having to write them down. By taking advantage of your calculator's storage capability, you can use all of the available digits in your intermediate steps. You can then round the final result to the desired number of digits, usually two or three digits to the right of the decimal.

Whatever method you use to carry out statistical calculations, you will find that it pays to be orderly and systematic. Lay out the raw data neatly and carefully, and label all of the quantities you derive from the data so that you can check your work when — not if, but when — the need arises.

Having found that the observed value of t in Table 9-3 exceeds the critical value at the .05 level, we reject H_0 in favor of H_1, the hypothesis that states that $\mu_1 > \mu_2$. A negative value of t less than -2.080, the lower critical value, would have led us to reject H_0 in favor of H_2, the second alternative hypothesis. Not only is our observed t greater than the critical value for a two-tailed test at the .05 level: Our t is also greater than the two-tailed critical value at the .02 level. Thus, we would report our results as significant at the .02 level, two-tailed.

Requirements for the t Test

The assumptions underlying the present t test — that is, the requirements for the test — are listed in Table 9-4 and are explained in the numbered sections below.

TABLE 9-4. **Requirements for Independent 2-Sample t Test.**

1. Interval or ratio scale.
2. Approximately normal distribution.
3. Unknown population variance, σ^2, estimated from S_1^2 and S_2^2.
4. Homogeneity of variance.
5. Each measurement of X_1 and X_2 must be independent of every other measurement in both samples.

1. Interval or Ratio Scale. As we have noted in our earlier discussions of t and Z, if the difference between means is to be quantitatively meaningful, then the measurements must constitute at least an interval scale.

2. Normal Distribution. Although a normally distributed population is one of the formal requirements for a t test, rather substantial departures from normality are of no great consequence under many conditions, as explained below in the section headed *Homogeneity of variance*.

3. Unknown Population Variance. The t test applies only where the population variance is unknown and must be estimated from the two observed sample variances. Where the population variance is known, a Z test is appropriate.

4. Homogeneity of Variance. In the formula for the t statistic, we use the variance of each sample, S_1^2 and S_2^2, to find the estimated variance of the population, S^2, in order to estimate the standard error of the difference between means, $S_{\bar{D}}$. Implicit in that procedure is the assumption of **homogeneity of variance,** the assumption that S_1^2 and S_2^2 do not differ from each other any more than the variances of two random samples from the same population might be expected to differ. (We will eventually develop a method of comparing two variances.) The assumption of homogeneity of variance would seem to be well founded, if indeed the two samples are random samples from the same population. Unfortunately, that assumption does not always hold.

Suppose, for example, that we want to study the effect of a high level of noise on the performance of a complex task, such as solving a number of moderately difficult problems requiring thought and consideration. We randomly select two groups of subjects from the same population, and we use one group as the control group and the other as the experimental group. The control group works in a quiet environment, and the experimental group is subjected to a high level of noise. Suppose that in the control group some subjects do very well, some perform moderately, and some very poorly, while in the experimental group nearly everyone does poorly. Thus, there is a difference between the means of the groups, and there is also a difference between the variances, since the scores in the control group range from high to low while the scores in the experimental group are nearly all low. Thus, the scores in the control group are more dispersed — spread out — and thus have a greater variance. The condition where the variances are unequal in the two samples is called **heterogeneity of variance.**

Using computer simulations of sampling experiments, Boneau (1960) has studied the effects of heterogeneity of variance and departures from normality on the t test. For small and *unequal* sample sizes, heterogeneity and nonnormality will each increase the probability of Type 1 errors in some cases and Type 2 errors in other cases. Thus, we might fail to detect the true difference between our control and experimental groups — making a Type 2 error — or in some other case we might erroneously reject a true null hypothesis — making a Type 1 error. In some situations, one-tailed tests are more error-prone than two-tailed tests. We have argued on other grounds that two-tailed tests are more often appropriate, so the present findings strengthen our argument that two-tailed tests are usually to be preferred. Where both samples are as large as 25 or 30, the effects of heterogeneity and nonnormality are essentially negligible. Tests that are not greatly impaired by a considerable degree of violation of their assumptions — requirements — are said to be **robust** (Box, 1953). Thus, the t test can be described as quite robust in many cases. To summarize, wherever possible use samples as large as 25 or 30; make the sample sizes as nearly equal as practicable, especially for small samples; and run two-tailed tests unless the logic of an experiment clearly demands a one-directional alternative hypothesis.

5. Independent Measurements. The two groups may be random samples drawn from the same population, or may consist of two randomized groups made up by dividing an existing group — a classroom, for example — using the procedures described earlier. In other cases, we may wish to compare naturally occurring classes of people — men and women, or Democrats and Republicans. In all of these cases, we have different subjects in the two groups, and we make sure that our choice of any particular subject is not influenced by our choice of any other subject. In Chapter 12, we will develop a procedure for dealing with matched groups of subjects, but the present independent 2-sample t test requires independent groups. We must also make sure that no subject's performance is allowed to influence any other subject's performance on our measurement of the dependent variable.

Ordinal Scales

The Mann-Whitney U Test

The test we are about to describe is usually attributed to Mann and Whitney (1947). Other workers, most notably Wilcoxon (1945), had proposed very similar test procedures earlier, but Mann and Whitney are usually credited with the more extensive development of these procedures.

The Mann-Whitney U test is used in comparing two independent groups of subjects where the measurements comprise an ordinal scale — that is, where the measurements consist of a set of ranks. The U test is also useful where measurements are on an interval or ratio scale, but where the requirements for the independent 2-sample t test cannot be met. For example, where there are very great departures from a normal distribution, or where the variances within groups differ grossly, the Mann-Whitney U is more appropriate than a t test.

In order to explain the logic of the U test, we will first consider a comparison between two very small groups, one having two subjects and the other having three. We will then extend those procedures to making comparisons between larger groups.

Logic of the U Test

Suppose an industrial psychologist wishes to compare job satisfaction in a group of three production workers and a group of two supervisors. The sample sizes here are of course unrealistically small, but will serve to introduce most of the features of the U test. The workers are designated Group A and the supervisors Group B. On the basis of interviews, the psychologist arranges the subjects in ascending rank order of their judged job satisfaction, as in Table 9-5, larger numbers indicating greater satisfaction. Notice that the

TABLE 9-5.   Job Satisfaction Among Workers (Group A) and Supervisors (Group B). High Ranks Mean Greater Satisfaction.

Ranks	1	2	3	4	5	$U_A = 1 =$ Number of times $A > B$
Subjects	A	A	B	A	B	$U_B = 5 =$ Number of times $B > A$

arrangement in rank order is without regard to group membership. For the present, we will assume that there are no ties between any of the measures of job satisfaction. Later, we will present a procedure for dealing with the ties that often occur in real data.

The Null and Alternative Hypotheses.   Under the null hypothesis in the U test, the two groups of subjects represent independent random samples drawn from a single population. If the null hypothesis is true, then the ranks of the subjects in Group A should not differ significantly from the ranks in Group B. In that case, the probability that the rank of any randomly chosen A will exceed that of a randomly chosen B is no greater than the probability that the rank of a B will exceed that of an A. Since we have ruled out — for the present — any ties between subjects, those two probabilities are both equal to 1/2. Thus, when the null hypothesis is true, the probability that the rank of any particular A exceeds that of any particular B, is equal to 1/2, but if the null hypothesis is *not* true, then that probability will either be greater than or less than 1/2. Thus, we can state the null and alternative hypotheses in the following ways:

H_0: $P(A > B) = .5$;

H_1: $P(A > B) > .5$;

H_2: $P(A > B) < .5$.

The above hypotheses appear quite different from the ones we have previously formulated for Z tests and t tests of the differences between sample means. Indeed, the null hypothesis for the U test is a probability statement, while for Z and t, H_0 is a statement that two population parameters are equal, that is, $\mu_1 = \mu_2$. Thus, in running Z and t tests, we are in effect estimating the values of population parameters — that is, the means of the populations from which the two samples were drawn. But the U test compares only the *ranks* of measurements in two independent groups. Since no population parameters are estimated or directly compared, the U test is often called a **nonparametric test.** The U test is also called a **distribution-free test,** since the test is free of the assumption of a normal distribution — or indeed, any assumption at all regarding the shape or variability of the distribution from which the two independent samples are drawn.

The Two U Statistics.   We can test the null hypothesis somewhat indirectly by finding the values of the following statistics: U_A, which is the number of times the rank of each A exceeds the rank of a B; and U_B, which is the number of times the rank of each B exceeds the rank of an A. We will refer to U_A and U_B as the **U statistics.** Sometimes, we will refer to U_A and U_B—either or both—simply as U.

In Table 9-5, in only one case does the rank of any A exceed that of any B: Rank 4 is occupied by an A, while Rank 3 is occupied by a B. Thus, the value of U_A is equal to 1. The value of U_B is equal to 5, since the B in Rank 3 exceeds the ranks of 2 As and the B in Rank 5 exceeds 3 As. It is always possible to find the values of U_A and U_B by the counting methods we have just described, but those methods become very tedious and error-prone for all but the smallest sample sizes. We will develop an easy method of calculating the U statistics, and then we will explain their use in hypothesis testing. As you may suppose, there are tables of critical values of U which we will explain shortly.

Calculating the U Statistics. Table 9-6 lists all of the 10 possible sequences of 3 As and 2 Bs that can be arranged. We let N_A and N_B, respectively, equal the number of subjects in Groups A and B, and we let R_A

TABLE 9-6. All Possible Sequences of 3 As and 2 Bs.

Sequence Number	Rank 1	2	3	4	5	Rank Sum R_A	R_B	Number of Times A > B U_A	Number of Times B > A U_B	$P(U_A)$	$P(U_B)$
1	A	A	A	B	B	6	9	0	6	.10	.10
2	A	A	B	A	B	7	8	1	5	.10	.10
3	A	B	A	A	B	8	7	2	4	.20	.20
4	A	A	B	B	A	8	7				
5	B	A	A	A	B	9	6	3	3	.20	.20
6	A	B	A	B	A	9	6				
7	B	A	A	B	A	10	5	4	2	.20	.20
8	A	B	B	A	A	10	5				
9	B	A	B	A	A	11	4	5	1	.10	.10
10	B	B	A	A	A	12	3	6	0	.10	.10
										1.00	1.00

N_A = Number of As $\qquad$ N_B = Number of Bs

R_A = Sum of A ranks $\qquad$ R_B = Sum of B ranks

$$U_A = R_A - \frac{N_A(N_A + 1)}{2} \qquad U_B = R_B - \frac{N_B(N_B + 1)}{2} \qquad U_A + U_B = N_A N_B$$

$$= R_A - 6 \qquad\qquad\qquad = R_B - 3 \qquad\qquad\qquad = 6$$

and R_B equal the sums of the ranks in those groups. In the first sequence in Table 9-6, the value of U_A is equal to zero, since none of the 3 As is greater than either B. But U_B is equal to 6 in that sequence, since each of the 2 Bs has a greater rank than each of the 3 As. In the tenth sequence, where each A exceeds every B, U_A equals 6 while U_B equals zero. Thus, there is a complementary relationship between U_A and U_B: When one is at its minimum value of zero, the other is at its maximum value of $N_A N_B$, regardless of sample sizes.

The relationships between U_A and R_A and between U_B and R_B make it possible to derive simple computational formulas for U_A and U_B. Table 9-6 shows that the value of U_A for every sequence is equal to R_A minus a constant, 6. That constant, 6, is the minimum possible value of the sum of any 3 ranks. The table shows that R_A, the sum of the 3 ranks of Group A, ranges from 6 through 12 inclusive; R_A is at its minimum value in Sequence 1 where the A ranks are at their lowest possible values, namely 1, 2, and 3. The table also shows that each value of U_B is equal to R_B minus a constant, 3, which is the minimum value of a sum of 2 ranks. R_B is at its minimum value of 3 in Sequence 10, where the B ranks are at their lowest possible values, namely, 1 and 2. Since any set of ranks, 1 through N inclusive, is an arithmetic progression whose sum is N(N + 1)/2, it follows that the minimum value of R_A is $N_A(N_A + 1)/2$, and the minimum value of R_B is $N_B(N_B + 1)/2$. Thus, we can write the following computational formulas for the U statistics:

$$U_A = R_A - \frac{N_A(N_A + 1)}{2};$$
(9-22)

$$U_B = R_B - \frac{N_B(N_B + 1)}{2};$$
(9-23)

Check Sum: $U_A + U_B = N_A N_B.$
(9-24)

The check sum, above, utilizes the complementary relationship between U_A and U_B. For each of the sequences in Table 9-6, the sum of U_A and U_B is equal to 6, which is equal to $N_A N_B$. If U_A and U_B do not add up to $N_A N_B$, then you have made an error in your calculations.

The Distribution of U.   We can find the probability of observing any value of U_A or U_B by considering the probabilities of observing the various sequences of As and Bs shown in Table 9-6. If the null hypothesis is true, then each sequence in Table 9-6 represents a possible outcome of a probability experiment consisting of randomly assigning the ranks 1 through 5 to the 3 subjects in Group A and the 2 subjects in Group B. We could carry out such a probability experiment in the following way.

Suppose we let 3 identical white marbles represent the subjects in Group A and 2 identical black marbles represent the subjects in Group B. We place the 5 marbles in an urn, and we randomly draw the marbles one at a time without replacement. The first marble which is drawn is assigned the rank of 1, the second the rank of 2, and so on until all the marbles are drawn. Each time a white marble is drawn, we write an A under the rank corresponding to that draw, and each time a black marble is drawn, we write a B under the rank corresponding to that draw. Our probability experiment consists of drawing all five marbles, and each time we perform the experiment we observe one of the sequences of As and Bs shown in Table 9-6.

Now consider the number of ways the 3 white marbles can occupy 3 of the 5 ranks. (When the white marbles occupy any particular combination of 3 ranks, the black marbles of course occupy the remaining 2 ranks.) The problem here is formally identical to the kind of problem we solved in connection with our development of the binomial probability experiment in Chapter 7. The number of ways that 3 white and 2 black marbles can be distributed among 5 ranks is exactly equal to the number of ways 3 heads and 2 tails can be distributed among 5 coins — that is, the number of combinations of 5 things taken 3 at a time. In general, if the number of As and Bs are N_A and N_B, then the number of different sequences of As and Bs is equal to the number of combinations of $(N_A + N_B)$ things taken N_A (or N_B) at a time. The number of combinations of N things taken S (or $N - S$) at a time is given by Formula 6-26:

$$C_S^N = \frac{N!}{S!(N - S)!}. \tag{6-26}$$

Letting $N = N_A + N_B$ and $S = N_A$ (or N_B), and substituting in 6-26, we have

$$
\begin{array}{l}
\text{Number of possible} \\
\text{sequences of} \\
N_A \text{ As and } N_B \text{ Bs}
\end{array}
= \frac{(N_A + N_B)!}{N_A!(N_A + N_B - N_A)!} = \frac{(N_A + N_B)!}{N_A! \, N_B!}. \tag{9-25}
$$

Besides representing the number of possible sequences of As and Bs in our present situation, Formula 9-25 gives in general the number of ways in which any set of objects can be divided between two categories when N_A of the objects are placed in one category and the remaining N_B objects are placed in the other category.

Using 9-25 to find the number of sequences of the 3 As and 2 Bs in Table 9-6 yields the following:

$$
\begin{array}{l}
\text{Number of} \\
\text{sequences}
\end{array}
= \frac{(3 + 2)!}{3!2!} = \frac{5!}{3!2!} = \frac{5 \cdot 4 \cdot \cancel{3} \cdot \cancel{2} \cdot \cancel{1}}{\cancel{3} \cdot \cancel{2} \cdot \cancel{1} \cdot 2 \cdot 1} = \frac{20}{2} = 10.
$$

Thus, Formula 9-25 yields the same number of sequences as we have listed in Table 9-7. Where the sample sizes are very small, it is fairly easy to list all of the possible sequences, but that procedure becomes tedious even for modest sample sizes. Formula 9-25 allows us to find the number of sequences very easily no matter how large the samples may be.

If the null hypothesis is true, then all 10 sequences of 3 As and 2 Bs are equally probable, and thus the probability of each sequence is .10. Each of the sequences in Table 9-6 yields a particular value of U_A, and also of U_B. Thus, whatever probability is associated with U_A is also associated with U_B in any particular sequence. Notice that in some cases 2 sequences yield the same value of U_A. Since we know the probability of each sequence, we can now find the probability associated with each value of U_A, as shown in Table 9-6. Where two different sequences result in the same value of U_A, the probability of observing that particular value is equal to the sum of the probabilities of the different sequences of As and Bs resulting in that value of U_A. Table 9-6 shows that U_A is a symmetrically distributed discrete random variable whose expected value is 3. As we noted earlier, the values of U_A and U_B are complementary, and thus the distribution of U_B has the same expected value and the same symmetrical shape as the distribution of U_A. In general, the expected value of U—and by this we mean U_A or U_B—is equal to $N_A N_B / 2$.

After all of the preceding developments, we are now in a position to test the significance of the observed difference in job satisfaction between workers and supervisors. In Table 9-5, supervisors are more satisfied, as indicated by their higher ranks. Indeed, U_B—the number of times a supervisor's rank exceeds that of a worker—is equal to 5, while U_A—the number of times a worker's rank exceeds that of a supervisor—is equal to 1. Referring to Table 9-6, the probability of observing a value of U as large or larger than 5 is .20. Since a 2-tailed test is appropriate, we must also take into account the probability of a value of U as small or smaller than 1, which is the complement of 5, and which represents a value in the lower tail of the U distribution. Thus, the probability of the results in Table 9-6 occurring just by chance is .40, and thus we cannot reject the null hypothesis. Indeed, the most extreme values of U that are possible in comparing such small groups—values of 0 and 6—would not allow the rejection of H_0, as you can see by noting the probabilities associated with those U values in Table 9-6. Thus, it would be pointless to design such a small study for real research purposes, but considering such a study has been instructive in developing some of the principles of the U test. We now consider a somewhat larger study.

Schizophrenia is the most prevalent category of psychosis, accounting for about 30% of first admissions to mental hospitals. In some cases, the onset of schizophrenia is slow, taking place over a period of months or years. In other cases the onset is rapid, occurring in a matter of days or weeks, perhaps in response to some traumatic event. The disorder has been called **process schizophrenia** where the onset is slow, and **reactive schizophrenia** where the onset is rapid (Higgins & Peterson, 1966). Is there any difference between the rate of recovery among process and reactive schizophrenics?

We can consider the length of a schizophrenic patient's hospitalization as an indication of the rate of recovery. Suppose we have a sample of four process and five reactive schizophrenics, all of whom were admitted to a particular mental hospital during a particular period of time. The patients were released after the lengths of time in months shown in Table 9-7. Since we have two independent groups of subjects, and since our dependent variable —elapsed time—is measured on a ratio scale,[1] it might occur to you to run a t

---

[1] Elapsed time has a meaningful, absolute zero, while calendar time does not. Thus, elapsed time is a ratio scale, while calendar time is an interval scale (see Chapter 1).

TABLE 9-7.   Hospitalization in Months for Process and Reactive Schizophrenics.

	Process	Reactive
	9	2
	14	3
	25	5
	58	6
		11
Mean	26.50	5.40
Median	19.50	5.00
Variance	485.67	12.30

test. But first, look at the data carefully. One of the scores in the Process group is much greater than any of the other scores in that group. The data in Table 9-7 show that the mean of the Process group is substantially greater than the median, and thus those scores are strongly positively skewed rather than normally distributed. The range of scores is considerably larger in the Process group, and indeed, the variance is more than 40 times as large as the variance of the Reactive group. Such grossly unequal variances would occur with a probability of less than .01 if the Process and Reactive groups were random samples drawn from a single normally distributed population of patients.[2] Although the t test is robust in most situations, our present data strongly violate the requirement of equality (homogeneity) of variances and appear to violate the requirement of normality as well.

Fortunately, the Mann-Whitney U test provides an excellent alternative to the t test in our present situation. The U test requires no assumption of normality or homogeneity of variance. Since the U test requires only that we be able to place our subjects in rank order, we can easily meet that requirement by reducing our ratio scale to an ordinal scale.

The four Process and five Reactive patients listed in Table 9-7 are arranged in ascending rank order of months of hospitalization in Table 9-8. The values of U_A and U_B are calculated by Formulas 9-22 and 9-23, and the check sum by 9-24. The final step in running a U test is to compare the observed value of U_A with the critical values, as in the lower portion of Table 9-8. In the next section, we will explain how those critical values are determined.

Critical Values of U.   Consider the number of possible sequences of 4 Ps and 5 Rs in the ranks of the 9 schizophrenic patients. Applying Formula 9-25 shows that there are 126 such sequences. Since all of the sequences are equally probable, the probability of each one is $1/126 = .007937$. Table 9-9 lists some selected sequences that are of special interest—that is, sequences yielding extreme value of U. For clarity, only the Ps are shown in that table. In each sequence, all of the 5 blank spaces are occupied by Rs. The sequences are listed in a systematic order beginning with the case where the rank of every P

---

[2] In a later chapter, we will explain the F ratio, a statistic for comparing two variances.

TABLE 9-8.   The Mann-Whitney U Test for Process (P) and Reactive (R) Schizophrenics. Length of Hospitalization in Months.

Months	2	3	5	6	9	11	14	25	58
Ranks	1	2	3	4	5	6	7	8	9
Subjects	R	R	R	R	P	R	P	P	P

Process group: $N_P = 4$ Reactive group: $N_R = 5$

$$U_P = R_P - \frac{N_P(N_P + 1)}{2}$$ $$U_R = R_R - \frac{N_R(N_R + 1)}{2}$$

$$= 29 - \frac{4(5)}{2}$$ $$= 16 - \frac{5(6)}{2}$$

$$= 29 - 10 = 19.$$ $$= 16 - 15 = 1.$$

Check sum: $U_A + U_B = N_A N_B$,
$$19 + 1 = 4(5),$$
$$20 = 20.$$

$H_0: P(P > R) = .5$ Two-tailed critical values from Table C: $LCV_{.05} = 1$, $UCV_{.05} = 19$.
$H_1: P(P > R) > .5$ Since $U_P = 19$, and since $19 \geq UCV_{.05}$, reject H_0 in favor of H_1
$H_2: P(P > R) < .5$ at the .05 level.

exceeds that of every R and ending with the sequence where no P exceeds any R. The two tails of the distribution of sequences are the most interesting parts, so we have omitted a great many sequences in the middle, namely, sequences 8 through 119. For each sequence, the table shows the value of R_A, the sum of the ranks for the P group. The values of U_A were found using Formula 9-22. As in our previous example, two or more sequences sometimes result in the same value of U_A. In every case, the probability associated with any value of U_A is

TABLE 9-9.   Some Selected Sequences of 4 Ps and 5 Rs. For Clarity, Ranks Occupied by Rs Are Left Blank.

Sequence	1	2	3	4	5	6	7	8	9	R_P	U_P	$P(U_P)$	$P(U_P$ or more)	$P(U_P$ or less)
1						P	P	P	P	30	20	.007937	.007937	
2				P			P	P	P	29	19	.007937	.015874	
3			P				P	P	P	28	18	.015874	.031748	
4				P	P			P	P	28				
5		P					P	P	P	27				
6			P		P			P	P	27	17	.023811	.055559	
7					P	P	P		P	27				
.														
.														
.														
120	P		P	P	P					13				
121	P	P		P		P				13	3	.023811		.055559
122	P	P	P				P			13				
123	P	P		P	P					12	2	.015874		.031748
124	P	P	P			P				12				
125	P	P	P		P					11	1	.007937		.015874
126	P	P	P	P						10	0	.007937		.007937

the sum of the probabilities of the sequences resulting in that value of U_A. (We could, of course, list the value of U_B for each of the sequences in Table 9-9, but that is unnecessary for our present purposes.)

Now consider Sequence 2 in Table 9-9, which corresponds to the observed ranking of the 9 schizophrenics. The value of U_A associated with that sequence is 19, and the table shows that the probability of observing a value of 19 *or more* is equal to .015874. Large values of U_A are associated with sequences where the ranks of large numbers of Ps exceed the ranks of Rs. Now consider Sequence 125. The value of U_A associated with that sequence is 1, and the probability of observing a value of 1 *or less* is also equal to .015874. Small values of U_A are associated with sequences where the ranks of small numbers of Ps exceed the ranks of Rs. Thus, the probability that U_A is *greater than or equal to 19* or *less than or equal to 1* is given by $2(.015874) = .031748$. The preceding relationship can be expressed more compactly in symbols:

$$P(U \geq 19) + P(U \leq 1) = .031748. \tag{9-26}$$

Now consider the probability that U is *greater than or equal to 18* or *less than or equal to 2*. That probability is given by $2(.031748) = .063496$. In symbols,

$$P(U \geq 18) + P(U \leq 2) = .063496. \tag{9-27}$$

Since Equation 9-26 is a probability less than .05 and 9-27 is greater than .05, it follows that the U_A values of 1 and 19 are critical values for a two-tailed test of the null hypothesis at the .05 level. The lower critical value ($LCV_{.05}$) of U defines a lower rejection region and the upper critical value ($UCV_{.05}$) defines an upper rejection region. For an observed value of U_A at or above the $UCV_{.05}$ we would reject the null hypothesis in favor of H_1, the alternative hypothesis that states that the length of hospitalization is greater for Process schizophrenics. For an observed value of U_A at or below the $LCV_{.05}$ we would reject H_0 in favor of H_2, the alternative hypothesis that the length of hospitalization is greater for Reactive schizophrenics. Critical values for the U test are listed in Table C. The margins of that table show the values of N_A and N_B. In the body of the table, there are two numbers presented for each combination of N_A and N_B. The smaller number is the LCV and the larger number is the UCV for a test at a given level of significance. Since U_A and U_B are complementary, if the observed value of U_A falls in one rejection region, then the observed value of U_B will fall in the other; and if U_A does not fall in one of the rejection regions, then neither will U_B. Thus, in so far as rejecting the null hypothesis is concerned, it does not matter whether you use U_A or U_B as your test statistic. But since U_A is the number of times that the rank of each P exceeds that of an R, and U_B the number of times each R exceeds a P, an observed value of U_A in the upper rejection region would lead us to accept the alternative hypothesis that *Process* schizophrenics are hospitalized significantly longer, while an observed value of U_B in the upper rejection region would lead us to accept an alternative hypothesis that *Reactive* schizophrenics are hospitalized significantly longer.

Wherever dashes appear in the U table, no decision is possible. For each level of significance covered by the table, there are some combinations of small sample sizes where it is not possible to carry out a test. For example, it is not possible to run a test at the .05 level where $N_A = 3$ and $N_B = 2$, as we found in our comparison of job satisfaction in workers and supervisors. Accordingly, Table C lists no critical values for those sample sizes. In planning an experiment where the U test will be run, Table C should be consulted in order to determine the sample sizes necessary for a test at the conventional significance level of .05 or less.

One- and Two-Tailed Tests. We can run either a one-tailed or a two-tailed U test, just as in every other test procedure we have described so far. Here, as in every other situation, the decision to run a one- or two-tailed test should be made before collecting the data — and once made, should be adhered to. The logic of an experiment or other kind of study will determine whether a one- or two-tailed test is appropriate.

Suppose for the moment that you are interested only in the question of whether Process schizophrenics require longer hospitalization. *Before* collecting your data, if you can be certain that you will have absolutely no interest in the possibility that *Reactive* schizophrenics might require longer hospitalization, then you are justified in running a one-tailed test, where H_1 is your single alternative hypothesis. In that case, Table 9-9 shows that the critical value of U_A for a one-tailed test at the .05 level is equal to 18, since

$$P(U_A \geq 18) = .031748 \qquad \text{and} \qquad P(U_A \geq 17) = .055559.$$

In the one-tailed U test, we place all of the significance probability under one tail of the U distribution, and thus we have a single rejection region. But in the two-tailed test, we divide the significance probability equally between the two tails of the distribution, and thus we have two rejection regions. As you can see, the same principles apply to one- and two-tailed U tests as apply to Z and t tests.

Tied Ranks. In a formal sense, the U test requires an ordinal scale where every subject has a unique rank. An interval or ratio scale can easily be reduced to such a set of ranks, provided there are no ties between any of the measurements. But in the real world, ties often occur in data measured on interval or ratio scales in cases where it may be desirable to use the U test. Fortunately, ties are of no consequence in some cases, and of little consequence in others — especially where the sample sizes are fairly substantial.

In the first section of Table 9-10, the months of hospitalization and the ranks of the schizophrenic patients are listed. There are no ties between any of the measurements on these subjects in the first section of the table. We will now examine the effects of ties between some of the measurements. Suppose that 2 subjects were hospitalized for 3 months, and 3 subjects for 58 months, as in the second section of the table. The procedure for dealing with ties is to assign to each of the tied subjects the average of the ranks those subjects

TABLE 9-10. Some Comparisons of Rank Sums and U Statistics With and Without Ties. Data Modified After Table 9-8.

| | \multicolumn{9}{c}{Ranks} | | | | |
	1	2	3	4	5	6	7	8	9	R_P	U_P	R_R	U_R
Months	2	3	5	6	9	11	14	25	58				
Subjects	R	R	R	R	P	R	P	P	P				
Ranks, no ties	1	2	3	4	5	6	7	8	9	29	19	16	1
Months	2	3	3	6	9	11	58	58	58				
Subjects	R	R	R	R	P	R	P	P	P				
Ranks, with ties	1	2.5	2.5	4	5	6	8	8	8	29	19	16	1
Months	2	3	5	6	6	11	14	25	58				
Subjects	R	R	R	R	P	R	P	P	P				
Ranks, with ties	1	2	3	4.5	4.5	6	7	8	9	28.5	18.5	15.5	1.5

would have in the absence of ties. Actually, that is easier to do than it sounds, as you can see by referring to Table 9-10. The ties we have just described have absolutely no effect on the values of U_A and U_B. Ties that occur *within* groups of subjects — within runs of Rs and Ps in our present example — never affect the value of U, providing the ties are dealt with in the way we have described.

It might occur to you that ties could be handled in a simpler appearing way. Perhaps the two subjects having scores of 3 months could be considered tied for second place in our list of ranks, and perhaps the three subjects having scores of 58 months could then be considered tied for sixth place. But in that case, the sums of the ranks in the two groups, R_A and R_B, would change, and so would the values of U.

Now consider the third section of Table 9-10. Here, there is a tie between a Reactive and a Process patient. Although we have handled the tie in the same way as before, the value of U_A is lower and the value of U_B is higher than before. The present tie reduces the value of U_A below the upper critical value and raises the value of U_B above the lower critical value, and thus the null hypothesis could not be rejected, were such a tie to occur. Ties that occur *between* groups of subjects — between runs of Rs and Ps in our present example — affect the value of U_A in such a way as to reduce the probability of rejecting the null hypothesis. In the presence of such ties, the effective α level is somewhat lower than the **nominal α level,** that is, the significance level associated with a particular critical value. Thus, when ties occur, the U test is more **conservative** in that we are less likely to make a Type 1 error, but we are more likely to make a Type 2 error. For the most part, our procedure for handling ties is adequate, but when large numbers of ties occur, other procedures are available (Siegel, 1956).

The U Test for Large Samples. Table C presents critical values of U for sample sizes where N_A and N_B are each as large as 20. For larger sample sizes, U is very nearly normally distributed. Thus, it is possible to develop a

normal approximation to U that is similar to our normal approximation to the binomial. Mosteller and Rourke (1973) present a normal approximation to U that is suitable for larger sample sizes.

Requirements for the U Test.   The assumptions underlying the U test are set out in Table 9-11. The test requires an ordinal scale, or an interval or ratio scale that is reduced to a set of ranks, preferably without ties. When ties occur, they can be dealt with by the procedures described earlier. Every measurement must be independent of every other measurement. For example, no subject can be measured twice—neither as a member of a single group, nor as a member of both groups. In Chapter 12, we will develop tests utilizing repeated measures on the same subjects, but the U test requires independent measurements.

TABLE 9-11.   Requirements for the Mann-Whitney U Test.

1. Ordinal measurement scale, or an interval or ratio scale reduced to a set of ranks.
2. Two independent groups, where every measure is independent of every other measure.

Comparing the U Test and the t Test.   The U test may require somewhat less arithmetic than a t test, but where the data meet the t requirements reasonably well, the t test is more powerful—that is more sensitive. If the measurements constitute an interval or ratio scale, then reducing those measurements to a set of ranks destroys some of the information contained in the data, as we have pointed out earlier. Running a U test where t is appropriate increases the probability of a Type 2 error. But if measurements on an interval or ratio scale are badly skewed, or if the measurements differ greatly from a normal distribution in some other way, or if the variances in the two samples are grossly unequal, then a U test is appropriate. In that case, running a t test would increase the probability of a Type 1 error under some conditions and a Type 2 error under other conditions.

Nominal Scales

Suppose we are interested in comparing the proportion of high-school graduates who enrolled in college in 1950 with the proportion who enrolled in 1975. We might approach this problem by comparing college attendance in the 1950 and 1975 graduating classes from a particular high school. Suppose that 80 out of 194 students in the 1950 class went to college, and 113 out of 217 went to college in 1975. Thus, .412 of the 1950 class and .521 of the 1975 class went on to college. The question is, Do these proportions differ significantly? Our observations constitute a nominal scale having only two categories, college and noncollege. Since those two categories are mutually exclusive and exhaustive, and since we have two independent groups of subjects, we can develop a suitable test of **independent proportions** based on the normal approximation to the binomial.

The Binomial Test of a Difference between Independent Proportions

We begin by listing one of the equations for the normal approximation to the binomial, which we developed earlier in Chapter 7:

$$Z_X = \frac{(X \pm .5) - Np}{\sqrt{Npq}}; \qquad \begin{array}{l} +.5 \text{ when } X \leq N_p, \\ -.5 \text{ when } X \geq N_p. \end{array} \qquad (7\text{-}16)$$

The .5 in the above equation is the correction for continuity, as explained in Chapter 7. The binomial random variable X is the number of successes observed in N binomial trials. Remember, a success occurs when the outcome of a trial falls into one of two mutually exclusive and exhaustive categories, and a failure occurs when the outcome falls into the other category. We can find the **observed proportion of successes,** designated capital P, by dividing X, the observed *number* of successes, by N. Similarly, dividing the expected number of successes, Np, by N yields the **expected proportion of success,** the binomial probability p. Dividing the numerator and denominator of Equation 7-16 by N yields the **normal approximation to a binomial proportion, Z_P:**

$$Z_P = \frac{\left(\dfrac{X}{N} \pm \dfrac{.5}{N}\right) - \dfrac{Np}{N}}{\sqrt{\dfrac{Npq}{N^2}}} = \frac{\left(P \pm \dfrac{.5}{N}\right) - p}{\sqrt{\dfrac{pq}{N}}}; \qquad \begin{array}{l} +\dfrac{.5}{N} \text{ when } P \leq p, \\[2ex] -\dfrac{.5}{N} \text{ when } P \geq p. \end{array} \qquad (9\text{-}28)$$

Do not confuse the capital P and the small p in Equation 9-28. The capital P is the *observed* proportion of successes, while the small p is the *expected* proportion — and also the probability of a success on a single binomial trial, as in our earliest discussion of the binomial distribution. Thus, P is an observed sample statistic, and p is a population parameter. The numerator of Equation 9-28 is the deviation between an observed proportion — corrected for continuity — and an expected proportion, and the denominator is the standard deviation of the observed binomial proportion P. Thus, Equation 9-28 is a critical ratio for testing an observed binomial proportion against its expected value under the null hypothesis.

Besides playing a role in our present development, Equation 9-28 is useful in its own right. When Np and Nq are both equal to 5 or more, Z_P — like Z_X — will be approximately normally distributed and can be evaluated for significance by referring to Table A. Wherever the normal approximation to the binomial is appropriate, as described in Chapter 7, the normal approximation to a binomial proportion is also appropriate and will produce identical results in terms of statistical significance.

Returning to the problem of testing the significance of a difference between two observed proportions, suppose we have two independent samples of sizes N_1 and N_2. It does not matter whether the sample sizes are equal or unequal. For each sample, we have an observed binomial proportion, corrected for continuity:

$$\text{Proportion}_1 = P_1 \pm \frac{.5}{N_1} \qquad \text{and} \qquad \text{Proportion}_2 = P_2 \pm \frac{.5}{N_2}.$$

The expected values of those proportions are

$$E(\text{Proportion}_1) = p_1 \qquad \text{and} \qquad E(\text{Proportion}_2) = p_2,$$

and their variances are

$$\sigma_1^2 = \frac{p_1 q_1}{N_1} \qquad \text{and} \qquad \sigma_2^2 = \frac{p_2 q_2}{N_2}.$$

Since we have expressions for the expected values and the variances of two independent binomial proportions, and since those proportions will be nearly normally distributed for moderate sample sizes, we are now able to devise a Z test for the difference between two binomial proportions. The present Z test is formally identical to the Z test of a difference between sample means which we developed earlier in this chapter. By analogy with Equation 9-7 we write

$$Z_{(P_1 - P_2)} = \frac{\left[\left(P_1 \pm \frac{.5}{N_1}\right) - \left(P_2 \pm \frac{.5}{N_2}\right)\right] - \left[p_1 - p_2\right]}{\sqrt{\dfrac{p_1 q_1}{N_1} + \dfrac{p_2 q_2}{N_2}}}, \tag{9-29}$$

where $Z_{(P_1 - P_2)}$ is the Z-score associated with the observed difference between P_1 and P_2.

The Null Hypothesis.   Under the null hypothesis, Sample 1 and Sample 2 are random samples drawn from the same population. Thus, we can state the null and alternative hypotheses symbolically as follows:

$H_0\colon p_1 = p_2;$

$H_1\colon p_1 > p_2;$

$H_2\colon p_1 < p_2.$

Under the null hypothesis, since $p_1 = p_2$, the quantity $(p_1 - p_2)$ is equal to zero and thus vanishes from the numerator of 9-29. In that respect, that equation is quite analogous to 9-7, where the quantity $(\mu_1 - \mu_2)$ also vanishes from the numerator. If we let p_c equal the probability of success in the **common,** single, population from which our two samples are drawn, then q_c

is the common probability of failure, and thus

$$p_1 = p_2 = p_C \quad \text{and} \quad q_C = 1 - p_C.$$

Substituting p_C and q_C in Equation 9-29,

$$Z_{(P_1-P_2)} = \frac{\left(P_1 \pm \dfrac{.5}{N_1}\right) - \left(P_2 \pm \dfrac{.5}{N_2}\right)}{\sqrt{\dfrac{p_C q_C}{N_1} + \dfrac{p_C q_C}{N_2}}}. \tag{9-30}$$

We can determine the value of p_C by combining the $N_1 + N_2$ observations in our two samples and then finding the total proportion of successes. Since there are X_1 successes in Sample 1 and X_2 successes in Sample 2,

$$p_C = \frac{X_1 + X_2}{N_1 + N_2} = \frac{N_1 P_1 + N_2 P_2}{N_1 + N_2}.$$

And since $p_C + q_C = 1$,

$$q_C = 1 - p_C.$$

Each correction for continuity in Equation 9-30 is made in the same way as in 9-28. The correction of $.5/N_1$ is added to or subtracted from P_1, depending on whether $P_1 \leq p_C$ or whether $P_1 \geq p_C$, and the correction for P_2 is made analogously. The net effect of the two corrections for continuity is to reduce the magnitude of the difference between P_1 and P_2, regardless of whether that difference is positive or negative. Thus, rearranging terms yields the computational formula for the **normal approximation to the difference between binomial proportions:**

$$Z_{(P_1-P_2)} = \frac{|P_1 - P_2| - .5\left(\dfrac{1}{N_1} + \dfrac{1}{N_2}\right)}{\sqrt{p_C q_C \left(\dfrac{1}{N_1} + \dfrac{1}{N_2}\right)}}; \tag{9-31}$$

where $p_C = \dfrac{X_1 + X_2}{N_1 + N_2}$, and $q_C = 1 - p_C$.

Returning to our example, the computational formula above was used to test the significance of the difference between the observed proportions of high-school graduates attending college in 1950 and 1975. The calculations are shown in Table 9-12. Clearly, we should run a two-tailed test, since we would be impressed by a significant increase or decrease in the proportion of high-school graduates attending college. When we reject the null hypothesis, we can decide between the alternative hypotheses by noting the relationship between P_1 and P_2, the observed proportions: When $P_1 > P_2$, accept H_1, the alternative that states that $p_1 > p_2$; and when $P_1 < P_2$, accept H_2. Remember, P_1 and P_2 are observed proportions — that is, sample statistics — while p_1 and

TABLE 9-12.   Z Test of a Difference Between Independent Binomial Proportions.

Group 1: 1950 graduates	Group 2: 1975 graduates
$N_1 = 194$	$N_2 = 217$
Number attending college $= X_1 = 80$	Number attending college $= X_2 = 113$
Proportion attending college $= P_1 = .412$	Proportion attending college $= P_2 = .521$

Applying Formula 9-31,

$$p_C = \frac{X_1 + X_2}{N_1 + N_2} = \frac{80 + 113}{194 + 217} = \frac{193}{411} = .470, \quad q_C = 1 - p_C = 1 - .470 = .530.$$

$$Z_{(P_1 - P_2)} = \frac{\left| P_1 - P_2 \right| - .5\left(\dfrac{1}{N_1} + \dfrac{1}{N_2}\right)}{\sqrt{p_C q_C \left(\dfrac{1}{N_1} + \dfrac{1}{N_2}\right)}} = \frac{\left| .412 - .521 \right| - .5\left(\dfrac{1}{194} + \dfrac{1}{217}\right)}{\sqrt{.470(.530)\left(\dfrac{1}{194} + \dfrac{1}{217}\right)}}$$

$$= \frac{\left| -.109 \right| - .5(.0098)}{\sqrt{.2491(.0098)}} = \frac{.109 - .0049}{\sqrt{.00244}} = \frac{.1041}{.0494} = 2.11.$$

$H_0: p_1 = p_2 = p_C$ Two-tailed critical values from Table A: $CV_{.05} = 1.96, CV_{.01} = 2.58.$
$H_1: p_1 > p_2$ Since $2.11 > 1.96$, $Z_{(P_1 - P_2)} > CV_{.05}$. Therefore, reject H_0 at the .05 level
$H_2: p_1 < p_2$ and accept H_2, since $P_1 < P_2$.

p_2 are expected proportions, population parameters. When we observe that P_1 is significantly less than P_2, as in our present example, we draw the inference that the population parameter p_1 is also less than the parameter p_2. In that case, it follows that our two samples are not drawn from a single population, but rather from two different populations having different values of p, the binomial probability of success.

Requirements for the Z Test of Binomial Proportions.   The requirements for the test are listed in Table 9-13 and are discussed below, where the numbered sections refer to corresponding portions of the table. The present test represents an extension of the binomial probability experiment, as you can see by comparing Table 9-13 with Table 7-1.

1. Independence.   Each observation (trial) must be independent of every other observation *within* each sample and *between* samples as well. An obvious way to violate that requirement — assumption — would be to observe some subjects twice, perhaps first as a member of one group and then as a member of the other group. That would of course be most unlikely in our example involving high-school graduates. We will develop procedures for dealing with repeated measures on the same subjects in Chapter 12. Our present test, however, requires independent observations.

TABLE 9-13. Requirements for the Z Test (Normal Approximation) of a Difference Between Independent Binomial Proportions.

1. Two independent samples consisting of N_1 and N_2 trials (observations) drawn from Population 1 and Population 2.
2. Each trial has two mutually exclusive and exhaustive possible outcomes, success and failure.
3. The probabilities — the expected proportions — of success and failure in Population 1 are respectively p_1 and q_1, and in Population 2, p_2 and q_2. Those probabilities do not change across trials, and further, $p_1 + q_1 = 1$, and $p_2 + q_2 = 1$.
4. The binomial random variables X_1 and X_2 are the observed numbers of successes in Samples 1 and 2; P_1 and P_2 are the *observed* proportions of successes.
5. The null hypothesis states that there is no difference between the values of p_1 and p_2 — that is, no difference between the *expected* proportions of success and failure in the two populations. In symbols, $p_1 = p_2 = p_C$.
6. The following products must all be greater than or equal to 5: $N_1 p_C$, $N_1 q_C$, $N_2 p_C$, and $N_2 q_C$,

where $p_C = \dfrac{X_1 + X_2}{N_1 + N_2}$ and $q_C = 1 - p_C$.

2. Nominal Measurement Scale. The present test, like the binomial probability experiment, depends on observing a success or a failure on each trial. Thus, the measurement scale is a **dichotomous** — two-valued — nominal scale. It is always possible to reduce any higher measurement scale to any lower one, and so the present test could be used with ordinal, interval, or ratio scales. For example, if we were interested in comparing the income of a group of women with the income of a group of men, we might **dichotomize** the income variable, in effect splitting the scale at some point into a High category and a Low category. We could then test the significance of any difference between the proportions of High incomes in the group of women and the group of men. But income is a ratio scale that contains a great deal more information than a nominal scale, and thus, dichotomizing a higher-caliber scale in order to use the present test would be wasteful, and would result in a loss of power.

3. The Probabilities of Success and Failure. These probabilities remain constant across trials, as the requirement of independence demands. For each population, the probabilities of success and failure sum to 1.00.

4. The Sample Statistics. The statistics of particular interest in the test of a difference between binomial proportions are P_1 and P_2, the *observed* proportions of success in the two samples. Since X_1 and X_2 are the numbers of successes in the two samples, dividing those statistics respectively by N_1 and N_2 yields P_1 and P_2.

5. The Null Hypothesis. If there is no difference between the two populations from which the two samples are drawn, then $p_1 = p_2 = p_C$. Since the variance of $(P_1 - P_2)$ depends on the actual value of p_C, that value must be determined as in Equation 9-34.

6. Some Limitations on the Use of the Test. The use of any Z test requires an approximately normal distribution. The difference between P_1 and P_2 will be normally distributed for moderate sample sizes, depending partly on the value of p_C, which in turn depends on the observed proportion of successes in both samples. *Each* of the four products listed in Table 9-13 must be at least as great as 5. (In that respect, the present test is quite comparable to the one-sample normal approximation to the binomial, which we developed in Chapter 7.) If any one of those four products is less than 5, then **Fisher's exact test** should be used (Siegel, 1956). Because of space limitations, that test cannot be presented here. Fisher's test is *exact* in the sense of determining actual binomial probabilities, rather than approximations to those probabilities, as the present test does. For smaller sample sizes, Fisher's exact test is a useful alternative to the present test.

Choosing a Test

The test procedures described in the present chapter, and earlier procedures as well, have been organized within the framework of the four kinds of measurement scales. Choosing a test turns out to be a matter of identifying the measurement scale — nominal, ordinal, interval, or ratio — and then finding a test procedure whose requirements best fit the nature of the data. The most powerful tests, Z and t, require the highest-caliber measurement scales, interval and ratio scales. Besides requiring an interval or ratio scale, those tests have other requirements, such as a normal distribution, and homogeneity of variances. When those other requirements are strongly violated, an interval or ratio scale can be reduced to an ordinal scale, and the Mann-Whitney U test can then be used. It is not necessary to derive an ordinal scale from a higher-caliber scale in order to use the U test; that test can be used wherever a set of measurements comprise an ordinal scale. The least powerful test — the binomial in its various forms — requires no more than a nominal scale, which is the lowest-caliber measurement scale.

There is a relationship between the power of a test — its ability to reject a false null hypothesis, that is, to detect a difference that truly exists — and the caliber of measurement scale that the test requires: More powerful tests require higher-caliber measurement scales. Thus, the process of "choosing" a test turns out to be less a matter of choice than a matter of finding the most powerful test whose requirements match the measurement scale and the other characteristics of the data. That is one of the reasons we have so strongly emphasized the requirements for the various kinds of tests.

Not only does the nature of the data determine the kind of test that can be run, but the kinds of tests that are available can — and should — influence the very nature of the data that are collected in experiments and observations. Before collecting any data, a researcher should carefully consider the kinds of statistical tests that are to be used. A little planning and forethought can pay great dividends. Indeed, we will devote considerable space to the topic of designing experiments and observations.

Terms and Symbols

Each of the four tests presented in the present chapter is designed to test the significance of a difference between two independent groups. Each test is most appropriate in a particular situation. Comparing and contrasting the following terms and symbols will help you to see the similarities and differences between these tests.

Independent groups	Normal approximation to
Expected value	binomial proportion
Observed value	Fisher's exact test
Correlation	$\overline{D}$
Standard error of the differ-	$Z_{\overline{D}}$
ence between means	$\mu_{\overline{D}}$
Critical ratio	$\sigma_{\overline{D}}$
Estimated standard error of	$E(\overline{D})$
difference between means	$S_{\overline{D}}$
Unbiased estimator of popula-	S
tion variance	$E(S^2)$
Sum of squares	df
Homogeneity of variance	SS
Heterogeneity of variance	ΣX^2
Robust	$(\Sigma X)^2$
Nonparametric test	N_G
Distribution-free test	U
Critical values	U_A and U_B
Tied ranks	R_A and R_B
Conservative test	P_1 and P_2
Normal approximation to U	p_1 and p_2
Independent proportions	p_c and q_c
Observed proportion	$Z_{(P_1-P_2)}$
Expected proportion	

EXERCISES AND STUDY QUESTIONS

1. The State Department of Education has developed a new test designed to assess primary reading skills in sixth-graders, the Basic Reading Achievement Test, or the BRAT. In a recent year, the mean and standard deviation were 50 and 10 for the population of pupils taking the test. At Pottersfield Acres Northwest Grade School, the 124 sixth-graders had a mean BRAT

score of 51.29, and at Pottersfield Acres Southeast, the mean was 53.60 for their 187 sixth-graders. Do those two schools differ significantly on their BRAT performance?

a. Justify the use of a Z test.

b. State the null and alternative hypotheses in words and symbols.

c. Is a 1 or 2-tailed test appropriate? Explain.

d. Do you reject H_0? If so, is it reasonable to conclude that one school does a better job teaching its pupils than the other?

2. Mr. Smith and Mr. Jones are sixth-grade teachers at Pottersfield Acres Northwest Grade School. By a strange coincidence, the mean of Jones's 30 sixth-graders on the BRAT was 51.29, identical to the mean of all the sixth-graders at Northwest. By a stranger coincidence, the mean of Smith's 28 sixth-graders was 53.60, identical to the mean BRAT score at Pottersfield Acres Southeast, as in Exercise 1 above. Therefore, Smith argues, if the pupils at Southeast are significantly better on the BRAT than the pupils at Northwest, then his pupils must be significantly better than Jones's. "Balderdash!" says Jones, who goes on to argue that only a naive, statistically unsophisticated person would draw such an unwarranted conclusion.

a. Who is right, Smith or Jones? Explain.

b. Carry out a test to settle the issue, stating the null and alternative hypotheses.

c. What bearing do the sample sizes have on the power of a test of a difference between means?

3. Before a midterm exam, a professor informed a class that no grades would be posted. Exam papers were to be graded and returned at the next meeting of the class. Who showed up at that meeting to claim their papers and get feedback on their performances as soon as possible? The scores of the students present and absent at the next meeting of the class are shown below. Is there any significant difference between the students who showed up and those who didn't?

Present:	64	59	40	52	56	68	85	83	77	68	70	80	71
Absent:	70	44	52	45	36	67							

a. Justify the use of a t test.

b. State the null and alternative hypotheses in words and symbols. Justify your use of a 1 or 2-tailed test.

c. Do you reject H_0?

d. Do the different levels of class attendance cause students to perform differently on exams, or do the different levels of exam performance cause the different levels of attendance?

e. Does this study represent an *experiment,* or a set of *observations*? Explain your answer, and explain what bearing this question has on the kinds of conclusions you can legitimately draw.

4. As some of your teachers may have told you, self-recitation is a prevalent study habit among more successful students. Self-recitation is not at all a matter of rote memorization, repeating something over and over to yourself until you have memorized it, but rather a process of comparing and contrasting ideas, asking yourself questions about the material to be learned, finding the answers to those questions, and so on. Does self-recitation really work? A researcher randomly assigns half of a class of 20 students to a self-recitation group and half to a nonrecitation group. (Randomization is described in detail in Chapter 13.) The nonrecitation group spends 1 hour reading and rereading a new chapter in introductory psychology without engaging in any self-recitation. For the self-recitation group, 10-minute periods of reading alternate with 10-minute periods of self-recitation during a total study time of 1 hour. Thus, for that group, 1/2 hour is spent in reading and 1/2 hour in self-recitation. After the 1-hour study period, all of the subjects take a 50-question multiple-choice exam covering the new chapter. Their scores are shown below.

Self-recitation group:	49	50	31	40	44	48	27	48	38	39
Nonrecitation group:	31	37	37	40	28	29	24	31	42	41

   a. Justify the use of a t test.
   b. State the null and alternative hypotheses in words and symbols, and justify your use of a 1 or 2-tailed test.
   c. Do you reject H_0?
   d. Is this study an experiment or an observation, and what difference would it make one way or the other?

5. Does violence on television influence children's behavior? An experimenter randomly assigns half of the 12 children in a preschool class to a control group and the other half to an experimental group, arranging things so that there are equal numbers of boys and girls in the two groups. (Such procedures are described and discussed in detail in Chapter 13.) The control group watches a 3-minute videotape showing children playing peacefully and cooperatively with a number of toys, while the experimental group watches a tape of the same children playing aggressively: Refusing to share, taking toys away from each other, engaging in verbal abuse, and finally pushing and shoving. After viewing the videotapes, all of the children are allowed to interact during a 15-minute period in a large room provided with a large number of various toys. The children are observed unobtrusively, and the number and kind of any aggressive behaviors are carefully noted by several observers. The researchers feel confident that they can fairly reliably place the children in rank order of aggressiveness, but because of the wide variety of aggressive behaviors, they have little confidence in their ability to achieve any higher caliber of measurements.

Suppose the results came out as shown below, where the subjects are arranged in increasing order of aggressiveness. Is there a significant difference between the control and experimental groups?

Ranks:	1	2	3	4	5	6	7	8	9	10	11	12
Subjects:	C	C	C	E	C	E	E	C	C	E	E	E

    a. Justify the use of a Mann-Whitney U test.

    b. Formulate the null and alternative hypotheses in words and symbols. Indicate whether a 1 or 2-tailed test is appropriate, and indicate whether you reject H_0.

    c. Is this study an experiment or an observation, and what difference does that distinction make?

6. The Aero Aces Flying School has very high standards, and also, unfortunately, a high failure rate. About 60% of its beginning students drop out before obtaining a Private Pilot's License. Slow-Roll Simmons, chief instructor at Aero Aces, has devised a new set of training procedures that he believes may increase the success ratio. Incoming students are randomly assigned, in equal numbers, to Slow-Roll's new training method and to the old method. Only 18 out of 50 students taught by the old method complete the program, but 30 out of 50 are successful under the new training method. Does the new method differ significantly from the old?

    a. Justify a Z test of binomial proportions.

    b. State the null and alternative hypotheses in words and symbols. Justify your use of a 1 or 2-tailed test, and indicate whether you reject H_0.

    c. How would you go about randomly assigning incoming students to the old and new methods in equal numbers?

    d. Is this study an experiment or an observation?

7. Suppose there were only 50 incoming students available at the Aero Aces Flying School, and suppose 9 out of 25 trained by the old method successfully completed the program while 15 out of 25 trained by the new method were successful.

    a. Compare the observed proportions of success under the two methods in the present exercise and in the preceding one.

    b. Do the methods differ significantly in the present exercise?

    c. What are the effects of the sample sizes on the power of a test of binomial proportions?

8. Is there a significant difference between the proportions of liberals and conservatives favoring the death penalty for felony murder, that is, murder committed during the perpetration of a robbery or other crime? Suppose there were 54 persons in a survey identifying themselves as liberals and 46 identifying themselves as conservatives. The number of persons favoring the death penalty were 28/54 liberals and 35/46 conservatives.

    a. Justify a Z test of binomial proportions.

b. State the null and alternative hypotheses in words and symbols. Indicate whether a 1 or 2-tailed test is appropriate, and indicate whether you reject H_0.

c. Is this study an experiment or an observation?

d. Does conservatism cause people to support the death penalty more strongly, or does strong support for the death penalty contribute to conservatism — that is, which is *cause,* and which is *effect?*

Correlation and Regression: Ratio and Interval Scales

10

We introduced some of the fundamental ideas of correlation in Chapter 1, and it is now time to consider those ideas in greater detail. The techniques described in this chapter are designed for use with the two highest-caliber measurement scales. Related techniques, adapted for use with ordinal and nominal scales, are described in the next chapter.

As we noted earlier, a **correlation** is a relationship between variables. For example, taller people tend to weigh more than shorter people, and thus the variables of height and weight are correlated, although not every tall person is heavier than every short person. Good students tend to do well on successive exams in a course, and also tend to perform well in different courses, although not every good Math student can also be expected to excel in English.

By **regression** we mean the process of estimating, or predicting, the value of one variable based on the observed value of some other variable. For example, we are often interested in using a test of academic aptitude to predict the future level of a high-school student's performance in college, or in using a battery of other aptitude tests to estimate a person's likelihood of success in a particular occupation. If there is a correlation between the scores on an aptitude test and the level of performance that we wish to predict in some situation — grade-point average in school, for example, or level of success in some occupation or profession — then we can often use that relationship to make useful predictions, within certain limitations.

To be useful, a psychological test must be *reliable* and *valid.* **Reliability** is the extent to which a test yields comparable measures when it is given a second time to the same subjects, perhaps days or weeks later. The correlation between the two test measures provides an indication of the reliability. **Validity** is the extent to which a test measures what it was designed to measure. For example, to be valid, a test of academic aptitude must correlate significantly with performance in school. Thus, correlations play a great role in the development of psychological tests.

We will begin by presenting some of the descriptive statistics of correlation and regression, that is, procedures for describing the magnitude and direction of relationships between variables observed in **samples.** We will then present some of the inferential statistics of correlation and regression, procedures for testing the statistical significance of observed correlations, and for drawing conclusions about relationships between variables in **populations.** Predicting the future value of some variable based on the present observation of some other variable is an exercise in inferential statistics that we will consider in detail.

Correlation

Figure 10-1 graphically illustrates a correlation between two variables, two successive examinations given in a course. We should ordinarily expect that students who do well on the first exam should also do well on the second, and

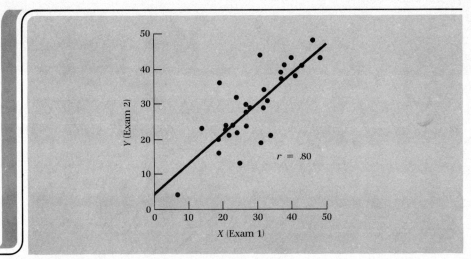

FIGURE 10-1. Scatter diagram showing correlation between two exams in a course. Straight line through swarm of points is regression line.

we should have analogous expectations for the students who perform poorly on the first exam. The display in Figure 10-1 is a **bivariate distribution,** since there are two variables, X and Y, respectively representing performance on Exam 1 and Exam 2. There is an X measure and a Y measure attached to each student in the class. Each point, each of the black dots, represents a single student. Since the points are scattered throughout such a display, such a presentation of a bivariate distribution is sometimes called a **scatter diagram,** or **scatter plot.**

We can regard the students in the scatter plot in Figure 10-1 as a sample drawn from an infinitely large population of students who might potentially have taken the two exams. Such a population does not exist, of course, but like other such conceptual populations, it will none the less prove to be useful. In a **bivariate population,** there is a value of X and a value of Y attached to each individual, and a **bivariate sample** is a collection of individuals chosen from such a population. After we have developed some methods of describing bivariate samples, we will present procedures for dealing with some of the inferential statistics of bivariate populations, for example, procedures for testing the statistical significance of an observed correlation.

The straight line passing through the swarm of points in Figure 10-1 is a **regression line,** a straight line that best expresses the relationship between the Y variable and the X variable. While the correlation between the two exams is not perfect, the upward — positive — slope of the regression line indicates that for the most part the scores on the two exams do tend to change together, to **covary.** As we move from lower to higher scores on the first exam, we also tend to move from lower to higher on the second. If we placed the students' names in ascending order in terms of their scores on the first exam, we would find as we moved through the list that the scores on the second exam would also tend to be in order, although the order of the second exam scores would not be perfect. While we cannot perfectly estimate a student's score on the second exam on the basis of the score on the first, we *can* predict that students will tend to perform similarly on the two exams.

The Pearson *r*

The **Pearson product-moment correlation coefficient,** symbolized *r*, is an index of linear relationship between two variables. Historically, the symbol *r* comes from *regression*, a term now used somewhat differently — as we will explain later. Equation 10-1 is the conceptual formula for *r*:

$$r = \frac{\Sigma(Z_X Z_Y)}{N},\tag{10-1}$$

where $Z_X = \dfrac{X - \bar{X}}{SD_X}$ and $Z_Y = \dfrac{Y - \bar{Y}}{SD_Y}.$

Notice that the Z-scores in the conceptual formula for *r* utilize the sample standard deviations, SD_X and SD_Y, rather than S_X and S_Y.

Table 10-1 demonstrates the use of the above formula in calculating *r* in the small distribution shown graphically in Figure 10-4. To use Formula 10-1, it is first necessary to find SD_X and SD_Y. A Z-score is then found for each value of X and for each value of Y. Notice that the sum of Z_X and Z_Y are both equal to zero, within rounding error, thus providing a check on your arithmetic. (It is easy to show that the sum of any set of Z-scores is zero, as we ask you to do in an exercise at the end of the chapter.) The two Z-scores for each subject are cross-multiplied, that is, multiplied by each other, and the cross-products are entered in the middle column of Table 10-1. The sum of that column is the sum of the cross-products, which gives the numerator of Formula 10-1. Dividing by N, the number of subjects yields *r*.

Formula 10-1 is tedious to use in a large distribution, since that formula requires finding all of the deviations between the scores and the X and Y means. As you may suppose, we will shortly develop a more convenient computational formula. But for the present, we will use the conceptual formula to explain some of the principles of correlation.

The Possible Values of *r*.   As we will show, *r* can take on any value between -1 and $+1$ inclusive, including the value of zero. Thus,

$$-1 \leq r \leq +1.$$

As a help in understanding the range of values of *r*, it will be useful to consider some properties of Z-scores. We can show that $\Sigma Z^2 = N$ (as we will ask you to do in an exercise). Now, consider Figure 10-2A, which shows a perfect correlation between two variables, X and Y. Indeed, each value of Y in that scatter diagram is exactly equal to the value of X for that subject. All of the points in that bivariate distribution fall precisely on the regression line. For each value of X, there is one and only one value of Y, and thus Y is a function of

TABLE 10-1. Calculation of the Pearson r Using the Conceptual Formula and the Raw-Score Computational Formula. Same Data as in Figure 10-4.

X^2	X	$\dfrac{X-\bar{X}}{SD_X}=$	Z_X	Z_XZ_Y	$Z_Y=$	$\dfrac{Y-\bar{Y}}{SD_Y}$	Y	Y^2	XY
1	1	$\dfrac{1-3}{1.41}=-1.42$		1.95	$-1.37=$	$\dfrac{1-2.4}{1.02}$	1	1	1
4	2	$\dfrac{2-3}{1.41}=-0.71$		0.28	$-0.39=$	$\dfrac{2-2.4}{1.02}$	2	4	4
9	3	$\dfrac{3-3}{1.41}=0.00$		0.00	$-0.39=$	$\dfrac{2-2.4}{1.02}$	2	4	6
16	4	$\dfrac{4-3}{1.41}=0.71$		1.11	$1.57=$	$\dfrac{4-2.4}{1.02}$	4	16	16
25	5	$\dfrac{5-3}{1.41}=1.42$		0.84	$0.59=$	$\dfrac{3-2.4}{1.02}$	3	9	15
55	15		0.00	4.18	0.01		12	34	42
$=\Sigma X^2$	$=\Sigma X$		$=\Sigma Z_X$	$=\Sigma Z_XZ_Y$	$=\Sigma Z_Y$		$=\Sigma Y$	$=\Sigma Y^2$	$=\Sigma XY$

$$\bar{X}=3 \qquad\qquad N=5 \qquad\qquad \bar{Y}=2.4$$

$$SD_X=\sqrt{\dfrac{\Sigma X^2-\dfrac{(\Sigma X)^2}{N}}{N}} \qquad\qquad SD_Y=\sqrt{\dfrac{\Sigma Y^2-\dfrac{(\Sigma Y)^2}{N}}{N}}$$

$$=1.41. \qquad\qquad =1.02.$$

By Conceptual Formula 10-1, $\quad r=\dfrac{\Sigma(Z_XZ_Y)}{N}=\dfrac{4.18}{5}=.84.$

By Computational Formula 10-5, $\quad r=\dfrac{\Sigma XY-\dfrac{\Sigma X\Sigma Y}{N}}{\sqrt{\left[\Sigma X^2-\dfrac{(\Sigma X)^2}{N}\right]\left[\Sigma Y^2-\dfrac{(\Sigma Y)^2}{N}\right]}}$

$$=\dfrac{42-\dfrac{15(12)}{5}}{\sqrt{\left[55-\dfrac{15^2}{5}\right]\left[34-\dfrac{12^2}{5}\right]}}=\dfrac{42-36}{\sqrt{10(5.2)}}=\dfrac{6}{\sqrt{52}}=\dfrac{6}{7.21}=.83.$$

X. Since $Y=X$, it follows that $Z_Y=Z_X$ for every individual in the bivariate distribution, and thus

$$r=\dfrac{\Sigma(Z_XZ_Y)}{N}=\dfrac{\Sigma Z_X^2}{N}=\dfrac{N}{N}=+1,$$

since $\Sigma Z_X^2=N$. When all of the points in a bivariate distribution fall on a single straight line, and when that line has a positive slope as in Figure 10-2A — sloping upward to the right — then there is a perfect **positive correlation** between X and Y, and r is equal to $+1.00$.

In Figure 10-2B, there is no regression line shown. There is no single straight line that can be drawn through all of the points in that scatter

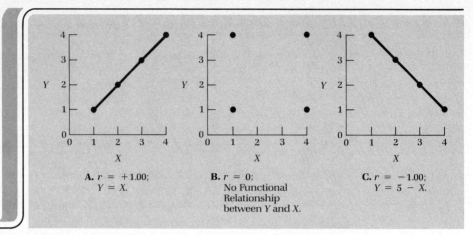

A. $r = +1.00$;
$Y = X$.

B. $r = 0$;
No Functional
Relationship
between Y and X.

C. $r = -1.00$;
$Y = 5 - X$.

FIGURE 10-2. A: Perfect positive correlation. **B:** No correlation. **C:** Perfect negative correlation. Equations in **A** and **C** express Y as a function of X.

diagram. Indeed, there is no relationship whatever between X and Y in that latter figure; thus, the value of r is equal to zero. Telling you a particular person's score on the X variable in Figure 10-2B gives you no information about that person's score on the Y variable. A person having an X score of 1 might have a Y score of 1 or 4, and so might a person having an X score of 4. But in Figure 10-2A, knowing anyone's X score allows you to know that person's Y score, since there is a perfect correlation between X and Y.

By considering the nature of the Z-scores in Figure 10-2B, we can see how it is that $r = 0$. For each X value of 1 or 4, there are two Y values of 1 and 4. Thus, for each Z_X there is a positive and a negative value of Z_Y. Since those Z_Y values are of the same magnitude but different in sign, the numerator of Equation 10-1 is equal to zero, and thus $r = 0$. This will become clear — if it isn't already — in an exercise at the end of the chapter.

In Figure 10-2C, all of the points fall on the regression line, but the line has a negative slope — downward to the right. In that bivariate distribution, as X goes up, Y goes down, and thus there is a **negative correlation.** Here, the negative correlation is perfect, and $r = -1.00$. The relationship between X and Y is just as "good" as the perfect positive relationship in Figure 10-2A, to the extent that knowing the value of X allows you to know the value of Y. But X and Y are **inversely related** — rather than **directly related** — in Figure 10-2C. When there is a perfect negative correlation, Y is just as surely a function of X as when there is a perfect positive correlation. Most of the correlations we have occasion to deal with will be positive, but we can easily find a number of negative correlations. For example, in a golf tournament, the players' winnings are negatively correlated with their total number of strokes. No doubt, you can think of some other negative correlations.

Where there is a perfect negative correlation, for each Z_X there is a Z_Y of the same magnitude but different sign. Thus, the numerator of Formula 10-1 is equal to $-N$ in that case, and $r = -1.00$. An exercise at the end of the chapter will make that clear.

Correlation coefficients are usually decimal numbers, but you should not suppose that an r of .75, for example, means that 75% of one variable is caused by the other, or that one variable causes the other 75% of the time. Remember, we cautioned you very early — in Chapter 1 — about drawing causal inferences from correlations. We will have more to say later about the meaning of the numerical values of r.

Computational Formula for r. Formula 10-1, the conceptual formula for r, is deceptive in its apparent simplicity. Using that formula requires finding Z-scores, and since the mean and standard deviation in a set of real data will usually have several decimal places, those Z-scores will have to be rounded to some manageable number of places. Rounding errors cannot ordinarily be eliminated, and furthermore, working with lots of decimals increases the likelihood of human errors, even if you are using a calculator of some kind. For those reasons, we will find it useful to develop raw-score computational formulas for r, just as we have developed computational formulas for other statistics in the past.

We begin by substituting for Z_X and Z_Y in Formula 10-1:

$$r = \frac{\Sigma(Z_X Z_Y)}{N} = \frac{\Sigma\left[\dfrac{(X - \bar{X})}{SD_X}\dfrac{(Y - \bar{Y})}{SD_Y}\right]}{N} = \frac{\Sigma(X - \bar{X})(Y - \bar{Y})}{N\,SD_X SD_Y}. \tag{10-2}$$

In the above manipulations, we make use of the fact that SD_X and SD_Y are constant within any given set of data, and can therefore be taken outside the summation operator.

Carrying out the multiplications in the numerator of 10-2, distributing the summation operator, and continuing,

$$r = \frac{\Sigma(X - \bar{X})(Y - \bar{Y})}{N\,SD_X SD_Y} = \frac{\Sigma(XY - X\bar{Y} - Y\bar{X} + \bar{X}\bar{Y})}{N\,SD_X SD_Y}$$

$$= \frac{\Sigma XY - \bar{Y}\Sigma X - \bar{X}\Sigma Y + N\overline{XY}}{N\,SD_X SD_Y} = \frac{\Sigma XY - \dfrac{\Sigma Y}{N}\Sigma X - \dfrac{\Sigma X}{N}\Sigma Y + N\dfrac{\Sigma X}{N}\dfrac{\Sigma Y}{N}}{N\,SD_X SD_Y}$$

$$= \frac{\Sigma XY - 2\dfrac{\Sigma X \Sigma Y}{N} + \dfrac{\Sigma X \Sigma Y}{N}}{N\,SD_X SD_Y}. \tag{10-3}$$

In the operations above, we apply the principles of summation from Chapter 4, noting that $\bar{X}$ and $\bar{Y}$ are constants. Collecting terms in Equation 10-3,

$$r = \frac{\Sigma XY - \dfrac{\Sigma X \Sigma Y}{N}}{N\,SD_X SD_Y}. \tag{10-4}$$

Formula 10-4 can be used as a computational formula for r, but that formula requires that we first calculate the standard deviations of X and Y. Since those calculations introduce rounding errors, it will be useful to derive a computational formula that will utilize the raw scores more directly. Substituting our computational formulas for SD_X and SD_Y in Equation 10-4,

$$r = \frac{\Sigma XY - \dfrac{\Sigma X \Sigma Y}{N}}{N \sqrt{\dfrac{\Sigma X^2 - \dfrac{(\Sigma X)^2}{N}}{N}} \sqrt{\dfrac{\Sigma Y^2 - \dfrac{(\Sigma Y)^2}{N}}{N}}}$$

$$= \frac{\Sigma XY - \dfrac{\Sigma X \Sigma Y}{N}}{\sqrt{N^2 \dfrac{\left[\Sigma X^2 - \dfrac{(\Sigma X)^2}{N}\right]\left[\Sigma Y^2 - \dfrac{(\Sigma Y)^2}{N}\right]}{N^2}}}.$$

Simplifying the denominator, above, yields a useful raw-score computational formula:

$$r = \frac{\Sigma XY - \dfrac{\Sigma X \Sigma Y}{N}}{\sqrt{\left[\Sigma X^2 - \dfrac{(\Sigma X)^2}{N}\right]\left[\Sigma Y^2 - \dfrac{(\Sigma Y)^2}{N}\right]}}. \tag{10-5}$$

Since the quantities in the denominator of 10-5 are the sums of squares for X and Y, that formula can be written more compactly in the following way:

$$r = \frac{\Sigma XY - \dfrac{\Sigma X \Sigma Y}{N}}{\sqrt{SS_X SS_Y}}. \tag{10-6}$$

Computational Formula 10-5, above, looks much more complicated than Conceptual Formula 10-1. But Formula 10-5 utilizes raw scores directly, while in order to use the simpler-appearing conceptual formula, scores must first be transformed into Z-scores. In all but the very simplest cases, the raw-score formula is far more useful for computational purposes than the deceptively simple-appearing conceptual formula. Table 10-1 demonstrates the use of Computational Formula 10-5. In using that formula, as in using other computational formulas in the past, remember that $(\Sigma X)^2 \neq \Sigma X^2$. The two values of r calculated in Table 10-1 differ slightly because of greater rounding errors in the conceptual formula.

Regression

By **linear regression** we mean the process of finding the equation of the straight line that best *estimates* or *predicts* the value of one variable from a given value of the other. Initially, we will confine ourselves to describing the relationship between X and Y in *bivariate samples*, groups of individuals each having an X score and a Y score. **Estimation** and **prediction**, as we will initially use those terms, are not directly concerned with foretelling the future, but are concerned instead with describing the relationship between X and Y in bivariate samples that are already in hand. We will first develop methods of describing such samples, and then we will extend those methods to the problems of predicting the future and assessing the magnitude of the errors that we are likely to make in such future predictions. We are often interested in predicting a person's future performance, based on some measurement made in the here-and-now, and we will develop procedures for doing so.

As we will see, regression and correlation are very closely related. The correlation coefficient is an index of the linear relationship between variables, while the regression equation offers a means of estimating the value of one variable based on knowledge of the other. In this text, we will be concerned only with **linear** relationships between variables — that is, relationships that can be expressed by *straight lines*. Sometimes, there are **curvilinear** relationships between variables, as in Figure 10-3. In Figure 10-3A, Y is a perfect quadratic (second-degree) function of X; and in 10-3B, Y is a perfect cubic (third-degree) function of X. But in both of those situations, $r = 0$, since there is no *linear* relationship between the variables. Confining ourselves to linear

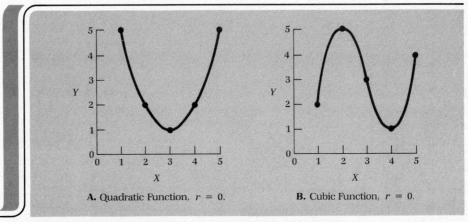

A. Quadratic Function, $r = 0$.   **B.** Cubic Function, $r = 0$.

FIGURE 10-3. Two perfect curvilinear relationships between Y and X. Since r is a measure of *linear* correlation, $r = 0$ in both cases.

relationships may appear terribly restrictive, but in fact linear correlation and regression can be applied to a very wide range of problems.

Estimating Y from X

The regression equation below is an equation of a straight line in slope-intercept form. That equation yields the best prediction, or estimate, of the value of Y based on any given value of X:

Regression equation: $Y' = a_Y + b_Y X,$ (10-7)

where Y' = estimated Y value, a_Y = Y intercept, and b_Y = slope. The **Y intercept** is the point at which the regression line cuts the Y axis, that is, the value of Y' where $X = 0$. The **slope** is the change in Y over the change in X as a point moves along the regression line, that is,

$$b_Y = \frac{Y_2 - Y_1}{X_2 - X_1} = \frac{\Delta Y}{\Delta X}.$$

Figure 10-4 shows the slope, intercept, and some other features of a regression line. Notice particularly that the regression line passes through the point having the coordinates $(\overline{X}, \overline{Y})$. The **regression coefficients,** a_Y and b_Y, are found using the two equations below.

Intercept = $a_Y = \overline{Y} - b_Y \overline{X},$ (10-8)

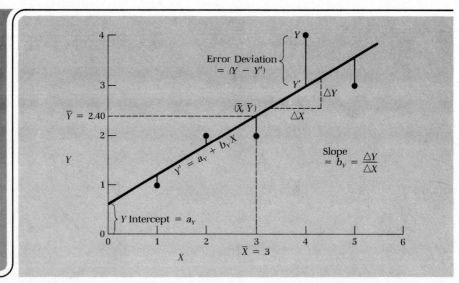

FIGURE 10-4. Regression line for predicting Y from X, slope, intercept, and regression equation. Only one error deviation is labeled, but there exists an error deviation for each subject in the scatter diagram.

$$\text{Slope} \ = \ b_Y \ = \ r\frac{SD_Y}{SD_X}. \tag{10-9}$$

The regression coefficients a_Y and b_Y represent two unknowns in the two simultaneous equations above. When the statistics, $\overline{Y}$, $\overline{X}$, r, SD_Y, and SD_X are calculated from a set of data, Equation 10-9 can be solved for b_Y, and then 10-8 · can be solved for a_Y. The resulting values of a_Y and b_Y are then substituted into the regression equation in 10-7. We will provide concrete examples of that process shortly, and we will explain how the equations for the regression coefficients are derived.

Error Deviation.   For each subject in a bivariate distribution, there is an observed value of Y and a Y' value found by solving the regression equation. When the regression coefficients a_Y and b_Y have been found, a subject's X score can be entered into Equation 10-7, which will then yield the Y' value for the subject. In the case of a perfect correlation, the Y' value for each subject will exactly equal the observed Y value, but where the correlation is less than perfect, there will be discrepancies between most of the predicted Y' values and the observed Y values. The **error deviation** for any particular subject is defined by the following equation:

$$\text{Error deviation} \ = \ Y - Y'. \tag{10-10}$$

Figure 10-4 shows the error deviations for all of the subjects in that bivariate distribution. The regression coefficients we find using Equations 10-8 and 10-9 result in a regression equation that minimizes the sum of the squared deviations from the regression line, that is, the sum of the squared error deviations:

$$\begin{matrix} \text{Sum of squared} \\ \text{error deviations} \end{matrix} \ = \ \Sigma(Y - Y')^2. \tag{10-11}$$

Referring to Figure 10-4, suppose we kept the slope of the regression line constant, but suppose we moved the line higher or lower. Those geometric operations are equivalent to holding b_Y constant and letting a_Y vary in the regression equation. If we moved the regression line much higher or lower, then all of the error deviations would become much larger in magnitude, and the sum of the squared deviations would increase. Similarly, if we kept the Y intercept constant, but changed the slope of the regression line (holding a_Y constant and letting b_Y vary), we would also increase the magnitude of the error deviations. The problem is to find the one straight line for estimating Y from X that minimizes the sum of the squared error deviations.

The Least-Squares Criterion.   A regression line that minimizes the sum of the squared error deviations in 10-11 is a **least-squares regression line.** It may not be entirely obvious why it is useful to find a regression line that minimizes the sum of the *squared* error deviations. Why not use a procedure that minimizes the sum of the error deviations, without any

✳ squaring? Notice that all of our regression lines pass through the point having the coordinates $(\overline{X}, \overline{Y})$, which implies that we would always predict a Y' value equal to $\overline{Y}$ for any subject having an X score equal to the mean of the Xs. It turns out that for *any* straight line passing through the point $(\overline{X}, \overline{Y})$ — whatever its slope — the sum of the error deviations is exactly zero. Some of the error deviations are positive and some are negative, and they all add up to zero for any such straight line. But the sum of the *squared* error deviations is greater than zero in all cases except where X and Y are perfectly correlated and all subjects fall precisely on the regression line. Where there is a correlation between X and Y, there is one and only one regression line for estimating Y from X that minimizes the sum of the squared error deviations. The situation here is analogous to our development of measures of dispersion in Chapter 4. The sum of the deviations from the mean is unsuitable as a measure of dispersion since that sum is always equal to zero. But the sum of the *squared* deviations from the mean is the sum of squares, SS, which is the numerator of the variance — a measure of dispersion which we have found useful in the past. Indeed, the sum of the squared error deviations from the regression line is also a measure of dispersion that will prove useful.

We have not as yet explained how it is that Equations 10-8 and 10-9 yield the exact values of a_Y and b_Y, which determine the least-squares regression line. We have developed those equations in Appendix C, using a little calculus. However, if you have not had any calculus, you should nevertheless be able to follow most of the material in that appendix. You will be able to utilize our correlation and regression procedures by using only a little basic algebra. Indeed, if you are sufficiently interested in the derivation of the least-squares regression equations, and have not had any calculus, see DuBois (1965, p. 129).

Estimating X from Y

So far, we have presented our development of regression in terms of estimating Y from X. In many situations, we are clearly more interested in estimating or predicting one of the variables from the other. For example, performance on many tasks increases with age during the developmental years. Thus, we would be more interested in estimating a child's reading achievement from the child's age than in estimating age from reading achievement. Ordinarily, we designate the variable we wish to estimate or predict as Y and the variable we wish to use as a predictor as X. But in some cases, we may be as interested in estimating X from Y as in estimating Y from X. If we were interested in the relationship between height and weight, for example, then we might be as interested in estimating height from weight as in estimating weight from height. Neither height nor weight "comes first" in the sense that age comes first when we are interested in the relationship between age and performance of some kind. You might suppose that we could predict X from Y by simply solving Equation 10-7 for X, but there are complications. There are *two* least-squares regression lines through any bivariate distribution, one for estimating Y from X and the other for estimating X from Y.

Figure 10-5 shows the regression line for estimating X from Y, and also shows the error deviations from that regression line. Notice that those error deviations are horizontal line segments, as opposed to the vertical error deviations from the regression line for predicting Y from X in Figure 10-4. The regression line for predicting X from Y minimizes the sum of the squared error deviations below.

$$\text{Sum of squared error deviations} = \Sigma(X - X')^2.$$

The regression equation and coefficients are shown below.

$$X' = a_X + b_X Y; \tag{10-12}$$

$$a_X = \bar{X} - b_X\bar{Y}; \tag{10-13}$$

$$b_X = r\frac{SD_X}{SD_Y}. \tag{10-14}$$

The equations for a_X and b_X were found by the same least-squares procedures as the equations for a_Y and b_Y (see Appendix C).

Figure 10-5 shows that the regression coefficient a_X is the **X intercept,** the point where the regression line cuts the X axis. The coefficient b_X is the change in X over the change in Y as a point moves along the regression line, that is, **$\Delta X/\Delta Y$.** Figure 10-6 shows the two regression lines. Every regression

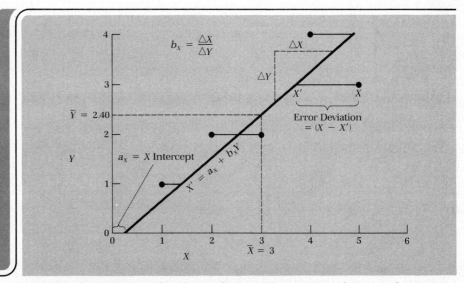

FIGURE 10-5. Regression line for predicting X from Y. Error deviations here are horizontal line segments. Compare with Figure 10-4.

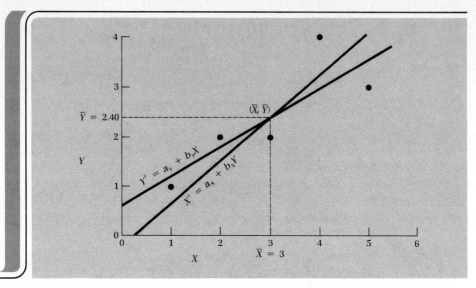

FIGURE 10-6. Regression lines and equations for predicting Y from X, and X from Y. The two regression lines cross at the point having the coordinates $(\overline{X}, \overline{Y})$.

line passes through the point having the coordinates $(\overline{X}, \overline{Y})$, and thus the two regression lines here cross at that point.

Table 10-2 demonstrates the procedures for finding the two regression lines shown in Figure 10-6. The data are shown in Table 10-1. After the correlation coefficient is calculated in that table, the quantities to be used in finding the regression equations are readily available. Thus, the procedures in Table 10-2 are quite straightforward.

TABLE 10-2.   Regression Equations for Predicting Y from X and X from Y. The Two Regression Lines are Shown in Figure 10-6. Data are Shown in Table 10-1.

$$r = .83$$

$\overline{X} = 3$	$\overline{Y} = 2.4$
$SD_X = 1.41$	$SD_Y = 1.02$

By Formulas 10-7, 10-8, and 10-9,

$$b_Y = r\frac{SD_Y}{SD_X} = .83\frac{1.02}{1.41} = .60.$$

$$a_Y = \overline{Y} - b_Y\overline{X}$$

$$= 2.4 - .60(3) = .60.$$

$$Y' = a_Y + b_Y X$$

$$= .60 + .60X.$$

By Formulas 10-12, 10-13, and 10-14,

$$b_X = r\frac{SD_X}{SD_Y} = .83\frac{1.41}{1.02} = 1.15.$$

$$a_X = \overline{X} - b_X\overline{Y}$$

$$= 3 - 1.15(2.4) = .24.$$

$$X' = a_X + b_X Y$$

$$= .24 + 1.15Y.$$

Proportion of Variance Accounted for

We have developed regression equations for predicting Y from X and X from Y, but our predictions are less than perfect for the most part. Actually, such a "prediction" is more in the nature of an *estimate* of the most likely value of one variable given some specific value of the other. Only where the correlation between X and Y is equal to $+1.00$ or -1.00 can we perfectly estimate either variable from the other. In all other cases most of the predicted X' and Y' values will differ from the observed values of X and Y. Indeed, in Figure 10-4, none of the observed Y values falls on the regression line. The process of predicting Y from X seems to suggest that Y is a function of X, but it is really Y' that is a linear function of X. There is one and only one value of Y' associated with each value of X, but there may be many different values of Y associated with a single X value. For example, in Figure 10-1 you can find subjects who have the same score on Exam 1 but different scores on Exam 2. But the regression equation estimates a single score on Exam 2 for everyone having any given score on Exam 1. Thus, whenever the correlation is less than perfect, there will be **errors of estimate** — failures of prediction, deviations between observed and estimated scores. We will develop methods of making probability statements about the size of those errors. Keep in mind that we are dealing for the present with estimation and "prediction" in bivariate *samples* where every subject already has an X value and a Y value. Later, we will extend the methods to making true predictions of the future — that is, where we estimate a person's future Y value based on the present observation of an X score. Predicting the future requires dealing with the concept of a bivariate population.

Error Variance and Explained Variance. We will develop the procedures in this section with regard to predicting Y from X. Later, we will extend these procedures to predicting X from Y. Since there will be no opportunity for confusion in our present development, we will write the regression equation as below, dropping the subscripts from a and b.

$$Y' = a + bX. \tag{10-15}$$

For each subject in a bivariate sample, there exists a **total deviation,** which is equal to the observed Y minus the Y mean; an **error deviation,** equal to the observed Y minus the predicted Y; and an **explained deviation,** equal to the predicted Y minus the Y mean. Those three deviations are shown for a single subject in Figure 10-7. The line segment representing the total deviation for that subject is the sum of the line segments representing the error deviation and the explained deviation. For other subjects, some of the deviations are positive and some are negative. For each subject, the total deviation is the algebraic sum, the sum with regard to sign, of the error deviation and the explained deviation.

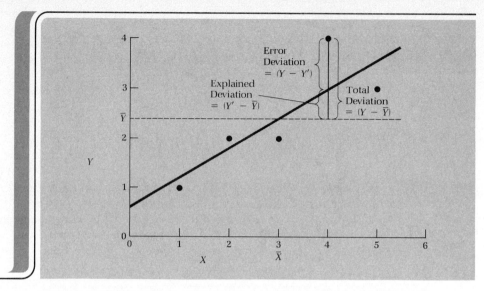

FIGURE 10-7. Deviations are shown for only one subject, but a set of such deviations exist for each subject in the scatter diagram.

Explanation and Causality. The explained deviation is the portion of a subject's total deviation—the deviation of the observed Y value from $\bar{Y}$—that can be accounted for by the correlation between Y and X. If there is a positive correlation between the two variables, then those subjects scoring high on the X variable will also tend to score high on the Y variable, and thus their total deviations will tend to be large and positive. The regression equation yields large Y' values for those subjects, and thus their deviations of Y' from the Y mean will also be large and positive. Since a portion of each subject's total deviation is explained—accounted for—by the regression equation, that portion of the total deviation is called the explained deviation. If some portion of the value of Y is accounted for by X, it sounds very much as though we are saying that X *causes* Y—but that is not the case. When there is a correlation between the two variables, knowing the value of X allows us to predict—estimate—the value of Y, but a predictive relationship does not mean that one variable necessarily causes the other. As we have noted earlier, both variables might be caused by some other variable. We will have more to say later about correlation and causality.

Partitioning the Total Variance of Y. As you know from our earlier treatment of measures of dispersion, the variance is a function of the squared deviations from the mean. Figure 10-7 shows that the total deviation can be **partitioned** into error deviation and explained deviation, that is, the total deviation can be divided into two mutually exclusive and exhaustive components. We show that partition for only a single subject, but such a partition exists for every subject in the distribution. Figure 10-8 shows the three

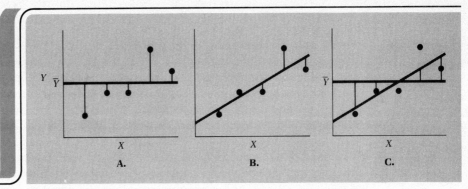

FIGURE 10-8. Same scatter diagram as Figure 10-7, reduced in size. **A:** Total deviations; **B:** error deviations; **C:** explained deviations.

varieties of deviations for all of the subjects in the distribution. The **total variance** of Y is the mean of the squared deviations of observed Y values from the Y mean. Those deviations are shown in Figure 10-8A. Thus, the *total variance* is defined exactly as we have defined the *variance* in the past. We are using the term total variance here because we will show that the variance of Y can be partitioned into two components, error variance and explained variance. The **error variance** is the mean of the squared deviations from the regression line. Figure 10-8B shows those deviations. The **explained variance** is the mean of the squared deviations of Y' values from the Y mean. Figure 10-8C shows those deviations. It is useful to be able to calculate those variances, and we will develop methods of doing so.

Referring to Figure 10-7, we can write the following equations, which partition the total deviation for a single subject:

$$\text{Total deviation} = \text{Error deviation} + \text{Explained deviation};$$

$$(Y - \bar{Y}) = (Y - Y') + (Y' - \bar{Y}). \tag{10-16}$$

Squaring and summing across all of the subjects in the distribution,

$$\Sigma(Y - \bar{Y})^2 = \Sigma[(Y - Y') + (Y' - \bar{Y})]^2$$

$$= \Sigma(Y - Y')^2 + 2\Sigma(Y - Y')(Y' - \bar{Y}) + \Sigma(Y' - \bar{Y})^2. \tag{10-17}$$

Equation 10-17 simplifies considerably, since the middle term is equal to zero, as we explain below. Thus,

$$\Sigma(Y - \bar{Y})^2 = \Sigma(Y - Y')^2 + \Sigma(Y' - \bar{Y})^2;$$

$$SS_{TOT} = SS_E + SS_{EXP}. \tag{10-18}$$

Each of the terms in 10-18 is a sum of squares, respectively the sum of the squared total deviations, error deviations, and explained deviations. That equation shows that the total sum of squares, SS_{TOT}, can be partitioned into two components, the error sum of squares and the explained sum of squares, SS_E and SS_{EXP}.

We will now explain why the middle term of 10-17 vanishes. That term is twice the sum of the cross-products of the error deviations and the explained deviations. Referring to Figure 10-8C, you can see that the explained deviations change systematically from negative values to larger and larger positive values as we move from left to right along the regression line. But the error deviations in Figure 10-8B do not change in any systematic way as we move along the regression line. Thus, the error deviations and the explained deviations are uncorrelated. The middle term of 10-17 is equal to twice the numerator of the correlation coefficient between the explained deviations and the error deviations, and since that correlation is equal to zero, that term vanishes from the equation. Appendix C offers a proof of this happy state of affairs under the heading *Partitioning the Total Variance* — which you can follow without any calculus.

Dividing Equation 10-18 by N yields the total variance, the error variance, and the explained variance. We introduce some new symbols, explained shortly, in the set of equations below:

$$\frac{\Sigma(Y - \bar{Y})^2}{N} = \frac{\Sigma(Y - Y')^2}{N} + \frac{\Sigma(Y' - \bar{Y})^2}{N}; \tag{10-19}$$

$$SD_Y^2 = SD_{Y|X}^2 + SD_{Y'}^2; \tag{10-20}$$

$$SD_{TOT}^2 = SD_E^2 + SD_{EXP}^2; \tag{10-21}$$

$$\text{Total variance} = \text{Error variance} + \text{Explained variance}. \tag{10-22}$$

Thus, we have partitioned the total variance of Y into an error component and an explained component.

In Equation 10-20, SD_Y^2 is simply the sample variance of Y, which can be calculated in the usual way by Formula 4-8. All of the variances in our present context are *sample* variances — not the unbiased estimators of population variances. The error variance, $SD_{Y|X}^2$, is also called the **variance of Y given X.** For any given value of X, there exists a value of Y' found by solving the regression equation. Thus, for each subject there exists a **deviation of Y given X** — that is, an error deviation, a deviation of the subject's observed Y value from the Y' value yielded by the regression equation. There is a close relationship between the deviation of Y given X and the conditional probability of one event given another. Thus, our use of the symbol $SD_{Y|X}^2$ for the error variance is no accident, a point that we will amplify later.

As we have noted, the error variance is the mean of the squared deviations from the regression line. Thus, the error variance is a measure of the dispersion of the observed Y values with respect to a straight line — in this case the regression line. Now consider the total variance of Y, the mean of the squared deviations of observed Y values from the Y mean. In Figure 10-8A, $\bar{Y}$ is shown as a straight line parallel to the X axis. Thus, like the error variance, the total variance of Y is a measure of the dispersion of the observed Y values with respect to a straight line — in this case the Y mean.

Proportion of Explained Variance. In Equation 10-21, the explained variance is that component of the total variance of Y which is accounted for by the correlation between X and Y. Rearranging 10-21,

$$SD^2_{EXP} = SD^2_{TOT} - SD^2_E. \tag{10-23}$$

Dividing 10-23 by SD^2_{TOT} yields the **proportion of explained variance,** or the **proportion of variance accounted for** — that is, the proportion of the total variance of Y that is accounted for by the correlation with X:

$$\begin{matrix} \text{Proportion} \\ \text{of explained} \\ \text{variance} \end{matrix} = \frac{SD^2_{EXP}}{SD^2_{TOT}} = \frac{SD^2_{TOT} - SD^2_E}{SD^2_{TOT}} = \frac{SD^2_Y - SD^2_{Y|X}}{SD^2_Y}. \tag{10-24}$$

We will now find an expression for the proportion of explained variance in terms of the correlation coefficient r.

Continuing from Equation 10-24,

$$\frac{SD^2_{EXP}}{SD^2_{TOT}} = \frac{SD^2_{EXP}}{SD^2_Y} = \frac{\dfrac{\Sigma(Y' - \overline{Y})^2}{N}}{SD^2_Y}.$$

Substituting the Regression Equation 10-15 for Y', and substituting Equation 10-8 for a,

$$\frac{\dfrac{\Sigma(Y' - \overline{Y})^2}{N}}{SD^2_Y} = \frac{\dfrac{\Sigma[(a + bX) - \overline{Y}]^2}{N}}{SD^2_Y} = \frac{\dfrac{\Sigma[(\overline{Y} - b\overline{X}) + bX - \overline{Y}]^2}{N}}{SD^2_Y}$$

$$= \frac{\dfrac{\Sigma[b(X - \overline{X})]^2}{N}}{SD^2_Y} = \frac{\dfrac{b^2\Sigma(X - \overline{X})^2}{N}}{SD^2_Y} = \frac{b^2 SD^2_X}{SD^2_Y} = b^2\frac{SD^2_X}{SD^2_Y}.$$

Substituting Equation 10-9 for b, and squaring,

$$b^2\frac{SD^2_X}{SD^2_Y} = r^2\frac{SD^2_Y}{SD^2_X}\frac{SD^2_X}{SD^2_Y} = r^2.$$

Thus, we have the important result that the proportion of variance accounted for, explained, is equal to the square of the correlation coefficient:

$$\begin{matrix} \text{Proportion} \\ \text{of explained} \\ \text{variance} \end{matrix} = r^2. \tag{10-25}$$

We cautioned you earlier against supposing that the correlation coefficient was to be interpreted as a proportion, but it turns out that the *square* of the correlation is the proportion of the variance of one variable that is accounted for by the other. We will make use of that fact to develop another expression for r. Substituting r^2 for the proportion of explained variance in Equation 10-24,

$$r^2 = \frac{SD_Y^2 - SD_{Y|X}^2}{SD_Y^2}; \qquad r = \sqrt{\frac{SD_Y^2 - SD_{Y|X}^2}{SD_Y^2}}. \tag{10-26}$$

Equation 10-26 is not a useful computational formula, but it expresses r as a function of the total variance of Y and the error variance. We will shortly make use of that relationship in some of our explanations.

The Sample Standard Error of Estimate

In this section we will develop **the sample standard error of estimate**, symbolized $\mathbf{SD_{Y|X}}$. As you can see, $SD_{Y|X}$ is the square root of the error variance, and thus is the standard deviation of observed Y values in a bivariate sample with respect to the *sample regression line*. Later, we will develop methods of making inferences about the dispersion of observed Y values with respect to the *population regression line*.

Rearranging Equation 10-21,

$$SD_E^2 = SD_{TOT}^2 - SD_{EXP}^2 = SD_{Y|X}^2 = SD_Y^2 - SD_{EXP}^2.$$

Dividing by SD_Y^2 expresses the above variances as proportions of the total variance.

$$\text{Proportion of error variance} = \frac{SD_{Y|X}^2}{SD_Y^2} = \frac{SD_Y^2}{SD_Y^2} - \frac{SD_{Y'}^2}{SD_Y^2}. \tag{10-27}$$

The rightmost term of 10-27 is the proportion of explained variance and is equal to r^2. Substituting,

$$\text{Proportion of error variance} = \frac{SD_{Y|X}^2}{SD_Y^2} = 1 - r^2. \tag{10-28}$$

Solving for the error variance,

$$\text{Error variance} = SD_{Y|X}^2 = SD_Y^2(1 - r^2). \tag{10-29}$$

We define the *sample standard error of estimate* as the square root of the error variance. Thus,

$$\text{Sample standard error of estimate} = \sqrt{\text{Error variance}} = SD_{Y|X} = SD_Y\sqrt{1 - r^2}. \tag{10-30}$$

The sample standard error of estimate above is to be used in connection with estimating Y given X. When estimating X from Y, the standard error of estimate is the following.

$$SD_{X|Y} = SD_X\sqrt{1 - r^2}. \tag{10-31}$$

TABLE 10-3. Calculating the Sample Standard Error of Estimate, $SD_{Y|X}$, Shown Graphically in Figure 10-9B.

$$r = .80$$

Exam 1: $\overline{X} = 29.00$ Exam 2: $\overline{Y} = 29.20$

$SD_X = 9.47$ $SD_Y = 10.26$

By Formula 10-30,   Sample standard error of estimate $= SD_{Y|X}\sqrt{1 - r^2}$

$$= 10.26\sqrt{1 - .80^2} = 6.16.$$

Regression equation:

By 10-7, $Y' = a + bX;$ By 10-9, $b = r\dfrac{SD_Y}{SD_X} = .80\dfrac{10.26}{9.47} = .87.$

$Y' = 3.97 + .87X.$ By 10-8, $a = \overline{Y} - b\overline{X} = 29.20 - .87(29) = 3.97.$

Table 10-3 demonstrates the calculation of the standard error of estimate for the distribution in Figure 10-9. That figure graphically illustrates the relationship between the standard deviation of Y and the standard error of estimate. Both of those statistics can be represented by vertical line segments, and thus each statistic represents a *distance* parallel to the Y axis. The standard error of estimate for predicting X from Y is a line segment parallel to the X axis, and so is the standard deviation of X. Whatever we say regarding $SD_{Y|X}$ can also be applied to $SD_{X|Y}$, with suitable translation.

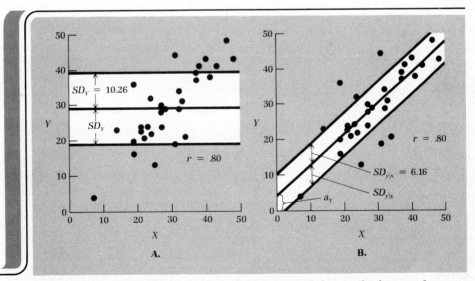

FIGURE 10-9. Comparing the standard deviation and the standard error of estimate (same data as Figure 10-1). **A:** All points in the shaded area are within 1 standard deviation of the Y mean. **B:** Shaded area is bounded by lines 1 standard error of estimate above and below regression line.

When there is a correlation between X and Y, the standard error of estimate is smaller than the standard deviation, as in Figure 10-9. In other words, the dispersion of the observed Y values with respect to the regression line is less than their dispersion with respect to the Y mean. Indeed, it is possible to interpret the correlation coefficient as a reduction in the error variance, as Equation 10-29 shows. The larger the value of r^2 in that equation, the smaller the value of the error variance and the standard error of estimate. When $r = 1$, Equation 10-30 shows that the standard error of estimate is equal to zero. When $r = 0$, the standard error of estimate for Y is exactly equal to the standard deviation of Y. In that case, knowledge of X is of no help in predicting Y. In the absence of a correlation, the best estimate of Y given any value of X is just the Y mean.

As you can see, there is a certain similarity between our present discussion of the standard error of estimate — that is, the standard deviation of Y and X — and our earlier discussion of conditional probability, the probability of event A given event B. Indeed, the standard error of estimate can be viewed as a kind of conditional standard deviation. The standard error of estimate is the standard deviation of Y around the regression line — that is, the standard deviation of Y given the relationship between X and Y. If there is a linear relationship between X and Y, then the standard deviation of Y given X will be different from the standard deviation of Y, as Figure 10-9 shows. In that case, X and Y are correlated and can be described as nonindependent. But if there is no linear relationship between X and Y, then the standard error of estimate will be equal to the standard deviation of Y. In that case, X and Y are uncorrelated and can be described as independent. Thus, we can write

For independent (uncorrelated) X and Y, $\qquad SD_{Y|X} = SD_Y$;

For nonindependent (correlated) X and Y, $\qquad SD_{Y|X} \neq SD_Y$.

Now, notice the similarity between the above equations and the following ones relating to conditional probability, presented in Chapter 6:

For independent events A and B, $\qquad\qquad P(A|B) = P(A)$; $\qquad$ (6-13)

For nonindependent events A and B, $\qquad\qquad P(A|B) \neq P(A)$. $\qquad$ (6-14)

The above equations indicate that for nonindependent events, knowing that event B has occurred changes our view of the probability of event A. Similarly, if X and Y are correlated (nonindependent), then knowing an individual's X score allows us to better estimate that individual's Y score. For example, a very high Y score is an event that has a low probability, but if we know that a particular individual has a high X score, then we will change our view of the probability that that individual also has a high Y score.

The Bivariate Normal Distribution.   When the following conditions hold, X and Y are *jointly normally distributed*, and their bivariate distribution is a **bivariate normal distribution:**

1. Taken separately, X and Y are *each* normally distributed.

2. For any and all values of X, the values of Y given X are normally distributed with equal variances.
3. For any and all values of Y, the values of X given Y are normally distributed with equal variances.

Condition 2, above, means that the variance around the regression line for predicting Y from X is equal for all values of X, and Condition 3 means that the variance around the regression line for predicting X from Y is equal for all values of Y. Figure 10-10A shows a distribution where the standard error of estimate, $SD_{Y|X}$, is the same for all values of X. Such a distribution is said to possess the property of **homoscedasticity** (the first c is pronounced as a k) — that is, equality of variance around the regression line for all values of X. The concept of homoscedasticity is closely related to homogeneity of variance, which we discussed in connection with t tests in the last chapter. As we will explain, homoscedasticity is important in interpreting the standard error of estimate.

Figure 10-10B shows a distribution lacking the property of homoscedasticity. For large values of X, the observed Y values are more widely scattered around the regression line than for small values of X. Since the variance of Y given X differs for different values of X, the distribution in Figure 10-10B is said to be **heteroscedastic.**

As we noted in Chapter 5, if a variable is normally distributed, then about 68% — roughly 2/3 — of the cases in a sample can be expected to lie within ± 1 SD of the mean. In Figure 10-9A, notice that about 2/3 of the cases fall in the shaded area, within 1 SD of the Y mean. If X and Y are jointly

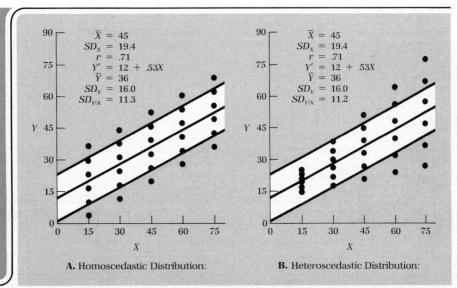

A. Homoscedastic Distribution: **B.** Heteroscedastic Distribution:

FIGURE 10-10. Distribution **A** displays homoscedasticity of Y values for all values of X; **B** displays heteroscedasticity. Shaded areas contain points within ± 1 $SD_{Y|X}$ of the regression lines for predicting Y from X.

normally distributed, then about 2/3 of the cases can also be expected to lie within ± 1 standard error of estimate of the regression line, as in Figure 10-9B. That means that if we use the regression equation to find a Y' value for any given X in the distribution, then the observed Y value will lie within 1 standard error of estimate of the predicted Y' about 68% of the time. Thus, there are close analogies between the standard deviation and the standard error of estimate. Indeed, the standard error of estimate *is* a standard deviation — the standard deviation of the errors made in predicting Y from X.

If a distribution is heteroscedastic — that is, if the variance of Y given X is not equal for all values of X — then we cannot use the standard error of estimate as a measure of prediction errors, as we did in Figure 10-9B. In the absence of homoscedasticity, we would need a different value of $SD_{Y|X}$ for each value of X. For example, in the heteroscedastic distribution in Figure 10-10B, for $X = 15$, all of the Y values are within ± 1 $SD_{Y|X}$ of the regression line, but only about 2/3 should fall in that region. For $X = 75$, 2/3 of the Y values are farther than 1 $SD_{Y|X}$ from the regression line, but only 1/3 should lie that far away. Thus, the standard error of estimate greatly underestimates prediction errors for some values of X in Figure 10-10B. Notice that the distributions in Figures 10-10A and B have the same regression equations and the same values of $SD_{Y|X}$. Indeed, those distributions are essentially identical except for the fact that one is homoscedastic and the other heteroscedastic. The absence of homoscedasticity in a distribution has great consequences for the use of the standard error of estimate in assessing the expected magnitude of prediction errors.

Estimation Errors and the Individual.   From one point of view, attempting to attach meaning to the error deviations from a regression line is a contradiction in terms. Except in the case of a perfect correlation, there will always be estimation errors in predicting one variable from another. Although we have treated those errors as random events in the past, we can nevertheless consider estimation errors in some other ways in some cases.

Consider, for example, the correlation between height and weight, which is substantial. As height increases, so does weight — though the relationship between those variables is not perfect. Now, visualize the regression line relating weight to height, and visualize a person whose weight is substantially above the regression line. Such a person is **fat.** There are short people who are fat, and tall people who are fat. Anyone whose weight is substantially greater than others of the same height is described as fat, and anyone whose weight is substantially less is described as **thin.** Thus, a person is fat if a large positive error is made in estimating weight from height, and thin if a large negative error is made.

Now consider a bivariate sample of academic aptitude test scores and school performance as measured by GPA. A student having a GPA substantially above the regression line has performed substantially better than we would estimate on the basis of the student's test score. Such a student can be described as an **overachiever,** a person who exceeds our expectations, perhaps through hard work, diligence, and good organization. On the other hand, a student having a GPA substantially below the regression line can be described as an **underachiever,** a person who fails to measure up to our expectations, perhaps through lack of application, poor organization, laziness, or some sort of handicap. A great many people feel uneasy, often with good reason, about pinning labels on other people. No doubt, labeling a student as an underachiever, or even as an overachiever, can sometimes have unhappy consequences. But on occasion, a student identified as an underachiever can sometimes be helped to perform at a much higher level — to the student's own benefit, and to everyone else's.

Some Inferential Statistics

Testing the Significance of r

Suppose we are interested in the correlation between height and weight in the population of adult males in the United States. We could in principle measure the height and weight of every member of that population, but in practice we must rely on the observation of samples from that very large population. Suppose we draw a sample of 20 men, and we observe that $r = .73$. If we drew another sample of 20 men, we should not expect to observe an r of *exactly* .73 in that second sample. The point is, r is a sample *statistic* that can be expected to vary from sample to sample, in much the way that the mean, standard deviation, and other statistics vary in different samples drawn from the same population. There exists of course a true value of the correlation between height and weight in our population of interest. The correlation coefficient in a population is a parameter symbolized by ρ (small Greek *rho*), and our best estimate of ρ is the sample statistic r.

Suppose we have a bivariate population where ρ, the correlation between the two variables, is zero. Would it be possible, just by chance, to draw a sample from that population and observe a substantial value of r? Clearly, the answer is yes. Even though there is no correlation between X and Y in the total population, it is nevertheless possible just through chance to draw a sample where the individuals having low X scores also happen to have low Y scores, and the individuals having high X scores also happen to have high Y scores. Such a sample would yield a substantial value of r, even though the value of ρ in the population is zero.

We will describe a test of the hypothesis that there is no correlation between X and Y in the population, that is, the null hypothesis that $\rho = 0$. The null and alternative hypotheses for such a test of r are listed below:

$H_0: \rho = 0$;

$H_1: \rho > 0$;

$H_2: \rho < 0$.

Like other sample statistics, r is a random variable having an expected value and a standard error. The expected value of r is ρ, and we estimate the standard error of r, S_r, from sample data. Thus, our test statistic follows the t distribution:

$$t = \frac{r - \rho}{S_r} = \frac{r}{\sqrt{\dfrac{1 - r^2}{N - 2}}}, \qquad \begin{array}{l} df = N - 2, \\[6pt] H_0 : \rho = 0. \end{array} \qquad (10\text{-}32)$$

The numerator of the t ratio, above, consists of the deviation of the observed value of a statistic from its expected value, and the denominator is an estimate of the standard error of the statistic. Thus, Equation 10-32 is analogous to the other t ratios we have used earlier.

The t ratio for testing the significance of an r is evaluated by finding the critical values associated with $N - 2$ degrees of freedom in Table B. We are more often interested in a two-tailed test, but if we are clearly interested in only one of the alternative hypotheses, then a one-tailed test is appropriate. If the observed value of t equals or exceeds the tabled critical value, then we reject the null hypothesis that $\rho = 0$ in favor of one of the alternative hypotheses.

We can best explain why there are 2 df associated with the above t ratio by considering a bivariate sample consisting of only two subjects. No matter what values of X and Y are attached to the two points representing the two subjects, it is always possible to connect those two points with a single straight line. Since there can be no dispersion around the regression line in such a distribution, the correlation will be perfect—either $+1$ or -1, depending on whether the slope of the line is positive or negative. Neither of the two points in such a distribution is free to vary from the regression line, and thus a correlation is always perfect when there are only two points. If there are three points in a distribution, then one point is free to vary from the regression line, since three points do not necessarily lie on a single straight line. Thus, there are $N - 2$ degrees of freedom associated with a correlation coefficient.

Formula 10-32 is usually written in the more compact form below:

$$t = \frac{r\sqrt{N - 2}}{\sqrt{1 - r^2}}, \qquad \begin{array}{l} df = N - 2, \\[6pt] H_0 : \rho = 0. \end{array} \qquad (10\text{-}33)$$

Formula 10-32, although less compact, is more clearly analogous to the other t ratios we have used in the past. Table 10-4 illustrates the use of Formula 10-33 in testing the significance of an r of .66, as observed in the distribution in Figure 10-12.

The preceding test of significance of an observed value of r can be used only to test the null hypothesis that $\rho = 0$. We are most often interested in the question of whether an observed r is significantly different from zero, but in some cases, we may be interested in testing other null hypotheses. For example, in the field of behavior genetics, it is sometimes possible to specify

TABLE 10-4.   Testing the Significance of a Pearson r of .66 where $N = 10$, as in Figure 10-12.

By Formula 10-33, $t = \dfrac{r\sqrt{N-2}}{\sqrt{1-r^2}}$;

$$df = N - 2$$
$$= 10 - 2 = 8.$$

$H_0: \rho = 0;$
$H_1: \rho > 0;$
$H_2: \rho < 0.$

$$t = \frac{.66\sqrt{10-2}}{\sqrt{1-.66^2}} = \frac{.66\sqrt{8}}{\sqrt{1-.44}} = \frac{.66(2.83)}{\sqrt{.56}} = \frac{1.87}{.75} = 2.49.$$

From Table B, $CV_{.05} = 2.306$; therefore reject H_0 at .05 level, accept H_1.

on theoretical grounds that the correlation between parents and children on some measure should be .50. In such a case, we would be interested in testing an observed r against an expected value of .50. In that case, and in any other situation where we wish to test an observed r against a nonzero expected value, it is necessary to use Fisher's r to Z transformation (see McNemar, 1969, p. 157). In other cases, we may be interested in testing the significance of the difference between two correlation coefficients. For example, does the correlation between height and weight differ between men and women? Fisher's r to Z transformation can also be used to test the significance of the difference between two rs.

Assessing Reliability and Validity

Before we can have any confidence in our ability to use a psychological test to predict anyone's future performance, we must first assess the reliability and validity of the test. In the case of a test of academic aptitude, we might assess the reliability by giving the test to the same subjects twice, making sure to allow a suitable interval of time to pass between the two administrations. We might then assess the validity by giving the test to a number of high-school seniors and observing the correlation between their test scores and grade-point averages at the end of their freshman year in college.

A test must be reliable in order to be valid, but reliability in itself offers no guarantee of the validity of a test. Thus, reliability is a necessary but not sufficient condition for validity. For example, suppose we have developed the hypothesis that larger people should have larger brains, and should therefore be brighter than smaller people, and thus do better in school. We can of course measure people's heights very reliably, though not perfectly so, because our heights decrease measurably over the course of a day. But if we correlated the heights of a group of students with their grade-point averages, we would find our very reliable height measurements lacking any validity in predicting academic performance in school. (On the other hand, height *is* a valid predictor in some other areas, for example, in predicting performance in some sports, and in occupations where size and strength are important factors.) It should be clear that a test cannot be valid without being reliable, since an unreliable test does not correlate with itself from one administration to another, and thus cannot be expected to correlate with anything else.

For a well-developed psychological test, the **reliability coefficient,** the correlation between two administrations of the test, may be as high as .95 or so. The **validity coefficient** is the correlation between the test and the **criterion,** the actual performance that we wish to predict. For a test of academic aptitude, for example, the validity coefficient may be on the order of .60, considerably lower than the typical reliability of such a test. Indeed, the validity coefficient for any test can never be significantly greater than the square of the reliability coefficient. If it is less than instantly obvious why that is so, and if you wish to delve more deeply into the important issues of reliability and validity, then see one of the following books on psychological testing: Anastasi (1968), or Cronbach (1970).

In order for a test to be useful for prediction or classification — or indeed, for any other purpose — the reliability coefficient must be on the order of .70 or higher. Although considerably lower values of r can be found statistically significant in large samples by Formula 10-33, a low reliability coefficient severely limits the possible magnitude of the validity coefficient, and that in turn greatly impairs the predictive value of the test. A low but statistically significant reliability coefficient can do nothing more than suggest that a researcher may be on the right path leading toward the development of a useful test.

A Subtle Problem: The Effect of a Truncated Range. What kind of subjects should we select in order to assess the validity of a psychological test, for example, a test of academic aptitude? Should we select a large random sample of entering freshmen, a sample that would very likely include some students of low aptitude, many of moderate aptitude, and some of very high aptitude? Or should we select a large sample of college freshmen who have done very well in high school, as measured by their grades? There is of course ample reason to believe that students who do well in high school will also tend to do well on our test — that is, if the test is any good. Intuitively, a sample of high-aptitude students may appear more desirable, but such a sample would be a very poor choice. Indeed, the correlation between test scores and college GPA is expected to be very low in such a group, even though our test might prove highly valid in a more representative sample.

If we have selected a sample of only the most capable entering freshmen, then we can indeed expect those students to have very high scores on our test. In that case, the range of test scores will be truncated — that is, cut off, in the sense that a portion of a geometric solid like a cone or pyramid can be truncated. The effects of a **truncated range** can be appreciated by referring to Figure 10-10A.

Suppose we truncated the range of the X variable in Figure 10-10A, leaving only the two highest values, 60 and 75. In doing so, we would also restrict the range of the Y values to just those Y scores associated with X values of 60 and 75. The total variance of Y, SD_Y^2, in that restricted set of Y scores would be substantially less than SD_Y^2 in the complete distribution. The standard error of estimate, however, is constant for all values of X when a distribution possesses homoscedasticity. Thus, the error variance, $SD^2_{Y|X}$, remains constant no matter how severely a distribution is truncated. Formula 10-26, which expresses r as a function of SD^2_Y and $SD^2_{Y|X}$, shows that r decreases when a distribution is truncated, since the value of the total variance of Y approaches that of the error variance.

Hardly anyone would be so naive as to attempt to validate a new test using a truncated distribution such as we have described, but occasionally the truncated range problem creates difficulties in some other contexts. For example, the Graduate Record Examination, a high-level test of academic aptitude, does not correlate as highly as some people might expect with grades or other measures of success in graduate school. Nor do grades earned in graduate school correlate very highly with the later productivity of research scientists. But graduate students represent a truncated distribution, and research scientists a more highly truncated one. Thus, we should not expect the correlations we have mentioned in those truncated distributions to be as high, for example, as the correlations between a test of academic aptitude and grade-point average among relatively unselected college freshmen.

Predicting the Future

So far, we have confined our discussion of prediction to the description of the relationship observed between two variables in a bivariate sample. Each individual in such a sample already has an X score and a Y score, so the process of "predicting" Y from X involves no consideration of the future, but rather involves the process of finding the regression line that best fits the *present* data, that is, the bivariate sample already in hand. Now, to what extent can we use the relationship that we have observed between X and Y in a bivariate sample to make predictions about the *future*?

Suppose, for example, that an industrial/organizational psychologist has developed a test designed to predict the level of proficiency among middle-management personnel in a small corporation. To assess reliability, the test is given to a group of 32 workers, and the reliability coefficient is .81. The psychologist then finds a significant correlation of .66 between the test and a measure of work proficiency among the 10 middle-level managers in the small corporation (see Table 10-4). Now suppose that the psychologist gives the test to a worker being considered for promotion to a management position. We can, of course, find the regression equation for estimating Y from X, that is, for estimating proficiency from test scores in our bivariate sample. But since we have only a test score on the new prospective manager, and not as yet a measure of work proficiency, that person is not a member of our bivariate sample. To what extent can we use the prospective manager's test score to predict that person's performance in a new job—that is, to what extent can we foretell the future? To answer that question, we will consider some of the relationships between bivariate samples and bivariate populations.

The Population Regression Line. Consider an infinite bivariate population where each individual has an X value and a Y value—for example, an infinite population of corporate managers, each having a test score and a measure of work proficiency in their jobs. There exists a **population regression line** that best expresses the relationship between X and Y in that bivariate population, and the equation of that regression line is the following:

$$\text{Population regression equation:} \qquad \mu_{Y|X} = \alpha + \beta X, \qquad (10\text{-}34)$$

where $\mu_{Y|X}$ is the mean of the Y values for any given value of X, α is the Y intercept, and β is the slope of the regression line. The following equations give the population regression coefficients:

$$\alpha = \mu_Y - \beta\mu_X \qquad \text{and} \qquad \beta = \rho\frac{\sigma_Y}{\sigma_X},$$

where μ_X and μ_Y are the mean of X and Y in the population, ρ is the Pearson correlation coefficient in the population, and σ_X and σ_Y are the population standard deviations.

The **sample regression line** has the following equation:

$$\text{Sample regression equation:} \qquad Y' = a + bX, \qquad (10\text{-}7)$$

$$\text{where } a = \bar{Y} - b\bar{X}, \qquad \text{and} \qquad b = r\frac{SD_Y}{SD_X}.$$

The above symbols are as defined previously for Equation 10-7.

Notice that the regression equations in a sample and in a population are of the same form. In keeping with our careful differentiation between samples and populations, we have used Roman letters for the observed values of regression coefficients in a bivariate sample and Greek letters for those coefficients in a bivariate population. In a sample, Y', a, b, r, SD_X, and SD_Y are *sample statistics*; and in a population, $\mu_{Y|X}$, α, β, ρ, σ_X, and σ_Y are *population parameters*.

If there is a positive correlation between X and Y in the population, then as X increases $\mu_{Y|X}$ also increases—that is, the mean of the Y value given X in the population is an increasing function of X when there is a positive correlation. Similarly, if there is a positive correlation between X and Y in a bivariate sample, then Y' is an increasing function of X. Thus, $\mu_{Y|X}$ is a population parameter that is analogous to the sample statistic Y', which is the estimated Y value in a sample for any given value of X.

The heavy line in Figure 10-11 is the population regression line in a bivariate population where there is a positive correlation between X and Y. The two lighter lines represent the sample regression lines in two small samples. Neither of those sample regression lines coincides with the population regression line, since the regression coefficients a and b are sample statistics—and thus random variables—that are expected to take different values in different samples. The dashed lines in Figure 10-11 are 1 $SD_{Y|X}$— that is, 1 sample standard error of estimate—above or below each of the

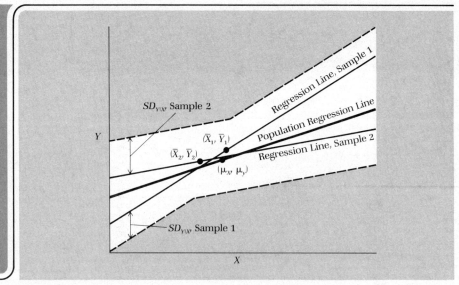

FIGURE 10-11. Population regression line (heavy line) and two sample regression lines (lighter solid lines). Dashed lines bound the region within ± 1 $SD_{Y|X}$ of either or both sample regression lines.

sample regression lines. The roughly hourglass-shaped area bounded by those dashed lines contains the observed Y values in both samples that lie within ± 1 $SD_{Y|X}$ of either sample regression line.

Now suppose we draw a very large number of samples of size 10, say, from the bivariate population illustrated in Figure 10-11. We find the sample regression equation in each sample, and we draw each of the sample regression lines. Most of those sample regression lines will cluster fairly closely around the population regression line. Indeed, the average location of the sample regression lines in the long run—that is, in an infinite number of samples—will precisely coincide with the population regression line.

A plot of the sample regression lines in such an exercise will look rather like the bundle of arrows in the American eagle's talons—that is, the regression lines will tend to cross each other near the center of the bivariate population. Using procedures that we will describe shortly, we can find a region surrounding the population regression line within which we expect 95% of the sample regression lines to lie. We will then develop a method of using the regression equation in a single bivariate sample to find the **confidence band for the population regression line,** a region that we expect to contain the population regression line with a particular level of confidence. For example, the inner pair of curved lines in Figure 10-12 define the 95% confidence band for the population regression line. That confidence band centers around the sample regression line observed in the illustrated bivariate sample of 10 cases, and has a probability of .95 of containing the population regression line.

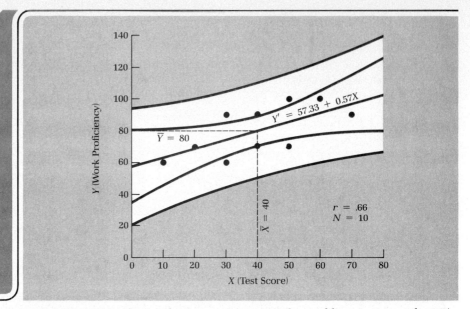

FIGURE 10-12. Predicting the future: Outer pair of curved lines represent the 95% confidence band for an individual predicted *Y* value, inner curved lines represent 95% confidence band for the population regression line. Significance of *r* is tested in Table 10-4.

Now consider the dashed lines in Figure 10-11. Any observed *Y* value falling within the region bounded by those dashed lines is within 1 sample standard error of estimate of either or both sample regression lines. If we plot the average location in a very large number of samples of the points within $\pm 1\, SD_{Y|X}$ of any of the sample regression lines, then those points will lie within a region bounded by curved lines similar to the outer pair of lines in Figure 10-12. We will use these ideas presently in predicting the future *Y* value for an individual for whom we have only an *X* score.

Standard Errors of Estimate.   In this section, we will develop three varieties of standard errors that are related to the sample standard error of estimate described earlier in this chapter. All of these standard errors will play a role in predicting the future *Y* values.

As we explained earlier, the error variance in a sample is the variance of the observed *Y* values with respect to the sample regression line, and the sample standard error of estimate, $SD_{Y|X}$, is the square root of that quantity. In a bivariate population the standard error of estimate is the standard deviation of *Y* values with respect to the population regression line, and is symbolized $\sigma_{Y|X}$. The sample error variance underestimates the population error variance by a factor of $N/(N-2)$, and thus multiplying the sample error variance in Equation 10-29 by that quantity yields an **unbiased estimate of the population error variance:**

$$S^2_{Y|X} = \frac{N}{N-2} SD^2_{Y|X} = \frac{N}{N-2} SD^2_Y(1-r^2). \tag{10-35}$$

The square root of the above quantity is the **corrected standard error of estimate:**

$$S_{Y|X} = SD_Y \sqrt{\frac{N}{N-2}(1-r^2)}. \tag{10-36}$$

Consider once again a large number of samples of some particular size drawn from a bivariate population where there is a correlation between X and Y. Suppose we find the regression equation in each sample. In all likelihood, those sample regression equations will differ from each other. Now suppose that we solve each regression equation for the Y' value associated with a given value of X, say an X value of 60. The different regression equations will yield many different Y' values—that is, many different estimated Y values—for that specific value of X, and indeed, for any given value of X. But in the population, there exists only one regression line, and thus only one estimated Y value—namely, $\mu_{Y|X}$—for any given X value. Thus, the Y' values found by the sample regression equations for any given value of X will be dispersed around the value of $\mu_{Y|X}$—that is, scattered around the population regression line. The standard deviation of those Y' values with respect to the population regression line is the **standard error of Y',** and is estimated by the following equation:

$$S_{Y'} = S_{Y|X} \sqrt{\frac{1}{N} + \frac{(X-\overline{X})^2}{NSD^2_X}}, \tag{10-37}$$

where $S_{Y'}$ is the standard error of Y', $S_{Y|X}$ is the standard error of estimate from Equation 10-36, N is the sample size, X is any given value of the X variable, and $\overline{X}$ and SD_X are the mean and standard deviation of the X values in the bivariate sample. Snedecor and Cochran (1980) and Working and Hotelling (1929) provide more extensive developments of these ideas.

Equation 10-37 allows us to estimate the standard error of Y' using a single bivariate sample of size N. In a later section, we will use $S_{Y'}$ to find the confidence band for the population regression line. We will then extend those ideas to finding a confidence band for a future Y value predicted for an individual having a given value of X.

We can best explain the nature of Equation 10-37 by squaring that equation and dealing with the resulting **error variance of Y':**

$$S^2_{Y'} = S^2_{Y|X} \left[\frac{1}{N} + \frac{(X-\overline{X})^2}{NSD^2_X} \right] = \frac{S^2_{Y|X}}{N} + \frac{S^2_{Y|X}}{N} Z^2_X, \tag{10-38}$$

remembering that $Z_X = (X-\overline{X})/SD_X$. Thus, the error variance of Y' is equal to $S^2_{Y|X}$ divided by N, plus a term that is a function of the square of the Z-score of a given X value. Equation 10-38 shows that $S^2_{Y'}$ differs for different given values of X. For example, when $X = \overline{X}$, $Z^2_X = 0$, and in that case $S^2_{Y'} = S^2_{Y|X}/N$.

But for a value of X above or below the sample mean, Z_X^2 will be positive, and the value of $S_{Y'}^2$ will be larger. Since the confidence band for the population regression line is found using $S_{Y'}$, as we will explain, that confidence band is bounded by curved lines that are closer together for values of X near the mean and farther apart for higher and lower given values of X. The inner pair of curved lines in Figure 10-12 are the boundaries of the 95% confidence band for the population regression line.

We now consider the problem of predicting the future Y score for an individual having at present only an X score. To make such a prediction of the future, we need to find a regression equation, and to do that, we need to have a bivariate sample already in hand. Now suppose that we have such a bivariate sample, where every member has an X score and a Y score already attached. We find the regression equation for predicting Y from X in that bivariate sample. However, the individual whose future we wish to predict is not a member of the bivariate sample already in hand, since that person has at present only an X score. But that person is a member of a bivariate *population* where we could in principle eventually obtain a measure of X and Y for every individual. Thus, predicting a future Y value based on the observation of an X value in the here-and-now requires drawing inferences about the characteristics of a bivariate population — that is, inferences about population parameters based on the observation of sample statistics in a bivariate sample.

To predict a future Y value given an individual's present X score, we begin by finding the regression equation in a bivariate sample using the same procedures described earlier in connection with Equation 10-7. We enter the individual's X score into the regression equation, and the resulting value of Y' is our best prediction of the individual's Y value to be observed in the future, Y_f. Now consider the error that we are likely to make in predicting that future Y value. It is highly unlikely that Y_f will fall precisely on the population regression line, or even precisely on the sample regression line. Thus, it is very unlikely that Y_f will be precisely equal to the predicted Y value, Y', or to $\mu_{Y|X}$, the point on the population regression line representing the mean of the Y values for any given value of X.

The error deviation of a future Y value from the population regression line is the sum of two other error deviations: The deviation of Y_f from Y', which is the deviation of the observed future Y value from the value predicted by the sample regression equation; and the deviation of Y' from $\mu_{Y|X}$, which is the deviation of the sample regression line from the population regression line at any given value of X. Thus,

$$(Y_f - \mu_{Y|X}) = (Y_f - Y') + (Y' - \mu_{Y|X}). \tag{10-39}$$

Equation 10-39 partitions the error deviations of a single future Y value from the population regression line into two components. But there are many possible future Y values associated with the value of Y' predicted by a regression equation based on a single bivariate sample — and in addition, there are many bivariate samples that can be drawn from a bivariate population. Thus, there are many error deviations of the form shown in Equation 10-39. We will square that equation and take the expected values of the squared error deviations:

$$E(Y_f - \mu_{Y|X})^2 = E(Y_f - Y')^2 + E(Y' - \mu_{Y|X})^2 + 2E[(Y_f - Y')(Y' - \mu_{Y|X})]. \quad (10\text{-}40)$$

The last term above is a function of the correlation between the error deviation within a sample and the deviation of the sample regression line from the population regression line. Since that correlation is zero, the last term in Equation 10-40 vanishes. Each of the remaining terms is a variance. The term on the left is the error variance of future Y values given X, that is, the variance of the future Y values with respect to the population regression line. The first term on the right is the error variance of the future Y values with respect to the sample regression line, and the second term is the variance of the *predicted* future Y values with respect to the regression line. Thus,

$$\sigma_{Yf}^2 = \sigma_{Yf|X}^2 + \sigma_{Y'}^2. \quad (10\text{-}41)$$

Based on the observation of a single bivariate sample, we can find estimates of the above variances. The variance of the future Y values with respect to the sample regression line is estimated by $S_{Y|X}^2$, as in Equation 10-35, and the variance of Y' values with respect to the population regression line is estimated by $S_{Y'}^2$, as in Equation 10-38. Substituting those estimates in Equation 10-41 yields an estimate of the variance of future Y values with respect to the population regression line:

$$S_{Yf}^2 = S_{Y|X}^2 + \frac{S_{Y|X}^2}{N} + \frac{S_{Y|X}^2}{N} Z_X^2$$

$$= S_{Y|X}^2 \left(1 + \frac{1}{N} + \frac{Z_X^2}{N} \right).$$

Taking the square root of the above equation yields the **standard error of Y_f**:

$$S_{Yf} = S_{Y|X} \sqrt{1 + \frac{1}{N} + \frac{Z_X^2}{N}}, \quad (10\text{-}42)$$

where S_{Yf} is the standard error of future Y values for a given value of X, $S_{Y|X}$ is the standard error of estimate from Equation 10-36, N is the sample size, and Z_X is the Z-score for a given value of X. Like the standard error of Y', the standard error of Y_f is at a minimum for a value of X equal to $\overline{X}$, increasing for larger and smaller given values of X. The outer pair of curved lines in Figure 10-12 are the boundaries of the 95% confidence band for a future Y value found by utilizing the standard error of Y_f in a procedure we will describe shortly.

Notice the terms under the radical in Equation 10-42. For a large sample, $1/N$ and Z_X^2/N both approach zero, the quantity under the radical approaches 1, and S_{Yf} aproaches $S_{Y|X}$, the standard error of estimate.

Confidence Band for the Population Regression Line.   In Chapter 8, we developed the idea of the sampling distribution, that is, the distribution of the means of all possible random samples of a given size that might be drawn from a population. We developed a procedure for estimating the standard deviation of the sampling distribution—the standard error of the mean—based on the observation of a single sample. We went on to find the confidence interval for the population mean utilizing information from a single sample, namely the observed value of the sample mean and an estimate of the standard error of the mean based on the observed standard deviation of the sample. In this section we will extend those ideas to finding the confidence band for the population regression line based on the observation of a single bivariate sample, and in the next section we will find the confidence band for a future predicted Y value.

The Y' value, which we calculate in a sample regression equation for any given value of X, is an unbiased estimate of $\mu_{Y|X}$, which is the mean of the Y values in the bivariate population for that given value of X. Thus, Y' bears essentially the same relationship to $\mu_{Y|X}$ that $\bar{Y}$ bears to μ_Y, or that $\bar{X}$ bears to μ_X. If we have a sample regression equation for a single bivariate sample, then we can use the calculated value of Y' for any given value of X to find a confidence interval for $\mu_{Y|X}$—that is, a range of Y values that we expect to contain $\mu_{Y|X}$ at a stated level of probability. The same reasoning that we used in developing the confidence interval for the mean in Chapter 8 applies to the present confidence intervals. The following equations give the confidence limits for $\mu_{Y|X}$:

$$LCL = Y' - t_{\alpha/2}S_{Y'},$$

$$UCL = Y' + t_{\alpha/2}S_{Y'},$$

$$df = N - 2, \tag{10-43}$$

where LCL and UCL are the lower and upper confidence limits, Y' is the predicted value for any given value of X in a sample regression equation, $t_{\alpha/2}$ is a 2-tailed t value, $S_{Y'}$ is the standard error of Y' from Equation 10-37, df is the degrees of freedom for the t value, and N is the number of pairs of observations in the sample.

Since Equation 10-37 shows that $S_{Y'}$ is larger for values of X that are farther away from $\bar{X}$, it follows that the confidence interval for $\mu_{Y|X}$ will also be larger for more deviant values of X. When we plot the confidence intervals for a large number of given X values on a bivariate distribution, and then connect all of the LCLs with each other, and similarly connect the UCLs, we then have the confidence band for the population regression line, the region between the inner pair of curved lines in Figure 10-12. The probability is .95 that the population regression line is contained within that region, which thus represents the 95% confidence band for the population regression line. Table 10-5 shows the calculation of the confidence limits for some selected values of X, and also the calculation of the necessary standard errors.

TABLE 10-5. Standard Errors of Estimate, Confidence Band for a Future Y Value, and Confidence Band for the Population Regression Line. Data are Shown Graphically in Figure 10-12.

X	Y
10	60
20	70
30	60
30	90
40	70
40	90
50	70
50	100
60	100
70	90

$\bar{X} = 40.00$; $\bar{Y} = 80.00$;

$SD_X = 17.32$; $SD_Y = 14.83$;

$r = .66$; $N = 10.$

Sample regression equation, by Formula 10-7:

$$Y' = a + bX; \qquad b = r\frac{SD_Y}{SD_X}; \qquad a = \bar{Y} - b\bar{X}.$$

$$b = .66\frac{14.83}{17.32} = .57.$$

$$a = 80 - .57(40) = 57.2.$$

$$Y' = 57.2 + .57X.$$

Sample standard error of estimate, by Formula 10-36:

$$S_{Y|X} = SD_Y\sqrt{\frac{N}{N-2}(1-r^2)} = 14.83\sqrt{\frac{10}{8}(1-.66^2)} = 12.43.$$

Standard error of Y' (predicted Y), by Formula 10-37:

$$S_{Y'} = S_{Y|X}\sqrt{\frac{1}{N} + \frac{(X-\bar{X})^2}{NSD_X^2}} = 12.46\sqrt{\frac{1}{10} + \frac{(X-40)^2}{10(17.32^2)}}.$$

95% confidence limits for $\mu_{Y|X}$ by Formula 10-43:

$$LCL = Y' - t_{\alpha/2}S_{Y'}; \qquad UCL = Y' + t_{\alpha/2}S_{Y'}. \qquad \text{For example, for } X = 60,$$

$$LCL = [57.2 + .57(60)] - 2.306\left[12.46\sqrt{\frac{1}{10} + \frac{(60-40)^2}{10(17.32^2)}}\right]$$

=	91.4	−	13.9	= 77.5;
$UCL =$	91.4	+	13.9	= 105.3.

For selected values of X,

X:	0	20	40	60	80
UCL	80.1	82.5	89.1	105.1	125.5
Y'	57.3	68.7	80.0	91.3	102.7
LCL	34.5	54.9	70.9	77.5	79.9

Note.   Connecting the LCLs and UCLs above yields the 95% confidence band for the population regression line, the inner pair of curved lines in Figure 10-12.

Standard error of Y_f (observed future Y values) by Formula 10-42:

$$S_{Yf} = S_{Y|X}\sqrt{1 + \frac{1}{N} + \frac{Z_X^2}{N}} = 12.46\sqrt{1 + \frac{1}{10} + \frac{Z_X^2}{10}}.$$

95% confidence limits for Y_f, by Formula 10-44:

$$LCL = Y' - t_{\alpha/2}S_{Yf}; \qquad UCL = Y' + t_{\alpha/2}S_{Yf}.$$

(continued)

TABLE 10-5.   *(continued)*

For example, for $X = 20$,

$$LCL = [57.2 + .57(20)] - 2.306\left[12.46\sqrt{1 + \frac{1}{10} + \frac{(20-40)^2}{10(17.32^2)}}\right]$$

$=$	68.6	$-$		31.9	$=$	36.7;
$UCL =$	68.6	$+$		31.9	$=$	100.5.

For selected values of X,

X:	0	20	40	60	80
UCL	93.9	100.5	110.1	123.3	139.5
Y'	57.2	68.6	80.0	91.4	102.8
LCL	20.5	36.7	49.9	59.5	66.1

Note. Connecting the *LCL*s and *UCL*s above yields the 95% confidence band for a future *Y* value, the outer pair of curved lines in Figure 10-12.

Confidence Limits for an Individual Future Y Value. Where we have an *X* score for a particular individual, and we have not yet observed the individual's *Y* score, we can use the sample regression equation to predict the future *Y* value. Solving the sample regression equation yields a value of *Y'*, which is our best predictor of Y_f, the individual's actual *Y* value to be observed at some time in the future. We can then use the standard error of Y_f, Equation 10-42, to find the confidence interval for the future *Y* value. The 95% confidence interval, for example, is a range of *Y* values centered at *Y'* which we expect to contain the future value of Y_f with a probability of .95. As in our earlier discussions, the lower and upper confidence limits are the bounds of the confidence interval:

$$LCL_{Yf} = Y' - t_{\alpha/2}S_{Yf},$$
$$UCL_{Yf} = Y' + t_{\alpha/2}S_{Yf},$$
$$df = N - 2, \tag{10-44}$$

where LCL_{Yf} and UCL_{Yf} are the lower and upper confidence limits for the future *Y* value, *Y'* is the predicted *Y* value for any given value of *X* in a sample regression equation, $t_{\alpha/2}$ is a 2-tailed *t* value, S_{Yf} is the standard error of future *Y* values in Equation 10-42, *df* is the degrees of freedom for the *t* value, and *N* is the number of pairs in the sample.

In working with confidence intervals, remember that

Confidence level $= 1 - \alpha$,   and $\alpha = 1 -$ confidence level.

Table 10-5 shows the calculation of several 95% and 99% confidence intervals for Y_f for different given values of *X*. Notice that the confidence intervals are larger for values of *X* that are farther away from $\overline{X}$, the sample mean of the *X* scores. Since S_{Yf} is larger for more deviant values of *X*, as we noted earlier, it follows that the confidence intervals are wider for future *Y* values associated with more deviant X values. Thus, we are more likely to make a larger error in predicting a future Y value from an X score that is very low or very high — that is, a score far below or far above the mean of the X scores.

Plotting the 95% confidence intervals for Y_f for a large number of given X values and then connecting the $LCLs$ and the $UCLs$ with each other yields the outer pair of curved lines in Figure 10-12. Those curved lines represent the 95% confidence band for a future Y value predicted from any given value of X. We can be 95% confident that any individual's Y_f value observed at some time in the future will fall within that confidence band.

Now consider the effects of the sample size on the shape of the confidence band for a future Y value. In Equation 10-44, the quantities $1/N$ and Z^2/N both approach zero as N becomes very large, and the expression under the radical then approaches 1. As a result S_{Yf} approaches $S_{Y|X}$ for any given value of X, and the curved boundaries of the confidence band approach straight lines located 1 standard error of estimate above and below the regression line. Indeed, in large samples of a hundred or so, the standard error of estimate in Equation 10-36 can be used to find the confidence interval for a future Y value with little loss of accuracy. But in attempting to predict a future Y value based on a small bivariate sample, confidence limits should be found using Equation 10-44. As you can see in Figure 10-12, the confidence band for Y_f is considerably wider for extreme values of X.

Whether a sample is large or small, we use the same procedure for predicting a future Y value given an individual's present X score. In either case, solving the sample regression equation for Y' yields a prediction of the future Y value. A regression equation based on a small sample might yield the same prediction of a future Y value as a regression equation in a large sample, but we are more likely to make a larger error in using the smaller sample. The procedures we have just described allow us to assess the magnitude of the errors that we are likely to make in predicting future Y values.

Some Final Words

There is probably no other statistical technique that has been so widely misunderstood, and even abused, as correlation. The existence of a correlation is too often taken as proof of a causal relationship between variables, but we have seen that correlation does not necessarily imply causality. It is also a mistake to suppose that a correlation means *nothing*, since there *may* be a causal relationship between variables that are correlated. We will end the present chapter on that cautionary note. In the next chapter, we will extend some of the procedures we have developed to situations involving ordinal and nominal scales.

Terms and Symbols

We have dealt with a rather substantial number of new terms and symbols in this chapter. As in the past, those are listed in the approximate order of their appearance in the text. Carefully compare and contrast these terms and the ideas they represent.

Sample and **population**
Bivariate distribution
Scatter diagram
Bivariate sample
Bivariate population
Regression line
Covary
Pearson product-moment correlation coefficient
Positive correlation
Negative correlation
Directly related
Inversely related
Linear regression
Prediction and **estimation**
Curvilinear relationship
Regression coefficient
Intercept
Slope
Least-squares criterion
Proportion of variance accounted for
Error variance
Explained variance
Total variance
Error deviation
Explained deviation
Total deviation
Partitioning
Variance of Y given X
Sample standard error of estimate
Sample regression line
Population regression line
Bivariate normal distribution
Homoscedasticity
Heteroscedastic
Fat and **thin**

Over- and **underachiever**
Significance of r
Predicting the future
Reliability and **validity**
Reliability coefficient
Validity coefficient
Unbiased estimator of population error variance
Corrected standard error of estimate
Confidence interval for Y'
Truncated range
r
Z_X and Z_Y
SS_X and SS_Y
Y'
a and b
ΔY and ΔX
$(\bar{X}, \bar{Y})$
SS_{TOT}, SS_E, and SS_{EXP}
SD_Y^2
$SD_{Y|X}^2$
SD_{EXP}^2
r^2
ρ
α
β
$\mu_{Y|X}$
μ_X and μ_Y
σ_X and σ_Y
$S_{Y|X}$
$S_{Y'}$
Y_f
S_{Yf}
σ_{Yf}^2
$\sigma_{Y'}^2$
$\sigma_{Y|X}^2$

EXERCISES AND STUDY QUESTIONS

1. Indicate whether you would expect to observe a positive or negative correlation in each of the following situations, and explain briefly.
   a. Words correct on a vocabulary test, and year in grade school.
   b. Running time for a 60-yard dash, and body weight in a group of 40-year-old men.
   c. Running *speed,* and body weight in the above group of men.
   d. Rank in class, and grade-point average.
   e. Magnitude of hand tremor, and marksmanship scores on a pistol range.
   f. Golf scores, and tournament winnings.
   g. Consumer Price Index by years, from 1965 through 1983.

2. Knowing some of the properties of Z-scores is very helpful in understanding several aspects of correlation and regression. Hence the following exercises:
   a. Show that $\Sigma Z = 0$ in general, that is, in every sample. Demonstrate algebraically that the above equation holds *in general,* not just in some particular distribution that you might devise.
   b. Find the value of ΣZ^2 in general. (Don't make the mistake of supposing that $\Sigma Z^2 = 0$ because $\Sigma Z = 0$.)

3. For each of the three bivariate distributions in Figure 10-2, make up a table similar to Table 10-1 showing the values of X, Y, X^2, Y^2, and so on.
   a. Using Conceptual Formula 10-1, calculate the value of r in each distribution. Notice particularly the roles that the Z-scores play.
   b. Using Computational Formula 10-5, find the value of r in each distribution.
   c. Which is easier to use, the simpler-appearing conceptual formula, or the more complicated-looking raw-score computational formula? Which is more accurate, and why?

4. The following data are the scores on two examinations in a statistics course:

Person:	1	2	3	4	5	6	7	8	9	10	11	12	13	14	15	16	17	18	19	20	21	22	23
Exam 1:	71	41	59	37	32	47	76	62	26	52	47	74	83	80	71	74	69	83	54	53	54	66	81
Exam 2:	84	53	70	62	28	35	64	71	59	57	56	78	81	89	76	78	71	61	45	61	57	56	87

   a. Draw a scatter diagram, treating Exam 1 as the X variable and Exam 2 as the Y variable. Estimate the value of r by looking at your scatter diagram. Compare your graph with Figure 10-1.
   b. Using Computational Formulas 10-5 and 10-6, find the correlation between the two exams.
   c. Is the observed value of r statistically significant? State the null and alternative hypotheses in words and symbols, indicate whether a 1 or 2-tailed test is appropriate, and indicate whether you reject H_0.

d. What proportion of the variance of Exam 2 is explained or accounted for by performance on Exam 1? What accounts for the rest of the variance? If Exam 1 accounts for a sizable proportion of the variance of Exam 2, does that mean that a high or low performance on the first exam tends to cause a high or low performance on the second?

e. Find the regression equation for predicting Exam 2 performance from the scores on Exam 1. (You will need SD_X and SD_Y for these calculations. As you can see by comparing Formulas 10-5 and 10-6, you have already found the sums of squares for X and Y, that is, SS_X and SS_Y, and thus it is easy at this point to find the required standard deviations.)

f. Plot the regression line on your scatter diagram, indicate the Y intercept, and indicate the point having the coordinates $(\overline{X}, \overline{Y})$.

g. Find the sample standard error of estimate using Formula 10-30. Plot a dashed line 1 $SD_{Y|X}$ above the regression line and plot another 1 $SD_{Y|X}$ below. What proportion of the distribution lies between those dashed lines? What proportion *should* lie within that region?

h. For Subject 9, find the predicted performance on Exam 2 based on the score on Exam 1. How would you describe that person, in terms of the discrepancy between the observed and predicted performance on the second exam? Do the same things for Subject 19. How might you account for the very different performances of these persons on Exam 2?

i. Suppose all of the students' scores on Exam 2 had been exactly 2 points higher than the actual scores shown above. How would that affect the value of the correlation between the two exams? (HINT: It is not necessary to recalculate r in order to answer this question. Consider, for example, what would happen to each of the Z-scores in Exercise 3 if you added a constant to each of the X values, or to the Y values, or to both, in one of your tables.)

j. Suppose everyone who failed to make a grade of C or better on the first exam dropped the course before taking the second exam. How would that most likely affect the correlation between the two exams? Explain.

k. Now suppose that everyone who made an A or a B on the first exam dropped the course because it wasn't challenging enough, and suppose that everyone else remained. How would that sort of exodus most likely affect the correlation between Exam 1 and Exam 2?

5. The baseball coach has designed a new test, the Baseball Aptitude Test (BAT), to aid in identifying and recruiting talented players. To assess the reliability of the BAT, the coach gives the test to 27 varsity baseball players on two occasions separated by a period of one week. Unfortunately, the reliability of the BAT was only .24, as measured by the test-retest correlation. In attempting to assess the validity of the BAT, the coach found a disappointing correlation of .06 between the players' scores on the first administration of the test and their batting averages in the season to date.

   a. Is the reliability coefficient of .24 statistically significant? State the null and alternative hypotheses in words and symbols. Indicate whether a 1 or 2-tailed test is appropriate, and indicate whether you reject H_0.

   b. Is the validity coefficient of .06 statistically significant?

   c. What advice would you give the coach regarding his new test?

6. A small manufacturing company considers the performance of its first-level supervisors crucial to its success. To improve the selection of capable supervisors, an industrial psychologist in consultation with management devises an objective measure of supervisors' performance on the job, and also designs a test to predict the future performance of supervisor candidates. The reliability of the test is .83 in a sample of 34 workers. Scores on the new test and actual job performance measures are shown below for the 12 supervisors currently employed:

Person:		1	2	3	4	5	6	7	8	9	10	11	12
Test score	(X):	62	33	21	12	42	45	54	43	51	71	57	73
Job performance	(Y):	74	67	62	49	72	67	89	63	80	83	60	66

   a. Is the reliability coefficient statistically significant?

   b. Carefully draw a scatter diagram showing the relationship between test scores and job performance.

   c. Find the validity coefficient, that is, the correlation between test scores and job performance using Formulas 10-5 and 10-6.

   d. Is the validity coefficient statistically significant? State the null and alternative hypotheses in words and symbols, and indicate whether a 1 or 2-tailed test is appropriate.

   e. Find the regression equation for predicting job performance from the test score.

   f. Find the 95% confidence band for the population regression line. Indicate this confidence band on your scatter diagram, and briefly explain its nature.

   g. Find the 95% confidence band for a future Y value predicted from an individual's test score. Indicate this confidence band on your scatter diagram, and explain briefly.

   h. Suppose we gave the test to 3 new supervisor candidates—that is, people not included in the original sample of 12 supervisors. Suppose the new candidates made test scores of 25, 47, and 72. Find the predicted job performance for each candidate, and find the 95% confidence interval for each prediction. Plot those confidence intervals on your scatter diagram, and explain how they relate to the 95% confidence band for a future Y value which you plotted previously.

7. Consider the confidence band for a future Y value, and for the population regression line, which you drew in the preceding exercise (also see Figure 10-12).
   a. For a constant sample size, what happens to the width and curvature of the confidence bands for different values of r?
   b. For a constant value of r, what happens to the width and curvature of the confidence bands in samples of different sizes?

8. Suppose we have a bivariate sample of 100 father-son pairs.
   a. If every son in our sample was exactly as tall as his father, what would be the observed value of the correlation between the heights of fathers and sons?
   b. Given the situation in a, above, what would you conclude regarding the relative contributions of heredity and environment in determining the height of sons?
   c. Now suppose that every son in our sample was exacty 1 inch taller than his father. In that case, what would be the observed value of the correlation between heights?
   d. Given the situation in c, above, what would you now conclude regarding the contributions of heredity and environment?

9. The actual correlation between the heights of fathers and sons is about .50, as predicted by genetic theory. But it is also true in the United States that sons have been about 1 inch taller than their fathers, on the average, over the last two generations.
   a. What does the correlation suggest, and the difference between generations suggest, regarding the heredity-environment issue?
   b. What bearing does the difference between generations have on the observed value of the correlation coefficient?
   c. What are some of the implications of a long-term increase in the size of the human species?

10. Parent-child correlations on intelligence tests are typically about .50.
   a. What can you conclude regarding the effects of heredity and environment on intelligence?
   b. Suppose there was a correlation of zero between the test performances of parents and children. What would you then conclude?

Measures of Association: Ordinal and Nominal Scales

11

In many instances, we may be interested in examining the correlation — association — between two variables that are measured on ordinal or nominal scales. Since the techniques we developed in the last chapter are most suitable for use with interval and ratio scales, we will develop additional procedures for use with the two lower-caliber measurement scales.

Ordinal Scales

Suppose two psychologists have developed a method of assessing aggression in school children. The method involves observing social interactions in a sample of children, and then placing the children in rank order of aggressiveness, assigning the rank 1 to the most aggressive and the rank N to the least aggressive child. The two researchers believe that their method will allow them to rank the children in aggressiveness, but they have no confidence in their ability to measure aggression on an interval or ratio scale. Thus, their measurements constitute only an ordinal scale. The questions of reliability and validity immediately arise: Does the method yield comparable results if the sample of children is assessed twice, and does the method measure what it was designed to measure — namely, aggression? We can answer those questions by proceeding much as we did in the last chapter, that is, we can assess the reliability by finding the correlation between two applications of the measurement method to the same children, and we can assess the validity by finding the correlation between the new measure and a standard measure of aggressive behavior, such as frequency and severity of antisocial behavior at school and elsewhere. But since we are dealing with measurements on an ordinal scale, we will need to develop a somewhat different variety of correlation coefficient.

Spearman's Rank-Order Correlation Coefficient, r_s

Spearman originally used the small Greek letter ρ *(rho)* to symbolize the statistic we are about to describe. For historic reasons, this correlation coefficient is sometimes called Spearman's *rho.* But in more recent years, most statisticians have come to use ρ to symbolize the value of the Pearson product-moment correlation coefficient in the population, in keeping with the customary use of Greek letters for population parameters and Roman letters for sample statistics. Thus, we will use r_s to symbolize the rank-order correlation coefficient. Furthermore, Spearman's rank-order correlation coefficient is a special case of the Pearson r, and thus our symbol r_s will serve as a reminder of the relationship between the two correlation coefficients. Indeed, r_s *is a Pearson* r where the X and Y variables are two sets of ranks.

Returning to the problem of assessing the reliability of the new method of measuring aggression, suppose that each of our two psychologists *independently* observes the same sample of 16 children, placing the children in

TABLE 11-1. Calculating r_s, Spearman's Rank-Order Correlation Coefficient.

Subject Number	$Rank_X$	$Rank_Y$	D	D^2	
1	1	2	−1	1	Applying Formula 11-1,
2	2	1	1	1	
3	3	3	0	0	$r_s = 1 - \dfrac{6\Sigma D^2}{N(N^2 - 1)}$
4	4	6	−2	4	
5	5	4	1	1	$= 1 - \dfrac{6(34)}{12(12^2 - 1)}$
6	6	8	−2	4	
7	7	7	0	0	$= 1 - \dfrac{204}{12(143)}$
8	8	5	3	9	
9	9	10	−1	1	$= 1 - \dfrac{204}{1716}$
10	10	12	−2	4	
11	11	11	0	0	$= 1 - .12 = .88.$
12	12	9	3	9	From Table D, $p < .01$, 1-tailed.
	78	78	0	34	

Arithmetic checks:
(1) $\Sigma R_X = \Sigma R_Y = N(N + 1)/2 = 78$;
(2) $\Sigma D = 0$.

rank order of aggressiveness, as in Table 11-1. For each child, **$Rank_X$** is the assessment by the first psychologist and **$Rank_Y$** is the assessment by the second psychologist. We now have two applications of the method to the same children, and thus we can assess the reliability of the method by noting the extent of agreement between the ranks which the two psychologists assigned to the children. As you can see, there is substantial — though not perfect — agreement between the two sets of ranks. Children ranked high in aggression by one psychologist also tend to be ranked high by the other, and similarly for children ranked low. Spearman's **rank-order correlation coefficient** is an index of the relationship between two variables measured on ordinal scales:

$$r_S = 1 - \frac{6\Sigma D^2}{N(N^2 - 1)}, \tag{11-1}$$

where $D = Rank_X - Rank_Y$, and $N =$ Number of subjects.

Table 11-1 demonstrates the calculation of r_S. The difference for each child, **D**, is found by subtracting $Rank_Y$ from $Rank_X$, always carrying out the subtraction in the same direction and retaining the sign. (We could just as well subtract $Rank_X$ from $Rank_Y$ as long as we were consistent.) The following arithmetic checks are very helpful:

$$\text{Arithmetic checks: } \Sigma Rank_X = \Sigma Rank_Y = \frac{N(N + 1)}{2}, \quad \text{and} \quad \Sigma D = 0.$$

Since the X and Y measures are two sets of ranks on the same number of subjects, the sums of ranks must be equal, as in the first arithmetic check above. Since a set of ranks is an arithmetic progression ranging from 1 through N, the sum of such a progression is $N(N + 1)/2$. (It is especially useful to check the value of the sum of the ranks when some of the ranks are tied, as in the next section.) Errors involving sign are very easy to make. The second arithmetic check, above, is very useful in detecting such errors.

Like the Pearson r, r_s can take on values between -1 and $+1$ inclusive. Referring to Formula 11-1, it is easy to see that $r_s = 1$ when there is perfect agreement between the two sets of ranks, since in that case $D = 0$ for every pair of ranks. Now consider the situation where there is the *least* agreement between the two sets of ranks — that is, where there is the maximum disagreement. In that case, the smallest $Rank_X$ will be paired with the largest $Rank_Y$, the next smallest $Rank_X$ with the next largest $Rank_Y$, and so on through the largest $Rank_X$ and the smallest $Rank_Y$. Thus, when there is maximum disagreement, there is a perfect negative correlation between the ranks, and the value of r_s is equal to -1.

The substantial value of r_s found in Table 11-1 indicates that the method of assessing aggression has a high degree of reliability since there is a high correlation between the assessments made by the two psychologists. The type of reliability here is called **interjudge reliability,** a measure of the extent to which two judges make comparable assessments of the same subjects using the same measurement technique. We will see that r_s is useful for other things besides finding interjudge reliability, and we should also note that interjudge reliability can be assessed in other ways than by calculating r_s — for example, by calculating a Pearson r if the data constitute an interval or ratio scale.

Relationship Between r and r_s.   Although the formulas for r and r_s appear very different, the two correlation coefficients are closely related. Indeed as we noted earlier, Spearman's r_s *is* a Pearson r calculated from data consisting of two sets of ranks. By utilizing the properties of two sets of ranks, Formula 11-1 can be derived from the Pearson r. Edwards (1967) offers an excellent derivation.

If r_s is directly derived from r, then it may not be entirely obvious that there is any advantage in using r_s. Why not simply calculate r, regardless of whether the data are measured on an ordinal scale or one of the higher-caliber measurement scales? There are two principal reasons why r_s is useful: First, when the data consist of ranks, r_s is much easier to calculate than r; and second, the procedure for testing the significance of r_s is different. The t test, which we presented earlier for testing the significance of r, requires at least an interval scale, and thus that procedure cannot be used with r_s without violating one of the t test requirements.

The Significance of r_s.   Suppose we have a sample of three subjects who are measured on two ordinally scaled variables, X and Y. Table 11-2 shows that there are exactly six ways that the three values of $Rank_X$ can be paired with the three values of $Rank_Y$. Since each set of ranks consists of three values, we are dealing here with the number of permutations of 3 things taken 3 at a time. If there is no correlation between X and Y, then each of the six possible pairings of ranks has the same probability of occurring, namely

TABLE 11-2.   Values of Spearman's r_s for All Possible Pairings of X and Y Ranks in a Sample of 3 Subjects.

Subject Number	$Rank_x$	Possible Permutations of Y Ranks					
		1	2	3	4	5	6
1	1	1	1	2	2	3	3
2	2	2	3	1	3	1	2
3	3	3	2	3	1	2	1
Probability of pairing R_X and R_Y		$\frac{1}{6}$	$\frac{1}{6}$	$\frac{1}{6}$	$\frac{1}{6}$	$\frac{1}{6}$	$\frac{1}{6}$
Value of r_s		1.00	.50	.50	−.50	−.50	−1.00
1-tailed probability of observing r_s as extreme as indicated value		$\frac{1}{6}$	$\frac{3}{6}$		$\frac{3}{6}$		$\frac{1}{6}$

1/6, as Table 11-2 shows. For each of the possible pairings of ranks, Table 11-2 shows the value of r_s, and also shows the one-tailed probability of observing a value as great or greater than the indicated value. Since there is only one way of observing an r_s of 1.00, the probability of observing that value is 1/6. But there are two ways of observing an r_s of .50, and so the probability of observing a value of .50 *or greater* is equal to 2/6 plus the probability of observing 1.00. Thus, the probability of observing .50 or greater is equal to 3/6, as the table shows. Similarly, the probability of observing a value of −.50 *or less* is also equal to 3/6.

Now, in a sample of three subjects, what value of r_s would we have to observe in order to reject the null hypothesis of zero correlation at the .05 level by a one-tailed test? Table 11-2 should convince you that no test of the significance of r_s can be carried out at the .05 level if there are only three subjects in our sample. The probability of observing a value of 1.00 (or −1.00) is 1/6 = .17, so there is *no* value of r_s that we could observe with a probability of .05 or less under the null hypothesis. Thus, it is not possible to carry out a test of r_s at the .05 level if we have a sample of only three cases.

Now consider a Pearson r in a sample of three subjects. Referring to Formula 10-33, which is an equation relating r and t, we note that r has 1 degree of freedom when $N = 3$. From Table B, the critical value of t for 1 df for a one-tailed test at the .05 level is 6.314. Entering that value into Formula 10-33 and solving the resulting equation for r yields a critical value of .988 for a one-tailed test at the .05 level. Thus, unlike r_s, there is a value of r that we might potentially observe in a sample of three subjects that would allow us to reject the null hypothesis by a one-tailed test at the .05 level. Although r_s is a Pearson r calculated on a set of ranks, the statistical significance of the two correlation coefficients must be tested by different methods because of the differences in the properties of their measurement scales. Table D gives critical values of r_s for one- and two-tailed tests of the null hypothesis that $\rho_s = 0$ in the population. The null hypothesis is rejected for an observed value of r_s greater than or equal to a tabled value for a given sample size and level of significance. For sample sizes larger than 30, which are not given in Table E, the significance of r_s can be tested using Formula 10-33, treating r_s in the same way as the Pearson r.

Tied Ranks. The derivation of Spearman's r_s is based on the assumption that there are no ties between any of the ranks within the X variable or within the Y variable. But in actual practice **tied ranks** often occur, so we will develop procedures for dealing with such situations.

As we noted in our early discussion of measurement scales in Chapter 1, we can convert any high-caliber measurement scale into any lower-caliber scale. Sometimes, there may be a considerable computational advantage in converting ratio or interval measurements into an ordinal scale. For example, suppose we want to find the correlation between weight and height in the sample of women shown in Table 11-3. Height in inches is a two-digit number and weight in pounds is a three-digit number for most adults. While each

TABLE 11-3.   Calculation of r_s With Tied Ranks.

Height (X)	Rank$_X$	Weight (Y)	R_Y	$R_X - R_Y = D$	D^2
69	1	140	1	0	0
67	2	135	2.5	−.5	.25
66	3.5	135	2.5	1	1
66	3.5	125	5	−1.5	2.25
65	5.5	120	6	−.5	.25
65	5.5	130	4	1.5	2.25
64	7.5	115	7	.5	.25
64	7.5	105	8.5	−1	1
63	9	100	10.5	−1.5	2.25
62	10	100	10.5	−.5	.25
61	11	105	8.5	2.5	2.25
60	12	96	12	0	0
	78		78	0	12

Arithmetic checks: (1) $\Sigma R_X = \Sigma R_Y = N(N+1)/2 = 12(12+1)/2 = 78$;
(2) $\Sigma D = 0$.

By Formula 11-1, $r_s = 1 - \dfrac{6\Sigma D^2}{N(N^2-1)} = 1 - \dfrac{6(12)}{12(144-1)} = .96.$

variable constitutes a ratio scale — the highest-caliber measurement scale — it may be more convenient to convert the variables to ordinal scales in order to calculate r_s rather than r. As you can see in Table 11-3, each value of D is at most a small two-digit number. Thus, calculating r_s involves squaring and summing a set of small numbers, while calculating r requires squaring and summing larger numbers, and also summing their cross-products. If you happen not to have a calculator at hand, r_s is often easier to calculate than r.

When we have a set of measurements on an interval or ratio scale, it often turns out that ties occur — that is, two or more subjects often have the same X, or Y, measurement. If two or more subjects have the same X measure, then they must be assigned the same $Rank_x$, namely the mean of the ranks they would be assigned in the absence of ties, as Table 11-3 shows. The procedures for dealing with ties here is identical to the procedure used in the Mann-Whitney U test in Chapter 8. Dealing with ties in this way insures that the sum of the rank differences will equal zero, and also insures that the sum of the ranks for the X and Y variables will be the same as in the absence of ties. Those conditions must be met if Formula 11-1 is to yield meaningful results.

Table 11-3 illustrates the calculation of r_s with tied ranks. The illustrated method of handling ties is quite adequate in most cases, but where there is a large proportion of tied ranks — substantially more than half — a better, but more complicated procedure is available (Siegel, 1956). Our simple procedure for handling ties leads to a slight underestimation of r_s, and thus our procedure is conservatively biased — that is, biased in the direction of decreasing the probability of a Type 1 error.

For purposes of comparison, the Pearson r calculated on the actual values of height and weight in Table 11-3 is .91. As you can see, r and r_s are closely comparable — though not identical. Since those two correlation coefficients differ somewhat, which one is *right?* The answer should be clear: Height and weight are measured on ratio scales, and when we reduce those measurements to the lower-caliber ordinal scale, we lose information, and thus we lose some precision. If our measurements constitute an interval or ratio scale, then r will be a more precise index of the correlation between variables. However, the small loss in precision in calculating r_s may be offset by the greater ease of calculation — especially if you do not have access to a fairly sophisticated calculator. The comparison between r and r_s in Table 11-3 should not lead you to suppose that the former coefficient is always smaller than the latter. Sometimes one coefficient is larger, and sometimes the other is.

Nominal Scales

There are a great many situations where we may be interested in assessing the association — correlation — between two variables measured on nominal scales. For example, is there any relationship between sex and employment in the professions of medicine and nursing? It may occur to you that we can ask that question in a slightly different way: Is there any difference between the proportion of women (or men) in the fields of nursing and medicine? We are dealing here with a *sex* variable having two categories — *levels*, or values — and a *profession* variable also having two levels. Applying a **two-way classification** procedure to a sample of nurses and physicians, classifying each person in terms of sex and profession, yields the sort of data shown in Table 11-4. When each variable has two levels, a two-way classification yields a **2 by 2,** or **fourfold, table** having four **cells,** each cell representing a sort of

TABLE 11-4. Association Between Sex and Profession: Calculating the ϕ Coefficient and Testing Its Significance.

		Profession: X Variable		
		(0) Physicians	(1) Nurses	
Sex: Y Variable	(0) Men	a 79	b 4	$83 = a + b$
	(1) Women	c 14	d 110	$124 = c + d$
		93 $= a + c$ $= N_1$	114 $= b + d$ $= N_2$	$207 = N$

Applying Formula 11-2, $\phi = \dfrac{ad - bc}{\sqrt{(a + b)(c + d)(a + c)(b + d)}}$

$$= \frac{79(110) - 4(14)}{\sqrt{83(124)(93)(114)}} = \frac{8,690 - 56}{\sqrt{109,115,784}} = \frac{8,634}{10,445.85} = .83.$$

Testing the significance of ϕ: H_0:   No association between variables;

                            H_1:   Variables are associated.

By Formula 9-34, $Z_{(P_1 - P_2)} = \dfrac{|P_1 - P_2| - .5\left(\dfrac{1}{N_1} + \dfrac{1}{N_2}\right)}{\sqrt{p_c q_c \left(\dfrac{1}{N_1} + \dfrac{1}{N_2}\right)}}$;

$P_1 = \dfrac{14}{93} = .151; P_2 = \dfrac{110}{114} = .965; p_C = \dfrac{(14 + 110)}{207} = .599; q_C = 1 - p_C = .401.$

$$Z_{(P_1 - P_2)} = \frac{|.151 - .965| - .5\left(\dfrac{1}{93} + \dfrac{1}{114}\right)}{\sqrt{.599(.401)\left(\dfrac{1}{93} + \dfrac{1}{114}\right)}} = 11.749. \qquad \text{Thus, reject } H_0 \text{ at .001.}$$

bin or box holding the indicated number of persons sharing a particular combination of sex and profession. Each person falls into one and only one of the cells labeled a through d. Cell a, for example, contains those 14 people who are women and physicians, while Cell b contains those 110 people who are women and nurses. We will deal with other aspects of Table 11-4 in a later section.

    Possible relationships between many other kinds of nominal variables may also be of interest. For example, is there any association between place of residence (urban, suburban, rural) and political party preference (Democratic, Republican, Independent, other)? The data required to answer such a question would appear in a 3 by 4 table having twelve cells since there is a *residence* variable having three levels and a *preference* variable having four. We might also examine the possible association between several racial or ethnic categories and political party preference, or the association between category of mental disorder and social class. There is almost no end to the number of such questions we can ask, and almost no end to the size of tables that such questions generate.

First, we will develop the ϕ coefficient (small Greek *phi*) as a measure of association in a 2 by 2 table. That measure is closely related to the Pearson *r* and also to the *Z* test of a difference between binomial proportions. We will then develop the *chi*-square (hard *ch*, as in *k*) test of association in a 2 by 2 table, and then extend that test to two-way tables of any size. We will use the symbol χ^2 (small Greek *chi*) to stand for the *chi*-square statistic.

The ϕ Coefficient

In Table 11-4, we have a total of 207 people who are measured on a *profession* variable *(X)* and a *sex* variable *(Y)*. We have assigned the male sex the value of 0 and the female sex the value of 1, but since we are dealing with a nominal scale where the numbers have no true quantitative meaning, we could just as well reverse those values, or the values assigned to the two levels of the *profession* variable. Table 11-5 is a partial list of the subjects appearing in Table 11-4. Subject 1 is a nurse who is a woman, 2 is a physician who is a man,

TABLE 11-5. Partial Listing of Subjects Appearing in Table 11-4.

Subject Number	Profession X	Sex Y	Cell in Table 11-4
1	1	1	*d*
2	0	0	*a*
3	0	1	*c*
4	1	1	*d*
.	.	.	.
.	.	.	.
.	.	.	.
207	1	0	*b*

and so on. To assess the relationship between *X* and *Y*, we could treat both variables as though they were measured on an interval or ratio scale, and then calculate a Pearson *r* using one of our computational formulas. But where the *X* and *Y* variables are both **dichotomous** — consisting of only two values, 0 and 1 — a much simpler procedure is available. The ϕ **coefficient,** defined by the formula below, is exactly equivalent to a Pearson *r* when *X* and *Y* are both dichotomous:

$$\phi = \frac{ad - bc}{\sqrt{(a + b)(c + d)(a + c)(b + d)}}, \qquad (11\text{-}2)$$

where *a, b, c,* and *d* are observed frequencies in a fourfold table. The ϕ coefficient is derived from the Pearson *r* in Appendix C, using only a little algebra.

Table 11-4 demonstrates the calculation of a ϕ coefficient. As you can see, Formula 11-2 involves considerably less arithmetic than calculating a Pearson r by one of our other computational formulas. Notice that each of the four terms in parentheses in the denominator of Formula 11-2 is one of the marginal totals in Table 11-4.

The Values of ϕ.   Like r, ϕ can take on all values from -1.00 through $+1.00$. A zero value indicates a complete absence of relationship — association — between the two variables, and values of -1.00 and $+1.00$ respectively indicate perfect negative and positive associations. However, the *sign* of a ϕ coefficient turns out to be arbitrary in many cases. For example, in Table 11-4, we arbitrarily assigned the value of 0 to men and 1 to women. Had we reversed those numbers, our ϕ coefficient would have had a negative sign, but the same magnitude.

In some cases, we can clearly attach quantitative meaning to the levels of dichotomous variables such as success and failure, presence and absence, or living and dead. In a drug study, for example, we might administer a drug to some subjects and a placebo to others, assigning the value of 0 to the placebo and 1 to the drug. We might then observe the subjects' performance on a behavioral test, assigning the value of 0 to failure and 1 to success. A positive value of ϕ would then indicate better performance under the drug, and a negative value would indicate a worse performance under the drug than under the placebo.

The value of ϕ in Table 11-4 indicates a strong association between sex and profession among the men and women in our sample. The relationship is highly statistically significant, as we will explain in a later section. Men are disproportionately represented in the profession of medicine and women in the profession of nursing. A randomly chosen physician is more likely to be a man, and a randomly chosen nurse more likely to be a woman. Thus, the profession variable is **contingent** — statistically dependent — on sex, and thus Table 11-4 can be called a **contingency table.**

The ideas of conditional probability, which we developed much earlier, apply directly to the interpretation of contingency tables. For example, what is the probability of randomly drawing a man from the 207 persons in Table 11-4? Since there are 83 men in that table,

$$P(\text{Man}) \;=\; \frac{83}{207} \;=\; .401.$$

Now, what is the probability of drawing a man from among the 93 physicians in Table 11-4? In other words, what is the probability that a person is a man, given that that person is a member of the medical profession? In order to apply Formula 6-16, we need to find the probability of the intersection of the events *Man* and *Physician* and the prior probability of the event *Physician*. Since there are 79 people who are men *and* physicians, $P(\text{Man} \cap \text{Physician}) = 79/207$, and since there are 93 physicians, $P(\text{Physician}) = 93/207$.

Applying 6-16 to find the conditional probability,

$$P(\text{Man}|\text{Physician}) = \frac{P(\text{Man} \cap \text{Physician})}{P(\text{Physician})} = \frac{79/207}{93/207} = .849.$$

Since $P(\text{Man}|\text{Physician}) \neq P(\text{Man})$, the events *Man* and *Physician* are nonindependent, and thus related. Similarly, the events *Man* and *Nurse* are also related, as are the events *Woman* and *Physician,* and *Woman* and *Nurse.* Since the events representing the levels of the *Sex* variable are related to the events representing the levels of the *Profession* variable, those variables are themselves associated.

A few more words about causality may be in order here. At the risk of tedious repetition, we again emphasize that a correlation does not necessarily imply that one variable causes the other. The association that we observe between sex and profession does not mean that sex necessarily causes — or even predisposes — men to become physicians and women to become nurses. Many other alternative explanations can be offered, some with a great many social and cultural implications.

The Statistical Significance of ϕ. The value of ϕ that we observed in Table 11-4 is very substantial, but as we have noted earlier in several other contexts, it is possible to observe an extreme value of a statistic just by chance. If there is an association between sex and profession, then the proportion of female physicians will differ significantly from the proportion of female nurses — or equivalently, we could state that the proportion of male physicians will differ significantly from the proportion of male nurses. In Table 11-4, the observed proportion of physicians who are women is $P_1 = 14/93 = .151$, and the observed proportion of nurses who are women is $P_2 = 110/114 = .965$. The Z test in Table 11-4 is a test of the significance of the difference between those binomial proportions, and thus constitutes a test of the significance of the observed ϕ coefficient. Since the observed value of Z greatly exceeds the two-tailed critical value at the .001 level, we reject the null hypothesis of no difference between the proportions of women in the professions of medicine and nursing in favor of the alternative hypothesis of a greater proportion of women in nursing. Rejecting that null hypothesis is equivalent to rejecting a null hypothesis of no association between sex and profession in favor of an alternative hypothesis stating there is an association between those variables.

Requirements for ϕ. The ϕ coefficient is based on the assumption that both variables are measured on nominal scales. Each variable is assumed to be a **true dichotomy,** a scale having only two values. In the human species, the male and female sexes represent a true dichotomy — if we exclude from consideration those rare abnormalities involving absence or reduplication of one or the other of the sex chromosomes. But if we were to classify a number of students into *high* and *low* aptitude categories on the basis of academic aptitude test scores and into *high* and *low* performance categories on the basis of grade-point averages, then we would create an **artificial dichotomy** on the aptitude variable and on the performance variable. As we have noted earlier, such variables represent continuous interval scales and also tend to be approximately normally distributed. Where two normally distributed variables are artificially dichotomized—degraded into nominal scales—a ϕ coefficient tends to underestimate the degree of correlation that would be observed if a Pearson r were calculated using the actual many-valued interval- or ratio-scale measurements of the variables. Where interval or ratio scales *are* dichotomized for some reason, the **tetrachoric correlation coefficient,** symbolized r_t, is a better estimate of the Pearson r than is the ϕ coefficient. For a more extended discussion of r_t than we can provide here, see McNemar (1969).

As a descriptive statistic, ϕ can be calculated in a sample of nearly any size. There would be little point in calculating ϕ where $N = 2$, since, like other correlation coefficients, ϕ can only take on the value of zero or one in that case. But in small samples of any modest size, ϕ can provide a descriptive measure of the relationship between two nominal variables. However, if the statistical significance of ϕ is to be assessed by the test of binomial proportions, as above, or by the *chi*-square test which we will develop shortly, then the sample-size requirements for those procedures must be met. The requirements for the test of binomial proportions are listed in Table 9-13, and the requirements for *chi*-square are presented in a later section. Where those sample-size requirements cannot be met, Fisher's exact test (Siegel, 1956) provides an alternative procedure for testing the significance of ϕ.

A Mixed Case: A Dichotomy and an Interval or Ratio Scale

The Point-Biserial Correlation Coefficient, r_{pb}.   Where one variable is a true dichotomy consisting of two levels on a nominal scale and the other is measured on an interval or ratio scale, **the point-biserial correlation coefficient, r_{pb},** provides a measure of association. There are a great many questions that can be asked regarding possible associations between variables measured in those ways. Is there any association between category of mental disorder—schizophrenia, manic-depressive psychosis—and age at onset? Is there any correlation between height in human males and the presence or absence of the XYY genetic syndrome? Is there any relationship between sex—male, female—and income in the medical profession?

It may strike you that we already have a method of answering the above questions. In each case, the dichotomous variable allows us to divide the subjects into two independent groups, each group possessing only one of the levels of that variable. If the interval or ratio scale is approximately normally distributed, and if the variances on that measurement scale are reasonably homogeneous in the two groups, then the requirements of the independent 2-sample t test are met. We can find the mean of the continuous variable for each group, and then test the difference between group means by the independent 2-sample t test. A statistically significant difference between means will establish the existence of an association between the dichotomous and the continuous variable.

The advantage of calculating a correlation coefficient in the present situation lies in the fact that r_{pb}, like the Pearson r, is a number between -1.00 and $+1.00$ inclusive. Thus, r_{pb} offers a more directly interpretable index of association than does a t ratio in a test of a difference between means.

To illustrate the use of r_{pb} we will consider the relationship between sex and height in a sample of young men and women. We will designate the dichotomous variable as X, assigning the values of 0 and 1, respectively, to women and men, and we will designate the other variable as Y. Figure 11-1 is a scatter diagram showing the sex and height of 13 men and 14 women. It is not necessary to have equal numbers in the two groups, but if inferences are to be drawn about a population based on a value of r_{pb} observed in a sample — that is, if the statistical significance of r_{pb} is to be tested — then the proportions of subjects in the dichotomous groups should approximate their proportions in the population. The proportions of *young* men and women are approximately equal in the population, and also in our sample of 27 people.

The scatter diagram in Figure 11-1 suggests a strong association between sex and height. There is some overlap between the two distributions — not every man is taller than every woman — but there is a strong tendency for

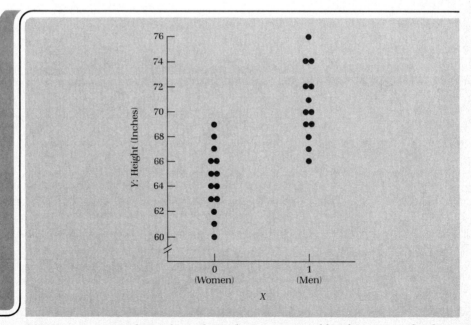

FIGURE 11-1. Point-biserial correlation between sex and height in a sample of 13 men and 14 women; $r_{pb} = .74$ (see Table 11-6).

men to be taller. The point-biserial correlation coefficient provides a numerical index of that tendency.

Figure 11-1 will help explain the origin of the term *point-biserial correlation*. The dichotomous *sex* variable is a discrete variable that can take only the *point* values of 0 and 1. Each of those point values is associated with a range — a *series* — of many values of the Y variable. There are two such series of Y values, each associated with one of the point values of X, hence the term *point-biserial correlation coefficient*.

The data shown graphically in Figure 11-1 are shown in tabular form in Table 11-6. The subjects are separated into two groups on the basis of the *sex*

TABLE 11-6.   Calculating r_{pb}, Point-Biserial Correlation Coefficient; X Is a Dichotomous Variable Having Values of 0 and 1, Y Is an Interval or Ratio Scale.

Group 1 (Women)		Group 2 (Men)		Applying Formula 11-3,
X	Y	X	Y	
0	66	1	69	$r_{pb} = \dfrac{(\bar{Y}_2 - \bar{Y}_1)\sqrt{N_1 N_2}}{NSD_Y}$
0	69	1	71	
0	64	1	70	$\quad = \dfrac{(70.62 - 64.50)\sqrt{13(14)}}{27(4.05)} = .76.$
0	64	1	69	
0	61	1	72	Null and alternative hypotheses:
0	65	1	66	
0	62	1	74	$H_0: \rho_{pb} = 0;\quad H_1: \rho_{pb} > 0;\quad H_2: \rho_{pb} < 0.$
0	68	1	74	Applying Formula 10-33,
0	63	1	67	
0	60	1	72	$t = \dfrac{r_{pb}\sqrt{N-2}}{\sqrt{1-r_{pb}^2}} = \dfrac{.76\sqrt{25}}{\sqrt{1-.76^2}} = 5.85.$
0	65	1	68	
0	67	1	76	2-tailed $CV_{.001} = 3.725;$
0	63	1	70	thus, reject H_0 at .001 level.
0	66			
$\bar{Y}_1 = 64.50$		$\bar{Y}_2 = 70.62$		

$$SD_Y = 4.05$$
$$N = 27$$

variable, X. Notice that all of the subjects within a group have the same value of the X variable, either 0 or 1. Since we have an X and a Y measure on each subject, we could treat the dichotomous variable *as though* it were an interval scale and then use one of our existing computational formulas to calculate a Pearson r as a measure of association. However, a simpler alternative procedure is precisely equivalent where one variable is a dichotomy and the other an interval or ratio scale. The following formula gives the point-biserial correlation coefficient:

$$r_{pb} = \frac{(\bar{Y}_2 - \bar{Y}_1)\sqrt{N_1 N_2}}{NSD_Y}, \qquad (11\text{-}3)$$

where $\bar{Y}_1$ and $\bar{Y}_2$ are group means, N_1 and N_2 are the numbers in Groups 1 and 2, N is the total number, and SD_Y is the standard deviation of *total* Y values without regard to group membership. Deriving Formula 11-3 from the Pearson r is straightforward, although we will spare you the algebra. For a derivation, see Guilford and Fruchter (1973, 5th ed., p. 483).

Notice that no quantity directly involving the X variable appears in the above formula. Since the values of X do not directly enter into the calculation of r_{pb}, it is not necessary to list those values as we have done in Table 11-6. We have done so to emphasize the idea that we are dealing with the *correlation* between X and Y, not merely with the difference between group means on the Y variable. Notice also that the **total standard deviation, SD_Y,** is the standard deviation of *all* the Y values without regard to the separate groups of subjects.

Table 11-6 demonstrates the calculation of r_{pb}. Like the Pearson r and the ϕ coefficient, r_{pb} can take on values between -1.00 and $+1.00$ inclusive; thus, the observed value of .76 represents a sizable correlation between sex and height. In many situations, the sign of r_{pb} turns out to be arbitrary. Had we chosen to designate women as Group 1 and men as Group 2, then the sign of our r_{pb} would be negative.

The Statistical Significance of r_{pb}. An observed value of r_{pb} is a statistic calculated in a sample drawn from a bivariate population where the parameter value of the point-biserial correlation is ρ_{pb}. Thus, the null and alternative hypotheses are the following:

$H_0: \rho_{pb} = 0;$

$H_1: \rho_{pb} > 0;$

$H_2: \rho_{pb} < 0.$

An observed r_{pb} can be transformed into a t ratio using Formula 10-33, which we have previously used in testing the significance of a Pearson r. Table 11-6 demonstrates the use of that procedure in testing the significance of an r_{pb}.

Requirements for r_{pb}. The point-biserial correlation coefficient is based on the assumption that one variable is a true dichotomy and the other an interval or ratio scale. Under some conditions, a variable may represent an artificial dichotomy. For example, suppose we were interested in the association between performance in college — as measured by GPA — and financial success in the real world — as measured by income five years after receiving the baccalaureate degree. We might classify students into high and low GPA categories, and then find the r_{pb} between that artificial dichotomy and annual income, a ratio scale. Where a normally distributed variable — such as grade-point average — is artificially dichotomized, r_{pb} tends to underestimate the correlation that would be observed if a Pearson r were calculated using the actual interval or ratio measurements. Where an interval or ratio scale *is* dichotomized for some reason and correlated with actual interval or ratio measurements on another variable, the **biserial correlation coefficient** —

symbolized r_b—is a better estimate of the Pearson r than is r_{pb}, the *point-biserial correlation coefficient* (see McNemar, 1969).

In order to use the t ratio as a test of the statistical significance of r_{pb}, the requirements of the *independent* 2-sample t test must be met. Those requirements are listed in Table 9-4.

The *Chi*-Square Test of Association in a 2 by 2 Table

Since we have already explained that the Z test of binomial proportions can be used to test the significance of an association in a 2 by 2 table, it may appear superfluous to develop yet another such test. But there are difficulties in attempting to apply the Z test in larger contingency tables. An **r by c contingency table** shows the association—if any—between two nominal variables, one having r levels and the other having c levels. The r levels of one variable comprise the *rows* of the table, and the c levels of the other comprise the *columns*. The data in Table 11-4, discussed earlier, are in the form of a contingency table where $r = 2$ and $c = 2$. The data in Table 11-10, to be discussed later, constitute a 2 by 3 contingency table where there are 2 rows and 3 columns. We will first develop the **chi-square test of association** in a 2 by 2 table and then extend that test to r by c contingency tables of any size.

The *chi*-square test of association was initially developed about 1900 by Karl Pearson. The following formula gives the value of *chi*-square in a 2 by 2 table:

For a 2 by 2 table, $$\chi_1^2 = \sum_r \sum_c \frac{(|f_o - f_e| - .5)^2}{f_e},$$

$$df = 1, \tag{11-4}$$

where f_o and f_e are the observed and expected frequencies in a particular cell; the summation across r and c represents the summation across the 2 rows and 2 columns of the table—that is, across all 4 cells; and df, the degrees of freedom, is equal to 1. The subtraction of .5 from the absolute value of each $f_o - f_e$ is a correction for continuity that is made only in the case where $df = 1$, as in all 2 by 2 contingency tables. The observed frequencies progress by integer steps, and thus the calculated value of a *chi*-square statistic is a discrete random variable. The significance of an observed *chi*-square is tested by comparison with a critical value from the continuous *chi*-square distribution—hence the correction for continuity. The quantities in the *chi*-square formula are explained in the following sections.

Observed and Expected Frequencies.   The data from Table 11-4 are presented in a slightly different way in Table 11-7. We have already found the value of the ϕ coefficient in that table, and tested its significance by a Z test of binomial proportions, but it will be instructive to use those same data in developing the present *chi*-square test.

For each cell in Table 11-7, the **observed frequency, f_o,** is the number

TABLE 11-7. *Chi*-Square Test of Association Between Sex and Profession. Whole Number in Each Cell Is Observed Frequency, f_o; Decimal Number Is f_e, Expected Frequency Under Assumption of No Association Between Variables. Cell Number (Row, Column) Is in Upper Left Corner.

		Profession	
		Physicians	Nurses	
Sex	Women	1,1 14 (55.71)	1,2 110 (68.29)	$124 = R_1$
	Men	2,1 79 (37.29)	2,2 4 (45.71)	$83 = R_2$
		$93 = C_1$	$114 = C_2$	$207 = N$

By Formula 11-4,

$$\chi_1^2 = \sum_r \sum_c \frac{(|f_o - f_e| - .5)^2}{f_e}$$

$$= \frac{(|14 - 55.71| - .5)^2}{55.71} + \frac{(|110 - 68.29| - .5)^2}{68.29}$$

$$+ \frac{(|79 - 37.29| - .5)^2}{37.29} + \frac{(|4 - 45.71| - .5)^2}{45.71}$$

$$= \frac{(41.71 - .5)^2}{55.71} + \frac{(41.71 - .5)^2}{68.29} + \frac{(41.71 - .5)^2}{37.29} + \frac{(41.71 - .5)^2}{45.71}$$

$$= 30.484 + 24.868 + 45.542 + 37.153 = 138.047.$$

From Table E, $CV_{.001} = 10.83$, thus reject H_0 at .001 level.

of persons falling in that cell. The **expected frequency, f_e,** is the number of persons expected to fall in a particular cell if the null hypothesis is true — that is, under the hypothesis of no association between variables. The *chi*-square test of association is based on the comparison between observed and expected frequencies. To find the necessary expected frequencies, we utilize the **marginal totals for rows, R_1 and R_2,** and the **marginal totals for columns, C_1 and C_2,** as shown in Table 11-7.

We begin by considering some probabilities. The probability of randomly drawing a person who is a woman from among the 207 people in our sample is

$$P(\text{Woman}) = \frac{R_1}{N} = \frac{124}{207} = .599.$$

In the above equation, R_1 is the row marginal for the first row — that is, the total number of women in our sample of 207 people.

The probability of randomly drawing a person who is a physician is

$$P(\text{Physician}) = \frac{C_1}{N} = \frac{93}{207} = .449.$$

Suppose now that the null hypothesis is true — that is, there is no association between sex and profession. In that case, the events *Woman* and *Physician* are independent, and the probability of randomly drawing a person who is a woman and a physician is the probability of the joint occurrence of those two independent events — that is, the probability of their intersect. Thus, when H_0 is true,

$$P(\text{Woman} \cap \text{Physician}) = P(\text{Woman})\,P(\text{Physician});$$

$$\frac{R_1}{N}\frac{C_1}{N} = \frac{R_1 C_1}{N^2} \tag{11-5}$$

In our earliest discussions of probability in Chapter 6, we pointed out that the probability of an event is the number of ways the event can occur divided by the total number of possible outcomes of a probability experiment. Thus, the probability of an event is the proportion of the total possible outcomes that result in the event. In our present situation, randomly drawing a person is a probability experiment having 207 possible outcomes, since there are 207 people in our sample. Thus, the probability in Equation 11-5 gives the proportion of the total outcomes that result in the event *Woman and Physician*. Thus, we can find the expected frequency of persons who are women and physicians by multiplying that proportion — that probability — by N. Thus,

$$f_{e(1,1)} = NP(\text{Woman})P(\text{Physician}) = N\frac{R_1 C_1}{N^2} = \frac{R_1 C_1}{N}, \tag{11-6}$$

where $f_{e(1,1)}$ is the expected frequency in Cell$_{1,1}$ — the cell in Row 1 and Column 1 — and the other symbols are as defined above.

The expected frequencies in the other three cells can be found analogously. Generalizing Equation 11-6,

$$f_{e(i,j)} = \frac{R_i C_j}{N}, \tag{11-7}$$

where $f_{e(i,j)}$ is the expected frequency in Cell$_{i,j}$ — the cell in Row$_i$ and Column$_j$; R_i and C_j are the marginal totals for Row$_i$ and Column$_j$; and N is the total number of subjects. In words, the expected frequency for any cell is equal to the product of the marginal totals of the row and column containing that cell divided by N. Equation 11-7 is a general expression for the expected frequency of any cell in any contingency table having any number of rows and columns, as we will explain in a later section.

Table 11-7 demonstrates the calculation of *chi*-square in a 2 by 2 table. The expected frequencies were found by Equation 11-7, above. Notice that the sums of the expected frequencies in the rows and columns of Table 11-7 are equal to the marginal totals, as are the sums of the observed frequencies. Also notice that the sum of the expected frequencies in all of the cells is equal to N. Those relationships make it possible to check the arithmetic accuracy of the expected frequencies — and that should certainly be done before proceeding any further. The value of *chi*-square was calculated by Formula 11-4.

Degrees of Freedom and Critical Values. The statistical significance of a test of association is assessed by comparing the observed — calculated — value of *chi*-square with a critical value that is determined by the number of degrees of freedom. In a 2 by 2 contingency table, the *chi*-square statistic has only 1 *df*, as we will explain. We regard the marginal totals as fixed in order to determine the expected frequencies. For example, consider Table 11-8, which shows only the marginal totals in a 2 by 2 contingency table. The expected frequency for each cell is 25, by Formula 11-7. Now, how

TABLE 11-8. Fixed Marginal Totals in a 2 by 2 Table. Observed Frequencies are Left Blank Within Cells. Entering a Permissible Observed Frequency in Any One Cell — A Number Between 0 and 50 Inclusive — Determines the Observed Frequencies in the Other Three Cells. Since the Observed Frequency is Free to Vary in Only One Cell, *df* = 1.

	Variable X		
	X_1	X_2	
Y_1			50
Y_2			50
	50	50	100

Variable Y

many of the *observed* frequencies in the four cells of that table are free to vary? The observed frequency in any particular cell might be as low as 0 or as high as 50 — no higher, since none of the marginal totals exceeds 50. Now suppose we have observed 30 cases in Cell$_{1,1}$. If we write the number 30 in that cell, we will have at once determined the observed frequencies in the other three cells. There is no special magic in Cell$_{1,1}$, since filling in a permissible observed frequency in any other cell also determines the observed frequencies in all the others. Only one cell in a 2 by 2 table is free to vary, and thus there is only 1 *df* in such a contingency table. Larger contingency tables have larger *df*s, as we will explain later.

The *chi*-square distribution is a family of curves determined by a single parameter, the degrees of freedom, *df*. We will not present the *chi*-square equation, which is rather complicated, but we have illustrated several members of the family of curves for several different *df*s in Figure 11-2. Since each term in the calculation of χ^2 is a squared quantity, values of χ^2 are all positive, ranging upward from zero without limit. Critical values for several levels of probability and many different *df*s are listed in Table E. All of those critical values are located in the right tails of the χ^2 distributions shown in Figure 11-2.

Hypothesis Testing. The null and alternative hypotheses for the *chi*-square test of association are the following:

H_0: No association between variables;

H_1: Variables are associated.

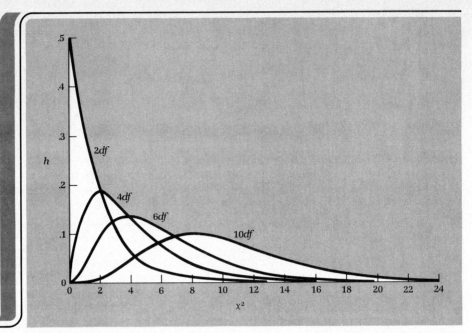

FIGURE 11-2. *Chi*-square distributions for several numbers of degrees of freedom, *df*.

Notice that there are no population parameters involved in the above statements of the null and alternative hypotheses. For that reason, the *chi*-square test is sometimes called a *nonparametric test*.

Critical values of *chi*-square are presented in Table E for several different numbers of degrees of freedom. We reject the null hypothesis in favor of the alternative when the observed — calculated — value of *chi*-square is greater than or equal to the tabled critical value for the appropriate *df*. As Figure 11-2 shows, large values are located in the right tail of each χ^2 curve. As in all probability distributions, the area under each *chi*-square curve is equal to 1.00. For any particular curve, corresponding to a particular *df*, the critical value is that value of χ^2 beyond which the area under the curve is equal to *alpha* — that is, the probability of observing a χ^2 as large or larger than the critical value. Figure 11-3 shows the *chi*-square distribution for 1 *df*.

Relationships Between χ_1^2, Z, and ϕ. We described the ϕ coefficient as a measure of association between two dichotomous variables. We tested the statistical significance of the observed association in Table 11-4 by using a Z test of independent binomial proportions, and we rejected the null hypothesis at the .001 level. We also tested the association between variables in the same data by using a *chi*-square test of association in Table 11-7, and again we rejected the null hypothesis at the .001 level. Thus, the *chi*-square test of association yielded the same results as the Z test of binomial proportions.

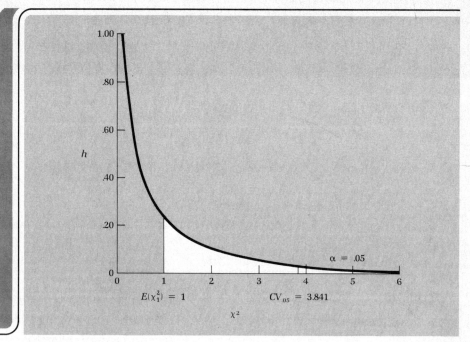

FIGURE 11-3. *Chi*-square distribution for 1 *df*. Shaded area, .05 of total area under curve, lies beyond critical value for testing H_0 at .05 level.

Indeed, we can show — through some rather tedious algebra which we will spare you — that

$$\chi_1^2 = Z^2. \tag{11-8}$$

Thus, the value of χ_1^2 — the *chi*-square statistic for 1 degree of freedom — is exactly equal to Z^2. Comparing the values of Z^2 and χ_1^2 from Tables 11-4 and 11-7,

$$Z^2 = 11.749^2 = 138.039;$$

$$\chi_1^2 \qquad = 138.047.$$

Thus, the calculated values of χ_1^2 and Z^2 agree within rounding error.

We can also show — again through some algebra that we will spare you — that the ϕ coefficient is closely related to χ_1^2. Thus,

$$\phi = \sqrt{\frac{\chi_{1(unc)}^2}{N}}, \tag{11-9}$$

where $\chi_{1(unc)}^2$ is the value of *chi*-square for 1 *df* uncorrected for continuity — that is, without the correction for continuity in Formula 11-4.

We will now consider the relationship between ϕ and the value of χ_1^2 *corrected* for continuity. As N increases in a 2 by 2 table, the magnitude of the correction for continuity becomes smaller. You can see this most easily by looking at the formula for the Z test of binomial proportions in Table 11-4. (Since $\chi_1^2 = Z^2$, and since both statistics require a correction for continuity, whatever is true of one is also true of the other.) In the Z formula, the correction for continuity is the quantity $.5(1/N_1 + 1/N_2)$, and that quantity decreases as N_1 and N_2 increase. Thus, as the total N increases in a 2 by 2 table, the correction for continuity decreases, and the value of the corrected chi-square approaches that of $\chi_{1(unc)}^2$. Thus,

$$\phi \simeq \sqrt{\frac{\chi_1^2}{N}}, \tag{11-10}$$

where the $\simeq$ sign means *approximately equals,* and χ_1^2 is the chi-square statistic with 1 df corrected for continuity.

Table 11-9 shows the relationship between ϕ and the corrected chi-square in three contingency tables. By Formula 11-2, the value of ϕ is .80 in each table. As you can see, the value of ϕ by Formula 11-10 closely approaches .80 as N increases.

TABLE 11-9. Relationship Between χ_1^2, Corrected for Continuity, and the ϕ Coefficient for Different Sample Sizes.

1	9	10	$\phi = .80 \simeq \sqrt{\chi_1^2/N} = \sqrt{9.800/20} = .700$	
9	1	10	$\chi_1^2 = 9.800$	$N\phi^2 = 12.800$
10	10	20 $= N$		$23.44\% =$ Discrepancy
10	90	100	$\phi = .80 \simeq \sqrt{\chi_1^2/N} = \sqrt{124.820/200} = .790$	
90	10	100	$\chi_1^2 = 124.820$	$N\phi^2 = 128.000$
100	100	200 $= N$		$2.48\% =$ Discrepancy
100	900	1000	$\phi = .80 \simeq \sqrt{\chi_1^2/N} = \sqrt{1276.802/2000} = .799$	
900	100	1000	$\chi_1^2 = 1276.802$	$N\phi^2 = 1280.00$
1000	1000	2000 $= N$		$0.25\% =$ Discrepancy

Since ϕ and chi-square are so closely related, it may appear as though one or the other of those statistics represents an unnecessary duplication. However, the value of chi-square is partly determined by N, as you can see in Table 11-8. On the other hand, the value of ϕ ranges between -1 and $+1$ regardless of the value of N. If there is no association between variables, then $\phi = 0$, and if there is a perfect association, then $\phi = \pm 1$. Thus, the ϕ coefficient is a useful index number that reflects the degree of association between two variables independently of the total N in a 2 by 2 contingency table. Neither chi-square nor Z can be so readily interpreted as a measure of association.

Chi-Square Tests of Association in Larger Contingency Tables

The following formula, an extension of 11-4, provides a *chi*-square test of association in an *r* by *c* contingency table where the number of degrees of freedom is greater than or equal to 2:

$$\chi^2_{df} = \sum_r \sum_c \frac{(f_0 - f_e)^2}{f_e},$$
$$df = (r - 1)(c - 1) \ge 2, \tag{11-11}$$

where *r* and *c* are the number of rows and columns. The above formula differs from 11-4 only in lacking the correction for continuity. When $df \ge 2$, that correction is neither necessary nor desirable.

If there are *r* rows and *c* columns in a contingency table, then there are *c* cells in each row and *r* cells in each column. As in our earlier example of a 2 by 2 table, we regard the marginal totals as fixed. Thus, in any particular row, if the observed frequencies of $c - 1$ cells are determined, then the frequency of the remaining cell in that row is also determined. Similarly, determining the observed frequencies in $r - 1$ of the cells in any column determines the frequency of the remaining cell in that column. Thus, in any *r* by *c* contingency table, $df = (r - 1)(c - 1)$, including the special case of a 2 by 2 table.

We will illustrate the application of the above formula to a set of data collected among students on a university campus. Is there any association between one's attitude toward regulating smoking in public and one's own smoking behavior? In a survey of 234 students, we asked the two following questions, among a number of other questions relating to smoking:

1. How should we regulate smoking in confined public places, such as classrooms, buses, and airplanes?
   A. Prohibit smoking.
   B. Allow only in smoking areas.
   C. Allow smoking anywhere.
2. Do you smoke?
   A. Yes.
   B. No.

In answering the two questions above, each person is classified on an *Attitude* variable having three levels and on a *Behavior* variable having two levels. Table 11-10 shows the resulting 2 by 3 contingency table, a **sixfold table** having six cells. As in our earlier 2 by 2 table, each person here also falls into one and only one cell. For example, $Cell_{1,1}$—the cell in the first row and first column—contains those 3 people who are smokers and who advocate prohibiting smoking in confined public places, while $Cell_{2,3}$ contains those 29 people who are nonsmokers and who advocate allowing smoking anywhere. The relationship between behavior and attitude may not be instantly obvious in Table 11-10, but there is indeed such a relationship, as we will see.

TABLE 11-10. Association Between Smoking Behavior and Attitude Toward Regulating Smoking in Confined Public Places. Cell Number (Row, Column) Is in Upper Left Corner of Each Cell. Other Numbers Are Observed and Expected Frequencies.

| | | How should we regulate smoking? | | | |
		Prohibit smoking	Allow in smoking areas	Allow smoking anywhere	Marginal totals for rows
Do you smoke?	Yes	1,1 3 (9.65)	1,2 33 (37.28)	1,3 25 (14.08)	$61 = R_1$
	No	2,1 34 (27.35)	2,2 110 (105.72)	2,3 29 (39.92)	$173 = R_2$
Marginal totals for columns		$37 = C_1$	$143 = C_2$	$54 = C_3$	$234 = N$

Expected frequencies by Formula 11-7,

$$f_e(1,1) = \frac{R_1 C_1}{N} = \frac{61(37)}{234} = \frac{2257}{234} = 9.65;$$

$$f_e(2,3) = \frac{R_2 C_3}{N} = \frac{173(54)}{234} = \frac{9342}{234} = 39.92.$$

Applying Formula 11-11, $\chi^2_{df} = \sum_r \sum_c \frac{(f_o - f_e)^2}{f_e}, \quad df = (r-1)(c-1) = 2.$

$$\chi^2_2 = \frac{(3 - 9.65)^2}{9.65} + \frac{(33 - 37.28)^2}{37.28} + \frac{(25 - 14.08)^2}{14.08}$$

$$+ \frac{(34 - 27.35)^2}{27.35} + \frac{(110 - 105.72)^2}{105.72} + \frac{(29 - 39.92)^2}{39.92}$$

$$= 4.58 + 0.49 + 8.47 + 1.62 + 0.17 + 2.99 = 18.32.$$

H_0: No association between behavior and attitude.

H_1: There is an association.

From Table E, $CV_{.01} = 9.210$.
Since $18.32 > 9.210$, reject H_0 at .01 level in favor of H_1.

You might be tempted to use the Z test of binomial proportions to compare the proportion of smokers among the people who would allow smoking anywhere ($25/54 = .463$) with the proportion among those who would establish smoking areas ($33/143 = .231$), and also with the proportion of smokers among those who would prohibit smoking ($3/37 = .081$). But there are difficulties in making such comparisons, especially in larger contingency tables. If we have a total of k such proportions to compare, then we can make $k(k-1)/2$ pairwise comparisons, which is equal to the number of combinations of k things taken 2 at a time — that is, C_2^k. In making a number of such comparisons in a large contingency table, the probability of making a Type 1 error on at least one test greatly increases over whatever α level you have chosen for the individual tests. For example, suppose the null hypothesis is true — that is, suppose there is no significant association between variables, no significant difference between proportions. If you choose an *alpha* level of .05 and run *one* test of proportions, then the probability of a Type 1 error is only .05. But if you run *three* such tests, then the probability of a Type 1 error on test 1 *or* 2 *or* 3 is substantially greater than .05. In the case of the three tests, the probability of a Type 1 error is the probability of the union of three events. Furthermore, those events — tests — are not independent. We will deal with some of these problems in more detail in a later chapter on comparing multiple groups. In our present situation, the χ^2 statistic provides a single test of the significance of an association between variables. If all of the *chi*-square requirements described in a later section are met, then the probability of a Type 1 error is no greater than the *alpha* probability associated with an observed value of χ^2.

Table 11-10 illustrates the use of Formula 11-11 in a 2 by 3 contingency table. Expected frequencies are found using Formula 11-7. Since the observed (calculated) value of χ_2^2 exceeds the critical value for 2 *df* at the .001 level, we reject the null hypothesis of no association in favor of the alternative hypothesis stating that there is an association between the *Behavior* and *Attitude* variables. The probability of a Type 1 error is no greater than our *alpha* level of .001, since we have run only a single statistical test.

The Nature of an Association in a Contingency Table. In our 2 by 2 contingency table, the nature of the association between sex and profession is clear. In Table 11-7, the differences between observed and expected frequencies are large and systematic: Women are underrepresented among physicians and overrepresented in nursing, while for men the under- and overrepresentations are reversed. The expected values in that table are based on the assumption that H_0 is true — that is, on the assumption that sex and profession are independent variables. To the extent that the observed and expected frequencies differ significantly, we reject that assumption of independence — no association. Indeed, the differences between observed and expected frequencies are so substantial, and the resulting value of χ_1^2 so large, that we reject the null hypothesis at the .001 level. Further, the large value of the ϕ coefficient in Table 11-4, .83, provides a numerical indication of the association between variables.

In a larger contingency table, the nature of the relationship between variables may be less clear. For example, in Table 11-10 there is a highly significant association between smoking behavior and attitude toward regulating smoking. In the main, smokers are more permissive than nonsmokers. Only three smokers would prohibit smoking in confined public places, whereas we would expect 9.65 smokers to hold that attitude if there were no association between variables. In Cell$_{1,3}$ 25 smokers advocate allowing smoking anywhere, versus an expected frequency of only 14.08. On the other hand, only 29 nonsmokers in Cell$_{3,3}$ — versus an expected frequency of 39.92 — would allow smoking anywhere. Among the people holding a moderate attitude toward smoking — those falling in Cell$_{1,2}$ and Cell$_{2,2}$ — there are no great differences between observed and expected frequencies. A contingency table must be studied carefully in order to discern the nature of an association after a significant χ^2 has been found.

Requirements for *Chi*-Square Tests of Association

The requirements for the χ^2 test of association — the assumptions underlying the test — are listed in Table 11-11 and are discussed in the numbered sections below.

TABLE 11-11.   Requirements for the *Chi*-Square Test of Association.

1. Nominal scales, including higher-caliber measurement scales that have been reduced to nominal scales.
2. N independent observations, each falling into one and only one cell in a contingency table.
3. Where $df = 1$, each cell must have an *expected* frequency of 5 or more.
4. Where $df \geq 2$, at least 80% of the cells must have *expected* frequencies of 5 or more, and there must be no expected frequency of zero.

1. Nominal Scales.   This requirement can always be met since we can reduce any higher-caliber measurement scale to a nominal scale. For example, income is a ratio scale, and so is level of education as measured by years of schooling. If we wanted to investigate the possible association between income and education, we might divide the income scale into *high, middle,* and *low* categories, and the education scale into categories of *less than high school, high-school graduate, some college,* and *college graduate.*

2. Independent Observations and Mutually Exclusive Categories.   Each observation of a person or other object must be independent of every other observation. It would not do to observe the same person twice, or to permit one person's response to influence another person's. The categories on each nominal scale are mutually exclusive and exhaustive in that each observation falls into one and only one category on each scale, and thus each observation falls into one and only one cell in a contingency table. For example, if we were interested in the possible association between place of residence (urban, suburban, rural) and political party preference (Democratic, Republican, other), we might find a person who preferred the Democratic candidate for the presidency, but a Republican candidate for the Senate. You might be tempted to count that person once as a Democrat and again as a Republican, but that would violate the requirements of independence of observations and exclusiveness of categories. A person who cannot express a preference for one of the major parties in such a study should be placed in the *other* category, which will include political independents, people who prefer other parties, and people who have no preference at all.

3. Expected-Frequency Requirements Where $df = 1$.   There is only one degree of freedom in a 2 by 2 contingency table, and thus each cell must have an *expected* frequency of 5 or more. We emphasize that this requirement applies to the *expected* frequency, not the observed frequency. Any observed frequency, including zero, is permissible in a contingency table. These requirements are closely related to the requirements for the Z test of a difference between binomial proportions in Table 9-13, where the following four quantities must all be at least as great as 5: N_1p_c, N_1q_c, N_2p_c, and N_2q_c. Those four quantities above are identical to the expected frequencies in a 2 by 2 contingency table. Only when these expected-frequency requirements are met does the *chi*-square probability distribution provide a good approximation to the probability associated with an observed χ_1^2. When these requirements cannot be met, Fisher's exact test (Siegel, 1956) provides an alternative to χ_1^2 and to the Z test of a difference between binomial proportions.

4. Expected Frequencies Where *df* > 1. We emphasize again that the requirements here apply to *expected* frequencies, not observed frequencies. Any observed frequency is permissible, including zero. In a contingency table having 2 or more *df*, at least 80% of the cells must have expected frequencies of 5 or more, and there must be no expected frequency of zero. In some cases where a set of data may not initially meet this requirement, categories can sometimes be combined in order to yield appropriate expected

TABLE 11-12. Top: Less Than 80% of Expected Frequencies Are 5 or Greater. Thus, a *Chi*-Square Test of Association Is Not Permissible. Bottom: By Combining Some Categories, All Expected Frequencies Are 5 or Greater.

			A		B	Grades C		D		F	
	Front		9		10	8		3		0	30
				(3)	(6)	(12)		(6)		(3)	
Seating Choice	Middle		1		7	24		7		1	40
				(4)	(8)	(16)		(8)		(4)	
	Rear		0		3	8		10		9	30
				(3)	(6)	(12)		(6)		(3)	
			10		20	40		20		10	100

		High (A and B)	Grades Average (C)	Low (D and F)	
	Front	19	8	3	30
		(9)	(12)	(9)	
Seating Choice	Middle	8	24	8	40
		(12)	(16)	(12)	
	Rear	3	8	19	30
		(9)	(12)	(9)	
		30	40	30	100

frequencies. For example, consider the possible relationship between grades in a course and the places in a classroom where students choose to sit — front, middle, and rear. Suppose an instructor observed where each member of a class had chosen to sit on a particular day, and then noted each person's grade on the last exam — A, B, C, D, or F. The data from such a hypothetical study are shown in Table 11-12 (top). Notice that only 9/15 — that is, only 60% — of the cells in the 3 by 5 table (top) have expected frequencies as great as 5. Thus, it would not be permissible to run a χ^2 test as the table stands. But if the grades of A and B are combined into a single *high* category, the grade of C designated as *average,* and D and F combined into a *low* category, then every expected frequency in the resulting 3 by 3 table — Table 11-12 (bottom) — is greater than 5. It is quite permissible to combine categories in this way when too many of the expected frequencies would otherwise be too small. However, care must always be taken to combine categories in as meaningful a way as possible. It would not be reasonable in the present case, for example, to combine the grade categories of A and F, since those grades represent two very different kinds of performances.

Choosing a Measure of Association

We have presented a great many different measures of association in the present chapter. However, all of these measures are similar in that they are all designed to assess the relationship — association, correlation — between variables. Indeed, some of our present measures are directly derived from the Pearson *r* and are thus closely related to each other. With such a large armamentarium of techniques, how should we go about choosing a measure of association? The answer is straightforward: Choose the measure of association that best matches the caliber of the measurement scales on which the data are measured. Such a technique will best utilize all of the information contained in the data. For example, in a set of measurements on ratio or interval scales, the Pearson *r* is the most appropriate measure of association.

TABLE 11-13. Measures of Association (Correlation) and Measurement Scales Listed in Descending Order of Caliber.

Measure of Association	Symbol	Measurement Scale
Pearson product-moment correlation coefficient	r	Ratio or interval
Spearman rank-order correlation coefficient	r_s	Ordinal
Point-biserial correlation coefficient	r_{pb}	Nominal on X (dichotomy), ratio or interval on Y
Phi coefficient	ϕ	Nominal (dichotomy)
Chi-square	χ^2_{df}	Nominal

In that situation the high-caliber measurement scales could be reduced — degraded — to ordinal or nominal scales, but some quantitative information would be lost. A lower caliber measure of association, such as r_s or ϕ, will be less precise than r when those measures are used with interval or ratio scales. Table 11-13 lists all of our measures of association and the measurement scales with which they can best be used.

Some Final Words

After studying this chapter, you should be able to see the material in Chapter 9 on differences between means in a new light. At first blush, the measures of association in the present chapter may seem to have nothing to do with any question of a difference between two independent groups. But we have shown that the ϕ coefficient and *chi*-square in a 2 by 2 table are closely related to the Z test of a difference between binomial proportions. Indeed, whenever there is a difference between means or proportions there is also an association between variables. For example, in a t test of the difference between the height of men and women, a significant difference implies an association between the dichotomous sex variable and the height variable. The point-biserial correlation coefficient, r_{pb}, will provide a measure of the association in that situation.

Measures of association are readily misinterpreted, especially where questions of causality are concerned. As we have pointed out repeatedly, correlation — association — does not necessarily imply a causal relationship, although one variable *may* be causally related to the other when we observe an association. In spite of our many admonitions and warnings, statistical associations are well worth knowing about and can add greatly to our understanding.

Terms and Symbols

The present chapter has presented several measures of association and tests of significance, and has stressed the relationships between those measures. Defining, comparing, and contrasting the terms and symbols that we have used are important steps in understanding the measures that we have presented, and understanding the relationships between them.

Rank-order correlation coefficient	**Two-way classification**
Interjudge reliability	**Fourfold table**
Tied ranks	**Dichotomous variable**
Rank$_x$ and Rank$_Y$	**Contingency table**
	True dichotomy

Artificial dichotomy	**Correction for continuity**
Tetrachoric correlation coeffi-	**Association** and **causality**
cient	r_s
Point-biserial correlation	D
coefficient	ϕ
Total standard deviation	χ^2_{df}
Biserial correlation coefficient	r_{pb}
Chi-square test of association	r_b
Observed frequency	f_o
Expected frequency	f_e
Marginal total	R_i and C_j
Test of binomial proportions	$\chi^2_{1(unc)}$

EXERCISES AND STUDY QUESTIONS

1. Identifying employees capable of advancing to management positions is a process vital to the continuing success of any organization, whether a business, educational institution, or an arm of government. The identification process often begins with an evaluation by a first-level supervisor. How reliable are such evaluations? Suppose two supervisors independently ranked a group of 14 workers on their judged likelihood of success as managers. The two sets of judgments are shown below, where each letter stands for a worker. The underlining indicates ties. For example, Supervisor 1 judged Worker F most promising, Workers J and H next most promising, and equally so, and so on.

Ranks:	1	2	3	4	5	6	7	8	9	10	11	12	13	14
Supervisor 1:	F	J	H	L	K	I	D	G	E	B	N	M	C	A
Supervisor 2:	J	H	I	F	G	L	K	M	B	E	D	N	A	C

   a. Plot a scatter diagram. Estimate the value of r_s from your scatter diagram, and then calculate it.
   b. Test the statistical significance of r_s and indicate whether a 1 or 2-tailed test is appropriate.
   c. What can we say about the reliability of the supervisors' judgments, and the possible value of those judgments in identifying future managers?

2. Suppose there were no ties in the judgments in Exercise 1, above. In that case, find the value of r_s and compare with the above value. What is the effect of ties in the present situation?

3. Is there an association between political opinion, as measured by the liberal-conservative dimension, and attitude toward gun control? Suppose

a number of subjects were asked the following questions in a public opinion survey:

1. Broadly speaking, should the state and federal governments follow more liberal or more conservative policies?
2. Would you advocate stronger gun-control laws?

Out of 64 liberals, 54 advocated stronger gun control, and 10 did not; and of 42 conservatives, 13 advocated stronger gun control, and 29 did not.

   a. Formulate the null and alternative hypotheses.
   b. Calculate the value of ϕ, and test its significance by a *chi*-square test.
   c. Prepare a table showing the percentages of liberals, conservatives, and of the total sample who advocate and do not advocate stronger gun control. (Summing across columns, the percentages in each row should add up to 100%.)
   d. Prepare another table showing the percentage of persons advocating stronger gun control who are liberals and conservatives, the percentages of persons not advocating stronger gun control who are liberals and conservatives, and the percentages of liberals and conservatives in the total sample. (Here, summing across rows, the percentages in each column should add up to 100%.)
   e. Given that a person is a liberal, what is the probability that that person also advocates stronger gun control?
   f. Given that a person is a conservative, what is the probability that that person advocates stronger gun control?
   g. Given that a person *does not* support stronger gun control what is the probability that that person is a liberal? Is a conservative?
   h. Describe the nature of the association between the two variables in this example.
   i. Does a person's advocacy of liberal or conservative policies determine the person's attitude toward gun control, or does the attitude toward gun control determine whether a person is liberal or conservative?

4. Is there a correlation between physical exercise and longevity? If greater physical activity leads to a longer life, then we should expect that very active people, such as athletes and coaches, should live longer than less active people, such as scientists and engineers. Each year, *The World Almanac* publishes brief obituaries of prominent persons who have died during the previous year. The following data are the ages at death of athletes and coaches, and scientists and engineers, listed in the 1975 *World Almanac:*[1]

Scientists and engineers:	101	76	76	80	84	82	72	80	67	78
	40	51	68	89	58	78	73	81	74	
Athletes and coaches:	59	68	88	63	59	59	53	35	69	46
	41									

[1] I am indebted to Professor Arthur L. Irion for calling my attention to this species of example.

a. Plot a scatter diagram, and estimate the value of r_{pb} before doing any calculations.

b. State the null and alternative hypotheses, and indicate whether a 1 or 2-tailed test is appropriate.

c. Calculate r_{pb} and test its significance.

d. What is the nature of the relationship between category of persons, athletes and coaches versus scientists and engineers — that is, does a more physically active lifestyle lead to a longer or shorter life? Offer some possible causal explanations of the observed correlation. (HINT: Consider the ages at which athletes and scientists are likely to become sufficiently prominent so that their passing will be noted in *The World Almanac*.)

5. Is there an association between the ethnicity of voters and their political party preference? Suppose the results of a voter survey turned out as shown below:

Ethnicity	Democratic	Republican	Independent and Other
White	56	37	31
Black	29	3	2
Hispanic	17	1	3
Asian	8	5	4
Other	6	2	1

a. Formulate the null and alternative hypotheses, and carry out a *chi*-square test. Pay attention to the number of cells having small expected frequencies.

b. Make up a table showing party preferences in percentages for each ethnic group, and for the total sample. Percentages within rows should sum to 100% within rounding error.

c. Make up a table showing ethnic groups in percentages for each preference category, and for the total sample. Here, percentages within columns should sum to 100% within rounding error.

d. Describe in words the nature of the association between ethnicity and party preference.

Comparing Two Correlated Measures: Repeated-Measures and Matched-Pairs Designs

12

In Chapter 9, we developed a number of procedures for testing the significance of a difference between measures made on two *independent* groups of subjects. In many situations, we may be interested in testing a difference between two measures made on the *same* subjects — for example, in a study comparing the effects of a drug and a placebo administered to the same group of subjects. When two measurements are made on the same subjects, it is true in a sense that we have two groups of measurements, but those two sets of measurements are **correlated** rather than independent.

Where more than one measurement is made on the same subjects, an experiment is called a **repeated-measures design.** In a repeated measures experiment, there is typically a substantial correlation between the two measures. For example, suppose a drug severely impairs performance on a motor-skills task. Everyone's performance may be greatly impaired under the influence of the drug, but those subjects who perform best without the drug will nevertheless tend to perform best under the drug condition. Thus, there will be a positive correlation between performance under the drug and under the placebo. Since correlated measures are not independent, a test requiring independence would not be appropriate in a repeated-measures experimental design.

In many cases, a repeated-measures design will provide a more powerful, sensitive test of the null hypothesis than a procedure requiring independent samples. Furthermore, in a repeated-measures experiment, each subject does "double duty," serving under both of the conditions in the experiment. Thus, a repeated-measures design requires fewer subjects than an independent-groups design. Although the repeated-measures procedure offers many advantages, there are also disadvantages, as we will explain in a later section.

A **matched-pairs design** utilizes two groups of subjects that are balanced as nearly as possible on the basis of comparable scores on a **matching variable.** For example, suppose we were interested in testing a new method of teaching reading by comparing a group of pupils taught by the new method with a control group taught by a standard method. Since we have reason to believe that intelligence influences reading ability, we might use intelligence as a matching variable in order to balance our two groups. We could match pairs of pupils as closely as possible on intelligence test scores, and we could then assign one member of each pair to the control group and the other to the experimental group. To the extent that the matching variable — intelligence — correlates with ability to learn to read, the control and experimental groups will be more nearly balanced on reading aptitude than if the subjects were randomly assigned to those groups. We will have more to say about the matched-pairs design when we have developed the repeated-measures procedure.

As in all of the other statistical tests we have developed, the kind of repeated-measures or matched-pairs test that can be used in a given situation depends on the nature of the measurement scale. Thus, the varieties of measurement scales provide a framework for this chapter.

Interval and Ratio Scales

The *t* Test for Correlated Measures

By **correlated measures** we mean measurements that are statistically related. As we noted earlier, repeated measurements made on the same subjects tend to be highly correlated, and thus repeated measures are correlated measures. In the matched-pairs design, the measurements of the dependent variable in the two groups are also correlated measures, to the extent that the matching variable correlates with the dependent variable. In the next section, we will explain the use of the correlated-measures *t* test in a repeated-measures design. In a later section, we will extend that test to the matched-pairs design.

Repeated-Measures Test.   We will consider a simple reaction-time experiment where we measure the time that passes between the onset of a stimulus and the occurrence of a response. The study of reaction times has a long history, and indeed, reaction times are still being measured in current studies of a great many psychological processes. Outside the laboratory, reaction times are of considerable importance to an active animal moving about the world — whether the animal is running, flying, or driving a car.

In our reaction-time experiment, we flashed a light, and the subject's task was to press a button as soon thereafter as possible. A few seconds before each presentation of the light, the subject received a ready signal. The time between the ready signal and the light varied randomly from trial to trial over a range of a few seconds. Is there a practice effect in such a simple task — that is, does the effect of performance on earlier trials carry over to later trials? In a learning experiment, for example, observing the practice effect — if any — is the principal point of the experiment. But in other kinds of repeated-measures designs, the presence of a carry-over effect raises serious problems, as explained in a later section.

Table 12-1 shows the visual reaction time in milliseconds — thousandths of a second — for a group of 10 subjects, 5 men and 5 women. Each subject received a total of 20 trials. The means of each subject's reaction times on the first 10 trials and on the second 10 trials are listed in Table 12-1. Thus, the data consist of two measures for each subject, a score on the first half of the trials and a score on the second half. If there is a significant practice effect, then there will be a significant difference between the means of those two scores across the group of subjects. A significant improvement — a decrease in mean reaction time in the last 10 trials — would constitute a practice effect, and so would a deterioration in performance — an increase in mean reaction time.

The question of a practice effect reduces to a comparison between the means for the first half and for the second half of the trials. The null and

$\Sigma X_1^2 = 1010060 \qquad \Sigma X_2^2 = 887293$ *(handwritten)*

TABLE 12-1. Repeated-Measures t Test. For Each Subject, X_1 and X_2 are, Respectively, the Mean Visual Reaction Times in Milliseconds for the First 10 and Last 10 Trials. Significant t Ratio Indicates a Significant Practice Effect.

Subject	X_1	X_1^2	X_2	X_2^2	D	D^2
1	309	95481	280	78400	29	841
2	313	97969	299	89401	14	196
3	255	65025	222	49284	33	1089
4	288	82944	296	87616	−8	64
5	284	80656	271	73441	13	169
6	382	145924	327	106929	55	3025
7	236	55696	250	62500	−14	196
8	363	131769	335	112225	28	784
9	430	184900	389	151321	41	1681
10	264	69696	276	76176	−12	144

$$\Sigma X_1 = 3124 \qquad \Sigma X_2 = 2945 \qquad \Sigma D = 179 \qquad \Sigma D^2 = 8189$$

$$\overline{X}_1 = 312.4 \qquad \overline{X}_2 = 294.5 \qquad \overline{D} = 17.9$$

Arithmetic check: $\overline{D} = \overline{X}_1 - \overline{X}_2 = 17.9.\checkmark$

By Formula 12-13,
$$t = \frac{\overline{D}}{\sqrt{\dfrac{\Sigma D^2 - \dfrac{(\Sigma D)^2}{N}}{N(N-1)}}} = \frac{17.9}{\sqrt{\dfrac{8189 - \dfrac{179^2}{10}}{10(10-1)}}} = \frac{17.9}{\sqrt{\dfrac{8189 - 3204.1}{90}}}$$

$df = N - 1 = 9.$

$H_0: \mu_D = 0;$

$H_1: \mu_D > 0;$

$H_2: \mu_D < 0.$

$$= \frac{17.9}{7.442} = 2.405.$$

2-tailed $CV_{.05} = 2.262.$

Since $2.405 \geq 2.262$, reject H_0 in favor of H_1.

---

alternative hypotheses can be stated in the same forms as in a test of a difference between the means of independent groups:

$H_0: \mu_1 = \mu_2;$

$H_1: \mu_1 > \mu_2;$

$H_2: \mu_1 < \mu_2.$

The null hypothesis, above, states that the mean of the population from which the first measures were drawn is equal to the mean of the population from which the second measures were drawn. The two alternative hypotheses state that the means of those two populations differ in the indicated ways.

It is possible, however, to state the null and alternative hypotheses in a way that will more clearly distinguish the correlated-measures test from the independent-groups procedure. In order to do so, we begin by defining a **difference score, D,** for each subject in our sample:

$$D = X_1 - X_2. \tag{12-1}$$

The above subtraction is always carried out in the same direction, and the sign is retained. It is easy to show that the sample mean of all the difference scores, $\overline{D}$, is equal to the difference between the observed means of X_1 and X_2. Thus,

$$\overline{D} = \overline{X}_1 - \overline{X}_2. \tag{12-2}$$

We let μ_D represent the expected value of D, that is, the mean of all of the difference scores in the population from which our sample was drawn. If the null hypothesis is true, then $\mu_D = 0$, and we can restate the null and alternative hypotheses in the following forms:

$H_0: \mu_D = 0;$

$H_1: \mu_D > 0;$

$H_2: \mu_D < 0.$

If the random variable $\overline{D}$ were normally distributed, and if we knew its standard deviation, then we could use the standard normal distribution to test the following critical ratio:

$$Z_{\overline{D}} = \frac{\overline{D} - \mu_{\overline{D}}}{\sigma_{\overline{D}}}. \tag{12-3}$$

In Chapter 9, we found the variance of a difference between sample means. Reproducing Equation 9-4 below,

$$\sigma_{\overline{D}}^2 = E(\overline{X}_1 - \mu_1)^2 + E(\overline{X}_2 - \mu_2)^2 - 2E[(\overline{X}_1 - \mu_1)(\overline{X}_2 - \mu_2)]. \tag{9-4}$$

We noted that the last term of 9-4 is a function of the correlation between sample means. For *independent* groups of subjects, there is no correlation between the X_1 and X_2 measures on individual subjects, and thus there is no correlation between $\overline{X}_1$ and $\overline{X}_2$, the means of the independent groups. But where we have repeated measures on the same subjects, the X_1 and X_2 measures will be correlated, and so will the means of those measures, $\overline{X}_1$ and $\overline{X}_2$. Thus, in the case of correlated measures, the last term of Equation 9-4 is not equal to zero. We now consider the nature of that term.

In a population of X_1 and X_2 measures, there exists a population correlation coefficient ρ_{12}, which is the correlation between Measure 1 and Measure 2, and which is defined as

$$\rho_{12} = \frac{E[(X_1 - \mu_1)(X_2 - \mu_2)]}{\sigma_1 \sigma_2}. \tag{12-4}$$

The above equation is very similar to one of the equations for the correlation coefficient observed in a sample. We reproduce Equation 10-2 below for comparison:

$$r_{12} = \frac{\Sigma[(X_1 - \overline{X}_1)(X_2 - \overline{X}_2)]}{NSD_1SD_2}. \tag{10-2}$$

We can rewrite Equations 12-4 and 10-2 in the following ways:

$$\rho_{12} = E(Z_1 Z_2), \quad \text{and} \quad r_{12} = \frac{\Sigma(Z_1 Z_2)}{N}.$$

Thus, the sample correlation r_{12} is the mean of the cross-products of Z-scores in a sample, and the population correlation ρ_{12} is the expected value of the cross-products of Z-scores in the population—that is, the average of the cross-products in the long run.

    It can be shown that the correlation between sample means is equal to the correlation between X_1 and X_2. Thus, the correlation between pairs of means of all possible samples of size N that might be drawn from an infinite bivariate population is

$$\rho_{12} = \frac{E[(\overline{X}_1 - \mu_1)(\overline{X}_2 - \mu_2)]}{\dfrac{\sigma_1}{\sqrt{N}} \dfrac{\sigma_2}{\sqrt{N}}}.$$

Solving for the numerator of the right side of the above equation,

$$E[(\overline{X}_1 - \mu_1)(\overline{X}_2 - \mu_2)] = \rho_{12} \frac{\sigma_1 \sigma_2}{N} \tag{12-5}$$

Substituting Equation 12-5 in 9-4, above,

$$\sigma_{\overline{D}}^2 = E(\overline{X}_1 - \mu_1)^2 + E(\overline{X}_2 - \mu_2)^2 - 2\rho_{12} \frac{\sigma_1 \sigma_2}{N},$$

$$= \frac{\sigma_1^2}{N} + \frac{\sigma_2^2}{N} - 2\rho_{12} \frac{\sigma_1 \sigma_2}{N}.$$

Taking the square root of the above expression yields $\sigma_{\overline{D}}$, the **standard error of the difference between correlated means,** which is the denominator of the critical ratio in Equation 12-3, above. Thus,

$$Z_{\overline{D}} = \frac{\overline{D} - \mu_{\overline{D}}}{\sqrt{\dfrac{\sigma_1^2}{N} + \dfrac{\sigma_2^2}{N} - 2\rho_{12} \dfrac{\sigma_1 \sigma_2}{N}}}. \tag{12-6}$$

    In actual practice, we seldom know the values of the population parameters σ_1 and σ_2 that are required in the Z test above. Where those parameters are unknown, they must be estimated from the sample data. The following equation yields $S_{\overline{D}}$, the **estimated standard error of the difference between correlated means:**

$$S_{\overline{D}} = \sqrt{\frac{S_1^2}{N} + \frac{S_2^2}{N} - 2r_{12} \frac{S_1 S_2}{N}} = \sqrt{\frac{S_1^2 + S_2^2}{N} - 2r_{12} \frac{S_1 S_2}{N}}. \tag{12-7}$$

    If 12-7 is substituted in 12-3, then the resulting critical ratio follows the t distribution, since the denominator is an estimated standard error. Thus,

$$t = \frac{\overline{D} - \mu_{\overline{D}}}{S_{\overline{D}}}. \tag{12-8}$$

Since $\mu_1 = \mu_2$ under the usual null hypothesis, it follows that $\mu_{\overline{D}} = 0$, and thus that term can be dropped from the above equation. Substituting 12-7 for $S_{\overline{D}}$ in Equation 12-8 yields the following expression for t:

$$t = \frac{\overline{D}}{\sqrt{\dfrac{S_1^2 + S_2^2}{N} - 2r_{12}\dfrac{S_1 S_2}{N}}}, \quad df = N - 1. \tag{12-9}$$

Notice the similarity between Formula 12-9 and Formula 9-21, the t test of a difference between the means of independent groups of the same size. That earlier formula is shown below for comparison:

$$t = \frac{\overline{D}}{\sqrt{\dfrac{S_1^2 + S_2^2}{N_G}}}, \quad df = 2(N_G - 1), \tag{9-21}$$

where N_G is the number of subjects in each of the independent groups. Equation 12-9 differs from 9-21 in two respects: There is a subtractive term in the denominator which is a function of the correlation between X_1 and X_2, and the number of degrees of freedom is only half as large as in 9-21. We will have more to say about other comparisons between those two t ratios in a later section.

Equation 12-9 will prove useful as a kind of conceptual formula, and while it would be possible to use that formula for computation, doing so would require finding the variances and standard deviations of X_1 and X_2, and also calculating the correlation between those measures. Fortunately, a more direct procedure is available. Since we have a difference measure D for each subject in Table 12-1, we can find the estimated standard error of $\overline{D}$ directly by applying Formulas 8-10 and 8-13. The unbiased estimate of the variance of D is

$$S_D^2 = \frac{\Sigma D^2 - \dfrac{(\Sigma D)^2}{N}}{N - 1}, \tag{12-10}$$

and the estimated standard error of $\overline{D}$ is

$$S_{\overline{D}} = \sqrt{\frac{S_D^2}{N}}. \tag{12-11}$$

Substituting 12-10 in 12-11,

$$S_{\overline{D}} = \sqrt{\frac{\Sigma D^2 - \dfrac{(\Sigma D)^2}{N}}{N(N - 1)}}. \tag{12-12}$$

Substituting 12-12 in 12-8 yields the **direct-difference computational formula** for the correlated-measures t test:

$$\text{Direct-difference formula: } t = \frac{\overline{D}}{\sqrt{\dfrac{\Sigma D^2 - \dfrac{(\Sigma D)^2}{N}}{N(N-1)}}}, df = N - 1, \qquad (12\text{-}13)$$

where N = number of pairs of measures. The denominator of 12-13 is exactly equivalent to the denominator of 12-9. Thus, the direct-difference formula saves a considerable amount of work.

Equation 12-13 is formally identical to Formula 8-16, the t test of a single mean under the null hypothesis that $\mu_0 = 0$. Indeed, the correlated-measures t test can also be viewed as a test of the null hypothesis that a single mean, $\overline{D}$, does not differ significantly from zero.

Table 12-1 shows the calculation of the correlated-measures t test in our visual reaction-time data. The first step in applying Formula 12-13 is to find the difference score, D, for each subject, always subtracting X_2 from X_1 and retaining the sign. Although the means of the X_1 and X_2 scores do not directly enter into the calculation of the correlated-measures t ratio by the direct-difference method, those means are of interest and should always be found. Furthermore, those means provide an arithmetic check, since $\overline{D} = \overline{X}_1 - \overline{X}_2$, as we show in Table 12-1. Our observed t of 2.405 is greater than the 2-tailed critical value at the .05 level, so we reject the null hypothesis that $\mu_D = 0$ in favor of the alternative hypothesis that $\mu_D > 0$. The fact that $\overline{D}$ is significantly greater than zero implies that $\overline{X}_1$ is significantly greater than $\overline{X}_2$, which in turn implies that reaction times decrease — improve — significantly with practice under the conditions of our experiment.

Comparing Correlated-Measures and Independent t Tests.   In order to demonstrate the greater power of the correlated-measures t test, we will now consider the results of *erroneously* running an independent 2-sample t test on the results of our repeated-measures experiment, treating those measurements as though they were made on two independent groups of 10 subjects each. Table 12-2 shows the correct application of the correlated-measures test and the erroneous application of the independent 2-sample t test using Formula 9-21. To help make this comparison as clear as possible, we have used Formula 12-9 for the correlated measures test, rather than the more convenient computational formula. Notice that Formulas 12-9 and 9-21 yield identical numerators for the t ratio — namely 17.90 — as we should expect, since we have noted earlier that $\overline{D} = \overline{X}_1 - \overline{X}_2$. If there were no correlation between the X_1 and X_2 measures, as in the case of independent groups, then those formulas would also yield identical denominators. But if there is a positive correlation between measurements — as in repeated measures — then the correlation serves to reduce the denominator of 12-9, thereby increasing the magnitude of the t ratio, resulting in a more powerful test. In Table 12-2, the observed t value resulting from the misapplication of the

TABLE 12-2. Comparing the Correlated-Measures t Test, Correctly Applied to the Repeated Measures in Table 12-1, with the Independent 2-Sample t Test *Erroneously* Applied to Those Data.

Correlated-measures t test:	Independent 2-sample t test:
$\bar{X}_1 = 312.40 \quad \bar{X}_2 = 294.50$	$\bar{X}_1 = 312.40 \quad \bar{X}_2 = 294.50$
$\bar{D} = 17.90$	$\bar{X}_1 - \bar{X}_2 = 17.90$
$S_1 = 61.57 \quad S_2 = 47.13$	$S_1 = 61.57 \quad S_2 = 47.13$
$r_{12} = .941$	$N_1 = 10 \quad N_2 = 10$
$N = 10$	$N_G = 10$
$df = N - 1 = 9$	$df = N_1 + N_2 - 2 = 2(N_G - 1) = 18$

Applying Formula 12-9,

$$
\begin{aligned}
t &= \frac{\bar{D}}{\sqrt{\dfrac{S_1^2 + S_2^2}{N} - 2r_{12}\dfrac{S_1 S_2}{N}}} \\[2mm]
&= \frac{17.90}{\sqrt{\dfrac{61.57^2 + 47.13^2}{10} - 2(.941)\dfrac{61.57(47.13)}{10}}} \\[2mm]
&= \frac{17.90}{\sqrt{\dfrac{6{,}012.1018}{10} - 546.1176}} \\[2mm]
&= \frac{17.90}{\sqrt{601.2102 - 546.1176}} \\[2mm]
&= \frac{17.90}{\sqrt{55.0926}} = \frac{17.90}{7.4224} = 2.412.^{a}
\end{aligned}
$$

$CV_{.05}$ (9 df) $= 2.262$; thus reject H_0.

Erroneously applying Formula 9-21,

$$
\begin{aligned}
t &= \frac{\bar{X}_1 - \bar{X}_2}{\sqrt{\dfrac{S_1^2 + S_2^2}{N_G}}} \\[2mm]
&= \frac{312.40 - 294.50}{\sqrt{\dfrac{61.57^2 + 47.13^2}{10}}} \\[2mm]
&= \frac{17.90}{\sqrt{\dfrac{6{,}012.1018}{10}}} \\[2mm]
&= \frac{17.90}{\sqrt{601.2102}} \\[2mm]
&= \frac{17.90}{24.5196} = 0.730.
\end{aligned}
$$

$CV_{.05}$ (18 df) $= 2.101$; thus do not reject H_0.

[a] t value here differs from value in Table 12-1 because of greater rounding error in Formula 12-9.

independent 2-sample test is far below the critical value required for rejection of the null hypothesis, although the value resulting from the proper application of the correlated-measures test allows the rejection of H_0 at the .05 level. In general, using an independent t test where a correlated-measures test is appropriate increases the probability of a Type 2 error—a failure to reject the null hypothesis when it is in fact false—and thus decreases the power of the test.

Some Difficulties in the Repeated-Measures Design. Although the repeated-measures test is usually more powerful than the independent t test, there are some situations where the repeated-measures design poses great difficulties. For example, in a study comparing performance under a drug with performance under a placebo, which condition should be given first? The effects of some drugs may be very long-lasting, so if the drug is given first, then the subjects' performance under the placebo condition may suffer from carry-over effects from the drug. It will probably occur to you that it might be wise to test the subjects under the placebo condition first, thereby eliminating any possible carry-over of drug effects. Such a procedure, however, would eliminate one kind of carry-over effect at the expense of introducing another.

Suppose we were interested in testing a new drug designed to enhance alertness. Such a drug might be expected to reduce simple reaction time. We might give a group of subjects a placebo, measure their reaction times to ten presentations of a light, and we might then measure ten reaction times under the influence — if any — of the drug. Suppose we found the mean reaction time significantly faster under the drug condition. Would you then conclude that the drug works as expected? Unfortunately, that conclusion would not be warranted. The drug might be totally ineffective, and the observed decrease in reaction time might be nothing more than a practice effect. Indeed, the data in Table 12-1 show just such a practice effect in simple reaction times. In our drug experiment, the two levels of the independent variable, *drug vs placebo,* are tied to the two levels of a temporal-order variable, *first ten vs second ten trials,* so that either the independent variable or the temporal order variable could account for the results. Thus, any effect of the independent variable is **confounded** with a possible practice effect. A partial solution to the problem might be to test half the subjects under the placebo first and the other half under the drug first, provided that enough is known about the duration of the drug effect to insure that any carry-over can be essentially eliminated. The matched-pairs design — described in the next section — completely eliminates carry-over effects, but at the expense of some of the power of the repeated-measures design. We will further discuss repeated-measures experiments in the chapter on experimental design.

Matched-Pairs Test.   A matched-pairs experimental design offers much of the power — sensitivity — of a repeated-measures design, and at the same time eliminates any carry-over effect from one condition to the other, since different subjects are used under each condition. Subjects are paired on a **matching variable,** some measure that is expected to correlate with the **dependent variable.** One member of each matched pair is then assigned to one experimental condition — to one level of the independent variable — and the other member is assigned to the other condition.

Suppose we wanted to assess the effects of a drug on simple reaction time. Our matching variable might consist of reaction times measured under a pretest condition without the drug *or* the placebo. Subjects having comparable reaction times would then be paired with each other, and one member of each pair would be assigned to the drug condition and the other to the placebo condition. In the experiment proper, the dependent variable consists of reaction times measured under the placebo and under the drug condition. A difference score would be found for each pair of subjects by subtracting reaction time under the drug from reaction time under the placebo, always retaining the sign of the difference. The significance of the difference would be tested by Formula 12-13.

We can best explain how it is that we would use the same formula for repeated-measures and matched-pairs tests by referring to Formula 12-9, which we remind you is precisely equivalent to 12-13. The use of the correlated-measures t test, which subsumes the test of matched pairs as well as repeated measures, is based on the assumption that r_{12} is greater than zero. As we noted earlier, r_{12} is the correlation between measures of the dependent variable under Conditions 1 and 2 in a repeated-measures experiment. In a matched-pairs experiment, r_{12} is also the correlation between two measures of the dependent variable, but here, each of those measures is made on a different member of a matched pair. If the matching variable correlates with the dependent variable, then the two measures of the dependent variable will also correlate with each other. In that case, the denominator of 12-9 will be reduced, and the correlated-measures test will be more powerful than the independent 2-sample t test that we should have to use in the absence of matching our subjects on a pretest measure. We will return to these points after presenting a detailed example of a matched-pairs test.

There are many situations besides drug experiments where it is inconvenient or impossible to make repeated measures on the same subjects. In some of those situations, it is very easy to use a matched-pairs design. Indeed, in some cases subjects can be matched on a variable that we would need to measure even in an independent-groups experiment. In such cases, a matched-pairs design may yield a more powerful test at a cost of very little additional work.

A Memory Experiment. Consider the nature of forgetting—the other side of the memory coin. We tend to forget material that we have learned but not used for some time. Does the memory trace passively decay through disuse over a period of time, or does new learning actively interfere with the recall of things learned in the past? The following experiment in verbal learning addresses this issue. An experimental group (E) learns word List A, learns List B, and is then tested for recall of List A. A control group (C) learns List A, rests while the experimental group is learning List B, and is then tested for recall of A at the same time as the experimental group. If the experimental group forgets more words from List A than does the control group, the difference in forgetting cannot be due to the mere passage of time, since the same amount of time passes for each group between original learning and test of recall. Thus, we attribute any difference in forgetting to the different treatment of the groups between original learning and recall. We argue that learning List B—that is, engaging in an **interpolated activity,** some activity occurring between original learning and recall—inhibits the recall of prior learning.[1] The interference we see here may give the appear-

---

[1] You might also argue that while the control groups is "resting," those subjects might very well be rehearsing the words from List A. If so, their superior performance on the recall test might be due to their having an opportunity for rehearsal that was not available to the experimental group. If you wish to pursue this argument, see Underwood (1957).

ance of working backward in time, and thus is called **retroactive inhibition.** The idea of **retroactive causality**—causality working backward in time—is of course preposterous. Nothing in the present can undo the past, but activities in the here-and-now can indeed alter our *recall* of past events. Table 12-3 illustrates the **retroactive inhibition paradigm,** the logic of an experiment on forgetting as a function of interpolated activity between learning and recall. That experimental paradigm has wide applications across many kinds of learning and retention situations.

TABLE 12-3.   Retroactive Inhibition Paradigm. Interpolated Activity, B, Interferes with Recall of Prior Learning, A.

	Original Learning	Interpolated Activity	Recall Test
Experimental group	A	B	A
Control group	A	—	A

It is possible to use two independent groups of subjects in an experiment on retroactive inhibition, but such an experiment also lends itself to the use of a match-pairs design, a procedure that will ordinarily yield a more powerful experiment. (It should be obvious that a repeated-measures design would be very difficult to use in the present situation, since it would not be feasible to have each subject learn List A under control and experimental conditions.) Notice that the control and experimental groups both learn List A. We should expect performance on the original learning of List A to be highly correlated with the recall test of A, and thus we have a matching variable—original learning of A—built into our experiment. Our experiment, described below in detail, is carried out in two stages. In the first stage, every subject learns List A. Subjects are then matched into pairs on the basis of their performance on List A. One member of each pair is assigned to the control group and the other member to the experimental group. In the second stage of the experiment, the groups are treated as shown in Table 12-3.

Sixteen subjects were tested in a matched-pairs experiment on retroactive inhibition. All of the subjects first learned List A, consisting of 15 common English words. Each subject studied the word list for 30 seconds, turned the list face down, and then wrote as many of the words as possible in 60 seconds on a slip of paper. The slip was then turned face down, the subject again studied List A for 30 seconds, and again wrote as many words as possible in 60 seconds. The subjects were given a total of five such learning trials on List A. Each subject's original learning score is the total number of words correct—without regard to order—on the five trials on List A. Original learning scores were then arranged in descending order, as in Table 12-4. The subjects having the two highest scores were paired, the two next highest were then paired, and so on through the remaining subjects. Unfortunately, only three pairs of subjects are perfectly matched. Thus, it would be possible to assign our subjects to the control and experimental groups in such a way that one group might contain a disproportionate number of better or poorer learners.

TABLE 12-4. Pairing Subjects on Original Learning Scores in Retroactive Inhibition Experiment; Assignment to Control Group (C) and Experimental Group (E).

Score	66	66	64	63	62	58	57	56	55	55	54	54	49	47	43	40
Group	C	E	E	C	C	E	E	C	C	E	E	C	C	E	E	C
Pair		1		2		3		4		5		6		7		8

Control group mean = 55.62
Experimental group mean = 55.50 } $t(7) = 0.168$

The following procedure yields groups that will usually be closely — if less than perfectly — matched: The subjects are assigned to the control and experimental groups in CEEC (or ECCE) order. Applying that procedure to data in Table 12-4 yields closely matched groups that do not differ significantly on original learning by a correlated-measures t test.

Assigning subjects to the control and experimental groups in CEEC or ECCE order results in more evenly matched groups than assigning subjects alternately in CECE or ECEC order, or randomly dividing each pair of subjects between the control and experimental groups. Since we arranged our 16 subjects in descending order of performance on original learning, and since we assigned subjects in CEEC order, the control group consisted of subjects having the following ranks (disregarding tied scores): 1, 4, 5, 8, 9, 12, 13, and 16. The experimental subjects had the following ranks (disregarding ties): 2, 3, 6, 7, 10, 11, 14, and 15. Thus, the means of the ranks are equal in the two groups, namely 8.5. If the groups do not differ in terms of mean ranks, then they should not differ substantially in terms of original learning scores. Now suppose we assigned subjects to the groups in CECE order. In that case, the mean ranks of the control and experimental groups would be 8 and 9 respectively. Now, does assigning subjects in CECE order, or in ECEC order, produce a significant difference between the control and experimental groups on their original learning scores? We will leave this question for you to answer in an exercise at the end of the chapter.

The procedure of assigning subjects to groups in CEEC or ECCE order represents a variety of **counterbalancing.** Within each block of four subjects, the order of assignment of subjects 1 and 2 is reversed for subjects 3 and 4. If the subjects are arranged in order on a matching variable, then counterbalancing will usually yield closely comparable control and experimental groups. It would be possible to assign randomly the subjects within each pair to the E and C groups, but counterbalancing leaves less to chance. Ideally, of course, all of the subjects in a matched-pairs experiment should be perfectly matched. But in practice, perfect matching can be achieved only by discarding large numbers of subjects — a procedure that makes good use of neither the subjects' nor the experimenter's time. Counterbalancing is also very useful in repeated-measures experiments where two or more measures are made on the same subjects. We will have more to say about counterbalancing in the chapter on experimental design.

In the second stage of our experiment, the control group rested while the experimental group learned List B, consisting of 15 common English words. The procedures for learning List B were the same as for List A. The words on List B were similar to those on List A — some synonyms, near-synonyms, and words that sound alike. As soon as the experimental group completed the interpolated activity, learning List B, both groups were asked to write as many words from List A as they could recall in 60 seconds. Thus, the recall test consisted of a single trial on List A. The results are shown in Table 12-5 for each subject. A difference score is found for each pair of subjects by subtracting the score of the experimental subject from that of the control subject. The

TABLE 12-5.   Correlated-Measures t Test in Matched-Pairs Experiment on Retroactive Inhibition. Words Correct on 1-Trial Recall Test of List A (15 Words).

| | Recall Test: List A | | | |
Pair	Control Group: X_1	Experimental Group: X_2	D	D^2
1	15	12	3	9
2	13	5	8	64
3	14	10	4	16
4	13	9	4	16
5	12	7	5	25
6	14	6	8	64
7	10	3	7	49
8	7	3	4	16

$\Sigma X_1 = 98 \quad \Sigma X_2 = 55 \quad \Sigma D = 43 \quad \Sigma D^2 = 259$

$\bar{X}_1 = 12.25 \quad \bar{X}_2 = 6.88 \quad \bar{D} = 5.38$

Arithmetic check: $\bar{D} = \bar{X}_1 - \bar{X}_2 = 12.25 - 6.88 = 5.37.\checkmark$ Checks within rounding error.

Applying Formula 12-13, $t = \dfrac{\bar{D}}{\sqrt{\dfrac{\Sigma D^2 - \dfrac{(\Sigma D)^2}{N}}{N(N-1)}}} = \dfrac{5.38}{\sqrt{\dfrac{259 - \dfrac{43^2}{8}}{8(8-1)}}} = 7.63.$

$H_0: \mu_D = 0;$

$H_1: \mu_D > 0;$ $\qquad df = N - 1 = 7.$

$H_2: \mu_D < 0.$

From Table B, 2-tailed $CV_{.001} = 5.405$; therefore reject H_0, accept H_1.

subtraction is always carried out in the same direction, and the sign of the difference is retained. Formula 12-13 provides a test of the null hypothesis that there is no difference between the mean recall of the control and experimental groups.

The correlated-measures t test is appropriate only where there is a correlation between X_1 and X_2, that is, where r_{12} is greater than zero. That requirement holds whether we use Formula 12-9, which explicitly contains r_{12}, or the equivalent direct-difference expression, Formula 12-13. Are we justified in using the correlated-measures test in our matched-pairs experiment? We argued earlier that we should expect a correlation between the dependent variable measures in our matched-pairs design if there is a correlation between the matching variable and the dependent variable — and we should certainly expect original learning scores to correlate with scores on the recall test. In fact, $r_{12} = .79$ in our experiment. Thus, matching subjects on original learning scores results in a substantial correlation between X_1 and X_2, the dependent variable measurements in the control and experimental groups. Thus, our correlated-measures test is more powerful than an independent two-sample t test in the present situation.

The retroactive inhibition paradigm illustrated in Table 12-3 has considerable generality. For example, in a human subject, if the interpolated activity between original learning and recall consists of receiving a head injury in an accident, then *retrograde amnesia* sometimes results. Memory for events occurring just prior to the injury may be greatly impaired, while recall of events progressively farther back in time may be less and less impaired.

Requirements for Correlated-Measures t Tests

The requirements — assumptions — listed in Table 12-6 apply equally to tests of repeated measures and matched pairs. The dependent variable must be measured on an interval or ratio scale. If this requirement cannot be met, then some other procedure should be used. Procedures suitable for use with nominal and ordinal scales are described later in this chapter.

TABLE 12-6. Requirements for Correlated-Measures t Tests.

1. Interval or ratio measurement scale.
2. Repeated measures on same subjects, or measures on matched pairs.
3. Approximately normal distribution of D, where $D = X_1 - X_2$.
4. X_1 and X_2 are positively correlated in the population, that is, $\rho_{12} > 0$.
5. The population standard deviation, σ_D, is unknown and must be estimated from S_D, the observed standard deviation of D.

The requirement of an approximately normal distribution of D usually poses no great difficulty. If X_1 and X_2 are approximately normally distributed, then D will also tend to be normally distributed. Like other t tests, the correlated-measures t is relatively robust, insensitive to most departures from normality.

In most repeated-measures experiments, it is fairly obvious that the X_1 and X_2 measures will very likely turn out to be positively correlated. It is of course possible to calculate the correlation between those measures after the experiment is completed, but it is not necessary to do so. Formula 12-13 takes the correlation between dependent measures into account by utilizing difference scores, thus saving us the work of calculating the correlation coefficient. But in a matched-pairs experiment, the correlation between X_1 and X_2 results from the correlation between the matching variable and the dependent variable. Here, too, we could calculate the correlation between X_1 and X_2 after the experiment, but that is ordinarily not done. Now, what happens in a matched-pairs or repeated-measures experiment if it turns out that there is no correlation between X_1 and X_2? In that case, the numerator of the t ratio remains the same, but the denominator increases in magnitude. If $r_{12} = 0$, then Formula 12-9 shows that the denominator of the correlated-measures t ratio is equal to that of the independent two-sample t test, and the correlated-measures t is then equal to the independent t ratio. But the correlated-measures t has only half as many degrees of freedom, and thus its critical value at any level of significance is higher than the critical value of the independent t. The upshot of all this is a loss of power if you use a correlated-measures t when there is no correlation between X_1 and X_2. In such a situation, you will increase the probability of a Type 2 error — that is, failing to detect a difference between $\overline{X}_1$ and $\overline{X}_2$ when a difference in fact exists.

The last requirement in Table 12-6, the assumption that the standard deviation of the population of difference scores is unknown, is analogous to the requirements of the other t tests described earlier. If we knew the value of σ_D, then we could use a Z test. Since we do not know the value of that population parameter, we must estimate its value from the observed value of S_D, and thus a Z test would be inappropriate.

Ordinal Scales

The procedures for comparing correlated measures that we have described so far require at least an interval measurement scale. In some cases, we may need to compare correlated measures that comprise only a nominal or ordinal scale. We will develop techniques for dealing with these lower-caliber measurement scales that are analogous in many respects to the correlated-measures t tests presented earlier.

The Sign Test

As described in the following sections, the **sign test** can be used equally well in repeated-measures or matched-pairs designs.

A Repeated-Measures Design.   Suppose a marketing researcher is interested in comparing two brands of coffee. Twelve subjects, six men and six women, are asked to sample both brands. The subjects are then asked to rate the taste of each brand on a five-point scale consisting of the categories *excellent, good, fair, poor,* and *very poor*. The number 1 is assigned to the *very poor* category and the number 5 to the *excellent* category. The numbers 1 through 5 represent ordinal measurements in this case, since we have no way of knowing whether the distance on our scale from 1 to 2, for example, corresponds to the same distance on the taste dimension as the interval from 3 to 4, or from 4 to 5. Our measurement scale thus lacks one of the characteristics of an interval scale, and thus a repeated-measures t test would not be entirely appropriate.

TABLE 12-7. Sign Test in a Repeated-Measures Design.

	Ratings on a 5-Point Scale		Sign of
Subject	Brand A	Brand B	A − B
1	4	3	+
2	4	4	0
3	5	3	+
4	4	2	+
5	3	2	+
6	2	1	+
7	5	5	0
8	3	2	+
9	5	4	+
10	1	3	−
11	3	2	+
12	4	1	+

$$X = \text{Number of} + \text{signs} = 9$$
$$\text{Number of} - \text{signs} = 1$$
$$N = 10$$

Applying Formula 7-22,
$$Z_X = \frac{|X - Np| - .5}{\sqrt{Npq}} = \frac{|9 - 10(.5)| - .5}{\sqrt{10(.5)(.5)}}$$

$$= \frac{4 - .5}{\sqrt{2.5}} = \frac{3.5}{1.58} = 2.214.$$

$H_0: p = .5;$
$H_1: p > .5;$
$H_2: p < .5.$

From Table A, 2-tailed $CV_{.05} = 1.96$; therefore reject H_0 and accept H_1.

The results of our survey are shown in Table 12-7. For each subject, we find the sign of the difference A − B, always carrying out the subtraction in that direction. As we have noted earlier in connection with other difference scores, it does not matter which measure is subtracted from which, as long as the subtraction is done in a consistent direction in a given set of data. The null hypothesis is the statement that there is no difference between the judgments of Brands A and B. If H_0 is true, then for any subject the probability of rating Brand A higher than Brand B is .5. If Brand A is rated higher by a particular subject, then the sign of A − B will be positive. For the two subjects who rated the brands equally, the difference between A and B is zero, and hence has no sign. If we discard those two subjects, then we can treat the remaining ten subjects as a binomial probability experiment where N is 10, p is the probability of a *plus*, q is the probability of a *minus*, and $p = q = .5$. Thus, we can state the following null and alternative hypotheses:

$H_0: p = .5;$

$H_1: p > .5;$

$H_2: p < .5.$

Are we justified in discarding the two subjects whose ratings of the brands were tied? The answer is straightforward: We *must* eliminate those subjects if we are to treat our results as the outcome of a binomial probability experiment, where each trial must result in success or failure — that is, a + or a − in the present context. Since Np and Nq are both as great as 5, we can use the normal approximation to the binomial to carry out our sign test, as shown in Table 12-7. As in other binomial tests, if either Np or Nq were less than 5, we should have to find the exact binomial probabilities by the procedures described in Chapter 7. Since p and q are always equal to .5 in the sign test, we can state a simple rule: The normal approximation to the binomial can be used in the sign test only when $N \geq 10$. For smaller N, the exact binomial probability must be used.

On the basis of our sign test in Table 12-7 we reject the null hypothesis. Since the number of +'s is greater than we would expect by chance, we accept the first alternative hypothesis, which states the probability is greater than .5 that any given subject will rate Brand A higher than Brand B. In most situations, we would be equally ready to reject the null hypothesis if there were fewer +'s than expected on the basis of chance. In that case, Brand B would be the higher-rated brand. In using the sign test, it is possible to carry out a one-tailed test — as in other kinds of tests. But a two-tailed test is usually more appropriate, as we have noted in many other contexts.

The Sign Test for Matched Pairs.   Like the correlated-measures t test, the sign test can be used in a matched-pairs as well as a repeated-measures design. Suppose, for example, a manufacturer wishes to pretest a new advertising campaign. Among other things, the manufacturer is interested in learning whether there is any difference between men and women in the perceived truthfulness of the proposed new advertising. It would of course be possible in such a study to use independent groups of women and men, but there are advantages in using matched pairs of husbands and wives. Indeed, husbands and wives are perfectly matched on some of the variables of interest in marketing research, since they share the same house, neighborhood of residence, and family income. Suppose the manufacturer presents the new advertising material to a group of 12 husband-wife pairs. Each subject then rates the perceived truthfulness of the advertising on an 11-point scale ranging from *very very low* to *very very high*, the numbers 1 and 11 representing, respectively, the lowest and highest amounts of perceived truthfulness. The results are shown in Table 12-8, where the sign test indicates that there is no significant difference in perceived truthfulness between men and women. Indeed, Table A shows that the two-tailed probability of observing a Z value as great as .60 just by chance is .5486. Thus the results of our sign test do not even approach statistical significance. Depending on the intended purpose of the new advertising campaign, those results might be viewed as disappointing or very encouraging.

Requirements for the Sign Test.   Table 12-9 lists the requirements for the test. As you can see, the sign test is a very straightforward extension of the binomial probability experiment developed in Chapter 7.

TABLE 12-8. Sign Test in a Matched-Pairs Design.

Pair	Ratings on an 11-Point Scale		Sign of A − B
	A (Husband)	**B (Wife)**	
1	3	10	−
2	2	6	−
3	3	2	+
4	2	11	−
5	1	9	−
6	3	7	−
7	8	5	+
8	1	6	−
9	11	9	+
10	4	4	0
11	8	7	+
12	3	9	−

$$X = \text{Number of} + \text{signs} = 4$$
$$\text{Number of} - \text{signs} = 7$$
$$N = 11$$

Applying Formula 7-22,

$$Z_X = \frac{|X - Np| - .5}{\sqrt{Npq}} = \frac{|4 - 11(.5)| - .5}{\sqrt{11(.5)(.5)}}$$

$$= \frac{|-1.5| - .5}{\sqrt{2.75}} = \frac{1}{1.66} = .60.$$

$H_0: p = .5;$

$H_1: p > .5;$ From Table A, 2-tailed $CV_{.05} = 1.96$; therefore do not reject H_0.

$H_2: p < .5.$

TABLE 12-9. Requirements for the Sign Test.

1. Ordinal measurement scale.
2. Repeated measures on same subjects, or measures on matched pairs.
3. For each subject, or each matched pair, the sign of the difference between measures A and B is found. Differences of zero are discarded.
4. Letting $p = P(+)$ and $q = P(-)$, $p = q = .5$.
5. Test statistic is the binomial random variable X, the *observed* number of + signs. Null hypothesis: $p = .5$.
6. To use the normal approximation to the binomial in the sign test, N must be at least as great as 10, where N is the number of *nonzero* differences between A and B.

A Difficulty with the Sign Test. If you look carefully at Table 12-8, you will see that most of the positive differences between pairs of husbands and wives are substantially smaller in magnitude than the negative differences between pairs. But the sign test uses only the *directions* of the differences between pairs — or between repeated measures on the same subjects — and ignores the *magnitudes* of those differences. Thus, the sign test does not utilize all of the information contained in our present data. In the next section, we will present a test that utilizes more of the information contained in measurements on an ordinal scale.

The Wilcoxon Signed-Ranks Test

The **Wilcoxon signed-ranks test** (Wilcoxon, 1945) takes advantage of the fact that a difference between a pair of measurements on an ordinal scale has a magnitude as well as a sign. Like the sign test, the Wilcoxon test applies to differences between matched pairs of subjects as well as to repeated measures on the same subjects. We have previously presented the Mann-Whitney U test, a test of a difference between independent groups measured on an ordinal scale. Since the present test utilizes correlated measures on an ordinal scale, the Wilcoxon signed-ranks test bears the same relationship to the Mann-Whitney U that the correlated-measure t bears to the t test of a difference between independent groups.

We will use the same data to illustrate the Wilcoxon test that we used to illustrate the sign test for matched pairs in Table 12-8. Applying different tests to the same data — perhaps in the hope of eventually finding a procedure that will yield significant results — is not to be recommended ordinarily, but in our present situation, doing so may help explain the Wilcoxon test. We will begin by presenting the mechanics of the test, and then we will explain the rationale.

Table 12-10 shows the quantities that we must find for each pair of subjects. The first four columns of that table are identical to Table 12-8. Column 5 shows the absolute value of the difference between the ratings by husbands and wives. The difference of zero — for subject 10 — is discarded, as

TABLE 12-10.   Wilcoxon Signed-Ranks Test. Same Data as in Table 12-8.

Pair	A (Husband)	B (Wife)	Sign of A − B	|A − B|	Rank of |A − B|	Signed rank
1	3	10	−	7	9	−9
2	2	6	−	4	5.5	−5.5
3	3	2	+	1	1.5	+1.5
4	2	11	−	9	11	−11
5	1	9	−	8	10	−10
6	3	7	−	4	5.5	−5.5
7	8	5	+	3	4	+4
8	1	6	−	5	7	−7
9	11	9	+	2	3	+3
10	4	4	0	0		
11	8	7	+	1	1.5	+1.5
12	3	9	−	6	8	−8

$$\Sigma R = 66 \qquad W = -46$$

Arithmetic check: $\Sigma R = \dfrac{N}{2}(N+1);$

$66 = \dfrac{11}{2}(11+1) = 66.\checkmark$

$H_0: \mu_A = \mu_B;$

$H_1: \mu_A > \mu_B;$

$H_2: \mu_A < \mu_B.$

From Table G, 2-tailed $CV_{.05} = 44$; since $|-46| \geq 44$, reject H_0, accept H_2.

in the sign test. The remaining 11 absolute differences are placed in ascending order and assigned the ranks shown in column 6. Notice that some of the absolute differences are tied. The two differences of 1 and the two differences of 4 are assigned the mean of the ranks those differences would have in the absence of ties. (The procedure here is identical to the method of dealing with ties in the Mann-Whitney U test in Chapter 9 and in calculating Spearman's r_s in Chapter 11.) At this point, you should carry out an arithmetic check before proceeding further. Since the sum of a set of ranks is equal to $(N/2)(N+1)$, the sum of the ranks of $|A - B|$ in column 6 should equal that quantity. Remember, N here is the number of pairs remaining after discarding any pairs whose ratings are tied. In the last column of Table 12-10 each rank is given the sign of $A - B$, which appears in column 4. Thus, the last column contains the **signed ranks** on which the test is based. The test statistic **W,** so designated in honor of Frank Wilcoxon, is the algebraic sum of the signed ranks.[1] The observed value of W is compared with the critical value in Table G for $N = 11$, the number of subjects remaining after discarding the pair having tied ratings. We reject the null hypothesis if the absolute value of our observed W is equal to or greater than the critical value. Thus, our results are significant at the .05 level by the Wilcoxon signed-rank test, although a sign test failed to achieve significance by a very wide margin.

Rationale for the Test. The null hypothesis states that $\mu_A = \mu_B$. Now consider the signed ranks in Table 12-9. If the null hypothesis is true, what is the expected value of the algebraic sum of the signed ranks? In our development of the sign test, we argued that if H_0 is true, then the number of +'s and —'s should be about equal. Thus, the rank of any particular difference, $|A - B|$, is expected to have a positive or negative sign with equal probability. It follows that the magnitudes of the positive ranks are expected to equal the magnitudes of the negative ranks, and thus the expected value of W, the sum of the signed ranks, is zero. Thus, the null hypothesis becomes less tenable the farther an observed W departs from the expected value of zero.

Table 12-11 shows the probability distribution of W for the case where $N = 3$. If the null hypothesis is true, then all of the eight arrangments of + and — signs are equally probable. Thus, each arrangement has a probability of 1/8, that is, .125. It is as though we let the toss of three coins determine the signs of our three ranks. (Indeed, you should be able to see many similarities between our present discussion and our introduction to the binomial probability experiment in Chapter 7.) When the null hypothesis is true, W is a random variable whose value is determined by the random distribution of positive and negative signs among the ranks. The last two columns of Table 12-11 give

---

[1] If you should wish to look up the treatment of this test in another textbook—a procedure that I recommend highly, for this test and others as well—you will probably find that a different test statistic is used, T rather than W. Wilcoxon (1945) defined T as the absolute value of the *smaller* of the sum of the positive or negative ranks. Most writers have followed Wilcoxon's lead, although the development of the W statistic is easier to follow than that of T. (For a clear treatment of both T and W, see Mosteller & Rourke, 1973.)

TABLE 12-11.   Distribution of Wilcoxon Statistic Where $N = 3$.

Signed Ranks			W	$P(W)$	$P(|W_{obs}| \geq |W|)$ One-Tailed	Two-Tailed
+1	+2	+3	6	.125	.125	.250
−1	+2	+3	4	.125	.250	.500
+1	−2	+3	2	.125	.375	.750
+1	+2	−3	0	.125	.500	1.000
−1	−2	+3	0	.125		
−1	+2	−3	−2	.125		
+1	−2	−3	−4	.125		
−1	−2	−3	−6	.125		

the one- and two-tailed probabilities of obtaining an observed W as large or larger than the value associated with each of the probabilities. Since the distribution of W is symmetrical, it is only necessary to present those probabilities for half the distribution, as we have also done for the Z distribution. Tables similar to Table 12-11 have been constructed for larger distributions, and critical values determined for one- and two-tailed tests at the usual levels of significance, as shown in Table G.

The Signed-Ranks Test in Large Samples.   Table G gives critical values of W for Ns as large as 50. While Table G is sufficiently large for most purposes, there may be times when a researcher has occasion to deal with a larger sample. For larger values of N, the distribution of W closely approaches the normal distribution, and thus a normal approximation to W is available (Mosteller & Rourke, 1973).

Requirements for the Signed-Ranks Test.   The requirements are listed in Table 12-12. As requirement 1 indicates, the Wilcoxon test is based on the assumption that measures A and B are on an ordinal scale, and also on the

TABLE 12-12.   Requirements and Procedures for the Wilcoxon Signed-Ranks Test.

1. Ordinal measurement scale. Applies to measures A and B, and to the absolute differences $|A - B|$.
2. Repeated measures on same subjects, or measures on matched pairs.
3. For each subject, or each matched pair, find the absolute difference $|A - B|$. Discard any difference of zero.
4. Rank the absolute differences, and give each difference the sign of $A - B$.
5. Test statistic is W, the algebraic sum of the signed ranks.
6. Null hypothesis: $\mu_A = \mu_B$. Reject H_0 when $|W_{obs}| \geq CV$ in Table G.

assumption that the absolute differences between A and B constitute ordinal measurements. As we pointed out in our early discussion of measurement scales in Chapter 1, the intervals between ordinal measurements are not necessarily equal—a property of an ordinal scale that has some bearing on our present discussion. Consider, for example, the absolute differences $|A - B|$ for pairs 7 and 9 in Table 12-10. The first difference is 3, between ratings of 8 and 5, and the second difference is 2, between ratings of 11 and 9. Even though we have assigned the difference of 3 a higher rank, it is very easy to conceive of a measurement scale having unequal intervals such that the difference between 5 and 8 would be *smaller* than the difference between 9 and 11. In most research situations, we seldom — if ever — have sufficient information to know whether the absolute differences truly constitute an ordinal scale. In actual practice, as long as measures *A* and *B* are on an ordinal scale, we must assume that the absolute differences also meet the ordinal requirement if we are to apply the Wilcoxon test.

Nominal Scales

A Test of Correlated Proportions

Can we change attitudes and opinions? Suppose a psychologist designs an experiment to investigate a possible method of changing people's attitudes toward the conservation of natural resources. Attitudes and behavior are certainly not one and the same, but surely a first step toward modifying wasteful behavior in the consumption of energy and other natural resources is to convince people that some of our resources will one day be exhausted. Suppose the researcher adopts a **before-after design,** where the opinions of a group of subjects are measured before and after an experimental treatment aimed at changing their attitudes. In the first phase of the study, the experimenter asks each subject, "Do you believe the United States will be faced with a severe shortage of energy before the end of this century unless we change our patterns of consumption?" The experimenter asks each subject to give a yes or no answer to that admittedly difficult question. Thus, the dichotomous yes-no responses constitute a nominal measurement scale. The experimental treatment is then administered to all the subjects, a one-hour film on the past history and future projections of the development of various energy resources in the United States and the world. After the experimental treatment, the experimenter asks the same question as before.

The results of the experiment are shown in Table 12-13. Before the film presentation, only .31 of the subjects answered yes, indicating a belief in a severe energy shortage by the end of the century. But after the presentation, .81 of those same subjects answered yes. Did the experimental treatment produce the change in proportion of positive responses, or might chance alone have been at work? It might occur to you to use the test of a difference between independent binomial proportions which we developed in Chapter 9. But that test applies to *independent* proportions, and since we have repeated measures on the same subjects, the proportions in our present situation are correlated, not independent. We will describe a procedure that McNemar (1947) has developed, a test of **correlated proportions** that can be viewed as an extension of the sign test.

TABLE 12-13. Results of Experiment on Opinion Change (See also Table 12-14). Repeated Measures on Same Subjects. Yes = 1, No = 0.

Subject	Do You Believe We Will Face Severe Energy Shortages?		Sign of Change
	X_1 (Before)	X_2 (After)	$X_2 - X_1$
1	$N = 0$	$Y = 1$	+
2	Y	Y	0
3	N	Y	+
4	Y	N	−
5	N	Y	+
6	N	Y	+
7	N	Y	+
8	Y	Y	0
9	N	Y	+
10	N	Y	+
11	Y	Y	0
12	Y	N	−
13	N	Y	+
14	N	Y	+
15	N	N	0
16	N	Y	+
Pr(Yes)	.31	.81	

$$\text{Number of } + \text{ signs} = 10$$
$$\text{Number of } - \text{ signs} = \underline{2}$$
$$N = 12$$

Consider the changes in the subjects' responses after the experimental treatment. Subject 1, for example, answered no before and yes after. We will consider that change to be positive, and thus we give that subject's change of opinion a + sign. Subject 4, on the other hand, changed from yes to no, and thus we give that change a − sign. It does not matter which kind of change we give which sign, as long as we are consistent. Our procedure here is equivalent to giving a yes response a value of 1, a no a value of 0, and then finding the sign of the difference $X_2 - X_1$. Several subjects made no change in their opinions after the experimental treatment. Those subjects have been given 0's in the column headed *Sign of Change* in Table 12-13. If there is no difference between the proportion of subjects answering yes before and after the experimental treatment, then the number of +'s should not differ significantly from the number of −'s, since the number of subjects changing in one direction must equal the number changing in the other direction if the proportions of yes responses are to remain equal before and after.

Before proceeding further, we will present the data more compactly in Table 12-14. Each subject in Table 12-13 has been tallied into one of the four cells in Table 12-14. Each cell in that fourfold table contains the subjects giving each of the four possible patterns of before-after responses. For example, Subject 1 goes in Cell *d*, Subject 2 goes in Cell *b*, Subject 4 in *a*, and Subject 15 goes in *c*. Since we are concerned only with those subjects whose opinions

TABLE 12-14.   Test of Correlated Proportions in Experiment on Opinion Change. Repeated Measures on Same Subjects. Data are Shown in a Different Format in Table 12-13. Positive Changes are in Cell *d*, Negative Changes in Cell *a*.

		X_2 (After)			
		No	Yes		
	Yes	*a* (−) 2	*b* (No change) 3	5	Before: Pr(Yes) = 5/16 = .31.
X_1 (Before)					
	No	*c* (No change) 1	*d* (+) 10 = X	11	
		3	13	16 = Total subjects	
			After: Pr(Yes) = 13/16 = .81.	N = a + d = 12; X = d = 10.	

Applying Formula 7-22,

$$Z_X = \frac{|X - Np| - .5}{\sqrt{Npq}} = \frac{|10 - 12(.5)| - .5}{\sqrt{12(.5)(.5)}}$$

$H_0: p = .5;$

$H_1: p > .5;$

$H_2: p < .5.$

$$= \frac{|4| - .5}{\sqrt{3}} = \frac{3.5}{1.73} = 2.02.$$

From Table A, 2-tailed $CV_{.05} = 1.96$; therefore reject H_0 and accept H_1.

have changed after the experimental treatment, we use only the subjects in cells *a* and *d* in our test. Thus, N is equal to the number of subjects in those cells, not the total number of subjects in the experiment. Applying Formula 7-22, we let *p* and *q*, respectively, equal the probability of a positive and negative change. Thus, under the null hypothesis $p = q = .5$. The null hypothesis $p = .5$, as stated in Table 12-14, is equivalent to the statement that there is no difference between the correlated proportions of yes responses before and after the experimental treatment. Since the observed value of the binomial random variable X is significantly greater than its expected value Np, we reject H_0 in favor of H_1. As in most situations, a two-tailed test is clearly more appropriate here than a one-tailed test, since we would be impressed by a change of opinion in either the positive or negative direction.

You may have detected a certain similarity between Table 12-14 and some of the tables we presented in our development of measures of association in Chapter 11. Indeed, in our present situation, we can ask whether there is any association between the responses before and after the experimental treatment. If there were a perfect association, then every subject's response would be the same before and after, and everyone would fall in Cells *b* and *c* in Table 12-14. In that case, there would be a perfect association between responses, and the value of the ϕ coefficient would be 1.00. (Note, however, that we would not be able to apply the *chi*-square test of association here, since some of the expected frequencies are too small.) If the association were perfect, then there would be no change in any subject's response, and thus the proportions of yes responses before and after would be equal. But if the association were less than perfect, then a test of association would not directly address the question of *differences* between proportions. In order to address that question, we must deal only with the subjects in Cells *a* and *d*, those subjects whose responses have changed after the experimental manipulation.

Other Uses of the Test. The test of correlated proportions can be used in many other situations besides the before-after design. The test is appropriate wherever we have two measurements on a nominal scale made on the same subjects or on matched pairs. For example, differences between the proportions of the same subjects passing two tests — or two test items — can be assessed. If two judges rate the same group of subjects on a two-point scale — high or low — the difference between the proportions of high ratings by the two judges can be tested. We could also match pairs of students on academic aptitude, for example, and then compare the proportions passing two different courses. Such a comparison would assess the relative difficulty of the courses.

Requirements for the Test of Correlated Proportions. Table 12-15 lists the requirements and procedures for the test. Notice that the requirements here are nearly identical to the requirements for the sign test in Table 12-9. Indeed, the test of correlated proportions is a straightforward extension of the sign test.

TABLE 12-15. Requirements and Procedures for the Test of Correlated Proportions.

1. Dichotomous nominal scale.
2. Repeated measures on the same subjects, or measures on matched pairs.
3. Assign values of 0 and 1 to the levels of the dichotomy. For each subject, or each matched pair, find the sign of the difference $X_1 - X_2$. Discard differences of zero. With data in the form of Table 12-14, use only Cells *a* and *d*; discard subjects in Cells *b* and *c*.
4. Letting $p = P(+)$ and $q = P(-)$, $p = q = .5$.
5. Test statistic is the binomial random variable X, the *observed* number of $+$ signs, that is, the number of subjects in Cell *d*. $H_0: p = .5$.
6. To use the normal approximation to the binomial, N must be at least as great as 10, where N is the number of nonzero differences between X_1 and X_2, that is, the difference between Cells *a* and *d*.

A Forward Look

We have now presented a great many statistical techniques in great detail in all of the preceding chapters. From time to time, we have discussed issues relating to experimental design, questions relating to the procedures used in gathering data. We have pointed out that flaws in the design or execution of an experiment or in carrying out a set of observations can render the results of any statistical test utterly meaningless — and therefore misleading. It is time now to consider experimental design in a more systematic way than we have in the past. The whole of the next chapter is devoted to this important topic.

Terms and Symbols

The list of new terms and symbols introduced in this chapter is rather short. Indeed, the tests in the present chapter represent straightforward extensions of procedures presented earlier.

Repeated-measures design
Matched-pairs design
Correlated measures
Standard error of the differ-
 ence between correlated
 means
Estimated standard error
Direct-difference formula
Confounding
Matching variable
Dependent variable

Counterbalancing
Sign test
Wilcoxon signed-ranks test
Correlated proportions
Before-after design
D and $\bar{D}$
ρ_{12}
$S_{\bar{D}}$
r_{12}
X_1 and X_2
W

EXERCISES AND STUDY QUESTIONS

1. In the Howard-Dolman apparatus for testing depth perception, two vertical rods are mounted on parallel tracks about an inch apart. As one rod moves toward the observer, the other moves away. The apparatus is located 15 feet from the observer, who aligns the rods using a string-and-pulley arrangement so they appear the same distance away. The results of an experiment comparing monocular and binocular depth perception are shown below. Each person made 8 adjustments using the right eye alone and 8 using both eyes. Monocular and binocular conditions were counterbalanced in *MBBM* order to control practice effects. The data below are the mean alignment errors in millimeters:

Subjects	1	2	3	4	5	6	7	8	9	10	11	12	13	14	15	16
Monocular	14	26	70	50	20	51	45	57	21	20	22	2	36	44	15	24
Binocular	24	45	20	25	23	10	17	38	13	8	8	6	12	9	17	9

a. Formulate the null and alternative hypotheses in words and symbols. Should this be a 1 or 2-tailed test?

b. Justify the use of a repeated-measures *t* test. Carry out the test and indicate whether you reject H_0, and explain what that means.

    c. Is binocular vision necessary for depth perception?

    d. This experiment could have been done using two independent groups, one group using monocular vision and the other binocular vision. What are the principal advantages and disadvantages of the repeated-measures and independent-groups designs in the present situation?

    e. We might also have used matched pairs of subjects in this experiment. Compare the relative advantages and disadvantages of the repeated-measures and matched-pairs designs in this context.

2. Suppose an industrial/organizational psychologist has designed a training program to promote greater responsibility among workers. Based on a composite measure of absenteeism, quality of workmanship, and supervisors' ratings, 32 workers are matched into 16 pairs. One member of each pair is randomly assigned to the Training Group and the other to the Control Group. Over a six-week period, the Training Group receives 1 hour of training per week dealing with ways of avoiding absenteeism and otherwise increasing responsible job behavior. The Control Group receives the same number of hours of instruction, but their training is specifically limited to increasing their job skills. Six months after the training period, the workers are rated in terms of *low*, *moderate*, or *high* responsibility. Suppose the results came out as below, where the number 3 represents the highest level of responsibility:

Pair	1	2	3	4	5	6	7	8	9	10	11	12	13	14	15	16
Training	3	3	2	3	2	2	3	3	3	2	1	2	1	3	3	2
Control	3	2	1	2	3	1	2	1	2	2	1	1	2	3	2	1

    a. Justify a sign test, state the null and alternative hypotheses, and carry out the test.

    b. This experiment might conceivably have used a repeated-measures design by assessing the same workers' responsibility before and after a training program. Compare and contrast such a procedure with the matched-pairs design in the present context.

3. Do repeat offenders, persons convicted of two or more misdemeanors or felonies, tend to increase or decrease the severity of their offenses? Suppose we classified the first and second convictions of a group of youthful offenders into 9 categories beginning with *shoplifting*, then *burglary*, and increasing in severity through *aggravated assault* and *murder*. In the following data, the numbers 1 through 9 represent the offenses in increasing order of severity:

Subject	1	2	3	4	5	6	7	8	9	10	11	12	13	14	15	16	17	18
1st offense	5	3	2	5	2	4	5	3	1	8	1	4	3	2	6	1	7	3
2nd offense	4	6	3	7	6	4	6	2	3	9	4	6	5	2	5	6	7	4

a. Justify using the Wilcoxon signed-ranks test. State the null and alternative hypotheses in words and symbols, and indicate whether you reject H_0.

4. A clinical psychologist has designed a program aimed at improving the chances of parolees making a satisfactory adjustment after release from prison. A group of young parolees are matched into pairs based on age and severity of offenses. One member of each pair is randomly assigned to the psychologist's treatment group, and the other to a control group receiving conventional parole supervision. After six months, adjustment is rated on a 9-point scale ranging from *unsatisfactory* through *excellent*. Suppose the results came out as below, where larger numbers indicate better adjustment:

Pair	1	2	3	4	5	6	7	8	9	10	11	12	13	14	15	16	17	18
Treatment	5	9	6	6	5	2	8	9	3	2	3	9	7	6	4	8	1	7
Control	1	3	1	9	6	2	4	3	6	4	1	1	4	1	4	5	2	9

a. Justify using the Wilcoxon signed-ranks test. State the null and alternative hypotheses, and indicate whether you reject H_0.
b. Why not use a repeated-measures design here?
c. Why not use an independent-groups design?
d. Are there particular pitfalls to avoid in the adjustment assessment procedure?

5. The State-Wide Educational Achievement Test (SWEAT) is given to all juniors and seniors at Greater Pottersfield High School. The results are shown below in terms of passing and failing for the 876 students who took the SWEAT both as juniors and seniors:

		As seniors:	
		Fail	Pass
As juniors:	Pass	7	546
	Fail	304	29

a. Justify using a correlated proportions test, state the null and alternative hypotheses, and do the test.
b. The principal at Greater Pottersfield is delighted with the statistical significance of the results, and goes on to point out that more than four times as many students changed their performances from failing to passing as from passing to failing over the course of their senior year. Comment on the principal's observations, and discuss the statistical significance of the results in relation to their practical importance in terms of the change in percentage of students passing as juniors and as seniors.

6. Has there been any change in the proportion of women receiving bachelor's degrees in the last generation? Suppose we survey the level of education in a sample of 113 women from 25 through 29 years old, and ask each subject also to indicate her mother's level of education. The results are below:

		Daughter graduated?	
		No	Yes
Mother graduated?	Yes	7	11
	No	76	18

a. Justify the use of a test of correlated proportions, state the null and alternative hypotheses, and do the test.

b. Make up a table showing the data in percentages by rows, including the marginal totals, and another table showing percentages by columns.

c. What percentage of the mothers, and what percentage of the daughters are college graduates?

d. Considering the mothers who were graduates, what percentage of their daughters were also graduates? Of the mothers who were *not* graduates, what percentage of their daughters *were*?

e. Considering the daughters who are graduates, what percentage of their mothers were also graduates? Of the daughters who are *not* graduates, what percentages of their mothers *were*?

Designing Experiments and Observations

13

Experimental design is the process of planning an experiment—choosing methods and procedures that can be expected to yield meaningful, interpretable results. Many of the principles of experimental design apply to the planning of observations as well. Like experiments, observations require careful planning and forethought if we are to make sense of the results.

An Overview

The preceding chapters have been largely concerned with the details of a great many statistical tests. Here and there, we have described some of the design problems that arise in applying specific tests, and it is now time to consider those issues more generally and systematically. Other statistical tests and procedures are yet to be presented, for example, multiple-group designs using three or more groups of subjects, where each group receives a different level of an independent variable. We will see that those procedures share many of the problems of the two-group designs that we have already described.

Some procedures—for example, multiple correlation and factor analysis—are presented only in broad outline, since the computational details are beyond the scope of this book. However, when you encounter those procedures in the psychological literature, the outlines presented here will help you understand the nature of the questions those techniques are designed to answer.

The present chapter will further develop our earlier discussions of design problems, and will then extend those ideas to statistical procedures that are to be presented later. Thus, this chapter stands as a bridge connecting the past and the future—treating design problems in applying tests that we have already described, and setting the stage for the knowledgeable application of procedures to be presented in the remaining chapters. We will first describe problems that are common to all kinds of designs, and then treat specific designs in detail.

Statistics and Experimental Design

In the present context, by **statistics** we mean the process of performing tests of significance. Although statistics and experimental design are closely related, those processes are not one and the same. For example, suppose an experimenter finds a statistically significant difference between a control group of children taught to read by a standard method and an experimental group taught by a new method. The results might be highly statistically significant, and yet utterly meaningless, if the experimenter had been so careless as to assign older pupils to one group and younger pupils to the other.

In such a case, the age variable—younger versus older—would be confounded with the independent variable—new versus standard teaching method. Thus, an adequate experimental design is essential if we are to place any credence in the results of an experiment, no matter how statistically significant those results may be.

Most of the designs in this chapter utilize statistical tests that we have already presented. Other designs utilize tests that we will present in later chapters. For the most part, the statistical tests yet to be presented represent extensions of techniques already described.

Choosing Research Problems and Strategies

A researcher's decision to work in a particular problem area is largely a matter of personal interest, preference, taste, and knowledge of the scientific literature. Some researchers, particularly those working in applied areas, are primarily motivated by the desire to solve problems directly bearing on human welfare, while others are primarily motivated by intellectual curiosity. No matter what your motivation, knowledge of the research literature is extremely useful in discovering problems that need to be solved, or that strike your fancy. Besides calling your attention to interesting areas, searching the scientific literature can also suggest promising research strategies. Before designing a study of your own, it is very useful to see how other researchers have approached similar problems.

Observation or Experimentation? We made several distinctions between the process of systematic observation and the experimental method as early as Chapter 1. In the first case, we observe values of variables as they are presented to us by nature, and in the second case, we manipulate the values of an independent variable in order to assess its effect on some dependent variable. At the risk of belaboring the point, note once again that we can draw far stronger inferences regarding causality from experiments than from observations. But in many cases, once a researcher has chosen to study a particular phenomenon, it is simply not possible to use the experimental method.

Many sociologists and social psychologists have noted the strong association between crime and socioeconomic deprivation, for example. On the basis of the correlations observed in a great many studies, deprivation cannot be ruled out as a possible cause—that is, we cannot **disconfirm** the hypothesis that deprivation produces crime and delinquency. But neither can we directly prove that hypothesis.

Could we bring the experimental method to bear on the question of whether deprivation causes crime and delinquency? The answer is yes, in principle, and clearly no in practice. We could never ethically carry out such an experiment where we might reasonably expect great harm to be done. Thus, we are forced to rely on observations in studying some of our most difficult and pressing problems.

Sampling Considerations

Whether a research problem lends itself to **experimentation** or to **observation,** sampling procedures must be given careful consideration. We undertake research in order to learn about the world in general — that is, we hope to generalize our research findings beyond the particular subjects studied in a particular experiment or set of observations. If we have somehow collected a sample that is not representative of the population, then the generality of our findings will be limited.

Random Samples.   Very early, we drew the distinction between a sample and a population, pointing out that everything we think we know about people in general — about the **population** of people — is based on experiments or observations involving **samples,** subsets of the population. The statistical tests that we have developed are based on the notion of a **random sample,** a sample drawn in such a way that every member of the population has the same probability of being chosen. Ideally, every sample should be a random sample from a well-defined population, but in practice, true random sampling is seldom achieved. If we were interested, for example, in studying some characteristic of young Americans 20 through 29 years old, we could in principle draw a random sample from that population. We would need a comprehensive list of such people, with their names and addresses, of course. Even if there were such a comprehensive directory in existence, you can well imagine the difficulty and expense of utilizing a random sample from such a population. Even a small sample would very likely consist of people scattered across the country. The researcher might need to travel far and wide in order to study the subjects, or perhaps all the subjects might have to be brought to a particular location. For most projects, the expense and difficulty of such procedures would be prohibitive.

Convenience Samples.   Most research projects make use of **convenience samples** consisting of subjects that are reasonably accessible to the researcher. A convenience sample might consist of an available class of school pupils, or college students. As you read the psychological research literature, you will see how much of our human research has utilized college and university students, and how much of our animal research has utilized the white rat. Indeed, some critics have defined experimental psychology as the study of the white rat and the college sophomore. Both kinds of subjects — sophomores and rats — are fairly accessible, but we may question whether either species is representative of its respective population — people in general, or rats in general. The white laboratory rat is very different from its wild gray cousin. The laboratory rat, for example, has poorer eyesight and is much less aggressive. College students may not differ in those particular ways from the general population of people, but they certainly differ in other ways. At the very least, students are people who have made the decision to go to school, and thus differ from nonstudents in terms of goals and perhaps values, if nothing else.

Thoughtful psychologists and other researchers have expressed many reservations about generalizing research findings beyond the kinds of subjects on which such findings are based. Nevertheless, virtually every research study uses a convenience sample of some sort. In an imperfect world, where the ideal of random sampling can seldom be attained, we simply do the best we can.

Sampling Bias. A **biased sample** differs significantly from the rest of a population in some way, perhaps in having a different mean or standard deviation, or perhaps differing in the direction or degree of skewness. A truncated distribution of bright students — a distribution having its lower end cut off — represents one kind of biased sample having a higher mean and a lower standard deviation than the general population of students. We have already seen in Chapter 10 the effect of a truncated distribution on the magnitude of the correlation coefficient. If we gave a test of academic aptitude to a group of very bright students, we would find a *lower* correlation between the test and their grade-point averages than we would find in a distribution of students having a greater range of abilities. Such a biased sample might lead to erroneous conclusions regarding the validity of a test, or the meaning of some other correlation, or the meaning of some other kind of result.

One of the most celebrated cases of sampling bias occurred during the presidential election campaign of 1936. Landon and Knox were running on the Republican ticket against Roosevelt and Garner on the Democratic ticket. The Literary Digest, a popular magazine of the day, conducted a public opinion poll, and predicted a Republican landslide. As a matter of convenience, the magazine sampled *several million* telephone subscribers and automobile owners. During the Great Depression, telephones and automobiles were much less widespread than today, and tended to be found in more affluent households. Thus, the people sampled were considerably more affluent than the rest of the population — and voted very differently. Since 1936, public opinion polls have become very much more sophisticated.

Biased samples can also affect the results of experiments as well as observations. Suppose, for example, that we wish to compare two methods of teaching reading, and suppose we have available a convenience sample of school pupils of higher than average ability. We manipulate the independent variable — the two levels of teaching method — by randomly assigning half the children to one method and half to the other method. (A later section treats the mechanics of this process in detail.) At the end of the experiment, suppose there is no significant difference in reading ability between the pupils taught by the two methods, as measured by a common reading test. Are we then justified in drawing the general conclusion that the methods do not differ? While the methods do not differ *for high-aptitude pupils*, we would not be justified in generalizing our results any further. Conceivably, the methods might differ if used with pupils of average or lower aptitude. There might be an *interaction* between the method variable and the aptitude variable — that is, the methods might differ at some levels of aptitude but not at other levels. If there were such an interaction, then we would need to take the ability variable into account in order to describe the effects of the method variable.

Sample Size and the Size of an Effect.   How large should a sample be? The answer is considerably less straightforward than the question: A sample should be large enough to detect the effect of an independent variable, where the effect is sufficiently large to be of interest. In an experiment involving two independent groups, for example, the **size of an effect** is the magnitude of the difference between the means of the control and experimental groups. Where an effect is very large, a small number of subjects will usually suffice — perhaps eight or ten subjects in each group — but where an effect is small, larger groups are required if the effect is to be detected. The magnitude of an effect is judged in relation to the estimated standard deviation of the population, and thus the size of an effect is not the same thing as the level of statistical significance. Indeed, a small effect may be highly statistically significant if the sample sizes are sufficiently large. A **small effect** is on the order of **.2S,** a **moderate effect** is about **.5S,** and a **large effect** is .8S or more, following Cohen's (1977) very readable discussion of the size of an effect.

The concept of the power of a test, developed in Chapter 8, extends to the present discussion. The power of a test is the probability of rejecting the null hypothesis, given that H_0 is false. Thus, power is the probability of detecting a difference between the means of the control and experimental groups when such a difference in fact exists. For any given size of effect, we can find the sample size required to achieve a desired level of power (Cohen, 1977). Since the power of a test increases with the sample size, smaller effects can be detected in larger samples. Then why not use a very large sample in every experiment? The answer here is straightforward: Some effects are too small to be worth the effort of detecting. For example, suppose a new teaching method produces a difference of one point between the performance of an experimental group and a control group on a test where the standard deviation is 20. Such a trivial effect might easily go undetected in a modest-sized experiment, and might not be worth the time and effort of detecting at all.

Perhaps you feel that this discussion of sample size and size of effect may be all well and good, but how do you know the size of an effect before you have done an experiment, and how do you go about determining the sample size before you know the size of the effect you are looking for? Cohen provides tables giving the sample sizes necessary to detect an effect of a given magnitude with a given probability, that is, with a particular level of power. For example, in an experiment using two independent groups, a large effect (.8S) can be detected with a probability of .50 if there are 13 subjects in each group, but a medium effect (.5S) requires 32 subjects per group in order to be detected with that probability. An experiment involving a modest number of subjects, 15 or 20 per group, will often provide a reasonably good estimate of the population standard deviation. Dividing that estimate into the observed difference between means will provide an estimate of the magnitude of effect. After carrying out such an experiment, if the null hypothesis cannot be rejected, you can then find the number of additional subjects required by consulting Cohen's tables. You can also decide whether the estimated size of the effect justifies the additional time and effort of enlarging your experiment.

The Number of Levels of an Independent Variable

So far, all of the experiments we have considered have involved a single **independent variable** having two **levels,** often the presence or absence of an experimental treatment. In a repeated-measures design, a single group is tested under both levels of the independent variable, while in an independent-groups or matched-pairs design, a different group of subjects is assigned to each level. Those designs can be extended to experiments and observations where the independent variable has several levels. For example, if there were several groups of subjects in a drug experiment, one group receiving a placebo and each of the others receiving a different amount of the drug, then it would be possible to learn something about the **dose-response relationship,** the effects of different levels of the drug. Such an experiment having a single independent variable is often called a **single-factor experiment.**

In the next chapter, we will develop the **analysis of variance,** a method of carrying out statistical tests where an independent variable has more than two levels. The analysis of variance represents an extension of the *t* test for two independent groups, or two correlated measures, to a situation having several independent groups, or several correlated measures.

The Number of Independent Variables

It is very useful in many situations to manipulate more than one independent variable in an experiment. For example, it is possible to study the effects of different levels of motivation on the performance of tasks of different levels of difficulty. Such an experiment would utilize two independent variables, a motivation variable and a task-difficulty variable, each having perhaps three levels. Nine independent groups of subjects might be used, each group under one of the possible combinations of levels of the two independent variables. Not only would such an experiment yield information about each independent variable considered separately, but also about the interaction between those independent variables — that is, information about any differences between the effects of one independent variable at different levels of the other.

An experiment or set of observations having more than one independent variable is a **factorial design,** and each independent variable is a **factor.** A factorial design may have several factors, each having several levels, although it is relatively uncommon for such a design to have more than three independent variables. A later section will describe factorial designs in more detail, and will illustrate some interactions between independent variables.

Reliability and Validity of an Experiment

We can describe **experimental design** as the art of arranging things so as to promote the **validity** of an experiment, the extent to which the independent variable can be said to produce an effect on the dependent variable. In Chapter 10, validity was defined as the extent to which a test measures what it is intended to measure. Thus, the present definition is fairly closely analogous to the earlier one.

Internal and External Validity. An experiment is designed to measure the effect of some specific independent variable on a dependent variable. If, instead, the results might be attributable to the effect of some uncontrolled variable that turns out to be confounded with the independent variable, then the experiment lacks **internal validity.** In that case, the results are invalid even for the specific subjects in the experiment. An experiment is also intended to yield results that can be generalized, extended to a population. The **external validity** of an experiment is the extent to which the results can be externalized — generalized — beyond the particular subjects in the experiment. Conceivably, an experiment can be internally valid and externally invalid, but the converse is not true. A biased sample is the most common threat to the external validity of an experiment.

As we describe specific research designs, we will indicate how particular strategies affect the internal and external validity of experiments and observations. Campbell and Stanley (1966) and Cook and Campbell (1979) provide more extended treatments of those topics, and highly readable discussions of the relationships between experiments and observations.

Reliability and Significance. The **reliability** of an experiment is equivalent to its statistical significance. Indeed, some researchers prefer to speak of **statistical reliability** rather than statistical significance. Chapter 10 defines reliability as the extent to which a test yields comparable measures when given a second time to the same subjects. When we say the results of an experiment are reliable — statistically significant — we mean that we would expect comparable results if the experiment were performed again and again under the same conditions — that is, using the same procedures and comparable subjects.

It is possible for an experiment — like a test — to be reliable but not valid. If the independent variable is confounded with some other variable, the results nevertheless may be highly significant — reliable — in the sense that we might observe quite consistent results if we performed the experiment again. We would attribute those reliable results to our manipulation of the independent variable, when in fact the results might be due entirely to the confounded extraneous variable and not at all to our manipulation. On the other hand, if an experiment is unreliable, then there can be no consistent effect of *any* variable.

Correlational Studies

Correlational methods are perhaps most closely identified with the development of psychological tests of intelligence, aptitude, and achievement. But those methods are also widely used in many other kinds of research. For example, a **time series** applies the ideas of correlation and regression to the study of a variable changing across time, often before and after an environmental change of some sort.

The correlational methods presented so far in this text have been limited to **bivariate correlation,** the relationship between two variables. Those ideas are extended to the study of relationships between several variables in *multiple correlation, partial correlation,* and *factor analysis.* While the computational details of those techniques cannot be presented here, you may find our brief discussions helpful when you encounter some of those ideas in the psychological literature.

Multiple and Partial Correlation

To some extent, a test of academic aptitude given in high school will predict freshman grade-point average in college, but that prediction can be improved by also taking high-school grades into account. A **multiple correlation** is the relationship between a single dependent variable and two or more predictor variables. The multiple correlation between college GPA and the predictor variables of test performance and high-school grades will ordinarily be higher than the correlation between college GPA and either predictor taken separately. **Multiple regression** is the process of expressing a dependent variable, such as GPA, as a function of two or more predictor variables in a single equation. Such an equation, having two or more predictor variables, is a **multiple regression equation.**

A **partial correlation** between two variables is a correlation that eliminates the effect of one or more other variables. For example, it can be argued that the correlation between education and income might be due entirely to a third variable, *ability.* If people of higher ability tend to get more education, and also tend to make more money, then education and income will be correlated — even though it is conceivable that education per se might have no direct effect on income. Guilford and Fruchter (1978) and Cohen and Cohen (1983) offer more extensive treatments of multiple and partial correlation than we can present here.

Time Series

A **time series** is a set of measurements of a particular variable made over a period of time. The techniques of correlation and regression can be adapted to the problem of determining the extent to which a variable changes across time. For example, the mean value of the Consumer Price Index year by year since 1967 is a time series. For many years — unfortunately — there has been a strong upward trend in the Consumer Price Index. Thus, that index has been highly correlated with the time variable. The mental age of a child, or of a group of children, measured by an intelligence test repeated at different chronological ages represents another time series. Many kinds of time series are of great interest in the field of developmental psychology.

Interrupted Time Series.   A series of observations of some variable across a period of time that brackets an important event of some kind is an **interrupted time series.** For example, Figure 13-1 shows the number of traffic fatalities in the United States per 100 million vehicle miles over a period of several years. In 1973, an Arab embargo on oil shipments to the United States substantially reduced our oil imports. To conserve oil, highway speed limits were reduced to 55 mph nationwide. Thus, imposing the new speed limit was an event that interrupted the time series shown in Figure 13-1. Did the lower speed limit save lives as well as gasoline?

Figure 13-1 shows a marked decline of 14.6% in the rate of fatalities from 1973 to 1974. But fatalities had already been declining steadily since 1966, so the question arises of whether the decline from 1973 – 74 might have occurred

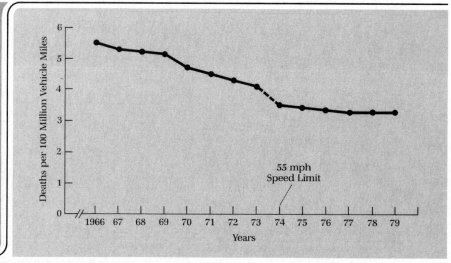

FIGURE 13-1. An interrupted time series. Rate of traffic deaths by years before and after introduction of 55 mph speed limit (data from *Statistical Abstract of the United States*).

in the absence of any change in the speed limit. We cannot fully develop the analysis of time series in the present context—although the ideas of correlation and regression presented in Chapter 10 represent the building blocks of such an analysis. Cook and Campbell (1979) and Campbell and Stanley (1966) offer good discussions of interrupted time series.

Factor Analysis

Besides being used to predict achievement, psychological tests have been used extensively as research tools in long-standing attempts to understand the nature of human abilities and intelligence. Shortly after the turn of the century, British psychologist Charles Spearman developed the fundamental ideas of factor analysis. Since many tests of different mental abilities tend to be moderately correlated—verbal skills and mathematical skills, for example—Spearman suggested that there was a single general intelligence factor, which has come to be called **Spearman's g,** and a number of specific factors underlying each mental ability. **Factor analysis** is a statistical procedure that attempts to account for the correlations observed in a set of tests or other measures. The techniques of factor analysis have played a great role in the development of theories of intelligence and abilities, as in Guilford's (1967) structure-of-intellect model, or Thurstone's (1938) earlier work on primary mental abilities. Guilford (1967) provides an excellent introduction to the area.

Single-Group Designs

In this section, we will describe several designs utilizing a single group of subjects. In some situations, the "group" is a single subject, as in a *case study,* or in the $N = 1$ experimental design.

Case Studies

A **case study** consists of the intensive observation of a single individual or of a group of subjects in a particular setting. Observing the responses of an individual in psychotherapy represents one kind of case study. The study of Eve, a case of multiple personality, is a vivid example (Thigpen & Cleckley, 1954). Other case studies may involve the responses of groups of subjects to treatments or services of various kinds, such as drug treatment programs, or summer job programs. Case studies of business management problems, for example, have been extensively used in teaching and research in schools of business administration. All of these varieties of case studies have many features in common—often involving very detailed study over protracted lengths of time.

Common Weaknesses.   Although a case study may generate great quantities of *descriptive* statistics — means, percentages, number of individuals in various categories, and the like — the results are very difficult to interpret, since there is no control group. Would the patient have improved anyway, without the psychotherapist's clinical skills? Would the major corporation's profits have increased anyway, without its reorganization of management? The lack of a control group makes these questions extremely difficult to answer with any degree of confidence. In some situations, a case study of a single individual can be converted into a true experiment using the $N = 1$ design to be described shortly. In other instances, a case study involving a group of subjects can be converted into a true experiment by incorporating a control group into the study, or by manipulating an independent variable in a repeated-measures design. Wherever possible, a contemplated case study should be turned into an experiment.

Before-After Design

In many instances, the **before-after design** is very similar to a case study involving a group of subjects. However, the term is usually applied to situations where subjects are measured before and after some well-defined experimental treatment is administered, as in the experiment on attitude change in the last chapter. Since the same subjects are measured twice in this design, the results must be analyzed by a repeated-measures test, as in Chapter 12. The appropriate test depends on the nature of the measurement scale — nominal, ordinal, interval, or ratio.

Weaknesses.   Since the same subjects are measured twice, it is conceivable that any before-after difference might be due to the repeated testing, and not at all to the experimental treatment. In this design, the possible effects of repeated testing are confounded with the possible effects of the experimental treatment. A two-group design — described in a later section — where only one group receives the experimental treatment, would overcome this threat to internal validity.

The before-after design always confounds the passage of time with the possible effects of the treatment. Where the subjects are tested in a single session immediately before and immediately after an experimental treatment, little time passes, and there is little opportunity for extraneous variables to influence performance. But where the experimental treatment may consist of administering a college education, or a long prison sentence, there are ample opportunities for extraneous variables to affect the outcome of a before-after design. Such a design, though economical in terms of its use of subjects, should be used very judiciously.

The $N = 1$ Design

In the $N = 1$ **experimental design,** a single subject is studied intensively under a number of conditions *manipulated by the experimenter.* The essential difference between a case study and the $N = 1$ experiment is the manipulation of an independent variable in the experiment. For example, a pigeon in a Skinner box is reinforced for pecking a key. When the key-pecking behavior is well established, a small light in the box is turned on from time to time, and key pecking is then reinforced only in the presence of the light. Rather quickly, the pigeon comes to peck the key overwhelmingly in the presence of the light. In operant conditioning terms, we would say that the pigeon's behavior has been brought under *stimulus control* (Holland & Skinner, 1961). The presence of the light has become a *positive discriminative stimulus* and its absence a *negative discriminative stimulus.* Now, is this a true experiment? Clearly it is, since there is an independent variable having two levels — reinforcement or no reinforcement, signalled by the presence or absence of a light — and that variable surely influences the pigeon's behavior. The experimenter manipulates the independent variable at will, turning the light on and off, signalling the availability of reinforcement, and the dependent variable changes with those manipulations.

The intensive experimental study of single organisms under very carefully controlled laboratory conditions is a strong tradition among psychologists involved in operant conditioning. However, the earliest systematic use of the $N = 1$ design appears to be the extensive studies of human learning by Ebbinghaus (1885) using himself as subject. The celebrated study of little Albert (Watson & Rayner, 1920) is another example of an experiment using a single subject. More recently, the $N = 1$ design has been used in studies of *behavior modification,* where operant techniques are brought to bear on a single subject's behavioral problems.

Counterbalancing.   Suppose we want to compare auditory and visual reaction times in a single subject. Our experiment involves repeated measures, and thus we have to consider the order of presentation of the auditory and visual stimuli. Since we saw in the last chapter that there is a practice effect in reaction times, it would not do to present a number of visual trials first and then a number of auditory trials, or vice versa. If we performed the experiment in that way, we might mistake a practice effect for a real auditory-visual difference, when in fact there might be no such real difference, or we might fail to detect a true difference because of a practice effect.

Suppose we give the subject four auditory and four visual trials. (A total of eight trials is really too small a number for an experiment of this sort. However, the principles that we are about to develop will apply to larger experiments as well.) We can deal with the question of order by supposing for the present that there is no difference between auditory and visual reaction time. (Auditory reaction times are really faster, but for our present discussion, we will assume there is no difference between auditory and visual reaction times.) Further, we suppose that there is equal and symmetrical transfer of practice effects within and between auditory and visual trials — that is, auditory or visual practice equally affects performance on subsequent trials, whether auditory or visual. In addition, we assume that there is no random variability in the measurements: On each trial, the observed performance is

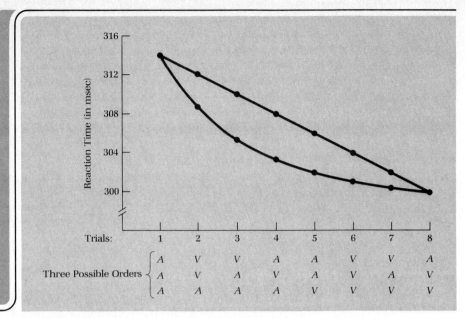

FIGURE 13-2. Linear and curvilinear practice effects in auditory and visual reaction times, assuming no auditory visual difference, and assuming symmetrical transfer of practice. Three possible orders of auditory and visual trials are shown. See also Table 13-1.

the sum of the true reaction time and some additional amount of time due to the need to practice. Under the above assumptions, Figure 13-2 shows the results of an experiment consisting of eight trials. Two curves are shown in that figure, one representing a linear practice effect, and the other a curvilinear practice effect. The linear practice effect is based on the assumption that each trial results in a decline of 2 milliseconds in reaction time, while the curvilinear effect is based on an exponential decline in reaction time as a function of practice. The auditory and visual stimuli are arranged in three possible orders under the trials in Figure 13-2. Table 13-1 shows the individual auditory and visual reaction times, and their means, for the three orders in Figure 13-2, under the assumptions of the illustrated linear and curvilinear practice effects. Since we stipulated that there was no difference between auditory and visual reaction times, there should be no difference between the observed auditory and visual means. But Table 13-1 shows that only the AVVA order yields the true difference of zero between those observed means, and that difference occurs only under the conditions of a linear practice effect. Thus, there seems to be a kind of special magic in the AVVA order which distributes a linear practice effect fairly and evenly across the auditory and visual trials. Interchanging the As and Vs produces another equally magical order, VAAV.

Presenting trials in AVVA or VAAV order is called **counterbalancing,** and those sequences of trials are called **counterbalanced orders.** We can

TABLE 13-1.   Effects of Different Orders on Auditory (A) and Visual (V) Reaction Times in Msec for Linear and Curvilinear Practice Effects Shown in Figure 13-2. True Difference Between Means is Assumed to be Zero, Observed Difference is $\overline{D}$.

	Practice Effect											
	Linear						Curvilinear					
Order:	AVVA		AVAV		AAAAVVVV		AVVA		AVAV		AAAAVVVV	
Stimulus:	A	V	A	V	A	V	A	V	A	V	A	V
	314	312	314	312	314	306	314	309	314	309	314	302
Trials	308	310	310	308	312	304	303	305	305	303	309	301
	306	304	306	304	310	302	302	301	302	301	305	301
	300	302	302	300	308	300	300	301	301	300	303	300
Mean	307	307	308	306	311	303	305	304	306	303	308	301
$\overline{D}$	0		2		8		1		3		7	

consider our counterbalanced order of eight trials as consisting of four blocks of two trials each, where each block has an auditory trial and a visual trial. In half the blocks, the trials are in AV order, and in VA in the other half of the blocks. Thus, in each AV block the visual trial benefits from the practice effect of the prior auditory trial, and in each VA block the auditory trial benefits from the prior visual practice. Since there are equal numbers of AV and VA blocks in our counterbalanced order, counterbalancing distributes the linear practice effect perfectly evenly across conditions. If counterbalancing is to be completely effective, the total number of trials must be a multiple of four, where there are two conditions — such as auditory and visual trials — to be arranged in order.

Notice that the AVAV order yields a higher mean auditory reaction time under the linear practice effect in Table 13-1. In each block of two trials in that order, the visual trial comes second, and thus the visual trial always benefits from the prior auditory practice. Presenting the trials in VAVA order would yield a higher mean visual reaction time. Thus, neither of those orders would yield the true difference of zero between auditory and visual means. Presenting all four auditory trials first, in AAAAVVVV order, would produce an even greater difference between means, as Table 13-1 shows.

So far, we have considered the effects of different orders only under the assumption of a linear practice effect. But in most situations, practice effects — that is to say, *learning curves* — are not straight lines, but curvilinear. Thus, the curvilinear practice effect shown in Figure 13-2 is more representative of most situations than is the linear practice effect. How well does our magic AVVA order fare under the assumption of a curvilinear practice effect? Under that assumption, Table 13-1 shows that the counterbalanced order yields the smallest difference between means — but that difference is not equal to zero, the true differences between means that we have assumed. Thus, counterbalancing does not distribute a curvilinear practice effect perfectly evenly across conditions in a single subject, although a counterbalanced order does minimize the observed difference between means.

Notice that presenting the trials in AVVA order produces a larger auditory mean under the assumption of a curvilinear practice effect. If the trials were presented in VAAV order, then the visual mean would be greater. Those two orders produce auditory-visual differences of the same magnitude, but opposite in sign. Thus, if we ran two subjects in our experiment, one in AVVA and the other in VAAV order, then the difference between auditory and visual means for that experiment would equal the true value of zero. The procedure we have just described is a variety of **between-subjects counter-balancing.** A later section provides further discussion of counterbalancing within and between subjects.

Up to this point, our discussion of counterbalancing has been based on the assumption of no true difference between auditory and visual reaction times. But what if there were a difference? Indeed, in most situations, auditory reaction times are faster. Would our counterbalancing procedures allow us to detect a true auditory-visual difference? Suppose the true visual reaction time for a well-practiced subject is 300 msec, and the true auditory reaction time is 200 msec, any observed times in excess of those values being due to the need to practice. If you subtract 100 msec from each auditory trial in Table 13-1, you will find that the difference between auditory and visual means is exactly 100 msec only for the AVVA order under the linear practice effect. Under all other combinations of orders and practice effects, the mean auditory-visual difference is greater than the true difference of 100 msec. Thus, when there is a difference between auditory and visual reaction times, the counterbalanced order yields the true value of that difference under a linear practice effect. Under a curvilinear practice effect, counterbalancing yields an auditory-visual difference that is closest to the true value of that difference.

Notice that in no case in Table 13-1 does an observed auditory or visual mean equal the true value of 300 msec that we assumed earlier. Thus, counterbalancing appears to yield at best the true value of a *difference* between means, not the true values of the means themselves. In principle, we could find the "true" value of a reaction time, or any other variable showing a practice effect, by giving a sufficiently large number of trials to allow performance to reach its best level and to stabilize at that level. We would then discard the series of trials showing a systematic improvement with time—the earliest several trials—and also discard any later series showing a systematic deterioration, retaining for analysis only those trials showing an essentially stable performance across time. In many experiments, the earliest trials are considered practice trials, and are not included in the data analysis. That procedure will often yield better estimates of the true value of a variable, and will also tend to reduce the variability of a set of measurements.

After this discussion of counterbalancing, you may wish to look back at the matched-pairs experiment described in the last chapter. By now, you may be able to see more clearly how it is that arranging subjects in descending order on a matching variable and then assigning them to the control and experimental groups in *ECCE* or *CEEC* order will result in well matched groups. Perhaps a review of that brief discussion of counterbalancing may enhance your understanding of the present discussion.

Strengths and Weaknesses of the $N = 1$ Design. The external validity of this design is certainly open to question — that is, the extent to which findings can be generalized from a single subject to a population. The internal validity may be threatened by the fact that repeated measures must be used if we are to present two levels of an independent variable. As we have noted earlier, there may be serious carry-over effects in using repeated measures in some situations. Like other repeated-measures designs, the $N = 1$ design should be used with care.

The economy of this design, in terms of the number of subjects used, is a strong point in its favor. Indeed, many a research project has started life as an $N = 1$ design, often with the experimenter or a colleague as the subject. Good **pilot work,** preliminary experiments or observations undertaken before launching a full-scale study, can often be done using this design.

Repeated Measures on a Group

This design has many of the features and problems of the $N = 1$ design. We might, for example, carry out an auditory-visual reaction time experiment in a group of several subjects, giving each subject visual and auditory trials. We could counterbalance the order of presentation within subjects and between subjects as well, giving half the subjects their trials in AVVA order, and the other half in VAAV order. As we pointed out earlier, counterbalancing between subjects will distribute a curvilinear practice effect evenly across the two levels of the independent variable, as long as the transfer of practice is symmetrical. In this respect, making repeated measures in a group of subjects offers a decided advantage over the $N = 1$ design, where between-subjects counterbalancing is not possible.

In some repeated-measures experiments, because of the amount of time required, or because of the difficulty of administering the experimental conditions, each subject may be measured only twice, once under each level of the independent variable. For example, in a drug experiment, each subject might be tested under the drug on one day and under a placebo on a different day. Half the subjects would receive the drug first and half the placebo first, and thus the order of treatments would be counterbalanced between subjects in DP and PD order. Since there can be no counterbalancing *within* subjects in this situation, the drug-placebo difference within any particular subject will be confounded with any possible practice effect or other kind of carry-over effect. But across all the subjects, the difference between the means under the drug and placebo treatments will be free of any symmetrical practice effect, due to the between-subjects counterbalancing.

In comparison with the two-group designs to be described shortly, the repeated-measures design is more economical in terms of number of subjects. However, practice effects and other carry-over effects must be considered carefully. In some cases, this design simply cannot be used. For example, if we wanted to measure the length of time required to learn a list of words under an experimental and a control condition, it would not be feasible to make repeated measures on the same subjects using the same words.

Two-Group Designs

Research designs using two groups of subjects represent one of the foundations — if not the cornerstone — of research in the field of psychology. Two-group designs are extensively used in systematic observations comparing natural groups, as well as in experiments where an independent variable is manipulated.

Natural and Manipulated Independent Variables

In some cases, an **experimental group** receives a treatment of some kind, while a **control group** receives no treatment. The independent variable in such an experiment has two levels, presence and absence of the experimental treatment. In other cases, each group receives a different nonzero amount of some experimental treatment. Each of those situations represents a true experiment having a **manipulated independent variable,** where the experimenter assigns a value of that variable to each subject. In a drug experiment, for example, some subjects are assigned to a drug condition and others to a **placebo,** or **sham treatment** condition at the will of the experimenter. Administering a placebo, an essentially inactive substance, equalizes the handling of the control and experimental groups, in that each receives a treatment of some kind.

Suppose we were interested in comparing men and women on a personality measure of some sort. In a systematic observation involving the comparison of two natural groups, each subject brings his or her own value of the independent variable to the study — in this case, the male or female gender. Here, we are dealing with a **natural independent variable** which is observed but not manipulated by the researcher. If we found a difference between men and women on some dependent variable, we would then say that that measure varies as a function of sex. In that sense, sex would be an independent variable — though a natural one, observed but not manipulated. Some examples of other natural independent variables are age, height, weight, socioeconomic status, racial or ethnic group membership, level of anxiety, and category of mental disorder.

Observing a significant difference between two natural groups on some dependent variable is equivalent to observing a correlation between that measure and a natural independent variable. Since a natural independent variable has not been manipulated, we are in no position to conclude that such a variable has caused the difference that we observe in the dependent variable. We will return to this issue of correlation and causality after we have dealt with two-group designs in more detail.

 Statistical Tests. Whether we are dealing with a true experiment involving a manipulated independent variable, or with an observation of two groups involving a natural independent variable, we would use the same procedure to test the significance of our results. Depending on the kind of measurement scale, one or another of the tests described in Chapter 9 would be appropriate for testing independent groups, or one of the tests in Chapter 12 would be appropriate for a matched-pairs design.

True Experiments: Manipulated Independent Variables

One of the principal problems in a true experiment is to eliminate or control extraneous variables in order to maintain the internal validity of the experiment. Some extraneous variables, such as noise, can be eliminated or minimized. Other extraneous variables — such as age, sex, and ability — cannot be eliminated but can be controlled by distributing their effects evenly across the levels of the independent variable. It may strike you that we have suddenly and arbitrarily designated age, sex, and ability as extraneous variables, while in other contexts those characteristics might represent natural independent variables of primary interest. But in a two-group experiment comparing two methods of teaching a foreign language, for example, teaching method is the independent variable, performance is the dependent variable, and any other variable is an extraneous variable — including age, sex, and ability. Two-group experiments may utilize independent groups or matched pairs of subjects. Each design has strengths and weaknesses that we will describe in the following sections.

Independent Groups.   This design represents perhaps the most straightforward procedure for conducting a true experiment. Different subjects are used in each of the two groups, and thus we avoid the problems of order effects that must be considered in a repeated-measures design, and the difficulties of finding a suitable matching variable in a matched-pairs design. Indeed, the independent-groups design appears so simple that it looks as though little could go wrong. But there are pitfalls.

Assignment biases, for example, can result in confounding extraneous variables with the independent variable. Suppose an experimenter wishes to assess the effects of social deprivation on the behavior of rats. A litter of 12 young rats are housed together in a large cage. Half the rats are to be assigned to a control group, to be reared together, and half to an experimental group, to be reared in individual cages, isolated from other rats. Suppose the experimenter opens the large cage, picks up the first six rats he can get his hands on, assigns those animals to the control group, and assigns the remaining six rats to the experimental group. At the end of the experiment, the experimental rats — reared in isolation — are shy, withdrawn, and fearful in the test situation, while the control rats — reared together — are more outgoing, bold, and self-possessed. Unfortunately, the way the animals were assigned to the control and experimental groups could account for the results of the experiment as well as the independent variable — the way the animals were reared.

The rats most likely to be picked up first are the rats nearest the cage door — the bolder, more outgoing animals — while the shy and fearful rats cowering in a far corner are more likely to be picked up last. Thus, the order of selection allows an extraneous variable to be confounded with the independent variable. Randomly assigning rats to the control and experimental groups, using procedures that we will describe, will avoid that kind of confounding.

Assignment biases can also occur in human experiments. Suppose that 16 subjects are to be run in a control group and 16 in an experimental group. If each subject must be measured individually, in a session lasting perhaps an hour, then such an experiment might take place over an extended length of time, over a period of weeks or months. Suppose the experimenter places the first 16 subjects to sign up in the control group and the last 16 in the experimental group, or vice versa. If the experiment were conducted in a college setting, where students are typically allowed to sign up for experiments at times largely of their own choosing, might there be differences between the subjects signing up earlier and later in the semester? While we might hesitate to compare the students signing up late with the reluctant rats cowering in the back of their cage, the possible differences between people participating early and late might be crucial — for example, if an experiment concerned some aspect of procrastination. Assigning subjects to the control and experimental groups in CEEC or ECCE order — randomly choosing one of those orders, perhaps by tossing a coin — would avoid the assignment bias we have described.

Balancing and Randomizing. By **balancing** we mean assigning subjects to groups in such a way that each group contains the same number of subjects having a particular level of a particular extraneous variable. For example, if we had a sample of 8 men and 8 women, we could balance the control and experimental groups with respect to sex by assigning half the men and half the women to each group. At the same time, we might also balance an ability variable by assigning half of the high-ability men to the control group and the other half to the experimental group, similarly dividing the low-ability men between the two groups, and assigning the women subjects in the same way.

Table 13-2 (top) shows how we might accomplish the balancing described above. The subjects are listed in four subgroups by sex and ability. First, we will deal with the subgroup of high-ability females. Using a table of random numbers, Table H, a two-digit random number is selected for each of the first three women in that subgroup. (We will explain the use of Table H shortly.) Subjects having odd and even random numbers are respectively assigned to the control and experimental groups. It is unnecessary to select a random number for the fourth subject, since two of the first three have been assigned to the control group, and thus the last subject must be assigned to the experimental group. In the second subgroup — the low-ability females — since the first two random numbers were odd, those two subjects were

TABLE 13-2. Balancing Sex and Aptitude (top), and Completely Randomizing (bottom). Subjects with Odd and Even Random Numbers are Respectively Assigned to Control (C) and Experimental (E) Groups.

Balancing Sex and Aptitude																
Subject number	1	2	3	4	5	6	7	8	9	10	11	12	13	14	15	16
Sex	F	F	F	F	F	F	F	F	M	M	M	M	M	M	M	M
Aptitude	H	H	H	H	L	L	L	L	H	H	H	H	L	L	L	L
Random number	42	19	33		25	63			19	00	88		85	26	75	
Group	E	C	C	E	C	C	E	E	C	E	E	C	C	E	C	E

Completely Randomized Assignment																
Subject number	1	2	3	4	5	6	7	8	9	10	11	12	13	14	15	16
Sex	M	M	M	M	M	M	M	M	M	M	M	M	M	M	M	M
Random number	06	58	88	40	97	09	83	78	38	93	49	64	89	24		
Group	E	E	E	E	C	C	C	E	E	C	C	E	C	E	C	C

assigned to the control group and the others to the experimental group — thus it was unnecessary to select a random number for either of the last two subjects.

To use a table of random numbers, you can enter the table anywhere at all, and you can read the numbers in any direction — up, down, left, right, or along any diagonal. Any sequence of random numbers read from such a table is as random as any other sequence. Indeed, you should enter Table H at a different point each time you use the table for **randomizing** a group of subjects, or for any other purpose, and you should vary the direction of reading the table. If you have a calculator with a random number routine, you will find it so convenient that you can dispense with Table H.

It may have occurred to you that there is a very simple way of randomly assigning subjects to two groups: Why not toss a coin for each subject, letting Heads assign the subject to one group and Tails to the other? Actually, there is nothing much wrong with coin tossing, if reasonable care is taken. However, we will shortly need to consider procedures for randomly assigning subjects to more than two groups, and methods of arranging several experimental conditions in several random sequences. A table of random numbers, or a random-number routine on a calculator, is easy to use in such situations, but coin tossing would be very cumbersome.

It might also occur to you to think up your own sequence of random numbers, thereby saving the time and effort of consulting Table H. Don't do it. People are very poor at generating random numbers. Cultivate the habit of using a table of random numbers, or a calculator, any time you need to randomize anything.

It is not necessary to have equal numbers of men and women, or boys and girls, in an experiment, although it is desirable for most purposes. An experiment that samples the sexes — or other naturally occurring categories of subjects — in the approximate proportions in which they occur in the population may provide results of greater generality. When there are unequal numbers of the sexes available as subjects, the sex variable can still be balanced by assigning the same number of males to each group, and similarly assigning the females. If there is an odd number of one sex, then subjects of that gender should be distributed as evenly as possible across the two groups.

The procedure of balancing sex and ability — and controlling other extraneous variables by randomizing — guarantees that we will have equal numbers of men and women, and high- and low-ability subjects, in the control and experimental groups. That procedure also guards against any kind of systematic bias in assigning subjects. Balancing any large number of extraneous variables would become very cumbersome, as you can see. In most experiments, the usual practice is to balance only one or two extraneous variables thought to be especially important. Ordinarily, the control of other extraneous variables is left to the process of randomizing.

In some situations, it may be known that the sex variable is of no consequence, and can thus be ignored as an extraneous variable. Other experiments may use only one kind of subject — all males, for example. In those cases, the control and experimental groups are completely randomized, as in the bottom portion of Table 13-2, with the restriction that we assign equal numbers of subjects to the two groups. Using a sequence of random numbers from Table H, subjects having odd and even random numbers are assigned respectively to the control and experimental groups, as in our earlier example. No random numbers were selected for subjects 15 and 16, since eight of the first 14 subjects were already assigned to the experimental group.

Strengths and weaknesses of the independent-groups experiment will be discussed after we have dealt with the matched-pairs design. We will then compare and contrast the problems in using those two designs.

Matched-Pairs Design. This experimental design offers many of the advantages of the repeated-measures design, while at the same time avoiding the problem of any carry-over effects. In many situations, **the matched-pairs design** may provide a more powerful, sensitive experiment than the independent-groups design. Where subjects can be paired on a matching variable that is expected to correlate with the dependent variable, a smaller number of subjects may yield as high a level of power as a larger number in an independent-groups design.

In an experiment designed to assess two methods of teaching reading, we might expect the more able pupils to learn better under either method. If we had some measure of ability on each pupil, perhaps an intelligence test, we might use that measure as a matching variable. We might form a number of perfectly matched pairs, where each pupil within a pair would have the same score on the matching variable, and then we might randomly assign one member of each pair to Method 1 and the other to Method 2. But if we insisted on perfect matching within pairs, then we would probably have to discard many potential subjects, since some pupils could not be perfectly matched. We could utilize more of the available subjects if we relaxed our matching criterion to allow mismatches of some specified magnitude. We could use all of the available pupils if we arranged them in order on the matching variable and then assigned them to methods in 1221 or 2112 order, thus counterbalancing the effect of the systematic change in ability from the most to the least able pupil.

An analogous procedure was described in detail in the last chapter. Whatever the matching procedure, we would expose each group to only one of the teaching methods. We would then measure each pupil's reading performance, find a difference score for each matched pair, and test the significance of the mean difference using the correlated-measures t test. Where an experiment can be conducted in two stages—as in the retroactive inhibition experiment in the last chapter—the matching procedure becomes very simple. That procedure is described in detail in Chapter 12.

Strengths and Weaknesses of True Experiments. All true experiments, whether involving independent groups, matched pairs, or repeated measures, share some strengths and weaknesses. The greatest strength of a true experiment lies in the causal inferences that we can draw from the results. For example, a statistically significant difference between two groups in an experiment—or between two repeated measures—allows us to reject the null hypothesis, and thus conclude that our manipulation of the independent variable *caused* the observed difference in the dependent variable. On the other hand, if we observe no significant difference between groups, we should be wary of concluding that the independent variable has no effect whatever. In that case, the best that we can say is that under the conditions of the experiment, the effect of the independent variable—if any—is too small to detect. The independent variable might in fact have produced a small effect, which we might detect in a more powerful experiment, having a larger number of subjects, for example.

In our early discussions of hypothesis testing, we were careful to speak of *rejecting* or *not rejecting* the null hypothesis, never speaking of *accepting* H_0. The distinction between *not rejecting* and *accepting* may strike you as utterly punctilious, but the concept of power provides a basis for that distinction. Under some conditions, we may be able to conclude that any possible effect of the independent variable is so small as to be trivial—not worthy of our notice. But we can never conclude that the effect of the independent variable is *exactly* zero, and thus we can never accept, confirm, or prove H_0—we can only reject or not reject that hypothesis. Cohen (1977, p. 16) provides an excellent brief discussion of "proving" the null hypothesis.

Perhaps the greatest shortcoming of the true experiment is its limited range of application. As we have noted earlier, there are many important problems that cannot be studied experimentally. However, there is a great deal to be learned through nonexperimental methods, although we are very limited in the causal inferences that we can draw.

Quasi-Experiments

In a **quasi-experiment**—a *seeming* experiment—each level of the independent variable is administered to a different **intact group,** a group of subjects already in existence before the experiment. Thus, a quasi-experiment is similar in some respects to a true experiment, the essential difference being the lack of control over the assignment of subjects to groups in the quasi-experiment. The experimenter can randomly assign the levels of the independent variable to the intact groups, but those groups were made up before the experimenter appeared on the scene, a fact that influences the conclusions to be drawn from a quasi-experiment.

In a school setting, for example, it might be very convenient to use existing third-grade classes to study the effectiveness of two different teaching methods. Such a quasi-experiment could be carried out with a minimum of physical disruption, since each class could be instructed by a different method. A true experiment might involve randomly dividing each class into control and experimental subjects, and periodically moving some of the pupils to a different room. In an industrial setting, a study of the effects of different incentives on productivity might utilize intact groups of workers with little disruption.

But there is a price to be paid for convenience. In conducting research, there is no free lunch — just as in other realms of life. Since the experimenter has played no role in assigning the subjects to the intact groups in a quasi-experiment, those groups may differ in some important way before the experimental treatment is administered, and thus preexisting group differences may be confounded with the independent variable. Thus, the internal validity of a quasi-experiment is always open to some question. By contrast, the internal validity of a true experiment can be more nearly assured by proper balancing, counterbalancing, randomizing, or random sampling.

The statistical significance of a quasi-experiment involving two groups can be tested using one of the procedures in Chapter 9, depending on the kind of measurement scale. Although we use the same statistical procedures in testing the results of quasi-experiments and true experiments, you should not make the mistake of supposing, therefore, that we can draw the same conclusions from the results in the two cases. Only in the case of the true experiment can we draw the clear inference that our manipulation of the independent variable has caused an observed difference in the dependent variable.

Wherever possible, a study should be designed as a true experiment, but where that is impossible or highly impractical, a quasi-experiment may be well worth doing. The researcher — and especially the consumer of research findings — should keep in mind the limitations of the quasi-experiment. Cook and Campbell (1979) offer examples of other kinds of quasi-experiments and discussions of problems in their interpretation.

Systematic Observations: Natural Independent Variables

We are often interested in comparing human or animal subjects that differ in terms of some natural characteristic, some natural independent variable. For example, developmental psychologists may be interested in comparing cognitive processes in younger and older children, or in middle age and old age. All such studies represent systematic observations rather than experiments, since a natural independent variable is only observed — not manipulated. You might want to argue that in a sense the researcher manipulates a natural independent variable by choosing one kind of subject for one group and a different kind for the other. A psychologist is certainly free to choose a group of four-year-olds and another of six-year-olds for use in a developmental study, but that researcher does not *cause* any particular subject to be four years old, or any other to be six years old. By contrast, in a true experiment the researcher has a collection of general-purpose subjects, any one of whom can be randomly assigned to a control or experimental group. But in a study involving a natural independent variable, there is no such thing as a general-purpose subject who can be made four years or six years old — or male or female — at the will of the researcher.

Systematic observations make use of independent groups and also matched pairs of subjects. In a study of sex differences in spatial perception, for example, pairs of subjects might consist of brothers and sisters, or parents and children. Depending on the measurement scale, one of the procedures in Chapter 9 or 12 will be a suitable test of significance in an independent-groups or matched-pairs design. Although identical tests of significance are used in experiments and observations, only in experiments can we conclude that the independent variable has caused an effect observed in the dependent variable.

Strengths and Weaknesses. The greatest strength of the process of systematic observation is its very wide range of application. There is almost no end to the kinds of observations that we can conceive of. But in every case, the internal validity of a systematic observation is threatened by extraneous variables over which the researcher has no control. Adult men and women, for example, have lived many years of their lives before falling into the clutches of a researcher interested in sex differences. If we observe a sex difference in some psychological process or other, how shall we interpret the finding? Do the sexes differ in that respect because of some genetic factor, or because of different treatment of the sexes in the social environment, or because of some interaction between genetic and environmental factors? The point is, statistically significant results in a systematic observation may be very interesting and well worth knowing about, but we can never be sure that the natural independent variable has caused those results. Therein lies the greatest weakness of systematic observation.

Multiple Groups: Single-Factor Designs

In this section, we will deal with situations where a single independent variable has more than two levels. In the present context, an independent variable is often called a **factor,** and thus a design having a single independent variable is called a **single-factor design.** In a later section, we will present **factorial designs,** where there are two or more independent variables, each having two or more levels. In a single-factor design, the different levels of the independent variable can be administered to independent groups, to matched groups, or to the same groups of subjects in a repeated-measures design. Strictly speaking, the last case represents a single-group design, but since there may be several levels of the independent variable, that case is more similar to the multiple-group designs in this section than to the single-group designs discussed earlier.

Multiple-group designs are highly flexible and are equally useful for true experiments, quasi-experiments, and systematic observations. The appropriate procedure for testing differences between means in most of these designs is the **analysis of variance,** which is described in Chapter 14. As you read the material in the present chapter, keep in mind that the analysis of *variance* is a procedure for testing *differences between means.* In some cases, depending on the measurement scale, a variety of *chi*-square test may be appropriate, as described in Chapter 15. Although the appropriate statistical tests are to be presented later, it will nevertheless be useful to describe some multiple-group designs in the present chapter.

True Experiments

Independent Randomized Groups.   Suppose an industrial psychologist wishes to assess the effects of three levels of illumination on the performance of assembly-line workers. Three independent groups are to be tested, each under a different level of illumination. Table 13-3 (top) demonstrates the random assignment of 15 subjects to three groups, using a sequence of random numbers from Table H, or from a calculator. The five subjects having

TABLE 13-3.   Assignment of Subjects to 3 Groups in 2 Different Designs (top, middle); and Assignment of the Order of 3 Treatments to a Single Group of Subjects (bottom).

Completely Randomized Design														
Subject number	1	2	3	4	5	6	7	8	9	10	11	12	13	14	15
Random number	16	26	18	40	06	13	77	17	32	82	59	46	45	08	66
Group	1	2	2	2	1	1	3	1	2	3	3	3	2	1	3

Randomized-Blocks Design														
Block (experience)		1			2			3			4			5	
Subject number	1	2	3	4	5	6	7	8	9	10	11	12	13	14	15
Random number	27	94	30	57	95	45	06	68	09	92	89	52	50	41	81
Group	1	3	2	2	3	1	1	3	2	3	2	1	2	1	3

Repeated-Measures Design														
Subject number		1			2			3			4			5	
Random number	61	26	20	40	68	77	93	20	96	24	57	99	45	07	55
Order	3	2	1	1	2	3	3	1	2	1	2	3	2	1	3

the lowest random numbers are assigned to Group 1, the five having the next highest random numbers are assigned to Group 2, and the remaining subjects are assigned to Group 3. This procedure yields a **completely randomized design.** Any number of independent groups can be used in this design, each receiving a different level of the independent variable, although a design using more than six or seven groups would be unusual. We say that an independent variable has an effect if there is any significant difference between the means of the dependent measures at any two levels of the independent variable, or at some combination of levels. When there is an effect, as indicated by an analysis of variance, then we can conclude that the experimenter's manipulation of the independent variable — illumination — caused the difference in performance.

At this point, you may wonder why we need a new technique to test the statistical significance of the results of this experiment. Why not simply compare all possible pairs of means — 1 and 2, 2 and 3, and 1 and 3 — using independent t tests? In a three-group experiment, there are only three such comparisons to make. But if the null hypothesis is true — if there is no difference between the effects of the three levels of illumination — then each additional t test increases the probability of a Type 1 error. The analysis of variance makes it possible to assess the statistical significance of a multiple-group experiment by running a single test, a procedure that avoids increasing the probability of a Type 1 error, as explained in detail in Chapter 14.

The completely randomized design, using multiple independent groups, is a straightforward extension of the two-group experiment using independent groups. As the next chapter will explain, the analysis of variance in a completely randomized design represents a kind of generalization of the independent two-sample t test to a situation having any number of independent samples. Details of the independent-groups analysis of variance are presented in Chapter 14.

Matched Groups and Repeated Measures. It is possible to extend the matched-pairs design to a situation where we have more than two levels of the independent variable. For example, consider the experiment on illumination levels described above. Workers differ in amount of work experience, and in some cases, more experienced workers may be more productive. The power of the completely randomized experiment might be increased by matching subjects on their amount of work experience. Since there are three levels of illumination in the present experiment, a **matched group** would consist of three workers of comparable experience. In the present context, a matched group is called a **block.** The three most experienced workers are placed in Block 1, the three next-most experienced are placed in Block 2, and so on. Although the workers in any particular block will probably not be perfectly matched in experience, they will be more comparable to each other than to the subjects in other blocks. Within each block, each subject is randomly assigned to one of the levels of illumination, as illustrated in Table 13-3 (middle). Thus, different subjects are tested under each level of the independent variable. The experimental design here is called a **randomized-blocks design,** where each matched group of subjects is considered a block. The results of such an experiment are tested by a randomized-blocks analysis of variance, a procedure that represents an extension of the correlated-measures t test.

The experiment on illumination levels could also be carried out as a **repeated-measures design.** Suppose an industrial psychologist has access to a group of well-experienced workers whose performances are not likely to change substantially through a practice effect. Each subject might then be tested under all three levels of illumination. The levels are presented in an order determined by a sequence of random numbers, as shown in Table 13-3 (bottom). The results of such an experiment can be tested by a repeated-measures analysis of variance, which represents an extension of the repeated-measures t test.

The repeated-measures analysis of variance—and the randomized-blocks design, to a lesser extent—are widely used in psychological research. However, we cannot present the computational details of those procedures because of space limitations. After you have studied the independent-groups analysis of variance in Chapter 14, you can extend those procedures to the repeated-measures designs in Winer (1971) and to the randomized-blocks designs in Kirk (1982).

Quasi-Experiments and Systematic Observations

Multiple-group designs are readily applied to quasi-experiments using intact groups. Our experiment on illumination levels might be carried out as a quasi-experiment using three intact groups of workers, or a study of three teaching methods might utilize three intact classes.

Systematic observations make extensive use of multiple-group designs. For example, a study of achievement motivation among industrial workers might utilize four groups of subjects: Executives, professionals, first-level supervisors, and production workers; or a study of the credibility of a proposed advertising campaign might utilize groups of subjects having low, middle, and high incomes. An independent-groups analysis of variance is used to test the statistical significance of a quasi-experiment or a set of observations based on multiple groups.

Factorial Designs

The experiments and observations discussed so far have all had a single independent variable. An experiment or systematic observation having more than one independent variable is called a **factorial design.** Manipulating more than one independent variable in an experiment yields information about the effects of different levels of each independent variable, as though each were manipulated in separate experiments, and in addition yields information about **interactions** between the independent variables. Including more than one natural independent variable in a systematic observation pays similar dividends. In some factorial designs, one independent variable may be manipulated and another may be a natural independent variable, as in the example described below.

Lucas (1952) measured the effects of anxiety on a simple learning task. A group of anxious subjects, as measured by the Taylor Manifest Anxiety Scale, and a group of nonanxious subjects were each randomly assigned to four subgroups. The experiment was conducted in two stages, a *preliminary task* consisting of learning six lists of ten consonant letters presented on a memory drum, and a *critical task* consisting of learning three new lists of ten consonants each. During the preliminary task, the four subgroups of anxious and nonanxious subjects received the following kinds of feedback on their performance: One subgroup received no feedback at all, and the three other subgroups were informed respectively that they had failed once, twice, or three times during the preliminary task. This experiment represents a **two-way factorial design,** since there are two independent variables: Factor *A,* number of failures; and Factor *B,* level of anxiety. More specifically, the experiment is a *four by two factorial,* since there are four levels of Factor *A* and two of *B.*

The experimenter hypothesized that the anxious subjects who were informed of failure more often during the preliminary task would subsequently perform more poorly during the critical task. The results in Figure 13-3 (upper left) support the experimenter's hypothesis regarding the performance of the anxious subjects, and in addition show that the performance of the nonanxious subjects *improves* as a function of number of failures experienced. Further, the mean performance of nonanxious subjects across all four subgroups — that is, their mean performance without regard to number of failures — was significantly higher than the mean performance of anxious subjects.

Main Effects

The upper right panel of Figure 13-3 shows the difference between anxious and nonanxious subjects, without regard to the failure variable. That difference represents a **main effect** of Factor *B,* that is, an effect of one independent variable that occurs without regard to any other independent variable. When we consider the main effect of a single independent variable in a factorial experiment, we view the other independent variable — for the moment — as if it were an extraneous variable balanced at each level of the independent variable under consideration. For example, in considering the main effect of anxiety, the number of failures on the preliminary task — 0, 1, 2, and 3 — are balanced across the two levels of the anxiety variable, Factor *B.* The lower left panel shows performance as a function of failure, without regard to the anxiety variable. Here, we consider anxiety to be an extraneous variable

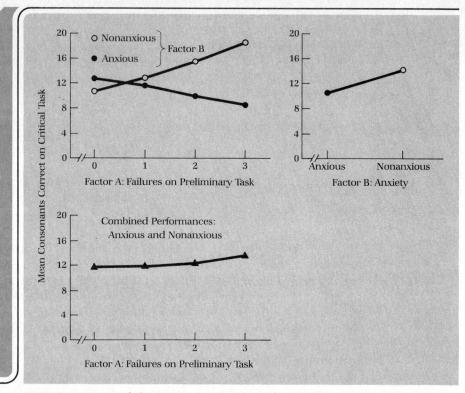

FIGURE 13-3. Top, left: *AB* interaction. Top, right: Significant main effect of Factor *B*. Bottom: Main effect of Factor *A*, not statistically significant. Modified after Lucas (1952); © 1952, 1980, by the Board of Trustees of the University of Illinois. Reprinted by permission of the University of Illinois Press.

balanced at each level of the failure variable. There is no significant difference between the dependent measures at any of the levels of failure, and thus there is no significant main effect of Factor *A*.

Interactions

Although there is no significant main effect of the failure variable, there is a *failure by anxiety interaction* — that is, an **interaction** between Factors *A* and *B*, or an ***AB* interaction.** The effect of the failure variable is different at each level of the anxiety variable (see Figure 13-3, upper left). Thus, we say that there are two different **simple effects** of failure, one for anxious subjects and another for nonanxious subjects. If we ask what effect failure has on subsequent performance, we must answer that question differently for anxious and nonanxious subjects. Or if we ask what effect anxiety has on performance, our answer depends on the number of failures that anxious and nonanxious subjects have experienced. Thus, when there is an interaction between independent variables, each factor must be taken into account in describing the effects of the other.

The significance of main effects and interactions in factorial designs are tested by an analysis of variance. Procedures for a single-factor analysis of variance are described in detail in Chapter 14. Those procedures can be extended to factorial designs, as in Winer (1971) or Keppel (1982) for example. Although factorial designs cannot be treated in detail in the present text, our limited discussion of those designs should allow you to understand some of their important features when you encounter them in the research literature.

In Conclusion

This chapter has attempted to consolidate the fundamental principles of designing experiments, planning observations, and interpreting the results of research. Although the problems of statistics and experimental design can be separated to some extent, no statistical test — no matter how highly significant — can be interpreted meaningfully in the absence of an adequate design. And no experimental design, no matter how elegantly conceived, can guarantee meaningful results if an inappropriate statistical test is applied. Indeed, statistics and experimental design represent two of the major pillars supporting the edifice of psychological research.

Terms and Symbols

The principles of experimental design in the present chapter lend themselves exceptionally well to the exercise of comparing and contrasting that I have recommended so often in the past. For example, what are the strengths and weaknesses of the various designs, and where are they most applicable? What are the conditions that promote — or threaten — the internal and external validity of experiments and observations? There is almost no end to the number of such questions that you can ask — and answer, I hope — regarding the contents of this important chapter.

Statistics	**Size of an effect**
Experimental design	**Independent variable**
Observation	**Level**
Experimentation	**Dependent variable**
Random sample	**Dose-response relationship**
Population	**Single-factor experiment**
Convenience sample	**Analysis of variance**
Sampling bias	**Factor**
Literary Digest poll	**Factorial design**

Internal validity
External validity
Statistical significance
Time series
Bivariate correlation
Multiple correlation
Partial correlation
Factor analysis
Multiple regression
Interrupted time series
Single-group design
Before-after design
Pilot experiment
$N = 1$ design
Counterbalancing
Between-subjects counterbalancing
Natural independent variable
Manipulated independent variable

Experimental group
Control group
Placebo
Sham treatment
Randomizing
Balancing
Matched-pairs design
Quasi-experiment
Intact group
Multiple groups
Randomized groups
Randomized-blocks design
Repeated-measures design
Two-way factorial design
Main effects
Interactions
.2S, .5S, and .8S
g
ECCE
ECEC

EXERCISES AND STUDY QUESTIONS

1. What do we mean by *statistics* and *experimental design* in the context of the present chapter? How are these processes related?

2. Differentiate between experiments and observations, paying attention to the roles of natural and manipulated independent variables. What is the essential importance of the distinction between those two ways of gaining knowledge?

3. What is random sampling, and why is it important?

4. What are statistical significance, reliability, internal validity, and external validity, and how are these constructs related?

5. Compare and contrast the ideas of statistical significance and the size of an effect.

6. Describe a situation where a time series might be useful.

7. What are multiple and partial correlation? Describe some situations where these techniques might be useful.

8. Briefly describe a factor analysis.

9. What is counterbalancing, and when is it useful?

10. In tests of motor skills, men tend to do better at making larger-scale movements involving the arms and hands, and women excel at smaller-scale movements of the fingers. Suppose a group of men and a group of women are tested on the tasks below, where the data represent their mean performance measures. The test of tweezer dexterity, of course,

principally involves the fingers, while the pursuit rotor requires large-scale arm and hand movements. Assume that larger numbers are better, and assume that all differences are statistically significant.

Task	Men	Women
Tweezer dexterity	10	50
Pursuit rotor	50	10

    a. Describe the experimental design.

    b. Draw a graph showing the results, and describe the results in words, making use of the ideas in this chapter.

    c. Is there any overall difference between men and women across the two tasks?

11. What are the principal advantages of a factorial design?

12. Describe a quasi-experiment using two intact groups and a true experiment using two randomized groups. What is the essential difference between these approaches, and what difference does it make in interpreting the results?

13. Assess the degree of reliability, internal validity, and external validity in the following situations. Where there is a particular difficulty, suggest a remedy.

    a. A psychologist is developing a new test of occupational stress. In a group of 27 air traffic controllers, widely considered a stressful occupation, the new test correlates .23 with a composite measure of physiological stress indicators, such as blood pressure and heart rate. Is the new test at all promising?

    b. A class of police cadets is given a test of interpersonal empathy early in their training program. After a course of sensitivity training, the cadets score significantly higher in empathy at the .01 level on a parallel form of the test. Was the sensitivity training responsible?

    c. In a study of local unemployment, a researcher surveys adults 20 through 29 years old at a supermarket on three successive weekday afternoons. In a sample of 217 people, local employment is significantly higher than the national figures at the .001 level. Do you trust these results?

    d. A cognitive psychologist has developed an experimental procedure designed to enhance problem solving. For convenience, all of the students in a Tuesday section of a Research Methods laboratory are tested under the experimental procedure, and the students in a Wednesday section are tested under a control procedure. The experimental group performs significantly and substantially better at the .05 level. Does the experimental procedure work?

Multiple Independent Groups

14

This chapter deals principally with the independent-groups analysis of variance, a set of procedures for use where the independent variable has several levels and where the dependent variable is measured on an interval or ratio scale. A procedure for use with ordinal scales is briefly described. Where a set of data consists of observed frequencies of cases falling in several nominal categories, the one-variable *chi*-square test is appropriate. That procedure is described in detail in the next chapter.

Consider a drug experiment designed to measure the effects of different doses of a particular drug. The independent variable in such an experiment consists of different levels of dosage, perhaps measured in milligrams per kilogram of body weight, or in some other convenient unit. Each level of the independent variable is administered to a different group of independent subjects. In such an experiment, the independent variable would be measured on a ratio scale. Now consider a different kind of drug study, an experiment designed to compare the effects of different drugs. Each drug represents a different level of the independent variable. Here, the independent variable would be measured on a nominal scale — that is, kind of drug.

In either of the above experiments, the dependent variable might be measured on any kind of measurement scale. For example, the experimenter might observe the frequency of animals surviving at each level of dosage in the single-drug experiment, or the number surviving after treatment with each different drug in the second experiment. In either case, the dependent variable would be measured on a nominal scale having two values — living or dead. In such a situation, a *chi*-square test of independent proportions — described in the next chapter — would be appropriate. In a human experiment, the drug effects might be assessed by having the subjects reproduce simple drawings, which the experimenter might then place in rank order of quality. Here, the dependent variable would be measured on an ordinal scale. The Kruskal-Wallis analysis of variance by ranks, briefly described in this chapter, would then be appropriate. If the drug effects were assessed by giving human subjects a standardized psychological test, then the dependent variable would be measured on an interval scale. Finally, if the effects on reaction time were measured, then the dependent variable would be measured on a ratio scale. In those last two cases, an independent-groups analysis of variance — described in detail in this chapter — would be appropriate.

As the above examples show, there is no necessary connection between the measurement scales of the independent and dependent variables. Either variable can be measured on any kind of scale — nominal, ordinal, interval, or ratio. But the nature of the dependent variable, especially, determines the kind of statistical test that can be applied most appropriately.

Analysis of Variance: Interval and Ratio Scales

As we mentioned in the last chapter, the **analysis of variance** is a procedure for testing the significance of differences between means in a multiple-group design. The term for this procedure may appear to be something of a misnomer, since the analysis of variance is used as a test of differences between *means*. But we saw in Chapter 9 that variances played a great role in determining the significance of a difference between the means of two independent groups, and we will see that the procedures in the present chapter will represent an extension of those earlier tests. Variances will play an even greater role in testing differences between the means of multiple independent groups, and thus analysis of variance is a rather apt term. The abbreviation ANOVA, pronounced as a word, is often used to stand for analysis of variance. The independent variable in an ANOVA design can be measured on any scale — nominal, ordinal, interval, or ratio — but the dependent variable must be measured on an interval or ratio scale.

A multiple-group experiment begins with the selection of the required number of independent groups of subjects. Each group may consist of a random sample of subjects drawn from the same population. Usually, however, the available subjects are divided into randomized groups by the procedure described in Chapter 13. Each group is then subjected to a different **treatment** consisting of the application of a particular level of the independent variable. The treatments might consist of different levels of drug dosage, amounts of practice on a learning task, different teaching methods, or almost anything else that we can conceive of.

In a systematic observation — as opposed to an experiment — the independent variable would be a naturally occurring one, rather than a variable manipulated by the experimenter. In such a case, all of the subjects in a particular group would share a common level of the natural independent variable — age, for example, or membership in a naturally occurring group of some sort. The dependent variable might consist of test scores, or any other kind of measurements on an interval or ratio scale.

The Effects of the Independent Variable

Figure 14-1 shows some possible outcomes of three hypothetical experiments, each using three independent groups of subjects. In each experiment, each group of subjects receives a different treatment, a different level of the independent variable. We assume that each group of three subjects is a random sample drawn from the same population. For purposes of the present discussion, we make the unrealistic assumptions that the means of the three groups are precisely equal in each case before the hypothetical experiment, and the variances within groups are also equal. Those assumptions are unrealistic because we have seen that the sample mean and variance are both random variables that are each unlikely to take precisely the same value in different random samples.

Panel A of Figure 14-1 represents an outcome where no level of the independent variable has any effect. In that case, the group means are the same after the experiment as they were before. The group means differ neither from each other nor from the **grand mean** $\overline{G}$, which is the mean of all the scores without regard to group membership. In Panel B, Level 1 of the

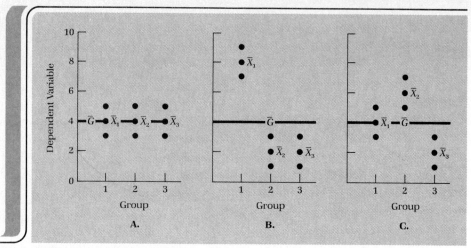

FIGURE 14-1. Three possible outcomes of a hypothetical experiment having 3 groups of 3 subjects each. Group means are $\bar{X}_1$, $\bar{X}_2$, and $\bar{X}_3$; grand mean is $\bar{G}$. **A:** Independent variable has no effect. **B:** Each level of independent variable has an effect. **C:** Levels 2 and 3 of independent variable have effects, Level 1 has none.

independent variable has the effect of adding 4 units to the score of each subject in Group 1, and Levels 2 and 3 have the effect of subtracting 2 units from each of the scores in Groups 2 and 3. After the experiment, all of the group means differ from the grand mean, and some of them differ from each other. In Panel C, Level 1 of the independent variable has no effect, but Level 2 has the effect of adding 2 units to the scores in Group 2, and Level 3 has the effect of subtracting 2 units from the scores in Group 3.

An **effect** is defined as a constant that is added to or subtracted from each of the scores in a group through the action of a particular level of the independent variable. Each effect is measured in relation to the grand mean, and thus the sum of all the effects is zero across all the levels of the independent variable. The assumption that the effect of any particular level of the independent variable falls equally on all the subjects within the group receiving that treatment, together with the assumption that the sum of all treatment effects is zero, represent the assumption of **additivity of effects** —a fundamental requirement in the analysis of variance.

The Null and Alternative Hypotheses.   The idea of an effect is used in the following statements of the null and alternative hypotheses:

H_0: The independent variable has no effect;

H_1: The independent variable has some effect.

Symbolically, the null hypothesis can be stated in the following form:

$$H_0: \mu_1 = \mu_2 = \ldots = \mu_k. \tag{14-1}$$

Expression 14-1 says that the means of the populations from which the k groups were drawn are all equal. Thus, the null hypothesis in ANOVA is of the same form as in the independent 2-sample t test, except here we are dealing with more than two groups. The alternative hypothesis in ANOVA is difficult to state symbolically, since there are a large number of possible alternatives when H_0 is false. For example, μ_1 and μ_2 might differ, and all the other means might be identical, or there might be some other difference between some combination of means. A later section discusses alternative hypotheses more extensively.

At this point, it may not be entirely clear why we need to introduce any new procedure to analyze the results of multiple-group experiments or observations, since it might appear that we could use independent 2-sample t tests to test the differences between all possible pairs of means. However, we briefly mentioned a problem in using such a procedure in the last chapter. Where there are k groups, the number of pairs of means is equal to the number of combinations of k things taken 2 at a time, that is,

$$\text{Number of possible pairs } = C_2^k = \frac{k(k-1)}{2}. \tag{14-2}$$

As you can see by Equation 14-2, the number of possible pairs increases greatly as k increases. For example, where $k = 5$, there are 10 possible pairs of means.

If the null hypothesis were perfectly true, and if we drew two random samples and tested the difference between their means, the probability of rejecting H_0 by a t test would be equal to our chosen *alpha* level. Now suppose we drew two additional random samples, and tested the difference between their means at the same *alpha* level. In that case, the probability of rejecting H_0 on either of the above tests—that is, on Test 1 *or* Test 2—would be considerably greater than α. Where two tests are independent,

$$
\begin{aligned}
P(\text{Rejecting } H_0 \text{ on Test 1 or Test 2}) &= P(\text{Test 1} \cup \text{Test 2}) \\
&= P(\text{Test 1}) + P(\text{Test 2}) - P(\text{Test 1} \cap \text{Test 2}) \\
&= \alpha + \alpha - \alpha^2 \\
&= 2\alpha - \alpha^2.
\end{aligned}
$$

Letting $\alpha = .05$,

$$P(\text{Rejecting } H_0 \text{ on Test 1 or Test 2}) = 2(.05) - .05^2 = .0975.$$

The situation becomes more complicated when we consider all of the possible pairwise comparisons that might be made between the means of several groups. But in any case, running a large number of t tests would greatly increase the probability of a Type 1 error, falsely rejecting a true null hypothesis, over and above the *alpha* level chosen for each test. ANOVA provides a single test of the null hypothesis, and thus avoids increasing the probability of a Type 1 error above the chosen α level.

Variance Within and Between Groups

The **variance within groups** is an unbiased estimate of the population variance based on the sample variance observed in each group. Where the groups are the same size, the within-groups variance is the mean of the sample variances observed in the k groups. The variance within groups is often called **error variance.** The **variance between groups** is based on the variance of the group means, as explained below. When the null hypothesis is true, the variance between groups is another unbiased estimate of the population variance. Those two estimates of the population variance, which are independent of each other, as we will also explain, are of central importance in the analysis of variance.

Table 14-1 shows the results of a hypothetical experiment using four independent groups of subjects. The independent variable might consist of four levels of age, or four teaching methods, and the dependent variable might consist of test performance, or any other kind of measure on an interval or ratio scale. Now consider the group means, which are located in the row labeled with the symbol $\bar{X}_j$, which stands for the mean of any one group in general. When we need to deal with the mean of some particular group, we can replace the j subscript with the number designating the group of interest. For example, the mean of Group 2 is $\bar{X}_2$, and its value is 4.25.

Any score in Table 14-1 is symbolized in general as X_{ij}, where the i and j subscripts, respectively, identify individuals and their groups. For example, X_{21} is a score of 7, representing the 2nd person in the 1st group, and X_{32} is a score of 5, representing the 3rd person in the 2nd group. Thus, the double subscripts are a set of addresses giving the locations of all the subjects in a table in terms of Row_i and Column_j.

$$\text{Variance within group}_j = S_j^2 = \frac{\sum_{i=1}^{n} X_{ij}^2 - \dfrac{\left(\sum_{i}^{n} X_{ij}\right)^2}{n}}{n-1}, \tag{14-3}$$

$$df_j = n - 1,$$

where the summation is across the n individuals in the jth group, n is the size of each group, and df_j is the degrees of freedom in each group. Since there are four groups in the example in Table 14-1, there are four variances of the above form. Since there are k such variances in general, we find the mean of the variances within groups by summing Expression 14-3 across the k groups and dividing by k. Thus,

$$\text{Variance within} = S_W^2 = \frac{\sum_{j=1}^{k} S_j^2}{k} = \sum_{j} \left[\frac{\sum_{i}^{n} X_{ij}^2 - \dfrac{\left(\sum_{i}^{n} X_{ij}\right)^2}{n}}{k(n-1)} \right], \tag{14-4}$$

$$df_W = k(n-1) = N - k,$$

TABLE 14-1.   Analysis of Variance, Four-group Experiment, Equal *ns* in All Groups.

A. Basic data:

	Group 1		Group 2		Group 3		Group 4		
	X_{i1}	X_{i1}^2	X_{i2}	X_{i2}^2	X_{i3}	X_{i3}^2	X_{i4}	X_{i4}^2	
	2	4	1	1	9	81	9	81	
	7	49	4	16	6	36	3	9	$k = 4$ groups
	5	35	5	25	7	49	7	49	
	9	81	7	49	7	49	10	100	$n = 8$ subjects
	6	36	1	1	9	81	6	36	per group
	6	36	2	4	12	144	5	25	
	4	16	4	16	9	81	6	36	$N = 32$ total subjects $= Kn$
	3	9	10	100	11	121	5	25	
$\sum_i X_{ij}$	42		34		70		51	$\sum_j \sum_i X_{ij} = G$	$= 197$
$\sum_i X_{ij}^2$		256		212		642		361	$\sum_j \sum_i X_{ij}^2$ $= 1471$
$\bar{X}_j$	5.25		4.25		8.75		6.38	$\sum_j \sum_i X_{ij}/N = \bar{\bar{G}}$	$= 6.16$
S_j^2	5.07		9.64		4.21		5.12	Mean(S_j^2)	$= 6.01$

B. Computational symbols from Formulas 14-32:

$$(1) = \frac{G^2}{N} \qquad = \frac{197^2}{32} \qquad = 1212.78$$

$$(2) = \sum_j \sum_i X_{ij}^2 \qquad = 256 + 212 + 642 + 361 = 1471$$

$$(3) = \sum_j \left(\sum_i X_{ij} \right)^2 / n_j = \frac{42^2}{8} + \frac{34^2}{8} + \frac{70^2}{8} + \frac{51^2}{8} = 1302.62$$

C. Computational Formulas 14-33:

$$SS_B = (3) - (1) = 1302.62 - 1212.78 = 89.84 \qquad\qquad df_B = k - 1 = 3$$
$$SS_W = (2) - (3) = 1471 \quad - 1302.62 = 168.38 \qquad\qquad df_W = N - k = 28$$
$$SS_T = (2) - (1) = 1471 \quad - 1212.78 = 258.22 \qquad\qquad df_T = N - 1 = 31$$

D. Summary of analysis of variance

Source	SS	df	MS	F
Treatment (Between groups)	89.84	3	29.95	4.98**
Error (Within groups)	168.38	28	6.01	
Total	258.22√	31 $= N - 1$√		

** $p < .01$

where *n* is the size of each group, **k** is the number of groups, and **N** is the total number of subjects. Where all groups are the same size, $N = kn$.

Since each of the *k* variances in 14-4 has $n - 1$ degrees of freedom, and since the variance within is based on all of those variances within groups, S_W^2 has $k(n - 1)$ degrees of freedom. The double summation in Equation 14-4 instructs us to do the following: Set *j* equal to 1, and then carry out the summation operations in the numerator across the *n* individuals in Group 1;

set $j = 2$, and sum across the n individuals in Group 2, and so on through all k groups, accumulating the sum as we go.

We now consider the variance between groups, an estimate of the population variance based on the observed variance of the sample means. Where the variance of the population is *known*, Equation 8-7 gives the variance of the sampling distribution — that is, the variance of the means of an infinite number of random samples of size n drawn from the population. Thus,

$$\sigma_{\bar{X}}^2 = \frac{\sigma_X^2}{n}, \tag{8-7}$$

where $\sigma_{\bar{X}}^2$ is the variance of the sampling distribution, σ_X^2 is the population variance, and n is the sample size. Solving 8-7 for the population variance,

$$\sigma_X^2 = n\sigma_{\bar{X}}^2. \tag{14-5}$$

Equation 14-5 shows that if we knew the variance of the sampling distribution, the variance of the sample means, then we could find the population variance by multiplying by n. But where the population variance is *unknown*, and must be estimated, substituting S_X^2 in Equation 8-7 yields an estimate of the variance of the sampling distribution:

$$S_{\bar{X}}^2 = \frac{S_X^2}{n}, \tag{14-6}$$

where $S_{\bar{X}}^2$ is an unbiased estimate of the variance of the sample means, and S_X^2 is the sample variance, an unbiased estimate of the population variance. Solving Equation 14-6 for S_X^2,

$$S_X^2 = nS_{\bar{X}}^2. \tag{14-7}$$

Equation 14-7 shows that if we had an unbiased estimate of the variance of the sampling distribution, then multiplying that quantity by the sample size would yield an unbiased estimate of the population variance. Treating each of the group means as a score, we can calculate the observed variance of the sample means, and that variance is an unbiased estimate of the variance of the sampling distribution. (Where the groups have unequal ns, things are a little more complicated — as explained later — but the principle remains the same.) Thus, where each group is a random sample from the same population — that is, where the null hypothesis is true — Equation 14-7 yields an unbiased estimate of the population variance.

Now consider the nature of the variance of the group means. If there were no differences whatever between the group means — if all the means were precisely equal — then the observed variance of the group means would be zero. Thus, the variance of the group means is determined by *differences between means*, and thus the unbiased estimate of the population variance that is based on the variance of the group means is designated the *variance between groups*. Since Equation 14-7 above yields that variance estimate,

Variance between $= S_B^2 = S_{\bar{X}}^2 = nS_{\bar{X}}^2.$ (14-8)

The term *between* in Equation 14-8 should remind you that S_B^2 is an estimate of the population variance based on the observed differences between group means.

The variance between can be found by the following procedure. Since the variance between is equal to n times the variance of the group means, we treat each mean as a score, find the variance of those scores, and then multiply by n. Adapting Formula 8-10 to our present needs,

$$\text{Variance between} = S_B^2 = nS_{\bar{X}}^2 = n \left[\frac{\sum\limits_{j=1}^{k} \bar{X}_j^2 - \dfrac{\left(\sum\limits_{j} \bar{X}_j\right)^2}{k}}{k-1} \right],$$ (14-9)

$$df_B = k - 1.$$

Since there are k means, the variance of the sample means has $k - 1$ degrees of freedom, and so does the variance between.

Comparing the Variance Between and Within.   The first question to be answered by an ANOVA is whether the independent variable had any effect — that is, whether any of the group means differ from each other or from the grand mean. Comparing the two independent estimates of the population variance — the variance between and within — will allow us to answer that question.

The group means in Table 14-1 are shown graphically in Figure 14-2. By Equations 14-4 and 14-9, the variance within is 6.01 and the variance between is 29.95. For reasons we will explain shortly, those variances are listed as *means squares* (MS) in Table 14-1D. Taking the square root of those variances yields S_W and S_B, the two estimates of the population standard deviation illustrated in Figure 14-2. Standard deviations are more useful for our present purposes, since those measures can be represented as linear distances on a graph while variances cannot.

If the independent variable has no effect — that is, if H_0 is true — then the dispersion of the group means in relation to the grand mean will be no greater than would be expected in the case of four random samples drawn from the same population. In that case, S_B and S_W should be closely comparable, since they are independent estimates of the population standard deviation. But if there is an effect, then the dispersion of the group means will be greater than expected under the null hypothesis, and S_B will be substantially greater than S_W.

In Figure 14-2, the heavy line is the grand mean — the mean of all the observations, or the mean of the group means where all the groups are the same size. The dashed lines are located 1 S_W above and below the grand mean, and the light solid lines are 1 S_B above and below the grand mean. The figure shows that S_B, the standard deviation based on the variance between groups,

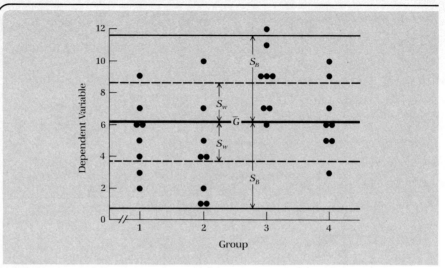

FIGURE 14-2. Data from Table 14-1 shown graphically. Each dot is a score. Solid heavy line is $\overline{G}$, grand mean. Lighter solid lines are 1 S_B above and below grand mean. Dashed lines are 1 S_W above and below grand mean. Since S_B is significantly greater than S_W, null hypothesis is rejected.

is considerably larger than S_W, the standard deviation based on variance within groups. Notice also that only about half of the total distribution, 17 of 32 cases, lie within ± 1 S_W of the grand mean. But if the four groups were random samples drawn from the same population — that being one of the requirements for ANOVA — and if the null hypothesis were true, then .6826 of the cases would be expected to fall within ± 1 S_W of the grand mean. Thus, it appears that S_W underestimates the dispersion actually observed in Figure 14-2. On the other hand, all but one case lie within ± 1 S_B of the grand mean, suggesting that the standard deviation based on the variance between groups overestimates the dispersion actually observed in the data. The F ratio, described in the next section, provides a test of the comparison between S_B^2 and S_W^2.

The F Ratio. The variance within groups is an unbiased estimate of the population variance, and where the null hypothesis is true — where the independent variable has no effect — the variance between groups is an independent unbiased estimate of the same population variance. the **F ratio,** defined in the following equation, is the ratio of the between-groups variance to the within-groups variance:

$$F = \frac{S_B^2}{S_W^2}.$$
(14-10)

Where the null hypothesis is true, both the numerator and denominator of the F ratio are unbiased estimates of the population variance, and thus the observed value of F should be close to 1.00. But where H_0 is false—where the independent variable has some effect—the variance between groups is expected to be larger than the variance within groups, and in that case the value of F will be larger.

Entering the variance within and between, calculated by Equations 14-4 and 14-9, into Equation 14-10 yields the F ratio for the data in Table 14-1:

$$F(3, 28) = \frac{S_B^2}{S_W^2} = \frac{29.95}{6.01} = 4.98,$$

$$df_B = 3, \quad df_W = 28.$$

The numbers in parentheses beside F in the above equation are the degrees of freedom for the numerator and denominator of the F ratio—that is, the df between and within.

To test the statistical significance of a calculated value of F, the observed F must be compared with a critical value listed in Table F. To find the appropriate critical value in that table, locate the column headed with the df for the numerator and the row labeled with the df for the denominator of the F ratio. Critical values of F at the .05 and .01 levels are listed at the intersection of that row and column. The null hypothesis is rejected if the observed, calculated, value of F is greater than or equal to the critical value listed in the table. The critical value of $F(3, 28)$ at the .01 level is 4.57, and thus we reject H_0 at that level.

Figure 14-3 shows the distribution of $F(3, 28)$, that is, the F curve for 3 and 28 degrees of freedom. The horizonal dimension shows the values of F,

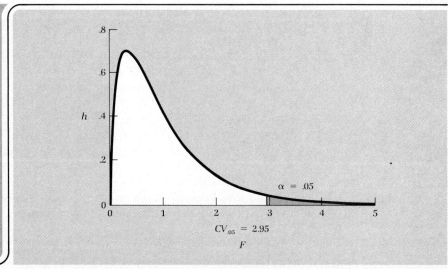

FIGURE 14-3. F distribution for 3 and 28 df. Shaded area, .05 of total area under curve, lies beyond critical value for testing H_0 at .05 level.

and the vertical axis shows the probability density h, the height or ordinate of the curve.

Since F is the ratio of two variances, all F values are positive, and range upward from zero without limit. The shaded area is equal to .05 of the total area under the curve. Thus, the lower bound of the shaded area is the critical value of F for a test of H_0 at the .05 level. The critical value at the .01 level is located farther out in the right tail. Since we are interested only in the situation where the variance between is greater than the variance within, we are concerned only with the right tail of the curve.

The probability distribution of the F statistic was derived by Sir Ronald A. Fisher, largely through his work in an agricultural research setting in Great Britain. Fisher called his statistic the *variance ratio,* but it was renamed the F ratio in his honor by an American statistician, Professor George W. Snedecor, at Iowa State University.

Rejection of the null hypothesis requires the acceptance of an alternative hypothesis stating that the independent variable had some effect on the dependent variable. But a significant F gives no indication of *which* levels of the independent variable have had *what* kinds of effects. In a later section, we will present methods of answering specific questions about which of the group means differ significantly.

Sums of Squares and Mean Squares

While the procedures described above can be used in the computation of an ANOVA, more convenient computational formulas can be derived by making use of the **sums of squares** — the sum of the squared deviations from a mean. Furthermore, some of the concepts in the analysis of variance can be clarified more easily by using the sums of squares. A **mean square,** symbolized **MS**, is a sum of squares divided by an appropriate number of degrees of freedom. Thus, the **mean square within, MS_W,** is an unbiased estimate of the population variance, and so is the **mean square between, MS_B,** when the null hypothesis is true. The sum of squares is an old idea introduced in connection with the 2-sample t test in Chapter 9, but the mean square is a new idea — at least a new term — that will be more fully explained shortly.

Partitioning the Total Sum of Squares.   In a multiple-group design, each subject's score has a **total deviation,** that is, a deviation from $\overline{G}$, the grand mean. For some scores, the total deviation is positive, for others negative, and the sum of the total deviations is equal to zero. Each subject's total deviation can be **partitioned** into two parts, the **deviation within,** that is, the deviation of the score from the mean of the subject's group, and the **deviation between,** the deviation of the mean of that group from the grand mean. The partition of the total deviation is illustrated for two specific subjects in the first two panels of Figure 14-4, and for any subject in general in the last panel. Each deviation is equal to a score minus a mean. The subtraction is always carried out in that order, and the sign of the deviation is

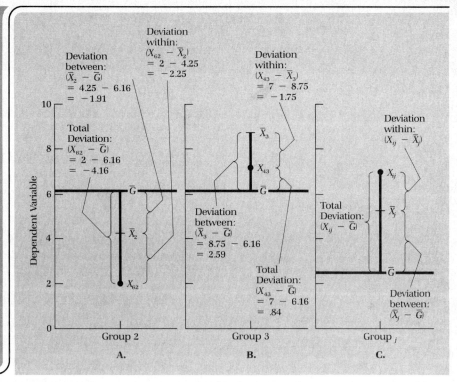

FIGURE 14-4. Partitioning the total deviation. **A**: Deviations for the 6th subject in Group 2, Table 14-1. **B**: Deviations for the 4th subject in Group 3, Table 14-1. **C**: General expressions for the deviations for any subject, i, in any group, j, in a multiple-group design.

retained. Thus, for each subject, the total deviation is the algebraic sum of the deviation within and the deviation between.

You may see some similarities between the present discussion of deviations within and between and the earlier treatment of error deviations and explained deviations in Chapter 10. Indeed, the deviation within is quite analogous to error deviation, and the deviation between is analogous to the explained deviation in the context of regression. There are many other similarities between ANOVA and regression, some of which will be discussed briefly in a later section.

Since the total deviation for a single subject is the algebraic sum of the deviations within and between, we can write the following equations:

Total deviation $=$ Deviation within $+$ Deviation between,

$$(X_{ij} - \overline{G}) \qquad = (X_{ij} - \overline{X}_j) + (\overline{X}_j - \overline{G}), \tag{14-11}$$

where the i and j subscripts identify individuals and groups, respectively.

There is an equation of the above form for each subject. Thus, squaring and summing Equation 14-11 across all subjects yields the **total sum of squares,** that is, the sum of the squared total deviations from the grand mean:

$$\sum_{j=1}^{k} \sum_{i=1}^{n_j} (X_{ij} - \overline{G})^2 = \sum_{j=1}^{k} \sum_{i=1}^{n_j} [(X_{ij} - \overline{X}_j) + (\overline{X}_j - \overline{G})]^2, \tag{14-12}$$

where n_j is the number of subjects in the jth group, and where n_j can differ across groups. Thus, our present development applies to cases with equal or unequal ns.

The double summation operators on the left side of the above equation instruct us to do the following: Across all of the groups from $j = 1$ through k, accumulate the sums of the squared total deviations across all of the individuals from $i = 1$ through n_j in each group. In other words, take each group, find the sum of the squared total deviations, and then find the sum of those sums for all the groups. It might appear that the double summation could be eliminated, since the total sum of squares is just the sum of every squared total deviation for each subject, but there are reasons for the double summation.

Expanding the square on the right side of 14-12 and distributing the summation operators,

$$\sum_j \sum_i (X_{ij} - \overline{G})^2 = \sum_j \sum_i (X_{ij} - \overline{X}_j)^2 - 2 \sum_j \sum_i (X_{ij} - \overline{X}_j)(\overline{X}_j - \overline{G})$$
$$+ \sum_j \sum_i (\overline{X}_j - \overline{G})^2. \tag{14-13}$$

Now that some of the details of double summation have been explained, the notation can be simplified a bit, as in Equation 14-13. The j subscripts indicate that the summation is across groups, and the i subscripts indicate summation across individuals within groups.

The middle term of the right side of 14-13 is equal to zero, as rewriting that term will show:

$$2 \sum_j \left[\sum_i (X_{ij} - \overline{X}_j)(\overline{X}_j - \overline{G}) \right] = 2 \sum_j (\overline{X}_j - \overline{G}) \left[\sum_i (X_{ij} - \overline{X}_j) \right]. \tag{14-14}$$

The expression $\sum_i (X_{ij} - \overline{X}_j)$ in 14-14 is the sum of the deviations of the individual scores in a group from the group mean. The quantity $(\overline{X}_j - \overline{G})$ is the deviation of a group mean from the grand mean, and that quantity is a constant for all of the individuals in a particular group. For each group, the right side of Equation 14-14 has the form

$$C_j \left[\sum_i (X_{ij} - \overline{X}_j) \right], \tag{14-15}$$

where C_j is the deviation of a particular group mean from the grand mean. For example, C_1—the deviation of $\overline{X}_1$ from the grand mean—is equal to $-.91$, and C_3 is equal to 2.59, as shown in Figure 14-3. Since the sum of the deviations of scores from the group mean is equal to zero for every group, the bracketed expression in Equation 14-15 is equal to zero, and so is 14-14, and thus the middle term of Equation 14-13 vanishes.

Now consider the last term of Equation 14-13. Since $(\overline{X}_j - \overline{G})$ is a constant for each individual in a particular group, summing the square of that constant across the n_j individuals in any group yields

$$\sum_i (\overline{X}_j - \overline{G})^2 = n_j(\overline{X}_j - \overline{G})^2. \tag{14-16}$$

Substituting the above expression in 14-13, and eliminating the middle term,

$$\sum_j \sum_i (X_{ij} - \overline{G})^2 = \sum_j \sum_i (X_{ij} - \overline{X}_j)^2 + \sum_j n_j(\overline{X}_j - \overline{G})^2,$$

$$SS_T \qquad = \qquad SS_W \qquad + \qquad SS_B, \tag{14-17}$$

where SS_T is the **total sum of squares, SS_W is the sum of squares within,** and SS_B is the **sum of squares between.**

The total sum of squares on the left of 14-17 is composed of the two parts on the right, SS_W and SS_B. The sum of squares within is the sum of the squared deviations of individual scores from their group means, and the sum of squares between is the sum of the squared deviations of group means from the grand mean weighted by the number of subjects in each group. Equation 14-17 shows that we have partitioned the total sum of squares into two nonoverlapping portions, SS_W and SS_B. The total degrees of freedom are also partitioned, and thus

$$df_T \quad = \quad df_W \quad + \quad df_B,$$

$$(N - 1) = (N - k) + (k - 1). \tag{14-18}$$

Expected Value of the Mean Square Within. This section demonstrates that the variance within is an unbiased estimate of the population variance, a statement made earlier without proof. In connection with the independent 2-sample t test in Chapter 9, we developed a method of arriving at a single estimate of the population variance by pooling the sample variances observed in two independent samples. We now extend that method to the development of a single estimate of the population variance based on the variances observed in k samples.

The mean square within is equal to the sum of squares within divided by the degrees of freedom within. Thus,

$$MS_W = \frac{SS_W}{df_W} = \frac{\sum_j \sum_i (X_{ij} - \overline{X}_j)^2}{N - k}, \tag{14-19}$$

where MS_W is the mean square within. Noting that $N - k = k(n - 1)$ when all groups are the same size, and rewriting 14-19 using Equation 8-10,

$$MS_W = \sum_j \left[\frac{\sum_i^n X_{ij}^2 - \frac{\left(\sum_i^n X_{ij} \right)^2}{n}}{k(n-1)} \right] = S_W^2 = \text{Variance within.} \qquad (14\text{-}20)$$

Since 14-20 is identical to 14-4, it follows that the mean square within is identical to the variance within. Indeed, in Chapter 4, we defined the variance as the mean of the squared deviations from the mean, so our present use of the term "mean square" for a variance is consistent with that early definition.

In Equation 14-19,

$$SS_W = SS_1 + SS_2 + \cdots + SS_k, \qquad \text{and}$$

$$df_W = N - k = (n_1 - 1) + (n_2 - 1) + \cdots + (n_k - 1).$$

Rewriting 14-19,

$$MS_W = S_W^2 = \frac{SS_1 + SS_2 + \cdots + SS_k}{(n_1 - 1) + (n_2 - 1) + \cdots + (n_k - 1)}. \qquad (14\text{-}21)$$

Since the sum of squares within any group is equal to $(n-1)$ times the sample variance within that group,

$$MS_W = \frac{(n_1 - 1)S_1^2 + (n_2 - 1)S_2^2 + \cdots + (n_k - 1)S_k^2}{(n_1 - 1) + (n_2 - 1) + \cdots + (n_k - 1)}.$$

Taking expected values,

$$E[MS_W] = \frac{(n_1 - 1)E[S_1^2] + (n_2 - 1)E[S_2^2] + \cdots + (n_k - 1)E[S_k^2]}{(n_1 - 1) + (n_2 - 1) + \cdots + (n_k - 1)}. \qquad (14\text{-}22)$$

In Chapter 8, we showed that the variance of a single sample is an unbiased estimate of the population variance — that is, the expected value of a sample variance is equal to the population variance. Substituting the population variance for the expected values in 14-22, and factoring,

$$E[MS_W] = \frac{[(n_1 - 1) + (n_2 - 1) + \cdots + (n_k - 1)]\sigma_X^2}{(n_1 - 1) + (n_2 - 1) + \cdots + (n_k - 1)} = \sigma_X^2. \qquad (14\text{-}23)$$

Thus, the expected value of the mean square within — that is, the variance within — is equal to the population variance.

Where all the groups are the same size, the ns are all equal in the above equations. In that case, those equations can be somewhat simplified. However, the above development shows that MS_W is an unbiased estimator of the population variance whether the ns are equal or not.

Expected Value of the Mean Square Between.   Consider the variance of the sample means in each of the panels in Figure 14-1. The variance of the group means is 0 in Panel A, 12.00 in B, and 4.00 in C. But the variance *within* all of the groups in all of the panels is exactly 1.00. Thus, the variance of the sample means is independent of the variance within groups — not only in the contrived example here, but in general. As noted earlier, when some level of an independent variable has an effect, the result is the algebraic addition of a constant to each of the scores in the group of subjects receiving that level of the independent variable. Thus, the variance of that group remains unchanged no matter what the direction or magnitude of the effect. (You may wish to review the section in Chapter 4 dealing with the noneffect that adding or subtracting a constant has on the variance.) You can also see graphically in Figure 14-1 that the dispersion of every group is the same whether the group mean is high or low.

We will now find the expected value of the mean square between. Beginning with the sum of squares between, from Equation 14-17,

$$SS_B = \sum_j n_j(\bar{X}_j - \bar{G})^2 = \sum_j n_j(\bar{X}_j^2 - 2\bar{G}\bar{X}_j + \bar{G}^2)$$

$$= \sum_j n_j \left(\bar{X}_j^2 - 2\bar{G}\frac{\sum_i X_{ij}}{n_j} + \bar{G}^2 \right),$$

where n_j is the number of subjects in the jth group. In our present development, the groups may be of different sizes.

Noting that

$$\bar{G} = \frac{\sum_j \sum_i X_{ij}}{N},$$

and distributing the summation operator,

$$SS_B = \sum_j n_j\bar{X}_j^2 - 2\bar{G}\sum_j \sum_i X_{ij} + \sum_j n_j\bar{G}^2 = \sum_j n_j\bar{X}_j^2 - 2N\bar{G}^2 + \sum_j n_j\bar{G}^2.$$

Since $\bar{G}^2$ is constant for all groups, and since $\Sigma n_j = N$,

$$SS_B = \sum_j n_j\bar{X}_j^2 - 2N\bar{G}^2 + N\bar{G}^2 = \sum_j n_j\bar{X}_j^2 - N\bar{G}^2. \tag{14-24}$$

Taking expected values,

$$E(SS_B) = \sum_j n_j E(\bar{X}_j^2) - NE(\bar{G}^2). \tag{14-25}$$

Since $\sigma_{\bar{X}}^2 = E(\bar{X} - \mu)^2 = E(\bar{X}^2) - \mu^2$, as in Equation 6-10, and since $\sigma_{\bar{G}}^2 = E(\bar{G}^2) - \sigma^2$, substituting for $E(\bar{X}_j^2)$ and $E(\bar{G}^2)$ in 14-25,

$$E(SS_B) = \sum_j n_j(\sigma_{\bar{X}}^2 + \mu^2) - N(\sigma_{\bar{G}}^2 + \mu^2)$$

$$= \sum_j n_j \left[\frac{\sigma_X^2}{n_j} + \mu^2 \right] - N \left[\frac{\sigma_X^2}{N} + \mu^2 \right]$$

$$= k\sigma_X^2 + N\mu^2 - \sigma_X^2 - N\mu^2$$

$$= k\sigma_X^2 - \sigma_X^2 = \sigma_X^2(k - 1). \tag{14-26}$$

Since 14-26 is the expected value of SS_B, dividing by $k-1$ yields the expected value of the mean square between:

$$E\left(\frac{SS_B}{k-1}\right) = E(MS_B) = \frac{\sigma_X^2(k-1)}{(k-1)} = \sigma_X^2. \tag{14-27}$$

Thus, *when the null hypothesis is true,* the mean square between provides an unbiased estimate of the population variance. Since the mean square within provides an independent estimate of the population variance, those mean squares should not differ significantly when H_0 is true. But when H_0 is false — that is, when the independent variable has an effect — some of the deviation between the group means and the grand mean will be due to the effect of the independent variable. In that case, the mean square between is expected to be significantly larger than the mean square within, and the resulting F ratio is expected to be significantly larger than 1.

Computational Formulas.   We can now express the F ratio more conveniently in terms of the mean squares:

$$F = \frac{S_B^2}{S_W^2} = \frac{MS_B}{MS_W} = \frac{SS_B/df_B}{SS_W/df_W},$$

$$df_B = k-1, \quad df_W = N-k. \tag{14-28}$$

The expressions in Equation 14-17 could be used to calculate the sums of squares, but more convenient computational formulas can readily be found. From Equation 14-17,

$$SS_T = \sum_j \sum_i (X_{ij} - \bar{G})^2 = \sum_j \sum_i X_{ij}^2 - \frac{\left(\sum_j \sum_i X_{ij}\right)^2}{N}; \tag{14-29}$$

$$SS_W = \sum_j \sum_i (X_{ij} - \bar{X}_j)^2 = \sum_j \left[\sum_i X_{ij}^2 - \frac{\left(\sum_i X_{ij}\right)^2}{n_j}\right]$$

$$= \sum_j \sum_i X_{ij}^2 - \sum_j \frac{\left(\sum_i X_{ij}\right)^2}{n_j}; \tag{14-30}$$

and from Equations 14-17 and 14-24,

$$SS_B = \sum_j n_j(\bar{X}_j - \bar{G})^2 = \sum_j n_j \bar{X}_j^2 - N\bar{G}^2$$

$$= \sum_j n_j \left[\frac{\sum_i X_{ij}}{n_j}\right]^2 - N\frac{\left(\sum_j \sum_i X_{ij}\right)^2}{N^2}$$

$$= \sum_j \frac{\left(\sum_i X_{ij}\right)^2}{n_j} - \frac{\left(\sum_j \sum_i X_{ij}\right)^2}{N}. \tag{14-31}$$

Notice that each term on the right side of each of the three equations above also occurs in one of the other equations. For example, $\sum\sum X_{ij}^2$ occurs in 14-29 and 14-30. Thus, in finding all of the sums of squares, it is necessary to calculate each of those terms only once. We can write the above computational formulas very compactly if we substitute the symbols (1), (2), and (3) for those recurring quantities, letting

$$\frac{\left(\sum_j \sum_i X_{ij}\right)^2}{N} = (1), \quad \sum_j \sum_i X_{ij}^2 = (2), \quad \text{and} \quad \sum_j \frac{\left(\sum_i X_{ij}\right)^2}{n_j} = (3). \qquad (14\text{-}32)$$

Substituting in Equations 14-29, 14-30, and 14-31,

$$SS_T = (2) - (1), \quad SS_W = (2) - (3), \quad \text{and} \quad SS_B = (3) - (1). \qquad (14\text{-}33)$$

We showed earlier that the total sum of squares was equal to the sum of squares within added to the sum of squares between. Adding the computational symbols in 14-33 above also yields that result.

Table 14-1 demonstrates the use of the computational formulas. The notation here is essentially that of Winer (1971). Symbol (1) is the total sum of the Xs, that quantity squared, divided by the total number of cases. Symbol (2) is the sum of the squared Xs, each score individually squared. Symbol (3) instructs us to find the sum of the scores for a particular group, square that sum, divide by the number of cases in that group, and sum the results of those operations across all of the k groups. The use of the above computational formulas in Table 14-1 yields the same value of F as found earlier by using the calculated values of the sample variances and the variance of the sample means. As a check on arithmetic, be sure that $SS_B + SS_W = SS_T$, as in the example in Table 14-1. The fact that each sum of squares is a sum of squared deviations provides another arithmetic check: A sum of squares can never be negative, nor can an F ratio.

The significant F ratio in Table 14-1 tells us only that the independent variable has some kind of effect, without providing any further information on the nature of the effect. Thus, a significant F is an overall indication that there is *something* significant in a set of data. After finding a significant F, we are always interested in knowing which levels of the independent variable produce what kinds of effects—for example, which levels of a drug are most effective, or which teaching method produces the greatest amount of learning. Thus, differences between group means are of great interest. A later section describes procedures for testing those differences.

Unequal Sample Sizes

The computational formulas above can be used whether or not the groups are of equal size. However, it is better to design experiments having equal ns. The analysis of variance requires a normal distribution and homogeneity of variance within groups, but the consequences of moderate violations of those assumptions are less troublesome when the groups are the same size. In this respect, ANOVA is quite analogous to the independent 2-sample t test.

Table 14-2 shows the results of an experiment having three groups of unequal size. While it is preferable to have the same number of subjects in all groups, that may not always be possible. If an experiment takes place over an extended period of time, then there may be unavoidable loss of some subjects. For example, student subjects may transfer to another school, or drop out, and animal subjects may die. Thus, for a great many reasons, experiments that start out with equal ns may not end up that way.

The ANOVA is carried out using Formulas 14-32 and 14-33. The only

TABLE 14-2.   Analysis of Variance, Three Groups, Unequal ns.

A.   Basic data:

	Group 1		Group 2		Group 3			
	X_{i1}	X_{i1}^2	X_{i2}	X_{i2}^2	X_{i3}	X_{i3}^2		
	9	81	12	144	1	1		
	6	36	12	144	7	49		
	7	49	8	64	3	9	N = Total subjects	
	10	100	11	121	7	49	= $\sum_j n_j$ = 18	
	9	81	5	25	3	9		
	4	16			6	36		
	13	169						
$\sum_i X_{ij}$	58		48		27		$\sum_j \sum_i X_{ij}$ = G	= 133
$\sum_i X_{ij}^2$		532		498		153	$\sum_j \sum_i X_{ij}^2$	= 1183
$\bar{X}_j$	8.29		9.60		4.50		$\sum_j \sum_i X_{ij}/N$ = $\bar{G}$ =	7.39
S_j^2	8.57		9.30		6.30			

B.   Computational symbols from Formulas 14-32:

$$(1) = \frac{G^2}{N} = \frac{133^2}{18} = 982.72$$

$$(2) = \sum_j \sum_i X_{ij}^2 = 532 + 498 + 153 = 1183$$

$$(3) = \sum_j \left(\sum_i X_{ij}\right)^2 / n_j = \frac{58^2}{7} + \frac{48^2}{5} + \frac{27^2}{6} = 1062.87$$

C.   Summary analysis of variance:

Source	Computational Formulas 14-33	SS	df	MS	F
Treatment (Between)	(3) − (1)	80.15	2	40.08	5.00*
Error (Within)	(2) − (3)	120.13	15	8.01	
Total	(2) − (1)	200.28✓	17 = $N - 1$✓		

* $p < .05$

difference between the present analysis and our earlier equal-n example in Table 14-1 is in the calculation of Quantity (3). Here, each group total is squared and divided by n_j, which is a different number for each group, while all of the ns were equal in the earlier example. The degrees of freedom for both of the mean squares are found by the same formulas, whether the ns are equal or unequal, and the analysis proceeds in the same way in both cases. Procedures for testing differences between means, described in a later section, are also very similar for equal and unequal ns.

Requirements for the Independent-Groups ANOVA

Table 14-3 shows the requirements, that is, the assumptions that must be met in using an independent-groups ANOVA and in using the multiple comparisons described below. These requirements are closely related to the requirements for the independent 2-sample t test listed in Chapter 9. The numbered sections below explain each requirement.

1. Interval or Ratio Scale. Since ANOVA is a test of differences between means, in order for any such differences to be quantitatively meaningful, measurements of the dependent variable must comprise an interval or ratio scale. (However, in spite of this requirement, there exists a variety of analysis of variance applicable to ordinal data, the Kruskal-Wallis procedure, briefly mentioned in a later section.)

2. Normal Distribution. The F ratio is based on the assumption of a normally distributed population, but the F test is relatively robust with respect to departures from normality. In this respect, the analysis of variance is comparable to the t test.

3. Unknown Population Variance. ANOVA is applicable to multiple-group experiments and observations where the population variance is unknown and must be estimated from the within-groups variance.

4. Homogeneity of Variance Within Groups. ANOVA is based on the assumption that each group is a random sample drawn from the same population. If that is indeed the case, then none of the variances within the different groups should be expected to differ significantly — that is, we should expect the variances to be homogeneous. Since the population variance is

TABLE 14-3.   Requirements for the Independent-Groups Analysis of Variance.

1. Interval or ratio measurement scale.
2. Approximately normally distributed population.
3. Unknown population variance, estimated from variance within groups.
4. Homogeneity of variance within groups.
5. Effects of independent variable are additive at all levels.
6. All measurements are independent.

estimated from the within-groups variances, if those variances were significantly different, then the denominator of the F ratio would be in error. Heterogeneity of variance usually tends to increase the probability of a Type 1 error, although in some cases the probability of a Type 2 error is increased. Moderate departures from normality and homogeneity of variance are not of great consequence as long as the sample sizes are equal, or as nearly so as possible.

Heterogeneity of variance can sometimes arise when the different levels of the independent variable have different effects on the dependent variable, as described in the discussion of t test requirements in Chapter 9. In some cases, heterogeneity of variance can be essentially eliminated by transforming the data in some way, for example, by taking logarithms of the dependent measures, or by taking square roots. Gross heterogeneity can usually be detected by inspection of the data, by comparing the dispersion of the scores in all the groups. If any of the groups appear to differ greatly in variability, then the homogeneity of the variances can be tested by procedures described in Winer (1971), and an appropriate transformation can be made if necessary. Ordinarily, it is not necessary to test for homogeneity of variance unless there is strong evidence for heterogeneity.

5. Additivity of Effects.   Analysis of variance is based on the assumption that, where the independent variable has some effect, the result is the algebraic addition of some constant to each of the scores in a group. As we have noted several times in the past, the addition of a constant to all of the scores in a group does not change the variance within the group. Thus, the effect of the independent variable—which adds different constants to the scores in different groups—results in no change in the variance within any group. If the variances are homogeneous in the different groups before the application of the different levels of the independent variable, then the variances will also be homogeneous at the end of the experiment—as long as the effects of the independent variable are additive. If the effects were multiplicative—that is, if the effect of each different level of the independent variable were to multiply the scores in each group by a different constant—then the variances within groups would be heterogeneous. Indeed, the requirement of additivity is implied by the requirement of homogeneity of variance, since variances can be homogeneous only where effects are additive.

6. Independent Measurements.   All measurements must be independent. No subject's response can be allowed to influence any other subject's response.

Repeated Measures

As noted earlier, the independent-groups ANOVA is an extension of the independent 2-sample t test. A repeated-measures ANOVA analogously extends the repeated-measures t test to a situation where there are more than two levels of the independent variable. For example, in a learning experiment, the performance of a group of subjects might be measured repeatedly after successively greater amounts of practice. The same basic procedures that we have developed in connection with the independent-groups ANOVA can be extended to the repeated-measures case. However, we will not be able to develop those procedures within the confines of the present text. Several varieties of repeated-measures analyses can be found in Winer (1971). You can easily extend the procedures described in this chapter to the calculation of a single-factor repeated-measures ANOVA.

Factorial Designs

The single-factor ANOVA described in this chapter can be extended to a factorial design having two or more independent variables, although the computational details cannot be presented here because of space limitations. The logic of a factorial design was described in Chapter 13. Factorial designs can utilize independent groups, or repeated measures. Although we have not developed the computational details, the material that we have presented should help you understand the major features of factorial designs when you find them reported in the psychological literature.

Testing Differences Between Means

Since a significant F in an ANOVA provides only an overall indication that there is something significant in the data — perhaps a difference between a single pair of means, or some combination of means — it is always useful to carry out additional tests after finding a significant F in order to learn the nature of the effects of the independent variable. Such tests are called **a posteriori,** or **post hoc tests** — meaning tests that are done after the fact, in a sense. We will describe procedures for *a posteriori* tests that will not raise the probability of a Type 1 error above our chosen *alpha* level.

In some cases, it is possible to formulate a hypothesis regarding a difference between one particular pair of means, or between a few specific pairs, **a priori** — that is, before the data are gathered and before an F ratio is calculated. *A priori* hypotheses, often called **planned comparisons,** can be tested whether or not the ANOVA yields a significant F. For example, suppose a researcher has devised a political attitude scale to measure the liberal-conservative dimension. Now suppose the researcher hypothesizes *a priori* that Democrats and Republicans will differ on that dimension, but has no notion whether Independents will differ from people preferring either major party. Since a planned comparison can be tested in the absence of a significant F, it might appear that it would be a waste of time to do an ANOVA. But the mean square within provides an estimate of the population variance that is used in making planned comparisons, as described below. Furthermore, if the ANOVA yields a significant F, then all remaining pairs of means can be tested *a posteriori* — that is, those means for which no comparisons were planned *a priori*.

In the absence of any *a priori* hypotheses, all pairs of means can nevertheless be tested *a posteriori*, provided that the ANOVA has yielded a significant F ratio. *A posteriori* tests are often called **unplanned comparisons.** In the above example, if the researcher had no specific *a priori* hypotheses regarding differences between particular groups, then after observing a significant F in an ANOVA, all possible pairs of means could be tested by the *a posteriori* procedures to be described.

A Priori Tests

Consider the above example, where a researcher hypothesizes *a priori* that Democrats and Republicans will differ on a liberal-conservative dimension, but has no specific hypothesis regarding Independent voters. The results of a hypothetical survey using three groups of subjects are shown in Table 14-4. Although the F ratio is significant — just barely — in the ANOVA, it would be appropriate to carry out a planned comparison even if the F were not significant. The appropriate test here is a 2-tailed t test based on the mean square within from the ANOVA. As explained below, such a t ratio is essentially identical to the independent 2-sample t test developed in Chapter 9.

The rationale for using MS_W in a t ratio is straightforward. By Formula 9-10, the independent 2-sample t test is

$$t = \frac{\overline{X}_a - \overline{X}_b}{\sqrt{S^2\left(\dfrac{1}{n_a} + \dfrac{1}{n_b}\right)}}. \tag{9-10}$$

In the above equation, S^2 is an unbiased estimate of the population variance based on the sample variance within the two groups. In an ANOVA design, there are k groups, and we have shown that MS_W is an unbiased estimate of the population variance based on the variance within those k groups. Thus, MS_W is a better estimate of the population variance than an estimate based on only two groups, since more information leads to a better estimate. Substituting MS_W for S^2 in Equation 9-10 yields the formula for an *a priori* t test of a difference between two means:

$$t = \frac{\overline{X}_a - \overline{X}_b}{\sqrt{MS_W\left(\dfrac{1}{n_a} + \dfrac{1}{n_b}\right)}}, \quad df = df_W = N - k, \tag{14-34}$$

where MS_W is the mean square within from an ANOVA, n_a and n_b are the sample sizes, and df is the degrees of freedom for MS_W.

TABLE 14-4.   Analysis of Variance, *a Priori* and *a Posteriori* Tests. Hypothetical Study, Liberalism and Political Party Preference; 3 Groups, 21 Subjects Per Group.

A. Analysis of variance: $k = 3$, $n = 21$, $N = 63$.

Source	SS	df	MS	F
Preference (Between groups)	186.14	2	93.07	3.15*
Error (Within groups)	1772.48	60	29.54	
Total	1958.62	62 $= N - 1$		

$* p < .05$

B. Group means arranged in order of magnitude:

		$\bar{X}_R$	$\bar{X}_I$	$\bar{X}_D$
		9.07	9.62	12.96
$\bar{X}_R$	9.07	—	0.55	3.89*
$\bar{X}_I$	9.62		—	3.34
$\bar{X}_D$	12.96			—

        $* p < .05$, *a priori*.

C. *A priori* test (planned comparison), Democrats versus Republicans:

By Formula 14-35,

$$t = \frac{\bar{X}_D - \bar{X}_R}{\sqrt{\dfrac{2MS_W}{n}}} = \frac{3.89}{\sqrt{\dfrac{2(29.54)}{21}}} = 2.319;$$

$$df = df_W = 60.$$

reject H_0, $p < .05$.

D. *A posteriori* tests (unplanned comparisons):

Entering the value of $r_\alpha(m, df)$ from Table I in Formula 14-36:

$$R_\alpha(m, df) = r_\alpha(m, df) \sqrt{\frac{MS_W}{n}};$$

$$R_{.05}(2, 60) = r_{.05}(2, 60) \sqrt{\frac{29.54}{21}} = 2.83(1.19) = 3.37.$$

		m = Number of means in range	
		2	3
Standardized range	$r_{.05}$	2.83	3.40
Critical range	$R_{.05}$	3.37	4.05

Comparing critical ranges here with differences in Section B, no *a posteriori* comparison is significant.

Formula 14-34 can be used for equal or unequal *n*s. For an *a priori* test with equal *n*s, the above formula simplifies to the following:

$$t = \frac{\bar{X}_a - \bar{X}_b}{\sqrt{\dfrac{2MS_W}{n}}}, \quad df = df_W = N - k, \tag{14-35}$$

where $n_a = n_b = n$.

The use of Formula 14-35 is demonstrated in the *a priori* test in Table 14-4C. The observed value of t exceeds the critical value at the .05 level for 60 df, and thus H_0 is rejected at the .05 level. To indicate that the difference between Democrats and Republicans is significant at the .05 level, a single asterisk is placed beside that difference in Table 14-3B.

After *a posteriori* tests are explained below, the *a posteriori* tests in Table 14-4D will be discussed.

A Posteriori Tests

We will use the data from the ANOVA in Table 14-1 to demonstrate the procedures for running *a posteriori* tests of the differences between all pairs of group means. All of the groups are the same size in that example. Later, we will demonstrate procedures for use with unequal *ns*.

After observing a significant *F* ratio in the ANOVA, the next step is to arrange the group means in order of magnitude, as in Table 14-5A. We then find the difference between each pair of means in that table. The problem now is to decide which of those differences is or are significant.

In carrying out an ANOVA, we assume that each group is a random sample from a normally distributed population. That assumption is one of the requirements described earlier. Now suppose that we have a normally distributed population, and suppose we draw two random samples from that population. In that case, the independent 2-sample *t* test provides a test of the significance of the difference between those two means. Now suppose we draw a third random sample. If we wish to test the difference between the largest and smallest of our three means, then a *t* test is no longer appropriate. Even when the null hypothesis is true — that is, when each group is indeed a random sample from the same population — if we draw more than two

TABLE 14-5. *A Posteriori* Tests of Differences Between Means, Equal *ns*, Data From Table 14-1

			$\bar{X}_2$	$\bar{X}_1$	$\bar{X}_4$	$\bar{X}_3$
			4.25	5.25	6.38	8.75
A.	Group means arranged in order of magnitude in margins of table. Body of table shows differences between means.	$\bar{X}_2$ 4.25	—	1.00	2.13	4.50**
		$\bar{X}_1$ 5.25		—	1.13	3.50*
		$\bar{X}_4$ 6.38			—	2.37
		$\bar{X}_3$ 8.75				—

* $p < .05$, ** $p < .01$.

			m = Number of means		
			2	3	4
B.	Standardized and critical ranges. See calculations below.	Standardized range[a] $r_{.05}$	2.90	3.51	3.87
		Critical range $R_{.05}$	2.51	3.05	3.37
		Standardized range[a] $r_{.01}$	3.91	4.48	4.84
		Critical range $R_{.01}$	3.40	3.90	4.21

[a] By interpolation in Table I.

C. Calculating some selected critical ranges for 28 *df* by Formula 14-36:

$$R_\alpha(m, df) = r_\alpha(m, df)\sqrt{\frac{MS_W}{n}}; \quad df = df_W = N - k = 28; \quad n = 8.$$

$$R_{.05}(2, 28) = r_{.05}(2, 28)\sqrt{\frac{6.01}{8}} = 2.90(.87) = 2.51$$

$$R_{.01}(4, 28) = r_{.01}(4, 28)(.87) = 4.48(.87) = 4.21.$$

random samples, then we are likely to observe greater differences between the largest and smallest means — just by chance — as the number of samples increases. Thus, if there are several groups in an ANOVA design, then a t test of the difference between the largest and smallest means — even when H_0 is true — will often yield a t ratio exceeding the critical value — thus increasing the probability of a Type 1 error.

The **Newman-Keuls procedure** (Newman, 1939; Keuls, 1952; Winer, 1971) takes the number of groups into account in testing the differences between all possible pairs of means. For each particular pair of means, the Newman-Keuls procedure utilizes a **critical range,** which is the smallest difference between that pair of means that can be judged statistically significant. Thus, the critical range is a critical value which a difference between a pair of means must equal or exceed in order to be significant.

The group means are arranged in ascending order across the top of Table 14-5A, and also down the left side of that table. The numbers in the body of that table are the differences between all of the possible pairs of means. Now consider the range of values between the smallest and largest means, that is, the values between 4.25 and 8.75 inclusive. Since there are four means falling within that range of values, $\bar{X}_2$, $\bar{X}_1$, $\bar{X}_4$, and $\bar{X}_3$, that region of the measurement scale is called the **range of 4 means.** Numerically, the range of the 4 means in Table 14-5A is 4.50, and that is the value of the largest difference in the top row of that table. The difference between the smallest and the next-to-the largest mean is 2.13, and that difference is a range of 3 means. The smallest difference in the top row is 1.00, the difference between the smallest and the next largest mean, representing a range of 2 means. The differences in the second row of the table represent ranges of 2 and 3 means, and the difference in the bottom row is a range of 2 means. Thus, there are three ranges of 2 means, two of 3 means, and one range of 4 means in Table 14-5A.

Each of the differences in Table 14-5A represents an **observed range** of 2, 3, or 4 means. Those observed ranges are compared with critical ranges found by the following formula:

$$\text{Critical range} = R_\alpha(m, df) = r_\alpha(m, df) \sqrt{\frac{MS_W}{n}}, \quad df = df_W = N - k, \quad (14\text{-}36)$$

where $R_\alpha(m, df)$ is the critical range for m means at an *alpha* level of .05 or .01, $r_\alpha(m, df)$ is a **standardized range** found in Table I, MS_W is the mean square within from an ANOVA, n is the number of subjects in each group, and df is the degrees of freedom for MS_W. After demonstrating the use of Formula 14-36, we will explain its rationale.

Values of $r_{.05}$ and $r_{.01}$ for ranges of 2, 3, and 4 means are listed in Table 14-5B. Those standardized ranges were found using Table I. The degrees of freedom are listed in the left margin of that table, and the number of means are listed across the top. In the present case, MS_W has 28 df, a number not listed in Table I. Thus, we must **interpolate** between the listed values for 24 and 30 *df*, as shown below for $r_{.05}(2, 28)$:

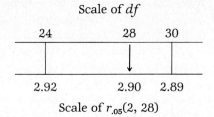

On the *df* scale above, 28 is 4/6 of the way from 24 toward 30, and thus the standardized range for 28 *df* is 4/6 of the way from 2.92 to 2.89. The values of the other standardized ranges are found similarly. This method of interpolation is quite general, and can be used in other kinds of tables.

Values of the critical ranges $R_\alpha(m, 28)$ listed in Table 14-5B were calculated by Formula 14-36, as demonstrated in Table 14-5C. A standardized range from Table I is a critical value of a difference between the means of two samples from a standard normal population, a distribution having a mean of 0 and a standard deviation of 1. Thus, Formula 14-36 transforms a standardized range into a critical range measured in raw-score units. Those critical ranges are then compared with the observed differences between means in Table 14-5A.

There is a particular order in which the observed differences between means must be tested. Using the values of $R_{.05}$, the differences in Row 1 are tested first, those in Row 2 next, and the difference in the bottom row is tested last. The largest difference in the first row, always the rightmost value, is tested first. Since there are four groups in the experiment, the largest difference covers a range of 4 means, the largest and smallest, and the two means lying between. Since 4.50 is greater than 3.37, the difference between $\overline{X}_2$ and $\overline{X}_3$ is significant at the .05 level, and is marked by an asterisk in Table 14-5A. The reason for the double asterisk is explained below.

If the largest difference between means had not been significant, no other differences in Table 14-5A would have been tested. But since the largest difference is significant, the next largest difference in Row 1 is then tested. That difference — covering a range of 3 means, $\overline{X}_2$, $\overline{X}_1$ and $\overline{X}_4$ — is compared with $R_{.05}(3)$. Since 2.13 is less than 3.05, the difference between $\overline{X}_2$ and $\overline{X}_4$ is not significant. When a nonsignificant difference is found in any row, no smaller difference is tested, such as the difference of 1.00 between $\overline{X}_2$ and $\overline{X}_1$. Since the value of $\overline{X}_1$ (5.25) lies within the range of values between $\overline{X}_2$ and $\overline{X}_4$ (4.25 – 6.38), if the difference between those last means is not significant, then it would not be reasonable to expect the range between $\overline{X}_2$ and $\overline{X}_1$ (4.25 – 5.25) to be significant. In rare instances, where two means lie within a range that has been found nonsignificant, those means can nevertheless appear to differ significantly if they are tested. Thus, to avoid that inconsistency, means lying within a nonsignificant range — $\overline{X}_2$ and $\overline{X}_1$, for example — are not tested.

The largest difference in Row 2, covering a range of 3 means — $\overline{X}_1$, $\overline{X}_4$, and $\overline{X}_3$ — is tested next. That difference is larger than 3.05, and thus is marked by a single asterisk indicating significance at the .05 level. Each of the remaining differences, 1.13 in Row 2 and 2.37 in Row 3, covers a range of 2 means. Neither of those differences is significant, since neither is as large as 2.51, the critical value of $R_{.05}(2)$.

The differences are now tested at the .01 level using the appropriate values of $R_{.01}(m, 28)$. Only those differences already found significant at the .05 level could possibly be significant at .01, and thus at this stage, only those differences already marked by a single asterisk are tested. Since 4.50 is greater than 4.21, that difference is now marked by a double asterisk, indicating significance at the .01 level. The other difference found significant at .05 is not significant at .01, since 3.50 is less than 3.90.

Some statisticians would argue that a single level of significance should be used for any collection of tests, whether the present multiple range tests or any other variety. However, the prevailing practice is to report the different levels of significance that may be found in a set of several comparisons. By convention, levels of probability numerically greater than .05 are not considered significant, and are not ordinarily reported.

Rationale for the Tests. Now that we have demonstrated the mechanics of testing the differences between means, we will further explain the rationale for those tests. Now consider the t ratio in Formula 14-35. In every t test, a calculated value of t is compared with a critical value of t. Thus, it follows that we can substitute a critical value of t in Formula 14-35, and then solve that equation for the critical value of the difference between the two means — that is, the smallest value of the difference that must be observed in order to reject H_0. Thus,

$$t_\alpha \sqrt{2} \sqrt{\frac{MS_W}{n}} = \text{Critical value of } (\overline{X}_a - \overline{X}_b) = R_\alpha(2, df);$$

$$df = 2(n - 1) = df_W = N - k. \tag{14-37}$$

Since there are only two means to be compared in a t test, the critical value of the difference between means in 14-37 is equal to the critical range of 2 means — that is, $R_\alpha(2, df)$. Referring now to Equation 14-36, letting $m = 2$, and substituting that expression for $R_\alpha(2, df)$ in 14-37,

$$t_\alpha \sqrt{2} \sqrt{\frac{MS_W}{n}} = r_\alpha(2, df) \sqrt{\frac{MS_W}{n}}, \qquad \text{and thus} \qquad r_\alpha(2, df) = t_\alpha \sqrt{2}. \tag{14-38}$$

The above equation shows that the standardized range of 2 means is equal to the critical value of t multiplied by the square root of 2. In Table B, the critical value of t for 28 df for a 2-tailed test at the .05 level is 2.048. Multiplying that t value by $\sqrt{2}$ yields 2.90, the value of $r_{.05}(2, 28)$ that we found by interpolation in Table I. That value is listed in Table 14-5B. Notice that both of the other standardized ranges at the .05 level, $r_{.05}(3)$ and $r_{.05}(4)$, are larger than $r_{.05}(2)$. As we noted earlier, the probability of observing a greater difference between the largest and smallest means increases as the number of means increases.

Thus, the critical values of the standardized ranges are made larger as the number of means increases in order to keep the probability of a Type 1 error no greater than α, regardless of the range of any two means that are compared. Since the standardized ranges are based on the t ratio, "Student's" t, the standardized ranges in Table I have been called **Studentized ranges,** after W. S. Gosset's pen name. Winer (1971) provides a more detailed discussion of the rationale underlying the Newman-Keuls procedure.

Unequal *ns*

Where the groups in an ANOVA are unequal in size, *a priori* tests—planned comparisons—use the t ratio in Formula 14-34. Except for the use of MS_W in place of S^2, that test is identical to the independent 2-sample t tests described in Chapter 9.

A *posteriori* tests involving unequal *ns* require critical ranges that take into account the differing numbers of subjects entering into each comparison between means. Standardized ranges are found in Table I using the number of means covered by each comparison and the df_W from the ANOVA. Formula 14-39 then gives the values of the critical ranges in raw-score units:

$$R_\alpha(m, df) = r_\alpha(m, df) \sqrt{\frac{MS_W}{2}\left(\frac{1}{n_a} + \frac{1}{n_b}\right)}; \quad df = df_W = N - k; \quad (14\text{-}39)$$

where n_a and n_b are the numbers of subjects in Groups a and b, and the other symbols are as defined in Formula 14-36.

As you can see, the *a posteriori* procedures are very similar for equal and unequal *ns*. Indeed, if $n_a = n_b = n$, then Formula 14-39 simplifies to 14-36, the formula for equal *ns*. An exercise at the end of the chapter will help clarify the above procedure for unequal *ns*.

Comparing *a Priori* and *a Posteriori* Tests

In order to compare these procedures, we return to the *a priori* test in Table 14-4 that was described above. As we found earlier, the planned comparison between Democrats and Republicans was significant. But what if the researcher had not decided *a priori* to test that difference—that is, had not decided before the experiment to make that test as a planned comparison? Since the F ratio in the ANOVA is significant, it would then be appropriate to test the differences between all pairs of means using the *a posteriori* procedures we have described. Thus, critical ranges are calculated in Table 14-4D using Formula 14-36. Since the difference between Democrats and Republicans is less than the value of $R_{.05}(3)$, that difference is not significant by an *a posteriori* test, nor is either of the other differences in Table 14-4A.

Since the *a priori* test in Table 14-4 leads to the rejection of the null hypothesis while the *a posteriori* test does not, it appears that the former procedure provides a more powerful, sensitive test. Indeed, it is true without exception that the planned comparisons that we have described are more powerful than the unplanned comparisons. Thus, if the null hypothesis is false, an *a priori* test is more likely to lead to the rejection of H_0 than is an *a posteriori* test, thus decreasing the probability of a Type 2 error. Now if that is the case, then why not decide before conducting a study to test all pairs of means using the more powerful *a priori* procedure? The answer is straightforward: An *a priori* test not only decreases the probability of a Type 2 error, but at the same time *increases* the probability of a Type 1 error.

At this point, it may be helpful to refer back to our discussion of **power** in Chapter 8, particularly to Figure 8-6. For our present purposes, suppose μ_0 in that figure represents the sampling distribution of the difference between the means of the Democrats and Republicans in Table 14-4 under the null hypothesis, and suppose μ_1 represents that distribution under the alternative hypothesis. Now suppose that CV_1 in that figure represents the critical range for an *a posteriori* test. Running an *a priori* test is equivalent to lowering CV_1 and that has the effect of increasing the power of the test, the area labeled $(1 - \beta)$, and also increasing the probability of a Type 1 error, the area labeled $\alpha/2$.

In a design having several groups of subjects, it would be most unusual for a researcher to have a clear basis *a priori* for expecting all possible pairs of means to differ significantly. In the absence of a clear rationale for such comparisons, running a large number of tests by *a priori* procedures greatly increases the Type 1 error rate. Thus, *a priori* tests — planned comparisons — should be judiciously limited to a small number of specific hypotheses, formulated before a study is undertaken, and supported by well defined reasoning. However, after a study is completed, some pairs of means that the researcher had not decided to test *a priori* may nevertheless differ significantly by *a posteriori* tests. The use of *a posteriori* procedures for those unplanned, *post hoc* comparisons guards against an excessive Type 1 error rate and still allows a researcher the opportunity of making unexpected discoveries in a set of data.

The Size of an Effect

The concept of the **size of an effect** was introduced in Chapter 13 in connection with discussions of appropriate sample sizes. Those ideas also extend to the analysis of variance. A large F ratio — yielding a low probability, and thus highly significant results — is not necessarily an indication that the independent variable has a large effect. A very small effect can produce a very large F ratio if the sample sizes are large.

As in our earlier development, the size of an effect can be measured in terms of the estimated standard deviation of the population. Since the error variance, the mean square within, is an unbiased estimate of the population variance, the square root of that quantity gives an estimate of the standard deviation. Dividing the largest difference between means by the standard deviation, that is, by $\sqrt{MS_W}$, gives a measure of that difference in standard deviation units, and gives a rough idea of the size of effect. For example, for the largest difference between means in Table 14-5,

$$\text{Size of effect} = \frac{D_{max}}{S} = \frac{D_{max}}{\sqrt{MS_W}} = \frac{4.50}{\sqrt{6.01}} = 1.84, \tag{14-40}$$

where D_{max} is the maximum difference between means, S is the estimated standard deviation, and MS_W is the error variance in the ANOVA. As we noted earlier in connection with the independent 2-sample t test, Cohen (1977) considers effects on the order of $.2S$, $.5S$, and $.8S$ to be small, moderate, and large respectively. Thus, a difference of $1.84S$ between the largest and smallest means — that is, 1.84 times as large as the standard deviation — is a large effect in those terms.

Other measures of the size of effect in the analysis of variance have also been proposed. Cohen offers another measure consisting of the standard deviation of the observed sample means divided by the estimated standard deviation of the population. That measure, as opposed to the measure based on D_{max}, takes all of the sample means into account. The size of an effect can also be measured in terms of the strength of association between the independent and dependent variables — that is, the extent to which different levels of the independent variable tend to produce different values of the dependent variable (see Hays, 1981).

Other Multiple Comparisons

A **multiple comparison** is a test of a difference between a pair of means, or between some combination of means, in a multiple-group experiment. The *a priori* and *a posteriori* procedures that we have described — planned and unplanned comparisons — represent two varieties of multiple comparisons. We will briefly describe some other multiple comparisons.

The Newman-Keuls procedure, which we described in detail, is only one of several *a posteriori* tests of differences between all pairs of means. **Duncan's new multiple-range test** is a widely used procedure that uses smaller critical ranges than the Newman-Keuls test. Thus, Duncan's test is less conservative — more prone to Type 1 errors — than the Newman-Keuls, but Duncan's test also yields a lower Type 2 error rate, and thus has greater power. Tukey's **HSD** (*honestly significant difference*) test uses a single critical value for testing the differences between all pairs of means. In the HSD test, that single critical value is identical to the critical range that would be found by the Newman-Keuls procedure for the largest difference between means. Thus, the HSD test is a very conservative procedure, but the low rate of Type 1 error is achieved at the expense of a loss of power — that is, at the cost of an increase in the Type 2 error rate. You can find more detailed comparisons between these tests in Kirk (1982) and Winer (1971). All things considered, I recommend the Newman-Keuls procedure to you most highly.

Trend Analysis.   As noted earlier, ANOVA is appropriate where the dependent variable is measured on an interval or ratio scale. The independent variable can consist of any kind of measurements—nominal, ordinal, interval, or ratio. Where the independent variable constitutes an interval or ratio scale, it is sometimes possible to see an orderly, systematic relationship between the independent and dependent variables. Indeed, in some cases it is possible to find a regression equation expressing predicted values of the dependent variable as a function of the independent variable. In the context of analysis of variance, the procedure for finding the nature of the relationship between the independent and dependent variables is called **trend analysis.**

Figure 14-5 shows a **linear trend,** a straight-line relationship between the dependent and independent variables in an ANOVA design. Each level of the independent variable was administered to a different group of subjects. The dependent measures are group means. The independent variable might consist of different levels of age, drug dosage, different amounts of practice on a learning task, or almost anything else we could conceive of that could be measured on an interval or ratio scale. The dependent variable might consist of trials to criterion, performance speed, or any other kind of interval or ratio measurement. The regression line fitted to the data in Figure 14-5 shows that the predicted values of the dependent variable are a linear function of the independent variable. Trend analysis can also be applied to curvilinear relationships between variables. Although trend analysis is no more complicated than other procedures that we have presented in detail, we will not be able to pursue this topic further because of time and space limitations. Extended treatments of trend analysis can be found in Kirk (1982) and Winer (1971).

Testing Combinations of Means. In some cases, a researcher may wish to make a single comparison involving more than two means. For example, in the study of the liberal-conservative dimension in Table 14-4, the

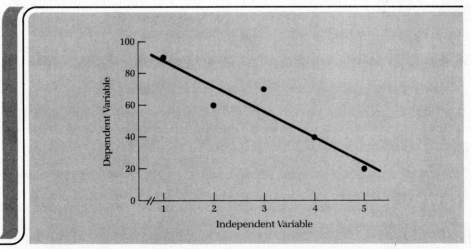

FIGURE 14-5. Linear trend in the group means in a multiple-group design. For a trend analysis, independent variable, as well as dependent variable, must be measured on an interval or ratio scale.

F ratio was significant in the ANOVA, but there was no significant difference between any of the group means by the *a posteriori* tests that we applied. However, by another *a posteriori* procedure, the combined mean of the Democrats and Independents differs significantly from the mean of the Republicans. Indeed, a significant overall *F* implies that there must be *some* significant difference somewhere in the data — a difference between a pair of means, or between some combination of means — that can be found by some *a posteriori* procedure. Such comparisons can readily be made, using procedures described in the references mentioned above.

Nominal and Ordinal Scales

The Kruskal-Wallis Analysis of Variance by Ranks

The Mann-Whitney *U* test, described in Chapter 9, is a test of the difference between two independent samples where the dependent variable is measured on an ordinal scale. The **Kruskal-Wallis analysis of variance by ranks** extends the Mann-Whitney procedure to situations where there are three or more independent groups. Thus, the Kruskal-Wallis procedure bears the same relationship to the Mann-Whitney *U* test as the independent-groups ANOVA bears to the independent 2-sample *t* test. An excellent description of the Kruskal-Wallis procedure can be found in Mosteller and Rourke (1973), and good computational examples in Siegel (1956).

One-Variable *Chi*-Square Tests: Frequencies and Proportions

In Chapter 7, we developed the binomial test of a difference between the frequencies of cases observed in two nominal categories — such as number of male and female births, or number of men and women in a sample of 80-year-olds. In many cases, we are interested in comparing the frequencies observed in three or more categories — for example, the frequencies of voters expressing the following political preferences: Democratic, Republican, Other, and None. The one-variable *chi*-square test, described in detail in the next chapter, provides an extension of the binomial to a test of differences between the frequencies observed in three or more categories. In all of those situations, each subject is classified into one and only one category — male, female, or one or another political preference — and is thus measured on a nominal scale.

Some Final Words

The procedures described in this chapter are being continually applied in a very wide range of research situations. Indeed, the analysis of variance is the most widely used procedure at the present time in the entire field of psychological research. Thus, it will certainly be to your advantage to understand these procedures. The one-variable *chi*-square test—to be developed in the next chapter—is less widely used in psychological research, though an important procedure nevertheless.

Terms and Symbols

As you review the following terms and symbols, and the ideas they represent, consider carefully the relationships between the procedures in the present chapter and the procedures we have dealt with earlier. I have emphasized many points of similarity, and you will be able to discover others for yourself.

Analysis of variance	**Studentized range**
Treatment	**Size of an effect**
Grand mean	**Power**
Additivity of effects	**Multiple comparisons**
Variance within groups	**Duncan's new multiple range**
Variance between groups	**test**
F ratio	**HSD test**
Sum of squares	**Trend analysis**
Mean square within	**Linear trend**
Mean square between	**Homogeneity of variance**
Partitioning	**Kruskal-Wallis analysis of**
Deviation within and **deviation**	**variance by ranks**
between	$\overline{G}$
Null hypothesis in ANOVA	X_{ij}
Alternative hypotheses in	n
ANOVA	k
A priori **test**	N
A posteriori **test**	S_W^2
Planned comparison	S_B^2
Unplanned comparison	F
Post hoc **test**	$E(MS_W)$
Newman-Keuls procedure	$E(MS_B)$
Critical range	$R_\alpha(m, df)$
Range of *m* **means**	$r_\alpha(m, df)$
Standardized range	D_{max}
Interpolation	

EXERCISES AND STUDY QUESTIONS

1. Suppose you have just calculated an *F* ratio in an ANOVA, and you have found that $F(2, 27) = -5.49$. What do you do now?

2. a. When is it permissible to make *a priori* and *a posteriori* comparisons in an ANOVA design?

   b. What are the consequences of making the above comparisons in situations where they should not be made, and failing to make them where they should be?

3. Suppose the data below represent the results of a study of the perceived quality of life in the workplace in a major corporation among workers in 5 categories of jobs: Unskilled labor, skilled labor, clerical, management, and professional. Quality of life was measured by a 40-item test assessing the workers' perceptions of adequacy and fairness of pay, caliber of supervision, job safety, and a number of other environmental variables. Higher numbers indicate higher perceived quality of life.

X_1	X_2	X_3	X_4	X_5
6	19	9	17	16
12	8	17	15	7
11	15	7	21	13
15	19	17	25	23
5	8	12	15	26
7	15	10	22	19
4	15	6	31	15
11	12	6	28	14
7	5	10	14	12
10	19	16	11	14

   a. Is this study an experiment or an observation? Briefly explain your answer, and explain why this distinction is important.

   b. Justify using an ANOVA. State the null hypothesis in words and symbols, and state the alternative hypothesis.

   c. Calculate the F ratio, indicate whether you reject the null hypothesis, and explain what your decision means.

   d. *A priori*, before gathering the data, suppose you had decided to test the perceptions of unskilled vs skilled laborers. Carry out an *a priori* test of the difference between those groups.

   e. Do an *a posteriori* test of each pair of means.

   f. After seeing the data, you notice that the difference between managers and professionals looks rather substantial, though not significant by an *a posteriori* test. Would it then be permissible to subject that difference to an *a priori* test?

   g. Based on the observed means, are we justified in concluding that managers on the average perceive their quality of life to be more than twice as high as that of unskilled laborers? Briefly explain your answer.

   h. Draw a graph showing the results.

   i. Are the observed differences between means large or small, in terms of the discussion of the size of an effect in Chapters 13 and 14?

4. So far, we have said nothing about the way the subjects were chosen in the above study. Comment on the difficulties that the following procedures would raise, particularly regarding internal and external validity.

a. To save time and effort, suppose the researcher decided to mail questionnaires to a random sample of 20 persons chosen from each category of worker.

b. Using the Personnel Department's roster of the 5 categories of workers, the researcher chooses the first ten names appearing in alphabetical order in each category.

c. On a typical workday, the researcher selects for participation the first 10 workers in each category appearing in the company cafeteria.

d. Suppose each worker must be tested individually, and suppose that the researcher can comfortably test no more than 10 subjects per day. For convenience, the researcher tests each group of subjects on successive days, moving from one department to another.

e. So that all of the subjects can be tested on the same day, the researcher enlists the aid of 5 assistants. Each assistant claims to feel most comfortable interacting with one or another of the categories of workers, and is thus allowed to test that particular category and no other.

5. Exactly how would you go about choosing a random sample of 10 workers from each category in the preceding problem? Don't just say, "Use a table of random numbers, or use a random-number routine on a calculator." Be specific.

6. In the interest of energy conservation, a human factors psychologist has designed a study of the effects of lower levels of lighting on productivity. In the final assembly stage on a computer production line, each worker's station is lighted by 4 40-Watt fluorescent tubes. The psychologist chooses a random sample of 40 workers and randomly assigns 10 subjects to each of the following levels of illumination: 1, 2, 3, or 4 tubes. Because of the large potential saving, the psychologist, and company management, are especially interested in comparing the lowest and highest levels of illumination. Suppose the data below represent the mean number of units, rounded to the nearest integer, assembled during an 8-hour workday over a period of 4 weeks. Unfortunately, some of the workers quit their jobs during the period of the study, hence the unequal ns.

X_1	X_2	X_3	X_4
16	15	21	17
15	17	22	17
18	20	24	18
17	18	22	21
14	16	21	21
19	21	18	22
16	17	17	21
18	15	18	16
14		17	20
17		21	

      a. Is this study an experiment or an observation?

      b. Justify an ANOVA. State the null and alternative hypotheses.

      c. Calculate the F ratio, and indicate whether you reject H_0.

      d. Justify an *a priori* test of $\bar{X}_1$ vs $\bar{X}_4$.

      e. Justify *a posteriori* tests of the differences between the other means, and do the tests.

      f. Draw a graph showing the results. Does there appear to be a trend in the data?

      g. How do you explain the observed difference between $\bar{X}_3$ and $\bar{X}_4$ favoring the lower level of illumination?

      h. In the light of the results, what would you advise company management to do, carefully considering the possible costs and benefits?

7. How is it that the analysis of *variance* turns out to be a test of differences between *means*? In answering this question, consider the nature of the independent estimates of the population variance, and the concept of an effect of the independent variable.

Frequencies and Proportions in Multiple Categories

15

We began the last chapter by noting that the independent-groups analysis of variance is an extension of the independent 2-sample t test to a situation having more than two levels of the independent variable. We begin this chapter in a similar vein, by noting that the **one-variable *chi*-square test** represents an extension of the binomial test to situations where there are more than two categories. Similarly, the **chi-square test of independent proportions** represents an extension of the binomial test of a difference between two proportions to situations where there are three or more proportions to be tested.

From one point of view, a *chi*-square test of independent proportions is similar to an independent-groups ANOVA, except for the fact that the dependent variable is measured on a nominal scale in the present situation. For example, an experimenter might administer a different level of drug dosage to each of several independent groups of animals, and then observe the proportions surviving at each level, or a researcher might observe the proportions of unemployment in three groups of workers. From another point of view, a test of proportions is a test of association between an independent variable and a dependent variable measured on a nominal scale. Thus, there are great similarities between the procedures to be described in the present chapter and procedures described earlier.

The One-Variable *Chi*-Square Test

This test applies in situations where a single variable has three or more levels — each level consisting of a category or classification — and where the data consist of the frequencies of independent observations falling in each category. Suppose, for example, a marketing researcher wants to choose the most appealing color of package for a product. Four hundred consumers are allowed to choose a red, green, yellow, or blue package. Thus, each consumer's response is measured on a nominal scale having the levels red, green, yellow, and blue. The data in such a study would consist of the **observed frequencies** of consumers falling in each category of color. Under the null hypothesis of no differences between color preference, the **expected frequencies** in all categories would be equal to 100 in our example. Test procedures are described in detail below.

In some cases, the expected frequencies in a one-variable *chi*-square test are not equal in the different categories. For example, consider the racial and ethnic composition of the students admitted to a particular university. Is there any significant difference between the proportions of the various racial/ethnic groups in the freshman class and the proportion of those groups in the population of the United States? Since the proportions of those groups are different in the population, their expected frequencies in the freshman class will be different. Test procedures are described below.

Equal Expected Frequencies

Returning to the marketing study briefly described above, each of 400 consumers is allowed to choose one and only one free sample of a product packaged in red, green, yellow, or blue. Conditions are arranged so that all choices are independent — that is, no person is allowed to see anyone else's choice of package. The results of such a hypothetical study are shown in Table 15-1. Each person falls in one and only one cell in that table, and thus the cells represent mutually exclusive and exhaustive categories.

It might occur to you that we already have a procedure for testing the consumers' preferences in this situation: Why not find the proportion of subjects choosing each of the colors, and then do a binomial test of the difference between those proportions for each pair of cells? No doubt, you have thought of the answer to that question: Such a procedure would increase the probability of a Type 1 error. The situation here is quite analogous to a multiple-group experiment having measurements on an interval or ratio scale, where running *t* tests on all possible pairs of means would also increase the Type 1 error rate. In the present situation, a variety of *chi*-square test will allow us to see if there is any significant difference between the preference for any of the colors without increasing the probability of a Type 1 error. In that respect, the present use of *chi*-square is analogous to the use of the *F* test in an ANOVA.

Null and Alternative Hypotheses. In the present context, the **null hypothesis** states that there is no difference between preferences for colors — that is, no difference between observed and expected frequencies. Thus, under the null hypothesis, equal numbers of choices are expected to fall in each category. The **alternative hypothesis** states that either there is a significant difference between the observed frequencies in at least two categories, or a significant difference within some combination of observed frequencies. Thus, there are many possible alternatives to the null hypothesis here, just as in an independent-groups ANOVA.

Observed frequencies are shown in the left portions of the cells in Table 15-1, and expected frequencies in the lower right corners. As in our earlier

Table 15-1. One-Variable *Chi*-Square Test of Consumer Color Preferences in a Hypothetical Marketing Study, Equal Expected Frequencies.

Red	Green	Yellow	Blue	
79	106	87	128	400 = N
(100)	(100)	(100)	(100)	

By Formula 15-1, $\chi^2_{df} = \sum \dfrac{(f_o - f_e)^2}{f_e}$, $df = k - 1 = 4 - 1 = 3$.

$$\chi^2_3 = \frac{(79 - 100)^2}{100} + \frac{(106 - 100)^2}{100} + \frac{(87 - 100)^2}{100} + \frac{(128 - 100)^2}{100}$$

$$= \quad 4.41 \quad + \quad .36 \quad + \quad 1.69 \quad + \quad 7.84 \quad = 14.30.$$

From Table E, $CV_{.01} = 11.341$;   therefore reject H_0 at .01 level.

chi-square tests of association, observed frequencies and expected frequencies as well must sum to N, the total number of observations.

The following formula gives the one-variable *chi*-square for three or more categories:

$$\chi^2_{df} = \sum \frac{(f_o - f_e)^2}{f_e}, \tag{15-1}$$

$$df = k - 1, \quad \text{for} \quad k > 2,$$

where f_o and f_e are observed and expected frequencies in a cell, the summation is across cells, df is the degrees of freedom, and k is the number of cells. Since the total number of observations is fixed, observed frequencies are free to vary in only $k - 1$ of the cells, hence the above expression for degrees of freedom. Where there are only 2 categories, a correction for continuity is needed, and Formula 15-2 — described below — should be used.

Table 15-1 demonstrates the calculation of a one-variable *chi*-square test in the hypothetical marketing study. The observed, calculated, value of χ^2_3 is 14.30. The null hypothesis is rejected when an observed value of *chi*-square equals or exceeds the critical value found in Table E. Since 14.30 is greater than 11.341, we reject H_0 at the .01 level.

Having now rejected the null hypothesis, what alternative hypothesis do we accept? For example, the observed frequencies of Red and Blue might differ significantly, or the combined frequencies of Red and Yellow might differ significantly from the combined frequencies of Green and Blue. The situation here is analogous to the state of affairs after observing a significant F in an ANOVA: A significant χ^2 is an overall indication that there is something significant somewhere in the data. Unfortunately, procedures for making *a posteriori* comparisons after finding a significant χ^2 are not so well developed as the analogous procedures for use after an ANOVA. (However, see Marascuilo and McSweeney, 1977, for some approaches to the problems of *post hoc* comparisons after finding a significant *chi*-square.) Guided by the observed frequencies in Table 15-1, our best judgment after observing a significant χ^2 is that Blue is the most preferred color.

Relationship Between χ^2 and Z. In a one-variable *chi*-square test, each observation falls into one and only one of k mutually exclusive and exhaustive categories. Thus, the one-variable *chi*-square test represents an extension of the binomial test to a situation having any number of categories. Indeed, where there are only two categories, *chi*-square and the binomial are equivalent tests yielding identical probabilities — although in that case a **correction for continuity** is required, since the *chi*-square has only one degree of freedom. Where there are only two categories, the following formula yields the value of *chi*-square:

$$\chi^2_1 = \sum \frac{(|f_o - f_e| - .5)^2}{f_e}, \tag{15-2}$$

$$df = 1,$$

where the summation is across the two cells in the design, and the other symbols are as defined in Formula 15-1. Subtracting .5 from the absolute value of each difference between an observed and expected frequency constitutes the correction for continuity.

A study of the number of male and female births in a sample of babies might utilize a one-variable *chi*-square having 1 *df*. Under the null hypothesis of equal numbers of males and females at birth, each expected frequency would be equal to $N/2$, and the observed frequencies would be equal to the number of births in each category. Alternatively, such a study might utilize the normal approximation to the binomial, described in Chapter 7. In that case, the binomial random variable X would equal the observed frequency of male or female births — the choice is arbitrary — and the binomial probabilities p and q would equal .5. Under all conditions, the probability associated with a value of χ_1^2 is exactly equal to the probability associated with a value of Z found by the normal approximation to the binomial. Indeed, those two statistics are functionally related, as noted in Chapter 11, since $\chi_1^2 = Z^2$. Although *chi*-square and the binomial yield identical probabilities where there are only two categories, it is probably better to use the binomial in that case, reserving the one-variable *chi*-square test for cases where there are three or more categories. Following that procedure relieves you of the necessity of deciding whether to make a correction for continuity in a one-variable *chi*-square test.

Requirements.   The requirements for the present test conform to those set out in Table 11-11 for the *chi*-square test of association. The present *chi*-square is a test of differences between the observed frequencies falling in different categories, rather than a test of association between two variables, but the same statistic is used in both cases.

To recapitulate briefly, *chi*-square applies where measurements are on a nominal scale. To be sure, we could attach a particular wavelength of light to each of the colors in the hypothetical marketing study — as might be done in a psychophysical experiment involving color — but for present purposes the color dimension is considered to consist of nominal categories. In other situations, a higher-caliber measurement scale — ordinal, interval, or ratio — may be divided into nominal categories, such as low, middle, and high socioeconomic class, or short, medium, and tall stature. However, as noted earlier, degrading a higher-caliber measurement scale results in some loss of information — although for some purposes that may be of little consequence.

Since all expected frequencies are equal in the present case, each *expected* frequency must be greater than or equal to 5. Observed frequencies may take any value between zero and N inclusive. All observations must be independent. The same subjects cannot be measured more than once, nor can a subject be allowed to fall into more than one cell, nor can one subject's response be allowed to influence another's.

Unequal Expected Frequencies

In some cases, there may be theoretical grounds for expecting different frequencies in some of the cells in a one-variable *chi*-square test. In the field of genetics, for example, if both parents are carriers of an autosomal recessive trait — a characteristic determined by a gene located on one of the non-sex chromosomes — then 1/4 of the offspring are expected to show the trait, 1/2 are expected to be carriers of the gene without expressing the trait, and 1/4 are expected to be completely free of the gene.

Now consider the racial and ethnic composition of entering freshman students admitted to a university in a recent year. For many years, there have been growing efforts to extend educational opportunities to minority students. How should we judge the results of those efforts? Clearly, we should not expect to observe equal frequencies of all racial and ethnic groups in the freshman class at any university, since the proportions of those groups differ greatly in the population. We might argue — at least as a first approach to the problem — that if educational opportunities are being extended equally to all, then the proportions of the different racial groups in the freshman class should not differ significantly from their proportions in the population of the United States.

Table 15-2 shows the proportions of the principal racial groups in the United States according to the 1980 census. The column headed p_e lists the proportion of each racial group in the population, and thus gives the *expected proportion* in our sample. The column headed f_o is the observed frequency of each racial group in a hypothetical freshman class of 2,780 students at

Table 15-2.   *Chi*-Square Test of Racial Proportions in Freshman Class at University A.

Group	Population Proportion p_e	Observed Proportion p_o	Observed Frequency f_o	Expected Frequency $f_e = Np_e$	$\dfrac{(f_o - f_e)^2}{f_e}$
White	.82	.83	2,301	2,279.6	.20
Black	.12	.13	361	333.6	2.25
Asian	.02	.02	43	55.6	2.86
Native American	.01	.01	15	27.8	5.89
Other	.03	.02	60	83.4	6.57
	1.00 $= \Sigma p_e$	1.01 $= \Sigma p_o$	2,780 $= \Sigma f_o = N$	2,780.0 $= \Sigma f_e = N$	17.77 $= \chi_4^2$

By Formula 15-1, $\chi_4^2 = \sum \dfrac{(f_o - f_e)^2}{f_e},$ $df = k - 1 = 4.$

$$\chi_4^2 = \frac{(2{,}301 - 2{,}279.6)^2}{2{,}279.6} + \frac{(361 - 333.6)^2}{333.6}$$

$$+ \frac{(43 - 55.6)^2}{55.6} + \frac{(15 - 27.8)^2}{27.8} + \frac{(60 - 83.4)^2}{83.4}$$

$$= .20 + 2.25 + 2.86 + 5.89 + 6.57 = 17.77.$$

From Table E, $CV_{.01} = 13.277;$ therefore reject H_0.

University A. The observed frequencies in this example are contrived, but the proportions of the racial groups in the population are real data from the 1980 census.[1] The expected frequency of each racial group in the freshman class, in the column headed f_e, is found by multiplying the proportion of each group in the population by N, the size of the class. The **observed proportion p_o** of each racial category in the freshman class, listed in parentheses, is found by dividing the observed frequency by N. Because of rounding error, the observed proportions sum to 1.01. Those observed proportions do not directly enter into the calculation of χ^2, but they will be discussed later.

In the present situation, the null hypothesis states that there is no significant difference between the observed proportions of the racial groups in the freshman class and their proportions in the population. However, Formula 15-1 uses observed and expected *frequencies* in the calculation of χ^2. Although it is possible to modify Formula 15-1 so that χ^2 can be calculated using observed and expected proportions or percentages, expected frequencies will usually have smaller rounding errors than expected proportions carried only to 2 or 3 decimal places, and thus will provide more accurate results. Indeed, the expected proportions in Table 15-2 do not quite sum to 1.00 because of rounding error. We will discuss those expected proportions further after describing the test.

The expected frequency of each group in Table 15-2 is found by multiplying the **population proportion p_e** by N. Each quantity in the last column of Table 15-2 is equal to $(f_o - f_e)^2/f_e$, and thus represents one of the terms in the *chi*-square formula. Thus, adding those terms yields the value of χ^2 by Formula 15-1, as shown in Table 15-2. Since there are 5 racial categories, there are 4 *df*, and thus the critical value of χ_4^2 at the .01 level is 13.277. Since the calculated value of χ_4^2 is 17.77, we reject H_0 at the .01 level.

As in our earlier example, the significant χ^2 here is an overall indication that there is something significant in the data. Having rejected H_0, we have ruled out the idea that only chance is at work in determining the differences between the observed proportions of the racial groups in the freshman class and their proportions in the population. Rejecting H_0 at the .01 level means that differences as large or larger than the ones observed would occur by chance no more than once in a hundred replications of our observations.

Now consider the nature of the differences between the observed and expected frequencies in Table 15-2. For two of the racial categories — Whites and Blacks — the observed frequencies are greater than the expected frequencies, and for the remaining categories, observed frequencies are smaller than expected. Thus, Whites and Blacks are *overrepresented* in the freshman class, and Asians, Native Americans, and Others are *underrepresented*. If a χ^2 is significant, then some category or categories will necessarily be overrepresented and some underrepresented — but a significant χ^2 gives no indication of the *reason* for the over- and underrepresentation.

Now consider the observed proportions of the racial groups in the freshman class, the column headed p_o in Table 15-2. Notice that the observed

[1] Any resemblance between the fictional composition of the freshman class at University A and that of any other institution, living or dead, is purely coincidental.

proportions are very close to the proportions in the population — indeed, in no case does an observed proportion differ by more than 1% from a population proportion. Thus, those differences are quite small, even though statistically significant overall. Although we did not use the observed proportions in our test, it is nevertheless instructive to compare observed and expected proportions as well as frequencies.

What are we to make of these data? Are we to conclude that University A has discriminated against Asians, Native Americans, and Others, while favoring the admission of Whites and Blacks? Such a conclusion would be unwarranted without *much* additional information. For example, most universities and colleges draw students disproportionately from surrounding geographic areas — especially public-supported institutions. Now if most of University A's entering freshmen are drawn from a single state, or from a region within a state, then it might not be reasonable to compare the racial composition of its students with the population of the entire United States, since all minorities are much more heavily represented in some geographical areas than in others. It would also be useful to take into account the number of students who were denied admission in the different racial groups.

Essentially, the data in Table 15-2 can be interpreted as showing a significant association between a racial variable and a variable measuring representation in the freshman class at University A. Some groups are significantly — though slightly — overrepresented, and some are underrepresented. But an association, a correlation, does not necessarily imply a causal relationship between variables, and it would be erroneous to conclude that a prospective freshman's race causes that student's admission or denial of admission. The data do not rule out such a possibility, but additional information is needed in order to draw causal inferences, as in other cases involving correlations and associations.

Requirements.   For equal or unequal expected frequencies, the requirements for the one-variable *chi*-square test are the same as those in Table 11-11 for the *chi*-square test of association. There must be no *expected* frequency of zero, and at least 80% of the expected frequencies must be greater than or equal to 5. All observations must be independent, and each person must be classified into one and only one category. That requirement can sometimes create problems in studies of racial and ethnic groups. For example, how should we classify a person of mixed White and Native American ancestry? Whether such a person is classified into one of those two categories, or placed in the *Other* category, it is essential not to count the person more than once.

The expected frequencies must be determined on theoretical grounds *a priori* — that is, before the results of a study are taken into account. Thus, the observed frequencies are not to be allowed to influence the calculation of expected frequencies. In this respect, the one-variable *chi*-square test differs from the *chi*-square test of association, where the observed marginal totals are used to calculate the expected frequencies within cells.

Interpreting a One-Variable *Chi*-Square Test

The one-variable *chi*-square test, for equal or unequal expected frequencies, is sometimes called a test of **goodness of fit.** Such a test is a measure of the extent to which a set of observed frequencies differs from the frequencies expected *a priori,* on some theoretical basis. Rejecting the null hypothesis leads to the conclusion that the data do not fit the theory. Not rejecting H_0 indicates that the data do not depart significantly from theoretical expectations — that is, that the observed frequencies do not differ significantly from the expected frequencies. In other words, an observed value of *chi*-square smaller than the critical value in Table E indicates that the data *fit, support,* and are *consistent with* the theory. Notice carefully that we have not said that the data *prove* the theory when H_0 is not rejected. Indeed, proving the theory would be equivalent to accepting the null hypothesis. As we have noted earlier, a nonsignificant value of a test statistic does not prove that H_0 is true, and thus does not allow us to accept that hypothesis. For a lucid discussion of "proving the null hypothesis" see Cohen (1977), as also suggested earlier.

Chi-Square Tests of Homogeneity of Proportions

In Chapter 9, we presented a test of a difference between two independent binomial proportions. In this section, we will extend that procedure to testing differences between binomial proportions in three or more independent groups. The null hypothesis in such a test is the statement that there is no significant difference between observed proportions. In other words, H_0 states that the proportions are **homogeneous,** and thus the test is described as a test of **homogeneity of proportions.** The alternative hypothesis states that the proportions are **heterogeneous** — that is, at least two proportions differ significantly, or there is a significant difference within some combination of proportions.

In a sense, both of the one-variable *chi*-square tests described earlier in this chapter are tests of proportions. Where the expected frequencies are equal, the same proportion of cases is expected to fall into each cell, namely $1/k$. Although the *chi*-square formula uses expected frequencies rather than expected proportions, each of those quantities is a direct function of the other. Where the expected frequencies are unequal, the one-variable *chi*-square test in effect compares observed and expected proportions falling in the different categories, even though the formula uses observed and expected frequencies for computational purposes.

First, we will present a test of homogeneity of three or more independent **binomial proportions** — that is, a test of *differences* between three or more binomial proportions. Then we will describe a test of homogeneity of independent **multinomial proportions.** For example, if several independent groups of subjects responded to a statement in a survey by indicating *Agreement, Disagreement,* or *Undecided,* then each response would fall into one of three mutually exclusive and exhaustive categories. If there were, say, four groups of subjects, we would be interested in the consistency — that is, the homogeneity — of the proportions of responses falling in the three categories across the four groups of subjects.

Binomial Proportions

Table 15-3 shows the frequencies of three major categories of crimes against persons in a recent year in which a gun was or was not used. Is there any significant difference between the proportions of murders, aggravated assaults, and robberies committed using guns? Before carrying out a test of homogeneity of those proportions, we will consider the data in terms of percentages, as shown in Table 15-4.

The percentage in each cell of Table 15-4 is found by dividing the observed frequency in Table 15-3 by the column marginal and multiplying by 100. For example, the percentage of murders committed using a gun is $100(13,582/21,456) = 63.3\%$. Notice that the percentages of crimes involving guns range from a high of 63.3% for murder to a low of 23.0% for aggravated assault. Thus, the proportions of cases falling in the binomial categories of

Table 15-3.   *Chi*-Square Test of Binomial Proportions, *Gun versus No Gun,* in Three Categories of Major Crimes Against Persons. Data From *Uniform Crime Reports for the United States, 1979,* Federal Bureau of Investigation, Washington, D.C.

	Murder	Aggravated Assault	Robbery	
Gun	13,582 (6,620.47)	141,269 (189,521.66)	185,352 (144,060.87)	340,203
No Gun	7,874	472,944 (424,691.34)	281,529 (322,820.13)	762,347
	21,456	614,213	466,881	1,102,550 $= N$

Expected frequencies by Formula 11-7, $f_{e(ij)} = \dfrac{R_i C_j}{N}$.

$$f_{e(11)} = \frac{340,203(21,456)}{1,102,550} = 6,620.47; \quad f_{e(12)} = \frac{340,203(614,213)}{1,102,550} = 189,521.66;$$

$$\cdots f_{e(23)} = \frac{762,347(466,881)}{1,102,550} = 322,820.13.$$

By Formula 11-11, $\chi^2_{df} = \sum_r \sum_c \dfrac{(f_o - f_e)^2}{f_e}, \quad df = (r-1)(c-1)$

$$= (2-1)(3-1) = 2.$$

$$\chi^2_2 = \frac{(13,582 - 6,620.47)^2}{6,620.47} + \frac{(141,269 - 189,521.66)^2}{189,521.66}$$

$$+ \cdots + \frac{(281,529 - 322,820.13)^2}{322,820.13}$$

$$= 7,320.16 + 12,285.24 + \cdots + 5,281.45 = 45,470.88.$$

From Table E, $CV_{.001} = 13.816$;   therefore reject H_0.

Table 15-4. Data from Table 15-3 in Percentages Falling in Binomial Categories *Gun* vs *No Gun*. Percentages Sum to 100 Within Each Category of Crime.

	Murder	Aggravated Assault	Robbery	Combined Crimes
Gun	63.3%	23.0%	39.7%	30.9%
No gun	36.7%	77.0%	60.3%	69.1%
	100.0%	100.0%	100.0%	100.0%
Frequencies	21,456	614,213	466,881	1,102,550

Gun and *No Gun* appear rather different across the three categories of crimes.

The combined percentage of all three crimes committed using a gun is found by dividing the marginal total for the first row of Table 15-3 by the total N and multiplying by 100. Thus, 30.9% of the total crimes across all three categories were committed with guns, and 69.1% were committed without. If the proportions of guns used were homogeneous within all three crimes, then we would not expect any of those percentages to differ significantly from the combined percentage of 30.9%. The *chi*-square test in Table 15-3, using observed and expected frequencies, is a test of homogeneity of binomial proportions within the three categories of crimes — that is, a test of the differences between those binomial proportions.

The expected frequencies in Table 15-3 are found using Formula 11-7. For any cell, the expected frequency is equal to the product of the row and column marginals divided by the total N. As in all *chi*-square tables, the observed frequencies must sum to N, and so must the expected frequencies — within rounding error. By Formula 11-11, the calculated value of χ_2^2 is 45,470.88. Since that value exceeds the critical value at the .001 level from Table E, we reject the null hypothesis.

The significant χ^2 indicates that the proportions in Table 15-4 are not homogeneous — that is, the proportion of crimes involving guns is not the same for all three categories of crimes against persons. A murder is much more likely to be committed with a gun than is an aggravated assault or a robbery — by a margin of 63.3% to 23.0% and 39.7%. These data suggest that more stringent gun control may have the greatest potential of reducing the most serious of the crimes against persons — the crime of murder. A very strong supporter of gun control might argue that 63.3% of all murders could potentially be eliminated through tighter gun control. But an opponent might argue that tighter gun control would not reduce murders at all, since a would-be murderer denied a gun could always find another weapon — a knife, an axe, or in a real pinch, bare hands. My own opinion is that the truth probably lies somewhere between those extremes — as we may find one day, if we should ever choose to exercise greater control over the use and availability of guns.

Test of Proportions and Association Between Variables. It is no accident that the formula used in the test of homogeneity of proportions is the same formula introduced in Chapter 11 as a test of *association between two* *variables* measured on nominal scales. Indeed, a test of proportions *is* a test of association, and vice versa. The significant difference between the proportions, or percentages, in Table 15-4 implies an association between a *Weapon* variable having two levels—Gun, No Gun—and a *Crime* variable having three levels. Overall, a gun was used in 30.9% of the crimes, and no gun was used in 69.1%, as the combined percentages show in Table 15-4. Thus, the prior probability of randomly drawing a crime committed with a gun from the 1,102,550 total crimes is .309, but the conditional probability of drawing a crime committed with a gun from among the 21,456 *murders* is .633. Thus,

$$P(\text{Gun}|\text{Murder}) \ = \ .633 > P(\text{Gun}) \ = \ .309,$$

and thus the events *Gun* and *Murder* are not independent by Formula 6-14. Since one of those events represents a level of the *Weapon* variable and the other a level of the *Crime* variable, those two variables are not independent, and thus are associated.

Now consider the prior probability of *Murder:*

$$P(\text{Murder}) \ = \ \frac{21,456}{1,102,550} \ = \ .019.$$

But the conditional probability of *Murder* given that a gun was used in a crime is

$$P(\text{Murder}|\text{Gun}) \ = \ \frac{13,582}{340,203} \ = \ .040,$$

a probability more than twice as great as the prior probability of *Murder*.

The data show a highly significant association between guns and murder, but a correlation does not *prove* the existence of a causal relationship—as we have noted so often in the past. However, the association here is very suggestive—if not compelling. What should we do—go on as in the past, enforce stricter gun control, arm ourselves to the teeth, or none of the above? Whatever we decide to do about gun control, our decisions will be based on observations, as opposed to experiments. Thus, the issue of gun control—like most other socially important issues—must be decided on the basis of weaker causal inferences than we should prefer. But decide we must, even if our decision is to do nothing different. I hope this textbook will provide you with some intellectual tools that may be useful in making such decisions.

Multinomial Proportions

Suppose a manufacturer wants to carry out a preliminary test of a proposed national advertising campaign using a new television commercial. The ultimate test of an advertising campaign, of course, is how well a product sells. But a national advertising campaign is very expensive, and thus it is very useful to have some preliminary indication of the probable success of a proposed campaign.

Table 15-5. *Chi*-Square Test of Multinomial Proportions—*Believable, Not Believable, Undecided*—in an Advertising Survey in Three Groups of Consumers.

		Consumers			
		Urban	Suburban	Rural	
	Believable	11	16	13	40
		(13.33)	(13.33)	(13.33)	
Responses:	Not believable	10	6	17	33
		(11.00)	(11.00)	(11.00)	
	Undecided	9	8	0	17
		(5.67)	(5.67)	(5.67)	
		30	30	30	$90 = N$

Expected frequencies by Formula 11-7, $\quad f_{e(ij)} = \dfrac{R_i C_j}{N}$.

$$f_{e(11)} = \frac{30(40)}{90} = 13.33; \quad f_{e(12)} = \frac{30(40)}{90} = 13.33;$$

$$\cdots f_{e(33)} = \frac{30(17)}{90} = 5.67.$$

By Formula 11-11, $\quad \chi^2_{df} = \sum_r \sum_c \dfrac{(f_o - f_e)^2}{f_e}, \quad df = (r-1)(c-1)$

$$= (3-1)(3-1) = 4.$$

$$\chi^2_4 = \frac{(11-13.33)^2}{13.33} + \frac{(16-13.33)^2}{13.33} + \cdots + \frac{(0-5.67)^2}{5.67}$$

$$= \quad .41 \quad + \quad .53 \quad + \cdots + \quad 5.67 \quad = 15.17.$$

From Table E, $CV_{.01} = 13.277$; therefore reject H_0.

A marketing researcher might show the proposed commercial to a group of *Urban, Suburban,* and *Rural* consumers, asking each person to rate the commercial as *Believable* or *Not believable,* or to respond as *Undecided.* The hypothetical results of such a marketing study are shown in Table 15-5. Expected frequencies are found by Formula 11-7. Although the observed frequency in one cell is zero, notice that the expected frequency for that cell is 5.67. An expected frequency of zero would violate one of the requirements for a *chi*-square test, but an observed frequency of zero is permissible.

Formula 11-11 is used to calculate the value of χ^2, as in our earlier test of homogeneity of binomial proportions. Since the observed value of χ^2_4 exceeds the critical value at the .01 level from Table E, we reject the null hypothesis at the .01 level. Thus, we conclude that the proportions of consumers falling in the multinomial categories of *Believable, Not believable,* and *Undecided* are not homogeneous across the *Urban, Suburban,* and *Rural* groups.

Table 15-6 shows the data in percentages. The commercial appears most believable to suburban consumers, and least believable to rural consumers. Depending on the nature of the product, and the nature of the expected market, the commercial might be viewed as disappointing or potentially very successful. Indeed, a sophisticated study would take those possible factors into account. Our contrived example is based on equal numbers of urban, suburban, and rural consumers, but a more realistic study might sample

Table 15-6. Advertising Survey Data From Table 15-5 in Percentages Falling in Multinomial Categories *Believable*, *Not Believable*, and *Undecided*. Percentages Sum to 100% Within Each Group of Consumers.

		Consumers: Urban	Suburban	Rural	Combined Percentages
	Believable	36.7%	53.3%	43.3%	44.4%
Responses:	Not believable	33.3%	20.0%	56.7%	36.7%
	Undecided	30.0%	26.7%	0.0%	18.9%
	Percentages	100.0%	100.0%	100.0%	100.0%
	Frequencies	30	30	30	90

those groups in accordance with their expected proportions of the potential market.

Observations and Experiments

There is almost no end to the kinds of studies that can be done using tests of homogeneity of proportions. For example, a political candidate running for state or national office is keenly interested in the proportions of supporters, nonsupporters, and undecided voters in different geographic areas, racial or ethnic groups, age groups, and socioeconomic levels. Public interest groups, and special interest groups as well, are heavily involved in assessing attitudes among various groups of voters.

The above examples all represent observations, as opposed to experiments. However, tests of proportions are quite useful in experiments where the data consist of frequencies falling in two or more categories, for example, the number of rats developing or not developing gastric ulcers under different kinds of approach-avoidance conflicts (Sawrey, Conger, & Turrell, 1956).

Requirements

The requirements for tests of homogeneity of binomial and multinomial proportions are identical to the requirements for the *chi*-square test of association in Table 11-11. As we noted earlier, a test of proportions *is* a test of association between variables. Indeed, after our present discussion, you may want to review the section in Chapter 11 on tests of association.

Some Closing Words

Now that we have come to the end of this text, some closing words are in order. I hope that this book, with the aid of your instructor, has helped you become a more critical, intelligent consumer of research findings. If your goal is to become a professional researcher, then I hope that your instructor and I have smoothed the way for you.

I strongly recommend keeping this book as a reference, and also keeping your class notes, homework, laboratory exercises, and reports. In writing this book, I have tried to keep in mind two principal functions of a textbook: First, the text was designed to teach, and second to serve as a useful reference after you have completed this course. Several features of this text should be very helpful in that latter respect: The statistical tables, extensive subject index, and concise descriptions of the requirements for each statistical test.

A textbook can be read, and reread, at several levels of understanding. For example, if you now reread the early chapters of this text, you will no doubt see things more clearly in the light of your present knowledge. I believe you will find it useful to review parts of this text from time to time, perhaps long after you have completed this course. I hope you will continue thinking critically, as a way of life, about the ideas and issues we have developed.

Terms and Symbols

This is an excellent time to begin the process of consolidating and integrating the ideas we have presented throughout this text. There is no better way to begin that process than by reviewing and carefully considering the terms and symbols listed at the end of each chapter.

One-variable *chi*-square	Multinomial proportions
Chi-square test of independent proportions	Association between variables
	Conditional probability
Observed frequency	Prior probability
Expected frequency	f_o
Equal expected frequencies	f_e
Unequal expected frequencies	df
Null hypothesis	p_e
Alternative hypothesis	p_o
Correction for continuity	$f_{e(i,j)}$
Population proportion	R_i and C_j
Observed proportion	r and c
Goodness of fit	$P(G|M)$
Homogeneity of proportions	$P(G)$
Binomial proportions	

EXERCISES AND STUDY QUESTIONS

1. Tortilla sales at Señor Juan's Mexican Bakery have gone rather flat recently. Señor Juan's vice-president for marketing suggests that their customers may have grown tired of the old, traditional round tortillas, and that a new improved shape might stimulate sales. A hundred customers are each offered a choice of 1 free package of tortillas from among four

different shapes. Suppose the data came out as below:

Round	Triangular	Square	Hexagonal
22	19	21	38

   a. Justify a *chi*-square test, and state the null and alternative hypotheses. Explain your choice of expected frequencies.
   b. Carry out the test. Indicate whether you reject H_0, and explain what that means.
2. Suppose the study above was conducted using the following procedures. Identify the problems that each procedure would raise, and suggest a remedy.
   a. The study is conducted over several days, and a few customers are allowed to choose a package of tortillas on more than one occasion.
   b. The bakery makes up 50 packages of each shape. All of the tortillas are stacked on a counter, sorted by shape, and each customer is allowed to select one and only one package.
   c. Midway in the preparation of the samples for the study, a problem develops in the automatic package-wrapping machine so that some of the points are blunted on the triangular tortillas, and some of the square ones are warped and twisted. Unfortunately, those occasional defects can be seen through the clear plastic wrapping.
3. Suppose the affirmative action officer at Academic State University has become concerned about the number of women faculty members in various areas in the College of Arts and Sciences. The faculty are listed below by sex and area.

Area	Men	Women
Math & Physical Sciences	71	8
Life Sciences	17	11
Psychology	18	9
Social Sciences	52	17
Humanities	139	24

   a. Justify a *chi*-square test of proportions. State the null and alternative hypotheses.
   b. Carry out the test, and indicate whether you reject H_0. Explain what that means.
   c. Some of the areas in this study represent several university departments. For example, the Departments of Mathematics, Computer Science, Chemistry, Physics, and Geology are grouped into the area designated *Math & Physical Sciences*. Why not present the data by departments, rather than larger areas?

4. **a.** Using the data in Exercise 3, make up a table showing the percentages of men and women in each area, and in the total sample. Here, the percentages in each row will sum to 100%.

   b. Make up another table showing the data in percentages by columns. Here, the percentages in each column will sum to 100%, including the column that contains the marginal totals for all the areas.

   c. Briefly describe the different information each of the percentage tables conveys.

5. Suppose the affirmative action officer concludes that the university has discriminated against women in hiring faculty in some areas, pointing out the small percentage of women in *Math & Physical Sciences*. Is that conclusion justified on the basis of the above data?

6. An automobile manufacturer is planning an advertising campaign to promote a new model. A marketing researcher randomly divides a sample of consumers into 3 groups. Each group is then shown a different set of advertising material emphasizing *price, economy,* or *style*. A response of *Yes, No,* or *Undecided* indicates whether a subject would seriously consider buying the new model, would rule it out, or cannot decide between those choices. Equal numbers of consumers were assigned to each set of material, but unfortunately some potential subjects failed to appear, hence the unequal *n*s below.

	Emphasis		
Response	**Price**	**Economy**	**Style**
Yes	20	13	8
Undecided	7	12	13
No	4	8	11

   a. Justify a *chi*-square test of proportions. State the null and alternative hypotheses.

   b. Carry out the test. Do you reject H_0? Explain what that means here.

   c. Make up a table showing the data in percentages by columns.

   d. What is the nature of the differences between responses across the categories of advertising material?

   e. Does this study represent a set of observations, or an experiment? What difference does that distinction make, if any, in the present situation?

Review of Basic Mathematics

A

As you study this text, you may come to think that statistics is all about squaring and taking square roots. To be sure, those operations do play a large role, but there are other things you will also need to know. Understanding some fundamentals of algebra is an essential prerequisite to understanding this text. Since you may have forgotten some of those fundamentals, this appendix provides a review of the basic operations you will need. Operations are first expressed in general terms, and numerical examples are then given.

The present material is far from comprehensive, and is intended only as a brief review. If anything is unclear, it may be useful to consult a college algebra text.

Algebraic Operations

Addition

The **commutative law of addition** says the order of addition does not matter. Thus,

$$a + b = b + a,$$

$$4 + 7 = 7 + 4.$$

The **associative law of addition** deals with the collection of additive terms into quantities:

$$(a + b) + c = a + (b + c),$$

$$(2 + 5) + 4 = 2 + (5 + 4),$$

$$7 + 4 = 2 + 9.$$

In words, the above equation says, the quantity a plus b added to c is equal to a added to the quantity b plus c.

Multiplication

The **commutative law of multiplication** says

$$ab = ba,$$

$$2(4) = 4(2).$$

The **associative law of multiplication** deals with the collection of multiplicative terms into quantities:

$$a(bc) = (ab)c,$$

$$3[2(4)] = [3(2)]4,$$

$$3[8] = [6]4.$$

Multiplication by zero yields zero. Thus,

$0(a) = 0,$ for any a, including $a = 0$.

The **distributive law** deals with the multiplication of a parenthetic expression. Thus,

$a(b + c) = ab + ac,$

$5(4 + 3) = 5(4) + 5(3) = 35.$

The above equation shows that the multiplier a is distributed over the terms in parentheses. However, when an expression of the above form consists of numerical values, as opposed to algebraic symbols, then it is better to carry out the operations inside the parentheses first. Thus,

$5(4 + 3) = 5(7) = 35.$

The distributive law also applies to expressions of the following form:

$(a + b)(c + d) = a(c + d) + b(c + d) = ac + ad + bc + bd,$

$(6 + 3)(2 + 5) = 6(2 + 5) + 3(2 + 5) = 12 + 30 + 6 + 15 = 63.$

In the above equation, the expression $(c + d)$ is distributed across the terms $(a + b)$. Distributing $(a + b)$ across $(c + d)$ would also yield the same result.

Once again, it is easier and less conducive to error to do the operations inside the parentheses first. Thus,

$(6 + 3)(2 + 5) = 9(7) = 63.$

Since we will use a great many expressions involving parentheses, it will pay you to become very familiar with these operations.

The Square of a Binomial

A **binomial** is an expression having two terms, such as $(a + b)$, or $(c - d)$. It is easy to find the square of a binomial by applying the distributive law above. However, we will have so many occasions to square binomials that it will be very useful to remember the expressions below:

$(a + b)^2 = (a + b)(a + b) = a^2 + ab + ba + b^2 = a^2 + 2ab + b^2.$

Where one of the terms has a negative sign,

$(a - b)^2 = (a - b)(a - b) = a^2 - ab - ba + b^2 = a^2 - 2ab + b^2.$

Notice that

$(a - b)^2 \neq a^2 - b^2,$ since

$a^2 - b^2 = (a + b)(a - b) = a^2 - ab + ba - b^2.$

The $\neq$ sign, above, means **not equal to.** In evaluating a squared binomial consisting of two numbers—as opposed to algebraic symbols—find the algebraic sum of the numbers and then square that quantity. Thus,

$$(5 + 1)^2 = 6^2 = 36,$$

$$(9 - 4)^2 = 5^2 = 25, \qquad \text{and}$$

$$(3 - 7)^2 = (-4)^2 = 16.$$

Division

There are several ways of expressing division:

$$a \div b = \frac{a}{b} = a/b, \qquad \text{for } b \neq 0;$$

$$6 \div 3 = \frac{6}{3} = 6/3 = 2.$$

The restriction that b, the divisor in the above equation, cannot equal zero is very important. Division by zero yields an undefined result that leads to absurdity. For example, if division by zero is allowed, then it is possible to prove that 1 equals 2, as we will do in a later section.

Although changing the order of terms in addition or multiplication has no effect on the result, interchanging the dividend and divisor—that is, the numerator and denominator of a fraction—does change the result, unless the terms are equal. Thus,

$$a \div b \neq b \div a, \qquad \frac{a}{b} \neq \frac{b}{a}, \qquad \text{unless } a = b;$$

$$\frac{8}{4} \neq \frac{4}{8},$$

$$2 \neq \frac{1}{2}.$$

Division can also be expressed in terms of the multiplication of the dividend by the reciprocal of the divisor:

$$a \div b = \frac{a}{b} = \frac{1}{b}(a),$$

$$8 \div 4 = \frac{8}{4} = \frac{1}{4}(8) = .25(8) = 2.$$

Operations Involving Different Signs

Multiplying or dividing two terms differing in sign yields a result having a negative sign. Thus,

$$-a(b) = -ab, \qquad \text{and} \qquad a(-b) = -ab;$$

$$-6(5) = -30, \qquad \text{and} \qquad 6(-5) = -30.$$

For division,

$$\frac{-a}{b} = -\frac{a}{b}, \qquad \text{and} \qquad \frac{a}{-b} = -\frac{a}{b};$$

$$\frac{-9}{3} = -3, \qquad \text{and} \qquad \frac{9}{-3} = -3.$$

Where two terms have the same sign, whether positive or negative, multiplication and division yield results having positive signs. Thus,

$$(-a)(-b) = ab, \qquad \text{and} \qquad \frac{-a}{-b} = \frac{a}{b}.$$

Where there are several multiplicative factors, as below, we can use the associative law of multiplication to group the terms and find the sign of the product. But there is a simpler rule: If there is an odd number of negative factors, then the product is negative; if there is an even number of negative factors then the product is positive. Thus,

$$(-a)(b)(-c)(d)(-e) = -abcde, \qquad \text{and} \qquad (a)(-b)(c)(-d)(e) = abcde.$$

Collection of Terms

It is often useful in dealing with an additive expression to collect the positive terms into one group and the negative terms into another. For example,

$$a - b + c - d + e = a + c + e - b - d = (a + c + e) - (b + d),$$

$$2 - 6 + 4 - 3 + 1 = 2 + 4 + 1 - 6 - 3 = (2 + 4 + 1) - (6 + 3)$$

$$= 7 - 9 = -2.$$

Notice that in collecting the negative terms, those terms are *added* inside the parentheses. A minus sign in front of a set of parentheses must be thought of as a **coefficient** of -1, that is, a multiplier that changes the sign of all the terms inside. A positive sign — or the absence of a negative sign — in front of parentheses can also be thought of as a coefficient of $+1$. But since multiplication by $+1$ has no effect on sign, a plus sign in front of a set of parentheses has no effect on the terms inside. Thus,

$$(a - b) - (c - d) = a - b - c + d = a + d - (b + c),$$

$$(3 - 5) - (4 - 8) = 3 - 5 - 4 + 8 = 3 + 8 - (5 + 4)$$

$$= 11 - 9 = 2.$$

Fractions

A fraction consists of a **numerator** divided by a **denominator.** The denominator of a fraction can be thought of as denoting — specifying — the size of the units of measurement, and the numerator can be thought of as *enumerating* — listing, or indicating — the number of units under consideration. A fraction is also the **ratio** of the numerator to the denominator, that is, the number of times the denominator goes into the numerator. Thus,

$$\frac{a}{b} = \text{ratio of } a \text{ to } b, \qquad \text{and} \qquad \frac{b}{a} = \text{ratio of } b \text{ to } a;$$

$$\frac{6}{3} = 2, \qquad \text{and} \qquad \frac{3}{6} = \frac{1}{2} = .5.$$

Addition

Where two or more fractions have the same denominator, addition is accomplished by algebraically adding their numerators. Thus,

$$\frac{a}{d} + \frac{b}{d} - \frac{c}{d} = \frac{a+b-c}{d};$$

$$\frac{1}{8} + \frac{7}{8} - \frac{3}{8} = \frac{5}{8}.$$

Notice, however, that fractions having the same *numerator* cannot be added so directly. Thus,

$$\frac{a}{b} + \frac{a}{d} \neq \frac{a}{b+d};$$

$$\frac{2}{3} + \frac{2}{5} \neq \frac{2}{3+5} \qquad \text{since} \qquad \frac{2}{3+5} = \frac{2}{8} = \frac{1}{4}.$$

In the equation above, since 2/3 and 2/5 are each greater than 1/4, their sum cannot equal 1/4. Procedures for adding fractions of the above form are described below.

In order to add two or more fractions, the fractions must have a **common denominator.** Usually, it is desirable to find the **lowest common denominator** for a set of fractions, that is, the smallest possible denominator for all of a set of fractions. The process is simple where one denominator is a multiple of another. For example,

$$\frac{1}{2} + \frac{3}{4} = \frac{2(1)}{2(2)} + \frac{3}{4} = \frac{2}{4} + \frac{3}{4} = \frac{5}{4}.$$

The procedure is to divide the smaller denominator into the larger, multiply the fraction having the smaller denominator by that quotient, and add the numerators of the fractions now having a common denominator.

The fact that the above result is 5/4 should not be disturbing, even though there are only four fourths in the whole of anything. The fraction 5/4 merely specifies that our unit of measurement is the *fourth,* and we have five of those units. If our fourth were a quarter of a year, for example, then we could talk about business earnings in five quarters, or a student's academic experience in five quarters. It is possible to express 5/4 as 1 1/4, but that is not desirable for most of our purposes.

Where the denominators of fractions to be added have no common multiple, the following procedure is used:

$$\frac{a}{b} + \frac{c}{d} = \frac{da}{db} + \frac{bc}{bd} = \frac{ad + bc}{bd};$$

$$\frac{1}{2} + \frac{2}{3} = \frac{3(1)}{3(2)} + \frac{2(2)}{2(3)} = \frac{3 + 4}{6} = \frac{7}{6}.$$

The above procedure can be extended to the addition of any number of fractions.

Multiplication

Multiplying both numerator and denominator by the same quantity does not change the value of a fraction. Indeed, we have already made use of that fact in some of the preceding developments. However, the multiplier in this case must not be zero, since that would result in a denominator of zero — and thus division by zero, which is not permissible. Thus,

$$\frac{\not{c}a}{\not{c}b} = \frac{a}{b}, \qquad \text{for any } c \neq 0.$$

In the above example, you can think of the c in the numerator and the c in the denominator as cancelling each other. Cancellation is a very useful technique in simplifying fractions.

To multiply the value of a fraction by a quantity, only the numerator is multiplied. Thus,

$$c\frac{a}{b} = \frac{ca}{b}, \qquad \text{for any value of } c, \text{ including } 0;$$

$$3\left(\frac{4}{5}\right) = \frac{3(4)}{5} = \frac{12}{5}.$$

As noted above, multiplication of an *entire* fraction by zero is permissible. Thus,

$$0\left(\frac{a}{b}\right) = 0,$$

$$0\left(\frac{4}{7}\right) = \frac{0(4)}{7} = \frac{0}{7} = 0.$$

Fractions are multiplied as below:

$$\frac{a}{b} \cdot \frac{c}{d} = \frac{ac}{bd},$$

$$\frac{2}{5} \cdot \frac{3}{4} = \frac{6}{20} = \frac{3}{10}.$$

Division

To divide one fraction by another, invert the divisor and multiply by the dividend. Thus,

$$\frac{a}{b} \div \frac{c}{d} = \frac{d}{c} \cdot \frac{a}{b} = \frac{ad}{bc},$$

$$\frac{1}{8} \div \frac{1}{4} = \frac{4}{1} \cdot \frac{1}{8} = \frac{4}{8} = \frac{1}{2}.$$

It is easy to see why the above rule works by expressing the division operation as a compound fraction:

$$\frac{a}{b} \div \frac{c}{d} = \frac{\dfrac{a}{b}}{\dfrac{c}{d}}.$$

Multiplying numerator and denominator of the compound fraction by d/c,

$$\frac{\dfrac{a}{b}}{\dfrac{c}{d}} = \frac{\dfrac{d}{c} \cdot \dfrac{a}{b}}{\dfrac{d}{c} \cdot \dfrac{c}{d}} = \frac{\dfrac{ad}{bc}}{1} = \frac{ad}{bc}.$$

To divide a fraction by a quantity, multiply the denominator by the quantity. Thus,

$$\frac{a}{b} \div c = \frac{a}{bc},$$

$$\frac{15}{64} \div 3 = \frac{15}{3(64)} = \frac{5}{64}.$$

The above division can also be carried out using a compound fraction:

$$\frac{a}{b} \div c = \frac{\dfrac{a}{b}}{\dfrac{c}{1}} = \frac{1}{c} \cdot \frac{a}{b} = \frac{a}{bc}.$$

Squares and Square Roots

The **square** of a quantity is equal to the quantity multiplied by itself. The terminology comes from plane geometry, where the area of a square is equal to the length of a side multiplied by itself.

$$a \cdot a = a^2,$$

$$3 \cdot 3 = 3^2 = 9.$$

Fractions are squared as below:

$$\left(\frac{a}{b}\right)^2 = \frac{a^2}{b^2},$$

$$\left(\frac{2}{3}\right)^2 = \frac{2^2}{3^2} = \frac{4}{9}.$$

The **square root** of a quantity, when multiplied by itself, equals the quantity. Thus,

$$\sqrt{n}\sqrt{n} = (\sqrt{n})^2 = n,$$

$$3 \cdot 3 = 3^2 = 9, \qquad \text{and thus} \qquad 3 = \sqrt{9}.$$

The above equations deal with the **positive square root** of n. For each positive number, there exist a positive and a negative square root. Thus,

$$(-\sqrt{n})(-\sqrt{n}) = n,$$

$$(-3)(-3) = 9, \qquad \text{and thus} \qquad -3 = \sqrt{9}.$$

However, we will have no occasion to use the negative square root of any quantity, so when we write $\sqrt{n}$, we will always mean the positive square root. Note carefully that $-\sqrt{n} \neq \sqrt{-n}$. The square root of a negative number is an imaginary number, since there does not exist a real number that yields a negative number when multiplied by itself. In this text, we will have no occasion to take the square root of a negative quantity. Indeed, if any of your operations result in an attempt to take the square root of a negative number, then you will have made a mistake. This fact provides a useful check on your arithmetic. But we will have many occasions to find the *square* of negative quantities. Squaring a negative number is perfectly permissible, so do not confuse the operations of squaring and taking square roots.

From the above, it follows that

$$\sqrt{b^2} = \sqrt{b \cdot b} = \sqrt{b}\sqrt{b} = b;$$

$$\sqrt{6^2} = \sqrt{6 \cdot 6} = \sqrt{6}\sqrt{6} = 6.$$

It is useful — for example — to be able to see that

$$\sqrt{197^2} = 197,$$

without having to calculate the value of the square under the radical.

Multiplication Under a Radical

Where the quantity under a radical consists of a product of a number of factors, any of the factors can be placed under separate radicals and multiplied together. Thus,

$$\sqrt{abc} = \sqrt{a}\sqrt{bc} = \sqrt{b}\sqrt{ac} = \sqrt{c}\sqrt{ab}.$$

The above relationships can be very useful. For example,

$$\sqrt{49(64)} = \sqrt{3{,}136}.$$

It may not be instantly obvious that the square root of 3,136 is 56. Thus, it is often useful to separate the factors under the radical:

$$\sqrt{49(64)} = \sqrt{49}\sqrt{64} = 7(8) = 56.$$

Addition Under a Radical

The following expression may appear counterintuitive:

$$\sqrt{a+b} \neq \sqrt{a} + \sqrt{b}.$$

In words, the above expression says that the square root of a sum of terms is not equal to the sum of the square roots of the terms. Using numbers, letting $a = 9$ and $b = 16$,

$$\sqrt{9 + 16} = \sqrt{25} = 5 \neq \sqrt{9} + \sqrt{16} = 3 + 4 = 7.$$

It follows from the above that

$$\sqrt{c^2 + d^2} \neq c + d,$$

$$\sqrt{5^2 + 6^2} = \sqrt{25 + 36} = \sqrt{61} = 7.81 \neq 5 + 6.$$

Placing a Multiplier Under a Radical

It is sometimes useful to be able to carry out the following operation:

$$a\sqrt{b+c} = \sqrt{a^2(b + c)},$$

$$2\sqrt{3 + 6} = \sqrt{2^2(3 + 6)} = \sqrt{4(9)} = \sqrt{36} = 6.$$

Exponents

Multiplication

An exponent indicates the number of times a quantity appears as a factor in a product. Thus,

$$a \cdot a = a^2, \quad \text{and} \quad b \cdot b \cdot b = b^3;$$

$$2 \cdot 2 = 2^2 = 4, \quad \text{and} \quad 4 \cdot 4 \cdot 4 = 4^3 = 64.$$

It is easy to see that

$$a^2a^3 = a^5, \quad \text{since}$$

$$a^2a^3 = (a \cdot a)(a \cdot a \cdot a)$$

$$= a \cdot a \cdot a \cdot a \cdot a = a^5.$$

In the above equations, a is the **base,** and the exponents 2, 3, and 5 are **powers** to which the base is **raised.** Where each factor in a product consists of the same base raised to a power, the power of the product is equal to the sum of the exponents. In general,

$$a^m a^n = a^{m+n}.$$

Anything raised to the first power is equal to itself. Thus,

$$a^1 = a, \quad \text{and} \quad b^3 = b^1 \cdot b^1 \cdot b^1 = b \cdot b \cdot b.$$

Division

To divide a base raised to some power by the same base raised to another power, subtract the exponent on the denominator from the exponent on the numerator. Thus,

$$\frac{a^5}{a^3} = \frac{\cancel{a} \cdot \cancel{a} \cdot \cancel{a} \cdot a \cdot a}{\cancel{a} \cdot \cancel{a} \cdot \cancel{a}} = a \cdot a = a^2.$$

Three of the as in the denominator cancel three in the numerator, and that is equivalent to raising the base to a power equal to the exponent on the numerator minus the exponent on the denominator. In general,

$$\frac{a^m}{a^n} = a^{m-n}.$$

Zero as an Exponent

Consider the following division:

$$\frac{a^2}{a^2} = \frac{\cancel{a} \cdot \cancel{a}}{\cancel{a} \cdot \cancel{a}} = 1.$$

Certainly, any quantity divided by itself is equal to 1 — unless the quantity is equal to zero, in which case the division is not a permissible operation. Now consider the above division from the standpoint of the exponents on the numerator and denominator. By the above rule,

$$\frac{a^2}{a^2} = a^{2-2} = a^0 = 1.$$

In general,

$$a^0 = 1, \quad \text{for any } a \neq 0.$$

Thus, any nonzero quantity raised to the zeroth power is equal to 1. We make use of that fact in dealing with permutations and combinations in Chapters 6 and 7.

Negative Exponents

Consider the quantity a^2/a^4. By subtracting the exponent in the denominator from the one in the numerator, as described above,

$$\frac{a^2}{a^4} = a^{(2-4)} = a^{-2}.$$

We can see the nature of a^{-2} by writing the above equation in another way:

$$\frac{a^2}{a^4} = \frac{\not{a} \cdot \not{a}}{\not{a} \cdot \not{a} \cdot a \cdot a} = \frac{1}{a \cdot a} = \frac{1}{a^2}.$$

Thus,

$$a^{-2} = \frac{1}{a^2}, \qquad \text{and in general,} \qquad a^{-n} = \frac{1}{a^n},$$

$$3^{-2} = \frac{1}{3^2} = \frac{1}{9}.$$

Factoring

The process of factoring plays a great role in simplifying, solving, and clarifying the meaning of equations. The additive terms in the expression below all share a common **factor,** that is, a common multiplier. **Factoring** is the process of extracting a common multiplier. Thus,

$$ab + ac - ade = a(b + c \div de),$$

$$2(3) + 2(7) - 2(6)(4) = 2[3 + 7 - 6(4)]$$

$$= 2(10 - 24) = 2(-14) = -28.$$

Factoring involves applying the distributive law in reverse. In the above equation, factoring the expression on the left requires finding a multiplier to distribute across the terms on the right so as to reproduce the terms on the left.
   Expressions of the following form can be factored readily:

$$ab^2 - b^2 = b^2(a - 1),$$

$$7(3^2) - 3^2 = 3^2(7 - 1) = 9(6) = 54.$$

   In the following equation, $(b + c)$ is the common multiplier. Thus,

$$a(b + c) + d(b + c) = (b + c)(a + d);$$

$$6(3 + 2) + 4(3 + 2) = (3 + 2)(6 + 4) = 5(10) = 50.$$

After you have factored an expression, always check your work by applying the distributive law to see if your result will reproduce the expression you began with.

Equations

An equation is a statement that two expressions are the same in a quantitative sense. You can think of an equation as a kind of scales balancing the quantities on the left and right sides of the **equals** sign. The operations in this section are especially useful in **solving** equations, that is, in expressing one variable as a function of another, or in finding the numerical value of a variable.

Addition

The same quantity can be added algebraically—that is, added to or subtracted from—both sides of an equation without destroying the balance. Thus,

$$(a + b)^2 = a^2 + 2ab + b^2, \quad \text{and}$$
$$(a + b)^2 + c = a^2 + 2ab + b^2 + c;$$
$$(3 + 4)^2 = 3^2 + 2(3)(4) + 4^2, \quad \text{and}$$
$$(3 + 4)^2 + 5 = 3^2 + 2(3)(4) + 4^2 + 5,$$
$$7^2 + 5 = 9 + 24 + 16 + 5,$$
$$49 + 5 = 54,$$
$$54 = 54.$$

Adding the same quantity to both sides of an equation is equivalent to adding two equations. If $a = b$, and if $c = d$, then we can add c to one side of the first equation and d to the other. Thus,

$$
\begin{array}{ll}
\text{Equation 1} & a = b \\
+ \ \text{Equation 2} & c = d \\
\hline
= \ \text{Equation 3} & a + c = b + d.
\end{array}
$$

Multiplication and Division

Multiplying or dividing both sides of an equation by the same quantity preserves the equality. Thus,

$$\text{if} \quad a = b, \quad \text{then} \quad ca = cb;$$
$$3 = \sqrt{9}, \quad \text{and} \quad 2(3) = 2\sqrt{9} = 6.$$

Dividing both sides of an equation by the same quantity is an especially useful operation in solving equations. Thus,

if $a + b = c,$ then $\dfrac{a + b}{d} = \dfrac{c}{d}.$

Squaring and Taking Square Roots

Squaring both sides of an equation preserves the equality, and so does taking the square root of both sides. Indeed, raising both sides to any given power, or taking any given root of both sides, also preserves the equality. Thus,

if $a + b = c + d,$ then $(a + b)^2 = (c + d)^2;$

$5 + 2 = 4 + 3,$ and $(5 + 2)^2 = (4 + 3)^2,$

$$7^2 = 7^2.$$

Taking the square root of both sides,

if $e + f = g,$ then $\sqrt{e + f} = \sqrt{g};$

$16 + 9 = 25,$ and $\sqrt{16 + 9} = \sqrt{25};$

$$\sqrt{25} = \sqrt{25}.$$

Solving Equations

Solving an equation means arranging things so that a single variable raised to the first power appears by itself on the left side. For example, to solve the following equation for b.

$a - 2b - c = d,$

begin by adding algebraically $-a$ and $+c$ to both sides. Those operations are equivalent to transposing a and c from one side to the other and changing their signs, yielding

$-2b = d - a + c.$

Dividing by 2,

$-b = \dfrac{d - a + c}{2}.$

Multiplying by -1 makes b positive, and yields the solution,

$b = \dfrac{a - c - d}{2}.$

Assigning numerical values to a, c, and d,

$11 - 2b - 4 = 1,$

$$-2b = 1 - 11 + 4,$$

$$b = \frac{11 - 4 - 1}{2} = \frac{6}{2} = 3.$$

Solving an equation for an unknown that is squared requires arranging things so that the squared unknown appears by itself on the left side of the equation. Taking the square root of both sides then yields the solution. For example, solving the following for a:

$$c^2 = a^2 + b^2, a^2 = c^2 - b^2, \quad \text{and} \quad a = \sqrt{c^2 - b^2};$$

$$5^2 = a^2 + 3^2, a^2 = 5^2 - 3^2, \quad \text{and} \quad a = \sqrt{5^2 - 3^2},$$

$$= \sqrt{25 - 9} = \sqrt{16} = 4.$$

Solving for an unknown under a radical requires squaring in order to remove the radical. To solve for c,

$$a = \sqrt{\frac{b^2}{c}}, \quad a^2 = \frac{b^2}{c}, \quad a^2 c = b^2, \quad \text{and finally} \quad c = \frac{b^2}{a^2};$$

$$4 = \sqrt{\frac{8^2}{c}}, \quad 4^2 = \frac{8^2}{c}, \quad 4^2 c = 8^2, \quad \text{and finally} \quad c = \frac{8^2}{4^2} = \frac{64}{16} = 4.$$

Inequalities

The following statements are inequalities: One is less than two, and five is greater than four. In symbols, we write

$$1 < 2, \quad \text{and} \quad 5 > 4,$$

where the $<$ sign means **less than** and the $>$ sign means **greater than.** If $a < 2$, then the following values of a—among many others—would satisfy the inequality: 1.99, 0, -1, and $-5,963$.

We will be especially concerned with inequalities of the following form:

$$a \leq b, \quad \text{and} \quad c \geq d,$$

where $\leq$ means **less than or equal to** and $\geq$ means **greater than or equal to.** If $c \geq 4$, then any value of c equal to 4 or more would satisfy the inequality. If $c \geq -4$, then the following values of c—as well as many other values— would satisfy the inequality: $-4, -2, 0, 1, 2$, and any other positive number.

We will often deal with the following kind of inequality,

$$c \leq a \leq b,$$

which is read "a is less than or equal to b and greater than or equal to c." The following are numerical examples:

$$1 \leq 1 \leq 2, \quad 1 \leq 2 \leq 2, \quad \text{and} \quad 1 \leq 2 \leq 3.$$

Addition and Subtraction

Algebraically adding the same quantity to both sides of an inequality preserves the relationship. Thus,

if $\quad b \leq a,\quad$ then $\quad c + b \leq a + c;$

since $\quad 3 \leq 4,\quad$ then $\quad 2 + 3 \leq 4 + 2,\quad$ and $\quad 5 \leq 6.$

In the case of subtraction,

since $3 \leq 4,\quad$ then $\quad -6 + 3 \leq 4 - 6,\quad$ and $\quad -3 \leq -2.$

The principle remains the same where the inequality is in the following form:

if $\quad d \leq e \leq f,\quad$ then $\quad d + g \leq e + g \leq f + g;$

since $\quad 5 \leq 7 \leq 8,\quad$ then $\quad 5 + 2 \leq 7 + 2 \leq 8 + 2;$

and $\quad 7 \leq 9 \leq 10.$

Multiplication

Multiplying an inequality by a *positive* quantity preserves the inequality. Thus,

if $\quad a \geq b,\quad$ then $\quad ca \geq cb,\quad$ for positive $c;$

since $\quad 3 \geq 2,\quad$ then $\quad 4(3) \geq 4(2),\quad$ and $\quad 12 \geq 8.$

Multiplying by a *negative* quantity requires reversing the direction of the inequality. Thus,

if $\quad a \geq b,\quad$ then $\quad -ca \leq -cb;$

since $\quad 3 \geq 2,\quad$ then $\quad -4(3) \leq -4(2),\quad$ and $\quad -12 \leq -8.$

Multiplying by -1, for example, yields the following result:

if $\quad a \leq b \leq c,\quad$ then $\quad -a \geq -b \geq -c;$

since $\quad 1 \leq 2 \leq 3,\quad$ then $\quad -1 \geq -2 \geq -3.$

Division by Zero

As we noted earlier, division by zero leads to mathematical absurdity, and is therefore not a permissible operation. We now illustrate one of the absurd consequences of dividing by zero.

Let $a = b.$

Adding b to both sides,

$a + b = 2b$.

Subtracting $2a$,

$a + b - 2a = 2b - 2a$.

Collecting terms and factoring,

$b - a = 2(b - a)$.

Dividing by $b - a$,

$$\frac{b - a}{b - a} = \frac{2(b - a)}{b - a}, \qquad \text{and thus} \qquad 1 = 2.$$

The fallacy in this demonstration lies in dividing by zero. Since $a = b$, $a - b = 0$, and thus dividing by $a - b$ is not permissible. All of the above operations are valid down to the point where division by $a - b$ occurs. If division by zero is allowed to occur, then all bets are off: We could prove all manner of nonsense if that forbidden operation were to be permitted. This demonstration was not intended to convince you that we can prove *anything* mathematically — no matter how nonsensical — but rather to show what can happen when one of the cardinal rules is violated.

As you study this text, you may find it helpful to refer to this math review from time to time. Some of these operations may become more meaningful as you work with them in the context of statistical ideas and problems.

Estimating the Population Variance

B

This appendix deals with ideas that are introduced in Chapter 8 in connection with hypothesis testing, when the population standard deviation and variance are unknown. Estimates of the population variance also play a direct role in the analysis of variance, a set of procedures presented in Chapter 14 for testing hypotheses about differences among the means of several groups. You can profitably study the present material in conjunction with the sections of Chapter 8 dealing with the t distribution, and you may want to refer to this material again when you are working with the analysis of variance.

Expected Value of the Sample Variance

We noted earlier that the sample mean, $\overline{X}$, is a random variable. In any particular sample, it is most unlikely that $\overline{X}$ will be precisely equal to μ, the population mean, although in a large number of random samples of size N, the sample means will tend to cluster around μ_x. We have shown in Chapter 8 that the expected value of the sample mean is equal to μ_x, and we have shown that the standard error of the mean — its standard deviation — is equal to $\sigma_x/\sqrt{N}$. Since the central limit theorem tells us that the sample means will be approximately normally distributed for "large" samples, we can use the Z test described in Chapter 8 to test hypotheses about the observed value of a sample mean.

But in many cases, more often than not, we do not know the value of the population standard deviation. Intuitively, we might expect to be able to use the standard deviation of a sample as an estimate of the population standard deviation — and indeed we can, after we make a small correction. We will show that the expected value of the sample variance is systematically smaller than the population variance, and we will develop methods of correcting the sample variance and standard deviation to yield better estimates of the corresponding population parameters.

Figure B-1 shows a sample of five values of a random variable arranged on a measurement scale. Since the sample mean is a random variable, $\overline{X}$ does not precisely coincide with μ in our example. The figure shows that the deviation of one of the values of X from μ is equal to the sum of the deviation of that value from $\overline{X}$ and the deviation of $\overline{X}$ from μ. In general, the deviation of any score, X_i, from the population mean is the algebraic sum of the deviation of the score from the sample mean and the deviation of the sample mean from the population mean. Thus, we write the following equation:

$$(X_i - \mu) = (X_i - \overline{X}) + (\overline{X} - \mu). \tag{B-1}$$

In effect, we have subtracted and added $\overline{X}$ to the right side of Equation B-1. Squaring, summing across the N values in a sample, and dividing by N, we have

$$\sum_{i=1}^{N} \frac{(X_i - \mu)^2}{N} = \sum_{i=1}^{N} \frac{(X_i - \overline{X})^2}{N} + 2 \sum_{i=1}^{N} \frac{(X_i - \overline{X})(\overline{X} - \mu)}{N} + \sum_{i=1}^{N} \frac{(\overline{X} - \mu)^2}{N}. \tag{B-2}$$

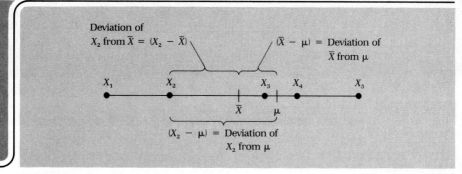

FIGURE B-1. Deviation of a particular score, X_2, from $\overline{X}$, the mean of a sample of 5 scores; deviation of $\overline{X}$ from μ, the population mean; and deviation of the score from the population mean.

Consider the middle term on the right side of Equation B-2. For any given sample, the deviation of the sample mean from the population mean is a constant, and thus we can rewrite the middle term, as below:

$$2(\overline{X} - \mu) \sum_{i=1}^{N} \frac{(X_i - \overline{X})}{N}. \tag{B-3}$$

It is easy to show that $\Sigma(X_i - \overline{X}) = 0$, which we left as an exercise in Chapter 4, and thus Expression B-3 is equal to zero. Returning to B-2, the first term on the right is the sample variance of X, that is, the variance observed in a sample of size N; the second term is zero; and the third term is a constant for each of the N values in a sample. Thus, we write

$$\sum_{i=1}^{N} \frac{(X_i - \mu)^2}{N} = SD_X^2 + \frac{N(\overline{X} - \mu)^2}{N} = SD_X + (\overline{X} - \mu)^2. \tag{B-4}$$

Equation B-4, above, applies to a single sample of size N drawn from the population. Now consider the infinite number of samples, each of size N, that could be drawn from the infinite population of values of X. Each of the quantities in B-4 has an expected value — that is, a mean in the long run, as we draw samples of size N again and again from the population. Taking expected values,

$$E\left[\sum_{i=1}^{N} \frac{(X_i - \mu)^2}{N} \right] = E(SD_X^2) + E(\overline{X} - \mu)^2;$$

$$\sum_{i=1}^{N} \frac{E(X_i - \mu)^2}{N} = E(SD_X^2) + \sigma_{\overline{X}}^2. \tag{B-5}$$

Since $E(X_i - \mu)^2$ is the population variance of the random variable X, and since that variance is a constant, the left side of B-5 is then

$$\sum_{i=1}^{N} \frac{E(X_i - \mu)^2}{N} = \sum_{i=1}^{N} \frac{\sigma_X^2}{N} = \frac{N\sigma_X^2}{N} = \sigma_X^2.$$

Substituting in B-5 and rearranging,

$$\sigma_X^2 = E(SD_X^2) + \sigma_{\bar{X}}^2, \quad \text{and} \quad E(SD_X^2) = \sigma_X^2 - \sigma_{\bar{X}}^2 \tag{B-6}$$

The above equation shows that the expected value of the sample variance is not equal to the population variance, but is smaller by an amount exactly equal to the variance of the sample mean. If we used the variance of a sample to estimate the unknown variance of a population, Equation B-6 shows that we would underestimate the population variance most of the time. We now correct the sample variance so that it will yield a better estimate of the population variance.

Correcting the Sample Variance

Expressing $\sigma_{\bar{X}}^2$ in B-6 as a function of σ_X^2, and continuing,

$$E(SD_X^2) = \sigma_X^2 - \frac{\sigma_X^2}{N} = \sigma_X^2\left(1 - \frac{1}{N}\right) = \sigma_X^2\left(\frac{N-1}{N}\right).$$

Multiplying by $N/(N-1)$,

$$E\left(\frac{N}{N-1}SD_X^2\right) = \sigma_X^2. \tag{B-7}$$

Thus, we have the important result that the expected value of the sample variance multiplied by a factor of $N/(N-1)$ is exactly equal to the population variance. Substituting Conceptual Formula 4-7 for the sample variance, SD_X^2, in Equation B-7,

$$E\left[\frac{N}{N-1}\frac{\Sigma(X-\bar{X})^2}{N}\right] = E\left[\frac{\Sigma(X-\bar{X})^2}{N-1}\right] = \sigma_X^2. \tag{B-8}$$

We will let the symbol S_X^2 stand for $N/(N-1)$ times the sample variance, and thus

$$S_X^2 = \frac{N}{N-1}SD_X^2 = \frac{\Sigma(X-\bar{X})^2}{N-1}. \tag{B-9}$$

Substituting S_X^2 in Equation B-8,

$$E(S_X^2) = \sigma_X^2. \tag{B-10}$$

Since the expected value of S_X^2 is equal to σ_X^2, S_X^2 is an **unbiased estimator** of the population variance. While it is true that S_X^2 is a random variable which will take on different values in different samples, its expected value — its average value in the long run — is exactly equal to the population variance. The sample variance as defined by Formula 4-7, SD_X^2, is a **biased estimator** of the population variance, since we have just shown that the expected value of SD_X^2 is less than σ_X^2. The simple expedient of multiplying that biased estimator by the correction factor $N/(N-1)$ removes the bias and provides an unbiased estimator of the population variance. For large values of N, the correction factor approaches 1, and is thus of little consequence, but for small samples, the correction is substantial.

Formula B-9 is the conceptual formula for the unbiased estimator of the population variance, but that formula is inconvenient for computational purposes. Multiplying Computational Formula 4-8 for the sample variance by $N/(N-1)$ yields the following computational formula:

$$\text{Unbiased estimator of population variance} = S_{\bar{X}}^2 = \frac{\Sigma X^2 - \dfrac{(\Sigma X)^2}{N}}{N-1}. \tag{B-11}$$

Taking the square root of the equation above,

$$\text{Corrected estimator of population standard deviation} = S_X = \sqrt{\frac{\Sigma X^2 - \dfrac{(\Sigma X)^2}{N}}{N-1}}. \tag{B-12}$$

To save words in our future discussions, we will usually refer to $S_{\bar{X}}^2$ and S_X as simply the variance and standard deviation, understanding that those sample statistics represent estimators of the corresponding population parameters.

Since $S_{\bar{X}}^2$ is an unbiased estimator of the population variance, and since S_X is the square root of $S_{\bar{X}}^2$, you might expect S_X to be an unbiased estimator of the population standard deviation, but that is not quite the case. The expected value of S_X is slightly less than the value of σ_X and thus S_X is a slightly biased estimator of the population standard deviation, although it is a better estimator than SD_X, the uncorrected sample standard deviation.

The expected value of $S_{\bar{X}}^2$ is the average value of that sample statistic in the long run. In Equation B-13 below, each S^2 is the variance of a particular sample, there are N such samples — each of a particular size that we do not need to specify — and N is very large. Keep in mind here that N is the number of samples, not the sample size.

$$\text{Population variance} = \sigma^2 = E(S^2) = \frac{1}{N}(S_1^2 + S_2^2 + \cdot \cdot \cdot + S_N^2), \tag{B-13}$$

where N is the number of samples, and N is very large. Since the population standard deviation is the square root of the population variance.

$$\text{Population standard deviation} = \sigma = \sqrt{\sigma^2} = \sqrt{E(S^2)} = \sqrt{\frac{1}{N}(S_1^2 + S_2^2 + \cdot \cdot \cdot + S_N^2)}. \tag{B-14}$$

Now consider the expected value of S, the average of that sample statistic in the long run;

$$E(S) = \frac{1}{N}(S_1 + S_2 + \cdot \cdot \cdot + S_N), \tag{B-15}$$

where N is the number of samples, and N is very large. If we can show that Expression B-15 is less than B-14, then we will have shown that the expected value of S underestimates the population standard deviation. Thus, if it is true that

$$\frac{1}{N}(S_1 + S_2 + \cdots + S_N) < \sqrt{\frac{1}{N}(S_1^2 + S_2^2 + \cdots + S_N^2)}, \tag{B-16}$$

then it follows that $E(S) < \sigma$. We will not show that the above inequality is true in general, but it is easy to see that the inequality holds for specific cases. In words, Inequality B-16 says that the mean of a set of numbers is less than the square root of the mean of the squares of the numbers. For example, substituting the numbers 1, 2, and 3 in B-16,

$$\frac{1}{3}(1 + 2 + 3) < \sqrt{\frac{1}{3}(1^2 + 2^2 + 3^2)},$$

$$\frac{6}{3} < \sqrt{\frac{1 + 4 + 9}{3}},$$

$$2 < \sqrt{4.67} = 2.16.$$

There is no special magic in the integers 1, 2, and 3, and thus you can easily show for yourself that Inequality B-16 holds for any set of real numbers you care to use — as long as the numbers are not all equal. (In a large number of random samples — an infinite number, for example — when would the observed values of the sample variances all turn out to be precisely equal?)

Eliminating the small amount of bias remaining in S is cumbersome. Fortunately, that small amount of bias is quite negligible for our purposes, and is ordinarily disregarded by most statisticians. We will find S, the corrected estimate of the population standard deviation, entirely adequate in our future developments.

Some Derivations in Correlation and Regression

C

The material in this appendix supplements the material on correlation and regression in Chapter 10, and on association between dichotomous variables in Chapter 11. The section headed *Fitting Least-Squares Regression Lines* uses a little calculus. However, DuBois (1965, p. 129) presents noncalculus derivations of the least-squares regression equations. You will not need any calculus at all to follow the sections in this appendix headed *Partitioning the Total Variance*, and *Deriving the ϕ Coefficient*.

Fitting Least-Squares Regression Lines

Predicting Y from X

The problem is to find the one straight line through the swarm of points in a bivariate distribution that will best express the relationship between Y and X. The equation of the regression line in Figure C-1 is of the following general form:

$$Y' = a_Y + b_Y X. \tag{C-1}$$

The above regression equation yields a value of Y' for each subject, that is, a predicted Y value. By a **predicted Y value** we mean an estimated value of Y based on the regression equation. Only in the case of a perfect correlation will the Y' values found by solving a regression equation precisely equal the observed Y values. Since the correlation between X and Y is not perfect in Figure C-1, there is an **error deviation** for each subject equal to the observed Y value minus the predicted value, Y'.

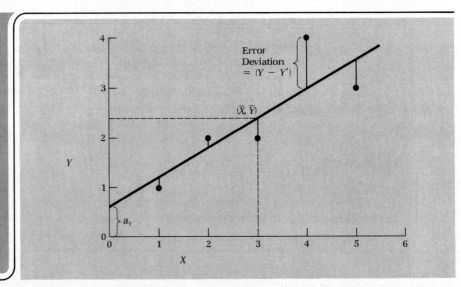

FIGURE C-1. Error deviation for one subject.

Error deviation $= Y - Y'$.

Only one of the error deviations is labeled in Figure C-1, but keep in mind that an error deviation exists for each subject in a bivariate distribution.

Under the least-squares criterion, the line of best fit — the regression line that best expresses Y as a function of X — is the one straight line that minimizes the sum of the squared error deviations, below. Squaring C-2 and summing across all of the subjects in the distribution yields the following:

$$\text{Sum of squared error deviations} = \Sigma(Y - Y')^2. \tag{C-2}$$

Substituting Regression Equation C-1 for Y' in C-2 above,

$$\Sigma(Y - Y')^2 = \Sigma[Y - (a + bX)]^2. \tag{C-3}$$

We have dropped the subscripts from a and b in Equation C-3 above. Since we are dealing only with the prediction of Y from X in this section, there will be no chance of confusion.

Our problem is to find those values of a and b that will minimize the sum of the squared error deviations in Equation C-3. We will treat the regression coefficients a and b as variables, which are determined by the observed values of X and Y in our set of data. We can then find the value of a by taking the partial derivative of the above equation with respect to a, setting the derivative equal to zero, and solving for a. Similarly, we can find the value of b by taking the partial derivative with respect to b, setting that derivative equal to zero, and solving for b. Before taking the partial derivatives, we will carry out the squaring operation on the right side of Equation C-3 and distribute the summation operator.

$$\begin{aligned}
\Sigma(Y - Y')^2 &= \Sigma[Y^2 - 2Y(a + bX) + (a + bX)^2] \\
&= \Sigma[Y^2 - 2aY - 2bXY + a^2 + 2abX + b^2X^2] \\
&= \Sigma Y^2 - 2a\Sigma Y - 2b\Sigma XY + Na^2 + 2ab\Sigma X + b^2\Sigma X^2. \tag{C-4}
\end{aligned}$$

In taking the partial derivative of Equation C-4 with respect to a, the variable b and all other terms are treated as constants:

$$\frac{\partial}{\partial a}[\Sigma(Y - Y')^2] = 0 - 2\Sigma Y - 0 + 2Na + 2b\Sigma X + 0$$

$$= -2\Sigma Y + 2Na + 2b\Sigma X. \tag{C-5}$$

Setting the partial derivative in Equation C-5 equal to zero,

$$-2\Sigma Y + 2Na + 2b\Sigma X = 0.$$

Solving for a, and simplifying,

$$2Na = 2\Sigma Y - 2b\Sigma X,$$

$$a = \frac{\Sigma Y}{N} - b\frac{\Sigma X}{N} = \bar{Y} - b\bar{X}. \tag{C-6}$$

In order to use Equation C-6 to find the value of a, the value of b must first be found. Taking the partial derivative of Equation C-4 with respect to b, treating a and the other terms as constants.

$$\frac{\partial}{\partial b}\Sigma(Y-Y')^2 = 0 - 0 - 2\Sigma XY + 0 + 2a\Sigma X + 2b\Sigma X^2$$

$$= -2\Sigma XY + 2a\Sigma X + 2b\Sigma X^2. \tag{C-7}$$

Setting Equation C-7 equal to zero and rearranging,

$$\Sigma XY = a\Sigma X + b\Sigma X^2. \tag{C-8}$$

We now have two simultaneous equations, C-6 and C-8, involving the two unknowns, a and b. All of the other terms and factors in those equations can be calculated from the data, so we are able to solve the simultaneous equations for the unknown regression coefficients, a and b.

Substituting C-6 for a in C-8, we have

$$\Sigma XY = (\bar{Y} - b\bar{X})\Sigma X + b\Sigma X^2$$

$$= \bar{Y}\Sigma X - b\bar{X}\Sigma X + b\Sigma X^2.$$

Solving for b,

$$b(\Sigma X^2 - \bar{X}\Sigma X) = \Sigma XY - \bar{Y}\Sigma X,$$

$$b\left[\Sigma X^2 - \frac{(\Sigma X)^2}{N}\right] = \Sigma XY - \frac{\Sigma X\Sigma Y}{N},$$

$$b = \frac{\Sigma XY - \dfrac{\Sigma X\Sigma Y}{N}}{\Sigma X^2 - \dfrac{(\Sigma X)^2}{N}}. \tag{C-9}$$

The numerator of Formula C-9 is exactly equal to the numerator of the computational formula for r, Formula 10-4, and the denominator of C-9 is equal to one of the terms in the denominator of 10-4. Thus, if you have already calculated r, you have the ingredients for calculating b. However, we will develop a more compact expression for b.

Noting that the denominator of Equation C-9 is the sum of squares of X, we write

$$b = \frac{\Sigma XY - \dfrac{\Sigma X\Sigma Y}{N}}{SS_X} = \frac{\Sigma XY - \dfrac{\Sigma X\Sigma Y}{N}}{N\,SD_X^2}. \tag{C-10}$$

Multiplying numerator and denominator of Equation C-10 by SD_XSD_Y/SD_XSD_Y,

$$b = \frac{\Sigma XY - \dfrac{\Sigma X\Sigma Y}{N}}{N\,SD_X^2}\frac{SD_XSD_Y}{SD_XSD_Y} = \frac{\Sigma XY - \dfrac{\Sigma X\Sigma Y}{N}}{N\,SD_XSD_Y}\frac{SD_Y}{SD_X}. \tag{C-11}$$

Since Equations 10-2 and 10-4 show that

$$\frac{\Sigma XY - \dfrac{\Sigma X \Sigma Y}{N}}{N\,SD_X SD_Y} = r,$$

Substituting in Equation C-11 yields the following expression:

$$b = r\frac{SD_Y}{SD_X}. \tag{C-12}$$

Equations C-6 and C-12 are presented in Chapter 10 as Equations 10-8 and 10-9. An example of the use of those equations is given in that chapter.

Predicting X from Y

As we noted in Chapter 10, there are times when we may be as interested in predicting X from Y as in predicting Y from X. The regression equation and coefficients for predicting X from Y are the following:

$$X' = a_X + b_X Y, \tag{C-13}$$

$$a_X = \overline{X} - b_X \overline{Y}, \tag{C-14}$$

$$b_X = r\frac{SD_X}{SD_Y}. \tag{C-15}$$

The regression coefficients above minimize the sum of the squared error deviations from the regression line:

$$\text{Sum of squared error deviations} = \Sigma(X - X')^2. \tag{C-16}$$

Notice that each of the error deviations in Equation C-16 is equal to $(X - X')$, while in Equation C-2 each deviation is equal to $(Y - Y')$. The equation for a_X is found by expanding the right side of Equation C-16, substituting Equation C-13 for X', taking the partial derivative with respect to a_X, setting the derivative equal to zero, and solving for a_X. A similar procedure yields the equation for b_X. Thus, the same least-squares procedures are used to find the regression equations for predicting X from Y or Y from X. However, a_X is the X intercept — that is, the point where the regression line cuts the X axis — and b_X is the slope of the regression line with respect to the Y axis — that is, $\Delta X/\Delta Y$, the change in X over the change in Y.

Partitioning the Total Variance

We will partition the total variance of Y in this section, but these procedures apply equally to the total variance of X. By **total variance** of Y, we simply mean the *variance* of Y, as we have defined that term in the past. In Chapter 10, we showed that

$$\begin{array}{ccc} \text{Total} \\ \text{deviation} \end{array} = \begin{array}{c} \text{Error} \\ \text{deviation} \end{array} + \begin{array}{c} \text{Explained} \\ \text{deviation} \end{array};$$

$$(Y - \bar{Y}) = (Y - Y') + (Y' - \bar{Y}).$$

Squaring and summing,

$$\Sigma(Y - \bar{Y})^2 = \Sigma(Y - Y')^2 + 2\Sigma(Y - Y')(Y' - \bar{Y}) + \Sigma(Y' - \bar{Y})^2. \qquad \text{(C-17)}$$

The middle term of Equation C-17 vanishes, thus considerably simplifying our further developments. We offered an intuitive explanation of that fact in Chapter 10. Here, we will demonstrate that the middle term of that equation is indeed equal to zero. To do so, we need to express the regression equation in a different form. Beginning with Equation C-1, substituting for a and simplifying,

$$Y' = a + bX = (\bar{Y} - b\bar{X}) + bX = \bar{Y} + b(X - \bar{X}). \qquad \text{(C-18)}$$

Substituting Equation C-18 for Y' in the middle term of Equation C-17, and continuing,

$$\begin{aligned} 2\Sigma(Y - Y')(Y' - \bar{Y}) &= 2\Sigma[Y - [\bar{Y} + b(X - \bar{X})]][[\bar{Y} + b(X - \bar{X})] - \bar{Y}] \\ &= 2\Sigma[(Y - \bar{Y}) - b(X - \bar{X})]b(X - \bar{X}) \\ &= 2\Sigma[b(X - \bar{X})(Y - \bar{Y}) - b^2(X - \bar{X})^2] \\ &= 2b\Sigma[(X - \bar{X})(Y - \bar{Y}) - b(X - \bar{X})^2]. \end{aligned}$$

Distributing the summation operator,

$$2b[\Sigma(X - \bar{X})(Y - \bar{Y}) - b\Sigma(X - \bar{X})^2] = 2b[\Sigma(X - \bar{X})(Y - \bar{Y}) - bSS_x]. \qquad \text{(C-19)}$$

From Equation C-10,

$$bSS_x = \Sigma XY - \frac{\Sigma X \Sigma Y}{N},$$

and from Equation 10-3 in Chapter 10,

$$\Sigma XY - \frac{\Sigma X \Sigma Y}{N} = \Sigma(X - \bar{X})(Y - \bar{Y}),$$

and thus $\qquad bSS_x = \Sigma(X - \bar{X})(Y - \bar{Y}).$

Substituting for bSS_x in Equation C-19,

$$2b[\Sigma(X - \bar{X})(Y - \bar{Y}) - \Sigma(X - \bar{X})(Y - \bar{Y})] = 0.$$

Thus, we have shown that the midterm of Equation C-17 is equal to zero. Dropping that term and dividing by N,

$$\frac{\Sigma(Y - \bar{Y})^2}{N} = \frac{\Sigma(Y - Y')^2}{N} + \frac{\Sigma(Y' - \bar{Y})^2}{N};$$

$$\begin{array}{ccc} \text{Total} \\ \text{variance} \end{array} = \begin{array}{c} \text{Error} \\ \text{variance} \end{array} + \begin{array}{c} \text{Explained} \\ \text{variance} \end{array} \qquad \text{(C-20)}$$

Thus, we have the important result showing that the total variance can be partitioned into error variance and explained variance. That result is used in further developments in Chapter 10.

Deriving the ϕ Coefficient

As we noted in Chapter 11, the ϕ coefficient is an index of association — correlation — between two dichotomous variables. The ϕ coefficient is appropriate only where each variable represents a true dichotomy, such as male and female, or living or dead. If two continuous variables have been artificially dichotomized — such as height into the categories of short and tall, or weight into light and heavy — then the tetrachoric correlation coefficient r_t is more appropriate (McNemar, 1969).

The ϕ coefficient derives directly from the Pearson r when one level of each dichotomy is arbitrarily assigned the value of 0 and the other level the value of 1. Table C-1 shows the symbols we will use in our derivation. Symbol a represents the number of persons having an X value of 0 and a Y of 1, b is the number having an X of 1 and a Y of 0, and c and d represent the numbers having the other two possible combinations of X and Y values. It will be convenient to use Computational Formula 10-6 in our derivation:

$$r = \frac{\Sigma XY - \dfrac{\Sigma X \Sigma Y}{N}}{\sqrt{SS_X SS_Y}}. \tag{10-6}$$

Now consider the sum of the cross-products, ΣXY, in Formula 10-6. If a subject has an X or a Y value of zero, then that subject's cross-product is zero, and thus makes no contribution to the value of ΣXY. If a subject has an X and a Y value of 1, then the subject's cross-product is 1. Since there are d such subjects in Table C-1, having cross-products of 1, and $a + b + c$ subjects having cross-products of zero, it follows that

$$\Sigma XY = d(1) + (a + b + c)(0) = d. \tag{C-21}$$

TABLE C-1.   Fourfold Table for Calculation of ϕ Coefficient

		X		
		0	1	
Y	0	a	b	$a + b$
	1	c	d	$c + d = \Sigma Y$
		$a + c$	$b + d$	$a + b + c + d = N$
			$= \Sigma X$	

Now consider the sum of the Xs and the sum of the Ys. Since there are $a + c$ subjects having an X value of 0 and $b + d$ having an X of 1, it follows that $\Sigma X = b + d$. The sum of the Ys is found similarly. Thus,

$$\Sigma X = b + d, \quad \text{and} \quad \Sigma Y = c + d. \tag{C-22}$$

We now have an expression for the numerator of Formula 10-6 in terms of the frequencies of cases in the cells of Table C-1. Dealing with the denominator, the following expressions are the computational formulas for the sums of squares:

$$SS_X = \Sigma X^2 - \frac{(\Sigma X)^2}{N}, \quad \text{and} \quad SS_Y = \Sigma Y^2 - \frac{(\Sigma Y)^2}{N}. \tag{9-13}$$

Since X and Y can take only the values of 0 and 1, it is true in our special case that $X^2 = X$, and $Y^2 = Y$. Thus, it follows that $\Sigma X^2 = \Sigma X$, and $\Sigma Y^2 = \Sigma Y$. Substituting from Equation C-22 in Equation 9-13, above,

$$SS_X = b + d - \frac{(b + d)^2}{N}, \quad \text{and} \quad SS_Y = c + d - \frac{(c + d)^2}{N}.$$

Putting the expression for SS_X over a common denominator and factoring,

$$SS_X = \frac{N(b + d) - (b + d)^2}{N} = \frac{(b + d)[N - (b + d)]}{N}. \tag{C-23}$$

Noting that N is equal to the sum of all the frequencies in Table C-1, and substituting for N in the numerator of Equation C-23,

$$SS_X = \frac{(b + d)[(a + b + c + d) - (b + d)]}{N} = \frac{(b + d)(a + c)}{N}. \tag{C-24}$$

Similarly,

$$SS_Y = \frac{(c + d)[(a + b + c + d) - (c + d)]}{N} = \frac{(a + b)(c + d)}{N}. \tag{C-25}$$

We have now defined all of the quantities in Formula 10-6 in terms of the frequencies in Table C-1. Substituting Expressions C-21 and C-22 in the numerator, and C-24 and C-25 in the denominator of Formula 10-6,

$$r = \frac{\Sigma XY - \dfrac{\Sigma X \Sigma Y}{N}}{\sqrt{SS_X SS_Y}} = \frac{d - \dfrac{(b + d)(c + d)}{N}}{\sqrt{\dfrac{(a + c)(b + d)(a + b)(c + d)}{N^2}}}$$

$$= \frac{dN - (b + d)(c + d)}{\sqrt{(a + b)(c + d)(a + c)(b + d)}}.$$

Substituting for N, and multiplying $(b + d)(c + d)$,

$$r = \frac{d(a + b + c + d) - bc - bd - cd - d^2}{\sqrt{(a + b)(c + d)(a + c)(b + d)}} = \frac{ad - bc}{\sqrt{(a + b)(c + d)(a + c)(b + d)}}.$$

Thus, where X and Y are true dichotomies, the computations of the Pearson r simplifies very greatly. Under those conditions, the symbol ϕ is used to stand for the correlation coefficient. Thus,

$$\phi = \frac{ad - bc}{\sqrt{(a+b)(c+d)(a+c)(b+d)}}. \tag{C-26}$$

Notice that each of the expressions in the denominator above is one of the marginal totals from Table C-1. Thus, the calculation of a *phi* coefficient is very straightforward. Formula C-26 is reproduced as Formula 11-2 in Chaper 11.

Answers to Study Questions and Exercises

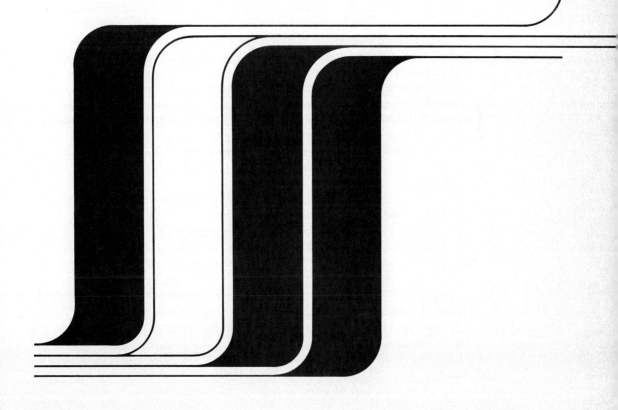

Chapter 1

1. Qualitative descriptions use verbal labels or categories, such as bright, average, and dull, or introvert and extravert. Quantitative descriptions attempt to attach numbers to people and their behaviors in meaningful ways. Psychological measurements, such as aptitude and achievement tests, and personality scales, represent attempts to describe people more quantitatively and precisely. Throughout the history of science, quantitative description has led to greater understanding of every aspect of the physical universe. In the field of psychology, quantitative description has led to better prediction, and promises to help us achieve higher levels of control and understanding.

2. In some instances, the arbitrary zero on an interval scale is a convenient point that is agreed upon by consensus, as in a scale of calendar time, or the Fahrenheit or Celsius temperature scales. Time did not begin with the birth of Christ, nor does temperature begin at 0° F or 0° C. The point is, the arbitrary zero on an interval scale does not correspond with the total absence of whatever is being measured. It is less obvious that a zero on an aptitude, achievement, or intelligence test is also an arbitrary zero. But a test score of zero does not necessarily correspond with the total absence of whatever the test attempts to measure, since there might be *some* way for a subject to demonstrate some slight amount of knowledge or ability — if only the tester were clever enough to devise a sufficiently easy question. On the other hand, an absolute zero does correspond with total absence of a characteristic. Zero height and zero weight, for example, represent highly meaningful, nonarbitrary points on their respective scales, even though heights and weights of zero are never directly observed. The fact that those absolute zero points exist conceptually allows us to make ratio comparisons between quantities measured on ratio scales. For example, a person 6 feet tall is twice as tall as a person 3 feet tall. We could not make that kind of comparison in the absence of an absolute, meaningful zero on the measurement scale.

3. Unfortunately, some things simply cannot be measured on ratio scales, and thus we do not always have a free choice of using the highest caliber scale.

4.   a. Since weight is a ratio scale, anyone who weighs twice as many pounds as another person is twice as heavy.

b. Model numbers sometimes represent an ordinal scale, where lower numbers indicate earlier models, and sometimes only a nominal scale, where the numbers merely stand for name tags. In either case, we cannot make ratio comparisons by dividing one model number into another.

c. The scale here is nominal. It is meaningless to ask questions about differences between numbers on a nominal scale.

d. The scale of model numbers here is ordinal, in the sense that the lower numbers represent earlier airplanes. It is meaningless to ask questions about the magnitude of differences between measurements on an ordinal scale.

e. Since IQ measurements represent interval measurements at best, we cannot divide one IQ into another meaningfully.

f. Scores on a course examination, like IQ measurements, represent interval measurements at best. We cannot make ratio comparisons on an interval scale.

g. The second rat is indeed pressing the bar at twice as great a rate as the first rat. Numbers of bar presses represent a ratio scale.

h. Yes, since weight is a ratio scale, regardless of what is being measured.

i. The gold, silver, and bronze medal winners comprise an ordinal scale. The situation here is analogous to the model numbers in b and d above. Based on the information given here, we have no way of comparing the differences between winners.

j. Reaction time, unlike calendar time, is measured on a ratio scale. Thus, the first person is twice as fast as the second, or we could say the second is twice as slow as the first.

k. If a subject reacts in response to a stimulus delivered by the experimenter, then there can be no reaction time of zero — since all physiological processes require at least a small amount of time. An apparent reaction time of zero, or a response *before* the delivery of the stimulus, could result only from the subject's "jumping the gun." The fact that we can never observe a real reaction time of zero does not at all impair the usefulness of the absolute zero on the reaction-time scale.

5. A carefully conducted experiment, where we have manipulated an independent variable, allows us to draw conclusions about causal relationships between variables. In an observation, where we have only observed variables as they occur, we cannot draw causal inferences so clearly. Thus, we should always prefer experiments to observations. But in many cases, for humane, ethical, or practical reasons, we cannot apply the experimental method. In those cases, we must rely on observations.

6. We observe a correlation here between population density and serious crime over a period of many years, but it would be a mistake to suppose that increasing population density necessarily caused the increase in crime. However, the correlation that we observe does not allow us to rule out the possibility of a causal relationship between population density and crime. The strongest statement that we can make, in the absence of much additional data, is that those variables *may* be causally related.

7. The independent variable is group size: 1, 2, or 3 people. Each of those group sizes represents a *level* of the independent variable. The dependent variable is the number of correct solutions.

8. Manipulating an independent variable means assigning the values —levels— of that variable to the subjects in an experiment. For example, in a drug experiment, the experimenter determines which subjects will receive a drug and which a placebo. The independent variable in such an experiment has two levels, which we can designate *D* and *P*, and it is the experimenter who determines which subjects will be assigned to level *D* and which to *P*. On the other hand, in a study of sex differences the researcher compares the performance of male and female subjects. Once again, there seems to be an independent variable having two levels—*M* and *F*—in such a study. But the experimenter has not *caused* the subjects in such a study to have their particular levels of the sex variable. Instead, the subjects have brought with them their own values of the sex variable. Only where an independent variable has been manipulated can we draw strong causal inferences. We will elaborate these ideas in later chapters, particularly in Chapter 13.

Chapter 2

1. First, list the heights in order and tally the number of men and women having each height, as below.

Height	60	61	62	63	64	65	66	67	68	69	70	71	72	73	74	75	76
Women	/	/	/	/	////	///	//	//		/							
Men								/	//	//	///	////	//	////		//	/

The histograms for men and women are shown in the following figure.

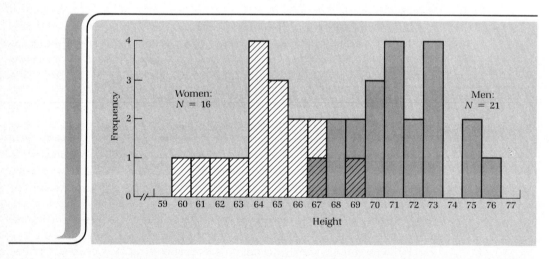

Since the two distributions overlap, the bars are cross-hatched in one histogram and shaded in the other. Notice that each histogram, taken separately, conforms approximately to the three-quarters rule—that is, the height of each histogram is approximately equal to 3/4 of its width. Also notice the break in the horizontal axis, indicating that the origin is not located at a height of zero. There is no break in the vertical axis since the frequency dimension begins at an origin of zero. Keep a supply of graph paper on hand for your frequency distributions and other figures that you will need to draw from time to time. Develop the habit of using a straightedge to draw all of your graphs as neatly as possible.

2. The frequency polygon below uses the frequencies tallied in Exer-

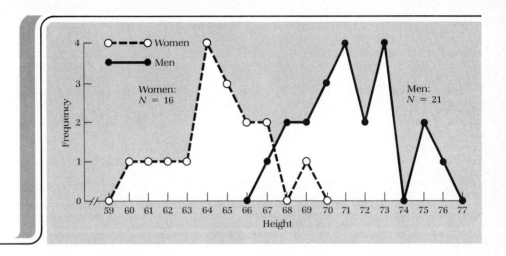

cise 1, above. A frequency polygon, like a histogram, should conform to the three-quarters rule. Notice that each frequency polygon shows a frequency of zero for the heights just below and just above the lowest and highest values actually represented in the distribution. Plotting those zero frequencies results in a closed figure in each frequency polygon having an area equal to N, the number of cases. As we noted earlier, we will make extensive use of the idea of the area of a frequency polygon in later developments.

Where two frequency polygons are plottted on the same axes, using filled circles and solid lines for one distribution and unfilled circles and dashed lines for the other will help you distinguish the distributions at a glance. As you can see by comparing the above figures, where two distributions overlap, frequency polygons convey information more clearly than histograms. We will have many occasions to display two distributions on the same axes.

3. The bar graph below shows the frequencies of major crimes committed with and without a gun. The filled bars indicate the use of a gun, and the unfilled bars indicate that no gun was used. It is often useful to let a filled symbol stand for the presence of something and an unfilled symbol stand for its absence, as in the present example.

There are many times more aggravated assaults and robberies than there are murders, and thus the lengths of the bars representing those crimes indicate their relative frequencies. But it would be a mistake to suppose that the very short bars for murder show that a negligible number of murders occurred during 1979. Indeed, those short bars represent 21,456 murders committed during that year.

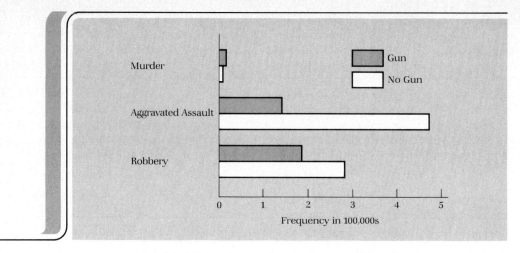

4. The table below shows the percentages of each category of crime committed with and without a gun. For each kind of crime, those percentages are found by dividing the respective frequencies in Exercise 3 by the column total for that crime. For example, the percentage of murders committed with a gun is $(13,582/21,456)100 = 63.3\%$. As a check on your arithmetic, the percentages within columns must all sum to 100%.

	Murder	Aggravated Assault	Robbery	Total Crimes
Gun	63.3%	23.0%	39.7%	30.9%
No gun	36.7%	77.0%	60.3%	69.1%
	100.0%	100.0%	100.0%	100.0%

The following bar graph shows the percentages in the table above. The length of the horizontal scale here is the same as in the bar graph in Exercise 3, but notice that the relative lengths of the bars are very different in the present bar graph.

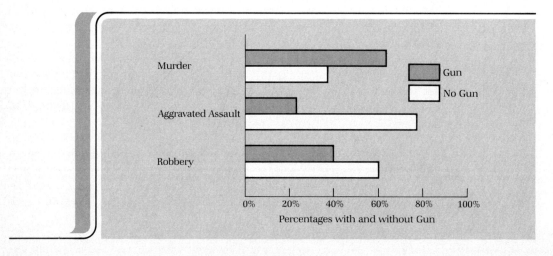

The present bar graph and the previous one convey different information, and thus each has its uses. For example, the previous bar graph shows that there are relatively few murders in comparison with aggravated assaults, but the present bar graph shows more clearly that a murder is far more likely to be committed with a gun than is an aggravated assault.

5.   There is a strong relationship between category of crime and the use of a gun. Nearly two-thirds of murders — but only about one-fourth of aggravated assaults, and 40% of robberies — are committed with guns. The bar graph showing percentages is most useful in displaying the association between kind of crime and the use or nonuse of a gun.

6.   The data show a very strong relationship, association, between the categories of major crimes against persons and the use of a gun. A murder, the most severe crime of all, is far more likely to be committed with a gun than is any other major crime. However, there are difficulties in attempting to draw cause-and-effect inferences based on correlations, or associations, as we have noted. Although nearly two-thirds of murders are committed using guns, it does not necessarily follow that eliminating guns would reduce the murder rate by two-thirds. No doubt, some murderers would find other means in the total absence of guns. Nor does it follow that eliminating guns would have *no* effect on the murder rate. It seems highly probable that *some* murders would not be committed in the absence of the readily available lethal force that a gun provides. We will have more to say about correlations and causal inferences in later chapters.

7.   To construct a pie chart, it is first necessary to find the central angles of all of the slices, as in the table below. Convert each percentage to a proportion, and multiply by 360°, the number of degrees in a full circle.

Category	Percentage	Central Angle
Alcoholic disorder	18%	$.18(360°) = 65°$
Brain syndromes	11	$.11(360°) = 40$
Depressive disorders	10	36
Personality disorders	10	36
Schizophrenia	30	107
All others	21	$.21(360°) = 76$
	100%	360°

Round each angle to the nearest degree. A small problem arises, since the central angle for schizophrenia turns out to be 108°, and the sum of the angles is then 361°. A reasonable solution is to decrease the angle of the largest slice by 1 degree. Using a protractor, compass, and straightedge, construct the pie chart as shown below.

8.   Begin by arranging the digits representing the 10s and 100s places of the scores along a vertical line, the stem, see bottom left figure p. 474. Then, for each score in the distribution, list the unit digit — the digit in the 1s place — on the same line as the 10s and 100s digits for that score. This operation is equivalent to tallying a distribution, except here you list the value of each unit digit instead of merely making a tally mark for each score. The

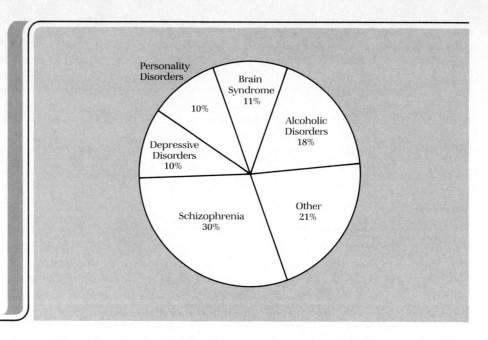

result is a variety of stem-and-leaf display, or digital histogram, where the unit digits are in a scrambled order on each line. Arranging the unit digits in order on each line, as in the figure on the right, makes a more pleasing display that is also more readily interpretable.

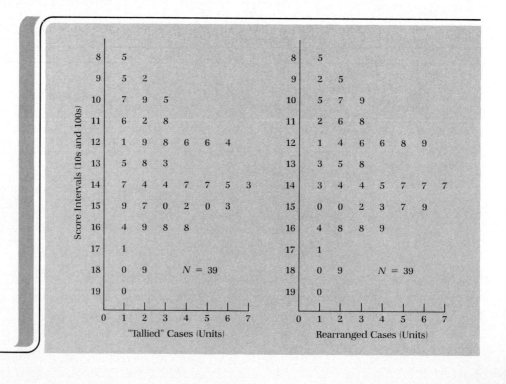

Chapter 3

1.   **a.** Mean $= \overline{X} = \dfrac{\Sigma X}{N} = (4 + 4 + 6 + \cdots + 5)/18 = 5.00$.

   b. The grouped frequency distribution is shown below. You should lay out your work approximately as shown in that table. Cultivating good work habits is very useful, and you will find that orderliness saves time and effort in the long run.

Index of Summation j	Score X_j	Simple Frequency f_j	Cumulative Frequency cf_j	Frequency Times Score $f_j X_j$
5	7	1	$18 = N$	7
4	6	4	17	24
3	$X_{LL} = 4.5 \rightarrow$ 5 $=$ Mode $\ f_w =$ 8		13	40
2	4	4	$cf_b = 5$	16
1	3	1	1	3

$$\sum_{j=1}^{5} f_j = N = 18 \qquad\qquad \sum_{j=1}^{5} f_j X_j = 90$$

By Formula 3-5, $\qquad \overline{X} = \dfrac{\sum\limits_{j=1}^{m} f_j X_j}{N} = \dfrac{\sum\limits_{j=1}^{5} f_j X_j}{18} = \dfrac{90}{18} = 5.00.$

By Formula 3-7, $\qquad Mdn = X_{LL} + i\left(\dfrac{\dfrac{N}{2} - cf_b}{f_w}\right) = 4.5 + 1\left(\dfrac{\dfrac{18}{2} - 5}{8}\right)$

$$= 4.5 + \dfrac{4}{8} = 4.5 + .5 = 5.00.$$

   c. Mean $= 5.00$ (see calculations in table above).

   d. Distribution is symmetrical, as you can see by the simple frequencies above.

   e. Mode $= 5$, the score having the highest simple frequency. Since the distribution is symmetrical and has only a single mode, the median and the mode are identical.

   f. By Formula 3-7, Mdn $= 5.00$ (see calculations above).

   g. See the frequency polygon on p. 476 (top). A vertical line is often erected at the mean to help us visualize the proportion of a distribution lying above and below that point, but you should not suppose that the mean — or the mode, or median — is located at the top of such a line. Each of those measures of central location is a point on the measurement scale, the horizontal axis, and not a point marking the peak of a frequency polygon. Since this distribution is symmetrical, the mean, mode, and median are identical.

2.   **a.** Mean $= \overline{X} = \dfrac{\Sigma X}{N} = (6 + 3 + 5 + \cdots + 7)/18 = 5.00$.

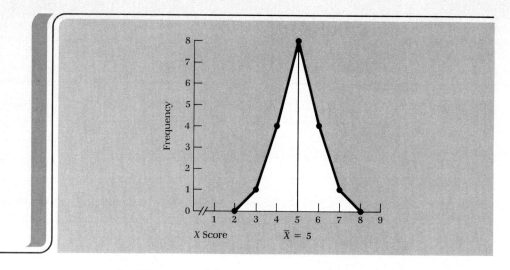

b. The grouped frequency distribution is shown below:

Score	1	2	3	4	5	6	7	8	9	
f	1	1	2	3	4	3	2	1	1	$\Sigma f = 18 = N$

c. The mode is 5, and since the distribution is symmetrical, and has only a single peak, the median is also 5.

d. The frequency polygon is shown below.

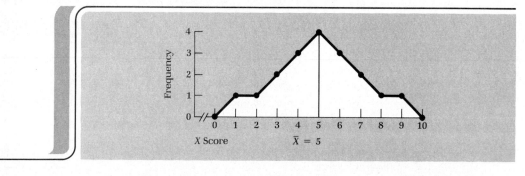

3. Distribution 2 has the best subject, and also the worst. Since the distributions have the same measures of central location, neither distribution is better overall than the other — that is, on the average, both groups of subjects perform equally well.

4. The above distributions have the same means, modes, and medians, and are thus identical in terms of their measures of central location. But the shapes of the distributions differ greatly. The scores in Distribution 1 are more tightly clustered around the central location while the scores in Distribution 2 are more widely dispersed. Thus, the distributions differ in their *dispersion*, an aspect of frequency distributions that we will develop extensively in the next chapter.

5. a. $\bar{X} = \dfrac{\Sigma X}{N} = (6 + 2 + \cdots + 3)/18 = 5.00.$

b. Grouped frequency distribution:

Index of Summation j	Score X_J	Simple Frequency f_j	Cumulative Frequency cf_j
7	7	4	18 = N
6	$X_{LL} = 5.5 \rightarrow$ 6	$f_w = 5$	14
5	5	3	$cf_b = 9$
4	4	2	6
3	3	2	4
2	2	1	2
1	1	1	1

$$\sum_{j=1}^{7} f_j = N = 18$$

By Formula 3-7, $Mdn = X_{LL} + i\left(\dfrac{\dfrac{N}{2} - cf_b}{f_w}\right) = 5.5 + 1\left(\dfrac{\dfrac{18}{2} - 9}{5}\right) = 5.5 + \dfrac{0}{5} = 5.5 + 0 = 5.5.$

c. *Mode* = 6.

d. The interval containing the median is the lowest score interval where the cumulative frequency exceeds $N/2$, or 9 in the present distribution. Thus, a score of 6 represents that interval. Applying Formula 3-7, above, yields a value of 5.5 for the median. It is also possible to find the median by inspection in this distribution. The cumulative frequency through a score of 5 is exactly equal to half the cases in the distribution, and thus the median corresponds to the upper limit of that score interval, namely 5.5.

e. The distribution is negatively skewed, since the quantity $(\bar{X} - Mdn)$ is negative.

f. The frequency polygon shows the direction of the skew graphically:

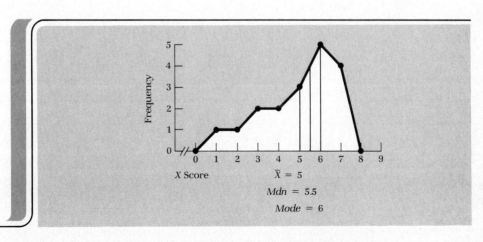

The distribution is skewed toward the lower tail. Vertical lines are erected at the mean, median, and mode. Remember, those measures are located on the horizontal axis, not at the tops of the vertical lines.

6. **a.** $\overline{X} = \dfrac{\Sigma X}{N} = (3 + 9 + \cdots + 5)/18 = 5.00.$

b. Grouped frequency distribution:

Index of Summation j	Score X_j	Simple Frequency f_j	Cumulative Frequency cf_j
7	9	1	18 = N
6	8	1	17
5	7	2	16
4	6	2	14
3	$X_{LL} = 4.5 \rightarrow \; 5$	$f_w = 3$	12
2	4 = $Mode$	5	$cf_b = 9$
1	5	4	4

$$\sum_{j=1}^{7} f_j \;=\; N \;=\; 18$$

By Formula 3-7, $\quad Mdn = X_{LL} + i \left(\dfrac{\dfrac{N}{2} - cf_b}{f_w} \right) = 4.5 + 1 \left(\dfrac{\dfrac{18}{2} - 9}{3} \right) = 4.5 + \dfrac{0}{3} = 4.5 + 0 = 4.5.$

c. $Mode = 4.$

d. Interval containing median is found as in Exercise 5 above.

e. Distribution is positively skewed since the quantity $(\overline{X} - Mdn)$ is positive.

f. The frequency polygon shows the direction of skew graphically, toward the upper end of the measurement scale.

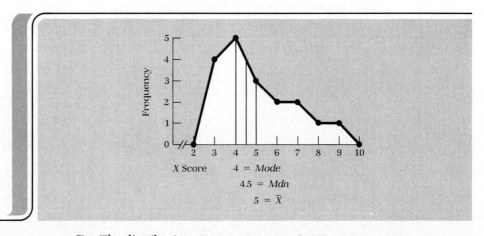

4 = Mode
4.5 = Mdn
5 = $\overline{X}$

7. The distributions in Exercises 5 and 6 above have the same mean, but different modes and medians. Both distributions are skewed, but in opposite directions. Overall, we might argue that the subjects in Distribution 5 performed better, since half of those subjects had scores above the median of

5.5, while half of Distribution 6 lies above a median of 4.5. On the other hand, the lowest score occurs in Distribution 5, and the highest in Distribution 6. But the higher value of the mode in Distribution 5 indicates that the most typical subjects in that distribution performed better than the most typical subjects in the other distribution.

8. In these particular skewed distributions, the mean is the least useful measure of central location. In most cases, the median is the most informative measure of central location in a skewed distribution.

9. **a.** Grouped frequency distribution:

Index of Summation j	Score X_j	Simple Frequency f_j	Cumulative Frequency cf_j
9	9	1	18 = N
8	8	2	17
7	7 = $Mode_2$	4	15
6	6	2	11
5	Mdn = 5	f_w = 0	9
4	4	2	cf_b = 9
3	3 = $Mode_1$	4	7
2	2	2	3
1	1	1	1

$$\sum_{j=1}^{9} f_j = N = 18$$

b. There are two modes, as shown above. The median is 5.00, the middle of the empty interval below which the cumulative frequency is $N/2$. Thus, half the distribution is located below and half above that point. Since the distribution is symmetrical, the mean and median are identical.

c. Using Formula 3-7 requires division by f_w. But in the present case, the median falls in an empty interval having a zero frequency, and thus $f_w = 0$. Since division by zero is not permissible (see Appendix A), Formula 3-7 cannot be used here or in any similar situation.

d. The frequency polygon is shown below:

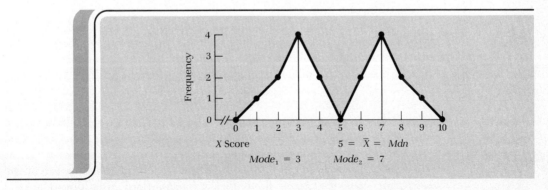

e. The distribution is bimodal. Two kinds of subjects, differing greatly in ability, might account for such a distribution. For example, if half of the 18 subjects were fourth-grade pupils and the other half eighth-graders, then we might expect a bimodal distribution. Bimodality can also arise in other ways, for example, where about half of the questions on an exam are rather easy and the other half rather difficult.

Note. By now, the distributions in the preceding exercises may look familiar. Indeed, all of those distributions are shown in Figure 2-11 in Chapter 2. Compare the frequency polygons you have drawn with the histograms in that figure. Frequency polygons are much easier to draw than histograms, and are quite adequate for most purposes.

10. The frequency distribution is shown below:

Index of Summation j	Score: Children X_j	Simple Frequency f_j	Cumulative Frequency cf_j	Frequency Times Score $f_j X_j$
7	6 or more	277,000	57,804,000	1,662,000
6	5	549,000	57,527,000	2,745,000
5	4	1,745,000	56,978,000	6,980,000
4	3	4,913,000	55,233,000	14,739,000
3	2	11,005,000	50,320,000	22,010,000
2	$X_{LL} = 0.5 \rightarrow$ 1	$f_w =$ 11,882,000	39,315,000	11,882,000
1	0 $= Mode$	27,433,000	$cf_b =$ 27,433,000	0

$$\sum_{j=1}^{7} f_j = N = 57,804,000 \qquad\qquad \sum_{j=1}^{7} f_j X_j = 60,018,000$$

By Formula 3-5,
$$\overline{X} = \frac{\sum_{j=1}^{m} f_j X_j}{N} = \frac{\sum_{j=1}^{7} f_j X_j}{57,804,000} = \frac{60,018,000}{57,804,000} = 1.04.$$

By Formula 3-7,
$$Mdn = X_{LL} + i\left(\frac{\frac{N}{2} - cf_b}{f_w}\right) = 0.5 + 1\left(\frac{\frac{57,804,000}{2} - 27,433,000}{11,882,000}\right)$$

$$= 0.5 + \frac{1,469,000}{11,882,000} = 0.5 + 0.12 = 0.62.$$

a. *Mode* $= 0$, the score having the largest simple frequency. *Mdn* $= 0.62$ (see calculations above).

b. $\overline{X} = 1.04$.

c. There are 277,000 households having 6 or more children under 18 years of age living at home, but the data provide no indication of the number of households having 6, 7, 8, 9, or perhaps 20 such children. However, the mode would still be zero, and the median would still be 0.62, even if all of those 277,000 households had 20 children each — or even some greater number. But the mean of 1.04, which you calculated under the assumption that each household in the 6+ category had exactly 6 children, represents the lowest possible value of the mean under an unrealistic assumption. Thus, 1.04 represents a lower limit for the true value of the mean. Now, can we arrive at some idea of a possible upper limit for the mean? If we make the unrealistic assumption that each household in the 6+ category had 10 children, then the mean would turn out to be 1.06. Thus, the mean is unlikely to be much greater than 1.04, and almost surely less than 1.06.

d. The distribution is positively skewed since the quantity $(\overline{X} - Mdn)$ is positive. Furthermore, the longer, lower tail of the frequency polygon—where the scores are farthest away from the mean, median, and mode—is located toward the high end of the measurement scale, indicating a positive skew.

e. The measures of central location should be indicated by vertical lines, as in your other frequency polygons.

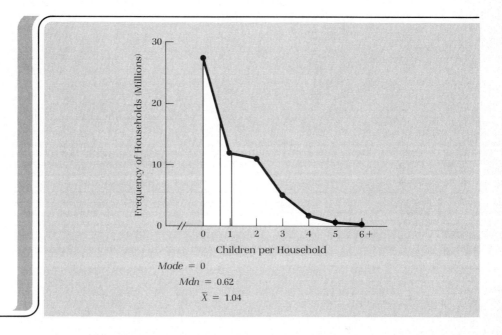

Mode = 0

Mdn = 0.62

$\overline{X}$ = 1.04

11.   a. *Mode.*   **b.** Mean (see Figure 3-3 in Chapter 3).   **c.**   Mean. **d.** *Mode.*   **e.** Median.   **f.** Mean.   **g.** *Mode* or median.   **h.** Mean.   **i.** Median.

12.   a. Postively skewed.   **b.** More than half are below the mean. **c.** Exactly half are below the median in any distribution, whether skewed or symmetrical.   **d.** The figure below illustrates the positively skewed distribution.

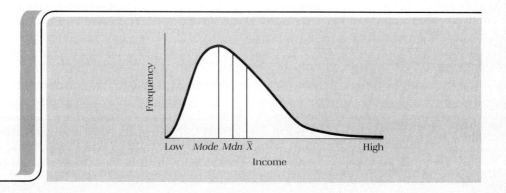

13. a. Negatively skewed. **b.** More than half are above the mean.
c. Exactly half are below the median, as in any distribution. **d.** The figure
below shows the negatively skewed distribution.

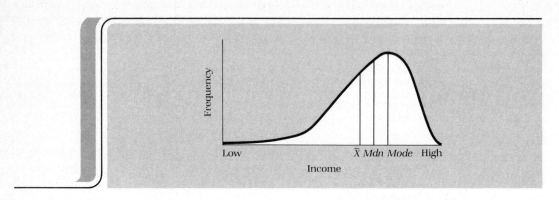

Chapter 4

1. The following table shows the distribution and computations:

Score	4	4	6	6	5	5	3	5	5	5	6	4	6	7	5	5	4	5	ΣX	=	90
$(X - \bar{X})$	−1	−1	1	1	0	0	−2	0	0	0	1	−1	1	2	0	0	−1	0	$\Sigma(X - \bar{X})$	=	0✓
$\lvert X - \bar{X}\rvert$	1	1	1	1	0	0	2	0	0	0	1	1	1	2	0	0	1	0	$\Sigma\lvert X - \bar{X}\rvert$	=	12
X^2	16	16	36	36	25	25	9	25	25	25	36	16	36	49	25	25	16	25	ΣX^2	=	466

By Formula 3-1,
$$\bar{X} = \frac{\Sigma X}{N} = \frac{90}{18} = 5.$$

By Formula 4-1,
$$AD = \frac{\Sigma\lvert X - \bar{X}\rvert}{N} = \frac{12}{18} = 0.67.$$

By Formula 4-5,
$$SD = \sqrt{\frac{\Sigma X^2 - \dfrac{(\Sigma X)^2}{N}}{N}} = \sqrt{\frac{466 - \dfrac{(90)^2}{18}}{18}} = \sqrt{\frac{466 - \dfrac{90(90)}{18}}{18}}$$

$$= \sqrt{\frac{466 - 5(90)}{18}} = \sqrt{\frac{16}{18}} = \sqrt{.8889} = .9429 = 0.94.$$

By Formula 4-8,
$$\text{Variance} = SD^2 = \frac{\Sigma X^2 - \dfrac{(\Sigma X)^2}{N}}{N} = .8889 = 0.89.$$

a. Range $= 7 - 3 + 1 = 5$.
b. To find the average deviation, it is first necessary to find the
mean. Then find for each score the quantity $(X - \bar{X})$. Notice that all of the
signs are retained at this stage, even though the calculation of the AD uses

absolute values. Retaining the signs provides a useful arithmetic check, since $\Sigma(X - \bar{X}) = 0$, as you will see in a later exercise. The absolute deviations, the magnitudes without regard to sign, are then summed and divided by N, yielding the *AD*.

  c. To find the *SD*, square each of the scores, and enter the sum of the squared scores into Formula 4-5. Square the sum of the scores, and enter that quantity into the formula, proceeding as in the table above. Remember, $\Sigma X^2 \neq (\Sigma X)^2$, that is, the sum of the squared scores is not equal to the squared sum of the scores. Since the mean is an integer in the present example, it may have occurred to you that it would be as easy to use our Conceptual Formula 4-3 to find the *SD* as to use the Computational Formula 4-5. But in most situations, the mean will be a decimal number, and each deviation will also be a decimal. Carrying out a large number of subtractions involving decimals is a very error-prone operation — even using a calculator — and in addition to human errors, the conceptual formula produces larger rounding errors that simply cannot be avoided.

  d. You have already found the variance, which is merely the square of the standard deviation. Thus, the variance is the quantity under the radical in Exercise 1c above.

  e. The frequency polygon appears below. Keep in mind the fact

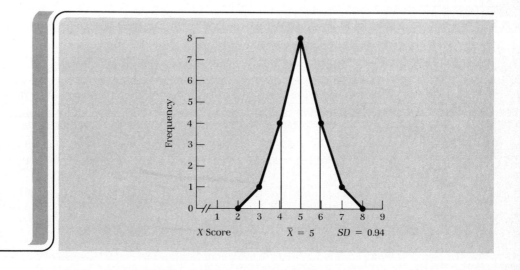

that the mean is a *point* on the horizontal axis, not at the top of the vertical line you drew. Remember also that the *SD* is a *distance* measured along the scale of scores, not a point on the horizontal axis, and certainly not a point at the top of either of the vertical lines you drew 1 *SD* above and below the mean. We will have much more to say about the nature of measures of dispersion beginning in the next chapter and continuing throughout the remainder of the book.

  2. **a.** The following table shows the grouped frequency distribution:

Score	1	2	3	4	5	6	7	8	9		
f	1	1	2	3	4	3	2	1	1	Σf	$= 18 = N$
fX	1	2	6	12	20	18	14	8	9	ΣfX	$= 90$
$(X - \bar{X})$	-4	-3	-2	-1	0	1	2	3	4		
$f(X - \bar{X})$	-4	-3	-4	-3	0	3	4	3	4	$\Sigma f(X - \bar{X})$	$= 0$
$\lvert X - \bar{X}\rvert$	4	3	2	1	0	1	2	3	4		
$f\lvert X - \bar{X}\rvert$	4	3	4	3	0	3	4	3	4	$\Sigma f\lvert X - \bar{X}\rvert$	$= 28$
X^2	1	4	9	16	25	36	49	64	81		
fX^2	1	4	18	48	100	108	98	64	81	ΣfX^2	$= 522$

By Formula 3-6, $\qquad \bar{X} = \dfrac{\Sigma fX}{N} = \dfrac{90}{18} = 5.$

By Formula 4-2, $\qquad AD = \dfrac{\Sigma f\lvert X - \bar{X}\rvert}{N} = \dfrac{28}{18} = 1.56.$

By Formula 4-6, $\qquad SD = \sqrt{\dfrac{\Sigma fX^2 - \dfrac{(\Sigma fX)^2}{N}}{N}} = \sqrt{\dfrac{522 - \dfrac{90^2}{18}}{18}}$

$$= \sqrt{\dfrac{522 - \dfrac{8100}{18}}{18}} = \sqrt{\dfrac{522 - 450}{18}} = \sqrt{\dfrac{72}{18}} = \sqrt{4} = 2.$$

By Formula 4-8, $\qquad$ Variance $= SD^2 = \dfrac{\Sigma fX^2 - \dfrac{(\Sigma fX)^2}{N}}{N} = 4.$

b. Range $= 9 - 1 + 1 = 9$.

c. $AD = 1.56$ (see table above). Before calculating the average deviation, find the sum of the deviations from the mean with regard to sign. As an arithmetic check, the sum of the signed deviations, $\Sigma f(X - \bar{X})$, must equal zero, as in Exercise 1.

d. $SD = 2$.

e. Variance $= SD^2 = 4$, which is the quantity under the radical.

f. You should indicate the location of the mean and the points 1 SD above and below the mean as in Exercise 1e above.

3. **a** and **b.** Compare the estimates here based on your frequency polygons with the more precise determinations in c and d below, based on the histograms in Figures 2-11A and 2-11B.

c. Referring to Figure 2-11A, the mean is 5 and the SD is 0.94. Thus, a point that is 1 SD above the mean falls at 5.94, which is 0.44 above the lower limit of the score interval of 6. It follows that .56 of the area of each unit square representing a score of 6 lies beyond the point 1 SD above the mean, and thus for the 4 scores of 6, the area lying beyond that point is $4(.56) = 2.24$. Adding the whole area of the score of 7, we have $2.24 + 1.00 = 3.24$. Since the total area of the histogram (and the frequency polygon as well) is equal to $N = 18$, the proportion of area lying beyond a point 1 SD above the mean is $2.24/18 = .12$. The situation is simpler in Figure 2-11B, since $SD = 2$. Referring to that figure, the point that is 1 SD above the mean exactly bisects the area of the two scores of 7. Adding the areas of the scores of 8 and 9, we have an area of 3.00, and dividing by 18 gives .17, the proportion of the total area lying beyond 1 *SD* above the mean. Since the distribution is symmetrical, the same proportion also lies below a point 1 *SD* below the mean. Areas of various portions of frequency distributions will be very important in several contexts, and we will develop refined methods of dealing with such areas beginning in the next chapter.

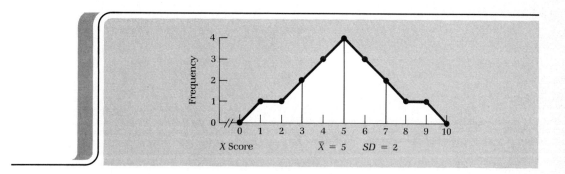

4.   a. Bowler A is the more consistent. A smaller *SD* indicates less dispersion, less spread, and thus greater consistency.

   b. Bowler B is more likely to bowl a 200 game. Both bowlers have the same mean score in their last 100 games, but since B has a greater *SD* — a greater spread — bowler B is more likely to bowl a high game. It also follows that B is more likely to bowl a very *low* game. Thus, greater dispersion is both good and bad in the present context.

   5.   For violinists A and B, the mean settings were respectively 0.2 Hz below and 0.2 Hz above the standard frequency of 440 Hz. Thus, in terms of their mean performance the violinists were equally proficient, the first playing very slightly flat, and the second very slightly sharp by an equal amount. But violinist B had the smaller average deviation, and thus made smaller errors on the average across the 50 trials. Indeed, the conditions of this experiment represent the *method of average error,* sometimes called the *method of adjustment,* one of the classical psychophysical methods. The *AD* can be taken as a measure of the *just noticeable difference,* the *JND,* which is the smallest difference between two stimuli that the observer can detect 50% of the time. Thus, violinist B has the smaller *JND,* and therefore the better pitch perception. For an extended discussion of psychophysical methods, see Schiffman (1982).

   6.   For each score in a distribution there is a deviation from the mean, $(X - \bar{X})$. Summing across all the scores,

Sum of deviations $= \Sigma(X - \bar{X})$.

Expanding the summation, dropping parentheses, and collecting terms,

$$\Sigma(X - \bar{X}) = (X_1 - \bar{X}) + (X_2 - \bar{X}) + \cdots + (X_N - \bar{X})$$

$$= \underbrace{X_1 + X_2 + \cdots + X_N}_{N \text{ terms}} \qquad + \underbrace{\bar{X} + \bar{X} + \cdots + \bar{X}}_{N \text{ terms}}$$

$$= \Sigma X \qquad\qquad + \qquad N\bar{X}.$$

Notice that there are no subscripts on the N instances of $\bar{X}$ in the above equation, since the mean takes on a single value in any given distribution. Thus, each deviation represents the subtraction of a constant from a particular score. Noting that $N\bar{X} = N(\Sigma X/N)$, substituting in the above equation yields

$$\Sigma(X - \bar{X}) = \Sigma X - N\bar{X} = \Sigma X - N\frac{\Sigma X}{N} = \Sigma X - \Sigma X = 0. \tag{1}$$

Thus, we have the important result that the sum of the deviations from the mean is equal to zero.

It is also possible to carry out the above demonstration slightly differently, using fewer steps. Distributing the summation operator across $(X - \bar{X})$, noting that the mean is a constant, and recalling that $\Sigma c = Nc$,

$$\Sigma(X - \bar{X}) = \Sigma X - N\bar{X}.$$

Proceeding as in Equation 1, above, completes the demonstration.

It is possible, of course, to create a distribution of specific scores, find the mean, and then show arithmetically that the sum of the deviations from the mean is equal to zero. But the algebraic proofs above show that *in general*— that is, ever and always—the sum of the deviations from the mean is equal to zero in any distribution of scores. An arithmetic demonstration using a specific distribution would not possess that level of generality. We will make extensive use of summation operations, and it will be very useful to understand the principles of summation.

7. Dividing by a constant is equivalent to multiplying by the reciprocal of the constant, as we point out in Appendix A, which is a review of basic mathematic operations. Thus, dividing by c is equivalent to multiplying by $1/c$. If c is a constant, so is the reciprocal. Thus, referring to Table 4-3,

$$Mean\left(\frac{X}{c}\right) = Mean\left(\frac{1}{c}X\right) = \frac{1}{c}Mean(X) = \frac{1}{c}\bar{X} = \frac{\bar{X}}{c};$$

$$Var\left(\frac{X}{c}\right) = Var\left(\frac{1}{c}X\right) = \frac{1}{c^2}Var(X) = \frac{1}{c^2}SD^2 = \frac{SD^2}{c^2};$$

$$SD\left(\frac{X}{c}\right) = SD\left(\frac{1}{c}X\right) = \frac{1}{c}SD(X) = \frac{1}{c}SD = \frac{SD}{c}.$$

8. The basis for answering each of these questions can be found in Table 4-3 and the accompanying discussion.

a. The mean on the final exam is 66.12, the *SD* is 6.20, and the variance is 38.44.

b. Each score on the final is equal to 1.5 times the midterm score. Thus, $\overline{X} = 1.5(36.12) = 54.18$; $SD = 1.5(6.20) = 9.30$; $SD^2 = 1.5^2(38.44) = 86.49$.

c. Since the final is twice as long as the midterm, if every student answers the same proportion of questions correctly, then each student's final exam score will be twice as large as the midterm score. Thus, $\overline{X} = 2(36.12) = 72.24$; $SD = 2(6.20) = 12.40$; and $SD^2 = 2^2(38.44) = 153.76$.

9. Under each condition in Exercise 8 above, we can write a simple equation expressing each student's final exam score as a function of the student's midterm score. In *a*, $X_F = X_{MID} + 30$; in *b*, $X_F = 1.5X_{MID}$; and in *c*, $X_F = 2X_{MID}$. In each case, knowing a student's midterm exam score allows us to calculate the student's performance on the final with no uncertainty, and thus the correlation, relationship, between midterm and final is perfect. Of course, we do not often observe perfect correlations in the real world, a point that we will amplify in later discussions. We will develop several measures of correlation and association in later chapters.

Chapter 5

1.   a. By Formula 5-3,

$$PR = \frac{N - R + .5}{N} = \frac{164 - 61 + .5}{164} = 63\text{rd.}$$

b. Since West Point cadets—and indeed, college students in general—are more highly selected than high-school students, General Eisenhower's performance represents a higher level of accomplishment than Private Schmidt's, even though both students had identical percentile ranks in graduating classes of the same size.

2.   a. The professional basketball player is more likely to be taller than the college player, even though both players are at the 50th percentile in their respective reference groups. Professional players are more highly selected on several dimensions, and are more likely to be taller than college players.

b. As the preceding examples show, comparing percentile ranks across different reference groups can be misleading. Comparing the percentiles of individuals *within* a reference group can be very informative, but comparisons *between* different groups are very hazardous.

3.   a. Although height is a ratio scale, converting a distribution of heights to percentile ranks results in an ordinal scale that lacks a meaningful zero. Thus, we cannot meaningfully divide one percentile into another, even though the percentiles here were derived from a ratio scale.

b. Money represents a ratio scale, but converting a distribution of incomes to percentiles degrades the scale to an ordinal scale that will not allow us to make ratio comparisons.

c. Since percentiles always represent an ordinal scale, the ratio comparison here cannot be made, regardless of the caliber of the measurement of aggression.

4. **a.** By Formula 5-11, $Z = \dfrac{X - \mu}{\sigma}$.

For an IQ of 98, $Z_{98} = \dfrac{98 - 100}{15} = \dfrac{-2}{15} = -0.13.$

In Table A, Column 3 gives the proportion of the total area below a Z-score of -0.13, namely .4483. Multiplying that proportion by 100 gives the percentage of cases below that Z-score. Thus, rounding to the nearest percentile the percentile rank is $PR_{98} = 45$th. For an IQ of 119,

$$Z_{119} = \dfrac{119 - 100}{15} = \dfrac{19}{15} = 1.27; \quad PR_{119} = 90\text{th}.$$

Since Z_{119} is positive, the proportion of total area below that Z-score is in Column 2 of Table A. Multiplying by 100 and rounding gives the percentile rank above.

b. To the extent that an IQ test measures intelligence, we can say that person B is brighter than person A. But since the IQ scale lacks a meaningful zero, we cannot divide 98 into 119 in order to find how many times brighter B is than A. Nor can we divide the 45th percentile into the 90th and conclude that B is twice as bright, although it is true that there are twice as many people below B as there are below A. We can also consider the number of people having *higher* IQs: Although 55% have IQs higher than A's and only 10% higher than B's, it would be a mistake to conclude that B is therefore 5 1/2 times as bright as A.

5. **a.** For bowler A,

$$Z_{194} = \dfrac{194 - 178}{16} = \dfrac{16}{16} = 1.00; \qquad PR_{194} = 84\text{th}.$$

$$Z_{200} = \dfrac{200 - 178}{16} = \dfrac{22}{16} = 1.38; \qquad PR_{200} = 92\text{nd}.$$

For bowler B,

$$Z_{194} = \dfrac{194 - 178}{22} = \dfrac{16}{22} = 0.73; \qquad PR_{194} = 77\text{th}.$$

$$Z_{200} = \dfrac{200 - 178}{22} = \dfrac{22}{22} = 1.00; \qquad PR_{200} = 84\text{th}.$$

b. The percentile rank of a score gives the percentage of scores in a distribution that are as low or lower. What we need here is the proportion of scores that are as high or higher than the given scores of 194 and 200 for each bowler. We can find the percentage of games at or above those scores by subtracting the percentile ranks from 100. Dividing the resulting percentages by 100 yields the proportion of games at or above 194 and 200.

For bowler A,
$$\text{Proportion at or above 194} = \frac{100 - PR_{194}}{100} = \frac{100 - 84}{100} = .16;$$

$$\text{Proportion at or above 200} = \frac{200 - PR_{200}}{100} = \frac{100 - 92}{100} = .08.$$

For bowler B,
$$\text{Proportion at or above 194} = \frac{100 - PR_{194}}{100} = \frac{100 - 77}{100} = .23;$$

$$\text{Proportion at or above 200} = \frac{100 - PR_{200}}{100} = \frac{100 - 84}{100} = .16.$$

The above calculations give the proportions of each bowler's last 100 games that were as high or higher than 194 and 200. Using past performance to predict the future, we might expect about .16 of Bowler A's games to be at or above 194, and about .08 to be at or above 200. Thus, Bowler A has a probability of .16 of bowling 194 or higher on the next game, and a probability of .08 of bowling 200 or higher. Similarly, Bowler B has a probability of .23 of bowling 194 or higher and a probability of .16 of bowling 200 or higher. We will explain in detail in the next chapter the relationships between probabilities and proportions.

6. The semi-interquartile range, Q, is half the difference between Q_1 and Q_3, the first and third quartiles. Q_1 is a point on the measurement scale that cuts off .25 of the total area in the lower tail of the curve, and Q_3 cuts off .25 in the upper tail. Now consider the average deviation. In a normal distribution, half the cases are within 1 AD of the mean, and half are farther away. Thus, the point on the measurement scale 1 AD below the mean cuts off .25 of the area in the lower tail of the curve, and the point 1 AD above the mean cuts off .25 in the upper tail. Thus, in a normal distribution Q and AD are identical measures of dispersion, but in a skewed distribution, those measures are not identical.

We can find the relationship between the AD and the SD by determining the value of Z that cuts off .25 of the area under the curve in the standard normal distribution. In Table A, Column 3 shows that .2514 of the area lies above a Z of .67, and .2483 lies above a Z of .68. Since the standard normal distribution has a standard deviation of 1.00, it follows that the AD is equal to .67 SD, rounding off to two decimal places. In any normal distribution, no matter what the values of the mean and standard deviation, the average deviation is equal to .67 SD.

7. The percentile ranks are useful here. By Formula 5-3, for the small graduating class,

$$PR_{51} = \frac{100 - 51 + .5}{100} = 49.50\text{th percentile.}$$

For the large graduating class,

$$PR_{51} = \frac{1,000 - 51 + .5}{1,000} = 94.95\text{th percentile.}$$

Since the students in the two graduating classes are equally able on the average, as their identical means indicate, and since the two distributions have equal measures of dispersion, it follows that equal ranks in those distributions represent very different levels of performance. Thus, a student ranking 51st in the large class is much higher in that distribution than is a student ranking 51st in the smaller class, as the calculated percentiles show. We will have much to say in later chapters about the relative standing of measures in different distributions.

8. We can compare your Psychology exam performance and your friend's performance in Political Science by using Z-scores to find percentile ranks. For your exam,

$$Z = \frac{81 - 72.40}{9.21} = \frac{8.60}{9.21} = 0.93; \quad PR = 82.38\text{th.}$$

For your friend's exam,

$$Z = \frac{81 - 72.40}{14.87} = \frac{8.60}{14.87} = 0.58; \quad PR = 71.90\text{th.}$$

The Z-scores and associated percentile ranks above show that your performance is better, in relation to your reference group of Psychology students, than your friend's performance, in relation to Political Science students. However, such a comparison says nothing about the relative difficulty of the two exams.

9. a. Short and fat. **b.** Average height and weight. **c.** Tall and thin. **d.** Small overall, short, and light in weight. **e.** Large overall, tall, and heavy.

10. The following table shows the frequency distribution in Figure 2-11F:

X	f	cum f	PR	Z	PR$_Z$
9	1	18 = N	97.22	2.27	98.84
8	1	17	91.67	1.70	95.54
7	2	16	83.33	1.14	87.29
6	2	14	72.22	0.57	71.57
5	3	12	58.33	0.00	50.00
4	5	9	36.11	−0.57	28.43
3	4	4	11.11	−1.14	12.71
	$\Sigma f = N = 18$		$\bar{X} = 5.00$		$SD = 1.76$

a. By Formula 5-5, $PR = \dfrac{cf_b + .5f_w}{N} \, 100.$

$$PR_3 = \dfrac{0 + .5(4)}{18} \, 100 \;=\; \dfrac{2}{18} \, 100 \;=\; 11.11;$$

$$PR_9 = \dfrac{17 + .5(1)}{18} \, 100 = \dfrac{17.5}{18} \, 100 = 97.22.$$

b. and **c.** By Formula 5-12, $Z = \dfrac{X - \overline{X}}{SD}.$

$$Z_3 = \dfrac{3 - 5.00}{1.76} = \dfrac{-2}{1.76} = -1.14; \quad PR_Z = 12.71.$$

$$Z_9 = \dfrac{9 - 5.00}{1.76} = \dfrac{4}{1.76} = \;\;2.27; \quad PR_Z = 98.84.$$

d. Since the present distribution is positively skewed, there are more cases below the mean than there are above. Since the procedure of using Z-scores to find percentile ranks is based on the assumption of an approximately normal distribution that is symmetrical, and since the present distribution is asymmetrical, there will be discrepancies between the percentiles found by Formula 5-5 and by Z-scores. For example, in a normal distribution, the mean is at the 50th percentile, but as your table will show, a score of 5 in the present distribution is at the 58.33rd percentile. Where a distribution is strongly skewed, Formula 5-5 will yield more accurate percentiles.

11.   a and **b.** The figures below show the raw-score and Z-score frequency polygons.

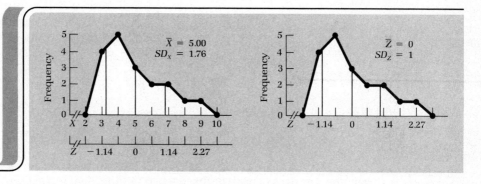

c. If you used the same horizontal scale for your frequency polygons — that is, the same distance between successive Z-scores as between successive raw scores — then your two frequency polygons will be identical in shape. Indeed, since every Z-score is a linear transformation of an X score, a raw-score frequency polygon *is* a Z-score frequency polygon. Thus, to show the distribution of Z-scores graphically, it is only necessary to list a Z-score under each raw score, as in the figure above.

d. There is an important general truth here: Transforming a set of raw scores to Z-scores does not change the shape of a distribution. Thus, if a distribution is skewed, then converting the raw scores to Z-scores will not convert the distribution into a normal distribution. It is true that the Z-scores in the standard normal distribution are normally distributed, having a mean of 0 and a standard deviation of 1, but that is true only because the *raw* scores (the X values) in that distribution are normally distributed. Several kinds of transformations will be useful in developing tests of statistical significance in later chapters.

Chapter 6

    1.   **a.** $P(5 \text{ boys}) = .51^5 = .035$.
        b. $P(5 \text{ girls}) = .49^5 = .028$.
        c. $P(5 \text{ children of same sex}) = P(5 \text{ boys or } 5 \text{ girls}) = P(5 \text{ boys} \cup 5 \text{ girls}) = P(5 \text{ boys}) + P(5 \text{ girls}) - P(5 \text{ boys} \cap 5 \text{ girls}) = .035 + .028 - 0 = .063$.
    2.   **a.** $P(3 \text{ deuteranopes}) = (1/2)^3 = 1/8$.
        b. $P(3 \text{ deuteranopes}|2 \text{ deuteranopes}) = 1/2$. The probability of a third deuteranopic son is independent of the prior birth of any other sons.
    3.   It is convenient to let the area of a rectangle 100 by 50mm represent the total population, as in the figure below. Since the population is

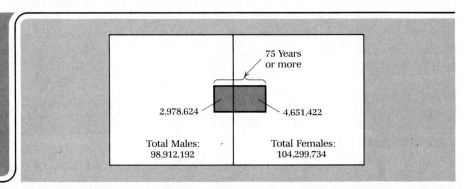

48.7% male and 51.3% female (see table), a vertical line 48.7mm from one end of the rectangle divides the total population into a set of males and a set of females. The area of each of those sets is proportional to the number of males and females in the population. To find the area of the small rectangle representing persons 75 years of age or older, we begin by noting that the area representing the total population is 100mm(50mm) = 5,000mm², that is, 5,000 square millimeters. Thus, an area of 50mm² represents 1% of the population. Since 3.8% of the population is 75 or older, the area of the rectangle representing those persons is 3.8(50mm²) = 190mm². Letting the length of that rectangle equal 20mm, for convenience, the height is then

190mm²/20mm = 9.5mm. Thus, a vertical slice of that rectangle 1 by 9.5mm contains 1/20th, or 5% of its area. Now 39.0% of the people 75 or older are males. Dividing 5% into 39.0% yields 7.8, and thus a vertical line 7.8mm from the end of the rectangle representing persons 75 or older partitions those people into male and female subsets. The area of each rectangle in the Venn diagram is directly proportional to the number of people that it represents.

4. a. $P(\text{Male}) = 98,912,192/203,211,926 = .487.$

b. $P(\text{Female}) = 104,299,734/203,211,926 = .513.$

c. $P(75 \text{ or older}) = 7,630,926/203,211,926 = .038.$

d. $P(\text{A male 75 or older}) = P(\text{Male} \cap 75 \text{ or older}) = \dfrac{2,978,624}{203,211,926} = $ .015.

e. $P(\text{A female 75 or older}) = \dfrac{4,651,422}{203,211,926} = .023.$

f. By Formula 6-15, $P(75 \text{ or older}|\text{Male}) = \dfrac{75 \text{ or older} \cap \text{Male}}{\text{Number of Males}} = \dfrac{2,978,624}{98,912,192} = .030.$

g. $P(75 \text{ or older}|\text{Female}) = \dfrac{75 \text{ or older} \cap \text{Female}}{\text{Number of Females}} = \dfrac{4,651,422}{104,299,734} = .045.$

h. The events *Female* and *75 or older* are not independent, since the prior probability of *75 or older* (in item c above) is not equal to the posterior probability of *75 or older* given that a *Female* was drawn (item g).

i. There is an association between sex and longevity, since the data show that women tend to live longer than men.

5. a. To find the probability of a hand consisting of 13 spades, we need to find the number of possible hands that can be dealt from a deck of 52 cards. The number of possible hands is the number of combinations of 52 things taken 13 at a time. Since only one of those combinations is all spades,

$$P(13 \text{ spades}) = \frac{1}{C_{13}^{52}} = \frac{1}{\dfrac{52!}{13!(52-13)!}} = \frac{13!39!}{52!}. \qquad (1)$$

Many small calculators will allow you to evaluate the factorial expression above without taking any numbers out of the machine. If you have such a calculator, your result will emerge in *scientific notation,* as a product of a power of 10, as we will explain. The number of combinations of 52 things taken 13 at a time is

$$C_{13}^{52} = 635,013,559,600 = 6.35013559600 \times 10^{11} = 6.35 \times 10^{11},$$

rounding to two decimal places. Thus,

$$P(13 \text{ spades}) = \frac{1}{6.35 \times 10^{11}} = \frac{1}{6.35} 10^{-11} = .157 \times 10^{-11}.$$

To express the above probability in conventional notation, move the decimal point 11 places to the left, an operation equivalent to dividing by 10^{11}, and then multiply by 10^{11}, thereby eliminating 10^{-11} as a factor. Thus,

$$P(13 \text{ spades}) = .157 \times 10^{-11} = .00000000000157.$$

Scientific notation is used extensively in dealing with numbers that are very small or very large.

There is another approach to the present problem that is especially useful if your calculator has no routine for directly handling factorials. If a hand is to consist of all spades, then the first spade can occur in 13 out of 52 ways. After the first spade is dealt, there are 12 remaining spades, and 51 remaining cards. The 2nd spade can occur in 12 out of 51 ways, the 3rd in 11 out of 50 ways, and so on through the 13th spade, which can occur in only 1 out of 40 ways. Thus, the probability of a spade on the first card is 13/52, the probability of a spade on the first *and* second cards is 13/52(12/51), and thus

$$P(13 \text{ spades}) = \frac{13}{52} \frac{12}{51} \frac{11}{50} \frac{10}{49} \frac{9}{48} \frac{8}{47} \frac{7}{46} \frac{6}{45} \frac{5}{44} \frac{4}{43} \frac{3}{42} \frac{2}{41} \frac{1}{40}. \tag{2}$$

It is fairly easy to find the above probability using chain division and multiplication on a small calculator. If you divide 13 by 52, multiply the result by 12, divide that result by 51, multiply by 11, divide by 50, and so on, then you can find the above probability without having to write down any of the intermediate steps.

It is easy to see that the probabilities in Equations 1 and 2 are identical. Noting that the numerator of Equation 2 is equal to 13!, and multiplying numerator and denominator by 39!, we have

$$P(13 \text{ spades}) = \frac{13 \cdot 12 \cdot 11 \cdot 10 \cdot 9 \cdot 8 \cdot 7 \cdot 6 \cdot 5 \cdot 4 \cdot 3 \cdot 2 \cdot 1 \cdot 39!}{52 \cdot 51 \cdot 50 \cdot 49 \cdot 48 \cdot 47 \cdot 46 \cdot 45 \cdot 44 \cdot 43 \cdot 42 \cdot 41 \cdot 40 \cdot 39!}$$

$$= \frac{13!39!}{52!} = \text{Equation 1.}$$

b. Since there are 4 suits, there are 4 combinations yielding hands where all 13 cards are of the same suit. Since each of those combinations has the probability found in a, above,

$$P(13 \text{ cards of the same suit}) = \frac{4}{C_{13}^{52}} = 4(.157 \times 10^{-11})$$

$$= .628 \times 10^{-11}.$$

c. There is 1 combination of 13 hearts and 1 of 13 diamonds, and thus

$$P(13 \text{ hearts or 13 diamonds}) = \frac{2}{C_{13}^{52}} = 2(.157 \times 10^{-11})$$

$$= .314 \times 10^{-11}.$$

We can also approach the present problem, and the one in item b, as an exercise in set operations. Applying Formula 6-20,

$$P(13H \text{ or } 13D) = P(13H \cup 13D) = P(13H) + P(13D) - P(13H \cap 13D).$$

Since a hand cannot consist of 13 hearts and 13 diamonds at the same time, those two events are mutually exclusive, and thus the probability of their intersect is zero. Thus,

$$P(13H \cup 13D) = P(13H) + P(13D)$$

$$= .157 \times 10^{-11} + .157 \times 10^{-11} = .314 \times 10^{-11}.$$

d. There are 26 red cards, 13 hearts and 13 diamonds. Thus, the number of possible red hands is the number of combinations of 26 things taken 13 at a time. Dividing by the total number of possible hands yields the required probability:

$$P(13 \text{ red cards}) = \frac{C_{13}^{26}}{C_{13}^{52}} = \frac{\dfrac{26!}{13!13!}}{\dfrac{52!}{13!39!}} = \frac{10,400,600}{635,013,559,600}$$

$$= .0000164 = .164 \times 10^{-4}.$$

In working with factorials, it is possible to do a great deal of cancelling, but do not suppose that $26!/13!$ is equal to 2.

6. **a.** There are 13 hearts, and since a poker hand consists of 5 cards,

$$\text{Number of heart flushes} = C_5^{13} = \frac{13!}{5!(13-5)!} = \frac{13!}{5!8!} = 1,287.$$

b. Dividing the number of possible heart flushes by the total number of possible poker hands yields the required probability:

$$P(\text{Heart flush}) = \frac{C_5^{13}}{C_5^{52}} = \frac{\dfrac{13!}{5!8!}}{\dfrac{52!}{5!47!}} = \frac{1,287}{2,598,960}$$

$$= .000495 = .495 \times 10^{-3}.$$

c. Since there are four suits, the probability of a flush in any unspecified suit — clubs, diamonds, hearts, spades — is equal to 4 times the probability of a heart flush in b, above. Thus,

$$P(\text{Any unspecified flush}) = 4(.000495)$$

$$= .00198.$$

When there are only a couple of zeroes to the right of the decimal, a probability is usually written conventionally rather than in scientific notation.

7. The player keeps 3 hearts and discards 2 diamonds, hoping to fill out a heart flush by drawing 2 hearts from the remaining 47 cards. There are 10 hearts among the remaining cards, and thus the probability of a heart on the first draw is 10/47 and on the second draw 9/46. Thus,

$$P(\text{Filling out flush}) = \frac{10}{47}\frac{9}{46} = \frac{90}{2,162} = .0416.$$

Would it make any difference in the above probability if we dealt the hand to a single player, keeping the remaining 47 cards in the deck, or if the hand were dealt to a player in a real poker game with several other players? In the latter situation, many of the remaining 47 cards will have been dealt, face down, to the other players in the game. But in finding the above probability, it makes no difference whether the unknown 47 cards are kept in the deck, in a single stack, or scattered face down through several spatial locations. The probability of two adjacent hearts being available to fill out the flush remains the same.

8. In Exercise 6b we were dealing with the prior, or *a priori*, probability of a heart flush. In Exercise 7 we dealt with the conditional, posterior, or *a posteriori* probability of a heart flush given 3 hearts in the original 5 cards. Those two probabilities are very different.

9. a. Null hypothesis:　　　　　Psychologists do not judge psychotics identically.

　　　　　Alternative hypothesis:　Psychologists judge psychotics identically.

b. The question here is the probability that the two psychologists could arrange the 5 paranoid schizophrenics in the same order just by chance alone, without any regard to severity of their symptoms. Suppose the first psychologist writes the letters *A* through *D*, representing the 5 psychotics, on slips of paper and randomly draws the slips in the following order:

Rank order	1	2	3	4	5
Person	B	E	C	A	D

Now suppose that the second psychologist randomly draws the slips. What is the probability of drawing the slips in the order *B E C A D*, the same order as the first psychologist? That probability is equal to 1 over the number of permutations of 5 things taken 5 at a time,

$$P(B\ E\ C\ A\ D) = \frac{1}{P_5^5} = \frac{1}{5!} = \frac{1}{120} = .00833.$$

Thus, if the psychologists have no real basis for agreeing on the severity of symptoms—that is, if only chance is at work—then the probability of a perfect agreement is less than 1/100. Thus, we reject the null hypothesis since the observed probability of .00833 is less than the conventional *alpha* level of .05.

c. Rejecting the null hypothesis means that the results are judged to be statistically significant, that is, meaningful in the sense that the results are probably not merely due to chance. In the present situation, if the results are not due to chance, then the two psychologists have reliably measured the severity of psychotic symptoms on an ordinal scale. You have no doubt recognized that there is a perfect correlation between the two sets of ordinal measures in the present case. We will have much more to say about correlations on ordinal scales, and other scales, in later chapters.

10. a. Null hypothesis: Psychologist cannot identify potential violators.

Alternative hypothesis: Psychologist can identify potential violators.

b. and **c.** The problem involves the number of combinations of 6 things taken 2 at a time. Since only one of those possible combinations consists of the two parole violators,

$$P(\text{Choosing 2 violators}) = \frac{1}{C_2^6} = \frac{1}{\dfrac{6!}{2!4!}} = \frac{1}{15} = .0667.$$

We cannot reject the null hypothesis because the above probability is *greater* than .05. But the method correctly identified the 2 violators in a sample of 6 parolees, and the probability of that result occurring just by chance is only .0667. Thus, a prudent researcher would suspend judgment on the usefulness of the method until more preparole records could be studied.

d. The probability above, .0667, is the probability that anyone could pick the names of the 2 violators at random, completely by chance.

Chapter 7

1. a. In words and symbols,

H_0: Equal proportions of left and right handers; $p = q.$

H_1: Greater proportion of left handers; $p > q.$

H_2: Greater proportion of right handers; $p < q.$

As in other situations, whether we let p stand for one binomial outcome or the other is entirely arbitrary.

b. A 2-tailed test is appropriate since it is logically conceivable that we might observe a greater proportion of left-handers, although such a result would run counter to our experience. But an anthropologist studying a remote people would be keenly interested in such a possibility. Thus, a 2-tailed test having two alternative hypotheses is clearly desirable, unless you are fully prepared to regard one of the possible alternatives as having no scientific interest, merit, or value whatever. The decision to run a 1- or 2-tailed test should always be made on logical grounds in advance of the data collection. In no case should a researcher decide to run a 1-tailed test after looking at the data. Such a procedure would increase the probability of rejecting a true null hypothesis, as we will explain further in Chapter 8.

  c. Since $p = q$, $p = .5$ and $q = .5$. Thus, $Np = 10(.5) = 5$ and $Nq = 10(.5) = 5$. The normal approximation to the binomial is thus justified since $Np \geq 5$ *and* $Nq \geq 5$ (see Table 7-1).

  d. By the normal approximation to the binomial, Formula 7-17,

$$Z = \frac{|X - Np| - .5}{\sqrt{Npq}} = \frac{|2 - 10(.5)| - .5}{\sqrt{10(.5)(.5)}} = \frac{|2 - 5| - .5}{\sqrt{10(.25)}}$$

$$= \frac{|-3| - .5}{\sqrt{2.5}} = \frac{3 - .5}{1.58} = \frac{2.5}{1.58} = 1.58.$$

Notice that p and q in the above equation are the *expected values* of those parameters — that is, their theoretical values under the null hypothesis — not the *observed values* of the proportions of left- and right-handers in the sample of 10 subjects.

  From Table A, the critical value of Z for a 2-tailed test at the .05 level is 1.96. Since the observed value of Z, above, is less than the critical value, we cannot reject the null hypothesis. Thus, the observed proportions of left- and right-handers do not differ significantly in the sample of 10 subjects.

  2. **a.** In the present situation, $N = 20$, $p = q = .5$, and thus Np and Nq are both as great as 5, as required for the normal approximation to the binomial.

  b. Applying the normal approximation, Formula 7-17,

$$Z = \frac{|X - Np| - .5}{\sqrt{Npq}} = \frac{|4 - 20(.5)| - .5}{\sqrt{20(.5)(.5)}} = \frac{|4 - 10| - .5}{\sqrt{20(.25)}}$$

$$= \frac{|-6| - .5}{\sqrt{5}} = \frac{6 - .5}{2.24} = \frac{5.5}{2.24} = 2.46.$$

Since the observed value of Z, 2.46, exceeds the critical value of 1.96 for a 2-tailed test at the .05 level (from Table A), we reject H_0 at the .05 level. We reject the notion that only chance is at work in determining our results, and thus we conclude that the proportions of left- and right-handers differ significantly in our sample of 20 subjects. Since the quantity $X - Np$ is negative, the number of left-handers in the sample is less than expected under the null hypothesis, and thus we accept H_2.

  c. It may seem puzzling initially that the results of a test based on a sample of 20 subjects is significant, while a test based on 10 subjects was not, even though the proportions of left- and right-handers were identical in the two samples. Examining Formula 7-17 will help explain why this is so. The numerator of that expression is a direct function of N, increasing as N increases; the denominator, $\sqrt{Npq}$, grows as a function of $\sqrt{N}$, and thus increases at a slower rate than the numerator. As a result, the value of Z in Formula 7-17 increases for larger sample sizes, since p and q are constant under the null hypothesis. Since a larger observed Z value is more likely to reach or exceed a critical value of Z, a larger sample is more likely to yield statistically significant results *when H_0 is false.* Thus, if the null hypothesis is false, a larger sample will more likely allow us to detect that fact and correctly reject H_0 in favor of a true alternative hypothesis. There is nothing special about the sample sizes of 10 and 20 in the present case, and indeed, there is nothing special about the normal approximation to the binomial in so far as the effects of sample sizes are concerned. In later chapters, we will see that, in general, larger samples lead to a higher probability of correctly rejecting a false null hypothesis, that is, a greater likelihood of detecting a true difference between the observed and expected values of a population parameter of some sort.

3. a. In words and symbols,

H_0: There is no illusion; $p = q$.
H_1: Horizontal dimension looks longer; $p > q$.
H_2: Vertical dimension looks longer; $p < q$.

The assignment of p to one of the binomial outcomes and q to the other is entirely a matter of choice, as in other contexts.

b. A 2-tailed test is clearly appropriate. Even though the vertical dimension of the Arch probably looks substantially longer to you, suppose you carried out a study and found that a statistically significant proportion of other subjects saw the *horizontal* dimension as longer. You would no doubt find such a result interesting, though perhaps puzzling. As we have noted earlier, a 2-tailed test is appropriate unless you have decided on logical grounds — before collecting the data — that one of the possible alternative hypotheses is of no interest whatever.

c. Since $p = q, p = .5$ and $q = .5$. Thus, $Np = 12(.5) = 6$ and $Nq = 12(.5) = 6$. The normal approximation to the binomial is thus justified since $Np \geq 5$ and $Nq \geq 5$.

d. By the normal approximation to the binomial,

$$Z = \frac{|X - Np| - .5}{\sqrt{Npq}} = \frac{|1 - 12(.5)| - .5}{\sqrt{12(.5)(.5)}} = \frac{|1 - 6| - .5}{\sqrt{12(.25)}}$$

$$= \frac{|-5| - .5}{\sqrt{3}} = \frac{5 - .5}{1.73} = \frac{4.5}{1.73} = 2.60.$$

Notice that p and q in the above equation are the *expected values* of those parameters — that is, their theoretical values under the null hypothesis — not the *observed values* of the proportions of horizontal and vertical responses in the sample of 12 subjects.

From Table A, the critical value of Z for a 2-tailed test at the .01 level is 2.58. Thus, we reject H_0 at the .01 level. Since the quantity $X - Np$ is negative, the number of horizontal responses is less than expected under the null hypothesis, and thus we accept H_2. Rejecting H_0 means that we reject the notion that only chance is at work in determining the observed results, and accepting H_2 means that we conclude that the vertical dimension of the Arch looks longer to most observers than the horizontal dimension. Thus, the Arch represents an instance of the *horizontal-vertical illusion,* a classical geometrical illusion observed in several other contexts. Indeed, the Arch has been called the world's largest horizontal-vertical illusion (Coren & Girgus, 1978).

    4. **a.** In a binomial probability experiment, there are two and only two mutually exclusive and exhaustive categories, but the responses of the present subjects fall into three categories, *horizontal, vertical,* and *equal,* thus violating one of the requirements for a binomial test. That requirement can be met by eliminating the subject who gave the *equal* response, thereby reducing the number of subjects to 11, all of whom now fall in one or the other of two categories. However, eliminating more than a very few subjects would not represent good practice. For example, if you tested 100 subjects and found 89 giving responses of *equal,* 1 *horizontal,* and 10 *vertical,* it would not be reasonable to exclude the great majority of such subjects in order to meet the binomial requirements for a very small minority. Any potential subjects eliminated for any reason should be noted in any written report of the results of a study. It should go without saying that a subject should never be eliminated because of giving a "wrong," or unexpected response — for example, for saying the horizontal dimension looks longer, when you have the conviction that everyone in the world should see the vertical as longer. Discarding subjects for any such reason would yield extremely biased, misleading results, and would represent a totally unacceptable practice.

    b. Having eliminated the subject who gave the *equal* response, the null and alternative hypotheses are formulated as above. Since $Np = 11(.5) = 5.5 \geq 5$ and $Nq = 11(.5) = 5.5 \geq 5$, the normal approximation is justified. By Formula 7-17,

$$Z = \frac{|X - Np| - .5}{\sqrt{Npq}} = \frac{|1 - 11(.5)| - .5}{\sqrt{11(.5)(.5)}} = \frac{|1 - 5.5| - .5}{\sqrt{11(.25)}}$$

$$= \frac{|-4.5| - .5}{\sqrt{2.75}} = \frac{4.5 - .5}{1.66} = \frac{4}{1.66} = 2.41.$$

From Table A, the critical value of Z for a 2-tailed test at the .05 level is 1.96. Thus, we reject H_0 in favor of H_2 at the .05 level.

    c. The present results are statistically significant at the .05 level while the results in Exercise 3, above, are significant at the .01 level. The present results are *less* statistically significant because of the smaller sample size due to the elimination of a subject.

    5. For a student who knows nothing about the subject matter, a 20-question true-false exam is a binomial probability experiment where $N = 20$ and $p = q = .5$. Thus, we treat the student's score as an observation of the binomial random variable X. Under the null hypothesis of no knowledge, the expected value of the binomial random variable X is $Np = 20(.5) = 10$. The student could have expected to make a score of 10 by randomly choosing answers without even reading the questions. Thus, a grade of F is justified.

The student claims to have guessed wrong on each of the 10 questions that he did not know. Suppose we assume, for the moment, that the student really knew the answers to 10 questions. If the student was guessing on the remaining 10 questions, then what is the probability of guessing all 10 wrong? As we noted above, the probability of guessing right on a true-false exam is equal to the probability of guessing wrong. Thus, for the 10 questions the student claims to have guessed, the expected number of questions guessed *right* is $Np = 10(.5) = 5$. Instead, the student claims to have guessed *no* questions right. Now what is the probability of being that unlucky? Applying the normal approximation,

$$Z = \frac{|X - Np| - .5}{\sqrt{Npq}} = \frac{|0 - 10(.5)| - .5}{\sqrt{10(.5)(.5)}} = \frac{4.5}{1.58} = 2.85.$$

Table A shows that the probability of a Z-score of 2.85 or greater is only .0022. Thus, given that the student guessed on 10 questions, the probability of guessing all 10 wrong is about 2 chances in 1,000. A 1-tailed test is appropriate here, since we are evaluating the student's claim that he guessed the 10 questions *wrong*. Which is now more credible, the student's claim that he really knew 10 questions and guessed the other 10 wrong, or the instructor's claim that the student knew nothing of the subject matter?

6. Each child's performance on the test problem represents a single binomial trial. There are 16 children, and thus $N = 16$. Since the test problem has 3 alternatives, only 1 of which is correct, $p = 1/3$ and $q = 2/3$. The null and alternative hypotheses are below.

a. H_0: Children have not learned oddity concept; $p = 1/3$.

H_1: Children have learned oddity concept; $p > 1/3$.

b. Learning requires choosing the correct object. If the children were so unlucky as to choose the odd object less frequently than we would expect by chance, we would still reach the conclusion that only chance was at work, and that no learning had occurred. Thus, a 1-tailed test is appropriate.

c. If the null hypothesis is true, then each child's performance on the test problem is determined by chance and is independent of every other child's performance—providing suitable precautions are taken in running the experiment. Even though the oddity problem has 3 alternatives, 2 of those are wrong and the other right. Thus, each trial has 2 mutually exclusive and exhaustive outcomes, success and failure, as required in a binomial probability experiment. The normal approximation is justified here since $Np = 16(1/3) = 5\ 1/3 \geq 5$, and $Nq = 16(2/3) = 10\ 2/3 \geq 5$.

d. By the normal approximation,

$$Z = \frac{|X - Np| - .5}{\sqrt{Npq}} = \frac{|13 - 16(.33)| - .5}{\sqrt{16(.33)(.67)}} = 3.84.$$

Since the observed value of Z exceeds the critical value for a 1-tailed test at the .001 level, we reject H_0 in favor of H_1. Rejecting the null hypothesis means that we reject the notion that the observed performance of 13 out of 16 correct occurred merely by chance and accept the alternative hypothesis stating that the children have learned the oddity concept. Although not every child demonstrated knowledge of the concept, a substantial and statistically significant number did.

7.   a. *Confounding* is the term that applies here, a concept discussed in Chapter 6. *Oddity* and *complexity* are said to be confounded, since either dimension provides a possible basis for solving the test problem.

b. For half the subjects, the test problem might be presented as illustrated, and for the other half, the odd object might be the less complex and the two matching objects the more complex. Better yet, several different test problems might be used, rather than a single problem for all subjects.

8.   a. There are now only 14 remaining subjects, since 2 of the original 16 were eliminated before finishing the experiment. Thus, $N = 14$, and since $Np = 14(1/3) = 4.67 < 5$, the normal approximation is not appropriate.

b. An alternative analysis uses the exact binomial probabilities. Equation 7-2 gives the probability of any observed number of correct responses, that is, any value of X:

$$P(X) = C_X^N p^X q^{(N-X)}. \tag{7-2}$$

To find the probability of a performance of 11 *or more*, we add the probabilities of 11, 12, 13, and 14, calculating the probability of each value of X by the formula above. Beginning with the probability of 11 correct,

$$P(11) = C_{11}^{14} \left(\frac{1}{3}\right)^{11} \left(\frac{2}{3}\right)^3.$$

If you have a calculator that will handle factorials and exponents, it may be possible to find the above probability without taking any numbers out of the machine. Otherwise, a bit of arithmetic is necessary. If your calculator will not do factorials directly, you can proceed in the following way, simplifying the factorial expression by cancelling:

$$C_{11}^{14} = \frac{14!}{11!(3!)} = \frac{14(13)(12)}{3!} = \frac{14(13)(12)}{6} = 14(13)(2) = 364.$$

Substituting in the above equation, and carrying out the exponential operations,

$$P(11) = 364(.00000565)(.29629630) \quad = .00060936.$$

Because of the small values, the above calculations are carried to 8 decimal places. Always use as many decimal places as your calculator permits in all of your intermediate calculations, and then round off your final result to a suitable number of places. Continuing,

$$P(12) = \frac{14!}{12!(2!)} \left(\frac{1}{3}\right)^{12}\left(\frac{2}{3}\right)^{2}$$

$$= \frac{14(13)}{2}(.00000188)(.44444444) = .00007604;$$

$$P(13) = \frac{14!}{13!(1!)} \left(\frac{1}{3}\right)^{13}\left(\frac{2}{3}\right)^{1}$$

$$= 14(.00000063)(.66666667) \qquad = .00000588;$$

$$P(14) = \frac{14!}{14!(0!)} \left(\frac{1}{3}\right)^{14}\left(\frac{2}{3}\right)^{0} = \left(\frac{1}{3}\right)^{14} = .00000021,$$

recalling that $0! = 1$. Adding the above probabilities,

$$P(11 \text{ or more}) = P(11) + P(12) + P(13) + P(14)$$

$$= .00060936 + .00007604 + .00000588 + .00000021$$

$$= .00069149.$$

The null and alternative hypotheses here are the same as in Exercise 8, above. Since the exact binomial probability of observing a performance of 11 or more just by chance is less than .001, the present results are also statistically significant at the .001 level, as were the results in the earlier exercise.

11. **a.** Since the probability of answering a question right is p and the probability of answering wrong is q, and since each question represents an independent binomial trial, the probability of Smith's particular pattern of answers is

$$P(\text{Smith's pattern}) = P(R\ W\ W\ R\ R\ W\ W\ R\ R\ R)$$

$$= p \cdot q \cdot q \cdot p \cdot p \cdot q \cdot q \cdot p \cdot p \cdot p = p^6 q^4.$$

Since $p = q = 1/2$ in a true-false exam,

$$P(\text{Smith's pattern}) = \left(\frac{1}{2}\right)^6\left(\frac{1}{2}\right)^4 = \left(\frac{1}{2}\right)^{10} = \frac{1}{2^{10}} = \frac{1}{1,024} = .000977.$$

Thus, Smith was correct in saying that the probability of his specific pattern of answers was less than .001.

Analogously, the probability of Jones's particular pattern is

$$P(\text{Jones's pattern}) = P(R\ R\ R\ R\ R\ R\ R\ R\ W\ R)$$

$$= p \cdot p \cdot p \cdot p \cdot p \cdot p \cdot p \cdot p \cdot q \cdot p = p^9 q^1$$

$$= \left(\frac{1}{2}\right)^{10} = .000977.$$

Once again, Smith was correct in calculating the probability of Jones's specific pattern of answers.

The binomial probability of Smith's score of 6 is

$$P(\text{Smith's score}) = P(6) = C_6^{10}p^6q^4 = C_6^{10}\left(\frac{1}{2}\right)^{10} = .205;$$

and the binomial probability of Jones's score of 9 is

$$P(\text{Jones's score}) = P(9) = C_9^{10}p^9q^1 = C_9^{10}\left(\frac{1}{2}\right)^{10} = .00977.$$

Thus, Jones's binomial probabilities of the particular exam scores are also correct, as far as they go.

b. Smith is correct in calculating the probabilities of his and Jones's specific patterns of answers, but as Jones argues, it is the number correct that matters on an exam. However, in finding the binomial probabilities of the two scores, using a single term of the binomial distribution for each, Jones misses the point that the probability of a particular score *or more* is of greater importance than the probability of the score itself.

12.   a. In a Y-maze, or in any other 2-choice situation where the alternatives are equally probable under the null hypothesis, $p = q = 1/2$. The probability of making 9 or more correct responses in 10 trials can be found using the normal approximation to the binomial:

$$Z = \frac{|X - Np| - .5}{\sqrt{Npq}} = \frac{|9 - 10(.5)| - .5}{\sqrt{10(.5)(.5)}} = 2.22.$$

Since the observed value of Z exceeds 1.65, the critical value for a 1-tailed test at the .05 level, the performance of an individual rat achieving 9 out of 10 correct is statistically significant. Thus, the choice of a 9-out-of-10 criterion is defensible on statistical grounds.

b. Suppose all of the rats reinforced for choosing the lighter door learn that response, and the rats reinforced for choosing the darker door also learn. Those results might suggest that the rats can discriminate the lighter and darker doors, but since the lighter door was always on the left and the darker on the right, all of the rats may have learned a spatial response, half learning to turn left and the other half learning to turn right. Thus, spatial location and shade of gray are confounded. The difficulty here could be avoided by randomizing the left-right locations of the lighter and darker doors, using procedures described in detail in Chapter 13.

c. Many animals prefer darker areas, and others prefer lighter. Reinforcing only the lighter or only the darker door for every animal would cloud the results of an experiment to some extent. If an animal strongly preferred a particular door, say the darker one, then reinforcing that door might result in a performance that an experimenter would take as evidence of discrimination learning, when in fact no learning had occurred. Here, the effects of reinforcement would be confounded with the animal's preexisting preference for the particular shade of gray.

Chapter 8

1.   In calculating the variance and standard deviation of a single sample, the mean is subtracted from each score in order to find a deviation. Since the mean has one and only one value in any given sample, the mean is a constant as long as we are dealing with a single sample, as in our development of computational formulas in Chapter 4. But where we are dealing with the sampling distribution — that is, the distribution of the means of all possible random samples of a particular size that might be drawn from a population, as in the present chapter — the sample mean is a random variable that can take on different values in different samples. Treating the sample mean as a constant in the first case and as a random variable in the second case should not appear inconsistent.

2.   The central limit theorem states that as N increases, the distribution of sample means closely approaches a normal distribution having a mean of μ_x and a variance of σ_x^2/N, regardless of the shape of the distribution of X. Every Z test requires an essentially normal distribution of whatever statistic is being tested. The central limit theorem assures us that the sampling distribution of $\overline{X}$s will be approximately normal for a reasonably large N no matter what the shape of the population of Xs.

3.   **a.** Test scores represent an interval scale, and are likely to be approximately normally distributed, as required for a Z test. Furthermore, the rather large sample size of 112 would provide an essentially normal distribution of sample means regardless of the shape of the distribution of test scores.

   b. $H_0: \mu = \mu_0 = 100$. The mean of the population from which the Boskydell East seniors were drawn is equal to the mean of the total population of seniors taking the SWEAT.

   $H_1: \mu > \mu_0$. Boskydell East seniors were drawn from a population having a higher mean than the total population of seniors.

   $H_2: \mu < \mu_0$. Boskydell East seniors were drawn from a population having a lower mean than the total population of seniors.

   c. A 2-tailed test is appropriate, since we would be interested in either direction of outcome. As in all other situations, the decision to run a 1- or 2-tailed test should be made before the data are gathered. The observed value of the sample mean, higher or lower than μ_0, must not be allowed to influence that decision.

   d. By Formula 8-9,

$$Z_{\overline{x}} = \frac{\overline{X} - \mu_0}{\dfrac{\sigma_x}{\sqrt{N}}} = \frac{103.49 - 100}{\dfrac{20}{\sqrt{112}}} = \frac{3.49}{1.89} = 1.85.$$

Since the observed value of Z, 1.84, is less than the critical value, 1.96, for a 2-tailed test at the .05 level, we do not reject H_0. However, notice that the observed Z is greater than the critical value for a 1-tailed test. Having decided on logical grounds that a 2-tailed test is appropriate, it would not be acceptable to change our minds in favor of a 1-tailed test after the fact, even though our observed Z exceeds the critical value of 1.65 for a 1-tailed test at the .05 level. Our failure to reject H_0 means that we cannot rule out the possibility that only chance is at work in determining the observed difference between the Boskydell East students and the total population of seniors.

e. By Equations 8-21 and 8-22,

$$LCL_{.95} = \overline{X} - Z_{.05/2}\sigma_{\overline{X}} = \overline{X} - Z_{.025}\frac{\sigma_X}{\sqrt{N}}$$

$$= 103.49 - 1.96\frac{20}{\sqrt{112}}$$

$$= 103.49 - 3.70 = 99.79;$$

$$UCL_{.95} = \overline{X} + Z_{.05/2}\sigma_{\overline{X}} = 103.49 + 3.70 = 107.19.$$

Thus, the 95% confidence interval for the mean extends from 99.79 to 107.19. The observed sample mean does not differ significantly from any point contained within the above confidence interval. That interval contains the value of 100, as it should, since we found earlier that the observed mean did not differ significantly from the population mean.

4. a. The null and alternative hypotheses are as in the preceding problem.

b. By Formula 8-9,

$$Z_{\overline{X}} = \frac{\overline{X} - \mu_0}{\dfrac{\sigma_X}{\sqrt{N}}} = \frac{103.49 - 100}{\dfrac{20}{\sqrt{201}}} = \frac{3.49}{1.41} = 2.48.$$

Thus, we reject H_0 at the .05 level since our observed Z exceeds the critical value of 1.96 for a 2-tailed test at the .05 level. Since the observed value of $\overline{X}$ is greater than the population mean, we accept H_1. Notice that our observed Z also exceeds the critical value of 2.33 for a 1-tailed test at the .01 level. However, having previously decided on logical grounds to run a 2-tailed test, it would not be appropriate to change our minds at this point.

c. By Equations 8-21 and 8-22,

$$LCL_{.95} = \overline{X} - Z_{.05/2}\sigma_{\overline{X}} = \overline{X} - Z_{.025}\frac{\sigma_X}{\sqrt{N}}$$

$$= 103.49 - 1.96\frac{20}{\sqrt{201}} = 103.49 - 2.76 = 100.73;$$

$$UCL_{.95} = \overline{X} + Z_{.05/2}\sigma_{\overline{X}} \qquad = 103.49 + 2.76 = 106.25.$$

Since we rejected H_0 at the .05 level, the 95% (.95) confidence interval should not contain 100, the value of μ_0.

d. By Equations 8-21 and 8-22,

$$LCL_{.99} = \bar{X} - Z_{.01/2}\sigma_{\bar{X}} = \bar{X} - Z_{.005}\frac{\sigma_X}{\sqrt{N}}$$

$$= 103.49 - 2.58\frac{20}{\sqrt{201}} = 103.49 - 3.64 = 99.85;$$

$$UCL_{.99} = \bar{X} + Z_{.01/2}\sigma_{\bar{X}} \qquad\qquad = 103.49 + 3.64 = 107.13.$$

Since we cannot reject H_0 at the .01 level, the 99% confidence interval should — and indeed, does — contain 100, the value of the population mean under the null hypothesis.

      e. The 99% confidence interval here is wider than the 95% confidence interval. Since the width of the 95% confidence interval is determined by the critical value of Z (or t, for example) for a 2-tailed test at the .05 level and the width of the 99% confidence interval determined by the critical value at the .01 level, it follows that the latter confidence interval is always wider in any given situation since the critical value is larger at the .01 level than at the .05 level.

      5.   **a.** Although the means are identical in the two schools, we nevertheless concluded that the smaller group of seniors did not differ significantly from the population mean while the larger group did. In general — ever and always — for any given difference between an observed and expected value of a statistic, a larger sample is more likely to result in rejection of the null hypothesis.

      b. The power of a statistical test is the probability of correctly rejecting H_0, that is, the probability of rejecting the null hypothesis under the condition that it is in fact false. Thus, power is the probability of detecting a significant difference between the observed and expected value of a statistic, given that such a difference exists. As we noted in a, above, a larger sample size increases the probability of detecting any such difference, and thus the power of a test increases with increasing sample size.

      c. In Exercise 3, where $N = 112$, the 95% confidence interval is wider than in Exercise 4, where $N = 201$. Indeed, inspection of Formulas 8-21 and 8-22 will show that the width of the confidence interval always decreases with larger sample sizes. A smaller confidence interval allows us to determine more precisely the probable location of the population mean.

      6.   **a.** Money represents a ratio scale having a highly meaningful zero. Thus, the measurement scale meets the requirement for either a Z or a t test. But since we do not know the standard deviation of scores — wins and losses — in the population of gamblers, we must estimate that parameter from our sample, and thus a t test is appropriate. We assume that the distribution of scores is approximately normal, and that assumption is reasonable under most conditions in a game of chance.

      b. $H_0 : \mu = \mu_0 = 0.$ Gamblers neither win nor lose in the long run.
             $H_1 : \mu > 0.$ Gamblers win.
             $H_2 : \mu < 0.$ Gamblers lose.

If gamblers neither win nor lose, then the expected value of the mean score in the population of gamblers is equal to zero, since we assigned a positive sign to wins and a negative sign to losses.

c. A 2-tailed test is justified since either direction of outcome, winning or losing, is of interest to us. Of course, we would be most unlikely to see a group of 12 gamblers come out ahead. Indeed, the gambling industry could not survive in the long run if its patrons were to win — even a little — on the average. Nevertheless, a 2-tailed test is appropriate.

d. By Formula 8-16,

$$t = \frac{\overline{X} - \mu_0}{\sqrt{\dfrac{\Sigma X^2 - \dfrac{(\Sigma X)^2}{N}}{N(N-1)}}} = \frac{-32.58 - 0}{\sqrt{\dfrac{39,279 - \dfrac{(-391)^2}{12}}{12(12-1)}}} = \frac{-32.58}{\sqrt{\dfrac{39,279 - 12,740.08}{132}}}$$

$$df = N - 1 = 11.$$

$$= \frac{-32.58}{\sqrt{201.05}} = \frac{-32.58}{14.18} = -2.30.$$

From Table B, the critical value of t for 11 df for a 2-tailed test at the .05 level is 2.201. Our observed value of $t(11)$ — which is read "t eleven," indicating the number of degrees of freedom — is -2.30. Since the absolute value of our observed $t(11)$ exceeds the critical value we reject H_0, and because of the negative sign we accept H_2.

e. In the present case, where σ is unknown, we use Formulas 8-25 and 8-26 to find the confidence intervals for the population mean. Those formulas require the value of $S_{\overline{x}}$, the estimated standard error of the mean, which is simply the denominator of the t ratio, as you can see by Equation 8-16. Substituting the value of the denominator for $S_{\overline{x}}$ in Formulas 8-25 and 8-26,

$$LCL_{.95} = \overline{X} - t_{.05/2}S_{\overline{x}} = -32.58 - 2.201(14.18) = -32.58 - 31.21 = -63.79;$$

$$UCL_{.95} = \overline{X} + t_{.05/2}S_{\overline{x}} \qquad\qquad = -32.58 + 31.21 = -1.37.$$

$$LCL_{.99} = \overline{X} - t_{.01/2}S_{\overline{x}} = -32.58 - 3.106(14.18) = -32.58 - 44.04 = -76.62;$$

$$UCL_{.99} = \overline{X} + t_{.01/2}S_{\overline{x}} \qquad\qquad = -32.58 + 44.04 = 11.46.$$

Since the results are significant at the .05 level, the 95% confidence interval should not contain zero. But the results are not significant at the .01 level, and thus the 99% confidence interval should contain zero, as it does in fact.

7. a. Treating the gamblers' wins and losses as a series of 12 binomial trials, $p = q = .5$. Thus, $Np = 12(.5) = 6$, $Nq = 12(.5) = 6$, and thus the sample size meets the requirements for the normal approximation to the binomial, since *both* Np and Nq are as great as 5. (Remember, the values of p and q are determined on logical grounds by the expected values of the probabilities of success and failure under the null hypothesis, not by the observed proportions of success and failure in our sample.)

b. $H_0: p = q = .5.$ The probability of winning is equal to the probability of losing.

$H_1: p > q.$ The probability of winning is greater than the probability of losing.

$H_2: p < q.$ The probability of winning is less than the probability of losing.

As we noted earlier, a 2-tailed test is appropriate here. The same arguments apply whether we use a t test or the binomial.

    c. By Equation 7-17,

$$Z = \frac{|X - Np| - .5}{\sqrt{Npq}} = \frac{|5 - 12(.5)| - .5}{\sqrt{12(.5)(.5)}} = \frac{|5 - 6| - .5}{\sqrt{3}}$$

$$= \frac{.5}{1.73} = 0.29.$$

Since the observed value of Z falls far short of the critical value for a 2-tailed test at the .05 level, we do not reject H_0. Is it useful here to compare the observed Z with the critical value at the .01 level?

    d. The normal approximation falls far short of achieving statistical significance even though the t test on the same data in the preceding exercise yielded significant results. In considering the observations as a set of binomial trials, we have discarded a great deal of information on the *magnitude* of each score, retaining only the *direction* of each subject's performance in terms of winning or losing. In degrading a set of measurements on a ratio scale — amount of money — to a nominal scale — success or failure — we lose not only information, but we sacrifice power as well. The t test is more appropriate here since it utilizes more of the information in the data than does the binomial. Ordinarily, the test that properly utilizes more information is more powerful, that is, more sensitive, more likely to lead to the correct rejection of H_0.

    We have run two different statistical tests on the same set of data only to demonstrate the consequences of using an inappropriate, less sensitive test. You should not suppose that it is permissible, or even ethical, to run every conceivable kind of test on the same data in the hope of eventually unearthing a statistically significant — and perhaps publishable — result.

    8.   **a.** Since we do not know the standard deviation of the measurements in the population, a t test is appropriate.

$H_0: \; \mu = \mu_0 = 30$ cm.   Comparison mean is equal to the standard, that is, there is no illusion.

$H_1: \; \mu > \mu_0.$ Comparison mean is greater than the standard; left line looks longer than right.

$H_2: \; \mu < \mu_0.$ Comparison mean is less than the standard; left line looks shorter than right.

    b. If there is no illusion, then the mean of the population of all possible comparison adjustments — that is, the mean adjustment in the population of all possible subjects that might in principle be measured — will be exactly equal to the standard length of 30 cm. Note particularly that μ_0, the expected value of the population mean under the null hypothesis, is not equal to zero in this situation, and in many other cases as well. Thus, you should not automatically assume that $\mu_0 = 0$.

c. By Formula 8-16,

$$t = \frac{\overline{X} - \mu_0}{\sqrt{\dfrac{\Sigma X^2 - \dfrac{(\Sigma X)^2}{N}}{N(N-1)}}} = \frac{33.03 - 30}{\sqrt{\dfrac{10{,}941.57 - \dfrac{330.3^2}{10}}{10(10-1)}}} = \frac{3.03}{0.59} = 5.13.$$

$df = N - 1 = 9.$

From Table B, the 2-tailed critical value of $t(9)$ is 4.781 at the .001 level. Thus, we reject H_0 at that level of significance. The positive sign on our observed t value leads us to accept H_1, and thus we conclude that the line on the left looks longer than the line on the right.

  d. Substituting the value of $S_{\overline{X}}$ from the t calculation, above, in Formulas 8-25 and 8-26,

$$LCL_{.99} = \overline{X} - t_{.01/2}S_{\overline{X}} = 33.03 - 3.250(.59) = 33.03 - 1.92 = 31.11;$$

$$UCL_{.99} = \overline{X} + t_{.01/2}S_{\overline{X}} \qquad\qquad\qquad = 33.03 + 1.92 = 34.95.$$

The 99% confidence interval does not contain 30, the value of μ_0. Since we rejected H_0 at the .001 level, it follows that the results are also significant at the .01 level, and thus the 99% confidence interval should not contain μ_0, the population mean under the null hypothesis. We could, of course, construct a 99.9% confidence interval using the critical value of t for a 2-tailed test at the .001 level. If we did, would 30 lie inside or outside that interval?

  9.   The results of the illusion study are highly statistically significant at the .001 level. Thus, it is most improbable that only chance is at work. There is little room for doubt that *something* caused the subjects to see the left line, the standard, as longer than the comparison. But the standard was always located on the left. As the experiment stands, it is conceivable that a line presented on the observer's left appears longer than a line presented on the right, without regard to the configuration of the inward- or outward-pointing fins. Thus, the left-right spatial location of the standard and comparison, rather than the configuration of the fins, might cause the comparison to look shorter than the standard, and thus location and fin configuration are confounded. To overcome this difficulty, the apparatus could be rotated 180 degrees for half the subjects, thereby switching the left-right locations of the standard and comparison. There have been many careful studies of the Müller-Lyer illusion using such procedures, and showing that the configuration of the fins does indeed cause the illusion (see Coren & Girgus, 1978, for example.) We will have much more to say about experimental design in later chapters — ways of avoiding confounding and other difficulties in interpreting the results of research.

  10.   **a.** Having made the decision to run a 2-tailed test on logical grounds, it would not be permissible — or even ethical— to run a 1-tailed test in order to see your theory supported.

  b. Discarding the present results and deciding *a priori* to run a

1-tailed test in a new study is hardly appropriate either. The logic of any such study still demands a 2-tailed test.

c. Running the same study over and over, using the same number of subjects and the same test instrument, discarding nonsignificant results and continuing until a study achieves "significance" is misleading and fraudulent. If the null hypothesis were perfectly true, then by chance alone you should expect to observe "significant" results in about 1 study out of 20. Running enough studies will practically guarantee that you will reject H_0 sooner or later, whether or not your theory has any merit. Research is simply not done that way.

d. Increasing the sample size reduces the size of $S_{\bar{x}}$, and that in turn increases the value of the t ratio for any given difference between $\bar{X}$ and μ_0. Thus, a larger sample size is more likely to result in statistically significant results, if in fact H_0 is false, and thus larger sample sizes provide greater power. Increasing the sample size, within reasonable limits, is an entirely legitimate procedure. However, with a huge sample, it is possible to judge very small differences between $\bar{X}$ and μ_0 as *statistically* significant, perhaps minute differences that have little or no *scientific* significance, meaning, or value. But that is not to say that a large sample will always necessarily result in the rejection of H_0. We will further discuss the effects of sample size under the heading of *Sampling Considerations* in Chapter 13.

e. Attempting to develop a more sensitive, powerful, measure of students' expectations is certainly a permissible and desirable alternative. But developing such a measure is easier said than done. Reducing the variance of the measures in some way would be one means of increasing the power of a statistical test.

f. If the results of a study are in the expected direction, then it may be useful to increase the sample size, or to refine the study in some way. Discarding a well-conceived theory on the basis of a single nonsignificant study, especially when the results are in the expected direction and approaching significance, may not always be wise. Prematurely abandoning a promising line of research may be costly, sometimes resulting in a Type 2 error — that is, failing to reject a false null hypothesis in favor of a true alternative, in this case, failing to confirm a possibly useful theory.

Chapter 9

1. **a.** Since the test scores represent interval measurements, and are expected to be approximately normally distributed, and since the standard deviation is known in the population of pupils taking the BRAT, a Z test of the difference between means is appropriate.

b. H_0: There is no difference between the means of the populations from which the pupils at Northwest and Southeast
are drawn; $\mu_1 = \mu_2$.

H_1: The mean of the population from which the pupils at
Northwest are drawn is greater than the mean of the
population from which the pupils at Southeast are drawn;
$\mu_1 > \mu_2$.

H_2: The mean of the population from which the pupils at
Northwest are drawn is less than the mean of the population from which the pupils at Southeast are drawn; $\mu_1 < \mu_2$.

c. A 2-tailed test is appropriate, since a difference in favor of either
school would be of interest.

d. By Formula 9-8,

$$Z = \frac{\overline{X}_1 - \overline{X}_2}{\sqrt{\sigma^2\left(\dfrac{1}{N_1} + \dfrac{1}{N_2}\right)}} = \frac{51.29 - 53.60}{\sqrt{10^2\left(\dfrac{1}{124} + \dfrac{1}{187}\right)}} = \frac{-2.31}{\sqrt{100(.0134)}} = \frac{-2.31}{1.158} = -1.99.$$

Since $|-1.99|$ is greater than the critical value of Z, 1.96, for a 2-tailed test at the
.05 level, we reject H_0. And since the sign of our observed Z is negative, we
accept H_2.

Having rejected H_0 and accepted H_2, we conclude that the pupils at
Pottersfield Acres Southeast are significantly better—as measured by their
BRAT scores—than the pupils at Pottersfield Acres Northwest. But it would
be a mistake to conclude, therefore, that the teachers at Southeast have done a
better job of educating their pupils. It is entirely possible that the pupils in the
two schools differed in reading-related skills even *before* entering school,
possibly because of differing levels of parental education in the two neighbor-
hoods, or a multiplicity of other sociocultural differences.

2.   a. Jones is right. Even though the difference between the means of
two small samples may be as large as a *significant* difference between the
means of two large samples, we have no assurance that the difference
between the small samples is necessarily significant. Since the standard error
of a sample mean is inversely related to the sample size, any given difference
between means is more likely to occur just by chance in the case of smaller
samples. By referring to Equation 9-6 and the surrounding text, you can also
see that the standard error of the difference between means is inversely
related to the sample sizes, and thus the value of the Z ratio increases with
larger sample sizes for any given difference between means.

b. H_0: Smith's and Jones's pupils are drawn from populations
having equal means; $\mu_s = \mu_J$.

H_1: Smith's pupils are drawn from a population having a
higher mean than Jones's; $\mu_s > \mu_J$.

H_2: Smith's pupils are drawn from a population having a lower
mean than Jones's; $\mu_s < \mu_J$.

Applying Formula 9-8,

$$Z = \frac{\bar{X}_s - \bar{X}_J}{\sqrt{\sigma^2\left(\dfrac{1}{N_s} + \dfrac{1}{N_J}\right)}} = \frac{53.60 - 51.29}{\sqrt{10^2\left(\dfrac{1}{28} + \dfrac{1}{30}\right)}} = \frac{2.31}{2.628} = 0.88.$$

Since the observed value of Z is less—indeed, substantially less—than the critical value for a 2-tailed test at the .05 level, we cannot reject H_0.

c. The power, sensitivity, of a test of a difference between means increases with larger sample sizes. The situation here is quite analogous to our earlier discussion of the power of a test of a single mean in Chapter 8. Larger sample sizes are more likely to result in the rejection of H_0 if in fact there is a difference between the means of the two populations.

3. **a.** Since we have no knowledge of the standard deviation of the population of students on the midterm exam—indeed, such a population of exam scores exists only as a theoretical construct, a figment of our imagination, but a useful one—we must estimate that population parameter, and thus a t test is appropriate. The measurements comprise an interval scale, and can be expected to be approximately normally distributed.

b. H_0: Students present and absent after an exam are drawn from populations having equal means; $\mu_P = \mu_A$.

H_1: Students present are drawn from a population having a higher mean than students absent; $\mu_P > \mu_A$.

H_2: Students present are drawn from a population having a lower mean than students absent; $\mu_P < \mu_A$.

A 2-tailed test is appropriate, since either direction of outcome is possible, and either would be of interest.

c. By Formula 9-15,

$$t = \frac{\bar{X}_P - \bar{X}_A}{\sqrt{\dfrac{\Sigma X_P^2 - \dfrac{(\Sigma X_P)^2}{N_P} + \Sigma X_A^2 - \dfrac{(\Sigma X_A)^2}{N_A}}{N_P + N_A - 2}\left(\dfrac{1}{N_P} + \dfrac{1}{N_A}\right)}}; \qquad \begin{aligned} df &= N_P + N_A - 2 \\ &= 13 + 6 - 2 = 17. \end{aligned}$$

$$t = \frac{67.15 - 52.33}{\sqrt{\dfrac{60{,}649 - \dfrac{873^2}{13} + 17{,}350 - \dfrac{314^2}{6}}{13 + 6 - 2}\left(\dfrac{1}{13} + \dfrac{1}{6}\right)}}$$

$$= \frac{14.82}{\sqrt{\dfrac{77{,}999 - 58{,}625.31 - 16{,}432.67}{17}\,(.244)}}$$

$$= \frac{14.82}{\sqrt{173.00(.244)}} = \frac{14.82}{\sqrt{42.212}} = \frac{14.82}{6.497} = 2.28.$$

Since the observed value of $t(17)$ exceeds the critical value of 2.110 for a 2-tailed test at the .05 level (see Table B), we reject H_0 and accept H_1.

d. It would of course be preposterous to argue that failing to attend class *after* an exam could have any conceivable influence on that particular exam performance. But we can argue that regular class attendance over a semester should be expected to promote better performance on exams. Thus, to the extent that a student's presence or absence on any particular day may reflect the student's usual style of attendance or nonattendance, the present results are consistent with the notion that class attendance is one of the causal factors determining the level of performance in a course. On the other hand, we can also argue that students who believe they have done poorly on an exam may be less eager to show up for exam feedback. Thus, it seems possible that exam performance may be a *cause,* and attendance after the exam an *effect,* rather than vice versa. We have no way of knowing the direction of causality in the present study, or indeed, whether attendance and exam performance *are* causally related in any direct way. Both of those variables may be caused by some other variable, such as level of ability, motivation, or interest, for example.

e. The present study represents an observation rather than an experiment. The researcher did not manipulate class attendance, or exam performance, but merely observed the values of those variables that were attached to the students in the class. Unless an independent variable is manipulated in an experiment, cause-and-effect inferences cannot be drawn with any degree of clarity. We discussed some of the differences between observations and experiments in Chapter 1, and we will consider these issues further in Chapter 13.

4.   a. The data constitute an interval scale, and the measurements can be expected to be approximately normally distributed. Since we do not know the population standard deviation, a *t* test is appropriate.

b. H_0: There is no significant difference between self-recitation and nonrecitation; $\mu_1 = \mu_2$.

H_1: Self-recitation produces superior results; $\mu_1 > \mu_2$.

H_2: Self-recitation produces inferior results; $\mu_1 < \mu_2$.

A 2-tailed test is clearly appropriate here.

c. Since there are equal numbers in the two groups, Formula 9-18 or 9-21 will be more convenient here, 9-21 especially if you have a calculator that has a routine for finding S^2. (Be sure that you know whether your calculator finds S^2, which is equal to $SS/(N-1)$, or SD^2, which is equal to SS/N.) By Formula 9-21,

$$t = \frac{\overline{X}_1 - \overline{X}_2}{\sqrt{\dfrac{S_1^2 + S_2^2}{N_G}}}; \qquad \begin{array}{l} \text{where } N_1 = N_2 = N_G, \\ \text{and } df = 2(N_G - 1) = 2(10 - 1) = 18. \end{array}$$

Finding each of the sample variances by Formula 8-10:

$$S_1^2 = \frac{\Sigma X_1^2 - \dfrac{(\Sigma X_1)^2}{N_1}}{N_1 - 1} = \frac{17{,}700 - \dfrac{414^2}{10}}{10 - 1} = \frac{560.40}{9} = 62.27;$$

$$S_2^2 = \frac{\Sigma X_2^2 - \frac{(\Sigma X_2)^2}{N_2}}{N_2 - 1} = \frac{11,906 - \frac{340^2}{10}}{10 - 1} = \frac{346.00}{9} = 38.44.$$

Substituting the variances in Formula 9-21,

$$t = \frac{41.4 - 34.0}{\sqrt{\frac{62.27 + 38.44}{10}}} = \frac{7.4}{\sqrt{10.071}} = \frac{7.4}{3.173} = 2.33.$$

Since the critical value of $t(18)$ is 2.101 for a 2-tailed test at the .05 level, we reject H_0 in favor of H_1.

  d. This study represents a true experiment, as opposed to an observation. By randomly assigning subjects to the control and experimental groups, the experimenter has manipulated the independent variable—that is, the experimenter has determined which subjects will engage in self-recitation and which will not. Under these conditions, we can conclude that the different treatment of the control and experimental subjects has caused the difference in their performance.

  5. **a.** Since the measurement scale is ordinal, a Mann-Whitney U test is appropriate.

    b. H_0: There is no significant difference between the judged aggressiveness of control and experimental children. Put differently, the probability that an experimental subject will be judged more aggressive than a control subject is equal to .5. In symbols, $P(E > C) = .5$, where E is the rank of an experimental subject and C the rank of a control subject.

    H_1: An experimental child is *more* likely to be judged more aggressive than a control child; $P(E > C) > .5$.

    H_2: An experimental child is *less* likely to be judged more aggressive than a control child; $P(E > C) < .5$.

  A 2-tailed test is appropriate, as in most situations. Although we might expect the aggressive videotape to produce more aggressive behavior, a significant result in the opposite direction would be of great interest. Applying Formulas 9-22 and 9-23,

$$U_E = R_E - \frac{N_E(N_E + 1)}{2} = 50 - \frac{6(6 + 1)}{2} = 29;$$

$$U_C = R_C - \frac{N_C(N_C + 1)}{2} = 28 - \frac{6(6 + 1)}{2} = 7.$$

Checking the U values by Formula 9-24,

$$U_E + U_C = N_E N_C; \quad 29 + 7 = 6(6) = 36. \checkmark$$

In Table C, the lower and upper critical values of U are 5 and 31 for a 2-tailed test at the .05 level. Thus, neither U_E nor U_C falls in the rejection region. Although we cannot reject H_0, the results are in the expected direction in that experimental children are judged more aggressive, but not significantly so.

c. This study represents an experiment, since the experimenter caused each child to view either an aggressive or a nonaggressive videotape. Had there been a significant difference between the judged aggressiveness of the control and experimental groups, then we could attribute that difference to the experimenter's manipulations — that is, we could conclude that viewing the different videotapes *caused* the observed difference in behavior.

6.   a. The data comprise a nominal measurement scale, thus meeting one of the requirements for a Z test of binomial proportions. We now deal with the sample-size requirements. The common proportion, or probability, of success in the combined independent groups is

$$P_C = \frac{X_1 + X_2}{N_1 + N_2} = \frac{18 + 30}{50 + 50} = \frac{48}{100} = .48.$$

The common proportion, or probability of failure is $q_C = 1 - p_C = .52$. In order to use a Z test here, all four of the following quantities must be at least as large as 5: $N_1 p_C$, $N_1 q_C$, $N_2 p_C$, and $N_2 q_C$. Since each of those quantities is at least as large as 24, the experiment meets the sample-size requirements.

  b. H_0: The probability of success under the new method is equal to the probability of success under the old; $p_N = p_O$.

  H_1: The probability of success under the new method is greater than under the old; $p_N > p_O$.

  H_2: The probability of success under the new method is less than under the old; $p_N < p_O$.

A 2-tailed test is appropriate. Instructors devise new teaching methods in the hope of improving their students' performance, but it would nevertheless be interesting if a new method turned out to be significantly worse than a standard procedure. Indeed, it might be very useful in some cases to know how *not* to teach flying! Applying Formula 9-34,

$$Z = \frac{|P_N - P_O| - .5\left(\dfrac{1}{N_N} + \dfrac{1}{N_O}\right)}{\sqrt{p_C q_C\left(\dfrac{1}{N_N} + \dfrac{1}{N_O}\right)}} = \frac{\left|\dfrac{30}{50} - \dfrac{18}{50}\right| - .5\left(\dfrac{1}{50} + \dfrac{1}{50}\right)}{\sqrt{.48(.52)\left(\dfrac{1}{50} + \dfrac{1}{50}\right)}}$$

$$= \frac{|.60 - .36| - .5(.04)}{\sqrt{.2496(.04)}} = \frac{.24 - .02}{\sqrt{.009984}} = \frac{.22}{.0999} = 2.20.$$

Since the observed value of Z exceeds the critical value of 1.96 in Table A for a 2-tailed test at the .05 level, we reject H_0; and since P_N is greater than P_O, we accept H_1, which states that the probability of success is greater under the new method.

  c. We could randomly assign students to the control and experimental groups by tossing a coin for every other subject, for subjects 1, 3, 5, and so on. If the coin comes up Heads, then Subject 1 is assigned to the control group and Subject 2 to the experimental group — or vice versa, if the coin comes up Tails. The other pairs of subjects, 3 and 4, 5 and 6, and so on, are treated analogously. If the members of each pair of subjects were of the same sex, then the sex variable would be balanced across groups. Chapter 13 deals with such procedures in greater depth.

    d. This study is an experiment, since the researcher assigned the subjects to groups, thereby manipulating the kind of instruction they received.

    7.   **a.** The observed proportions of success under the two methods in the present exercise are $P_N = 15/25 = .60$ and $P_O = 9/25 = .36$, just as in the preceding exercise.

    b. Applying Formula 9-34 to the present results,

$$p_c = \frac{X_N + X_O}{N_N + N_O} = \frac{24}{50} = .48, \quad q_c = 1 - p_c = .52,$$

and

$$Z = \frac{|P_N - P_O| - .5\left(\dfrac{1}{N_N} + \dfrac{1}{N_O}\right)}{\sqrt{p_c q_c\left(\dfrac{1}{N_N} + \dfrac{1}{N_O}\right)}} = \frac{|.60 - .36| - .5\left(\dfrac{1}{25} + \dfrac{1}{25}\right)}{\sqrt{.48(.52)\left(\dfrac{1}{25} + \dfrac{1}{25}\right)}}$$

$$= \frac{.24 - .5(.08)}{\sqrt{.2496(.08)}} = \frac{.20}{\sqrt{.01997}} = \frac{.20}{.1413} = 1.42.$$

The difference between the two methods is not statistically significant in the present situation.

    c. Like other tests, a Z test of binomial proportions becomes more powerful with increasing sample sizes, that is, more likely to detect a difference between p_1 and p_2, the proportions of success in the two binomial populations, if in fact there *is* any difference between those population parameters.

    8.   **a.** The common proportion of success, favoring the death penalty, is

$$p_c = \frac{X_L + X_C}{N_L + N_C} = \frac{28 + 35}{54 + 46} = .63, \quad \text{and} \quad q_c = 1 - p_c = .37.$$

The smallest of the four quantities $N_1 p_c$, $N_1 q_c$, $N_2 p_c$, and $N_2 q_c$ is equal to 22.08. All of those quantities are at least as great as 5, thus meeting the sample-size requirements for the Z test of binomial proportions.

    b. H_0: The proportion of liberals favoring the death penalty is equal to the proportion of conservatives favoring the death penalty; $p_L = p_C$.

        H_1: The proportion of liberals favoring the death penalty is greater than the proportion of conservatives; $p_L > p_C$.

        H_2: The proportion of liberals favoring the death penalty is less than the proportion of conservatives; $p_L < p_C$.

Since either direction of outcome would be of interest, a 2-tailed test is appropriate. By Formula 9-34,

$$Z = \frac{|P_L - P_C| - .5\left(\dfrac{1}{N_L} + \dfrac{1}{N_C}\right)}{\sqrt{p_c q_c \left(\dfrac{1}{N_L} + \dfrac{1}{N_C}\right)}} = \frac{\left|\dfrac{28}{54} - \dfrac{35}{46}\right| - .5\left(\dfrac{1}{54} + \dfrac{1}{46}\right)}{\sqrt{.63(.37)\left(\dfrac{1}{54} + \dfrac{1}{46}\right)}}$$

$$= \frac{|.519 - .761| - .5(.019 + .022)}{\sqrt{.2331(.019 + .022)}} = \frac{|-.242| - .5(.041)}{\sqrt{.009557}}$$

$$= \frac{.242 - .0205}{.09776} = \frac{.2215}{.09776} = 2.27.$$

Since the observed value of Z exceeds the critical value for a 2-tailed test at the .05 level, and since the observed proportion of liberals favoring the death penalty is less than the proportion of conservatives, we accept H_2. Whether you consider a response favoring the death penalty as a *success* or *failure* is entirely arbitrary, or perhaps a matter of personal preference. As we have noted in other contexts, it does not matter which of the binomial outcomes is designated a success, as long as we are consistent across all of the binomial trials.

c. This study represents an observation, since the researcher does not cause the subjects to be liberal or conservative.

d. As we have pointed out many times, an observation — as opposed to an experiment — does not allow valid cause-and-effect inferences to be drawn. It is possible that a conservative outlook may be one of the factors leading a person to support the death penalty, and it is also possible that supporting the death penalty may be one of the factors leading a person to consider himself a conservative. Thus, we are left with a kind of chicken-and-egg problem that cannot be solved without much additional research.

Chapter 10

1. a. Positive correlation; children's vocabularies tend to develop across time. **b.** Positive; heavier men, particularly those overweight, tend to take longer to run a given distance. **c.** Negative; speed is distance covered per unit time. **d.** Negative; Rank 1 is assigned to the student with the highest GPA, Rank 2 to the next highest, and so on. (Notice that ranks comprise an ordinal scale. In the next chapter, we will develop simple methods for dealing with correlations involving ordinal variables.) **e.** Negative; people with steady hands, low magnitude of tremor, tend to have higher marksmanship scores. **f.** Negative; higher golf scores mean lower performances. **g.** Positive; prices have been rising over a period of many years.

2. a. Since $Z = \dfrac{X - \bar{X}}{SD_X}$, $\Sigma Z = \Sigma\left(\dfrac{X - \bar{X}}{SD_X}\right)$, and since SD_X is a constant in any given sample, $\Sigma Z = \dfrac{1}{SD_X} \Sigma(X - \bar{X})$. Distributing the summation operator, and recalling that $\bar{X}$ is a constant in any given sample,

$$\Sigma(X - \bar{X}) = \Sigma X - \Sigma \bar{X} = \Sigma X - N\bar{X} = \Sigma X - N\frac{\Sigma X}{N} = \Sigma X - \Sigma X = 0.$$

Thus, $\Sigma Z = \dfrac{1}{SD_X}(0) = 0.$

b. $\Sigma Z^2 = \Sigma \left(\dfrac{X - \bar{X}}{SD_X}\right)^2 = \dfrac{\Sigma(X - \bar{X})^2}{SD_X^2} = \dfrac{1}{SD_X^2}\Sigma(X - \bar{X})^2.$

Since $SD_X^2 = \dfrac{\Sigma(X - \bar{X})^2}{N}$, $\Sigma(X - \bar{X})^2 = NSD_X^2$. Substituting,

$$\Sigma Z^2 = \frac{1}{SD^2}\Sigma(X - \bar{X})^2 = \frac{1}{SD_X^2}NSD_X^2 = N.$$

3. The three distributions in Figure 10-2 are shown in the table below.

Exercise 3, Values of r.

A. Data from Figure 10-2A.

X^2	X	$\dfrac{X - \bar{X}}{SD_X}$	$=$	Z_X	$Z_X Z_Y$	Z_Y	$=$	$\dfrac{Y - \bar{Y}}{SD_Y}$	Y	Y^2	XY
1	1	$\dfrac{1 - 2.5}{1.12}$	$= -1.34$		1.80	-1.34	$=$	$\dfrac{1 - 2.5}{1.12}$	1	1	1
4	2	$\dfrac{2 - 2.5}{1.12}$	$= -.45$		.20	$-.45$	$=$	$\dfrac{2 - 2.5}{1.12}$	2	4	4
9	3	$\dfrac{3 - 2.5}{1.12}$	$= .45$		.20	$.45$	$=$	$\dfrac{3 - 2.5}{1.12}$	3	9	9
16	4	$\dfrac{4 - 2.5}{1.12}$	$= 1.34$		1.80	1.34	$=$	$\dfrac{4 - 2.5}{1.12}$	4	16	16
30 $= \Sigma X^2$	10 $= \Sigma X$ $\bar{X} = 2.5$			0.00 $= \Sigma Z_X$	4.00 $= \Sigma Z_X Z_Y$	0.00 $= \Sigma Z_Y$			10 $= \Sigma Y$ $\bar{Y} = 2.5$	30 $= \Sigma Y^2$	30 $= \Sigma XY$

$N = 4$

$$SD_X = \sqrt{\frac{\Sigma X^2 - \dfrac{(\Sigma X)^2}{N}}{N}}$$

$$= 1.12.$$

$$SD_Y = \sqrt{\frac{\Sigma Y^2 - \dfrac{(\Sigma Y)^2}{N}}{N}}$$

$$= 1.12$$

By Conceptual Formula 10-1, $r = \dfrac{\Sigma(Z_X Z_Y)}{N} = \dfrac{4}{4} = 1.00.$

By Computational Formula 10-5, $r = \dfrac{\Sigma XY - \dfrac{\Sigma X \Sigma Y}{N}}{\sqrt{\left[\Sigma X^2 - \dfrac{(\Sigma X)^2}{N}\right]\left[\Sigma Y^2 - \dfrac{(\Sigma Y)^2}{N}\right]}}$

$$= \frac{30 - \dfrac{10(10)}{4}}{\sqrt{\left[30 - \dfrac{10^2}{4}\right]\left[30 - \dfrac{10^2}{4}\right]}} = \frac{5}{\sqrt{5(5)}} = \frac{5}{5} = 1.00.$$

(*continued*)

Exercise 3 (*Continued*)

B. Data from Figure 10-2B.

X^2	X	$\dfrac{X - \bar{X}}{SD_X}$ = Z_X	$Z_X Z_Y$	Z_Y = $\dfrac{Y - \bar{Y}}{SD_Y}$	Y	Y^2	XY
1	1	$\dfrac{1 - 2.5}{1.50} = -1.00$	1.00	$-1.00 = \dfrac{1 - 2.5}{1.50}$	1	1	1
1	1	$\dfrac{1 - 2.5}{1.50} = -1.00$	-1.00	$1.00 = \dfrac{4 - 2.5}{1.50}$	4	16	4
16	4	$\dfrac{4 - 2.5}{1.50} = 1.00$	-1.00	$-1.00 = \dfrac{1 - 2.5}{1.50}$	1	1	4
16	4	$\dfrac{4 - 2.5}{1.50} = 1.00$	1.00	$1.00 = \dfrac{4 - 2.5}{1.50}$	4	16	16
34 $= \Sigma X^2$	10 $= \Sigma X$	$= \Sigma Z_X$ 0.00	0.00 $= \Sigma Z_X Z_Y$	0.00 $= \Sigma Z_Y$	10 $= \Sigma Y$	34 $= \Sigma Y^2$	25 $= \Sigma XY$

$$\bar{X} = 2.5 \quad SD_X = 1.50 \qquad N = 4 \qquad \bar{Y} = 2.5 \qquad SD_Y = 1.50$$

By Conceptual Formula 10-1, $\quad r = \dfrac{\Sigma(Z_X Z_Y)}{N} = \dfrac{0}{4} = 0.$

By Computational Formula 10-5,

$$r = \dfrac{\Sigma XY - \dfrac{\Sigma X \Sigma Y}{N}}{\sqrt{\left[\Sigma X^2 - \dfrac{(\Sigma X)^2}{N}\right]\left[\Sigma Y^2 - \dfrac{(\Sigma Y)^2}{N}\right]}} = \dfrac{25 - \dfrac{10(10)}{4}}{\sqrt{\left[34 - \dfrac{10^2}{4}\right]\left[34 - \dfrac{10^2}{4}\right]}} = \dfrac{0}{\sqrt{9(9)}} = 0.$$

C. Data from Figure 10-2C.

X^2	X	$\dfrac{X - \bar{X}}{SD_X}$ = Z_X	$Z_X Z_Y$	Z_Y = $\dfrac{Y - \bar{Y}}{SD_Y}$	Y	Y^0	XY
1	1	$\dfrac{1 - 2.5}{1.12} = -1.34$	-1.80	$1.34 = \dfrac{4 - 2.5}{1.12}$	4	16	4
4	2	$\dfrac{2 - 2.5}{1.12} = -.45$	$-.20$	$.45 = \dfrac{3 - 2.5}{1.12}$	3	9	6
9	3	$\dfrac{3 - 2.5}{1.12} = .45$	$-.20$	$-.45 = \dfrac{2 - 2.5}{1.12}$	2	4	6
16	4	$\dfrac{4 - 2.5}{1.12} = 1.34$	-1.80	$-1.34 = \dfrac{1 - 2.5}{1.12}$	1	1	4
30 $= \Sigma X^2$	10 $= \Sigma X$	$= \Sigma Z_X$ 0.00	-4.00 $= \Sigma Z_X Z_Y$	0.00 $= \Sigma Z_Y$	10 $= \Sigma Y$	30 $= \Sigma Y^2$	20 $= \Sigma XY$

$$\bar{X} = 2.5 \quad SD_X = 1.12 \qquad N = 4 \qquad \bar{Y} = 2.5 \qquad SD_Y = 1.12$$

By Conceptual Formula 10-1, $\quad r = \dfrac{\Sigma(Z_X Z_Y)}{N} = \dfrac{-4}{4} = -1.00.$

By Formula 10-5, $\quad r = \dfrac{20 - \dfrac{10(10)}{4}}{\sqrt{\left[30 - \dfrac{10^2}{4}\right]\left[30 - \dfrac{10^2}{4}\right]}} = \dfrac{-5}{\sqrt{5(5)}} = -1.00.$

a. Notice that where $r = 1$, the values of Z_X and Z_Y are equal for each subject. Thus, cross-multiplying those scores and finding the sum of the cross products, $\Sigma Z_X Z_Y$, is equivalent to squaring and summing the values of Z_X or Z_Y. Since $\Sigma Z^2 = N$, as you found in the preceding exercise, the conceptual formula shows that $r = 1$ under these conditions. You should not suppose that X and Y must always be equal within each pair of scores in order for r to take on its maximum value of 1; it is only necessary that the Z-scores for X and Y have the same value within each pair.

b. The table above illustrates the use of Computational Formula 10-5 in the present cases.

c. Using the conceptual formula requires much more arithmetic, since Z-scores must be found and cross-multiplied for each pair of scores, a procedure that is prone to human error, and also to the inescapable effects of rounding errors. Particularly in larger distributions, the computational formula is much more convenient.

4. a. The figure below shows the scatter diagram. The dispersion of points here is comparable to the dispersion in Figure 10-1, and thus you might expect the correlation coefficients to be comparable in the two distributions.

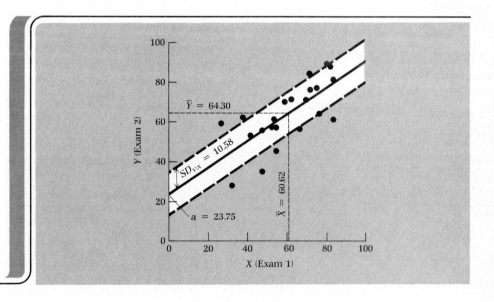

b. $\Sigma X = 1392 \quad \Sigma XY = 93727 \quad \Sigma Y = 1479$
$\Sigma X^2 = 90504 \quad N = 23 \quad \Sigma Y^2 = 100509$

By Formulas 10-5 and 10-6,

$$r = \frac{\Sigma XY - \dfrac{\Sigma X \Sigma Y}{N}}{\sqrt{\left[\Sigma X^2 - \dfrac{(\Sigma X)^2}{N}\right]\left[\Sigma Y^2 - \dfrac{(\Sigma Y)^2}{N}\right]}} = \frac{\Sigma XY - \dfrac{\Sigma X \Sigma Y}{N}}{\sqrt{SS_X SS_Y}}$$

$$= \frac{93727 - \dfrac{1392(1479)}{23}}{\sqrt{\left[90504 - \dfrac{1392^2}{23}\right]\left[100509 - \dfrac{1479^2}{23}\right]}} = \frac{93727 - 89511.65}{\sqrt{6257.74(5402.87)}} = .72.$$

c. $H_0: \rho = 0$. $H_1: \rho > 0$. It is so nearly inconceivable that two exams in the same course could be negatively correlated that a 1-tailed test is appropriate. Applying Formula 10-33,

$$t = \frac{r\sqrt{N-2}}{\sqrt{1-r^2}} = \frac{.72\sqrt{23-2}}{\sqrt{1-.72^2}} = \frac{.72\sqrt{21}}{\sqrt{1-.5184}} = \frac{3.30}{\sqrt{.4816}} = \frac{3.30}{.69} = 4.78;$$

$df = N - 2 = 21$.

Therefore, reject H_0 at the .001 level and accept H_1. Thus, the two exams are significantly and rather substantially correlated, as we should expect.

d. By Formula 10-25, Proportion of explained variance $= r^2 = .72^2 = .52$. The remainder of the variance in Exam 2 is unexplained, unaccounted for, and thus represents error variance. Although Exam 1 accounts for a sizable proportion of the variance in Exam 2, it is not appropriate to suppose that the level of performance on one exam *causes* the level of performance on another. For example, if all the students quit studying and quit coming to class after the first exam, then their performance on the second exam would be essentially random, and there would be little or no correlation between the two exams. Thus, performance on Exam 1, in and of itself, can hardly be considered the cause of performance on Exam 2.

e. To find the regression equation, the standard deviations of X and Y can be found using the sums of squares in b, above, and the means can be found using the sums of X and Y.

$$SD_X = \sqrt{\frac{SS_X}{N}} = \sqrt{\frac{6257.74}{23}} = 16.49; \quad SD_Y = \sqrt{\frac{SS_Y}{N}} = \sqrt{\frac{5402.87}{23}} = 15.33.$$

By Formula 10-9, $\quad b = r\dfrac{SD_Y}{SD_X} = .72\dfrac{15.33}{16.49} = .67.$

$$\bar{X} = \frac{\Sigma X}{N} = \frac{1392}{23} = 60.52; \quad \bar{Y} = \frac{\Sigma Y}{N} = \frac{1479}{23} = 64.30.$$

By Formula 10-8, $a = \bar{Y} - b\bar{X} = 64.30 - .67(60.52) = 23.75$. Thus, the regression equation is $Y' = 23.75 + .67X$.

f. Since the regression line must pass through the point having the coordinates $\bar{X}, \bar{Y}$, the line can be drawn most easily by connecting that point and the Y intercept, which is equal to a.

g. By Formula 10-29,

$$SD_{Y|X} = SD_Y\sqrt{1-r^2} = 15.33\sqrt{1-.72^2} = 15.33\sqrt{.4816} = 10.58.$$

Plotting dashed lines 1 $SD_{Y|X}$ above and below the regression line shows that $14/23 = .6087$ of the distribution lies within ± 1 standard error of estimate of the regression line. Table A shows that .6826 of a bivariate normal distribution should lie within that region.

　　h. By the regression equation,

$$Y' = 23.75 + .67X$$

$$= 23.75 + .67(26) = 41.17.$$

The performance of Subject 9 on the second exam is much higher than predicted based on Exam 1, thus representing a kind of *overachievement,* perhaps through harder work and better application.

For Subject 19,　　$Y' = 23.75 + .67(54) = 59.93.$

Subject 19 performed worse than expected on Exam 2, representing a kind of *underachievement,* perhaps through complacency or lack of application. Of course, other explanations are possible.

　　i. The correlation would remain the same. Adding a constant to each score in a distribution has no effect on the standard deviation, and thus no effect on the Z-scores. By looking at Conceptual Formula 10-1, and referring to your tables of Z-scores and cross-products in Exercise 3, you should be able to see that any transformation of the X or Y scores, or both, that leaves the Z-scores unchanged will also leave the correlation unchanged.

　　j. The correlation would probably decrease, since we would have a truncated distribution.

　　k. Again, the correlation would probably decrease. Truncating a distribution at either end, or at both ends, is expected to result in a lower correlation.

　　5.　a. $H_0: \rho = 0$; $H_1: \rho > 0$. A 1-tailed test is appropriate, since we would have no interest whatever in a test having a negative reliability.

By Formula 10-33,　　$t = \dfrac{r\sqrt{N-2}}{\sqrt{1-r^2}} = \dfrac{.24\sqrt{27-2}}{\sqrt{1-.24^2}} = 1.24.$

Since the critical value of $t(25) = 1.708$ for a 1-tailed test at the .05 level, we cannot reject H_0.

　　b. If a test is not reliable, then it cannot be valid. Furthermore, in the present example, since the reliability coefficient of .24 was not statistically significant, it follows that no lower value of r in a group of 27 subjects could be significant. Thus, it is not necessary to test the observed validity coefficient of .06.

　　c. In attempting to assess the reliability and validity of the BAT, using the varsity baseball team, the coach is dealing with a highly truncated distribution. If the test were given to all entering freshmen, for example, then it might prove to be of value in identifying potentially talented baseball players, in spite of its poor correlation with the batting averages of the varsity players.

6. a. By Formula 10-33, $t = \dfrac{.83\sqrt{34-2}}{\sqrt{1-.83^2}} = 8.42;$ $df = 32.$

Thus, we reject H_0 at the .001 level. In most cases in the real world, reliability coefficients will be highly statistically significant.

b. The scatter diagram is shown in the figure below.

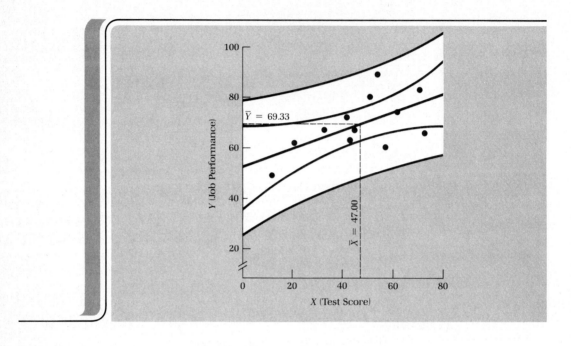

c. $\Sigma X = 564$ $\Sigma XY = 40454$ $\Sigma Y = 832$
$\Sigma X^2 = 30292$ $N = 12$ $\Sigma Y^2 = 59018$

By Formulas 10-5 and 10-6,

$$r = \frac{\Sigma XY - \dfrac{\Sigma X \Sigma Y}{N}}{\sqrt{\left[\Sigma X^2 - \dfrac{(\Sigma X)^2}{N}\right]\left[\Sigma Y^2 - \dfrac{(\Sigma Y)^2}{N}\right]}}$$

$$= \frac{\Sigma XY - \dfrac{\Sigma X \Sigma Y}{N}}{\sqrt{SS_X SS_Y}}$$

$$= \frac{40454 - \dfrac{564(832)}{12}}{\sqrt{\left[30292 - \dfrac{564^2}{12}\right]\left[59018 - \dfrac{832^2}{12}\right]}} = \frac{40454 - 39104}{\sqrt{3784(1332.67)}} = .60.$$

d. H_0: Test has no validity, no correlation with criterion; $\rho = 0$.
H_1: Test has validity, correlates with criterion; $\rho > 0$.

A 1-tailed test is appropriate since we can specify the direction of the expected correlation between a test and the criterion, the performance that we wish to predict. By Formula 10-33,

$$t = \frac{r\sqrt{N-2}}{\sqrt{1-r^2}} = \frac{.60\sqrt{12-2}}{\sqrt{1-.60^2}} = 2.37; \quad df = N - 2 = 10.$$

Since the observed value of $t(10)$ exceeds the 1-tailed critical value of 1.812, we reject H_0 at the .05 level. Thus, the observed validity coefficient of .60 is statistically significantly greater than zero.

e. Using SS_X and SS_Y in Item c, above, to find SD_X and SD_Y,

$$SD_X = \sqrt{\frac{SS_X}{N}} = \sqrt{\frac{3784}{12}} = 17.76, \quad \text{and} \quad SD_Y = \sqrt{\frac{SS_Y}{N}} = \sqrt{\frac{1332.67}{12}} = 10.54.$$

By Formula 10-9, $\quad b = r\dfrac{SD_Y}{SD_X} = .60\dfrac{10.54}{17.76} = .36.$

By Formula 10-8, $\quad a = \bar{Y} - b\bar{X} = 69.33 - .36(47.00) = 52.41.$

Thus, the regression equation is $\quad Y' = 52.41 + .36X.$

f. The first step is to find the corrected standard error of estimate by Formula 10-36:

$$S_{Y|X} = SD_Y\sqrt{\frac{N}{N-2}(1-r^2)} = 10.54\sqrt{\frac{12}{12-2}(1-.60^2)} = 9.24.$$

We now find the equation for the standard error of Y' using Formula 10-37.

$$S_{Y'} = S_{Y|X}\sqrt{\frac{1}{N} + \frac{(X-\bar{X})^2}{NSD_X^2}} = 9.24\sqrt{\frac{1}{12} + \frac{(X-47)^2}{12(17.76^2)}}.$$

We then solve the above equation for several values of $S_{Y'}$, at selected values of X, use the regression equation to find the Y' value associated with each of those X values, and then find the LCL and UCL for $\mu_{Y|X}$ at each of those points, as in Table 10-5. For example, for $X = 20$,

$$S_{Y'} = 9.24\sqrt{\frac{1}{12} + \frac{(20-47)^2}{12(17.76^2)}} = 4.85. \quad \text{Applying the regression equa-}$$

tion, $Y' = a + bX = 52.41 + .36(20) = 59.61$; and applying Formula 10-43,

$$LCL_{.95} = Y' - t_{.025}S_{Y'} = 59.61 - 2.228(4.85)$$
$$= 59.61 - 10.81 = 48.80;$$

$$UCL_{.95} = Y' + t_{.025}S_{Y'}$$
$$= 59.61 + 10.81 = 70.42.$$

Connecting the points representing the *LCL*s and *UCL*s for *Y'* at several values of *X* with smooth curves, as in the figure in b, above, yields the 95%, or .95, confidence band for the population regression line. That confidence band encloses a region which we expect to contain the population regression line with a probability of .95.

g. Having found $S_{Y|X}$ in Item f, above, we begin here by finding the equation for the standard error of a future *Y* value by Formula 10-42.

$$S_{Yf} = S_{Y|X}\sqrt{1 + \frac{1}{N} + \frac{Z_X^2}{N}} = 9.24\sqrt{1 + \frac{1}{12} + \frac{Z_X^2}{12}}.$$

For an *X* of 20, for example, $\qquad Z_X^2 = \dfrac{(20-47)^2}{17.76^2} = 2.31.$

Substituting in the above equation,

$$S_{Yf} = 9.24\sqrt{1 + \frac{1}{12} + \frac{2.31}{12}} = 10.44.$$

Since we found the *Y'* value for an *X* of 20 in Item f, above, substituting that value in Formula 10-44, we have

$$LCL_{.95} = Y' - t_{.025}S_{Yf} = 59.61 - 2.228(10.44) = 59.61 - 23.26 = 36.35;$$

$$UCL_{.95} = Y' + t_{.025}S_{Yf} \qquad\qquad\qquad = 59.61 + 23.26 = 82.87.$$

Connecting the *LCL*s and *UCL*s for Y_f at several values of *X*, as in the figure in b, above, yields the .95 confidence band for a future *Y* score for a subject having any particular given value of *X*. Any future *Y* value that we predict using the regression equation is expected to lie within that confidence band with a probability of .95.

h. If you have found the *LCL* and *UCL* for a future *Y* value at several different values of *X*, say 0, 20, 40, 60, and 80, and if you have drawn the confidence band carefully, then the confidence limits for Y_f for the *X* scores of 25, 47, and 72 should coincide with the curved lines defining the confidence band, as in the figure.

7.   a. For a constant sample size, as *r* increases, the confidence bands for the regression line and for a future predicted *Y* value both decrease in width and curvature, finally coinciding with the sample regression line when *r* reaches its maximum value of 1. The width and curvature of both confidence bands depend partly on the value of $S_{Y|X}$, and Formula 10-36 shows that that quantity approaches zero as *r* approaches 1.

b. For a constant value of *r*, Formula 10-42 shows that S_{Yf} approaches $S_{Y|X}$ as *N* increases, since the quantities $1/N$ and Z_X^2/N approach zero for large values of *N*. Thus, the confidence band for a future *Y* value decreases in width and curvature as *N* increases. Formula 10-37 shows that the confidence band for the population regression line also decreases in width and curvature as *N* increases. Since both terms under the radical are divided by *N*, the entire expression approaches zero for very large values of *N*. Indeed, if the sample size were so large as to encompass the whole of a very large population, then the confidence band would become vanishingly small, and in that case the sample regression line would precisely coincide with the population regression line.

8.   a. $r = 1$.

b. Given the observed correlation of 1.00, many people would conclude—too hastily—that height was entirely determined by heredity. Before you, too, reach such a conclusion, consider the situation in c, below.

c. Here, $r = 1$ also. Adding a constant to each of the scores in a distribution has no effect on the standard deviation, and no effect on the Z-scores, and thus no effect on the correlation with some other variable. To clarify, consider the nature of Conceptual Formula 10-1, and the role of Z-scores in determining the value of r, as in Exercise 3.

d. If every son was exactly 1 inch taller than his father, then we would attribute the difference in height to environmental differences between generations, perhaps to improved diet and medical care. Although it might be tempting to attribute the correlation between fathers and sons entirely to heredity, the environments of fathers and sons tend to be similar, and thus there is a strong argument for the presence of environmental effects in determining the correlation as well as the difference between generations.

9.   a. The correlation indicates that there *may* be genetic factors in determining height, and the difference between generations rather strongly implies the presence of environmental factors.

b. A difference between generations has no bearing on the correlation, as noted in the previous exercise.

c. Consider the formula for the volume of a cube: $V = L^3$, where L is the length of a side. For example, doubling the linear dimensions of a cube multiplies the volume, and the weight, by a factor of 8, since $2^3 = 8$. Although the human body is hardly a cube, it is true that multiplying all of the linear dimensions of any solid by some factor will increase the volume, and weight, by the cube of that factor. To the extent that the food consumption of an organism is directly related to body weight, some of the implications of a long-term increase in human size are obvious.

10.   a. The correlation suggests the possibility of genetic factors in determining intelligence and aptitudes, but there are no doubt environmental factors at work as well. Consider the musically gifted children of Johann Sebastian Bach, for example, C. P. E. Bach and P. D. Q. Bach, among numerous others. Did the Bach children inherit their musical gifts, or did their father provide a superb environment in which great musical ability could hardly fail to develop, or was there an interaction between heredity and environment? By contrast, several generations of the Jukes and Kallikak families—fictitious names, but real people—were overpopulated with criminals and ne'er-do-wells. Did the children in those families inherit their antisocial tendencies, or did those tendencies grow out of the miserable environments which their parents provided? To summarize, and oversimplify, the observed correlations show clearly that parents have *something* to do with the intelligence of their children, but the precise nature of the parents' contributions — genetic, environmental, and perhaps a complex mixture of those sets of factors — remains elusive.

　　b. If there were a correlation of zero between parents and children, then we could draw the strong conclusion that parents have no influence whatever on their children's intelligence.

Chapter 11

1.　a.

	Rank X		Rank Y			
Worker	W/O ties	W ties	W/O ties	W ties	*D*	*D²*
F	1	1	4	4	−3	9
J	2	2.5	1	1.5	1	1
H	3	2.5	2	1.5	1	1
L	4	4	6	6	−2	4
K	5	5	7	7	−2	4
I	6	7	3	3	4	16
D	7	7	11	11	−4	16
G	8	7	5	5	2	4
E	9	9	10	10	−1	1
B	10	10	9	8.5	1.5	2.25
N	11	11	12	12	−1	1
M	12	12	8	8.5	3.5	12.25
C	13	13	14	13.5	−0.5	0.25
A	14	14	13	13.5	0.5	0.25
Sums	105	105	105	105	0✓	72

Arithmetic check: $\Sigma R = \dfrac{N(N + 1)}{2}$

$$= \dfrac{14(14 + 1)}{2} = 105.✓$$

Notice that the sums of the ranks are all equal, with or without ties, and also notice that $\Sigma D = 0$. The scatter diagram is shown on p. 592. In estimating r_s, compare with Figure 10-1.

　　b. $H_0: \rho_s = 0$. Evaluations are unreliable.

　　　　$H_1: \rho_s > 0$. Evaluations are reliable.

By Formula 11-1,

$$r_s = 1 - \dfrac{6\Sigma D^2}{N(N^2 - 1)} = 1 - \dfrac{6(72)}{14(196 - 1)} = 1 - \dfrac{450}{2,730}$$

$$= 1 - .16 = .84.$$

Since we are concerned here with the reliability of an assessment procedure, a 1-tailed test is appropriate. Consulting Table D, the critical value of r_s is .715 at

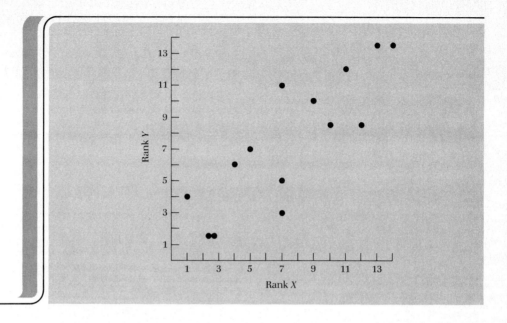

the .005 level. Thus, we reject the null hypothesis of a zero correlation in favor of the alternative of a positive correlation between the two supervisors' judgments.

      c. The reliability of these judgments is substantial, although not so high as that of a well-constructed and carefully standardized test. However, the value of those judgments in identifying future managers involves a question of *validity*, which can only be answered by correlating assessments with managerial success.

      2.   Using the ranks without ties in the above table, the value of ΣD^2 is 74. Entering that value in Formula 11-1, $r_s = .84$. Thus, the values of r_s with and without ties are identical here to 2 decimal places. In other cases, tied ranks will have a greater effect, and in any event should be handled in the way we have described. Where there are large numbers of ties involving, say, more than half of the ranks, the procedure described in Siegel (1956) should be used. Alternatively, a Pearson r can be calculated. In that case, the significance of the resulting r should be tested using Table D, treating the correlation coefficient as though it were r_s.

      3.

Stronger Gun Control?

	Yes	No	Totals

Liberal	*a*
	54
	    (40.45)
		b
		10
		    (23.55)
			64

Conservative	*c*
	13
	    (26.55)
		d
		29
		    (15.45)
			42

	67	39	106

a. H_0: No association between liberal-conservative dimension and advocacy of gun control.

H_1: There is an association.

b. By Formula 11-2,

$$\phi = \frac{ad - bc}{\sqrt{(a + b)(c + d)(a + c)(b + d)}} = \frac{54(29) - 10(13)}{\sqrt{64(42)(67)(39)}} = .54.$$

Testing the statistical significance of the observed correlation by a *chi*-square test first requires finding the expected value in each cell in the above table by Formula 11-7. In Cell a, for example,

$$f_{e(a)} = \frac{R_1 C_1}{N} = \frac{64(67)}{106} = 40.45.$$

By Formula 11-4, $\chi_1^2 = \sum_r \sum_c \frac{(|f_o - f_e| - .5)^2}{f_e}$

$$= \frac{(|54 - 40.45| - .5)^2}{40.45} + \frac{(|10 - 23.55| - .5)^2}{23.55}$$

$$+ \frac{(|13 - 26.55| - .5)^2}{26.55} + \frac{(|29 - 15.45| - .5)^2}{15.45}$$

$$= 4.21 + 7.23 + 6.41 + 11.02 = 28.87.$$

Since $CV_{.001} = 10.827$, reject H_0 at the .001 level.

c. Percentages within rows:

Stronger Gun Control?

	Yes	No	Totals
Liberal	a 84.4%	b 15.6%	100.0%
Conservative	c 31.0%	d 69.0%	100.0%
	63.2%	36.8%	100.0%

d. Percentages within columns:

Stronger Gun Control?

	Yes	No	Totals
Liberal	a 80.6%	b 25.6%	60.4%
Conservative	c 19.4%	d 74.4%	39.6%
	100.0%	100.0%	100.0%

e. Referring to the table in Item c above, converting the percentage in Cell a to a proportion yields the probability that a person who is a liberal will also support stronger gun control. Thus, $p = .84$.

f. Given that a person is conservative, the probability of supporting stronger gun control is .31.

g. From Item d, $P(\text{Liberal}|\text{No}) = .26$, and $P(\text{Conservative}|\text{No}) = .74$.

h. Liberals tend to support stronger gun control, and conservatives do not.

i. As we have noted many times, a correlation does not necessarily indicate a causal relationship between variables.

4.   a. The figure below shows the scatterplot. Comparing with Figure 11-1, the point-biserial distribution of heights of men and women, the present scatterplot shows a greater amount of overlap among the two series of Y values. Thus, r_{pb} will be lower in the present case.

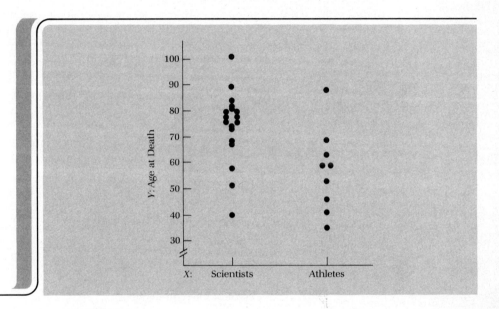

b. $H_0: \rho_{pb} = 0$; $H_1: \rho_{pb} > 0$; $H_2: \rho_{pb} < 0$.

A 2-tailed test is appropriate, since longevity could be greater in either group.

c. By Formula 11-3, $$r_{pb} = \frac{(\bar{Y}_2 - \bar{Y}_1)\sqrt{N_1 N_2}}{N S D_Y},$$

where SD_Y is the standard deviation of all Y values without regard to group membership, and N_1 and N_2 are the numbers of subject in Groups 1 and 2. Finding SD_Y by Formula 4-5, and entering in the above equation,

$$r_{pb} = \frac{(58.18 - 74.11)\sqrt{19(11)}}{30(15.50)} = -.49.$$

Testing the significance by Formula 10-33,

$$t = \frac{r_{pb}\sqrt{N-2}}{\sqrt{1-r_{pb}^2}} = \frac{-.49\sqrt{30-2}}{\sqrt{1-(-.49)^2}} = -3.01;$$

$$df = N - 2 = 28; \quad CV_{.01} = 2.763.$$

Therefore reject H_0 at the .01 level in favor of H_2. The negative sign on r_{pb} and on t merely indicates that $\bar{Y}_1$ is greater than $\bar{Y}_2$. Had we chosen to designate the athletes as Group 1 and the scientists as Group 2, then the sign of the correlation would have been positive in that case. Thus, the sign of a point-biserial correlation is essentially arbitrary.

d. It is clear that the prominent scientists and engineers were significantly older at death than the prominent athletes and coaches in our two samples. To the extent that athletes are more active and scientists more sedentary, our data might suggest (1) that physical activity is harmful; or (2) that a quieter lifestyle promotes longevity; or both (1) and (2). But there is a simpler explanation. Consider the usual age at which an athlete becomes famous, perhaps through winning a world championship or an Olympic medal. Now consider the age at which a scientist is likely to become famous, through making a major discovery, or winning a Nobel prize. The athlete is likely to become prominent at a much earlier age than the scientist, perhaps at 20 or so versus 50 or more. Now, if we randomly selected a group of ordinary 20-year-olds and a group of ordinary 50-year-olds, which group would more likely be older on the average at death? Not all of the younger group can be expected to survive to the age of 50, while all of the 50-year-olds have already attained that age, and are thus expected to be older at death, on the average, than the group that was selected for observation at an earlier age. We see here another situation where unwarranted causal inferences might be drawn.

5. **a.** H_0: No association between ethnicity and voter preference.
   H_1: There is an association.

Political Party Preference:

Ethnicity:	Democratic	Republican	Independent and Other	
White	56 (70.17)	37 (29.03)	31 (24.80)	124
Black	29 (19.24)	3 (7.96)	2 (6.80)	34
Hispanic	17 (11.88)	1 (4.92)	3 (4.20)	21
Asian	8 (9.62)	5 (3.98)	4 (3.40)	17
Other	6 (5.09)	2 (2.11)	1 (1.80)	9
	116	48	41	205

A problem immediately arises, since 6/15 of the cells have expected frequencies less than 5, while a *chi*-square test requires that no more than 20% of the cells (3/15 here) have such low expected frequencies. The problem can be solved by combining the two smallest ethnic categories, *Asian* and *Other* into a single category designated *Other*. Doing that results in the table below, where only 2/12 of the cells have expected frequencies of less than 5. Notice that it is only necessary to recalculate expected frequencies in the newly constituted *Other* category, since the row and column totals are unchanged in the remainder of the table.

Political Party Preference:

Ethnicity:	Democratic	Republican	Independent and Other	
White	56 (70.17)	37 (29.03)	31 (24.80)	124
Black	29 (19.24)	3 (7.96)	2 (6.80)	34
Hispanic	17 (11.88)	1 (4.92)	3 (4.20)	21
Other	14 (14.71)	7 (6.09)	5 (5.20)	26
	116	48	41	205

When working with a *chi*-square table, be sure that the observed and expected frequencies sum to the same values within rows and columns, and sum to N overall. Expected frequencies are found by Formula 11-7, as in the previous example. By Formula 11-11,

$$\chi^2_{df} = \sum_r \sum_c \frac{(f_o - f_e)^2}{f_e}; \quad \begin{aligned} df &= (r-1)(c-1) \\ &= 3(2) = 6. \end{aligned}$$

$$\chi^2_6 = \frac{(56 - 70.17)^2}{70.17} + \frac{(37 - 29.03)^2}{29.03} + \cdots + \frac{(5 - 5.20)^2}{5.20}$$

$$= 23.87; \quad CV_{.001} = 22.457; \text{ therefore reject } H_0.$$

b. **Political Party Preference:**

Ethnicity:	Democratic	Republican	Independent and Other	
White	45.2%	29.8%	25.0%	100.0%
Black	85.3%	8.8%	5.9%	100.0%
Hispanic	81.0%	4.8%	14.3%	100.1%
Other	53.8%	26.9%	19.2%	99.9%
	56.6%	23.4%	20.0%	100.0%

The above table might be of interest to a political party in determining where its strengths and weaknesses lie among the different ethnic groups. The bottom row of numbers, the marginal totals for columns, shows the percentages of the different party preferences in the total sample.

c.   **Political Party Preference:**

Ethnicity:	Democratic	Republican	Independent and Other	
White	48.3%	77.1%	75.6%	60.5%
Black	25.0%	6.3%	4.9%	16.6%
Hispanic	14.7%	2.1%	7.3%	10.2%
Other	12.1%	14.6%	12.2%	12.7%
	100.1%	100.1%	100.0%	100.0%

The table above shows the ethnic composition of each category of preference. The marginal totals for rows show the ethnic composition of the total sample.

d. In this sample, the greatest strength of the Republican party is among White voters. Among the other ethnic groups, the Democratic party is much stronger. The tables in Items b and c both show that association, each in a slightly different way. Each of those tables in percentages shows the association between ethnicity and voter preference more clearly than the raw data, the observed frequencies.

Chapter 12

1. **a.** $H_0: \mu_{\bar{D}} = 0$, or $\mu_1 = \mu_2$; the mean difference is zero, or Mean 1 equals Mean 2.

$H_1: \mu_{\bar{D}} > 0$, or $\mu_1 > \mu_2$; mean difference is greater than zero, or Mean 1 is greater than Mean 2.

$H_2: \mu_{\bar{D}} < 0$, or $\mu_1 < \mu_2$; mean difference is less than zero, or Mean 1 is less than Mean 2.

A 2-tailed test is appropriate, since a difference in either direction would be of interest.

b. Since monocular and binocular acuity tend to be comparable in the same individual, those measures are correlated, thus justifying the repeated-measures t test.

Subjects	1	2	3	4	5	6	7	8	9	10	11	12	13	14	15	16
Monocular	14	26	70	50	20	51	45	57	21	20	22	2	36	44	15	24
Binocular	24	45	20	25	23	10	17	38	13	8	8	6	12	9	17	9
D	−10	−19	50	25	−3	41	28	19	8	12	14	−4	24	35	−2	15

By Formula 12-13,

$$t = \frac{\bar{D}}{\sqrt{\dfrac{\Sigma D^2 - \dfrac{(\Sigma D)^2}{N}}{N(N-1)}}}; \qquad \begin{aligned} df &= N - 1 \\ &= 15. \end{aligned}$$

$$t = \frac{14.56}{\sqrt{\dfrac{8871 - \dfrac{233^2}{16}}{16(16-1)}}} = \frac{14.56}{\sqrt{\dfrac{8871 - 3393.06}{240}}} = \frac{14.56}{\sqrt{22.82}} = 3.05.$$

Since $CV_{.01} = 2.947$, reject H_0 and accept H_1. Errors are greater for monocular viewing, and thus binocular depth perception is better.

   c. It is a common misconception that depth perception depends entirely on binocular vision. However, there are numerous monocular depth cues. Two eyes are indeed better than one, as the data indicate, but comparing the monocular and binocular means (32.31 and 17.75) shows that the average error is less than twice as large under monocular conditions. Certainly, some monocular depth perception occurs.

   d. It is very convenient to switch from monocular to binocular viewing, so this is an easy experiment to do using repeated measures. Furthermore, any practice or fatigue effects should be expected to transfer symmetrically from one experimental condition to the other, and the counter-balancing procedure can be expected to distribute those effects essentially equally across conditions. In this situation, the repeated-measures design offers greater power and sensitivity than the independent-groups design, at no cost in greater difficulty or inconvenience in running the experiment. The independent-groups design would eliminate the possibility of any carry-over effect from one condition to the other, but at the cost of using a greater number of subjects to achieve the same level of power. We will discuss the problem of choosing an appropriate experimental design at greater length in Chapter 13.

   e. A matched-pairs design would require the premeasurement of some sort of matching variable, at the cost of additional time and effort. Furthermore, a matched-pairs design would require twice as many subjects. In the present situation, where measurements under one condition are not expected to greatly influence measurements under the other, there is no real advantage in the matched-pairs design. But in a learning experiment, for example, it would obviously not be feasible to have the same subjects learn the same material under two different conditions.

   2.   a. The subjects were matched initially, and since the subsequent measures constitute an ordinal scale, the sign test is appropriate. Symboli-cally, the null and alternative hypotheses are as stated in the previous problem.

Pair	1	2	3	4	5	6	7	8	9	10	11	12	13	14	15	16
Training	3	3	2	3	2	2	3	3	3	2	1	2	1	3	3	2
Control	3	2	1	2	3	1	2	1	2	2	1	1	2	3	2	1
Sign $(T - C)$	0	+	+	+	−	+	+	+	+	0	0	+	−	0	+	+

X = Number of + signs = 10
Number of − signs = 2
N = 12

Applying Formula 7-22, discarding differences of zero,

$$Z_x = \frac{|X - Np| - .5}{\sqrt{Npq}} = \frac{|10 - 12(.5)| - .5}{\sqrt{12(.5)(.5)}} = \frac{3.5}{\sqrt{3}} = 2.02.$$

Since the observed value of Z exceeds the critical value of 1.96 for a 2-tailed test at the .05 level, reject H_0 in favor of H_1.

b. A repeated-measures design would provide no protection against the possibility of a change resulting from the effects of some extraneous variable or variables. In the matched-pairs design, the effects of any such variables can be expected to fall on the control group as well as the treatment group; thus, any differences between groups after the experiment can be attributed to the effects of training.

3. The severity of crimes constitutes an ordinal scale, and since we have repeated measures, the Wilcoxon test is appropriate.

$H_0\colon \mu_1 = \mu_2$; 1st and 2nd offenses are equally severe.

$H_1\colon \mu_1 > \mu_2$; 1st offense is more severe.

$H_2\colon \mu_1 < \mu_2$; 1st offense is less severe.

Sub-ject	(A) 1st Offense	(B) 2nd Offense	Sign of $A - B$	$|A - B|$	Rank of $|A - B|$	Signed Rank
1	5	4	+	1	4	+4
2	3	6	−	3	12.5	−12.5
3	2	3	−	1	4	−4
4	5	7	−	2	9.5	−9.5
5	2	6	−	4	14	−14
6	4	4		0		
7	5	6	−	1	4	−4
8	3	2	+	1	4	+4
9	1	3	−	2	9.5	−9.5
10	8	9	−	1	4	−4
11	1	4	−	3	12.5	−12.5
12	4	6	−	2	9.5	−9.5
13	3	5	−	2	9.5	−9.5
14	2	2		0		
15	6	5	+	1	4	+4
16	1	6	−	5	15	−15
17	7	7		0		
18	3	4	−	1	4	−4
					$\Sigma R = 120$	$W = -96$

Arithmetic check: $\Sigma R = \dfrac{N}{2}(N + 1)$

$$= \frac{15}{2}(15 + 1) = 120. \checkmark$$

Since the absolute value of W exceeds the critical value of 90 from Table G for a test at the .01 level, reject H_0; and since W is negative, accept H_2. Notice that differences of zero are discarded, and thus $N = 15$, not 18.

4. a. Since the parolees were matched on the severity of their offenses, and since the adjustment ratings comprise an ordinal scale, the Wilcoxon test is appropriate. Symbolically, the null and alternative hypotheses are as in the previous example.

Sub-ject	(A) Treatment	(B) Control	Sign of $A - B$	$|A - B|$	Rank of $|A - B|$	Signed Rank
1	5	1	+	4	10.5	+10.5
2	9	3	+	6	14.5	+14.5
3	6	1	+	5	12.5	+12.5
4	6	9	−	3	7.5	−7.5
5	5	6	−	1	1.5	−1.5
6	2	2		0		
7	8	4	+	4	10.5	+10.5
8	9	3	+	6	14.5	+14.5
9	3	6	−	3	7.5	−7.5
10	2	4	−	2	4	−4
11	3	1	+	2	4	+4
12	9	1	+	8	16	+16
13	7	4	+	3	7.5	+7.5
14	6	1	+	5	12.5	+12.5
15	4	4		0		
16	8	5	+	3	7.5	+7.5
17	1	2	−	1	1.5	−1.5
18	7	9	−	2	4	−4

$$\Sigma R = 136 \qquad W = 84$$

Arithmetic check: $\Sigma R = \dfrac{N}{2}(N + 1)$

$$= \dfrac{16}{2}(16 + 1) = 136.\checkmark$$

Reject H_0 and accept H_1 since the observed value of W exceeds the critical value of 78 from Table G for a 2-tailed test at the .05 level.

     b. For a group of parolees just released from prison, it would be difficult to find a measure of adjustment that could be administered at once and then compared meaningfully with a second administration after some months of living on the outside. Thus, a repeated-measures design would not suit the present study as well as a matched-pairs design.

     c. This study could have been done using independent groups. But we might expect a parolee's adjustment outside prison to be related to the severity of previous offenses. In this case, the matched-pairs design takes good advantage of a readily available matching variable, thus providing a more powerful experiment.

     d. After the treatment program, it would be highly desirable to have a blind assessment of the parolees' adjustment, an independent assessment made by a person having no knowledge of a subject's membership in the treatment or control group. Such a procedure would guard against any unconscious bias that might otherwise cloud the judgment of the best-intentioned and most intellectually honest researcher.

    5.   **a.** Repeated test performances tend to be correlated, so a test of correlated proportions is appropriate here.

H_0: $p = .5$; probability of a change from failing to passing is .5.

H_1: $p > .5$; probability of changing from failure to passing is greater than .5.

H_2: $p < .5$; probability of changing from failing to passing is less than .5.

As Seniors:

		Fail	Pass	
As Juniors:	Pass	$a\ (-)$ 7	b (No change) 546	553
	Fail	c (No change) 304	$d\ (+)$ $29 = X$	333
		311	575	886 = Total

$$N = a + d = 36$$

By Formula 7-22,

$$Z_X = \frac{|X - Np| - .5}{\sqrt{Npq}} = \frac{|29 - 36(.5)| - .5}{\sqrt{36(.5)(.5)}} = \frac{10.5}{3} = 3.50.$$

Since the observed Z exceeds the critical value of 3.30 from Table A for a 2-tailed test at the .001 level, reject H_0 and accept H_1.

    b. To evaluate the principal's enthusiastic reception of the results, we find the percentages of students passing over the two years, using the marginal totals from the table above. The percentages passing as juniors and seniors are

$$100(553/886) = 62.4\%, \quad \text{and} \quad 100(575/886) = 64.9\%.$$

Although the results are highly statistically significant, a change of 2.5% in the students passing from one year to the next is hardly earthshaking—although an increase is certainly better in this context than a decrease. If the numbers are large enough in an observation or experiment, very small differences of little practical importance can often turn out to be highly significant statistically. We will have more to say about this kind of issue in our discussion of sample sizes in Chapter 13.

    6. **a.** Since each mother and daughter have shared a common socio-economic environment, they constitute a pair of subjects that are matched on several variables that we expect to be correlated with the probability of graduating from college. Thus, a test of correlated proportions is appropriate.

Daughter Graduated?

		No	Yes	
Mother Graduated?	Yes	$a\ (-)$ 7	b (No change) 11	18
	No	c (No change) 76	$d\ (+)$ $18 = X$	94
		83	29	112 = Total

$$N = a + d = 25$$

By Formula 7-22,

$$Z_x = \frac{|X - Np| - .5}{\sqrt{Npq}} = \frac{|18 - 25(.5)| - .5}{\sqrt{25(.5)(.5)}} = \frac{5}{2.5} = 2.00.$$

Reject H_0 in favor of H_1, since the observed value of Z exceeds the critical value of 1.96 from Table A for a 2-tailed test at the .05 level.

b. Percentages by rows:

		Daughter Graduated?		
		No	Yes	
Mother Graduated?	Yes	38.9%	61.1%	100%
	No	80.9%	19.1%	100%
		74.1%	25.9%	100%

c. Percentages by columns:

		Daughter Graduated?		
		No	Yes	
Mother Graduated?	Yes	8.4%	37.9%	16.1%
	No	91.6%	62.1%	83.9%
		100%	100%	100%

c. Mothers, 16.1% graduated; daughters, 25.9%.

d. Referring to the first table above, given the mothers that graduated, 61.1% of their daughters also graduated. But among the mothers who were not graduates, only 19.1% of their daughters were.

e. Referring to the second table above, taking the daughters who were graduates, 37.9% of their mothers were also, but among the daughters who were not graduates, only 8.4% of their mothers were.

Chapter 13

1. In this context, *statistics* is the process of testing the significance of results, assessing the likelihood that only chance is at work. *Experimental design* is the process of arranging conditions so that the results of an experiment can be attributed to an independent variable rather than to some uncontrolled extraneous variable.

2. In an experiment, the researcher manipulates an independent variable by assigning its values to subjects, that is, by assigning the subjects to the different levels of the independent variable. But in an observation, the subjects bring with them their own values of a naturally occurring independent variable. We can draw causal inferences much more securely in an experiment.

3. In a random sample, every member of the population has an equal chance of being represented. Thus, a random sample is by definition unbiased. Furthermore, most of our statistical tests are based on the assumption of random sampling.

4. The level of statistical significance is the probability that the results of an experiment or observation are due to chance. A low significance probability gives us great confidence that the results are *not* due to chance, and thus repeatable, or *reliable*. Internal validity is the extent to which the results can be attributed to the independent variable, and not to some uncontrolled extraneous variable. External validity is the extent to which the results can be extended, generalized, beyond the particular subjects and context at hand. Without statistical significance, which is a form of reliability, there can be no internal validity, and without internal validity, there can be no external validity.

5. Statistical significance is not synonymous with the scientific significance, or importance, of a research finding. In a very large sample, a minute difference between means can sometimes turn out to be highly statistically significant, even though the independent variable has little effect on the dependent variable. Such a result may be of little scientific or practical value or interest.

6. A time series is useful wherever a variable changes across time, as in the number of social interactions on the part of an autistic child, for example, after successive therapy sessions.

7. A multiple correlation expresses the relationship between a variable that we wish to predict and two or more other variables. For example, the length of hospitalization of a schizophrenic can be predicted better from the severity of symptoms and rapidity of onset than from either of those variables alone. A partial correlation expresses the relationship between two variables after eliminating the effects of other specified variables. For example, we might examine the correlation between success in business and achievement motivation, eliminating the effects of ability and level of education.

8. Beginning with a set of bivariate correlations between several tests or other measures, a factor analysis attempts to find a set of underlying variables — factors — that will account for the observed correlations. Factor analysis has been used most widely in the development and evaluation of psychological tests.

9. Counterbalancing consists of presenting experimental conditions in a repeated-measures design in a particular order that will tend to distribute fatigue or practice effects evenly across conditions.

10. a. This is a repeated-measures factorial design where each man and woman is tested on the 2 tasks. The design could also have used 4 independent groups, 2 of men and 2 of women, each group being tested on a single task. In this situation, the repeated-measures design would probably be more advantageous.

b. The graph shows the results. There is an interaction between the sex variable and the task variable (compare with Figure 13-3). There is no main effect of either variable. The mean performance for the combined sexes

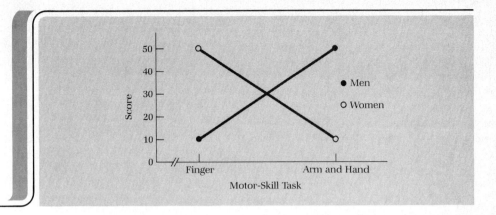

on the tweezer task, 30, is identical to the mean performance on the pursuit rotor; and the mean for men across both tasks is also 30, and so is the mean for women.

    c. The mean for men across the 2 tasks is identical to the mean for women.

    11.　The principal advantage of a factorial experiment lies in the information it provides on interactions between independent variables.

    12.　A quasi-experiment would utilize two intact groups, such as two existing classes of students. To compare two teaching methods, for example, each group would be taught by a different method. Unfortunately, any preexisting differences between intact groups before an experiment would be confounded with the possible differences between teaching methods, or between the levels of any other independent variable. In a true experiment, subjects would be randomly assigned to groups, thereby decreasing the likelihood of mistaking the systematic effects of some extraneous variable for the possible effects of the independent variable. We can draw causal inferences much more securely where we have randomly assigned subjects.

    13.　**a.** Since reliability and statistical significance are equivalent, testing the significance of the correlation by Formula 10-33,

$$t = \frac{r\sqrt{N-2}}{\sqrt{1-r^2}} = \frac{.23\sqrt{27-2}}{\sqrt{1-.23^2}} = 1.18; \quad df = 25.$$

The correlation is not significant, the observation lacks reliability, and thus there can be no internal or external validity. Since air traffic controllers are in a highly stressful occupation, we are dealing here with a truncated distribution, which might be expected to result in a low correlation (see Chapter 10). Thus, the new test might be more promising than the correlation in this sample would suggest.

    b. The results are statistically significant, and thus reliable, but there is a serious question regarding the internal validity of the observations. The before-after design here confounds the sensitivity training with other aspects of the cadets' regular training program, and with the passage of time. The difficulty could be remedied by using a control group. As the experiment stands, the question of external validity cannot be addressed in the absence of a design that guarantees internal validity.

c. The results are highly statistically significant, and thus highly reliable. If the survey were done again with a sample from the same population, we should expect comparable results with a high level of confidence. But a question arises regarding the nature of the population that was sampled. Who is most likely to visit a supermarket on a workday afternoon, someone who is employed, or unemployed? No doubt, you can think of other sources of bias that might influence the results of such a survey. Any selection bias strongly threatens the external validity of an observation or experiment.

d. The results are reliable at the .05 level. However, the study constitutes a quasi-experiment utilizing 2 intact groups, two existing laboratory sections. At first blush, there might appear to be no great difficulty here, but there may be substantial differences between students in sections of the same course meeting at different times. The possible effects of the independent variable are confounded with any such preexisting differences, and thus we cannot say with confidence that the experimental procedure worked.

Chapter 14

1. An *F* ratio is a ratio of two variances, each of which is equal to a sum of squared deviations divided by an appropriate number of *df*. Thus, a variance can never be negative, nor can an *F* ratio. Redo your calculations if your *F* value comes out negative.

2. **a.** *A priori* comparisons are decided upon *before* the data are gathered and are then carried out regardless of whether an ANOVA yields a significant *F* ratio. *A posteriori* comparisons between all possible pairs of means are made after finding a significant *F*.

b. For either kind of comparison, a sin of *com*mission, making the comparison where it should not be made, increases the probability of a Type 1 error. A sin of *o*mission, neglecting to make an appropriate comparison, guarantees a Type 2 error, if the null hypothesis that you fail to test is in fact false.

3. **a.** This study utilizes a naturally occurring independent variable, categories of workers, and thus represents an observation rather than an experiment. It may be very useful to know how different categories of workers perceive the quality of life in their working environments, but we cannot conclude that the independent variable has *caused* the significant differences observed in the dependent variable.

b. We ordinarily consider test scores to be essentially normally distributed, and to comprise an interval scale. By inspection, the standard deviations, and hence the variances, do not appear greatly different from one group to another. Thus, our data meet the requirements for an ANOVA.[1]

---

[1] There are of course tests for homogeneity of variance, and there are procedures for dealing with variances that are grossly heterogeneous, for example, where the largest variance within any group is many times the smallest. Winer (1971) discusses these issues at greater length.

H_0: $\mu_1 = \mu_2 = \mu_3 = \mu_4 = \mu_5$; population means of all categories are equal.

H_1: Population means are not all equal.

c. Analysis of variance.

	Un-skilled	Skilled	Cleri-cal	Manage-ment	Profes-sional		
	X_1	X_2	X_3	X_4	X_5		
$\sum_i X_{ij}$	88	135	110	199	159	$\sum_j \sum_i X_{ij} = G = 691$	
$\sum_i X_{ij}^2$	886	2055	1380	4351	2801	$\sum_j \sum_i X_{ij}^2 = 11473$	
$\overline{X}_j$	8.80	13.50	11.00	19.90	15.90	$\dfrac{\sum_j \sum_i X_{ij}}{N} = \overline{G} = 13.82$	
S_j	3.52	5.08	4.35	6.59	5.51		

$k = 5$ groups, $n = 10$ subjects/group, $N = kn = 50$ Total subjects.
Computational symbols, Formulas 14-32:

$$(1) = \frac{G^2}{N} = \frac{691^2}{50} = 9549.62;$$

$$(2) = \sum_j \sum_i X_{ij}^2 = 11473;$$

$$(3) = \frac{\sum_j \left(\sum_i X_{ij}\right)^2}{n_j} = \frac{88^2}{10} + \frac{135^2}{10} + \frac{110^2}{10} + \frac{199^2}{10} + \frac{159^2}{10} = 10295.10.$$

Summary of analysis of variance:

Source	Formula	df	SS	MS	F
Categories (between)	$(3) - (1)$	$k - 1 = 4$	745.48	186.37	7.12**
Error (within)	$(2) - (3)$	$N - k = 45$	1177.90	26.18	
Total	$(2) - (1)$	$N - 1 = 49$	1923.38		

**$p < .01$.

Since the observed value of $F(4,45)$ exceeds the critical value of 3.77 (by interpolation in Table F), reject H_0 at the .01 level. Thus we conclude that the independent variable has an effect, that is, at least one of the population means differs from the others. Do not confuse the *statistical* effect of the independent variable with the notion of *causality* here, since we are dealing with an observation and not an experiment.

d. Planned comparison, *a priori* test, by Formula 14-35:

$$t = \frac{\overline{X}_2 - \overline{X}_1}{\sqrt{\dfrac{2MS_W}{n}}} = \frac{4.70}{\sqrt{\dfrac{2(26.18)}{10}}} = 2.05; \quad df = 45.$$

Reject H_0 since the observed $t(45)$ exceeds the 2-tailed *CV* at the .05 level.

e. *A posteriori* tests (unplanned comparisons):

		X_1	X_3	X_2	X_5	X_4
		8.80	**11.00**	**13.50**	**15.90**	**19.90**
X_1	**8.80**	—	2.20	4.70	7.10*	11.10**
X_3	**11.00**		—	2.50	4.90	8.90**
X_2	**13.50**			—	2.40	6.40*
X_5	**15.90**				—	4.00
X_4	**19.90**					—

*$p < .05$; **$p < .01$.

By Formula 14-36,

$$R_\alpha(m,df) = r_\alpha(m,df) \sqrt{\frac{MS_w}{n}}.$$

Finding the standardized range for 5 means at the .05 level by interpolation in Table I, and entering the value below,

$$R_{.05}(5,45) = r_{.05}(5,45) \sqrt{\frac{26.18}{10}} = 4.02(1.62) = 6.51.$$

Other critical ranges are found similarly. For example,

$$R_{.01}(3,45) = 4.35(1.62) = 7.05.$$

Significant differences are marked with asterisks above.

Notice that the difference between Means 1 and 2 is not significant by an *a posteriori* test, but is significant by a planned comparison utilizing a *t* test. It is not always true that a planned comparison will yield significant results when an unplanned comparison will not, but failing to run an appropriate *a priori* test will indeed increase the probability of a Type 2 error.

f. It is not appropriate to run an *a priori* test after looking at the data. A planned comparison must be decided upon in advance, before collecting the data.

g. We cannot say that the managers perceive their quality of work life to be twice as high as that of unskilled laborers, even though the mean of the former group is indeed numerically more than twice as high as that of the latter. We are dealing with test scores here, an interval scale lacking a meaningful zero. As we noted in Chapter 1, we cannot make ratio comparisons on an interval scale.

h. The graph is shown on p. 545.

i. To assess the size of the effect of the independent variable, we need an estimate of the standard deviation of the population. The MS_w in the ANOVA is an unbiased estimate of the population variance, so taking the square root yields our estimate of the population standard deviation:

$$S = \sqrt{MS_w} = \sqrt{26.18} = 5.12.$$

The largest difference between any pair of means, D_{max}, can be found among the differences listed above. By Formula 14-40:

$$\text{Size of effect} = \frac{D_{max}}{5.12} = \frac{11.10}{5.12} = 2.17.$$

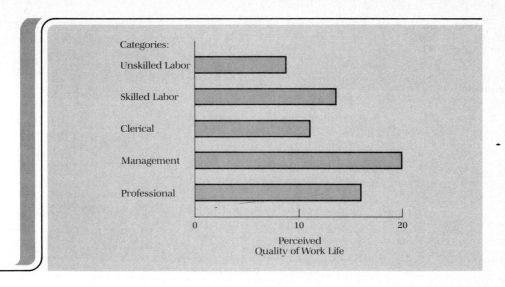

Thus, the independent variable produced a difference between the largest and smallest means that was more than twice as large as the standard deviation, a very substantial effect.

4. **a.** A mail questionnaire would practically guarantee unequal *n*s. Furthermore, a researcher can usually count on a response rate of about 50% in a mail survey. What kinds of people respond, and what kinds do not? Possible self-selection biases would undermine the external validity of the study. When subjects are directly available, as in the present study, mail questionnaires are to be avoided.

b. Choosing the first 10 names from an alphabetic roster would entail the risk of choosing people having the same surname, perhaps relatives, or husbands and wives, whose views would not be entirely independent. This procedure would call the internal validity of the study into question. A random sample of each category of worker would avoid this problem.

c. In choosing the first workers to come into the company cafeteria for lunch, there are many opportunities for self selection to result in biased samples of workers, thereby threatening the external validity of the study. Self-selection biases can be avoided by using random samples.

d. Testing different categories of workers on different days exposes the study to the possible effects of a host of extraneous variables. For example, suppose the national news media announced a sharp increase, or decrease, in the Consumer Price Index while the data were being collected, or perhaps a sharp change in the level of unemployment. Any such extraneous event would be confounded with the comparisons between groups tested before and after the event, thus weakening the internal validity of the study. The remedy here is to test all of the workers on the same day if at all possible.

e. If there are 5 research assistants, each interviewing a single category of workers, then any effects of the different interviewers are confounded with the possible differences between categories. The internal validity of such a study would be seriously threatened. An appropriate procedure would be to assign 2 workers from each category to each research assistant, thereby balancing any interviewer effects across groups.

5. To choose a random sample of 10 workers from each of 5 categories, assign a random number to every worker using a table of random numbers, or a random-number routine on a calculator, and then select the 10 workers in each category having the lowest (or highest) numbers. In a small organization having a few tens of workers in each category, 2-digit random numbers are sufficient, but where there are hundreds or thousands of workers involved, it is helpful to use 3- or 4-digit numbers to avoid excessive duplication.

6. **a.** The independent variable is manipulated, so this study is an experiment where causal inferences may be drawn.

b. The data constitute a ratio scale, thus justifying an ANOVA. The null and alternative hypotheses are as in the earlier example above.

c. The analysis of variance is shown below. Reject H_0 at the .01 level since the observed $F(3,33) = 5.98$, exceeding the critical value of 4.44 found by interpolation in Table F.

	Number of Tubes					
	1	**2**	**3**	**4**		
	X_1	X_2	X_3	X_4		
$\sum_i X_{ij}$	164	139	201	173	$\sum_j \sum_i X_{ij} = G = 677$	
$\sum_i X_{ij}^2$	2716	2449	4093	3365	$\sum_j \sum_i X_{ij}^2 = 12623$	
n_j	10	8	10	9	$\Sigma n_j = N = 37$	
$\overline{X}_j$	16.40	17.38	20.10	19.22	$k = 4$ groups	
S_j	1.71	2.20	2.42	2.22		

Computational symbols, Formulas 14-32:

$$(1) = \frac{G^2}{N} = \frac{677^2}{37} = 12387.27;$$

$$(2) = \sum_j \sum_i X_{ij}^2 = 12623;$$

$$(3) = \frac{\sum_j \left(\sum_i X_{ij} \right)^2}{n_j} = \frac{164^2}{10} + \frac{139^2}{8} + \frac{201^2}{10} + \frac{173^2}{9} = 12470.27.$$

Summary of analysis of variance:

Source	Formula	df		SS	MS	F
Categories (between)	(3) − (1)	$k - 1 =$	3	83.00	27.67	5.98**
Error (within)	(2) − (3)	$N - k =$	33	152.73	4.63	
Total	(2) − (1)	$N - 1 =$	36	235.73		

**$p < .01$.

d. Planned comparison, *a priori* test, by Formula 14-35:

$$t = \frac{\overline{X}_4 - \overline{X}_1}{\sqrt{\dfrac{2MS_W}{n}}} = \frac{2.82}{\sqrt{\dfrac{2(4.63)}{10}}} = 2.93; \quad df = 33.$$

Thus, reject H_0 at the .01 level.

e. *A posteriori* tests (unplanned comparisons):

		X_1	X_2	X_4	X_3
		($n = 10$)	($n = 8$)	($n = 10$)	($n = 9$)
		16.40	17.38	19.22	20.10
X_1 ($n = 10$)	16.40	—	0.98	2.82*	3.70**
X_2 ($n = 8$)	17.38		—	1.84	2.72*
X_4 ($n = 10$)	19.22			—	0.88
X_3 ($n = 9$)	20.10				—

*$p < .05$; **$p < .01$.

By Formula 14-39, for unequal ns,

$$R_\alpha(m,df) = r_\alpha(m,df) \sqrt{\frac{MS_W}{2}\left(\frac{1}{n_a} + \frac{1}{n_b}\right)}; \quad df = df_W = N - k.$$

Finding the critical range for 4 means at the .05 level,

$$R_{.05}(4,33) = r_{.05}(4,33) \sqrt{\frac{4.63}{2}\left(\frac{1}{10} + \frac{1}{9}\right)} = 3.83(0.70) = 2.68.$$

There are 2 comparisons covering a range of 3 means, $\overline{X}_1$ vs $\overline{X}_4$, and $\overline{X}_2$ vs $\overline{X}_3$. Since the ns are equal in the first comparison and unequal in the second, the critical ranges for those comparisons must be calculated separately. For example,

$$R_{.05}(3,33) = r_{.05}(3,33) \sqrt{\frac{4.63}{2}\left(\frac{1}{8} + \frac{1}{9}\right)} = 3.48(0.74) = 2.58.$$

Other critical ranges are found similarly. Significant differences are marked with asterisks above.

f. The graph on p. 548 shows an increase in productivity with increasing levels of illumination. Thus, there appears to be a linear trend in the data, even though the highest level of the dependent variable is associated with the second highest level of the independent variable.

g. The difference between $\overline{X}_3$ and $\overline{X}_4$, favoring the lower level of illumination, is not significant by the *a posteriori* test above. Thus, by our best judgment, the difference between those means is a matter of random variability.

h. Decreasing the level of illumination to 3 tubes resulted in no decrease in productivity. Indeed, there was a slight but not significant increase. Thus, it would be profitable to decrease the illumination to that level. More information would be needed to justify any further decrease, since there was a significant difference between the effects of 2 tubes and 3 or 4. The energy savings would need to be weighed carefully against the increased assembly costs due to the lower productivity under lower illumination.

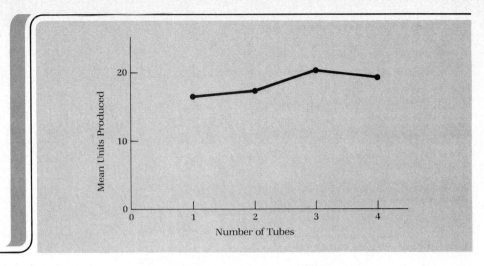

7. If the independent variable has an effect, then the group means will differ. In that case, the variance of the group means will be greater than in the absence of an effect. We use the variance of the means to derive an estimate of the variance of the population, and we derive a second independent estimate of the population variance using the observed variance within groups. That second estimate is independent of any difference between means, that is, it is free of any effect of the independent variable. The F ratio in an ANOVA is the ratio of the first variance, above, to the second. Thus, the greater the differences between means, the greater the ratio of those variances, and the greater the value of F.

Chapter 15

1. a. The shapes of the tortillas comprise a nominal scale, each customer's choice falls in one and only one category, and the expected frequencies are sufficiently large to justify a *chi*-square test.

H_0: Shapes are preferred equally.

H_1: Shapes are not preferred equally.

The choice of equal expected frequencies follows from the nature of the null and alternative hypotheses.

b.

Round	Triangular	Square	Hexagonal	
22	19	21	38	100
(25)	(25)	(25)	(25)	

By Formula 15-1, $\chi^2_{df} = \sum \dfrac{(f_o - f_e)^2}{f_e}$; $df = k - 1$.

$$\chi^2_3 = \dfrac{(22 - 25)^2}{25} + \ldots + \dfrac{(38 - 25)^2}{25} = 9.20.$$

Since the critical value of *chi*-square in Table E is 7.815 at the .05 level, we reject H_0. Thus, we conclude that the 4 shapes of tortillas are not preferred equally. Only the hexagonal shape was chosen more frequently than expected.

2. **a.** Counting the same customers more than once results in observations that are nonindependent, thus violating one of the *chi*-square assumptions. Furthermore, such a procedure would result in a biased sample. It would be desirable to see that each customer is counted only once.

b. If one of the shapes happens to be chosen more frequently in the early stage of the study, later customers may be influenced by those early choices if they are allowed to see the number of packages remaining in each stack. The requirement of independence would again be violated, and possible biases would again be introduced. Showing each customer a single instance of each shape would eliminate the problem here.

c. Here, the accidental damage of some tortillas is confounded with two of the shapes, which fussy customers might tend to avoid. The remedy is to make sure that all of the tortillas are as nearly comparable as possible in all respects other than their shapes.

3. **a.** Since we are concerned with the proportions of men and women in 5 categories, this situation involves a *chi*-square test of binomial proportions.

H_0: Equal proportions in all areas.

H_1: Some proportions are not equal.

b.

Area	Men		Women		
Math & Physical Sciences	71	(64.11)	8	(14.89)	79
Life Sciences	17	(22.72)	11	(5.28)	28
Psychology	18	(21.91)	9	(5.09)	27
Social Sciences	52	(55.99)	17	(13.01)	69
Humanities	139	(132.27)	24	(30.73)	163
	297		69		366

By Formula 11-11,

$$\chi^2_{df} = \sum_r \sum_c \frac{(f_o - f_e)^2}{f_e}; \quad df = (r-1)(c-1).$$

$$\chi^2_4 = \frac{(71 - 64.11)^2}{64.11} + \ldots + \frac{(24 - 30.73)^2}{30.73} = 18.59.$$

Since the critical value of *chi*-square at the .001 level is 18.465, we reject H_0 at that level of significance. Thus, we conclude that there are highly significant differences between the proportions of men and women across the 5 areas.

    c. Some departments are relatively small, so if the data were broken down to that level in every case, then some of the expected frequencies would be too small. Combining departments into larger areas overcomes that difficulty. However, in any such situation, categories must be combined carefully and thoughtfully. For example, combining the Departments of Physics and Home Economics might cloud the issue a bit in a study of sex differences.

4. a.

Area	Men	Women	
Math & Physical Sciences	89.9%	10.1%	100%
Life Sciences	60.7%	39.3%	100%
Psychology	66.7%	33.3%	100%
Social Sciences	75.4%	24.6%	100%
Humanities	85.3%	14.7%	100%
	81.1%	18.9%	100%

b.

Area	Men	Women	
Math & Physical Sciences	23.9%	11.6%	21.6%
Life Sciences	5.7%	15.9%	7.7%
Psychology	6.1%	13.0%	7.4%
Social Sciences	17.5%	24.6%	18.9%
Humanities	46.8%	34.8%	44.5%
	100.0%	99.9%	100.1%

    c. The table in Item a shows the proportions of men and women by areas. For example, in *Math & Physical Sciences* only 10.1% of the faculty members are women, while in *Life Sciences* women make up 39.3% of the faculty. The marginal totals at the bottom show the percentages of men and women in the total sample. The table in b shows the separate distributions of men and women across areas. The marginal totals in that table show the percentages of the total sample falling in the various areas. Thus, each table provides somewhat different, though related, information.

    5. Concluding on the basis of the above information that the university has discriminated against women requires drawing a causal inference from an association between variables. As we have noted repeatedly, a correlation is no guarantee of a causal relationship. Although the small percentage of women in *Math & Physical Sciences* appears consistent with a sex-discrimination hypothesis, there are other factors to consider, for example, the number of women holding advanced degrees in those areas.

6. **a.** In comparing the proportions of subjects answering Yes, No, and Undecided across the categories of advertising material, we are concerned with a test of homogeneity of multinomial proportions. No expected frequency is less than 5, so a *chi*-square test is appropriate.

H_0: Proportions of subjects answering Yes, No, and Undecided are equal across categories.

H_1: Proportions are not equal.

b.

Response	Price	Emphasis Economy	Style	
Yes	20 (13.24)	13 (14.09)	8 (13.67)	41
Undecided	7 (10.33)	12 (11.00)	13 (10.67)	32
No	4 (7.43)	8 (7.91)	11 (7.67)	23
	31	33	32	96

By Formula 11-11,

$$\chi^2_{df} = \sum_r \sum_c \frac{(f_o - f_e)^2}{f_e}; \quad df = (r - 1)(c - 1).$$

$$\chi^2_4 = \frac{(20 - 13.24)^2}{13.24} + \ldots + \frac{(11 - 7.67)^2}{7.67} = 10.59.$$

Reject H_0, since the observed value of *chi*-square exceeds the critical value of 9.488 at the .05 level. Thus, proportions are not homogeneous — that is, not equal — across age groups.

c. Percentages by columns.

Response	Price	Emphasis Economy	Style	
Yes	64.5%	39.4%	25.0%	42.7%
Undecided	22.6%	36.4%	40.6%	33.3%
No	12.9%	24.2%	34.4%	24.0%
	100.0%	100.0%	100.0%	100.0%

d. The material emphasizing price is clearly superior. That category has the largest proportion of subjects who would seriously consider buying the new model, the smallest proportion ruling it out, and the smallest proportion of undecided responses.

e. This study is an experiment, since the researcher determined which subjects would be exposed to which categories of advertising material. Thus, we conclude that the different kinds of material have caused the observed differences in the subjects' responses. Had the study used 3 intact groups, any observed differences would then be confounded with possible preexisting group differences. Most of our examples of *chi*-square tests have involved observations, but these procedures are also useful in experiments wherever the results consist of frequencies.

Statistical Tables and Sources

E. Critical Values of *Chi*-Square   564

Abridged from Table IV, R. A. Fisher & F. Yates, *Statistical Tables for Biological, Agricultural and Medical Research,* 6th Edition. London: Longman Group Ltd. (previously published by Oliver & Boyd Ltd., Edinburgh). Reprinted by permission of the authors and publishers.

F. Critical Values of *F*   565

Reprinted by permission from *Statistical Methods* by G. W. Snedecor & W. G. Cochran, Seventh Edition. © 1980 by The Iowa State University Press, 211 South State Avenue, Ames, Iowa 50010.

G. Critical Values of Wilcoxon's *W*   569

Adapted from the following publications: F. Wilcoxon, S. K. Katti, & R. A. Wilcox, *Critical Values and Probability Levels for the Wilcoxon Rank Sum Test and the Wilcoxon Signed Rank Test.* Pearl River, NY: Lederle Laboratories Division, American Cyanamid Company, 1963. F. Wilcoxon and R. A. Wilcox, *Some Rapid Approximate Statistical Procedures.* Pearl River, NY: Lederle Laboratories Division, American Cyanamid Company, 1964. Reproduced with the permission of the American Cyanamid Company.

H. Random Numbers   570

Reprinted from Pages 1 and 2 of *A Million Random Digits with 100,000 Normal Deviates,* by the RAND Corporation. New York: The Free Press, 1955. Copyright 1955, 1983 by the RAND Corporation. Used by permission.

I. Standardized (Studentized) Ranges   572

Abridged from Table 29, E. S. Pearson & H. O. Hartley (Editors), *Biometrika Tables for Statisticians,* Volume 1. Cambridge, England: Cambridge University Press, 1970. Reprinted by permission of the *Biometrika* Trustees.

Using Table A: Areas of the Normal Distribution

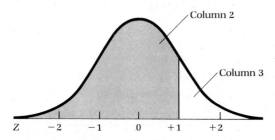

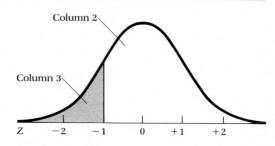

(Column 2) = Area below +Z.
(Column 3) = Area above +Z.
Areas are probabilities:
For example, $P(Z \leq 1) = .8413$.

Finding percentile ranks:
$PR(+Z) = 100(\text{Column 2})$.
For example,
$PR(+1) = 100(.8413) = 84.13\text{th}$.

(Column 3) = Area below −Z.
(Column 2) = Area above −Z.
Areas are probabilities:
For example, $P(Z \leq -1) = .1587$.

Finding percentile ranks:
$PR(-Z) = 100(\text{Column 3})$.
For example,
$PR(-1) = 100(.1587) = 15.87\text{th}$.

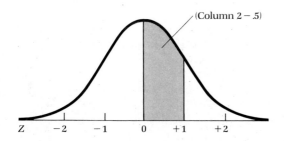

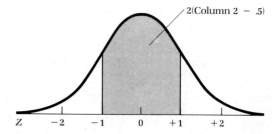

Area between mean and +Z or −Z
is equal to (Column 2) − .5000.
For example,
Area between mean and +1.00
$= .8413 - .5000 = .3413$.

Area between −Z and +Z, that is,
within ±Z units of the mean,
is equal to 2(Column 2 − .5000).
For example,
Area between −1 and +1
$= 2(.8413 - .5000) = .6826$.

Critical values for tests at several significance levels are shown in **boldface** type in Table A and identified in footnotes. An observed Z is significant if its absolute value is greater than or equal to one of those critical values, that is, if $|\pm Z| \geq CV$.

TABLE A: Areas and Critical Values of the Normal Distribution

(1) +z	(2) Area Below +z / Area Above -z	(3) Area Above +z / Area Below -z	(1) +z	(2) Area Below +z / Area Above -z	(3) Area Above +z / Area Below -z	(1) +z	(2) Area Below +z / Area Above -z	(3) Area Above +z / Area Below -z
-z			-z			-z		
0.00	.5000	.5000	0.55	.7088	.2912	1.10	.8643	.1357
0.01	.5040	.4960	0.56	.7123	.2877	1.11	.8665	.1335
0.02	.5080	.4920	0.57	.7157	.2843	1.12	.8686	.1314
0.03	.5120	.4880	0.58	.7190	.2810	1.13	.8708	.1292
0.04	.5160	.4840	0.59	.7224	.2776	1.14	.8729	.1271
0.05	.5199	.4801	0.60	.7257	.2743	1.15	.8749	.1251
0.06	.5239	.4761	0.61	.7291	.2709	1.16	.8770	.1230
0.07	.5279	.4721	0.62	.7324	.2676	1.17	.8790	.1210
0.08	.5319	.4681	0.63	.7357	.2643	1.18	.8810	.1190
0.09	.5359	.4641	0.64	.7389	.2611	1.19	.8830	.1170
0.10	.5398	.4602	0.65	.7422	.2578	1.20	.8849	.1151
0.11	.5438	.4562	0.66	.7454	.2546	1.21	.8869	.1131
0.12	.5478	.4522	0.67	.7486	.2514	1.22	.8888	.1112
0.13	.5517	.4483	0.68	.7517	.2483	1.23	.8907	.1093
0.14	.5557	.4443	0.69	.7549	.2451	1.24	.8925	.1075
0.15	.5596	.4404	0.70	.7580	.2420	1.25	.8944	.1056
0.16	.5636	.4364	0.71	.7611	.2389	1.26	.8962	.1038
0.17	.5675	.4325	0.72	.7642	.2358	1.27	.8980	.1020
0.18	.5714	.4286	0.73	.7673	.2327	1.28	.8997	.1003
0.19	.5753	.4247	0.74	.7704	.2296	1.29	.9015	.0985
0.20	.5793	.4207	0.75	.7734	.2266	1.30	.9032	.0968
0.21	.5832	.4168	0.76	.7764	.2236	1.31	.9049	.0951
0.22	.5871	.4129	0.77	.7794	.2206	1.32	.9066	.0934
0.23	.5910	.4090	0.78	.7823	.2177	1.33	.9082	.0918
0.24	.5948	.4052	0.79	.7852	.2148	1.34	.9099	.0901
0.25	.5987	.4013	0.80	.7881	.2119	1.35	.9115	.0885
0.26	.6026	.3974	0.81	.7910	.2090	1.36	.9131	.0869
0.27	.6064	.3936	0.82	.7939	.2061	1.37	.9147	.0853
0.28	.6103	.3897	0.83	.7967	.2033	1.38	.9162	.0838
0.29	.6141	.3859	0.84	.7995	.2005	1.39	.9177	.0823
0.30	.6179	.3821	0.85	.8023	.1977	1.40	.9192	.0808
0.31	.6217	.3783	0.86	.8051	.1949	1.41	.9207	.0793
0.32	.6255	.3745	0.87	.8078	.1922	1.42	.9222	.0778
0.33	.6293	.3707	0.88	.8106	.1894	1.43	.9236	.0764
0.34	.6331	.3669	0.89	.8133	.1867	1.44	.9251	.0749
0.35	.6368	.3632	0.90	.8159	.1841	1.45	.9265	.0735
0.36	.6406	.3594	0.91	.8186	.1814	1.46	.9279	.0721
0.37	.6443	.3557	0.92	.8212	.1788	1.47	.9292	.0708
0.38	.6480	.3520	0.93	.8238	.1762	1.48	.9306	.0694
0.39	.6517	.3483	0.94	.8264	.1736	1.49	.9319	.0681
0.40	.6554	.3446	0.95	.8289	.1711	1.50	.9332	.0668
0.41	.6591	.3409	0.96	.8315	.1685	1.51	.9345	.0655
0.42	.6628	.3372	0.97	.8340	.1660	1.52	.9357	.0643
0.43	.6664	.3336	0.98	.8365	.1635	1.53	.9370	.0630
0.44	.6700	.3300	0.99	.8389	.1611	1.54	.9382	.0618
0.45	.6736	.3264	1.00	.8413	.1587	1.55	.9394	.0606
0.46	.6772	.3228	1.01	.8438	.1562	1.56	.9406	.0594
0.47	.6808	.3192	1.02	.8461	.1539	1.57	.9418	.0582
0.48	.6844	.3156	1.03	.8485	.1515	1.58	.9429	.0571
0.49	.6879	.3121	1.04	.8508	.1492	1.59	.9441	.0559
0.50	.6915	.3085	1.05	.8531	.1469	1.60	.9452	.0548
0.51	.6950	.3050	1.06	.8554	.1446	1.61	.9463	.0537
0.52	.6985	.3015	1.07	.8577	.1423	1.62	.9474	.0526
0.53	.7019	.2981	1.08	.8599	.1401	1.63	.9484	.0516
0.54	.7054	.2946	1.09	.8621	.1379	1.64	.9495	.0505

Table A (Concluded)

(1) +z / −z	(2) Area Below +z / Area Above −z	(3) Area Above +z / Area Below −z	(1) +z / −z	(2) Area Below +z / Area Above −z	(3) Area Above +z / Area Below −z	(1) +z / −z	(2) Area Below +z / Area Above −z	(3) Area Above +z / Area Below −z
1.65[a]	.9505	.0495	2.20	.9861	.0139	2.75	.9970	.0030
1.66	.9515	.0485	2.21	.9864	.0136	2.76	.9971	.0029
1.67	.9525	.0475	2.22	.9868	.0132	2.77	.9972	.0028
1.68	.9535	.0465	2.23	.9871	.0129	2.78	.9973	.0027
1.69	.9545	.0455	2.24	.9875	.0125	2.79	.9974	.0026
1.70	.9554	.0446	2.25	.9878	.0122	2.80	.9974	.0026
1.71	.9564	.0436	2.26	.9881	.0119	2.81	.9975	.0025
1.72	.9573	.0427	2.27	.9884	.0116	2.82	.9976	.0024
1.73	.9582	.0418	2.28	.9887	.0113	2.83	.9977	.0023
1.74	.9591	.0409	2.29	.9890	.0110	2.84	.9977	.0023
1.75	.9599	.0401	2.30	.9893	.0107	2.85	.9978	.0022
1.76	.9608	.0392	2.31	.9896	.0104	2.86	.9979	.0021
1.77	.9616	.0384	2.32	.9898	.0102	2.87	.9979	.0021
1.78	.9625	.0375	2.33[c]	.9901	.0099	2.88	.9980	.0020
1.79	.9633	.0367	2.34	.9904	.0096	2.89	.9981	.0019
1.80	.9641	.0359	2.35	.9906	.0094	2.90	.9981	.0019
1.81	.9649	.0351	2.36	.9909	.0091	2.91	.9982	.0018
1.82	.9656	.0344	2.37	.9911	.0089	2.92	.9982	.0018
1.83	.9664	.0336	2.38	.9913	.0087	2.93	.9983	.0017
1.84	.9671	.0329	2.39	.9916	.0084	2.94	.9984	.0016
1.85	.9678	.0322	2.40	.9918	.0082	2.95	.9984	.0016
1.86	.9686	.0314	2.41	.9920	.0080	2.96	.9985	.0015
1.87	.9693	.0307	2.42	.9922	.0078	2.97	.9985	.0015
1.88	.9699	.0301	2.43	.9925	.0075	2.98	.9986	.0014
1.89	.9706	.0294	2.44	.9927	.0073	2.99	.9986	.0014
1.90	.9713	.0287	2.45	.9929	.0071	3.00	.9987	.0013
1.91	.9719	.0281	2.46	.9931	.0069	3.03	.9988	.0012
1.92	.9726	.0274	2.47	.9932	.0068	3.05	.9989	.0011
1.93	.9732	.0268	2.48	.9934	.0066	3.08	.9990	.0010
1.94	.9738	.0262	2.49	.9936	.0064	3.09	.9990	.0010
1.95	.9744	.0256	2.50	.9938	.0062	3.10[e]	.99903	.00097
1.96[b]	.9750	.0250	2.51	.9940	.0060	3.11	.9991	.0009
1.97	.9756	.0244	2.52	.9941	.0059	3.14	.9992	.0008
1.98	.9761	.0239	2.53	.9943	.0057	3.18	.9993	.0007
1.99	.9767	.0233	2.54	.9945	.0055	3.22	.9994	.0006
2.00	.9772	.0228	2.55	.9946	.0054	3.27	.99946	.00054
2.01	.9778	.0222	2.56	.9948	.0052	3.30[f]	.99952	.00048
2.02	.9783	.0217	2.57	.9949	.0051	3.33	.9996	.0004
2.03	.9788	.0212	2.58[d]	.9951	.0049	3.40	.9997	.0003
2.04	.9793	.0207	2.59	.9952	.0048	3.49	.9998	.0002
2.05	.9798	.0202	2.60	.9953	.0047	3.62	.9999	.0001
2.06	.9803	.0197	2.61	.9955	.0045	3.87	.99995	.00005
2.07	.9808	.0192	2.62	.9956	.0044	4.00	.99997	.00003
2.08	.9812	.0188	2.63	.9957	.0043			
2.09	.9817	.0183	2.64	.9959	.0041			
2.10	.9821	.0179	2.65	.9960	.0040			
2.11	.9826	.0174	2.66	.9961	.0039			
2.12	.9830	.0170	2.67	.9962	.0038			
2.13	.9834	.0166	2.68	.9963	.0037			
2.14	.9838	.0162	2.69	.9964	.0036			
2.15	.9842	.0158	2.70	.9965	.0035			
2.16	.9846	.0154	2.71	.9966	.0034			
2.17	.9850	.0150	2.72	.9967	.0033			
2.18	.9854	.0146	2.73	.9968	.0032			
2.19	.9857	.0143	2.74	.9969	.0031			

Critical Values

	1-Tailed	2-Tailed
a.	$p < .05$	$p < .10$
b.	$p < .025$	$p < .05$
c.	$p < .01$	$p < .02$
d.	$p < .005$	$p < .01$
e.	$p < .001$	$p < .002$
f.	$p < .0005$	$p < .001$

TABLE B: Critical Values of t

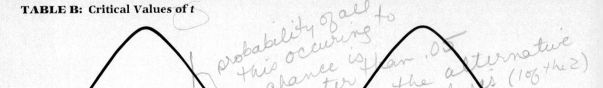

probability of all this occuring to chance is greater than .05

As the alternative hypothesis (1 of the 2) is correct

5.40   *2.101*

An observed t *is significant if* $|\pm t| \geq$ CV, *that is, if the absolute value is greater than or equal to the critical value for the appropriate degrees of freedom,* df.

df	Significance Probability (α) for One-Tailed Test								
	.25	**.20**	**.15**	**.10**	**.05**	**.025**	**.01**	**.005**	**.0005**
	Significance Probability (α) for Two-Tailed Test								
df	**.50**	**.40**	**.30**	**.20**	**.10**	**.05**	**.02**	**.01**	**.001**
1	1.000	1.376	1.963	3.078	6.314	12.706	31.821	63.657	636.619
2	.816	1.061	1.386	1.886	2.920	4.303	6.965	9.925	31.598
3	.765	.978	1.250	1.638	2.353	3.182	4.541	5.841	12.924
4	.741	.941	1.190	1.533	2.132	2.776	3.747	4.604	8.610
5	.727	.920	1.156	1.476	2.015	2.571	3.365	4.032	6.869
6	.718	.906	1.134	1.440	1.943	2.447	3.143	3.707	5.959
7	.711	.896	1.119	1.415	1.895	2.365	2.998	3.499	5.408
8	.706	.889	1.108	1.397	1.860	2.306	2.896	3.355	5.041
9	.703	.883	1.100	1.383	1.833	2.262	2.821	3.250	4.781
10	.700	.879	1.093	1.372	1.812	2.228	2.764	3.169	4.587
11	.697	.876	1.088	1.363	1.796	2.201	2.718	3.106	4.437
12	.695	.873	1.083	1.356	1.782	2.179	2.681	3.055	4.318
13	.694	.870	1.079	1.350	1.771	2.160	2.650	3.012	4.221
14	.692	.868	1.076	1.345	1.761	2.145	2.624	2.977	4.140
15	.691	.866	1.074	1.341	1.753	2.131	2.602	2.947	4.073
16	.690	.865	1.071	1.337	1.746	2.120	2.583	2.921	4.015
17	.689	.863	1.069	1.333	1.740	2.110	2.567	2.898	3.965
18	.688	.862	1.067	1.330	1.734	2.101	2.552	2.878	3.922
19	.688	.861	1.066	1.328	1.729	2.093	2.539	2.861	3.883
20	.687	.860	1.064	1.325	1.725	2.086	2.528	2.845	3.850
21	.686	.859	1.063	1.323	1.721	2.080	2.518	2.831	3.819
22	.686	.858	1.061	1.321	1.717	2.074	2.508	2.819	3.792
23	.685	.858	1.060	1.319	1.714	2.069	2.500	2.807	3.767
24	.685	.857	1.059	1.318	1.711	2.064	2.492	2.797	3.745
25	.684	.856	1.058	1.316	1.708	2.060	2.485	2.787	3.725
26	.684	.856	1.058	1.315	1.706	2.056	2.479	2.779	3.707
27	.684	.855	1.057	1.314	1.703	2.052	2.473	2.771	3.690
28	.683	.855	1.056	1.313	1.701	2.048	2.467	2.763	3.674
29	.683	.854	1.055	1.311	1.699	2.045	2.462	2.756	3.659
30	.683	.854	1.055	1.310	1.697	2.042	2.457	2.750	3.646
40	.681	.851	1.050	1.303	1.684	2.021	2.423	2.704	3.551
60	.679	.848	1.046	1.296	1.671	2.000	2.390	2.660	3.460
120	.677	.845	1.041	1.289	1.658	1.980	2.358	2.617	3.373
∞	.674	.842	1.036	1.282	1.645	1.960	2.326	2.576	3.291

TABLE C, PART 1: Critical Values of U at the .05 Level (One-Tailed) or the .10 Level (Two-Tailed)

An observed U is significant if it is less than or equal to the smaller critical value, or greater than or equal to the larger critical value for the appropriate sample sizes N_A and N_B. Dashes indicate no test is possible for some sample sizes at the significance levels given above.

Each cell gives the smaller / larger critical value.

N_B \ N_A	1	2	3	4	5	6	7	8	9	10	11	12	13	14	15	16	17	18	19	20
1	—	—	—	—	—	—	—	—	—	—	—	—	—	—	—	—	—	—	0 / 19	0 / 20
2	—	—	—	—	0 / 10	0 / 12	0 / 14	1 / 15	1 / 17	1 / 19	1 / 21	2 / 22	2 / 24	2 / 26	3 / 27	3 / 29	3 / 31	4 / 32	4 / 34	4 / 36
3	—	—	0 / 9	0 / 12	1 / 14	2 / 16	2 / 19	3 / 21	3 / 24	4 / 26	5 / 28	5 / 31	6 / 33	7 / 35	7 / 38	8 / 40	9 / 42	9 / 45	10 / 47	11 / 49
4	—	—	0 / 12	1 / 15	2 / 18	3 / 21	4 / 24	5 / 27	6 / 30	7 / 33	8 / 36	9 / 39	10 / 42	11 / 45	12 / 48	14 / 50	15 / 53	16 / 56	17 / 59	18 / 62
5	—	0 / 10	1 / 14	2 / 18	4 / 21	5 / 25	6 / 29	8 / 32	9 / 36	11 / 39	12 / 43	13 / 47	15 / 50	16 / 54	18 / 57	19 / 61	20 / 65	22 / 68	23 / 72	25 / 75
6	—	0 / 12	2 / 16	3 / 21	5 / 25	7 / 29	8 / 34	10 / 38	12 / 42	14 / 46	16 / 50	17 / 55	19 / 59	21 / 63	23 / 67	25 / 71	26 / 76	28 / 80	30 / 84	32 / 88
7	—	0 / 14	2 / 19	4 / 24	6 / 29	8 / 34	11 / 38	13 / 43	15 / 48	17 / 53	19 / 58	21 / 63	24 / 67	26 / 72	28 / 77	30 / 82	33 / 86	35 / 91	37 / 96	39 / 101
8	—	1 / 15	3 / 21	5 / 27	8 / 32	10 / 38	13 / 43	15 / 49	18 / 54	20 / 60	23 / 65	26 / 70	28 / 76	31 / 81	33 / 87	36 / 92	39 / 97	41 / 103	44 / 108	47 / 113
9	—	1 / 17	3 / 24	6 / 30	9 / 36	12 / 42	15 / 48	18 / 54	21 / 60	24 / 66	27 / 72	30 / 78	33 / 84	36 / 90	39 / 96	42 / 102	45 / 108	48 / 114	51 / 120	54 / 126
10	—	1 / 19	4 / 26	7 / 33	11 / 39	14 / 46	17 / 53	20 / 60	24 / 66	27 / 73	31 / 79	34 / 86	37 / 93	41 / 99	44 / 106	48 / 112	51 / 119	55 / 125	58 / 132	62 / 138
11	—	1 / 21	5 / 28	8 / 36	12 / 43	16 / 50	19 / 58	23 / 65	27 / 72	31 / 79	34 / 87	38 / 94	42 / 101	46 / 108	50 / 115	54 / 122	57 / 130	61 / 137	65 / 144	69 / 151
12	—	2 / 22	5 / 31	9 / 39	13 / 47	17 / 55	21 / 63	26 / 70	30 / 78	34 / 86	38 / 94	42 / 102	47 / 109	51 / 117	55 / 125	60 / 132	64 / 140	68 / 148	72 / 156	77 / 163
13	—	2 / 24	6 / 33	10 / 42	15 / 50	19 / 59	24 / 67	28 / 76	33 / 84	37 / 93	42 / 101	47 / 109	51 / 118	56 / 126	61 / 134	65 / 143	70 / 151	75 / 159	80 / 167	84 / 176
14	—	2 / 26	7 / 35	11 / 45	16 / 54	21 / 63	26 / 72	31 / 81	36 / 90	41 / 99	46 / 108	51 / 117	56 / 126	61 / 135	66 / 144	71 / 153	77 / 161	82 / 170	87 / 179	92 / 188
15	—	3 / 27	7 / 38	12 / 48	18 / 57	23 / 67	28 / 77	33 / 87	39 / 96	44 / 106	50 / 115	55 / 125	61 / 134	66 / 144	72 / 153	77 / 163	83 / 172	88 / 182	94 / 191	100 / 200
16	—	3 / 29	8 / 40	14 / 50	19 / 61	25 / 71	30 / 82	36 / 92	42 / 102	48 / 112	54 / 122	60 / 132	65 / 143	71 / 153	77 / 163	83 / 173	89 / 183	95 / 193	101 / 203	107 / 213
17	—	3 / 31	9 / 42	15 / 53	20 / 65	26 / 76	33 / 86	39 / 97	45 / 108	51 / 119	57 / 130	64 / 140	70 / 151	77 / 161	83 / 172	89 / 183	96 / 193	102 / 204	109 / 214	115 / 225
18	—	4 / 32	9 / 45	16 / 56	22 / 68	28 / 80	35 / 91	41 / 103	48 / 114	55 / 123	61 / 137	68 / 148	75 / 159	82 / 170	88 / 182	95 / 193	102 / 204	109 / 215	116 / 226	123 / 237
19	0 / 19	4 / 34	10 / 47	17 / 59	23 / 72	30 / 84	37 / 96	44 / 108	51 / 120	58 / 132	65 / 144	72 / 156	80 / 167	87 / 179	94 / 191	101 / 203	109 / 214	116 / 226	123 / 238	130 / 250
20	0 / 20	4 / 36	11 / 49	18 / 62	25 / 75	32 / 88	39 / 101	47 / 113	54 / 126	62 / 138	69 / 151	77 / 163	84 / 176	92 / 188	100 / 200	107 / 213	115 / 225	123 / 237	130 / 250	138 / 262

TABLE C, PART 2: Critical Values of U at the .025 Level (One-Tailed) or the .05 Level (Two-Tailed)

An observed U is significant if it is less than or equal to the smaller critical value, or greater than or equal to the larger critical value for the appropriate sample sizes N_A and N_B. Dashes indicate no test is possible for some sample sizes at the significance levels given above.

Each cell shows the smaller critical value / larger critical value.

N_B \ N_A	1	2	3	4	5	6	7	8	9	10	11	12	13	14	15	16	17	18	19	20
1	—	—	—	—	—	—	—	—	—	—	—	—	—	—	—	—	—	—	—	—
2	—	—	—	—	—	—	—	0/16	0/18	0/20	0/22	1/23	1/25	1/27	1/29	1/31	2/32	2/34	2/36	2/38
3	—	—	—	—	0/15	1/17	1/20	2/22	2/25	3/27	3/30	4/32	4/35	5/37	5/40	6/42	6/45	7/47	7/50	8/52
4	—	—	—	0/16	1/19	2/22	3/25	4/28	4/32	5/35	6/38	7/41	8/44	9/47	10/50	11/53	11/57	12/60	13/63	13/67
5	—	—	0/15	1/19	2/23	3/27	5/30	6/34	7/38	8/42	9/46	11/49	12/53	13/57	14/61	15/65	17/68	18/72	19/76	20/80
6	—	—	1/17	2/22	3/27	5/31	6/36	8/40	10/44	11/49	13/53	14/58	16/62	17/67	19/71	21/75	22/80	24/84	25/89	27/93
7	—	—	1/20	3/25	5/30	6/36	8/41	10/46	12/51	14/56	16/61	18/66	20/71	22/76	24/81	26/86	28/91	30/96	32/101	34/106
8	—	0/16	2/22	4/28	6/34	8/40	10/46	13/51	15/57	17/63	19/69	22/74	24/80	26/86	29/91	31/97	34/102	36/108	38/114	41/119
9	—	0/18	2/25	4/32	7/38	10/44	12/51	15/57	17/64	20/70	23/76	26/82	28/89	31/95	34/101	37/107	39/114	42/120	45/126	48/132
10	—	0/20	3/27	5/35	8/42	11/49	14/56	17/63	20/70	23/77	26/84	29/91	33/97	36/104	39/111	42/118	45/125	48/132	52/138	55/145
11	—	0/22	3/30	6/38	9/46	13/53	16/61	19/69	23/76	26/84	30/91	33/99	37/106	40/114	44/121	47/129	51/136	55/143	58/151	62/158
12	—	1/23	4/32	7/41	11/49	14/58	18/66	22/74	26/82	29/91	33/99	37/107	41/115	45/123	49/131	53/139	57/147	61/155	65/163	69/171
13	—	1/25	4/35	8/44	12/53	16/62	20/71	24/80	28/89	33/97	37/106	41/115	45/124	50/132	54/141	59/149	63/158	67/167	72/175	76/184
14	—	1/27	5/37	9/47	13/57	17/67	22/76	26/86	31/95	36/104	40/114	45/123	50/132	55/141	59/151	64/160	67/171	74/178	78/188	83/197
15	—	1/29	5/40	10/50	14/61	19/71	24/81	29/91	34/101	39/111	44/121	49/131	54/141	59/151	64/161	70/170	75/180	80/190	85/200	90/210
16	—	1/31	6/42	11/53	15/65	21/75	26/86	31/97	37/107	42/118	47/129	53/139	59/149	64/160	70/170	75/181	81/191	86/202	92/212	98/222
17	—	2/32	6/45	11/57	17/68	22/80	28/91	34/102	39/114	45/125	51/136	57/147	63/158	67/171	75/180	81/191	87/202	93/213	99/224	105/235
18	—	2/34	7/47	12/60	18/72	24/84	30/96	36/108	42/120	48/132	55/143	61/155	67/167	74/178	80/190	86/202	93/213	99/225	106/236	112/248
19	—	2/36	7/50	13/63	19/76	25/89	32/101	38/114	45/126	52/138	58/151	65/163	72/175	78/188	85/200	92/212	99/224	106/236	113/248	119/261
20	—	2/38	8/52	13/67	20/80	27/93	34/106	41/119	48/132	55/145	62/158	69/171	76/184	83/197	90/210	98/222	105/235	112/248	119/261	127/273

TABLE C, PART 3: Critical Values of U at the .01 Level (One-Tailed) or the .02 Level (Two-Tailed)

An observed U is significant if it is less than or equal to the smaller critical value, or greater than or equal to the larger critical value for the appropriate sample sizes N_A and N_B. Dashes indicate no test is possible for some sample sizes at the significance levels given above.

Each cell shows the smaller critical value / larger critical value.

$N_B \backslash N_A$	1	2	3	4	5	6	7	8	9	10	11	12	13	14	15	16	17	18	19	20
1	—	—	—	—	—	—	—	—	—	—	—	—	—	—	—	—	—	—	—	—
2	—	—	—	—	—	—	—	—	—	—	—	—	0/26	0/28	0/30	0/32	0/34	0/36	1/37	1/39
3	—	—	—	—	—	—	0/21	0/24	1/26	1/29	1/32	2/34	2/37	2/40	3/42	3/45	4/47	4/50	4/53	5/55
4	—	—	—	—	0/20	1/23	1/27	2/30	3/33	3/37	4/40	5/43	5/47	6/50	7/53	7/57	8/60	9/63	9/67	10/70
5	—	—	—	0/20	1/24	2/28	3/32	4/36	5/40	6/44	7/48	8/52	9/56	10/60	11/64	12/68	13/72	14/76	15/80	16/84
6	—	—	—	1/23	2/28	3/33	4/38	6/42	7/47	8/52	9/57	11/61	12/66	13/71	15/75	16/80	18/84	19/89	20/94	22/98
7	—	—	0/21	1/27	3/32	4/38	6/43	7/49	9/54	11/59	12/65	14/70	16/75	17/81	19/86	21/91	23/96	24/102	26/107	28/112
8	—	—	0/24	2/30	4/36	6/42	7/49	9/55	11/61	13/67	15/73	17/79	20/84	22/90	24/96	26/102	28/108	30/114	32/120	34/126
9	—	—	1/26	3/33	5/40	7/47	9/54	11/61	14/67	16/74	18/81	21/87	23/94	26/100	28/107	31/113	33/120	36/126	38/133	40/140
10	—	—	1/29	3/37	6/44	8/52	11/59	13/67	16/74	19/81	22/88	24/96	27/103	30/110	33/117	36/124	38/132	41/139	44/146	47/153
11	—	—	1/32	4/40	7/48	9/57	12/65	15/73	18/81	22/88	25/96	28/104	31/112	34/120	37/128	41/135	44/143	47/151	50/159	53/167
12	—	—	2/34	5/43	8/52	11/61	14/70	17/79	21/87	24/96	28/104	31/113	35/121	38/130	42/138	46/146	49/155	53/163	56/172	60/180
13	—	0/26	2/37	5/47	9/56	12/66	16/75	20/84	23/94	27/103	31/112	35/121	39/130	43/139	47/148	51/157	55/166	59/175	63/184	67/193
14	—	0/28	2/40	6/50	10/60	13/71	17/81	22/90	26/100	30/110	34/120	38/130	43/139	47/149	51/159	56/168	60/178	65/187	69/197	73/207
15	—	0/30	3/42	7/53	11/64	15/75	19/86	24/96	28/107	33/117	37/128	42/138	47/148	51/159	56/169	61/179	66/189	70/200	75/210	80/220
16	—	0/32	3/45	7/57	12/68	16/80	21/91	26/102	31/113	36/124	41/135	46/146	51/157	56/168	61/179	66/190	71/201	76/212	82/222	87/233
17	—	0/34	4/47	8/60	13/72	18/84	23/96	28/108	33/120	38/132	44/143	49/155	55/166	60/178	66/189	71/201	77/212	82/224	88/234	93/247
18	—	0/36	4/50	9/63	14/76	19/89	24/102	30/114	36/126	41/139	47/151	53/163	59/175	65/187	70/200	76/212	82/224	88/236	94/248	100/260
19	—	1/37	4/53	9/67	15/80	20/94	26/107	32/120	38/133	44/146	50/159	56/172	63/184	69/197	75/210	82/222	88/235	94/248	101/260	107/273
20	—	1/39	5/55	10/70	16/84	22/98	28/112	34/126	40/140	47/153	53/167	60/180	67/193	73/207	80/220	87/233	93/247	100/260	107/273	114/286

TABLE C, PART 4: Critical Values of U at the .005 Level (One-Tailed) or the .01 Level (Two-tailed)

An observed U is significant if it is less than or equal to the smaller critical value, or greater than or equal to the larger critical value for the appropriate sample sizes N_A and N_B. Dashes indicate no test is possible for some sample sizes at the significance levels given above.

N_B \ N_A	1	2	3	4	5	6	7	8	9	10	11	12	13	14	15	16	17	18	19	20
1	—	—	—	—	—	—	—	—	—	—	—	—	—	—	—	—	—	—	—	—
2	—	—	—	—	—	—	—	—	—	—	—	—	—	—	—	—	—	—	0/38	0/40
3	—	—	—	—	—	—	—	—	0/27	0/30	0/33	1/35	1/38	1/41	2/43	2/46	2/49	2/52	3/54	3/57
4	—	—	—	—	—	0/24	0/28	1/31	1/35	2/38	2/42	3/45	3/49	4/52	5/55	5/59	6/62	6/66	7/69	8/72
5	—	—	—	—	0/25	1/29	1/34	2/38	3/42	4/46	5/50	6/54	7/58	7/63	8/67	9/71	10/75	11/79	12/83	13/87
6	—	—	—	0/24	1/29	2/34	3/39	4/44	5/49	6/54	7/59	9/63	10/68	11/73	12/78	13/83	15/87	16/92	17/97	18/102
7	—	—	—	0/28	1/34	3/39	4/45	6/50	7/56	9/61	10/67	12/72	13/78	15/83	16/89	18/94	19/100	21/105	22/111	24/116
8	—	—	—	1/31	2/38	4/44	6/50	7/57	9/63	11/69	13/75	15/81	17/87	18/94	20/100	22/106	24/112	26/118	28/124	30/130
9	—	—	0/27	1/35	3/42	5/49	7/56	9/63	11/70	13/77	16/83	18/90	20/97	22/104	24/111	27/117	29/124	31/131	33/138	36/144
10	—	—	0/30	2/38	4/46	6/54	9/61	11/69	13/77	16/84	18/92	21/99	24/106	26/114	29/121	31/129	34/136	37/143	39/151	42/158
11	—	—	0/33	2/42	5/50	7/59	10/67	13/75	16/83	18/92	21/100	24/108	27/116	30/124	33/132	36/140	39/148	42/156	45/164	48/172
12	—	—	1/35	3/45	6/54	9/63	12/72	15/81	18/90	21/99	24/108	27/117	31/125	34/134	37/143	41/151	44/160	47/169	51/177	54/186
13	—	—	1/38	3/49	7/58	10/68	13/78	17/87	20/97	24/106	27/116	31/125	34/135	38/144	42/153	45/163	49/172	53/181	56/191	60/200
14	—	—	1/41	4/52	7/63	11/73	15/83	18/94	22/104	26/114	30/124	34/134	38/144	42/154	46/164	50/174	54/184	58/194	63/203	67/213
15	—	—	2/43	5/55	8/67	12/78	16/89	20/100	24/111	29/121	33/132	37/143	42/153	46/164	51/174	55/185	60/195	64/206	69/216	73/227
16	—	—	2/46	5/59	9/71	13/83	18/94	22/106	27/117	31/129	36/140	41/151	45/163	50/174	55/185	60/196	65/207	70/218	74/230	79/241
17	—	—	2/49	6/62	10/75	15/87	19/100	24/112	29/124	34/136	39/148	44/160	49/172	54/184	60/195	65/207	70/219	75/231	81/242	86/254
18	—	—	2/52	6/66	11/79	16/92	21/105	26/118	31/131	37/143	42/156	47/169	53/181	58/194	64/206	70/218	75/231	81/243	87/255	92/268
19	—	0/38	3/54	7/69	12/83	17/97	22/111	28/124	33/138	39/151	45/164	51/177	56/191	63/203	69/216	74/230	81/242	87/255	93/268	99/281
20	—	0/40	3/57	8/72	13/87	18/102	24/116	30/130	36/144	42/158	48/172	54/186	60/200	67/213	73/227	79/241	86/254	92/268	99/281	105/295

TABLE D: Critical Values of Spearman's r_s

An observed r_s is significant if $|\pm r_s| \geq CV$, that is, if the absolute value is greater than or equal to the critical value for the appropriate number of pairs, N. Dashes indicate no tests are possible at some levels of significance and values of N.

	Significance Probability (α) for One-Tailed Test					
	.10	.05	.025	.01	.005	.001
	Significance Probability (α) for Two-Tailed Test					
N	.20	.10	.05	.02	.01	.002
4	1.000	1.000	—	—	—	—
5	.800	.900	1.000	1.000	—	—
6	.657	.829	.886	.943	1.000	—
7	.571	.714	.786	.893	.929	1.000
8	.500	.619	.714	.833	.881	.952
9	.483	.600	.700	.783	.833	.917
10	.455	.564	.648	.745	.794	.879
11	.427	.536	.618	.709	.764	.855
12	.406	.503	.587	.678	.734	.825
13	.385	.484	.560	.648	.703	.797
14	.367	.464	.538	.626	.679	.771
15	.354	.446	.521	.604	.657	.750
16	.341	.429	.503	.585	.635	.729
17	.328	.414	.488	.566	.618	.711
18	.317	.401	.474	.550	.600	.692
19	.309	.391	.460	.535	.584	.675
20	.299	.380	.447	.522	.570	.660
21	.292	.370	.436	.509	.556	.647
22	.284	.361	.425	.497	.544	.633
23	.278	.353	.416	.486	.532	.620
24	.271	.344	.407	.476	.521	.608
25	.265	.337	.398	.466	.511	.597
26	.259	.331	.390	.457	.501	.586
27	.255	.324	.383	.449	.492	.576
28	.250	.318	.375	.441	.483	.567
29	.245	.312	.369	.433	.475	.557
30	.240	.306	.362	.426	.467	.548

TABLE E: Critical Values of χ^2

An observed χ^2 is significant if $\chi^2 \geq CV$, that is, greater than or equal to the critical value for the appropriate degrees of freedom, df.

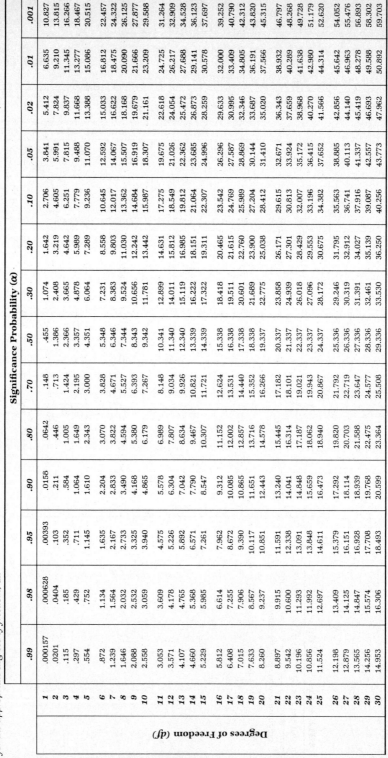

Degrees of Freedom (df)	Significance Probability (α)													
	.99	.98	.95	.90	.80	.70	.50	.30	.20	.10	.05	.02	.01	.001
1	.000157	.000628	.00393	.0158	.0642	.148	.455	1.074	1.642	2.706	3.841	5.412	6.635	10.827
2	.0201	.0404	.103	.211	.446	.713	1.386	2.408	3.219	4.605	5.991	7.824	9.210	13.815
3	.115	.185	.352	.584	1.005	1.424	2.366	3.665	4.642	6.251	7.815	9.837	11.345	16.266
4	.297	.429	.711	1.064	1.649	2.195	3.357	4.878	5.989	7.779	9.488	11.668	13.277	18.467
5	.554	.752	1.145	1.610	2.343	3.000	4.351	6.064	7.289	9.236	11.070	13.388	15.086	20.515
6	.872	1.134	1.635	2.204	3.070	3.828	5.348	7.231	8.558	10.645	12.592	15.033	16.812	22.457
7	1.239	1.564	2.167	2.833	3.822	4.671	6.346	8.383	9.803	12.017	14.067	16.622	18.475	24.322
8	1.646	2.032	2.733	3.490	4.594	5.527	7.344	9.524	11.030	13.362	15.507	18.168	20.090	26.125
9	2.088	2.532	3.325	4.168	5.380	6.393	8.343	10.656	12.242	14.684	16.919	19.679	21.666	27.877
10	2.558	3.059	3.940	4.865	6.179	7.267	9.342	11.781	13.442	15.987	18.307	21.161	23.209	29.588
11	3.053	3.609	4.575	5.578	6.989	8.148	10.341	12.899	14.631	17.275	19.675	22.618	24.725	31.264
12	3.571	4.178	5.226	6.304	7.807	9.034	11.340	14.011	15.812	18.549	21.026	24.054	26.217	32.909
13	4.107	4.765	5.892	7.042	8.634	9.926	12.340	15.119	16.985	19.812	22.362	25.472	27.688	34.528
14	4.660	5.368	6.571	7.790	9.467	10.821	13.339	16.222	18.151	21.064	23.685	26.873	29.141	36.123
15	5.229	5.985	7.261	8.547	10.307	11.721	14.339	17.322	19.311	22.307	24.996	28.259	30.578	37.697
16	5.812	6.614	7.962	9.312	11.152	12.624	15.338	18.418	20.465	23.542	26.296	29.633	32.000	39.252
17	6.408	7.255	8.672	10.085	12.002	13.531	16.338	19.511	21.615	24.769	27.587	30.995	33.409	40.790
18	7.015	7.906	9.390	10.865	12.857	14.440	17.338	20.601	22.760	25.989	28.869	32.346	34.805	42.312
19	7.633	8.567	10.117	11.651	13.716	15.352	18.338	21.689	23.900	27.204	30.144	33.687	36.191	43.820
20	8.260	9.237	10.851	12.443	14.578	16.266	19.337	22.775	25.038	28.412	31.410	35.020	37.566	45.315
21	8.897	9.915	11.591	13.240	15.445	17.182	20.337	23.858	26.171	29.615	32.671	36.343	38.932	46.797
22	9.542	10.600	12.338	14.041	16.314	18.101	21.337	24.939	27.301	30.813	33.924	37.659	40.289	48.268
23	10.196	11.293	13.091	14.848	17.187	19.021	22.337	26.018	28.429	32.007	35.172	38.968	41.638	49.728
24	10.856	11.992	13.848	15.659	18.062	19.943	23.337	27.096	29.553	33.196	36.415	40.270	42.980	51.179
25	11.524	12.697	14.611	16.473	18.940	20.867	24.337	28.172	30.675	34.382	37.652	41.566	44.314	52.620
26	12.198	13.409	15.379	17.292	19.820	21.792	25.336	29.246	31.795	35.563	38.885	42.856	45.642	54.052
27	12.879	14.125	16.151	18.114	20.703	22.719	26.336	30.319	32.912	36.741	40.113	44.140	46.963	55.476
28	13.565	14.847	16.928	18.939	21.588	23.647	27.336	31.391	34.027	37.916	41.337	45.419	48.278	56.893
29	14.256	15.574	17.708	19.768	22.475	24.577	28.336	32.461	35.139	39.087	42.557	46.693	49.588	58.302
30	14.953	16.306	18.493	20.599	23.364	25.508	29.336	33.530	36.250	40.256	43.773	47.962	50.892	59.703

TABLE F: Critical Values of F

An observed F is significant if F ≥ CV, that is, greater than or equal to the critical value for the appropriate degrees of freedom, df.

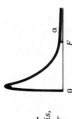

*Critical values at .05 level in light type and at .01 level in **boldface**.*

Degrees of Freedom for Numerator

df for Denominator		1	2	3	4	5	6	7	8	9	10	11	12	14	16	20	24	30	40	50	75	100	200	500	∞
1		161	200	216	225	230	234	237	239	241	242	243	244	245	246	248	249	250	251	252	253	253	254	254	254
		4,052	**4,999**	**5,403**	**5,625**	**5,764**	**5,859**	**5,928**	**5,981**	**6,022**	**6,056**	**6,082**	**6,106**	**6,142**	**6,169**	**6,208**	**6,234**	**6,261**	**6,286**	**6,302**	**6,323**	**6,334**	**6,352**	**6,361**	**6,366**
2		18.51	19.00	19.16	19.25	19.30	19.33	19.36	19.37	19.38	19.39	19.40	19.41	19.42	19.43	19.44	19.45	19.46	19.47	19.47	19.48	19.49	19.49	19.50	19.50
		98.49	**99.00**	**99.17**	**99.25**	**99.30**	**99.33**	**99.36**	**99.37**	**99.39**	**99.40**	**99.41**	**99.42**	**99.43**	**99.44**	**99.45**	**99.46**	**99.47**	**99.48**	**99.48**	**99.49**	**99.49**	**99.49**	**99.50**	**99.50**
3		10.13	9.55	9.28	9.12	9.01	8.94	8.88	8.84	8.81	8.78	8.76	8.74	8.71	8.69	8.66	8.64	8.62	8.60	8.58	8.57	8.56	8.54	8.54	8.53
		34.12	**30.82**	**29.46**	**28.71**	**28.24**	**27.91**	**27.67**	**27.49**	**27.34**	**27.23**	**27.13**	**27.05**	**26.92**	**26.83**	**26.69**	**26.60**	**26.50**	**26.41**	**26.35**	**26.27**	**26.23**	**26.18**	**26.14**	**26.12**
4		7.71	6.94	6.59	6.39	6.26	6.16	6.09	6.04	6.00	5.96	5.93	5.91	5.87	5.84	5.80	5.77	5.74	5.71	5.70	5.68	5.66	5.65	5.64	5.63
		21.20	**18.00**	**16.69**	**15.98**	**15.52**	**15.21**	**14.98**	**14.80**	**14.66**	**14.54**	**14.45**	**14.37**	**14.24**	**14.15**	**14.02**	**13.93**	**13.83**	**13.74**	**13.69**	**13.61**	**13.57**	**13.52**	**13.48**	**13.46**
5		6.61	5.79	5.41	5.19	5.05	4.95	4.88	4.82	4.78	4.74	4.70	4.68	4.64	4.60	4.56	4.53	4.50	4.46	4.44	4.42	4.40	4.38	4.37	4.36
		16.26	**13.27**	**12.06**	**11.39**	**10.97**	**10.67**	**10.45**	**10.29**	**10.15**	**10.05**	**9.96**	**9.89**	**9.77**	**9.68**	**9.55**	**9.47**	**9.38**	**9.29**	**9.24**	**9.17**	**9.13**	**9.07**	**9.04**	**9.02**
6		5.99	5.14	4.76	4.53	4.39	4.28	4.21	4.15	4.10	4.06	4.03	4.00	3.96	3.92	3.87	3.84	3.81	3.77	3.75	3.72	3.71	3.69	3.68	3.67
		13.74	**10.92**	**9.78**	**9.15**	**8.75**	**8.47**	**8.26**	**8.10**	**7.98**	**7.87**	**7.79**	**7.72**	**7.60**	**7.52**	**7.39**	**7.31**	**7.23**	**7.14**	**7.09**	**7.02**	**6.99**	**6.94**	**6.90**	**6.88**
7		5.59	4.74	4.35	4.12	3.97	3.87	3.79	3.73	3.68	3.63	3.60	3.57	3.52	3.49	3.44	3.41	3.38	3.34	3.32	3.29	3.28	3.25	3.24	3.23
		12.25	**9.55**	**8.45**	**7.85**	**7.46**	**7.19**	**7.00**	**6.84**	**6.71**	**6.62**	**6.54**	**6.47**	**6.35**	**6.27**	**6.15**	**6.07**	**5.98**	**5.90**	**5.85**	**5.78**	**5.75**	**5.70**	**5.67**	**5.65**
8		5.32	4.46	4.07	3.84	3.69	3.58	3.50	3.44	3.39	3.34	3.31	3.28	3.23	3.20	3.15	3.12	3.08	3.05	3.03	3.00	2.98	2.96	2.94	2.93
		11.26	**8.65**	**7.59**	**7.01**	**6.63**	**6.37**	**6.19**	**6.03**	**5.91**	**5.82**	**5.74**	**5.67**	**5.56**	**5.48**	**5.36**	**5.28**	**5.20**	**5.11**	**5.06**	**5.00**	**4.96**	**4.91**	**4.88**	**4.86**
9		5.12	4.26	3.86	3.63	3.48	3.37	3.29	3.23	3.18	3.13	3.10	3.07	3.02	2.98	2.93	2.90	2.86	2.82	2.80	2.77	2.76	2.73	2.72	2.71
		10.56	**8.02**	**6.99**	**6.42**	**6.06**	**5.80**	**5.62**	**5.47**	**5.35**	**5.26**	**5.18**	**5.11**	**5.00**	**4.92**	**4.80**	**4.73**	**4.64**	**4.56**	**4.51**	**4.45**	**4.41**	**4.36**	**4.33**	**4.31**
10		4.96	4.10	3.71	3.48	3.33	3.22	3.14	3.07	3.02	2.97	2.94	2.91	2.86	2.82	2.77	2.74	2.70	2.67	2.64	2.61	2.59	2.56	2.55	2.54
		10.04	**7.56**	**6.55**	**5.99**	**5.64**	**5.39**	**5.21**	**5.06**	**4.95**	**4.85**	**4.78**	**4.71**	**4.60**	**4.52**	**4.41**	**4.33**	**4.25**	**4.17**	**4.12**	**4.05**	**4.01**	**3.96**	**3.93**	**3.91**

Table F (Continued)

										Degrees of Freedom for Numerator														
	1	2	3	4	5	6	7	8	9	10	11	12	14	16	20	24	30	40	50	75	100	200	500	∞
11	4.84	3.98	3.59	3.36	3.20	3.09	3.01	2.95	2.90	2.86	2.82	2.79	2.74	2.70	2.65	2.61	2.57	2.53	2.50	2.47	2.45	2.42	2.41	2.40
	9.65	**7.20**	**6.22**	**5.67**	**5.32**	**5.07**	**4.88**	**4.74**	**4.63**	**4.54**	**4.46**	**4.40**	**4.29**	**4.21**	**4.10**	**4.02**	**3.94**	**3.86**	**3.80**	**3.74**	**3.70**	**3.66**	**3.62**	**3.60**
12	4.75	3.88	3.49	3.26	3.11	3.00	2.92	2.85	2.80	2.76	2.72	2.69	2.64	2.60	2.54	2.50	2.46	2.42	2.40	2.36	2.35	2.32	2.31	2.30
	9.33	**6.93**	**5.95**	**5.41**	**5.06**	**4.82**	**4.65**	**4.50**	**4.39**	**4.30**	**4.22**	**4.16**	**4.05**	**3.98**	**3.86**	**3.78**	**3.70**	**3.61**	**3.56**	**3.49**	**3.46**	**3.41**	**3.38**	**3.36**
13	4.67	3.80	3.41	3.18	3.02	2.92	2.84	2.77	2.72	2.67	2.63	2.60	2.55	2.51	2.46	2.42	2.38	2.34	2.32	2.28	2.26	2.24	2.22	2.21
	9.07	**6.70**	**5.74**	**5.20**	**4.86**	**4.62**	**4.44**	**4.30**	**4.19**	**4.10**	**4.02**	**3.96**	**3.85**	**3.78**	**3.67**	**3.59**	**3.51**	**3.42**	**3.37**	**3.30**	**3.27**	**3.21**	**3.18**	**3.16**
14	4.60	3.74	3.34	3.11	2.96	2.85	2.77	2.70	2.65	2.60	2.56	2.53	2.48	2.44	2.39	2.35	2.31	2.27	2.24	2.21	2.19	2.16	2.14	2.13
	8.86	**6.51**	**5.56**	**5.03**	**4.69**	**4.46**	**4.28**	**4.14**	**4.03**	**3.94**	**3.86**	**3.80**	**3.70**	**3.62**	**3.51**	**3.43**	**3.34**	**3.26**	**3.21**	**3.14**	**3.11**	**3.06**	**3.02**	**3.00**
15	4.54	3.68	3.29	3.06	2.90	2.79	2.70	2.64	2.59	2.55	2.51	2.48	2.43	2.39	2.33	2.29	2.25	2.21	2.18	2.15	2.12	2.10	2.08	2.07
	8.68	**6.36**	**5.42**	**4.89**	**4.56**	**4.32**	**4.14**	**4.00**	**3.89**	**3.80**	**3.73**	**3.67**	**3.56**	**3.48**	**3.36**	**3.29**	**3.20**	**3.12**	**3.07**	**3.00**	**2.97**	**2.92**	**2.89**	**2.87**
16	4.49	3.63	3.24	3.01	2.85	2.74	2.66	2.59	2.54	2.49	2.45	2.42	2.37	2.33	2.28	2.24	2.20	2.16	2.13	2.09	2.07	2.04	2.02	2.01
	8.53	**6.23**	**5.29**	**4.77**	**4.44**	**4.20**	**4.03**	**3.89**	**3.78**	**3.69**	**3.61**	**3.55**	**3.45**	**3.37**	**3.25**	**3.18**	**3.10**	**3.01**	**2.96**	**2.89**	**2.86**	**2.80**	**2.77**	**2.75**
17	4.45	3.59	3.20	2.96	2.81	2.70	2.62	2.55	2.50	2.45	2.41	2.38	2.33	2.29	2.23	2.19	2.15	2.11	2.08	2.04	2.02	1.99	1.97	1.96
	8.40	**6.11**	**5.18**	**4.67**	**4.34**	**4.10**	**3.93**	**3.79**	**3.68**	**3.59**	**3.52**	**3.45**	**3.35**	**3.27**	**3.16**	**3.08**	**3.00**	**2.92**	**2.86**	**2.79**	**2.76**	**2.70**	**2.67**	**2.65**
18	4.41	3.55	3.16	2.93	2.77	2.66	2.58	2.51	2.46	2.41	2.37	2.34	2.29	2.25	2.19	2.15	2.11	2.07	2.04	2.00	1.98	1.95	1.93	1.92
	8.28	**6.01**	**5.09**	**4.58**	**4.25**	**4.01**	**3.85**	**3.71**	**3.60**	**3.51**	**3.44**	**3.37**	**3.27**	**3.19**	**3.07**	**3.00**	**2.91**	**2.83**	**2.78**	**2.71**	**2.68**	**2.62**	**2.59**	**2.57**
19	4.38	3.52	3.13	2.90	2.74	2.63	2.55	2.48	2.43	2.38	2.34	2.31	2.26	2.21	2.15	2.11	2.07	2.02	2.00	1.96	1.94	1.91	1.90	1.88
	8.18	**5.93**	**5.01**	**4.50**	**4.17**	**3.94**	**3.77**	**3.63**	**3.52**	**3.43**	**3.36**	**3.30**	**3.19**	**3.12**	**3.00**	**2.92**	**2.84**	**2.76**	**2.70**	**2.63**	**2.60**	**2.54**	**2.51**	**2.49**
20	4.35	3.49	3.10	2.87	2.71	2.60	2.52	2.45	2.40	2.35	2.31	2.28	2.23	2.18	2.12	2.08	2.04	1.99	1.96	1.92	1.90	1.87	1.85	1.84
	8.10	**5.85**	**4.94**	**4.43**	**4.10**	**3.87**	**3.71**	**3.56**	**3.45**	**3.37**	**3.30**	**3.23**	**3.13**	**3.05**	**2.94**	**2.86**	**2.77**	**2.69**	**2.63**	**2.56**	**2.53**	**2.47**	**2.44**	**2.42**
21	4.32	3.47	3.07	2.84	2.68	2.57	2.49	2.42	2.37	2.32	2.28	2.25	2.20	2.15	2.09	2.05	2.00	1.96	1.93	1.89	1.87	1.84	1.82	1.81
	8.02	**5.78**	**4.87**	**4.37**	**4.04**	**3.81**	**3.65**	**3.51**	**3.40**	**3.31**	**3.24**	**3.17**	**3.07**	**2.99**	**2.88**	**2.80**	**2.72**	**2.63**	**2.58**	**2.51**	**2.47**	**2.42**	**2.38**	**2.36**
22	4.30	3.44	3.05	2.82	2.66	2.55	2.47	2.40	2.35	2.30	2.26	2.23	2.18	2.13	2.07	2.03	1.98	1.93	1.91	1.87	1.84	1.81	1.80	1.78
	7.94	**5.72**	**4.82**	**4.31**	**3.99**	**3.76**	**3.59**	**3.45**	**3.35**	**3.26**	**3.18**	**3.12**	**3.02**	**2.94**	**2.83**	**2.75**	**2.67**	**2.58**	**2.53**	**2.46**	**2.42**	**2.37**	**2.33**	**2.31**
23	4.28	3.42	3.03	2.80	2.64	2.53	2.45	2.38	2.32	2.28	2.24	2.20	2.14	2.10	2.04	2.00	1.96	1.91	1.88	1.84	1.82	1.79	1.77	1.76
	7.88	**5.66**	**4.76**	**4.26**	**3.94**	**3.71**	**3.54**	**3.41**	**3.30**	**3.21**	**3.14**	**3.07**	**2.97**	**2.89**	**2.78**	**2.70**	**2.62**	**2.53**	**2.48**	**2.41**	**2.37**	**2.32**	**2.28**	**2.26**
24	4.26	3.40	3.01	2.78	2.62	2.51	2.43	2.36	2.30	2.26	2.22	2.18	2.13	2.09	2.02	1.98	1.94	1.89	1.86	1.82	1.80	1.76	1.74	1.73
	7.82	**5.61**	**4.72**	**4.22**	**3.90**	**3.67**	**3.50**	**3.36**	**3.25**	**3.17**	**3.09**	**3.03**	**2.93**	**2.85**	**2.74**	**2.66**	**2.58**	**2.49**	**2.44**	**2.36**	**2.33**	**2.27**	**2.23**	**2.21**
25	4.24	3.38	2.99	2.76	2.60	2.49	2.41	2.34	2.28	2.24	2.20	2.16	2.11	2.06	2.00	1.96	1.92	1.87	1.84	1.80	1.77	1.74	1.72	1.71
	7.77	**5.57**	**4.68**	**4.18**	**3.86**	**3.63**	**3.46**	**3.32**	**3.21**	**3.13**	**3.05**	**2.99**	**2.89**	**2.81**	**2.70**	**2.62**	**2.54**	**2.45**	**2.40**	**2.32**	**2.29**	**2.23**	**2.19**	**2.17**

Degrees of Freedom for Denominator

Table F *(Continued)*

Degrees of Freedom for Numerator

Degrees of Freedom for Denominator

df	1	2	3	4	5	6	7	8	9	10	11	12	14	16	20	24	30	40	50	75	100	200	500	∞
26	4.22	3.37	2.98	2.74	2.59	2.47	2.39	2.32	2.27	2.22	2.18	2.15	2.10	2.05	1.99	1.95	1.90	1.85	1.82	1.78	1.76	1.72	1.70	1.69
	7.72	**5.53**	**4.64**	**4.14**	**3.82**	**3.59**	**3.42**	**3.29**	**3.17**	**3.09**	**3.02**	**2.96**	**2.86**	**2.77**	**2.66**	**2.58**	**2.50**	**2.41**	**2.36**	**2.28**	**2.25**	**2.19**	**2.15**	**2.13**
27	4.21	3.35	2.96	2.73	2.57	2.46	2.37	2.30	2.25	2.20	2.16	2.13	2.08	2.03	1.97	1.93	1.88	1.84	1.80	1.76	1.74	1.71	1.68	1.67
	7.68	**5.49**	**4.60**	**4.11**	**3.79**	**3.56**	**3.39**	**3.26**	**3.14**	**3.06**	**2.98**	**2.93**	**2.83**	**2.74**	**2.63**	**2.55**	**2.47**	**2.38**	**2.33**	**2.25**	**2.21**	**2.16**	**2.12**	**2.10**
28	4.20	3.34	2.95	2.71	2.56	2.44	2.36	2.29	2.24	2.19	2.15	2.12	2.06	2.02	1.96	1.91	1.87	1.81	1.78	1.75	1.72	1.69	1.67	1.65
	7.64	**5.45**	**4.57**	**4.07**	**3.76**	**3.53**	**3.36**	**3.23**	**3.11**	**3.03**	**2.95**	**2.90**	**2.80**	**2.71**	**2.60**	**2.52**	**2.44**	**2.35**	**2.30**	**2.22**	**2.18**	**2.13**	**2.09**	**2.06**
29	4.18	3.33	2.93	2.70	2.54	2.43	2.35	2.28	2.22	2.18	2.14	2.10	2.05	2.00	1.94	1.90	1.85	1.80	1.77	1.73	1.71	1.68	1.65	1.64
	7.60	**5.42**	**4.54**	**4.04**	**3.73**	**3.50**	**3.33**	**3.20**	**3.08**	**3.00**	**2.92**	**2.87**	**2.77**	**2.68**	**2.57**	**2.49**	**2.41**	**2.32**	**2.27**	**2.19**	**2.15**	**2.10**	**2.06**	**2.03**
30	4.17	3.32	2.92	2.69	2.53	2.42	2.34	2.27	2.21	2.16	2.12	2.09	2.04	1.99	1.93	1.89	1.84	1.79	1.76	1.72	1.69	1.66	1.64	1.62
	7.56	**5.39**	**4.51**	**4.02**	**3.70**	**3.47**	**3.30**	**3.17**	**3.06**	**2.98**	**2.90**	**2.84**	**2.74**	**2.66**	**2.55**	**2.47**	**2.38**	**2.29**	**2.24**	**2.16**	**2.13**	**2.07**	**2.03**	**2.01**
32	4.15	3.30	2.90	2.67	2.51	2.40	2.32	2.25	2.19	2.14	2.10	2.07	2.02	1.97	1.91	1.86	1.82	1.76	1.74	1.69	1.67	1.64	1.61	1.59
	7.50	**5.34**	**4.46**	**3.97**	**3.66**	**3.42**	**3.25**	**3.12**	**3.01**	**2.94**	**2.86**	**2.80**	**2.70**	**2.62**	**2.51**	**2.42**	**2.34**	**2.25**	**2.20**	**2.12**	**2.08**	**2.02**	**1.98**	**1.96**
34	4.13	3.28	2.88	2.65	2.49	2.38	2.30	2.23	2.17	2.12	2.08	2.05	2.00	1.95	1.89	1.84	1.80	1.74	1.71	1.67	1.64	1.61	1.59	1.57
	7.44	**5.29**	**4.42**	**3.93**	**3.61**	**3.38**	**3.21**	**3.08**	**2.97**	**2.89**	**2.82**	**2.76**	**2.66**	**2.58**	**2.47**	**2.38**	**2.30**	**2.21**	**2.15**	**2.08**	**2.04**	**1.98**	**1.94**	**1.91**
36	4.11	3.26	2.86	2.63	2.48	2.36	2.28	2.21	2.15	2.10	2.06	2.03	1.98	1.93	1.87	1.82	1.78	1.72	1.69	1.65	1.62	1.59	1.56	1.55
	7.39	**5.25**	**4.38**	**3.89**	**3.58**	**3.35**	**3.18**	**3.04**	**2.94**	**2.86**	**2.78**	**2.72**	**2.62**	**2.54**	**2.43**	**2.35**	**2.26**	**2.17**	**2.12**	**2.04**	**2.00**	**1.94**	**1.90**	**1.87**
38	4.10	3.25	2.85	2.62	2.46	2.35	2.26	2.19	2.14	2.09	2.05	2.02	1.96	1.92	1.85	1.80	1.76	1.71	1.67	1.63	1.60	1.57	1.54	1.53
	7.35	**5.21**	**4.34**	**3.86**	**3.54**	**3.32**	**3.15**	**3.02**	**2.91**	**2.82**	**2.75**	**2.69**	**2.59**	**2.51**	**2.40**	**2.32**	**2.22**	**2.14**	**2.08**	**2.00**	**1.97**	**1.90**	**1.86**	**1.84**
40	4.08	3.23	2.84	2.61	2.45	2.34	2.25	2.18	2.12	2.07	2.04	2.00	1.95	1.90	1.84	1.79	1.74	1.69	1.66	1.61	1.59	1.55	1.53	1.51
	7.31	**5.18**	**4.31**	**3.83**	**3.51**	**3.29**	**3.12**	**2.99**	**2.88**	**2.80**	**2.73**	**2.66**	**2.56**	**2.49**	**2.37**	**2.29**	**2.20**	**2.11**	**2.05**	**1.97**	**1.94**	**1.88**	**1.84**	**1.81**
42	4.07	3.22	2.83	2.59	2.44	2.32	2.24	2.17	2.11	2.06	2.02	1.99	1.94	1.89	1.82	1.78	1.73	1.68	1.64	1.60	1.57	1.54	1.51	1.49
	7.27	**5.15**	**4.29**	**3.80**	**3.49**	**3.26**	**3.10**	**2.96**	**2.86**	**2.77**	**2.70**	**2.64**	**2.54**	**2.46**	**2.35**	**2.26**	**2.17**	**2.08**	**2.02**	**1.94**	**1.91**	**1.85**	**1.80**	**1.78**
44	4.06	3.21	2.82	2.58	2.43	2.31	2.23	2.16	2.10	2.05	2.01	1.98	1.92	1.88	1.81	1.76	1.72	1.66	1.63	1.58	1.56	1.52	1.50	1.48
	7.24	**5.12**	**4.26**	**3.78**	**3.46**	**3.24**	**3.07**	**2.94**	**2.84**	**2.75**	**2.68**	**2.62**	**2.52**	**2.44**	**2.32**	**2.24**	**2.15**	**2.06**	**2.00**	**1.92**	**1.88**	**1.82**	**1.78**	**1.75**
46	4.05	3.20	2.81	2.57	2.42	2.30	2.22	2.14	2.09	2.04	2.00	1.97	1.91	1.87	1.80	1.75	1.71	1.65	1.62	1.57	1.54	1.51	1.48	1.46
	7.21	**5.10**	**4.24**	**3.76**	**3.44**	**3.22**	**3.05**	**2.92**	**2.82**	**2.73**	**2.66**	**2.60**	**2.50**	**2.42**	**2.30**	**2.22**	**2.13**	**2.04**	**1.98**	**1.90**	**1.86**	**1.80**	**1.76**	**1.72**
48	4.04	3.19	2.80	2.56	2.41	2.30	2.21	2.14	2.08	2.03	1.99	1.96	1.90	1.86	1.79	1.74	1.70	1.64	1.61	1.56	1.53	1.50	1.47	1.45
	7.19	**5.08**	**4.22**	**3.74**	**3.42**	**3.20**	**3.04**	**2.90**	**2.80**	**2.71**	**2.64**	**2.58**	**2.48**	**2.40**	**2.28**	**2.20**	**2.11**	**2.02**	**1.96**	**1.88**	**1.84**	**1.78**	**1.73**	**1.70**
50	4.03	3.18	2.79	2.56	2.40	2.29	2.20	2.13	2.07	2.02	1.98	1.95	1.90	1.85	1.78	1.74	1.69	1.63	1.60	1.55	1.52	1.48	1.46	1.44
	7.17	**5.06**	**4.20**	**3.72**	**3.41**	**3.18**	**3.02**	**2.88**	**2.78**	**2.70**	**2.62**	**2.56**	**2.46**	**2.39**	**2.26**	**2.18**	**2.10**	**2.00**	**1.94**	**1.86**	**1.82**	**1.76**	**1.71**	**1.68**

Table F (Continued)

Degrees of Freedom for Numerator

df (denom)	1	2	3	4	5	6	7	8	9	10	11	12	14	16	20	24	30	40	50	75	100	200	500	∞
55	4.02	3.17	2.78	2.54	2.38	2.27	2.18	2.11	2.05	2.00	1.97	1.93	1.88	1.83	1.76	1.72	1.67	1.61	1.58	1.52	1.50	1.46	1.43	1.41
	7.12	**5.01**	**4.16**	**3.68**	**3.37**	**3.15**	**2.98**	**2.85**	**2.75**	**2.66**	**2.59**	**2.53**	**2.43**	**2.35**	**2.23**	**2.15**	**2.06**	**1.96**	**1.90**	**1.82**	**1.78**	**1.71**	**1.66**	**1.64**
60	4.00	3.15	2.76	2.52	2.37	2.25	2.17	2.10	2.04	1.99	1.95	1.92	1.86	1.81	1.75	1.70	1.65	1.59	1.56	1.50	1.48	1.44	1.41	1.39
	7.08	**4.98**	**4.13**	**3.65**	**3.34**	**3.12**	**2.95**	**2.82**	**2.72**	**2.63**	**2.56**	**2.50**	**2.40**	**2.32**	**2.20**	**2.12**	**2.03**	**1.93**	**1.87**	**1.79**	**1.74**	**1.68**	**1.63**	**1.60**
65	3.99	3.14	2.75	2.51	2.36	2.24	2.15	2.08	2.02	1.98	1.94	1.90	1.85	1.80	1.73	1.68	1.63	1.57	1.54	1.49	1.46	1.42	1.39	1.37
	7.04	**4.95**	**4.10**	**3.62**	**3.31**	**3.09**	**2.93**	**2.79**	**2.70**	**2.61**	**2.54**	**2.47**	**2.37**	**2.30**	**2.18**	**2.09**	**2.00**	**1.90**	**1.84**	**1.76**	**1.71**	**1.64**	**1.60**	**1.56**
70	3.98	3.13	2.74	2.50	2.35	2.23	2.14	2.07	2.01	1.97	1.93	1.89	1.84	1.79	1.72	1.67	1.62	1.56	1.53	1.47	1.45	1.40	1.37	1.35
	7.01	**4.92**	**4.08**	**3.60**	**3.29**	**3.07**	**2.91**	**2.77**	**2.67**	**2.59**	**2.51**	**2.45**	**2.35**	**2.28**	**2.15**	**2.07**	**1.98**	**1.88**	**1.82**	**1.74**	**1.69**	**1.62**	**1.56**	**1.53**
80	3.96	3.11	2.72	2.48	2.33	2.21	2.12	2.05	1.99	1.95	1.91	1.88	1.82	1.77	1.70	1.65	1.60	1.54	1.51	1.45	1.42	1.38	1.35	1.32
	6.96	**4.88**	**4.04**	**3.56**	**3.25**	**3.04**	**2.87**	**2.74**	**2.64**	**2.55**	**2.48**	**2.41**	**2.32**	**2.24**	**2.11**	**2.03**	**1.94**	**1.84**	**1.78**	**1.70**	**1.65**	**1.57**	**1.52**	**1.49**
100	3.94	3.09	2.70	2.46	2.30	2.19	2.10	2.03	1.97	1.92	1.88	1.85	1.79	1.75	1.68	1.63	1.57	1.51	1.48	1.42	1.39	1.34	1.30	1.28
	6.90	**4.82**	**3.98**	**3.51**	**3.20**	**2.99**	**2.82**	**2.69**	**2.59**	**2.51**	**2.43**	**2.36**	**2.26**	**2.19**	**2.06**	**1.98**	**1.89**	**1.79**	**1.73**	**1.64**	**1.59**	**1.51**	**1.46**	**1.43**
125	3.92	3.07	2.68	2.44	2.29	2.17	2.08	2.01	1.95	1.90	1.86	1.83	1.77	1.72	1.65	1.60	1.55	1.49	1.45	1.39	1.36	1.31	1.27	1.25
	6.84	**4.78**	**3.94**	**3.47**	**3.17**	**2.95**	**2.79**	**2.65**	**2.56**	**2.47**	**2.40**	**2.33**	**2.23**	**2.15**	**2.03**	**1.94**	**1.85**	**1.75**	**1.68**	**1.59**	**1.54**	**1.46**	**1.40**	**1.37**
150	3.91	3.06	2.67	2.43	2.27	2.16	2.07	2.00	1.94	1.89	1.85	1.82	1.76	1.71	1.64	1.59	1.54	1.47	1.44	1.37	1.34	1.29	1.25	1.22
	6.81	**4.75**	**3.91**	**3.44**	**3.14**	**2.92**	**2.76**	**2.62**	**2.53**	**2.44**	**2.37**	**2.30**	**2.20**	**2.12**	**2.00**	**1.91**	**1.83**	**1.72**	**1.66**	**1.56**	**1.51**	**1.43**	**1.37**	**1.33**
200	3.89	3.04	2.65	2.41	2.26	2.14	2.05	1.98	1.92	1.87	1.83	1.80	1.74	1.69	1.62	1.57	1.52	1.45	1.42	1.35	1.32	1.26	1.22	1.19
	6.76	**4.71**	**3.88**	**3.41**	**3.11**	**2.90**	**2.73**	**2.60**	**2.50**	**2.41**	**2.34**	**2.28**	**2.17**	**2.09**	**1.97**	**1.88**	**1.79**	**1.69**	**1.62**	**1.53**	**1.48**	**1.39**	**1.33**	**1.28**
400	3.86	3.02	2.62	2.39	2.23	2.12	2.03	1.96	1.90	1.85	1.81	1.78	1.72	1.67	1.60	1.54	1.49	1.42	1.38	1.32	1.28	1.22	1.16	1.13
	6.70	**4.66**	**3.83**	**3.36**	**3.06**	**2.85**	**2.69**	**2.55**	**2.46**	**2.37**	**2.29**	**2.23**	**2.12**	**2.04**	**1.92**	**1.84**	**1.74**	**1.64**	**1.57**	**1.47**	**1.42**	**1.32**	**1.24**	**1.19**
1000	3.85	3.00	2.61	2.38	2.22	2.10	2.02	1.95	1.89	1.84	1.80	1.76	1.70	1.65	1.58	1.53	1.47	1.41	1.36	1.30	1.26	1.19	1.13	1.08
	6.66	**4.62**	**3.80**	**3.34**	**3.04**	**2.82**	**2.66**	**2.53**	**2.43**	**2.34**	**2.26**	**2.20**	**2.09**	**2.01**	**1.89**	**1.81**	**1.71**	**1.61**	**1.54**	**1.44**	**1.38**	**1.28**	**1.19**	**1.11**
∞	3.84	2.99	2.60	2.37	2.21	2.09	2.01	1.94	1.88	1.83	1.79	1.75	1.69	1.64	1.57	1.52	1.46	1.40	1.35	1.28	1.24	1.17	1.11	1.00
	6.63	**4.60**	**3.78**	**3.32**	**3.02**	**2.80**	**2.64**	**2.51**	**2.41**	**2.32**	**2.24**	**2.18**	**2.07**	**1.99**	**1.87**	**1.79**	**1.69**	**1.59**	**1.52**	**1.41**	**1.36**	**1.25**	**1.15**	**1.00**

Degrees of Freedom for Denominator

TABLE G: Critical Values of Wilcoxon's *W*

W is the algebraic sum of the signed ranks of differences between pairs of measures. An observed W is significant if |± W| ≥ CV, that is, if the absolute value is greater than or equal to the critical value for the appropriate number of pairs, N. Dashes indicate no tests are possible at some levels of significance for some values of N.

N	Level of Significance for One-Tailed Test			
	.05	.025	.01	.005
	Level of Significance for Two-Tailed Test			
	.10	.05	.02	.01
5	15	—	—	—
6	17	21	—	—
7	22	24	28	—
8	26	30	34	36
9	29	35	39	43
10	35	39	45	49
11	40	46	52	56
12	44	52	60	64
13	49	57	67	73
14	55	63	75	81
15	60	70	82	90
16	66	78	90	98
17	71	85	99	107
18	77	91	107	117
19	84	98	116	126
20	90	106	124	136
21	97	115	133	147
22	103	123	143	157
23	110	130	152	168
24	118	138	162	178
25	125	147	173	189
26	131	155	183	201
27	140	164	194	212
28	146	174	204	224
29	155	183	215	235
30	163	191	225	247
31	170	202	236	260
32	178	210	248	272
33	187	221	259	285
34	195	231	271	299
35	204	240	284	312
36	212	250	296	324
37	221	261	307	339
38	229	271	319	353
39	238	282	332	366
40	248	292	344	380
41	257	303	357	395
42	265	315	371	409
43	274	326	384	424
44	284	336	398	438
45	293	349	411	453
46	303	359	425	467
47	314	372	438	484
48	324	384	452	498
49	333	395	467	515
50	343	407	481	529

TABLE H: Random Numbers

Enter this table at a randomly chosen location and read up or down, left or right, or in any diagonal direction.

Row	1	2	3	4	5	6	7	8	9	10
						Column				
00	10097	32533	76520	13586	34673	54876	80959	09117	39292	74945
01	37542	04805	64894	74296	24805	24037	20636	10402	00822	91665
02	08422	68953	19645	09303	23209	02560	15953	34764	35080	33606
03	99019	02529	09376	70715	38311	31165	88676	74397	04436	27659
04	12807	99970	80157	36147	64032	36653	98951	16877	12171	76833
05	66065	74717	34072	76850	36697	36170	65813	39885	11199	29170
06	31060	10805	45571	82406	35303	42614	86799	07439	23403	09732
07	85269	77602	02051	65692	68665	74818	73053	85247	18623	88579
08	63573	32135	05325	47048	90553	57548	28468	28709	83491	25624
09	73796	45753	03529	64778	35808	34282	60935	20344	35273	88435
10	98520	17767	14905	68607	22109	40558	60970	93433	50500	73998
11	11805	05431	39808	27732	50725	68248	29405	24201	52775	67851
12	83452	99634	06288	98083	13746	70078	18475	40610	68711	77817
13	88685	40200	86507	58401	36766	67951	90364	76493	29609	11062
14	99594	67348	87517	64969	91826	08928	93785	61368	23478	34113
15	65481	17674	17468	50950	58047	76974	73039	57186	40218	16544
16	80124	35635	17727	08015	45318	22374	21115	78253	14385	53763
17	74350	99817	77402	77214	43236	00210	45521	64237	96286	02655
18	69916	26803	66252	29148	36936	87203	76621	13990	94400	56418
19	09893	20505	14225	68514	46427	56788	96297	78822	54382	14598
20	91499	14523	68479	27686	46162	83554	94750	89923	37089	20048
21	80336	94598	26940	36858	70297	34135	53140	33340	42050	82341
22	44104	81949	85157	47954	32979	26575	57600	40881	22222	06413
23	12550	73742	11100	02040	12860	74697	96644	89439	28707	25815
24	63606	49329	16505	34484	40219	52563	43651	77082	07207	31790
25	61196	90446	26457	47774	51924	33729	65394	59593	42582	60527
26	15474	45266	95270	79953	59367	83848	82396	10118	33211	59466
27	94557	28573	67897	54387	54622	44431	91190	42592	92927	45973
28	42481	16213	97344	08721	16868	48767	03071	12059	25701	46670
29	23523	78317	73208	89837	68935	91416	26252	29663	05522	82562
30	04493	52494	75246	33824	45862	51025	61962	79335	65337	12472
31	00549	97654	64051	88159	96119	63896	54692	82391	23287	29529
32	35963	15307	26898	09354	33351	35462	77974	50024	90103	39333
33	59808	08391	45427	26842	83609	49700	13021	24892	78565	20106
34	46058	85236	01390	92286	77281	44077	93910	83647	70617	42941
35	32179	00597	87379	25241	05567	07007	86743	17157	85394	11838
36	69234	61406	20117	45204	15956	60000	18743	92423	97118	96338
37	19565	41430	01758	75379	40419	21585	66674	36806	84962	85207
38	45155	14938	19476	07246	43667	94543	59047	90033	20826	69541
39	94864	31994	36168	10851	34888	81553	01540	35456	05014	51176
40	98086	24826	45240	28404	44999	08896	39094	73407	35441	31880
41	33185	16232	41941	50949	89435	48581	88695	41994	37548	73043
42	80951	00406	96382	70774	20151	23387	25016	25298	94624	61171
43	79752	49140	71961	28296	69861	02591	74852	20539	00387	59579
44	18633	32537	98145	06571	31010	24674	05455	61427	77938	91936
45	74029	43902	77557	32270	97790	17119	52527	58021	80814	51748
46	54178	45611	80993	37143	05335	12969	56127	19255	36040	90324
47	11664	49883	52079	84827	59381	71539	09973	33440	88461	23356
48	48324	77928	31249	64710	02295	36870	32307	57546	15020	09994
49	69074	94138	87637	91976	35584	04401	10518	21615	01848	76938

Table H (Concluded)

Row	1	2	3	4	5	6	7	8	9	10
						Column				
50	09188	20097	32825	39527	04220	86304	83389	87374	64278	58044
51	90045	85497	51981	50654	94938	81997	91870	76150	68476	64659
52	73189	50207	47677	26269	62290	64464	27124	67018	41361	82760
53	75768	76490	20971	87749	90429	12272	95375	05871	93823	43178
54	54016	44056	66281	31003	00682	27398	20714	53295	07706	17813
55	08358	69910	78542	42785	13661	58873	04618	97553	31223	08420
56	28306	03264	81333	10591	40510	07893	32604	60475	94119	01840
57	53840	86233	81594	13628	51215	90290	28466	68795	77762	20791
58	91757	53741	61613	62269	50263	90212	55781	76514	83483	47055
59	89415	92694	00397	58391	12607	17646	48949	72306	94541	37408
60	77513	03820	86864	29901	68414	82774	51908	13980	72893	55507
61	19502	37174	69979	20288	55210	29773	74287	75251	65344	67415
62	21818	59313	93278	81757	05686	73156	07082	85046	31853	38452
63	51474	66499	68107	23621	94049	91345	42836	09191	08007	45449
64	99559	68331	62535	24170	69777	12830	74819	78142	43860	72834
65	33713	48007	93584	72869	51926	64721	58303	29822	93174	93972
66	85274	86893	11303	22970	28834	34137	73515	90400	71148	43643
67	84133	89640	44035	52166	73852	70091	61222	60561	62327	18423
68	56732	16234	17395	96131	10123	91622	85496	57560	81604	18880
69	65138	56806	87648	85261	34313	65861	45875	21069	85644	47277
70	38001	02176	81719	11711	71602	92937	74219	64049	65584	49698
71	37402	96397	01304	77586	56271	10086	47324	62605	40030	37438
72	97125	40348	87083	31417	21815	39250	75237	62047	15501	29578
73	21826	41134	47143	34072	64638	85902	49139	06441	03856	54552
74	73135	42742	95719	09035	85794	74296	08789	88156	64691	19202
75	07638	77929	03061	18072	96207	44156	23821	99538	04713	66994
76	60528	83441	07954	19814	59175	20695	05533	52139	61212	06455
77	83596	35655	06958	92983	05128	09719	77433	53783	92301	50498
78	10850	62746	99599	10507	13499	06319	53075	71839	06410	19362
79	39820	98952	43622	63147	64421	80814	43800	09351	31024	73167
80	59580	06478	75569	78800	88835	54486	23768	06156	04111	08408
81	38508	07341	23793	48763	90822	97022	17719	04207	95954	49953
82	30692	70668	94688	16127	56196	80091	82067	63400	05462	69200
83	65443	95659	18288	27437	49632	24041	08337	65676	96299	90836
84	27267	50264	13192	72294	07477	44606	17985	48911	97341	30358
85	91307	06991	19072	24210	36699	53728	28825	35793	28976	66252
86	68434	94688	84473	13622	62126	98408	12843	82590	09815	93146
87	48908	15877	54745	24591	35700	04754	83824	52692	54130	55160
88	06913	45197	42672	78601	11883	09528	63011	98901	14974	40344
89	10455	16019	14210	33712	91342	37821	88325	80851	43667	70883
90	12883	97343	65027	61184	04285	01392	17974	15077	90712	26769
91	21778	30976	38807	36961	31649	42096	63281	02023	08816	47449
92	19523	59515	65122	59659	86283	68258	69572	13798	16435	91529
93	67245	52670	35583	16563	79246	86686	76463	34222	26655	90802
94	60584	47377	07500	37992	45134	26529	26760	83637	41326	44344
95	53853	41377	36066	94850	58838	73859	49364	73331	96240	43642
96	24637	38736	74384	89342	52623	07992	12369	18601	03742	83873
97	83080	12451	38992	22815	07759	51777	97377	27585	51972	37867
98	16444	24334	36151	99073	27493	70939	85130	32552	54846	54759
99	60790	18157	57178	65762	11161	78576	45819	52979	65130	04860

TABLE I: Standardized (Studentized) Ranges
Critical Values at .05 Level (Light Type) and .01 Level (Boldface)

See Chapter 14 for instructions on using this table.

df	Number of Means (m) Covered in Range								
	2	**3**	**4**	**5**	**6**	**7**	**8**	**9**	**10**
1	17.97	26.98	32.82	37.08	40.41	43.12	45.40	47.36	49.07
	90.03	**135.0**	**164.3**	**185.6**	**202.2**	**215.8**	**227.2**	**237.0**	**245.6**
2	6.08	8.33	9.80	10.88	11.74	12.44	13.03	13.54	13.99
	14.04	**19.02**	**22.29**	**24.72**	**26.63**	**28.20**	**29.53**	**30.68**	**31.69**
3	4.50	5.91	6.82	7.50	8.04	8.48	8.85	9.18	9.46
	8.26	**10.62**	**12.17**	**13.33**	**14.24**	**15.00**	**15.64**	**16.20**	**16.69**
4	3.93	5.04	5.76	6.29	6.71	7.05	7.35	7.60	7.83
	6.51	**8.12**	**9.17**	**9.96**	**10.58**	**11.10**	**11.55**	**11.93**	**12.27**
5	3.64	4.60	5.22	5.67	6.03	6.33	6.58	6.80	6.99
	5.70	**6.98**	**7.80**	**8.42**	**8.91**	**9.32**	**9.67**	**9.97**	**10.24**
6	3.46	4.34	4.90	5.30	5.63	5.90	6.12	6.32	6.49
	5.24	**6.33**	**7.03**	**7.56**	**7.97**	**8.32**	**8.61**	**8.87**	**9.10**
7	3.34	4.16	4.68	5.06	5.36	5.61	5.82	6.00	6.16
	4.95	**5.92**	**6.54**	**7.01**	**7.37**	**7.68**	**7.94**	**8.17**	**8.37**
8	3.26	4.04	4.53	4.89	5.17	5.40	5.60	5.77	5.92
	4.75	**5.64**	**6.20**	**6.62**	**6.96**	**7.24**	**7.47**	**7.68**	**7.86**
9	3.20	3.95	4.41	4.76	5.02	5.24	5.43	5.59	5.74
	4.60	**5.43**	**5.96**	**6.35**	**6.66**	**6.91**	**7.13**	**7.33**	**7.49**
10	3.15	3.88	4.33	4.65	4.91	5.12	5.30	5.46	5.60
	4.48	**5.27**	**5.77**	**6.14**	**6.43**	**6.67**	**6.87**	**7.05**	**7.21**
11	3.11	3.82	4.26	4.57	4.82	5.03	5.20	5.35	5.49
	4.39	**5.15**	**5.62**	**5.97**	**6.25**	**6.48**	**6.67**	**6.84**	**6.99**
12	3.08	3.77	4.20	4.51	4.75	4.95	5.12	5.27	5.39
	4.32	**5.05**	**5.50**	**5.84**	**6.10**	**6.32**	**6.51**	**6.67**	**6.81**
13	3.06	3.73	4.15	4.45	4.69	4.88	5.05	5.19	5.32
	4.26	**4.96**	**5.40**	**5.73**	**5.98**	**6.19**	**6.37**	**6.53**	**6.67**
14	3.03	3.70	4.11	4.41	4.64	4.83	4.99	5.13	5.25
	4.21	**4.89**	**5.32**	**5.63**	**5.88**	**6.08**	**6.26**	**6.41**	**6.54**
15	3.01	3.67	4.08	4.37	4.59	4.78	4.94	5.08	5.20
	4.17	**4.84**	**5.25**	**5.56**	**5.80**	**5.99**	**6.16**	**6.31**	**6.44**
16	3.00	3.65	4.05	4.33	4.56	4.74	4.90	5.03	5.15
	4.13	**4.79**	**5.19**	**5.49**	**5.72**	**5.92**	**6.08**	**6.22**	**6.35**
17	2.98	3.63	4.02	4.30	4.52	4.70	4.86	4.99	5.11
	4.10	**4.74**	**5.14**	**5.43**	**5.66**	**5.85**	**6.01**	**6.15**	**6.27**
18	2.97	3.61	4.00	4.28	4.49	4.67	4.82	4.96	5.07
	4.07	**4.70**	**5.09**	**5.38**	**5.60**	**5.79**	**5.94**	**6.08**	**6.20**
19	2.96	3.59	3.98	4.25	4.47	4.65	4.79	4.92	5.04
	4.05	**4.67**	**5.05**	**5.33**	**5.55**	**5.73**	**5.89**	**6.02**	**6.14**
20	2.95	3.58	3.96	4.23	4.45	4.62	4.77	4.90	5.01
	4.02	**4.64**	**5.02**	**5.29**	**5.51**	**5.69**	**5.84**	**5.97**	**6.09**
24	2.92	3.53	3.90	4.17	4.37	4.54	4.68	4.81	4.92
	3.96	**4.55**	**4.91**	**5.17**	**5.37**	**5.54**	**5.69**	**5.81**	**5.92**
30	2.89	3.49	3.85	4.10	4.30	4.46	4.60	4.72	4.82
	3.89	**4.45**	**4.80**	**5.05**	**5.24**	**5.40**	**5.54**	**5.65**	**5.76**
40	2.86	3.44	3.79	4.04	4.23	4.39	4.52	4.63	4.73
	3.82	**4.37**	**4.70**	**4.93**	**5.11**	**5.26**	**5.39**	**5.50**	**5.60**
60	2.83	3.40	3.74	3.98	4.16	4.31	4.44	4.55	4.65
	3.76	**4.28**	**4.59**	**4.82**	**4.99**	**5.13**	**5.25**	**5.36**	**5.45**
120	2.80	3.36	3.68	3.92	4.10	4.24	4.36	4.47	4.56
	3.70	**4.20**	**4.50**	**4.71**	**4.87**	**5.01**	**5.12**	**5.21**	**5.30**
∞	2.77	3.31	3.63	3.86	4.03	4.17	4.29	4.39	4.47
	3.64	**4.12**	**4.40**	**4.60**	**4.76**	**4.88**	**4.99**	**5.08**	**5.16**

References

Bracketed page numbers indicate where each reference is first cited in the text. To find any subsequent citations, please consult the *Index*.

Anastasi, A. *Psychological testing* (3rd ed.). New York: Macmillan, 1968. [264]

Auble, D. Extended tables for the Mann-Whitney statistic. *Bulletin of the Institute of Educational Research at Indiana University,* 1953, *1*(Whole No. 2). [Table C]

Bachrach, A. J. *Psychological research: An introduction* (4th ed.). New York: Random House, 1981. [3]

Boneau, C. A. The effects of violations of assumptions underlying the *t* test. *Psychological Bulletin,* 1960, *57,* 49–64. [212]

Box, G. E. P. Non-normality and tests on variance. *Biometrika,* 1953, *40,* 318–335. [212]

Campbell, D. T., & Stanley, J. C. *Experimental and quasi-experimental designs for research.* Chicago: Rand-McNally, 1966. [350]

Cohen, J. *Statistical power analysis for the behavioral sciences* (Rev. ed.). New York: Academic Press, 1977. [348]

Cohen, J., & Cohen, P. *Applied multiple regression/correlation analysis for the behavioral sciences.* Hillsdale, NJ: Erlbaum, 1983. [351]

Cook, T. D., & Campbell, D. T. *Quasi-experimentation: Design and analysis issues for field settings.* Chicago: Rand-McNally, 1979. [350]

Coren, S., & Girgus, J. *Seeing is deceiving: The psychology of visual illusions.* Hillsdale, NJ: Erlbaum, 1978. [500]

Cronbach, L. J. *Essentials of psychological testing* (3rd ed.). New York: Harper & Row, 1970. [264]

DuBois, P. H. *An introduction to psychological statistics.* New York: Harper & Row, 1965. [248]

Ebbinghaus, H. [Memory] (H. A. Ruger & C. E. Bussenius, Trans.). New York: Dover, 1964. (Originally published, 1885.) [355]

Edwards, A. L. *Expected values of discrete random variables and elementary statistics.* New York: Wiley, 1967. [284]

Federal Bureau of Investigation. *Uniform crime reports for the United States, 1979.* Washington, DC: 1979. [38]

Fisher, R. A. *The design of experiments.* Edinburgh: Oliver & Boyd, Ltd., 1935. [127]

Fisher, R. A., & Yates, F. *Statistical tables for biological, agricultural and medical research* (6th ed.). London: Longman Group Ltd., 1974. (Previously published by Oliver & Boyd Ltd., Edinburgh.) [Table B]

Gazzaniga, M. S., & LeDoux, J. E. *The integrated mind.* New York: Plenum Press, 1978. [2]

Glaser, R., & Bond, L. (Eds.). Testing: Concepts, policy, practice, and research. *American Psychologist,* 1981, *36*(Whole No. 10). [7]

Glasser, G. J., & Winter, R. F. Critical values of rank correlation for testing the hypothesis of independence. *Biometrika,* 1961, *48,* 444–448. [Table D]

Gosset, W. S. [Student, pseudonym].

The probable error of a mean. *Biometrika*, 1908, *6*, 1–25. [178]

Guilford, J. P. *The nature of human intelligence.* New York: McGraw-Hill, 1967. [353]

Guilford, J. P., & Fruchter, B. *Fundamental statistics in psychology and education* (5th ed.). New York: McGraw-Hill, 1973. (See also 6th ed., 1978.) [295]

Hammond, E. C. Smoking in relation to mortality and morbidity. Findings in first thirty-four months of follow-up in a prospective study started in 1959. *Journal of the National Cancer Institute*, 1964, *32*, 1161–1188. [122]

Harlow, H. F. The formation of learning sets. *Psychological Review*, 1949, *56*, 51–65. [159]

Hays, W. L. *Statistics* (3rd ed.). New York: Holt, Rinehart and Winston, 1981. [168]

Hebb, D. O. *Textbook of psychology* (3rd ed.). Philadelphia: Saunders, 1972. [2]

Hempel, C. G. *Philosophy of natural science.* Englewood Cliffs, NJ: Prentice-Hall, 1966. [4]

Higgins, J., & Peterson, J. C. Concept of process-reactive schizophrenia: A critique. *Psychological Bulletin*, 1966, *66*, 201–206. [218]

Holland, J. G., & Skinner, B. F. *The analysis of behavior.* New York: McGraw-Hill, 1961. [355]

Keppel, G. *Design and anslysis: A researcher's handbook* (2nd ed.). Englewood Cliffs, NJ: Prentice-Hall, 1982. [373]

Keuls, M. The use of the "Studentized range" in connection with an analysis of variance. *Euphytica*, 1952, *1*, 112–122. [403]

Kirk, R. E. *Experimental design: Procedures for the behavioral sciences* (2nd ed.). Monterey, CA: Brooks/Cole, 1982. [370]

Lucas, J. D. The interactive effects of anxiety, failure, and intra-serial duplication. *American Journal of Psychology*, 1952, *65*, 59–66. [371]

Mann, H. B., & Whitney, D. R. On a test of whether one of two random variables is stochastically larger than the other. *Annals of Mathematical Statistics*, 1947, *18*, 50–60. [213]

Marascuilo, L. A., & McSweeney, M. *Nonparametric and distribution-free methods for the social sciences.* Monterey, CA: Brooks/Cole, 1977. [418]

McNemar, Q. Note on the sampling error of the difference between correlated proportions or differences. *Psychometrika*, 1947, *12*, 153–157. [335]

McNemar, Q. *Psychological statistics* (4th ed.). New York: Wiley, 1969. [263]

Mood, A. M. *Introduction to the theory of statistics.* New York: McGraw-Hill, 1950. [94]

Mosteller, F., & Rourke, R. E. K. *Sturdy statistics.* Reading, MA: Addison-Wesley, 1973. [224]

Newman, D. The distribution of range in samples from a normal population, expressed in terms of an independent estimate of standard deviation. *Biometrika*, 1939, *31*, 21–30. [403]

Ornstein, R. E. *The psychology of consciousness.* San Francisco: Freeman, 1972. [2]

Pearson, E. S., & Hartley, H. O. (Eds.). *Biometrika tables for statisticians* (3rd ed.). Cambridge, England: Cambridge University Press, 1970. [Table A]

RAND Corporation. *A million random digits.* New York: The Free Press, 1955. [Table H]

Sawrey, W. L., Conger, J. J., & Turrell, E. S. An experimental investigation of psychological factors in the production of gastric ulcers in the rat. *Journal of Comparative and Physiological Psychology*, 1956, *49*, 457–461. [428]

Schiffman, H. R. *Sensation and preception: An integrated approach* (2nd ed.). New York: Wiley, 1982. [485]

Siegel, S. *Nonparametric statistics.* New York: McGraw-Hill, 1956. [223]

Skinner, B. F. *Beyond freedom and dignity.* New York: Knopf, 1971. [2]

Smoking and health: A report of the Surgeon General (US Public Health Service Publication No. 79-50066). Washington, DC: US Government Printing Office, 1979. [123]

Snedecor, G. W., & Cochran, W. G. *Statistical methods* (7th ed.). Ames, IA: The Iowa State University Press, 1980. [269]

Stapp, J., & Fulcher, R. The employment of APA members. *American Psychologist,* 1981, *36,* 1263–1314. [Table 2-1]

Statistical abstract of the United States, 1979. Washington, DC: Government Printing Office, 1979. [Figure 2-3]

Stevens, S. S. Mathematics, measurement, and psychophysics. In S. S. Stevens (Ed.), *Handbook of experimental psychology.* New York: Wiley, 1951. [8]

Student. (See Gosset, W. S.)

Thigpen, C. H., & Cleckley, H. M. A case of multiple personality. *Journal of Abnormal and Social Psychology,* 1954, *49,* 135–151. [353]

Thorndike, E. L. *Human nature and the social order.* New York: MacMillan, 1940. [7]

Thurstone, L. L. *Primary mental abilities.* Chicago: University of Chicago Press, 1938, (new impression 1969). [353]

Tukey, J. W. *Exploratory data analysis.* Reading, MA: Addison-Wesley, 1977. [34]

Underwood, B. J. Interference and forgetting. *Psychological Review,* 1957, *64* 49–60. [323]

Walker, H. M. Degrees of freedom. *Journal of Educational Psychology,* 1940, *31,* 253–269. [180]

Watson, J. B. Psychology as the behaviorist views it. *Psychological Review,* 1913, *20,* 158–177. [2]

Watson, J. B., & Rayner, R. Conditioned emotional reactions. *Journal of Experimental Psychology,* 1920, *3,* 1–14. [355]

Wilcoxon, F. Individual comparisons by ranking methods. *Biometrics Bulletin,* 1945, *1,* 80–83. [213]

Wilcoxon, F., Katti, S. K., & Wilcox, R. A. *Critical values and probability levels for the Wilcoxon rank sum test and the Wilcoxon signed rank test.* Pearl River, NY: American Cyanamid Company, Lederle Laboratories Division, 1963. [Table G]

Wilcoxon, F., & Wilcox, R. A. *Some rapid approximate statistical procedures.* Pearl River, NY: American Cyanamid Company, Lederle Laboratories Division, 1964. [Table G]

Winer, B. J. *Statistical principles in experimental design* (2nd ed.). New York: McGraw-Hill, 1971. [370]

Working, H., & Hotelling, H. Application of the theory of error to the interpretation of trends. *Journal of the American Statistical Association,* 1929, *24,* 73–85. [269]

Index